Published by
Rajneesh Foundation International
Rajneeshpuram, Oregon 97741 U.S.A.

THE BOOK

An
Introduction
to the
Teachings
of
**Bhagwan
Shree
Rajneesh**

Series III from R to Z

Edited by: Academy of Rajneeshism
          Swami Krishna Prem, D.Phil.M. (RIMU), Acharya
Design: Ma Prem Tushita
Direction: Ma Yoga Pratima, D.Phil.M. (RIMU), Arihanta
Copyright: © 1984 Rajneesh Foundation International
Published by:
   Ma Anand Sheela, D.Litt.M. (RIMU), Acharya
   Rajneesh Foundation International, President
   P.O. Box 9, Rajneeshpuram,
   Oregon 97741, U.S.A.

First Edition: March 1984 — 10,000 copies

Printed in U.S.A.
ISBN 0-88050-704-7
Library of Congress Catalog Card Number 84-42616

INTRODUCTION

"What's your philosophy?"

As a disciple of Bhagwan Shree Rajneesh, I have been asked this question countless times. It's an understandable question—people are accustomed to equating religion and philosophy. Most of them have grown up with a set of beliefs, whether from the Bible, *the Koran, the Gita, Das Kapital* or whatever. They would like a neat package of words presented to them so that they can agree or disagree.

"Words are very troublesome," says Bhagwan in this third volume of *The Book*, "because they carry the past, they are made by the past. And for me the problem is to use the words which come from the past—because there are no other words—but to give them such a twist and turn that they can give you a little insight into a new meaning. The words are old, the bottles are old, but the wine is new."

"What's your philosophy?" To be with Bhagwan is to find oneself dropping philosophies, dropping the neat packages of beliefs about reality that keep one from experiencing life as fresh and new each moment. It is to find oneself getting drunk on His new wine. Philosophy? Who needs it!

Whether you come to this book out of curiosity or as a confirmed drunkard, you will find that it contains a rich variety of tastes to be savored—relationship, sex, relaxation, religion, search, sadness, technology, women—each subject illuminated by the beauty of His vision in such a way that it will never look quite the same again. And all so inviting, so temptingly bottled that you'll find yourself drinking again and again.

Cheers!

Ma Deva Sarito

R

RAIN You are walking and suddenly it starts raining. Now, you can make a problem out of it or you can enjoy it. Both are dependent on your attitude.

You can start thinking, "My clothes will become wet. Now I am in new shoes and they will be destroyed." Or, "I am going to meet someone; now it will be a problem." You become worried—and you are missing something tremendously beautiful. Or you can just relax and let the rain fall. You can start enjoying the music, the raindrops falling on you . . . the touch, the coolness and the freedom—and a totally new scene surrounds you. You relax and start enjoying it . . . you cherish it. Something inside your heart starts opening and you are not worried about stupid things like shoes getting wet or that you may catch cold, or this and that . . . just stupid things.

Such a beauty is pouring on you. So much is available if you can relax and simply watch what is happening and can start tasting the joy of it. Suddenly the whole vision has changed. Now you may come across the pleasure that you have never known. Then you may start waiting for it—for when it rains and you can go out, and walk in the rain. Sometimes you may even catch cold; that's nothing. It is worth it. And if you are not thinking about catching cold, you may not catch it. So just start looking at things in a very very happy way.

Try to find, in whatsoever is happening, the something beautiful that must be there. Uncover it, discover it. A person who never asks for anything always gets many gifts from God.

DANCE YOUR WAY TO GOD

RAJNEESHISM Rajneeshism is not a religion like Christianity, Hinduism, Mohammedanism, Buddhism, etc. The name should not be misunderstood. It simply shows a poverty of language—to be exactly true, Rajneeshism is a religionless religion.

In other words it is a kind of religiousness, not a dogma, cult or creed but only a quality of love, silence, meditation and prayerfulness. Hence it can never end.

It is not beginning with me. It has always existed and it will always exist. It is the very essence of human evolution, of culture consciousness.

Buddha, Jesus or Krishna are nothing but expressions of this spirit, but it was not possible in those days for religion to be manifested as well as it can be now. Because Jesus did not know about Buddha, Buddha did not know about Lao Tzu, and Krishna was also unaware of Lao Tzu, etc.

I have traveled all the paths and have looked at truth from all the windows. What I am saying is going to last forever because nothing more could be added to it.

Buddha was not so sure of his religion. He said that his religion would last for five thousand years, and that too only if he didn't allow women to join his commune. And when women entered his commune he said, "Now the religion will only last five hundred years." All of these people have talked about some aspect of truth and their disciples have understood it as the whole truth. I am talking about the whole truth so the future of my religion is infinite. All other religions will disappear into it as all the rivers disappear into the ocean.

RAJNEESHISM: AN INTRODUCTION TO
BHAGWAN SHREE RAJNEESH AND HIS RELIGION

Our religion should not be categorized with any other religion of the world because it has no tradition or dogma and it allows everybody without any discrimination into its religious fold.

Rajneeshism does not ask anyone to renounce their religion and does not have any conflict with Buddha, Christ, Krishna, Lao Tzu, etc. Basically Rajneeshism has the essential core of all religiousness.

The other religions are against each other's traditions and attitudes. In fact, these other religions are fanatic and each believes and fights that theirs is the true religion and others are false.

This is not the case with me or Rajneeshism. A Christian can become a Rajneeshee and he is not asked to drop his love for Jesus, in fact he finds Jesus in me. The same is true for a Buddhist or a Mohammedan.

Our commune consists of people from all religions who have found their religion's truth in me.

We have thousands of Christians, Buddhists, Jainas, Hindus and Jews who are Rajneeshees. We have people from every country, every race and every religion and there is no discrimination.

Even an atheist is absolutely accepted and loved in our religion. Rajneeshism is a way of life. It has nothing to do with hocus-pocus or heaven and hell.

My whole emphasis is in finding the center of the cyclone—the emptiness that is between you and existence and the eternal nothingness.

In this nothingness the flower of enlightenment blooms. You cannot condemn us like Christians, Jews, Hindus or Jainas as we do not discriminate against anyone.

Reported in THE RAJNEESH TIMES, Friday, October 28, 1983

The ecclesiastical organization of the religion is overseen by the Academy of Rajneeshism.

There are three categories of ministers: *Acharyas, Arihantas* and *Siddhas.* The category into which a candidate is placed depends on the particular type of energy he or she possesses: introverted, extroverted, or a synthesis of the two.

Ministers whose basic energy is outgoing, extroverted, reach the state of godliness through serving others. Known as *Arihantas*, they may perform marriage and birth ceremonies for sannyasins and non-sannyasins.

Those whose energy is basically introverted, who work on themselves for personal transformation and reach godliness in this way, are known as *Siddhas.* They are empowered to perform the death ceremony for sannyasins and non-sannyasins.

Those whose energy is both active and inactive, introverted and extroverted, work on themselves and help others too. They have the ability to be alone and to reach out— and it is through this synthesis that they attain the state of godliness. These ministers, who are called *Acharyas*, may perform birth, marriage and death ceremonies for sannyasins and non-sannyasins, and are also empowered to initiate new disciples into neo-sannyas.

To be eligible for the ministry, a person must have the following experience and training: a minimum of
—two years as a neo-sannyasin
—two years of participation and practice in meditation
—two years of participation in religious discourses and teachings with guidance
—one year of worship-meditation or apprenticeship in Rajneeshism
—specific orientation for the ministerial duties.

These religious-training activities may run concurrently.

RAJNEESHISM: AN INTRODUCTION TO
BHAGWAN SHREE RAJNEESH AND HIS RELIGION

See also Teacher

RATIONAL   See Reason

RATIONALIZATION   See Bullshit, 1st Series

REACTION   Be awake. Just see what you are doing, just see what your life consists of. Is there any awareness or is it just an unconscious play of unconscious forces? Are you just a victim of forces you are not aware of—from where they come, what they are doing to you? Are you going to die in this way?

The Master endures
Insults and ill treatment
Without reacting.

The Master cannot react. He responds, but he never reacts. Reactions come from the past, response is spontaneous; it is in the present. The slave reacts, the Master responds. The unconscious mind reacts, the conscious man responds. He has no ready-made answers. He encounters the situation, he reflects the situation. He accepts the challenge of the situation—and he acts accordingly. His action is born out of the present.

And remember one fundamental secret of life: if the action is born out of the present it is never binding; if it comes out of the past it is binding, it is karma. If the action comes out of your present awareness it is not karma, it is not binding. You do it and it is finished, you do it and get out of it; it never accumulates in you.

The Master never accumulates the past; he dies every moment to the past. He is born anew every moment.

> *The Master endures*
> *Insults and ill treatment*
> *Without reacting.*
> *For his spirit is an army.*

He need not react. Insults cannot insult him, ill treatment only brings his compassion, because he knows his awareness is a citadel, is a shelter which cannot be broken. It is an ultimate protection; he is ultimately secure in his awareness.

THE BOOK OF THE BOOKS, Vol. XII

We always react from our past. It has always worked, so we think it is going to work in every situation, but one day a situation arises where your past is simply irrelevent; it doesn't work. That is real crisis . . . and real opportunity too . . .

We always think out of the past. That is how *everybody* reacts. That is the meaning of reaction. That is the difference between reaction and response. A response means seeing that the situation is so new that you cannot have any answer from the past; seeing this, you respond to the situation. You go with the situation, you don't think of the past.

THE WISDOM OF THE SANDS, Vol. I

READING Reading is good after meditation, very good, but before it, it can be dangerous. If you read too much you can become addicted to books and they destroy you, because then information goes on being piled up and it becomes a heavy burden. Then it creates confusion, because you can read the Bible and the Koran and the Gita, and they are different languages, such different attitudes, so opposite to each other, diametrically opposite to each other. Your mind

simply starts falling into parts. You don't know what is true
and what is right and what to do. Then a person becomes
just a head, and goes on spinning. That is not going to help
much; it can be very destructive.

Books are good when you have been meditating. Then you
can see the point. If you read the Gita you will be able to
see that it is only a different language; it is the same thing
as the Bible. Then you read Buddha and you see it is exactly
the same thing as the Gita. You can go on reading a thousand and one books but you always fall upon your own
experience. You have something like a touchstone, a
criterion; you can fall upon it and you can judge through
it. Then things are never going apart, they start falling into
a harmony—but that is possible only when you have your
own experience.

Reading is not going to give you that experience, but if
you have the experience, reading can give you much con-
firmation that you are on the right track, that you are not
groping in the darkness. Scriptures can become witnesses
to you—that many have passed and many have come to
know, and you are not alone. It can give you great courage
and confidence. Otherwise it will give you conflict. So reduce
reading a little and put the same energy towards meditation . . . and meditation is totally different.

Reading means thinking and meditation means no-
thinking. It is a totally different dimension of consciousness—where thoughts have to be dropped and one
has to attain to a pure, silent space—the zero space, where
no object is. One is simply conscious but not conscious of
anything . . . pure subjectivity—as if a lamp is burning in
total emptiness. Light is there but nothing is lighted by it.
It is not falling on anything . . . there is nothing. In that state
of consciousness you will start experiencing something. And
only experience is going to give you truth—not logic, not
argument, not reading.

Reading can give you philosophy, but meditation can give
you truth.

DANCE YOUR WAY TO GOD

In India, when somebody is reading an ordinary book it
is called "reading"; but whenever somebody is reading Gita

we have a special term for it: we call it *path* . Literally translated it will mean "lesson". Ordinary reading is just reading— mechanical; but when you read, so deeply absorbed in it that the very reading becomes a lesson, then the very reading goes deep in your being and is not only part of your memory now but has become part of your being. You have absorbed it, you are drunk with it. You don't carry the message in so many words, but you have the essence in you. The very essential has moved into your being. We call it *path*.

THE SEARCH

Thoughts are figures, consciousness is the background. Mind consists of figures and no-mind is the background. Just start looking into the gaps. Fall in love with the intervals! Go deeper into them, search more into them—they have real secrets in them. The mystery is hidden there. It is not in the words that pass in your mind; those words are trivia, impressions from the outside. But see on what they pass, those ripples; look into that consciousness. And it is infinite. It is your being.

That consciousness is called no-mind.

That is the meaning of the English expression "reading between the lines". Read between the lines and you will become a wise man. Read the lines and you will become an ugly scholar, a pundit, a parrot, a computer, a memory—a mind. Read between the lines an you will become a no-mind.

And no-mind is herenow.

WALK WITHOUT FEET, FLY WITHOUT WINGS,
THINK WITHOUT MIND

REALITY This is attaining to reality: when you don't ask why, when you drop the longing, the neurotic longing for meaning. That neurotic longing is driving you to such despair that life has become almost impossible; it is a miracle how you go on living. Yes, Freud may be right as far as you are concerned: "Human life is more a matter of endurance than of enjoyment." He himself never enjoyed life; he endured.

But that is ugly: to endure, to endure such benediction in which you can disappear, in which you need not remain separate, in which you can become part of the dance and the song . . .

This is reality: dropping the question why, dropping philosophical attitudes towards life, dropping the longing for meaning, then you attain to reality.

THE SUN RISES IN THE EVENING

As far as objective reality is concerned, modern science agrees more with Buddha than with anybody else. Hence Buddha has a great future, because science will come closer and closer to Buddha every day. Science is going to speak in the same language as Buddha. Science says there is energy but no matter. That's what Buddha is saying about the inner world: There is energy, movement, processes, but no entity, no ego.

"Know thyself" means: Know that you are not. Great courage is needed to know this. People want to know that they are immortal souls. Then they are very happy—"We are immortal souls." And Buddha says, "Don't talk nonsense. You simply are not. Immortality is there, but you are not immortal. When *you* disappear completely, whatsoever is left behind—that cleanliness, that purity, that innocence, that nobodiness, that nothingness, that *shunya*—that is immortal. It has no beginning and no end, no birth and no death". . .

That's what all the Buddhas have been saying: The moment you understand that "I am ignorant," the first glimpse of knowing has happened. The moment you say, "I am not," for the first time, real existence has penetrated you. The first time you say, "I don't possess anything," the whole world is yours. The first time you say, "I am not separate, I am one with the whole," you become the whole. The dewdrop does not really disappear; it becomes the ocean. By knowing one's emptiness, one's egolessness, one loses nothing, one gains all.

THE BOOK OF THE BOOKS, Vol. VIII

Misery is not as big as you make it. So the first thing is to reduce it to the right proportion . . . Be very factual. If you really want to transform your life, be factual. You cannot get out of fictions, but you can get out of facts. Facts can be tackled, but fictions cannot be tackled.

But this is the way of the mind, the way of the ego: to

magnify everything. It makes everything look big and then, of course, you start suffering in a big way. The cause is not so big, but the effect can be very big; it depends on you.

Look again, consider again, reconsider the whole situation. What is it that you are calling "utterly miserable"? And then you will find ordinary facts of life. But we don't want to be ordinary. The ego hankers to be extraordinary. Even if it is misery we would like to be extraordinary . . .

The first thing for you is to bring things down to the level of reality. It is difficult, particularly for a woman. They live in fancy. When you fall in love you think you have fallen in love with a Greek god—and by the time the honeymoon is finished you know he is nothing but a goddamned Greek! Within seven days the Greek god is nothing but a goddamned Greek. And again it will happen; again you will fall in love and again you will create a great fancy. You will create projections. And all your projections are going to be shattered sooner or later because reality has no obligation to fulfill your projections.

So first bring your idea of misery down to the factual, to the real, and then it is not difficult to get out of it.

Then the second thing is to be aware of it. Just be aware of it—*and* you are out of it! Because you can be aware only if you are not in it. That is the miracle of awareness: when you observe something, one thing is certain, absolutely certain: that you are not in it. The observer is never the observed. The observed is there as an object confronting you; you are the observer, you are the subject. So misery is there, pain is there, or pleasure, or whatsoever experience is there . . . You are not it—you *are* out of it . . .

These two steps: first bring your misery to the level of reality and then watch it—because only reality can be observed, fictions cannot be observed; you become identified with them. Once the reality is there it is objective—watch it. And suddenly a great realization happens: you are the watcher, you are out of it . . .

You are out of it . . . right *now* you are out of it. It is only an illusion that you are in it. If you want to believe you can go on believing that you are in it; otherwise you can snap

out of it *any* moment. Try—try to snap out of it! Snap your
fingers and slap your face and wake up!

THE BOOK OF THE BOOKS, Vol. XI

REAPING It takes a little time for the seed to grow and
become a sprout, and the sprout to grow and become a tree.
And the tree also takes time, the right season, to grow
flowers, and then fruits come. It takes time. When you sow
the seeds you don't see the flowers or the fruits.

Be watchful when you are sowing your seeds, because once
sown you will have to suffer the consequences. whatsoever
you sow you will have to reap. It is just that the time gap
creates illusions in people's minds. They think they can
escape; that they can sow wrong seeds and can reap right
crops. That is impossible—that is against the eternal law.

THE BOOK OF THE BOOKS, Vol. V

REASONING Pseudo reasoning, rationalizations, explanations, excuses. All are borrowed. Not a single one is your
own authentic experience, but they give a kind of satisfaction. You think you are a very rational being. You cannot
become rational by accumulating borrowed arguments and
proofs. The real reason arises only when you are intelligent.
And remember, there is a difference between an intellectual and the man whom I call intelligent. The intellectual
is hidden behind the pseudo reasoning. His reasoning may
be very logical but it can never be reasonable. His reason
is just pseudo, it appears like reason . . .

The pseudo reasoning is just apparent reasoning, it is not
knowing. It is more for the sake of finding excuses; it is more
for the sake or argumentation. In this kind of deceiving, the
male mind is very expert. This is the male mind's expertise. He has learned the art very deeply . . .

Real reasoning arises only when pseudo reasoning has
been dropped. What is real reason?

Karl Jaspers has defined it perfectly. He says: Reason is
openness, reason is clarity, reason is the will to unity. Reason
uses logic, its methods and categories of understanding, just
to transcend them. Reason is the ultimate flowering of
wisdom.

But not pseudo reasoning. Beware of the pseudo. The

pseudo always creates a filter and the real always becomes a door. The real is always a bridge and the pseudo is always a block.

SUFIS: THE PEOPLE OF THE PATH, Vol. II

REBELLION See Dropout, 1st Series.
Reform

REBIRTH The moment you are awake, the whole becomes a mystery. Suddenly all knowledge evaporates like dewdrops in the early morning sun. For the first time your eyes are full of wonder like a child. It is a second birth! In India we have called the man who comes to know the mystery of existence, *dwij*—twice-born.

Jesus says to Nicodemus, "Unless you are born again you will not enter into my kingdom of God." He also says, "Unless you are like a child you will not enter into my kingdom of God." What does he mean? He simply means that a rebirth is needed.

GUIDA SPIRITUALE

RECEIVING This has been my observation: It is difficult for people to love, but there is one thing which is even more difficult than to love, and that is to receive love. To love is difficult, but to receive love is almost impossible. Why?— because to love is in a way simple, and one can do it because it is not against the ego. When you love somebody you are giving something, and the ego feels enhanced. You have the upper hand, you are the giver, and the other is at the receiving end. You feel very good; your ego feels enhanced, puffed up. But when you receive love, you can't have the upper hand. Receiving, your ego feels hurt. Receiving love is more difficult than giving love. And one has to learn both—to give and to receive.

And to receive is going to transform you more than giving can do, because in receiving love your ego starts disappearing.

Have you watched it in yourself? If not, then observe. When somebody gives love to you, you become a little resistant, you protect. You create a wall—a subtle wall; you show as if you are not much interested. You *are* interested. Who is not interested in love? Love is such a nourishment, but you don't want to show that you need it. You pretend that "It's okay. If you are giving, I will oblige you by receiving, otherwise I don't need . . . I am enough unto myself." You may not say so, but that's what you pretend. That's what your eyes show, your face shows. You become a little resistant, you withdraw.

This always happens to couples. If the woman is very loving, the man starts withdrawing. If the man is very loving, the woman starts withdrawing. Couples come almost every day to me, and this is one of the basic problems that if one is too much in love, the other starts escaping. What is the matter? It is very rare that a couple comes to me who are both in love and nobody is withdrawing. It *never* happens. It is so rare.

Why can't it happen? For a certain basic reason. If the woman is too loving, the man becomes afraid—"Now she is gaining the upper hand." And if he shows love then he will become a dependent, then he will become a slave. And she is so maternal that she will surround him from every side, she will become a prison to him, and he will not find any escape. He starts escaping before it is too late. He starts managing how to get out of it, or at least to keep a little distance, a little space, so that if the time arises he can escape. And the same happens to the woman. If the man is too loving and surrounds her from everywhere, she feels suffocated, she starts feeling that something is wrong, that she is no more free, that this man is too much.

Both want love, both need love, but the ego does not allow you to receive. And if you become incapable of receiving, you will become incapable of giving—that is a logical corollary. If you become incapable of receiving, if you are so much afraid when somebody is giving love to you, a natural consequence will be that you will become afraid of giving, because now you know how people become afraid when somebody gives love. When somebody gives love to you, you become afraid. Now you know that if you give too much love the other will become afraid. You don't give too much: you become a miser. You become a cripple, a paralyzed person.

You need not ask for my help, just be ready to receive it; it is already available. The moment you become a sannyasin, you become my responsibility. Then it is not only your life, it is my life too. It is part of me.

THE RAINBOW BRIDGE

Don't be a miser in receiving. People are miserly in giving, they are miserly in receiving too. When great gifts descend on you, you shrink away, you back away; you become afraid because those great gifts are so great that you feel you may be drowned. When bliss comes to you it is like a flood.

Hence Buddha says: *Do not turn away what is given you.* Because if you turn away you will miss the opportunity, and it may not knock on your door again for a long time. One never knows when the moment will come again. So whenever something happens to you in meditation, open up your heart. Even if you are afraid of the unknown, still go into the unknown. And go dancing, go joyously, because in meditation nothing wrong can ever happen to you. In meditation, only blessings are possible.

THE BOOK OF THE BOOKS, Vol. II

RECEPTIVITY God is searching . . . we need not search for him at all. And even if we search, we cannot find, because we don't know where he is, who he is. And even if he comes just in front of you, you will not be able to recognize him, because recognition is possible only when cognition has happened before. Recognition means that you are seeing somebody again—but you have not seen God before so how can you seek and how can you recognize?

Truth cannot be sought—one can simply be receptive, that's all. One can open the doors and wait . . . and wait prayerfully. One can say only this much, "If you come, you will be received, welcomed. I don't know who you are, and I don't know your address and I cannot even send an invitation. But whosoever you are, and whomsoever it concerns, if you come, my doors will be open—you will not find them closed." That's all that a seeker can do . . . that's all that is needed to be done. More than that is not possible and is not needed.

So let this posture be your deep attitude. One has to

become receptive. Hence I go on emphasizing that the search for truth is not a male search; it is a feminine search—just like feminine energy . . . receptive. Not like a male—aggressive.

The male mind has created science. Science is aggressive. It is almost a rape on nature. It is a violent effort to force nature to yield its secrets. It is not graceful. There is no prayer in it. There is conflict. Hence they call it the "conquest of nature", "conquering nature". But this is absurd! How can you conquer nature?—you are part of it. How can my hand conquer me?—the hand is part of me. How can a leaf conquer the tree? Foolish, just foolish!

And out of that foolishness we have created a whole civilization which is trying to conquer everything. It is the male-dominated world. And when I say male-dominated, I mean the aggressive mind. A woman can be male if she has an aggressive mind and a man can be feminine if he has a receptive mind. Science is male, religion is female.

Religion is simply a deep receptivity . . . a readiness, an open door. If God comes as a guest he will not be refused, that's all, and he will be received with great gratitude, he will be a welcome guest.

So meditate, dance and sing, but remain deep inside with a welcoming heart. And everything will come in its own right time . . . nothing happens before its right time. And it is good—it should not happen before the right time has come. If it happens before its time you will never be able to understand it, to digest it. It will never become part of you, it will even become a burden—may prove poisonous.

THE SHADOW OF THE WHIP

Receptivity is a state of no-mind. When you are utterly empty of all thought, when consciousness has no content, when the mirror reflects nothing, it is receptivity. Receptivity is the door to the divine. Drop the mind and be.

In the mind, you are miles away from being. The more you think, the less you are. The less you think, the more you are. And if you don't think at all, those are the moments when being asserts itself in its totality.

Receptivity simply means dropping the garbage that you go on carrying in your head. And much garbage is there, utterly useless. The mind means the past. Now the past is no more of any use; it has happened, and it is never going to happen again, because in reality nothing ever repeats . . .

When I say become receptive, I mean become a child again.

Remember Jesus, who goes on saying to his disciples: Unless you are like small children you will not be able to enter into my kingdom of God. What he is saying is exactly the meaning of receptivity. The child is receptive because he knows nothing; not knowing anything, he is receptive. The old man is not receptive because he knows too much; knowing too much, he is closed. He has to be reborn, he has to die to the past and become a child again—not in the body, of course, but the consciousness should always be like a child; not childish, remember, but like a child, grown-up, mature, but innocent.

And that's how one learns, learns the truth that is presented to you every moment of your life, learns to know the guest which comes and knocks on your doors every moment, day in, day out, year in, year out. But you are so surrounded by your own inner talk, by your own inner procession of thoughts, that you don't hear the knock.

Do you hear the distant call of the cuckoo? Do you hear the birds chirping? This is receptivity. It is an existential state of silence, utter silence; no movement, nothing stirs, and yet you are not asleep, and yet you are alert, and yet you are absolutely aware. When silence and awareness meet, mingle and become one, there is receptivity. Receptivity is the *most* important religious quality.

Become a child. Start functioning from the state of not-knowing, and then silence will come of its own accord, and great awareness. And then life is a benediction.

THE GUEST

RECOGNITION How does one become a disciple? A vague recognition, a fragrance that has touched you, a love that has moved your heart, something of the beyond. It is a feeling, it is not knowing. You cannot be absolutely certain about it; it is mysterious.

As you become more and more meditative you will become more and more clear about it. It is a faraway call of the cuckoo—yes, exactly the call of a cuckoo—a distant call. You hear it and it is no more there, but it lingers around you, it hangs around you for a while, as if in a dream. But this much *is* possible, and only this much is possible. If you ask more than that, in a state of *un*enlightenment, then you are asking for the impossible.

You cannot be absolutely certain who I am unless you know who you are. But the moment you are absolutely certain, you don't need me. You need me only because you are not absolutely certain. But something in you is triggered, something in you starts growing . . .

Your understanding, your knowledge, your mind, cannot recognize, but your feeling, your love—not your logic—can have a vague sense. It can smell, it can taste something of the divine. It can have an encounter with a faraway distant call. If you move in the direction from where the call has come you may arrive to the third plane of your being where knowing happens, when you are also in the some space as I am. Then it explodes totally. Then you know it. It is no more knowledge; it is your experience. You see it, and seeing is transforming, knowing is transforming . . .

And what I am you can be. I am simply your future. What has happened to me can happen to you. That day will come the total and absolute, unconditional, irrevocable recognition. Before that it is not possible.

GUIDA SPIRITUALE

Do you think you would have recognized Buddha? Now, of course, because now twenty-five centuries have passed and Buddha has become bigger and bigger, so huge. He looms large on the horizon like a beautiful sunrise. You cannot believe that people could have missed him—but they were missing him! Even his own father could not recognize him, that he was enlightened; even his own wife could not recognize him, that he was enlightened. There were only a very few people who had the courage to recognize him—because to recognize him means you have to change your lifestyle, to recognize him means you can't remain the same any more. To recognize a Buddha means you are waking up . . .

People are living in such unconsciousness. What to say about recognizing a Buddha—you don't even know who you are!

It is possible to miss the perfect jewel if you are not aware. But if you are aware then it is impossible. It all depends on your awareness . . .

Many people have asked me why I kept silent although I became enlightened in 1953. For almost twenty years I never said anything about it to anybody, unless somebody suspected it himself, unless somebody said to me on his own: "We feel that something has happened to you. We don't know what it is, but one thing is certain: that something has happened and you are no more the same as we are—and you are hiding it."

In those twenty years not more than ten people asked me, and even then I avoided them as much as I could unless I felt that their desire was genuine. And I told them only when they had promised to keep it a secret. And they all fulfilled it. Now they are all sannyasins, but they all fulfilled it, they kept it a secret. I said, "You wait, you wait for the right moment; only then will I declare it."

I have learned much from the past Buddhas. If Jesus had kept a little quieter about his being the son of God it would have been far more beneficial to humanity. I had made it a point that until I stopped traveling in the country I was not going to declare it, otherwise I would have been killed—you would not have been here. Once I finished with traveling, mixing with the masses, moving from one town to another . . . For twenty years continuously I was moving, and there was not a single bodyguard . . . And I was in constant danger. Stones were being thrown at me, shoes were being thrown at me.

I would reach a town after traveling for twenty-four hours in a train and the crowd wouldn't allow me to get down at the station; they would force me to go back. A fight would ensue between those who wanted me to get down from the train and those who did not want me to get down, in *their* town at least.

If I had declared it I would have been killed very easily. There would have been no problem in it; it would have been so simple. But for twenty years I kept absolutely silent about it. I declared it only when I saw that now I had gathered enough people who would understand it. I had gathered enough people who were mine, who belonged to me. I declared it only when I knew that now I could create my own small world and I was no more concerned with the crowds and the masses and the stupid mob.

THE BOOK OF THE BOOKS, Vol. XI

RECREATION If one meditates on one's sexuality, one starts understanding great secrets of life; they are hidden there. Sex is holding the very key. It is not only the key to reproduce children, it is also the key to recreate yourself again. It is not only reproduction, it is really recreation.

In English the word "recreation": has lost its original meaning. Now "recreation" means enjoying a holiday, enjoying fun, playing around. But in fact, whenever you are playing and you are on a holiday, something is created in you—it is actually *recreation,* it is not just fun. Something that dies in work and in the day-to-day world, is born again. And sex has become the most recreational act in people's lives. That is their recreation. But on a higher plane it is *really* recreation, it is not just fun. It holds great secrets in it, and the first secret is—if you meditate you will see it—that joy comes because sex disappears. And whenever you are in that moment of joy, time also disappears—if you meditate on it—the mind also disappears. And these are the qualities of meditation.

My own observation is that the first glimpse of meditation in the world must have come through sex; there is no other way. Meditation *must* have entered into life through sex, because this is the most meditative phenomenon—if you understand it, if you go deep into it, if you just don't use it like a drug. Then slowly slowly as more understanding grows, the more the hankering disappears, and one day comes of great freedom when sex no more haunts you. Then one is quiet, silent, utterly oneself. The need for the other has disappeared. One can still make love as one chooses to, but there is no need.

Then it will be a kind of sharing.

HALLELUJAH!

RED   I have chosen the color red with all its shades for my sannyasins. It symbolizes sunrise, the reddening of the eastern horizon just before the sun arrives. The East becomes full of colors, but they are all shades of red. It is getting ready to welcome the sun. The night is over, the birds have started singing, the flowers have started opening, the people and the animals and the trees are waking up. Life is going through a new birth. The night has been a small death; the sun heralds the beginning of a new day. Again life will celebrate and dance and sing, again there will be love and joy and all that is beautiful and alive.

Sannyas is sunrise in the inner world, the early morning, the dawn, the declaration that the night is over and that the day is just close by, at hand—get ready to welcome it!

IS THE GRASS REALLY GREENER ON THE OTHER SIDE OF THE FENCE?

To me sannyas is an awakening, not an escape. It is an awareness of the whole phenomenon of life—that it is a game.

If it is a game, play it well, that's all. Play it beautifully, and while it lasts, enjoy it. Don't cling to it, because it is a game; don't get mad about it, because it is a game. And when you understand that it is a game, why not let it be colorful?

Red is a basic color. In nature only two colors exist: red and green. They are the basic colors. Hindus have chosen red, Mohammedans have chosen green. Only two basic colors exist. All the trees are green and all the flowers are red.

When I was thinking what color I was going to give to my sannyasins, green was also a competitor, green was also a candidate. But then I decided on red, because in red the green is involved, but in green the red is not involved.

I will have to explain it to you: a tree can be without flowers, but flowers can't be without trees. In every flower the whole tree is involved. So behind my red there is green; behind all my teachings—even if the formulation is Hindu— the Mohammedan is hidden. So I talk about the Upanishads and I give examples from Sufis; I give you a meditation— three steps of the meditation come from the Hindu world and one step comes from the Mohammedan world . . .

I have chosen red because red is the culmination of the whole tree, red is the flowering, the last thing. You cannot defeat Hindus: of course they were first in the world of religion. They have chosen the best, they have not left anything behind—they have chosen the color red.

Red is the flower. Red is the blood. Red is the sun. From everywhere red surrounds you, and in red everything is implied, involved, because it is the flowering.

Let your life be colorful, I don't want you to become colorless. No. I would like you to become like rainbows, all seven colors. And when all the seven colors are there, there comes a moment when they meet and become one. That is white light. This is a miracle—white light can be divided into seven colors; and the seven colors of a rainbow if they meet together, if the alchemy happens, become white. When all the seven colors meet they become white, and when all the seven types of man meet they become white—just a white light, and nothing is left.

Play the game as beautifully as you can; but it is a game—don't get serious about it. And even if sometimes seriousness is needed, let it be a game, nothing more. Sometimes it is needed. It gives a taste to life. Sometimes you need to be serious also. Be serious, but never become serious, let that also be a game. Let everything be a game.

And sannyas is the last game. Beyond it the whole world of game disappears. Then there is reality. so this is just the last thing you are going to do. Do it as perfectly as possible—delight in it, dance in it, let it be a deep singing, a rejoicing.

TAO: THE THREE TREASURES, Vol. II

See also Orange, 2nd Series

REFLECTION "Reflecting" is nothing but a beautiful word for "thinking". The blind man can go on thinking about light; he can arrive at certain conclusions too, but those conclusions cannot be right. Howsoever right they appear to be, they are bound to be false, untrue.

The moon in the sky is one thing and the moon reflected in the silent lake is totally another. One exists, the other is only a reflection. If you jump into the silent lake you will not be able to catch hold of the moon; on the contrary, you may even disturb the reflection because the lake will be disturbed.

The more you think, the more you are creating waves and ripples in the mind. The real thing for the blind man to do is not to think about light but to heal his eyes, for the deaf man, not to reflect on music but to go through some alchemical processes which can make him hear.

ZEN: ZEST, ZIP, ZAP AND ZING

Buddha says:
Quieten your mind.

He is really saying: Go beyond mind, drop the mind, be finished with it. And what is the way? How has it to be done?

Reflect.

This is the first fundamental. Remember, by "reflect" he does not mean contemplate, think. No, by "reflect" he *actually* means reflect—like a mirror. The mirror reflects; whatsoever comes in front of the mirror, it reflects it. It does not think about it, it does not contemplate it; it simply reflects. When it has moved, the reflection disappears.

This should be the fundamental: reflect things and when they have disappeared, let them disappear. Don't go on carrying the past. Don't become a photo-plate; remember to remain a mirror. The photo-plate also reflects, but it becomes attached to the reflection, it becomes obsessed with the reflection. It clings to it, it becomes imprinted with it. The mirror remains clean; it is not imprinted by what it reflects. It does not become beautiful when a beautiful face is reflected; it does not become ugly . . .

So should be the seeker. When success comes, reflect; don't become attached to it. When failure comes, reflect; don't be disturbed by it. When you are in a palace, reflect the palace; and when you are in a hut, reflect the hut. Don't become attached either to the palace or to the hut. Let everything come and pass, and you simply be a mirror.

If you are a mirror you cannot carry the past with you, and if you don't carry the past you will remain fresh, you will remain you, you will remain in a continuous process of birth. Each moment you will be born anew.

THE BOOK OF THE BOOKS, Vol. X

REFORM   Man's evolution passes through three stages: the reform, the revolution and the rebellion. The reform is the most superficial: it only touches the surface, it never goes more than skin-deep. It changes nothing but the dressing of man; it changes man's formalities. It gives man etiquette, manners, a kind of civilization—without changing anything essential in his being. It paints man, it polishes man, and yet deep down man remains the same. It is a delusion. It is fiction. It gives respectability, and makes everybody a hypocrite. It gives good manners, but they are against the inner core. The inner core has not even been understood. But for the society it creates smoothness.

Reform functions like a lubricant. It keeps the status quo going, it helps thing remain the same—which will look paradoxical, because the reformist claims that he is changing society, but in fact all that he does is paint the old society in new colors. And the old society can exist more easily in new colors than it could have ever done with the old ones. The old were getting rotten. Reform is a kind of renovation. The house is falling, the supports are falling, the foundations are shaking, and you go on giving new props to it. And you can keep the house from falling a little longer. Reform is in the service of the status quo: it serves the past not the future.

The second thing is revolution; it goes a little deeper. Reform only changes ideas, it does not even change policies. Revolution goes and touches the structure, but only the outer, not the inner.

Man has two structures, man lives on two planes. One is the physical, another is the spiritual. The revolution only goes to the physical structure—to the economic, to the political—they all belong to the physical. It goes deeper than reform, it destroys many old things, it creates character. Reform creates manner, etiquette, civilization: the formal behavior of the man is changed. Revolution changes man's outer structure—really changes; it brings a new structure, but the inner blueprint remains the same, the inner consciousness is not touched. It creates a split.

The first, the reform, creates hypocrisy. The second, the revolution, creates schizophrenia, it makes man unbridgeable. Man starts falling into two beings, the bridge is broken. That's why revolutionaries go on denying the soul. Marx and Engels and Lenin and Stalin and Mao—they go on denying the soul. They have to deny it, they can't accept it, because if they accept it, then their whole revolution seems to be very superficial, then their revolution is not total.

The reformist does not deny the soul, remember; he accepts it because it makes no problem for him—he never goes up to that point. That point is not a problem. Gandhi accepts the soul, Manu accepts the soul—they are reformists. They never say no to anything, they are people who go on saying yes; they are polite people. Unless it becomes absolutely necessary they will not deny anything, they will accept. But revolutionaries deny the soul. They have to deny, otherwise their revolution looks partial.

The third thing is rebellion. Rebellion is from the very essential core: it changes consciousness—it is radical; it transmutes—it is alchemical. It gives you a new being, not only a new body, not only new dresses, but a new being. A new man is born.

I SAY UNTO YOU, Vol. II

REFUGE   The Buddhists have what they call three refuges. The first refuge they call refuge in the Buddha, in the awakened one. That is becoming a disciple, surrendering to a Master. And the second refuge they call taking refuge in the commune, taking refuge in the family of the Master— not only surrendering to the Master but surrendering to the commune that is happening around the Master. And the third they call taking refuge in *dhamma*, in the ultimate law of life.

A Buddha is a Buddha because he has become one with the ultimate law of life. His commune is a commune of a Buddha because the people who have gathered around him are trying to reach to the ultimate law of life. So the ultimate refuge, the final refuge is in *dhamma*, in the universal law. These are the true refuges. Not refuge in war, but refuge in peace, refuge in love, refuge in bliss, refuge in God.

DANCE TIL THE STARS
COME DOWN FROM THE RAFTERS

Buddham Sharanam Gachchhami
I go to the feet of the Awakened One
Sangham Sharanam Gachchhami
I go to the feet of the Commune of the Awakened One
Dhammam Sharanam Gachchhami
I go to the feet of the Ultimate Truth of the Awakened One

Buddham Sharanam Gachchhami

Unless you are in contact with one who has realized, it is almost impossible for you to grow. Unless you are in the company of someone who knows the way, who has traveled the way, who has arrived, it is almost impossible for you to reach. Unless your hands are in the hands of someone whom you can trust and surrender to, you are bound to go astray. The Master is such a magnetic force that your surrender to the Master becomes your protection.

Sangham Sharanam Gachchhami

And the second thing is the commune. Each Buddha creates a commune, because without a commune a Buddha cannot function. The commune means his energy field, the commune means the people who have become joined with him, the commune means an alternative society . . . a small oasis in the desert of the world. That is what a commune created by a Buddha is meant to be: a small oasis in which life is lived with a totally different gestalt, with a totally different vision, with a totally different goal; where life is lived with purpose and meaning; where life is lived prayerfully, alert, aware, awake; where life is not just accidental, where life starts becoming more and more a growth in a certain direction, towards a certain destination, where life is no more like driftwood.

Dhammam Sharanam Gachchhami

And *dhamma* means the truth. A Buddha represents the *dhamma* in two ways. One is through his communication—verbal; and the second is through his presence, through his silence, through his communion—non-verbal. The non-verbal is an energy communication. Verbally he communicates with the students; non-verbally, through silence, through energy, he communicates with the disciples. And

then there comes the ultimate unity where neither communication nor communion is needed, but oneness has
been achieved—where the Master and the disciple become
one, when there is no separation.

THE BOOK OF WISDOM, Vol. II

REINCARNATION   Jesus knew perfectly well about reincarnation. There are indirect hints spread all over the
gospels. Just the other day I was quoting Jesus: "I am before
Abraham ever was." And Jesus says, "I will be coming back."
And there are a thousand and one indirect references to reincarnation. He knew about it perfectly well, but there is some
other reason why he did not talk about it, why he did not
preach it.

Jesus had been to India and he had seen what had happened because of the theory of reincarnation. In India for
almost five thousand years before Jesus the theory was
taught. And it is a truth, it is not only a theory; the theory
is based in truth. Man has millions of lives. It was taught
by Mahavira, by Buddha, by Krishna, by Rama; all the Indian
religions agree upon it. You will be surprised to know: they
don't agree on anything else except this theory.

Hindus believe in God and the soul. Jainas don't believe
in God at all but only in the soul. And Buddhists don't
believe in the soul or God either. But about reincarnation
all three agree—even Buddhists agree, who don't believe in
the soul. A very strange thing . . . then who reincarnates?
Even *they* could not deny the phenomenon of reincarnation, although they could deny the existence of the soul;
they say the soul does not exist but reincarnation exists.
And it was very difficult for them to prove reincarnation
without the soul; it seems almost impossible. But they found
a way—of course it is very subtle and very difficult to com-
prehend, but they seem to be closer, the closest to the truth.

It is easy to understand that there is a soul and when you
die the body is left on the earth and the soul enters into
another body, into another womb; it is a simple, logical,
mathematical thing. But Buddha says there is no soul but
only a continuum. It is like when you kindle a candle in
the evening and in the morning when you are blowing it
out a question can be asked of you: "Are you blowing out

the same light that you started in the evening?" No, it is
not the same light, and yet a continuity is there. In the night
when you lit the candle . . . that flame is no more there,
that flame is continuously disappearing; it is being replaced
by another flame. The replacement is so quick you can't see
the gaps, but with sophisticated scientific instruments it is
possible to see the gaps: one flame going out, another coming up, that going out, another coming up. There are bound
to be small intervals, but you can't see them with bare eyes.

Buddha says that just as the candle flame is not the same—
it is changing constantly, although in another sense it is the
same because it is the same continuum—exactly like that,
there is no soul entity in you like a thing but one like a
flame. It is continuously changing, it is a river.

Buddha does not believe in nouns, he only believes in
verbs, and I perfectly agree with him. He has come closest
to the truth; at least in his expression he is the most
profound.

But why did Jesus, Moses, Mohammed—the sources of all
the three religions that have been born outside India—not
talk about reincarnation directly? For a certain reason, and
the reason is that Moses was aware . . . Because Egypt and
India have been in constant contact. It is suspected that once
Africa was part of Asia and that the continent has slowly
shifted away. India and Egypt were joined together, hence
there are so many similarities. And it is not strange that south
India is black; it has partly Negro blood in its veins, it is
negroid—not totally, but if Africa was joined with Asia then
certainly the mingling of the Aryans with the Negroes must
have happened, and then South India became black.

Moses must have been perfectly aware of India. You will
be surprised that Kashmir claims that both Moses and Jesus
are buried there. The tombs are there, one tomb for Moses
and one tomb for Jesus. They saw what happened to India
through the theory of reincarnation . . .

The theory of reincarnation made India very lethargic, dull.
It made India utterly time-unconscious. It helped people to
postpone. And if you can postpone for tomorrow, then today
you will remain the same as you have been and the tomorrow never comes. And India knows how to postpone not
only to tomorrow but even to the next life.

Moses and Jesus both visited India, both were aware. Mohammed never visited India but was perfectly aware, because he was very close to India and there was constant traffic between India and Arabia. They decided that it was better to tell people, "There is only one life, this is the *last* chance—the first and the last—if you miss it, you miss forever." This is a device to create intense longing, to create such intensity in people that they can be transformed easily.

Then the question arises: Were Mahavira, Buddha and Krishna not aware? Were they not aware that this theory of reincarnation would create lethargy? They were trying a totally different device. And each device has its time; once it is used . . . it cannot be used forever. People become accustomed to it. When Buddha, Mahavira and Krishna tried the device of reincarnation they were trying it from a totally different angle.

India was a very rich country in those days. It was thought to be the golden country of the world, the richest. And in a rich country the real problem, the greatest problem, is boredom. That is happening now in the West. Now America is in the same situation, and boredom has become the greatest problem. People are utterly bored, so bored that they would like to die.

Krishna, Mahavira and Buddha used this situation. They told people, "This is nothing, one life's boredom is nothing. You have lived for many lives, and remember, if you don't listen you are going to live many more lives; you will be bored again and again and again. It is the same wheel of life and death moving."

They painted boredom in such dark colors that people who were already bored with even one life became really very deeply involved with religion. One has to get rid of life and death; one has to get out of this wheel, this vicious circle of birth and death. Hence it was relevant in those days.

Then India became poor. Once the country became poor boredom disappeared. A poor man is never bored, remember; only a rich man can afford boredom, it is a rich man's privilege . . .

The moment India became poor the theory of reincarnation became an escape, a hope—rather than a boredom it became a hope, a possibility to postpone. "I am poor in this life. Nothing to be worried about; there are many lives. Next life I am going to strive a little harder and I will be richer. This life I have got an ugly woman. Nothing to be worried about; it is only a question of one life. Next time I am not going to make the same mistake again. This time I am suffering from my past karmas. This life I will not commit any wrong things so that I can enjoy the coming life." It became a postponement.

Jesus saw it, that the device was no longer working, no longer working in the way it was meant to work. The situation had changed. Now Jesus had to create another device: there is only one life—so if you want to be religious, if you want to meditate, if you want to become a sannyasin, be one right now—because the tomorrow is not reliable. There may be no tomorrow.

Hence the West has become too conscious of time; everybody is in a hurry. This hurry is because of Christianity. The device has again failed. No device can work forever.

My own experience is that a particular device works only while the Master is alive, because he is the soul of it; he manages it in such a way that it works. Once the Master is gone, the device falls out of use or people start finding new interpretations for it . . .

I am creating many devices because others have failed. I know perfectly well that my devices will function only while I am here; they are bound to fail as every other device has failed. I am not living in any fool's paradise thinking that my devices will remain as I create them forever. When I am not here, people are going to distort them. But that is natural, it has to be accepted; there is nothing to worry about.

Hence those who are here, please be alert and use these devices as deeply as possible. While I am here these devices will function perfectly well. In my hands they can be great situations for inner transformation, but once my hands are no more visible these same devices will be in the hands of the pundits and the scholars, and then the same story will be repeated as has been in the past.

Beware, be watchful. Don't waste time.

BE STILL AND KNOW

I will tell you a small story that will explain my attitude towards reincarnation.

Suramallo explains to the rabbi the theory of reincarnation: "Let's say, your holiness, that you die tomorrow. A flower blooms on your grave after a few days. A cow comes and eats the flower. The next morning the cow has a good shit. I go for a walk, see the shit and say, 'Ah, your holiness, you haven't changed a bit!'"

WALKING IN ZEN, SITTING IN ZEN

REJECTION The Hindus and the Jews both became dominated by the pundits, the scholars, theologians, rabbis. They lost track of the enlightened Masters. Even though sometimes enlightened people happened in spite of the rotten tradition, they were not accepted, they were rejected.

Hinduism rejected Buddha, and Buddha was the peak of the whole Hindu consciousness, the greatest peak, the Everest. But Hindus rejected him for the simple reason that if he had been accepted that would have meant the death of the whole establishment, the exploitation and oppression by the priests, and they had great vested interests in it.

The same has been true of Judaism. Jesus was the peak, but the Jews rejected Jesus. In that very rejection they rejected their own flowering; they remained a tree without flowers, in fact even without foliage—just a dead tree with no leaves, with no greenery, with no flowers, with no birds singing, no shade for travelers to sit underneath.

Whenever enlightened Masters are rejected by any tradition that is an indication that the tradition is absolutely dead; it cannot absorb any fresh new insight. The living tradition is that which is capable of absorbing new insights. And they are always coming—God is not finished yet with creation. The idea that God finished within six days and then rested on the seventh is sheer nonsense. God is not a person but creativity, not a creator but creativity. It goes on and on; God is still working . . .

The Hindu priest says that God has given his message in the Vedas and that was the end of it. He has given all that was needed by man; nothing more is needed at all. And the Jews think that the Old Testament is the end of the story.

It is only the beginning, not the end. And beginnings cannot be very great, remember; they are bound to be childish.

Remember the difference between childlike and childish: to be childlike is to be a sage, to be childish is not to be a sage. To be childish means to be immature; it needs much improvement, growth, maturity.

Judaism and Hinduism both have remained immature. They had the opportunity to become mature. Buddha could have transformed the whole Hindu world, he could have given it splendor, but he was rejected; the priests would not allow him entry. The Jews would have been the most significant people on the earth if Jesus had been absorbed. But strange are the ways of man, very strange: the Jews had been waiting and waiting for centuries for this same man Jesus to come. They were waiting for the messiah to come, and when he came they rejected him—they rejected him absolutely.

The priesthood is like cancer to every religion. The priesthood destroys every religious possibility, the very potential; it poisons the source.

COME, COME, YET AGAIN COME

REJOICING   Rejoicing is better than joy, because joy means that something has ended, is finished, completed; the full stop has been put there.

Rejoicing is on-going, riverlike; it knows no stopping, the full stop never comes. And life is more like rejoicing than like joy, because the moment joy ends, you will fall into its polar opposite. You will become sad, you will be in despair, you will start longing for joy again. You will start remembering the beauties of joy, the nostalgia, and the despair that it is no more.

Rejoicing—that is closer to life; that's how life is and should be. One goes on flowing from one peak to another, and the flow is a continuum. It is possible only to make your life a continuous flow if sadness is also absorbed in your joy, otherwise not. If sadness is against joy, then joy will end and sadness will have its say, will have its time. Just as night follows day, joy will be followed by sadness.

Rejoicing is an art. It means that the dance continues. Whether it is day or night doesn't matter: one enjoys the day and the sun and the light; and when the night comes, one enjoys the darkness, the depth of it, the velvety touch of it. But the dance continues. In success, in failure, young, old, alone, together, in life, in death, rejoicing continues.

So my emphasis is more on rejoicing than on joy. Rejoicing is far more comprehensive: it contains the polar opposites in it, hence it has more totality. And whatsoever is total is divine, whatsoever is partial is no more divine.

WON'T YOU JOIN THE DANCE?

Jesus says again and again to his disciples, "Rejoice, rejoice, I say to you rejoice!" But I don't think that his disciples understood him; I don't think they were able to rejoice. In fact the Christian church says that Christ never laughed. That is simply ridiculous, saying that about a man like Jesus who continuously says to people "Rejoice!", and who rejoices in every small thing; who rejoices in eating, in drinking, who rejoices in meeting people, who rejoices in ordinary humanity—the carpenters, the farmers, the gardeners, even the gamblers, the prostitutes, even the tax collectors. He rejoices in everybody! He was a feast, a festival—and for two thousand years these fools have been telling the world he never laughed!

You will not see a single picture of Christ laughing, or even smiling—laughter is far away. They have created the image of a Christ so miserable, so sad, that sometimes I wonder whether they are more interested in Christ or in the cross.

THE MIRACLE!

I always love to relate a story about a Hassid fakir's last moments. Zusya was dying—and for his whole life he laughed and joked and danced . . . I love that kind of person; to have such a man as company is a blessing. But the elders of the society were worried about him.

When he was dying somebody asked him, "Zusya, have you made your peace with God? Or have you wasted your life dancing, singing, joking, fooling around?" Zusya opened his eyes and he said "But I have never quarrelled with him, so why should I make peace with him? I have never quarrelled with him; we have always been on good terms. Sometimes I tell jokes—he laughs; sometimes he tells jokes—*I* laugh. Things have been going very well.

"And I have saved a few jokes which I have never told anybody; they are especially for him, because I know when I arrive there he will ask 'Zusya, what have you brought?' I have saved a few jokes especially for him! I am a poor man," Zusya said, "what else I can keep, to take with me as an offering? Prayers he has heard enough of, serious people he must have seen enough of."

Nobody knows how Zusya was received, but I can say with absolute authority that nobody has been received with such a joy as Zusya!

This is the way of a truly religious man.

THE GOLDEN WIND

RELATING   There are two kinds of surrender. One is when you are forced to surrender—that is ugly. Never allow that to happen. It is better to die than to surrender because you are forced to surrender. But there is a totally different kind of surrender: you are not forced to surrender, you simply feel like merging, melting, becoming one with somebody or with the whole of existence.

Of course it always begins as a relationship—that is natural. The first step of love is relationship, the second state of love is relating—and there is a vast difference between the two. In relationship you exclude everybody, you focus on one person. It is kind of concentration of the heart. But all concentration becomes a concentration camp! Basically it is fascist. To begin with it is okay but one should not start living there, in a concentration camp . . .

So love also starts as a concentration camp—a one-to-one affair, exclusive. Both are prisoners and both are the jailers; they function in both ways. Each is imprisoned by the other and each is a jailer in his own right. It is a beautiful game! But one should not remain there, otherwise life is wasted. One should learn the lesson, the beauty of it, the ugliness of it—both have to be learned. And the ugliness has to be dropped and the beauty has to be preserved.

That's what relating is; you drop all that is ugly in love— possessiveness, exclusiveness, domination, suspicion, doubt, every effort to curtail the other's freedom. When all these are dropped and your love becomes just a relating, not a relationship, closer to friendship . . . You can have many friends, you can also have many lovers—and one should start growing from one to many, but that too is not the goal.

The third state is when love is just a quality. You are not attached to one or to many; love is just like breathing—it is your nature—so to whoever you come in contact with, you are loving. This is the third stage: very few have attained to the third. And there is a fourth state which only so few people have attained that they can be counted on fingers.

The fourth is when your very being is love—it is not a quality, your very existence is love. You have forgotten all about love. Because you yourself are love there is no need to remember it; now you act out of it, simply, naturally, spontaneously. At that fourth point one is surrendered to existence.

At the first you are surrendered to a person, but there is a condition—he should be surrendered to you—so the surrender is not total, it is conditional. In the second you are surrendered to many people. It is better than the first because now surrender is not focused; it has more freedom, it has grown a few new dimensions, it has grown wings. In the third you are simply surrendered to existence, to the trees, to the mountains, to the stars, to all that is. And in the fourth you become surrender itself. In the fourth love means surrender: it is equivalent to it, synonymous with it. And this is the state of being of a Buddha or a Christ.

Nothing is higher than that. One who achieves that has achieved all. His life is fulfilled, he has come home.

IS THE GRASS REALLY GREENER
ON THE OTHER SIDE OF THE FENCE?

RELATIONSHIP A living relationship between a man and a woman is bound to be a little bit crazy. Man cannot drive the woman crazy because his argument, his way of thinking is logical. The woman's way of thinking is illogical, but that is her way: that's how she is made. She functions instinctively at the lowest and intuitively at the highest. Man functions intellectually at the lowest and intelligently at the highest. The way of instinct and intuition is the way of illogic. Logic cannot drive the illogical person crazy; if anything is going to happen it is going to happen to the logical mind.

Craziness is part of the logical mind. Craziness simply means your logic is no more functioning and you are at a loss as to what to do. You love the woman, you would not like to lose her at any cost. You feel for her, you try in every way to understand her. But whatsoever you do you are also helpless—you can act only logically. And logically she is not comprehensible; that way she is mysterious, very mysterious. You can devote your whole life to studying a single woman and you will not be able to figure out what is what.

She never tries to understand you. The illogical functioning of the psyche is not interested in understanding; it simply reaches the conclusions without any procedures—it jumps to the conclusions. And the miracle is that the woman is almost always right and you are almost always wrong. That drives you crazy! And you have been functioning so logically, mathematically, step by step; still your conclusion is not right.

One woman won a lottery. When her husband came he was surprised; he asked how she managed.

She said, "I had a dream, and in the dream the figure seven appeared three times. So I figured out that three times seven means twenty-eight."

The husband was aghast. He said, "Then what happened?"

She said, "I purchased the ticket of the number twenty-eight and I won the lottery."

The husband said, "But three times seven is not twenty-eight, it is twenty-one!"

The woman said, "Then you be the mathematician, but I have won the lottery!"

Who cares about mathematics? The real thing is the conclusion. She never tries to understand man—no woman ever tries—she understands already. In fact, they are always puzzled why men go on trying to understand women. For centuries man has been doing that. I think woman must have been the ancientmost subject of his enquiries—naturally; even before God he must have enquired about woman . . .

If you stop trying to understand her and just enjoy her she cannot drive you crazy. If you try to understand her, naturally, you will stop enjoying her, and then she is bound to drive you crazy. Rejoice in her! Rejoice in her differences, rejoice in her different approaches towards life. Rejoice that she is not a man but a woman. She does not think like you; not only is her body different from you, her psyche is also different from you. And once you forget trying to understand her, there is no way for her to drive you crazy.

When you are with your woman, put your mind aside. Become more existential and less intellectual. Love her, dance with her, sing with her, but don't try to argue with her. As far as argument is concerned, always agree with her and you will never be at a loss. And anyway, even if you argue, finally you will have to agree with her . . .

Be a little more meditative. In fact, meditation has been discovered as a defense. It is not the discovery of women, remember. Many people have asked me, "Why have women not discovered meditation?" Why should they discover it? They have no reason to discover it; it is man's discovery. Surrounded by his meditative energy he is protected. Nobody, not even a woman, can drive him crazy.

ZEN: THE SPECIAL TRANSMISSION

D.H. Lawrence was a poet and had the quality of a mystic, but only once in a while; otherwise he was very intellectual, very argumentative . . . He was very argumentative, very much in the head, but once in a while he slipped out of the head and then there were great insights.

This must have been such an insight:

It is easy, he says, *to see why man kills the thing he loves . . .* because when you love someone, some deep instinct in you starts hankering to know the person. And remember, knowledge is always an effort to conquer, to possess. Because you want to possess the person you love you want to know all the secrets, because that is the only way to possess. If something of the person remains unknown, that unknown part is not in your possession.

That's why husbands and wives and lovers go on playing detective with each other: they want to know everything. They go on goading each other, "Open your heart. Say it, whatsoever it is. Bring it out!" That is really ugly because you may be able to know a little more about the person, but at the same time the love is dying because love can exist only between two mysteries—two persons who are mysteries to each other . . .

Never try to know. Never try to penetrate the ultimate secret of the person; leave it free. Love gives freedom—it is not a question of conquering. And the more freedom you give the more *knowing* happens—but it is not knowledge. It is a feeling, it is intuitive . . . because the woman is far more mysterious than the man, in fact the most mysterious phenomenon in the whole existence, and very delicate, very fragile. Love is always very fragile—handle it with care . . .

Never try to know the woman you love, because the moment you start the effort to know her you have already started destroying her. Soon she will be reduced to a wife, but then she is not the woman you had loved in the first place. The mystery has disappeared—and *you* are the cause of it.

THEOLOGIA MYSTICA

Three things. The first: two consciousnesses can relate in three ways. The first way is the way of I-it. That's how millions of people relate: they reduce the other to a thing. Somebody becomes a husband or a wife; then it is an I-it relationship. Then the other is not respected as a person but used as a commodity. An I-it relationship remains a relationship of possession; it is the ugliest relationship. Science functions in the world of I-it, that's why science cannot believe that there is soul, that there is God. There are only things, matter; it reduces everything to matter. I-it is the world of the scientist.

The second relationship is of I-thou. That's how lovers relate. The other is respected, respected tremendously. The other is not reduced to a thing, the other is not used; in fact both enhance each other, both enrich each other.

In the first, the I-it relationship, you take; your whole concern is how to take more and more. In the second, you give; the whole concern is how to give more and more. It is not that by giving you don't get—you get a thousandfold, but that is a different matter, that is not your motive.

The second is the world of art; the artist lives in the world of I-thou. And many religions of the world, particularly religions born out of Judaism—Judaism, Christianity,

Mohammedanism—have not gone beyond I-thou. Hence they have not been able to develop meditation—only prayer. Prayer is an I-thou relationship; God is the other. Great respect is there, but still the other is the other; there is a separation. There is closeness, but not bridged yet—very close, intimate, but not one yet.

The third relationship is really not a relationship at all. It is very paradoxical; it is neither I-it nor I-thou. The two persons don't exist in it as two, they start functioning as one. They become one organic unity, they become one orgasmic joy. That's the state the mystic lives in, and that is the state the meditator tries to attain.

WON'T YOU JOIN THE DANCE?

Love has nothing to do with relationship. It is more a state of being. You have to become a loving person. It is not a question of being in relationship. I am not saying not to be in relationship; be in as many relationships as possible because each relationship has its own uniqueness and each relationship has its own beauty and each relationship contributes its own joy and of course its own suffering, its own pain. It has its own dark nights and its own beautiful days. But that's how one grows: through darkness, through light, through sweetness, through bitterness.

NO MAN IS AN ISLAND

There is a rhythm: sometimes enjoy relationship, sometimes enjoy aloneness. Enjoying both again and again, one day you will come to the understanding that there is no need to be in a relationship and there is no need to be alone. You can be in relationship and alone and you can be alone and in relationship. Then you have become wise. Then they are not two opposites. You are not to choose, both are there; one remains in relationship and yet one remains alone. One knows one's aloneness is eternal, it cannot be broken; still one shares one's joys with the other but one doesn't feel related in any way.

When two aloneness exist together in deep love without creating any imprisonment for the other, then something immensely valuable has happened. But before that happens you will have to go through these two stages again and again; one learns only by experience. But see how the human mind is foolish: when you were in relationship, you must have been hankering to be alone and free. Now you are alone and free you are thinking that you should be sad, you should feel miserable. Again you will be in relationship and again you will think you should be alone and happy; how beautiful it was!

We go on missing the point and we go on thinking of something else which was not the case; this is how the foolish mind functions. Enjoy the moment, and whatsoever the moment makes available to you, be enriched by.

DON'T BITE MY FINGER, LOOK WHERE I'M POINTING

We go on fulfilling some holes in our being by the other, the object of love. And we go on looking into the other's eyes for our image. So when the lover or the beloved disappears, suddenly there is a hole. Because you miss the mirror in which you could see your face, you miss your face . . .

That is the real problem when lovers separate. They have invested too much in each other. That's why many people continue to remain together even though love has disappeared long ago—they cannot afford to lose the other. Husbands and wives cling, knowing well that now they are clinging to nothing; there is nothing to hold it together. Love has disappeared long ago, or maybe it had not been there in the first place. And they *know* it, they are aware of it, and they feel miserable about it, but they cannot do anything. A thousand and one times they think to separate, but the very idea of separation brings fear because the image is in the hands of the other. Once the other is no more there, you don't know who you are. Suddenly you lose your identity. You lose your soul, your self. Suddenly everything becomes messy . . .

This time start living with your aloneness. That is the hole. This time don't try to fill it. Let it be. Difficult, hard, arduous . . . you will feel very sad, depressed; let it be, but learn to live alone. I am not saying to be alone for your whole life, but first learn to live alone and then find a partner. Then the relationship will be on a totally different plane; it will not be a mirror. You can live alone, and only then can you love. Then love is no more a neurotic need. It is no more something on which you have to depend for your definition. You can be alone. You know now, without your love, who you are. Love becomes a sharing. Then, because you have, you want to share. Then love is not a need but a luxury. And when love is a luxury, it is beautiful.

DANCE YOUR WAY TO GOD

You have to remember a few things. One is that every man needs a space of his own. If you want to love a man and love him forever, and if you want him to love you, never fill his space completely. At least a part, one fourth, has to be given to him. The poor man needs that much!

And that's the difference between the feminine mind and the male mind. The feminine mind can be full with love, the woman's whole being can move into love, but a man has other loves also. The love for the woman is only one of his loves. He may also love poetry, music, painting, hunting, and a thousand and one foolishnesses. For a woman, one love is enough.

Once she finds a lover she surrounds him from everywhere. She wants to fill every part and every crevice of his being. But then the lover becomes afraid because he would like some independence; he would like to be alone somewhere, to be himself. So one fourth you have to leave if you want three fourths. This is a bargain!

Otherwise one day you will lose the whole. For a woman, love is her whole being. And this is a natural thing and has to be understood—a maturity is needed. If the woman had the capacity, she would make her lover a small child again and put him in her womb so she could surround him and have no fear of him escaping. But that cannot be done, so she creates a psychological womb around him—that is what home is.

And even if he is reading, she becomes afraid that he is more interested in reading than in her. Or if he is playing on his flute, she is afraid he is more interested in it. Everything seems to be competitive. She wants his total attention. But this is impossible for a man, and if you force him too much he will escape—or surrender, but then he will be dead.

If a man surrenders totally to a woman he is dead; a husband and no more a lover—he is a slave. Then the woman is not satisfied, because who is satisfied with a slave? She wants someone to whom she can surrender, not someone to surrender to her—he will be useless. So this is the dichotomy, the dilemma: that a woman wants the husband to be hers completely, but when he becomes hers, she is not interested.

HAMMER ON THE ROCK

And the last thing to remember always is: in the relationship of love, you always blame the other if something goes wrong. If something is not happening as it should, the other is responsible. This will destroy the whole possibility of future growth.

Remember: you are always responsible, and change yourself. And drop those qualities which create trouble. Make love a self-transformation.

MY WAY: THE WAY OF THE WHITE CLOUDS

RELATIONSHIPS, EXTRAMARITAL Once in a while just a little taste of a new woman, a new man, revives your interest in the old woman and the old man. You start thinking, "After all, she is not so bad." A little change is always good.

I am not against extramarital relationships. The people who are against them are really teaching you possessiveness in an indirect way. When I say I am not against extramarital relationships I am teaching you non-possessiveness. Just see the point: if I talk about non-possessiveness people think, "That's spiritual, that's religious—that's great!" But if I talk about extramarital relationships, the spiritual and the religious are immediately offended.

But I am saying the *same* thing. Talking about non-possessiveness is abstract, talking about extramarital relationship is concrete. And you cannot live with abstractions, you have to live with concrete life. And what wrong can it do? If a man is tired of the same woman—the same contours, the same geography, the same topography—once in a while a little bit different geography, a little bit different landscape . . . and he comes home again interested in exploring the old woman. It gives a break—a coffee break. And after each coffee break you can again get involved in the same work, the same files, and you open them and you start working . . . The coffee break helps you . . .

If people want to live together in deep intimacy, they should not be possessive. They should allow freedom. And that's what extramarital relationship is—freedom . . .

Extramarital relationships are very significant, immensely helpful to psychological growth and maturity, because when you start moving with another woman or man for a day or two, or a few days, a distance is created between you and your old lover. And that distance is very helpful. When you are exactly at the same distance as you were before you fell in love with each other, again a honeymoon is possible. That space will allow a new honeymoon. And you will become interested, again you will start reconsidering, rethinking the whole matter.

And being with the new man and the new woman, you will see that after all they are not so different. So what is the point of destroying a certain intimacy that has developed? What is the point of destroying it? And intimacy is far more fulfilling than any sexual relationship can ever be.

If two persons are really intimate they will allow absolute freedom, because they know that intimacy is far *more* beautiful, far *more* significant—they have experienced it. So any sexual relationship is just a little diversion, nothing can go wrong just because of it.

PHILOSOPHIA ULTIMA

RELATIONSHIPS, PREMARITAL Unless a man or a woman has lived in many premarital relationships there is no possibility of choosing a right partner. This is such a simple phenomenon! Unless you have experienced many women and men in your life, how can you choose who is going to be the right person to live with? But they don't allow any premarital relationships, so people start falling in love at first sight—which is nonsense. Then, of course, the same people say love is blind. First they throw acid in your eyes and then they say love is blind! You see the strategy? Don't allow boys and girls to meet and mingle with each other so that they can experience many people before they decide—don't allow them. Suffocate their sexual energy!

Boys and girls become sexually mature at thirteen and

fourteen, but they will get married after their twenty-fifth year, nearabout thirty. For these fifteen, sixteen years, when they have been sexually the *most* potent . . . because the boy is the most sexually powerful at the age of seventeen and eighteen. Never again will he have the same power, never again will he have the same youth, vigor. By the time he gets married he is already old; then you start calling him a dirty old man. Strange logic! When he is young you don't allow him; because you don't allow him his whole sexuality starts getting into his head, it becomes cerebral . . . It is in the unconscious part of the mind that it accumulates.

By the time you allow, he is so obsessed with sex that he falls in love at first sight. Just keep anybody hungry for fifteen years, and then do you think he will think, "What food to choose?" Any food, any rotten banana . . .

Premarital relationship is a very scientific phenomenon. It has to be allowed, it has to become part of human rights. It should be one of the basic rights of every human being to have love relationships before one decides for some intimacy, to live with somebody for a longer period. I will not say for your whole life, because who knows?—life is a big thing!—but for a longer period. Tomorrow you may find a far more beautiful woman, a far more beautiful man; then your intelligence will say that it is better to choose. Then why go on being tortured by your past? Remain free for the future, open to the future. So I say only for a longer period, then you decide.

When you have enjoyed many relationships you will be able to choose, you will be able to judge what kind of woman or man suits you, what kind of woman or man is a nourishment.

I am all for premarital relationships. Without them man will remain insane.

PHILOSOPHIA ULTIMA

RELATIVITY Philosophy idolizes the absolute. Bradley, Hegel, Shankara, they idolize the absolute and they deny the relative. The relative means it is illusory; the absolute is true and whatsoever is relative is illusory . . .

Science emphasizes the relative. Albert Einstein discovered

the theory of relativity. Jainism has a little bit of the scientific attitude, hence Jainas were the first to contemplate on the theory of relativity. Albert Einstein without knowing it is a Jaina! Before Albert Einstein, twenty-five centuries before him Jainas discovered *sayadvada; sayadvada* means the theory of relativity. Einstein says everything is relative. *Sayadvada* can literally be translated as "perhapsism": everything is just a perhaps; nothing is absolutely certain, just a perhaps.

If you asked Mahavira, "Does God exist?" he would say, "Perhaps." If you asked him, "Are you absolutely sure about it?" he would say, "Perhaps." He would never budge from his perhaps. Everything is only a perhaps, because everything is relative. Nothing can be said absolutely, certainly, categorically. It depends, and one thing can be seen from many standpoints.

Sayadvada—"perhapsism"—has seven standpoints. If you ask about God, Mahavira will give you seven statements. He will confuse you more than you were ever confused before! He will say, "Perhaps God is"—his first statement. "Perhaps God is not"—his second statement. "Perhaps God is both"—his third statement. "Perhaps God is and is inexpresible"—his fourth. "Perhaps God is not and is inexpressible"—fifth. "Perhaps God is and is not both, *and* also is inexpressible." You may have come to him with a little bit of understanding for or against, but he will destroy all your standpoints. He will give you the whole perspective, all the standpoints.

That's what Albert Einstein has done, of course in a more scientific way; Mahavira's way is far more philosophical. Albert Einstein used to say, "At the most only one dozen people in the whole world understand what I am saying." Not that there are not many more intelligent people in the world, but the very idea of relativity has something fundamentally wrong about it.

Something can be relative only if you accept the absolute. If you *don't* accept the absolute, then what do you mean by relative? Even the meaning of the word "relative" loses all significance; it loses meaning. Relative simply means that which is not absolute, but what is absolute? According to

Albert Einstein there is nothing absolute, all is relative. And according to the absolutists there is nothing relative, all is absolute. Then what do you mean by absolute? The very term has meaning only in contrast to the relative . . .

Never choose, remain choicelessly aware and accept life as it is. Don't impose any choice of your own. The absolute is there, the relative is there. Your mind is relative, but your consciousness is absolute. Your body changes, your mind changes—they are like a wheel—but your witnessing consciousness is like an axle; it remains always the same, never changing. It is on that axle that the mind-and-the-body wheel moves. And they are not against each other; they are supporting each other, they are complementary to each other.

I AM THAT

A man who was frightened of dentists delayed seeing one until he had only six teeth left in his mouth.

The dentist examined him and said "These teeth are finished. Let me pull them out. Let me do root canal work and all those other things that I do, and you'll have a complete new set of choppers in your mouth. Beautiful you'll look, and chewing problems you'll no longer have."

The man was dubious. "I'm a physical coward, Doctor. I can't stand pain."

"Who said anything about pain? I'm a painless dentist!"

"You say it, but how do I know if it's true?"

"Not to worry" the dentist said. "I did a job exactly like this for another man. I'll give you his name and you can phone him right now. Ask if I cause him any pain."

So the man telephoned George Kaplan in Brooklyn.

"Mr. Kaplan" he said "My name is Al Goldstein. You don't know me, but I'm in the office of your dentist and he says he did a big job on your teeth. Is that correct?"

"Correct it is" Kaplan agreed.

"Okay" said Goldstein. "Now I want you to tell me the honest truth. Did it hurt? Tell me, yes or no?"

"A yes or no I can't give you" said Kaplan. "But I can give you a fr'instance. Every Sunday I go rowing in Prospect Park."

"So?" said Goldstein.

"So" said Kaplan, "Our dentist finished with me in

December. Now it's June and it's Sunday, and as usual I'm in my rowboat on the Prospect Park lake. Suddenly, one of the oars slips away. When I reach over to grab it, my balls get caught in the oarlock. Would you believe it, Mr. Goldstein, it was the first time in six months that my teeth didn't hurt!"

That's what the theory of relativity is.

                                        UNIO MYSTICA, Vol. II

RELAXATION   First, the nature of activity and the hidden currents in it have to be understood, otherwise no relaxation is possible. Even if you want to relax, it will be impossible if you have not observed, watched, realized the nature of your activity, because activity is not a simple phenomenon.

Many people would like to relax, but they cannot relax. Relaxation is like a flowering: you cannot force it. You have to understand the whole phenomenon—why you are active so much, why so much occupation with activity, why you are obsessed with it.

Remember two words: one is "action", the other is "activity". Action is not activity; activity is not action. Their natures are diametrically opposite. Action is when the situation demands it, you act, you respond. Activity is when the situation doesn't matter, it is not a response; you are so restless within that the situation is just an excuse to be active.

Action comes out of a silent mind—it is the most beautiful thing in the world. Activity comes out of a restless mind—it is the ugliest. Action is when it has a relevance. Activity is irrelevant. Action is moment to moment, spontaneous. Activity is loaded with the past. It is not a response to the present moment, rather, it is pouring your restlessness, which you have been carrying from the past, into the present. Action is creative. Activity is very very destructive—it destroys you, it destroys others . . .

This is the subtle point to be understood: activity has to go, but not action—and both are easy. You can drop both and escape to the Himalayas, that's easy. Or, the other thing is easy: you can continue in the activities, and force yourself every morning, or every evening, for a few minutes to relax.

You don't understand the complexity of the human mind, the mechanism of it. Relaxation is a state. You cannot force it. You simply drop the negativities, the hindrances, and it comes, it bubbles up by itself . . .

What is relaxation? It is a state of affairs where your energy is not moving anywhere, not to the future, not to the past—it is simply there with you. In the silent pool of your own energy, in the warmth of it, you are enveloped. *This* moment is all. There is no other moment. Time stops—then there is relaxation. If time is there, there is no relaxation. Simply, the clock stops; there is no time. This moment is all . . .

Relaxation means this moment is more than enough, more than can be asked or expected. Nothing to ask, more than enough, more than you can desire—then the energy never moves anywhere.

It becomes a placid pool. In your own energy, you dissolve. This moment is relaxation. Relaxation is neither of the body nor of the mind, relaxation is of the total.

That's why Buddhas go on saying, "Become desireless," because they know that if there is desire, you cannot relax. They go on saying, "Bury the dead," because if you are too much concerned with the past, you cannot relax. They go on saying, "Enjoy this very moment."

Jesus says, "Look at the lilies. Consider the lilies in the field—they toil not and they are more beautiful, their splendor is greater than King Solomon's. They are arrayed in a more beautiful aroma than King Solomon was ever. Look, consider the lilies!"

What is he saying? He is saying, "Relax! You need not toil for it—in fact everything is provided." Jesus says, "If he looks after the birds of the air, animals, wild animals, trees and plants, then why are you worried? Will he not look after you?" This is relaxation. Why are you so worried about the future? Consider the lilies, watch the lilies, and become like lilies—then you relax. Relaxation is not a posture; relaxation is a total transformation of your energy.

Energy can have two dimensions. One is motivated, going somewhere, a goal somewhere; this moment is only a means and the goal is to be achieved somewhere else. This is one dimension of your energy, this is the dimension of activity, goal-oriented— then everything is a means; some-how it has to be done and you have to reach the goal, then you will relax. But for this type of energy the goal never comes, because this type of energy goes on changing every present moment into a means for something else, into the future. The goal always remains on the horizon. You go on running, but the distance remains the same.

No, there is another dimension of energy: that dimension is unmotivated celebration. The goal is here, now; the goal is not somewhere else. In fact, you are the goal. In fact, there is no other fulfillment than that of this moment—consider the lilies. When you are the goal and when the goal is not in the future, when there is nothing to be achieved, rather, you are just celebrating it, then you have already achieved it, it is there. This is relaxation, unmotivated energy . . .

Remember, activity is goal-oriented, action is not. Action is an overflowing of energy; action is in this moment, a response, unprepared, unrehearsed. The whole existence meets you, confronts you, and a response simply comes. The birds are singing and you start singing—it is not an activity. Suddenly it happens. Suddenly you find it is happening, that you have started humming—this is action.

And if you become more and more involved in action, and less and less occupied in activity, your life will change and it will become a deep relaxation. Then you "do" but you remain relaxed. A Buddha is never tired. Why? Because he is not a doer. Whatsoever he has he gives, he overflows.

TANTRA: THE SUPREME UNDERSTANDING

RELICS Grow in consciousness and every cell is penetrated. And the moment your consciousness touches the cells, it is different. The very quality changes. A man is asleep; the sun rises and the man is awakened. Is he the same man who was asleep? Is his sleep and awakening the same? There was a closed, dead bud, and the sun has risen, and the bud opens and becomes a flower. Is this flower the same? Something new has penetrated. An aliveness, a capacity to grow and blossom, has appeared. A bird was just asleep, as if dead, as if just dead matter, but the sun comes up and the bird is on the wing. Is it the same bird? It is a different phenomenon. Something has touched and the bird has become alive. Everything was silent, and now everything is singing. The morning is a song.

The same phenomenon happens inside the cells of a Buddha's body. It is known as *Buddha-kaya*—the body of an enlightened one, of a Buddha. It is a different body. It is not the same body as you have, not even the same body as Gautam had before he became a Buddha.

Buddha is just on the verge of death, and someone asks him, "Are you dying? Then where will you be?" Buddha says, "The body that was born will die. But there is another body—the *Buddha-kaya,* the body of a Buddha, which is neither born, nor can it die. I have left that body which was given to me, that came to me from my parents. Just as a snake leaves the old body every year, I have left it. Now there is the *Buddha-kaya,* the Buddha-body."

What does he mean? *Your* body can become a Buddha-body. When your consciousness reaches to every cell, the very quality of your being changes, becomes transmuted, because then every cell is alive, conscious, enlightened . . .

Buddhists have preserved some bones of Buddha. People think they are just superstitious. They are not, because those are not ordinary bones. They are not! The cells, the particles, the electrons of those bones, have known something which happens rarely. In Kashmir, in a mosque, one hair of Mohammed is preserved. That is no ordinary hair. It is not just superstition. That hair has known something.

Just try to understand it in this way: a flower which has never known any sunrise and a flower which has known, encountered the sun, are not the same, cannot be the same. The flower that has never known a sunrise has never known a light to rise in it, because it rises when the sun rises. That flower is just dead—a potentiality. It has never known its own spirit. A flower which has seen the sunrise has also seen something rise in itself. It has known a soul. Now the flower is not just a flower. It has known a deep stirring inside. Something has stirred; something has become alive in it.

So the hair of Mohammed is a different thing; it has a different quality. It has known a man, it has been with a man who has an inner sun, an inner light. This hair has taken a deep bath in something mysterious which rarely happens. To be established in this inner light is the only lamp worth taking to the altar of the deity. Nothing else will do.

THE ULTIMATE ALCHEMY, Vol. II

RELIGION I teach the total man. One of the greatest problems that humanity is facing today is the fragmentary man. For centuries we have divided life into compartments. We have tried to make those compartments absolutely separate, so much so that one expert, one specialist knows nothing about anything else. He becomes very much informed, knowledgeable about one aspect of life at the cost of the whole. His vision becomes lopsided.

They define science as knowing more and more about less and less. The problem now is how to make all these experts understand each other, how to create bridges, because man is not compartmentalized; man is one organic unity. Life is not divided, but we look at it *as if* it is divided; that "as if" is a fiction.

A man is not only a father; he is also a husband, he is also a son, he is also an uncle, he is also a brother. He is so many things! You cannot define him by labeling him as father, as son, as brother. That will be absolutely unjustified and absurd. A man has a multi-dimensional being.

Religion, in fact, is not one-dimensional. Religion is a very comprehensive view of the whole of life.

I am not a politician, and I am sticking to my pursuit—but religion is multi-dimensional, religion *has* to be all-inclusive. A politician may not be able to make any statement about religion, because he is working in a one-dimensional pursuit. Politics is one-dimensional, science is one-dimensional, art is one-dimensional, philosophy is one-dimensional. That's where religion is totally different from all pursuits. It is not one of the pursuits; it is a vision that includes all. Hence a religious man has to be aware about the whole.

That's why sometimes I make statements about art, about science, about politics and about so many things. But up to now religious people have also thought that their pursuit is one-dimensional. After me they will have to redefine religion! I don't believe in that definition. And I would like to say that I am strictly sticking to my pursuit, but my pursuit is not *one* of the pursuits—it includes all.

Religion is like a bird's-eye view: the hills, the rivers, the trees, the people, all are included. That's the beauty of religion: it is not a specialized field.

GUIDA SPIRITUALE

Religion arises in wonder and awe. If you can feel wonder, if you can feel awe, you are religious. Not by reading the Bible or the Gita or the Koran, but by experiencing awe. When you see the sky full of stars, do you feel a dance in your heart? Do you see a song arising in your being? Do you feel a communion with the stars? Then you are religious. You are not religious by going to the church or by going to the temple and repeating borrowed prayers which have nothing to do with your heart, which are just head affairs.

Religion is a love affair—a love affair with existence.

ZEN: THE SPECIAL TRANSMISSION

What is religion? It is not the howling of the wolves at the moon, but that's what it has become to the masses. If the masses are right, then animals have a great religious sense—wolves howling, dogs barking at the moon, at the distant, at the faraway.

Paul Tillich has defined religion as the ultimate concern. It is exactly the opposite: it is the immediate concern, not the ultimate concern. In fact, the immediate is the only ultimate there is.

Religion is not a desire for the distant, a curiosity for the faraway. It is an inquiry into one's own being.

TAKE IT EASY, Vol. I

There are religions—Hinduism, Christianity, Buddhism, Jainism—and many more. But they are religions, not *the* religion. They are the reflections of the moon in many kinds of minds. They are not the real moon.

The moon is one but it can be reflected in millions of lakes. Reflections differ, but the reflected is one.

Mind is a mirror. When religion is reflected through the mind a Hinduism is born, or a Mohammedanism or a Jainism.

When the religion is not a reflected one, when one comes

face to face with reality without any mind whatsoever, when there is no mind between you and the truth, then there is born *the* religion.

Hassidism is *the* religion. Sufism is *the* religion. Zen is *the* religion.

THE TRUE SAGE

The word "religion" is very beautiful. It comes from a root *religere*, which means to rejoin, to reunite. With whom? With yourself, with the source of your being. And why reunite? Because with the source you are already united— it is a reunion. It is not that you are reaching to the source for the first time; otherwise, from where will you come? You have come from the source. Deep down you are still in the source. Just on the periphery, as if the branches have forgotten about the roots . . . not that they are broken from the roots, because then they cannot live. They have simply forgotten. In their ego, in their height in the sky, with the moon, in their romance, they have completely forgotten that they have roots underground—which nourish them, which sustain them, without which they cannot exist for a single moment. And all this greenery, and all these flowers, and all these fruits, will simply disappear like dreams once they are cut from the root. That's how it happens to man. You move in the branches, farther away from the roots. You come to many flowers. You are enchanted. The world is beautiful all around you. You completely forget about the roots. But it is not that you are uprooted. Forgetfulness is just forgetfulness.

That is the meaning of religion: to reunite, to remember again. This word "remember" is also beautiful. It means to become the member again, re-member—to become part of the source again, to go to the source and become the member again of it.

Religion is reuniting with your own source. Religion is remembering, becoming again a part of the organic unity that you are. It is nothing to do with others. The ego is always concerned with the others, this way or that. When you become totally concerned with yourself, ego simply drops. There is no point for it to exist.

Alone you have no ego. Try it! When you are sitting, totally

alone, not even thinking of others, is there any ego left?
There is no possibility. The ego needs two to exist. Just like
a bridge cannot exist if there are not two banks to the river;
the bridge needs two to be supported. The ego exists as a
bridge between you and the other. So, in fact, the ego is not
in you—it is just between you and the other.

This is something to be remembered always: the ego is
not in you. It cannot be there. It is always between you and
the other— the husband and wife, the friend, the enemy—
always the other. So when you go deep inside, there is no
ego. In your total loneliness, ego simply drops. That's why
ego goes on playing tricks. Even if you start searching and
seeking for truth, the ego says, "Help others"; the ego says,
"transform others". And religion is again missed. It becomes
a mission . . .

Religion is not a mission. You need not force anybody
towards it. When the urge arises, it arises. It cannot be artificially created. Nobody can create an artificial religious urge.
That is impossible. It is just like artificially creating a sexual urge in a small child. Even if a child asks questions about
sex, he is not interested in sex. Even if he asks from where
babies are coming, you misunderstand him if you think that
he is interested in sex. He is simply curious about babies,
from where they are coming. He is not interested in sex at
all. And don't start teaching him about sex, because he will
be simply bored. It will be nonsense to him, because when
the urge is not there, when he is not sexually mature,
anything you say about sex just goes above his head.

And the same happens with the spiritual urge. It is very
similar to the sexual urge. One comes to a maturity, a
spiritual maturity, something has ripened within you, and
then the search starts. Nobody can enforce it. But all the
religions have tried to enforce it, and they have killed the
very possibility of the urge.

The world is so irreligious because of the missionaries,
the priests. The world is so irreligious because you have
taught too much religion, without even thinking whether the
urge exists there or not. People are fed up with your
teachings. Churches simply bore. And beautiful words like
"God", "prayer", "love", "meditation", have become ugly. The
greatest words have become the dirtiest—because of the

missionaries. They have been forcing these beautiful words on you. And when something beautiful is forced, it becomes ugly. You can participate in beauty, but you cannot be forced towards it—then it becomes violence.

Religion is not concerned with other. It is concerned with you, absolutely with you. Religion is personal. It is not a social phenomenon. In fact, there cannot be any sociology of religion; there can only be a psychology. Society is a totally different matter—where peripheries meet. Religion is when you are so alone that there is nobody left to be met. In that total, virgin aloneness, the suprememost ecstasy is born. But you have to come to a ripeness.

Remember, ripeness is all. before it nothing can be done. And you may be thinking that you are ready, or somebody else may be thinking that he is ready; your curiosity may give you a wrong feeling, a notion that you are ready—but readiness only means that you are ready to stake your life; otherwise it is not a readiness.

Religion is higher than life because life is life with others, life is a relationship, and religion is a non-relationship. It is higher than life. It is the capacity to be alone. It is total independence from the other. Unless you are ready to sacrifice life to it, unless you are ready to die completely as you have been up to now, you are not ready. In that readiness, a small message can become so powerful that it can transform you.

Religion is not concerned with others. And, finally, religion is not concerned with scriptures, words. Wise words are there, but for those words you are not the target; they were never addressed to you. Krishna talked to Arjuna; it was a personal dialogue. Jesus talks to his disciples—a small group of disciples, a personal dialogue—he knows everybody; he knows what he is saying; he knows to whom he is saying it. But the Bible becomes dead, the Gita becomes dead.

Religion is not like a broadcast on the radio. You don't know to whom you are talking. In the air you talk. The face of the listener is not there. The center of the listener is not there. There is nobody. It may be, it is possible, that nobody is listening to the broadcast and you are talking in a vacuum. Religion is like a personal letter. You write it to somebody and *only* to somebody; it is meant for somebody. That's why

I have never tried to write anything—except letters. Unless you are here, alive centers, receptive, listening, I cannot say anything. It is impossible. To whom to say it? It is not a dead word. When there is a listener, the dialogue becomes alive; then it has significance which no scripture can ever have.

So everybody has to seek alive Masters. You can read the Gita—it is beautiful; you can read the Bible—it is wonderful; but they are pieces of literature—beautiful as literature, poetry, prose, but not as religion. Religion happens only between two persons: one who knows, and one who does not know but is ready to know. Suddenly religion is born.

UNTIL YOU DIE

See also Cult, 1st Series
         Rajneeshism

RELIGIOUSNESS   What I am teaching is not a religion but a religiousness. A religion is a creed, a dogma, an ideology; it is intellectual. You can be convinced about it—arguments can be given, proofs can be supplied—you can be silenced. Argumentation is a kind of violence, a very subtle violence. It is an attempt to manipulate you, control you, enslave you. And all the religions have been doing that for thousands of years; it is a subtle strategy to create mental slavery.

What I am doing here has nothing to do with religion at all. It is a kind of religiousness: no belief, no dogma, no church. It is a love affair—you cannot be convinced of it . . . Nobody can convince anybody else about his love affair. It is far deeper than the intellect, it is of the heart, and the heart knows no arguments, no proofs; it is simply so . . .

The people who have gathered around me are lovers, not intellectually convinced of what I am saying but *existentially* convinced of what I am. It is a question not to be decided by the mind but something to be felt . . .

They know perfectly well that it is not their intellects that have made them part of my Buddhafield, it is their hearts. Something has started ringing in their hearts—a bell has started ringing in their hearts. Their hearts have felt a new release of energy, a new dance; a new melody has been heard—not a new argument but a new melody. Their hearts were asleep, now they are awake. Their hearts were like a desert, now the spring has come, now roses are flowering, bees are humming. Their inner beings are transformed. It is religiousness.

Religiousness happens only when a Buddha or a Krishna or a Mahavira or a Christ is alive. When Christ dies there is religion. Religion is the corpse of religiousness; it only *looks* like the real person. When a person dies he looks exactly like he was when he was alive, just something very small is missing—he is no longer breathing—otherwise everything is perfectly good! . . .

When religiousness dies, religion is born. Religiousness breathes, religion is a corpse. But many people feel good with religion, in fact the majority; ninety-nine point nine percent of people feel good with religion, because it is not dangerous at all. What can the corpse do to you? You can do anything to the corpse, but the corpse cannot do anything to you; the corpse in is your hands.

But when religion is alive and breathing—that's what I mean by religiousness—then you are *possessed* by it, you cannot possess it. You cannot possess Buddha or Lao Tzu or Zarathustra, you cannot possess Bahauddin, Jalaluddin, Al-Hillaj Mansoor—no, that is not possible. These are people who have known the ultimate freedom, how can you possess them? They cannot fulfill your expectations, they cannot move according to you; they will have their own way. If it suits you, *you* have to be with them, you will not be able to force them to be with you; there is no possible way.

The truth cannot be with you—*you* have to be with the truth. But the lie is in your hands: you can manipulate it, you can make it look the way you want it to look, you can give it colors, you can cut it, you can give it form and shape, you can make it fit with your unconscious life. You can be a Hindu; it does not disturb your consciousness. You can be a Mohammedan; it makes no transformation in you. You can be a Buddhist with no trouble at all, with no danger, with no insecurity. But to be with a Buddha is to walk on fire! All that is non-essential in you will be burned and only the essence will survive—and the essential is very small in you. So much of you is false, and it is going to die.

To be with a Buddha means a death. Life comes afterwards, but death comes first. Resurrection first is not possible; it can follow only if crucifixion has happened—it comes after the crucifixion. To be with a Master is to be ready to die and ready to be born anew.

Religion is consolation, conformation. Religiousness is revolution, rebellion.

COME, COME, YET AGAIN COME

REMEDY   See Methods, 2nd Series

REMEMBERING   The word "enlightenment" is beautiful. We come from the source, the ultimate source of light—we are small rays of that sun—and howsoever far away we may have gone, our nature remains the same. Nobody can go against his real nature: you can forget about it, but you cannot lose it. Hence "attaining it" is not the right expression; it is not attained, it is only remembered.

That's why Buddha had called his method sammasati: sammasati means right remembrance of that which is already there. Nanak, Kabir, Raidas, they have all called it surati; surati means remembering the forgotten, but not the lost. Whether you remember or not it is there—it is there exactly the same. You can keep your eyes closed to it, it is there; you can open your eyes, it is there. You can keep it behind your back, it is there; you can take a one-hundred-and-eighty-degree turn and see it, it is there. It is the same.

George Gurdjieff used to call his method "self-remembering". Nothing has to be achieved, nothing at all, but only to be discovered. And the discovery is needed because we go on gathering dust on our mirrors. The mirror is there covered by dust. Remove the dust, and the mirror starts reflecting the stars, the beyond.

Krishnamurti calls it awareness, alertness, attentiveness. These are different expressions for the same phenomenon. They are to remind you that you are not to go anywhere, not to be somebody else, you just have to find out who you are. And the finding is not difficult because it is your nature—just a little reshuffling inside, a little cleaning . . .

COME, COME, YET AGAIN COME

Think over the word "remembering." It really means becoming part again of the whole, becoming a member again of the family that existence is: "re-member". It means that we suddenly learn the language that we had forgotten. It is like a name forgotten: you see somebody on the road, you recognize him, you feel that you know who he is, but you cannot remember his name. You have forgotten, although you can remember this much: that you have known him before. You say, "His name is just on the tip of my tongue." But if it is on the tip of your tongue, then why is it not coming? You feel absolutely certain, the name is just on the tip of your tongue. And then you try hard: the harder you try, the more difficult it becomes, because whenever you try to do something very hard you become tense, you become closed. Your consciousness becomes narrower and narrower. And it becomes more and more difficult in such tension, in such anxiety, to remember.

Then you drop the whole project, thinking that it is not possible. You forget all about it. You start listening to music or you go into the garden and you sit under a tree, or you start doing something else, sipping tea or talking to somebody . . . and then suddenly from nowhere the name surfaces.

This is the whole secret of enlightenment: it happens in relaxation, it happens in a deep state of rest. Surrender means relaxing. Ego means tension, carrying a load of anxiety, and unnecessarily.

GUIDA SPIRITUALE

It is an ancient habit; for many, many lives you have practiced it. You have put so much energy into it, into forgetting yourself. You remember money, you remember others, you remember the world. To remember all these things— all these things which Taoists call "the ten thousand and one things" . . . If you want to remember these ten thousand and one things, you will have to forget yourself, because your eyes will be focused on things, on people, on the world, and of course you will fall in the shadow.

It is a long, long habit—just a habit. You are there; you can turn in. But turning in seems to be difficult because your neck has become paralyzed. For how many lives have you remained in this forgetfulness? Now suddenly, you want to remember.

At the most, for one or two seconds you can remember; again you will forget. But those one or two seconds open the door of hope. Don't be worried: if you can remember only for a single moment, that's enough, the key is with you. You are never given more than a single moment at a single time; you are never given two moments together. If you can remember for a single moment, that's enough, the key is there; now you can work it out. After this moment is gone another moment will be given to you, and you know how to be alert, aware, in a single moment—be alert and aware in that.

THE GUEST

It is very significant to understand the word "remembrance". The whole religion is contained in that small word. God is not lost but only forgotten. We have only to remember him. It is not a question of seeking and searching. He is already here, he is with us, he is our very life, our very being. We cannot lose him, there is no way to lose him. The only possibility is that we can forget all about him and he is so close that it is very easy to forget him. There is no distance, hence we become oblivious.

All meditations, all prayers, all methods developed down the ages are nothing but devices to make you remember that which you have forgotten. The moment you remember it you cannot believe how for so long you remained in darkness while the light was waiting within you. How did it happen in the first place that you remained a beggar when the whole kingdom of God was yours? It is the ultimate puzzle, with no solution. But it is a fact that we have forgotten.

Buddha was asked again and again, "*How* have we forgotten?" He said, "Don't ask that, ask how to remember." When you have remembered then you can enquire how you forgot because nobody knows how we have forgotten. But there are methods to remember. And that is the real thing.

Sannyas means now it is going to be a twenty-four-hour-a-day remembrance, in every possible way. Seeing a flower, remember God.

EIGHTY-FOUR THOUSAND POEMS

RENUNCIATION There are foolish people who renounce the world in search of silence. The world does not disturb you; what disturbs is your mind—and they don't renounce the mind. When a Hindu becomes a monk he still remains a Hindu. Do you see the absurdity? He has renounced the Hindu society, but he still carries the idea of being a Hindu! If you have renounced the Hindu society . . . this idea of being a Hindu was given by the same society, how can you carry it?

Somebody becomes a Christian monk, but he still remains a Christian—a Catholic, a Protestant . . . The mind is so stupid; if you look at its stupidities you will be surprised, amazed! How can you be a Catholic if you have renounced the world? But people renounce the world, they don't renounce the mind—and the mind is a byproduct of the world! . . .

I don't teach you to renounce the world, I teach you to renounce the *mind*. And that's what is meant by this immensely beautiful Zen saying:

> *Sitting silently,*
> *doing nothing,*
> *The spring comes and the grass grows by itself.*

All that is needed on your part is just to be absolutely silent. And that's exactly the meaning of the word *upanishad*: sitting silently, doing nothing, by the side of the Master— that means by the side of spring—allowing the spring to possess you, to take you along with it like a tidal wave.

Your inner being is not something that has to be developed; it is already perfect. No spiritual development is needed, it only has to be discovered. And once silence falls over you, you start discovering it. It is the noise and the dust that the mind creates that goes on hindering the discovery.

I AM THAT

REPENT The word "repent" has to be understood; it has been misunderstood down the ages. "Repent" is repeated again and again by Jesus; he says again and again, "Repent! Repent! Because the end of the world is close by." From the

Greek, when Jesus' statements were translated into English, a great misfortune happened—too many words. This word "repent" is one that has suffered the most. It is a translation of a Greek word *metanoia; metanoia* means turning in, *metanoia* means meditation. "Repent" also means return—return to the source. It has nothing to do with the idea of repentance that you have been taught in your churches, that your priests have been telling you. "Repent" has nothing to do with repentance. "Repent" means: Turn in! Return back! Come to the source of your being! Come to the very core of your being!

THE FISH IN THE SEA IS NOT THIRSTY

REPRESSION Repression is not the way, cannot be the way. All that you have repressed is waiting for its opportunity. It has simply gone into the unconscious; it can come back any moment. Any provocation and it will surface. You are not free of it. Repression is not the way to freedom. Repression is a far worse kind of bondage than indulgence, because through indulgence one becomes tired sooner or later, but through repression one never becomes tired.

See the point: indulgence is *bound* to tire you and bore you; sooner or later you will start thinking how to get rid of it all. But repression will keep things alive. Because you have not *lived*—how can you be bored? You have not lived— how can you be fed up? Because you have not lived, the charm continues, the hypnosis continues. Deep down, it waits.

And the people who indulge are in a way normal compared to the people who repress. The repressing person becomes pathological; the indulgent is at least natural. That's how nature has made you, but to repress is to become unnatural. It is easy to go from lower nature to higher nature. It is very difficult to go from being unnatural to higher nature. Buddha calls the ultimate truth "ultimate nature"— *ais dhammo sanantano*. This is the ultimate nature, the ultimate law, he declared. What is the ultimate law? the eternal, the undying, the pure consciousness.

THE BOOK OF THE BOOKS, Vol. II

Gurdjieff used to say that all your centers are overlapping

each other, are misplaced, are interfering with each other, are trespassing, and you don't know what is what. Each center in its own functioning is beautiful, but when it starts interfering into somebody else's functioning, then there is great difficulty; then the whole system goes neurotic.

For example, if your sex center functions as a sex center, it is perfectly good. But people have been repressing it so much that in many people the sex center does not exist in their genitals, it has moved into their head. This is what overlapping is. Now they make love through the head— hence the great importance of pornography, visualization. Even while making love to your woman you may be thinking of some beautiful actress—that you are making love to her. Then suddenly you become interested in making love to your woman. In fact, your own woman is non-existential. It is a kind of masturbation. You are not making love to her, you are making love to somebody else who is not there. You go on fantasizing in the head.

Religious repression has disturbed all your centers. It is very difficult even to see that your centers are separate. And functioning in its own field, each center is perfectly right. When it interferes with another field, then problems arise. Then there is a confusion of your totality. Then you don't know what is what.

Sex can be transformed when it is confined to its own center, it cannot be transformed from the head. It has created a pseudo center in the head . . .

Watch and observe. Let the head function as reason, let the heart function as feeling, let the sex center function as sex. Let everything function in its own way. Don't allow mechanisms to mix into each other, otherwise you will have corrupted instincts.

When instinct is natural, untabooed, spontaneous, without any inhibition, there is a clarity in your body, a harmony in your body. There is a humming sound in your organism.

SUFIS: THE PEOPLE OF THE PATH, Vol. II

Kabir has looked deep into the human mind and its workings, its subtle cunning ways. And he has found exactly the whole process of inner alchemy. If you repress, this is how things happen.

I pulled back my sexual longings,
and now I discover that I'm angry a lot.

If you repress sex you will become angry; the whole energy that was becoming sex will become anger. And it is better to be sexual than to be angry. In sex at least there is something of love; in anger there is only pure violence and nothing else. If sex is repressed, the person becomes violent—either to others he will be violent, or to himself. These are the two possibilities: either he will become a sadist and will torture others, or he will become a masochist and will torture himself. But torture he will.

Do you know, down the ages, the soldiers have not been allowed to have sexual relationships? Why? Because if soldiers are allowed to have sexual relationships they don't gather enough anger in them, enough violence in them. Their sex becomes a release, they become soft, and a soft person cannot fight. Starve the soldier of sex and he is bound to fight better. In fact, his violence will be a substitute for his sexuality.

And Sigmund Freud is again right when he says that all our weapons are nothing but phallic symbols: the sword, the knife, the bayonet—they are nothing but phallic symbols. The soldier has not been allowed to enter into somebody's body, into some woman's body. Now he is going crazy to enter; now he can do anything. A great perverted desire has entered into his being now. Repressed sex—he would like to enter into somebody's body through a bayonet, through a sword . . .

Down the ages, the soldier was forced to repress his sexual desires . . .

Just allow all the armies of the world to be sexually satisfied and there will be peace. Just allow people sexual satisfaction, and there will be less Hindu-Mohammedan riots, less Christian and Mohammedan crusades—all that nonsense will disappear—both cannot exist together.

Kabir is exactly right. He says:

I pulled back my sexual longings,
and now I discover that I'm angry a lot.

THE FISH IN THE SEA IS NOT THIRSTY

Repression is to live a life that you were not meant to live. Repression is to do things which you never wanted to do. Repression is to be the fellow that you are not.

Repression is a way to destroy yourself.

Repression is suicide—very slow of course, but a very certain, slow poisoning.

Expression is life; repression is suicide.

This is the Tantra message: Don't live a repressed life, otherwise you will not live at all. Live a life of expression, creativity, joy. Live the way God wanted you to live; live the natural way. And don't be afraid of the priests. Listen to your instincts, listen to your body, listen to your heart, listen to your intelligence. Depend on yourself, go wherever your spontaneity takes you, and you will never be at a loss. And going spontaneously with your natural life, one day you are bound to arrive at the doors of the divine.

Your nature is God within you. The pull of that nature is God's pull within you. Don't listen to the poisoners, listen to the pull of nature. Yes, nature is not enough—there is a higher nature too—but the higher comes through the lower. The lotus grows out of the mud. Through the body grows the soul. Through sex grows *samadhi*.

Remember, through food grows consciousness. In the East we have said: *annam Brahm*: food is God. What type of assertion is this that food is God? God grows out of food: the lowest is linked with the highest, the shallowest is linked with the deepest.

Now the priests have been teaching you to repress the lower. And they are very logical. Only they have forgotten one thing—that God is illogical. They are very logical and it appeals to you. That's why you have listened down the ages and followed them. It appeals to reason that if you want to attain to the higher, don't listen to the lower—it looks logical. If you want to go high, then you cannot go low; then don't go low, go high—it is very rational. The only trouble is that God is not rational.

THE TANTRA VISION, Vol. II

See also Sexuality

REPRODUCTION   The life of each one of us shows that

we do not know anything about life at all. Otherwise, how come there is so much despair, so much misery, so much anxiety?

I say the same thing as far as our knowledge of sex is concerned. We do not know anything about it. Perhaps you will not agree. You will argue, "It is quite possible we do not know anything about the soul or God, but how can you say we do not know anything about sex?" You will probably reply that you have a wife and that you have children. And yet I dare to tell you that you do not know anything about sex although it may be difficult for you to agree with what I say. You may have gone through sexual experiences, but you know no more about sex than an animal. To go through a process mechanically is not enough to know it . . .

Anybody can marry. Anybody can produce children. It has nothing to do with an understanding of sex. Animals procreate, but it does not mean they know anything about sex.

The truth of the matter is that sex has not been studied scientifically. No philosophy or science of sex has developed because everyone believed he knew about sex. No one has seen the need for a scripture of sex. This is a very grave mistake by mankind.

The day we fully develop a scripture, a science, a complete system of thought on sex, we will produce a new race of humans. Then, there won't be the production of such ugly, insipid, lame and feeble human beings. Sick, weak, dull men won't be seen any more on this earth . . .

We never go deeply into the subject of sex, never reflect upon the practice of sex, never try to get to the bottom of it, never meditate on it—because of the delusion that we know everything there is to know about it. When everybody already knows everything, what need is there to ponder the subject? And in the same breath, I wish to tell you that there is no deeper mystery, no deeper secret, no deeper subject than sex—in this world and in life itself.

FROM SEX TO SUPERCONSCIOUSNESS

See also Recreation

RESOLUTION   Buddha says:

Do what you have to do
Resolutely . . .

But by "resolution" he does not mean will, as it ordinarily means in the dictionaries. Buddha is compelled to use your words, but he gives a new meaning to his words. By "resolution" he means out of a resolved heart—not out of will power but out of a resolved heart. And remember, he emphasizes the word "heart", not "mind". Will power is part of the mind. A resolved heart is a heart without problems, a heart which is no more divided, a heart which has come to a state of stillness, silence. That's what he calls a resolved heart.

Do what you have to do
Resolutely, with all your heart.

Remember the emphasis on the heart. Mind can never be one; by its very nature it is many. And the heart is always one; by its very nature it cannot be many. You cannot have many hearts but you can have many minds. Why?—because the mind lives in doubt and the heart lives in love. The mind lives in doubt and the heart lives in trust. The heart knows how to trust; it is trust that makes it one. When you trust, suddenly you become centered.

Hence the significance of trust. It does not matter whether your trust is in the right person or not. It does not matter whether your trust will be exploited or not. It does not matter whether you will be deceived because of your trust or not. There is every possibility you will be deceived—the world is full of deceivers. What matters is that you trusted. It is out of your trust that you become integrated, which is far more important than anything else.

THE BOOK OF THE BOOKS, Vol. IX

The mind is always indecisive. That is one of the basic characteristics of the mind, indecisiveness. The moment a resolution arises in you the mind disappears. To be decisive is to go beyond the mind; to remain indecisive, hesitant, divided, is to live in the mind.

Resolution means totality, commitment, involvement, a quantum leap into something, into something which is not yet clearly known. Taking a risk is resolution. But the mind is a coward. It avoids risks; it seeks security, safety. Resolution is one of the ways to go beyond misery, schizophrenia.

Ordinarily man is a crowd, a thousand and one desires dividing him. When all these desires become a single pool of energy, that is resolution. Sannyas is resolution; it is a total effort to get out of the mind. And if one really strives to get out of the mind—difficult though it is, but not impossible . . . And life gains significance only when you know something which is beyond the mind.

THE IMPRISONED SPLENDOR

RESPECT   Twenty-two centuries of slavery in India. Who is the cause of all this? Your saints, your mahatmas, your so-called sages, who escape to the monasteries, who escape to the Himalayan caves, to the forests, to the jungles—and you have worshipped them, you have respected them. When you respect somebody it means deep down you would also like to be *like* him—that's what respect means.

The word "respect" is beautiful; it means seeing again and again—"respect". When you pass a beautiful woman, if she is really beautiful you will have to look again and again. That is respect: *seeing* again and again. You will walk slowly, you will find excuses to go back, you will enter into the same shop the woman has entered, you will start asking for the same commodities she is purchasing so that you can be at the same counter. You will not be looking at *things,* you will be looking at *her.* This is respect—the literal meaning of the word!

When you respect a person it means you are fascinated, infatuated. You would like to be like him. And the East still goes on respecting the same fools who are the cause of its misery, its starvation, its whole ugly state.

I AM THAT

We have been taught to condemn ourselves; we have been taught that we are worthless. We have been told in a thousand and one ways that we are dirt, and that has become part of our conditioning.

The first step in sannyas is: Respect yourself, because if you don't respect yourself you cannot respect anybody else in the world. Not even God can be respected, because even God comes number two.

Love yourself. If you can't love yourself you cannot love anybody else. And if *you* cannot love yourself, who is going to love you? And when there is no love and no respect for one's being life becomes a desert, because it is only through love and respect that one makes a garden out of one's being, that one starts learning how to play on one's own heart's harp. Then one starts learning how to be more and more poetic, graceful, aesthetic, sensitive . . . because life is such a great opportunity, it has not to be missed. It is such a treasure, it has not to be wasted.

So the first step and the most fundamental step is: Love yourself, respect yourself. And that does not mean to become an egoist. Loving yourself is not creating an ego. The trees love themselves and there is no ego; the birds love themselves and there is no ego.

> SNAP YOUR FINGERS, SLAP YOUR FACE
> AND WAKE UP

RESPONSE   What is response? Response is unprogrammed experiencing in the moment. You look at a flower, you really look at the flower, with no ideas covering your eyes. You look at *this* flower, the *this-ness* of it, all knowledge put aside. Your heart responds, your mind reacts. Responsibility is of the heart. You may not say anything; in fact, there is no need to say, "This is beautiful."

I have heard . . .

Lao Tzu used to go for a morning walk. A neighbor wanted to be with him. Lao Tzu said, "But remember, don't be talkative. You can come along, but don't be talkative."

Many times the man wanted to say something, but knowing Lao Tzu, looking at him, he controlled himself. But when the sun started rising and it was so beautiful, the temptation was so much that he forgot all about what Lao Tzu had said. He said, "Look! What a beautiful morning!"

And Lao Tzu said, "So, you have become talkative? You are too talkative! You are here, I am here, the sun is here, the sun is rising—so what is the point in saying to me 'The sun is beautiful?' Can't I see? Am I blind? What is the point of saying it? I am also here." In fact, the man who said "The morning is beautiful" was not there. He was repeating, it was a reaction.

When you respond words may not be needed at all, or sometimes they may be needed. It will depend on the situation, but they will not necessarily be there; they may be, they may not be.

Response is of the heart. Response is a feeling, not a thought. You are thrilled: seeing a rose flower something starts dancing in you, something is stirred at the deepest core of your being. Something starts opening inside you. The outer flower challenges the inner flower, and the inner flower responds: this is responsibility of the heart. And if you are not engaged in trivialities, you will have enough energy, abundant energy, to have this inner dance of the heart. When energy is dissipated in thoughts, your feelings are starved. Thoughts are parasites: they live on the energy which is really for the feelings, they exploit it.

Thought are leakages in your being: they take your energy out. Then you are like a pot with holes—nothing can be contained in you, you remain poor. When there are no thoughts your energy is contained inside, its level starts rising higher and higher. You have a kind of fullness. In that fullness the heart responds.

THE SECRET OF SECRETS, Vol. II

RESPONSIBILITY Responsibility means: ability to respond. It does not mean a duty.

Responsibility—go to the root meaning of the word: it means to be responsive. Love is a response! When the other calls, you are ready. When the other invites, you enter the other. When the other is not inviting, you don't interfere, you don't trespass. When the other sings, you sing in response. When the other gives you her or his hand, you take it with deep response.

Responsibility means openness, readiness to respond. Somebody is calling and you don't respond, you remain closed. Somebody wants to love you but you don't help, you don't cooperate; rather, you create barriers. If this is the thing you are doing—and the majority of lovers go on doing this—when the other calls you don't respond, then when you call the other does not respond. Because when the other calls you see that this would be a good ego-enhancing thing—not to respond. Then you feel your own master: nobody can push you, and nobody can pull you into something which you were not going into already; you don't follow anybody.

Comes your beloved—and she is happy, and she would like to be in a deep silence with you, but you remain closed. Then when *you* call, there is no answer. Have you seen birds calling each other?—that is responsibility. A cuckoo calls; there is silence; and then another cuckoo responds. By their sounds, by their song, they answer. They may be far away in farther away trees, then they start flying closer; they have responded. By and by they come to the same tree, then they are sitting together, loving.

When the other's being calls *Ready!* —be ready; respond with your totality. Don't be a miser—that is the meaning of responsibility.

But in your sense love has no responsibility. The word has been corrupted, destroyed, poisoned. A mother says to the child, "I am your mother, you have to be responsible for me." A husband says, "I am your husband, and I work hard for you. You have to be responsible for me." A father says to the son, "Don't be irresponsible! Whenever you do something always think of me." This is not responsibility, you have corrupted a beautiful word. It has become ugly. Responsibility has become almost synonymous with duty. And duty is an ugly word.

TAO: THE THREE TREASURES, Vol. III

The first step toward Buddhahood, towards the realization of your infinite potential, is to recognize that up to now you have been wasting your life, that up to now you have remained utterly unconscious.

Start becoming conscious; that is the only way to arrive. It is arduous, it is hard. To remain accidental is easy: it needs no intelligence, hence it is easy. Any idiot can do it—all the idiots are already doing it. It is easy to be accidental because you never feel responsible for anything that happens. You can always throw the responsibility onto something else: fate, God, society, the economic structure, the state, the church, the mother, the father ... You can go on throwing the responsibility onto somebody else, hence it is easy.

To be conscious means to take the whole responsibility on your own shoulders. To be responsible is the beginning of Buddhahood.

When I use the word "responsible" I am not using it in the ordinary connotation of being dutiful. I am using it in its real, essential meaning: the capacity to respond—that's my meaning. And the capacity to respond is possible only if you are conscious. If you are fast asleep, how can you respond? If you are asleep, the birds with go on singing but you will not hear, and the flowers will go on blooming and you will never be able to sense the beauty, the fragrance, the joy, that they are showering on existence.

To be responsible means to be alert, conscious. To be responsible means to be *mindful*. Act with as much awareness as you can find possible. Even small things— walking on the street, eating your food, taking your bath— should not be done mechanically. Do them with full awareness.

Slowly slowly, small acts become luminous, and by and by those luminous acts go on gathering inside you, and finally the explosion ... The seed has exploded, the potential has become actual. You are no more a seed but a lotus flower, a golden lotus flower, a one-thousand-petalled lotus flower. And that is the moment of great benediction; Buddha calls it *nirvana*. One has arrived. Now there is no more to achieve, nowhere to go. You can rest, you can relax—the journey is over. Tremendous joy arises in that moment, great ecstasy is born.

But one has to begin from the beginning.

THE BOOK OF THE BOOKS, Vol. III

They say "You reap as you sow." If we are miserable that simply means that we have been sowing misery. Nobody else creates misery for you. Of course there is a gap between sowing and reaping, and because of the gap we think that somebody else is responsible. The gap deceives us. We have no idea of what we have been doing to ourselves in so many past lives, so when suddenly we have to reap something and we don't know from where it is coming, naturally we start looking for some outer cause. If we cannot find one we invent something. But this is the whole theory of karma, that whatsoever we are reaping we have sown.

Take the whole responsibility for your life. If it is ugly feel responsible for it. If it is nothing but anguish take responsibility for it. In the beginning it is hard to accept that "I am the cause of my own hell" . . . but only in the beginning. Soon it starts opening doors of transformation, because if I am responsible for my hell, then I can create my heaven too. If I have created so much anguish for myself I can create so much ecstasy too. Responsibility brings freedom and responsibility brings creativity.

The moment you see that whatsoever you are is your own creation, you are freed from all outer causes and circumstances. Now it is up to you: you can sing a beautiful song, you can dance a beautiful dance, you can live a life of celebration, your life can be a constant festival; nobody can disturb it. This is human dignity. God is a great respector of individuals, and a person becomes individual only when he takes the whole responsibility for himself upon himself.

SCRIPTURES IN SILENCE AND SERMONS IN STONE

See also Duty, 1st Series

REST So learn to sit silently, doing nothing—just sitting resting in yourself. It takes a little time because we have been brought up to be restless, we have been brought up by people who have been restless themselves. They have poisoned us, they have corrupted us, not knowingly, not intentionally—they may have been good people, they may have even tried to help you, but they were unconscious, and unconscious people cannot help, they can only harm. In spite of all their good intentions they are bound to harm. They have made everybody restless, fidgety. Everybody is always running, rushing, not knowing where, not knowing why, for what. Speed in itself has become important, as if it has some intrinsic value.

I used to live with a professor when I was a student in the university. He was a very busy man and always rushing from this university to that, from this country to that. He was a visiting professor of many universities all over the world, on many consulting boards . . . always on the run.

Whenever he was at home he would play chess, playing-cards, Monopoly—stupid things. I used to ask him why. And he would say, "To kill time."

I said "This is strange: you don't go by train when you have to go to another town, you rush by airplane to *save* time. And when time is saved you play Monopoly to kill time! And you think you are a professor of logic and philosophy—you are a fool! If this is for what time is to be saved, then why save it in the first place? Then go by bullock cart! You will enjoy the scenery and the villages and so many things on the way. Journeying by airplane is not really a journey. You enter a capsule in one place, you get out of the capsule in another place, to save time—and then what do you do with the time?"

He said "You always create trouble for me. In fact in talking with you I feel afraid that you will create some trouble. Now I know that I cannot answer you, you are right."

He died in a plane crash finally. I had been telling him again and again "You will die . . . " because in India, only a bullock cart is safe! " . . . You are running unnecessarily." He had enough money and I would ask him "Why do you go on like this?" "To earn money." And I said "You don't have any child."

He used to give me money and I would waste his money. I told him "I don't believe in money or anything—I simply waste it. If you give me money I will waste it. Never ask me 'What happened to it?' "

To earn money he was going to New York and to Washington and to London, and he had no child, his wife was divorced. I was the only person who was living with him so he had to give money to me—what else could he do with the money?

I said to him "This is stupid: you have enough money—you can retire, you can enjoy your life and play cards and chess and whatsoever you want." But he continued. It was just the old rut, the old habit.

A meditator has to learn to do only the essential and not

to waste one's life in the unessential. A meditator has to learn to relax, how to rest, and enjoy rest. And slowly slowly one settles into one's own center. And the moment you touch your own center you have touched eternity, you have touched timelessness, you have tasted nectar for the first time.

The whole of religion exists for this experience. If religion is not going to give you the experience of the immortal, of the eternal, then it is absolutely pointless.

My sannyasins are going to taste it. They are moving slowly deeper and deeper into it, relaxing into it. That's what sannyas is all about: an exploration of eternity.

THE GOLDEN WIND

RESURRECTION If you are not afraid of death, who bothers about resurrection? It is fear. In fact, if it is proved absolutely that there had been no resurrection in Jesus' life, ninety-nine percent of Christians will drop being Christians, because then what is the point? They have been hanging around this person with the idea that he knows the secret of resurrecting himself, somehow he will impart his secrets and keys to them. Or maybe, if he does not show the art, at least he can do the miracles for them; he can save them. It is fear of death.

If it is proved absolutely that Jesus never did any healing miracles, then you will not find many Christians in the world; they will disappear. They are not interested in Jesus at all. Their whole interest is in how to protect themselves from illness, and finally, from death.

Rather than thinking of resurrection and healing powers, go deep inside yourself and look into your fear of death. There is no resurrection, but if you go deep into your fear of death, it disappears. And with the fear of death, death disappears. Then you know you are eternal life. There is no resurrection. Resurrection is possible only if *first you die!* You never die. Nobody has ever died. Death is a myth!

The word myth comes from a Sanskrit root *mithya*. *Mithya* means false. Death is a falsity. Death has never happened— never is going to happen. It cannot happen in the very case. Life is eternal, only forms change. You die here, your flame disappears in this body, and it becomes embodied in some other body, you are born in some other womb. And so on and so forth. And even when there is no more birth, you disappear into God. But life lives . . .

Form is a flux. *You* never die! Form dies every day. But the problem arises because you have become too identified with the form. You think "I am the form." You think "I am this body." Then the fear of death arises.

You need not learn the art of resurrection. You have simply to learn that death does not exist; there is no need to resurrect because you cannot die in the first place! Rather than being intrigued by Jesus' miracles, perform a miracle: go into yourself. That is the only miracle. Go into your fear of death, and go on deeper into it, and see *where* it is, *what* it is. Watch it.

And don't rationalize, and don't bring theories borrowed from the outside to console yourself. Don't say that "soul is eternal", no; you don't know yet. I am saying it is eternal, but that is not your knowledge. Don't make it your consolation.

You have to go trembling, you have to go with fear, you have to descend the staircase of death. You have to go to the very end. You have to see the whole possibility of death—what it is. In that very seeing you will be surprised that you are not it. You are not the body, you are not even the mind. You are just pure life energy, you are a witness. In that witnessing is the real miracle.

I SAY UNTO YOU, Vol. II

RETIREMENT   This is what retirement is. You have earned the bread today, now retire.

But you don't know how to retire: you go on earning the bread in your dreams also. You lie down and you plan for tomorrow, and nobody knows whether the tomorrow is going to come or not. In fact it never comes. It is always today.

You are planning for the future, not knowing that death will destroy all future. Be wise. Remain in the moment. Live it as totally as possible and then you will know no death. A man who is not worried about tomorrow, knows no death. He becomes deathless, because death is tomorrow—life is today.

Death is in the future, life is always in the present—this is the meaning of retire. If you would like me to translate this word "retire", I will call it sannyas. You don't retire in the end of life, you retire every day, retire every moment. When you have enjoyed a moment it is retirement, it is through retirement, it is sannyas. When you come back from the office to your house, leave the office in the office. Don't carry it in your head, otherwise the head will have a headache, bound to have, such a big thing, the office, you carry in your head! It is heavy! The whole market in your head is heavy! . . .

Retirement every day, retirement every moment . . . The very word "retirement" does not look good to us because it gives a feeling of old age, inability. Somewhere beyond sixty-five, when death comes near, one retires. No, the word "retire" is very beautiful. It is the meaning of sannyas. Retire means rest. The work is done, now retire, enjoy it.

Don't postpone enjoyment, that is the meaning of the word "retire". Enjoy here and now.

TAO: THE THREE TREASURES, Vol. I

RETURN   See Coming back, 1st Series

REVERENCE   Meditation creates ecstasy in you, such joy that you cannot contain it. It starts overflowing. It is so much that you disappear in it. You are no more—there is only joy. That is rapture. The ego drowns in the rapture and is never found again: it dissolves, disappears, evaporates. You are left with only a deep joy in the heart, a joy which is not of time, a joy which is not of this earth, a joy which belongs to the beyond, to the farther shore. And only out off that joy, that rapture, that ecstasy, does reverence arise: reverence for existence.

In religious terms you can call it reverence for God. Reverence is far more important than God itself. Without reverence there is no God. If there is reverence, God is bound to happen. It is inevitable.

So my effort here is not to prove God to you. It needs no proof: God is. We cannot make the question and it cannot be answered in any way, positively or negatively. There is no proof for or against. It is beyond proofs, beyond logic.

My effort is to create reverence in you. If reverence arises in your heart, God is: suddenly you start feeling his presence everywhere, all around, within and without. In the moment of reverence the whole existence is transformed into godliness. Then trees are divine and rocks are divine. Wherever you look with a heart full of reverence you can only find God and nothing else. Without reverence, everything is there except God. With reverence only God is there and nothing else.

EIGHTY-FOUR THOUSAND POEMS

REVOLUTION Revolution is possible only in the individual soul. The social revolution is a pseudo phenomenon, because the society has no soul of its own. Revolution is a spiritual phenomenon. There can be no political revolution, no social revolution, no economic revolution. The only revolution is that of the spirit; it is individual. And if millions of individuals change, then the society will change as a consequence, not vice versa. You cannot change the society first and hope that individuals will change later on.

That's why revolutions have been failing: because we have taken revolution from a very wrong direction. We have thought that if you change the society, change the structure, economic or political, then one day the individuals, the constituent elements of the society, will change. This is stupid. Who is going to do this revolution?

For example, in 1917 a great so-called revolution happened in Russia. But who is going to take charge of this revolution? Who is going to become powerful? Joseph Stalin became powerful. Now Joseph Stalin had not gone through any revolution himself; he was a byproduct of the same society that he was changing or was trying to change. He proved a far more dangerous czar than the czars that he had destroyed, because he was created by those czars. He was a byproduct of a feudal society. He tried to change the society, but he himself was a dictatorial mind. He imposed his dictatorship on the country, revolution became counter-revolution—and this has been the misfortune of all the revolutions that have happened in the world because the revolutionary is the same type of person. He has been created by the past, he is not new. What is he going to do?—he will repeat the past. Labels will be new—he will call it communism, socialism, fascism; that doesn't matter. You can have fancy names; fancy names only befool people . . .

We go on giving fancy names, but deep down the reality remains the same. Nothing happened in 1917 . . .

Secondly, once a revolution has succeeded we have to destroy the revolutionaries, because the revolutionaries are dangerous people. They have destroyed the first society, they will destroy the second, because they are addicted to revolution. They know only one thing, they are experts only in one thing: in throwing governments—they don't care what government. Their whole expertise and their whole power is in throwing governments. Once a revolution succeeds the first work of the people who come in power is to destroy all the remaining revolutionaries—and they had succeeded because of them! So each revolution turns to counter-revolution because the people who had brought them into power are more dangerous people . . .

So those who are in power have to destroy all the remaining revolutionaries. Each revolution kills its own father—it has to be done—and once those fathers are killed, the revolution has turned into a counter-revolution. It is no more revolutionary, it is anti-revolutionary . . .

That's why I say the events that happen every day are almost meaningless, because the moment they happen, immediately they disappear because their context changes. Political revolutions have been happening and disappearing: they are bubbles, soap bubbles. Maybe for a moment they look very beautiful, but they are not eternal diamonds.

The eternal diamond is the inner revolution. But the inner revolution is difficult because the inner revolution needs creativity and the outer revolution needs destructiveness. Hate is easy, love is difficult. To destroy is easy. To create a Taj Mahal takes years—it took forty years and fifty thousand persons working every day—but how many days will you take to destroy it? Just take a bulldozer and within a day the land will be flat . . .

My work here is of creativity. I am not provoking you into any destruction, I am not telling you to blame others for your misery. I am telling you you are responsible, so only those who have the guts to take this responsibility can be with me. But this is a real revolution. If you take the responsibility for your life you can start changing it. Slow will be the change, only in the course of time will you start moving into the world of light and crystallization, but once you are crystallized you will know what real revolution is. Then share your revolution with others; it has to go that way, from heart to heart . . .

That's why I don't call my sannyasins revolutionary but rebellious—just to make the differentiation. Revolution has become too contaminated with the social idea. Rebellion is individual.

Rebel! Take responsibility for your life.

THE SECRET OF SECRETS, Vol. II

I say religion is the only revolution because it changes man. It changes man's consciousness, it changes man's heart. It depends on the individual, because the individual is real and concrete. It does not bother about the society. If the individual is different you will have a different society and a different world automatically. And you cannot change the inner by changing the outer, because the outer is on the periphery. But you can change the outer by changing the center, the inner, because the inner is at the very core of it. By changing the symptoms you will not change the disease. You will have to go deep into man. From where comes this violence? From where comes this exploitation? From where come all these ego-trips? From where? They all come from unconsciousness. Man lives asleep, man lives mechanically. That mechanism has to be broken, man has to be re-done. This is the religious revolution that has not been tried.

THE WISDOM OF THE SANDS, Vol. II

See also Reform

REWARD Love is when the rock of the ego is removed. Then your life's juices start flowing. That's what love is all about: your life juices. And they come with such a flood that you start overflowing with them. You have to share. And when you share your love energy with anybody, it is not that you are obliging the other person, in fact, just the contrary is the case: you feel obliged to the other because he accepted your love. You don't ask for anything in return because love in itself is such a joy, who cares for any reward?

Rewards are meant for purposes where the process itself is that of misery—then a reward is needed. So the reward is like a carrot hanging in front of you and to get the carrot you can pass through all kinds of miseries. The Nobel Prize, the gold medals in universities, the presidencies, the prime ministerships of the world—these are just prizes. They are very childish because to hanker for a prize is childish, to ask for a reward is childish.

The really mature person lives in such a way that each moment in itself is a reward. It is not that the reward will be coming later on. The mature person has such an insight into things that the journey and the goal are no more separate, so each step of the journey is a goal in itself—tremendously blissful, beautiful. Who cares about the goal? Every moment is such a benediction that one enjoys it as an end unto itself; it is not a means to anything.

When a man has come to this state, when everything is an end unto itself, only then has he lived his life truly, he has become really grownup. Growing old has nothing to do with you, it is not to your credit. Every donkey becomes old, it does not need any intelligence. But to be grownup needs great intelligence, great courage, and a heart which is ready to risk, gamble.

One can be my sannyasin only if one is ready to gamble, if one is ready to risk without holding anything back. When one is ready to be totally committed, then only is some transformation possible. But it brings infinite grace, it brings celebration to your life. Flowers start showering on you, the whole existence rejoices in your joy.

JUST THE TIP OF THE ICEBERG

RICHNESS   I have been poor. I have lived in utter poverty. I have lived in richness. And, believe me, richness is far better than poverty. I am a man of very simple interests: I am utterly satisfied with the best of everything. I don't ask for more.

THE WILD GEESE AND THE WATER

RIGHTNESS "The eightfold path" is simply a way of expressing his experience, of giving you a certain direction. The essence of the eightfold path is in the word "rightness". Buddha uses the word "rightness" about everything. He divides life into eight parts and he uses "rightness" about each part: right food, right effort, right mindfulness, right *samadhi*, and so on and so forth. And it is not only a question of eight things; if you understand, then it has to be used as a direction.

Whatsoever you are doing can be done in a wrong way or in a right way; both alternatives are always there. So you have to understand what he means by "rightness"—the essence of it. You have to taste the flavor of rightness, then you can apply it in everything that you are doing. You are walking; you can walk in the right way and you can walk in the wrong way. You are talking; you can talk in the right way, you can talk in the wrong way. You are listening; you can listen in the right way, you can listen in the wrong way.

If you are listening with all kinds of prejudices, that is a wrong way of listening; it is really a way of not listening. You appear to be listening, but you are only hearing, not listening. Right listening means you have put your mind aside. It does not mean that you become gullible, that you start believing whatsoever is said to you. It has nothing to do with belief or disbelief. Right listening means: "I am not concerned right now whether to believe or not to believe. There is no question of agreement or disagreement at this moment. I am simply trying to listen—whatsoever it is. Later on I can decide what is right and what is wrong. Later on I can decide whether to follow or not to follow."

And the beauty of right listening is this: that truth has a music of its own. If you can listen without prejudice, your heart will say it is true. If it is true, a bell starts ringing in your heart. If it is not true you remain aloof, unconcerned, indifferent—no bell rings in your heart, no synchronicity happens. That is the quality of truth: that if you listen to it with an open heart, it immediately creates a response in your being. Your very center is uplifted. You start growing wings. Suddenly the whole sky is open.

It is *not* a question of deciding logically whether what is being said is true or untrue; on the contrary, it is a question of love, not of logic. Truth immediately creates a love in your heart; something is triggered in you in a very mysterious way.

But if you listen wrongly—that is, full of your mind, full of your garbage, full of your knowledge—then you will not allow your heart to respond to the truth. You will miss the tremendous possibility, you will miss the synchronicity. Your heart was ready to respond to truth . . . It responds only to truth, remember, it never responds to the untrue. With the untrue it remains utterly silent, unresponsible, unaffected, unstirred. With the truth it starts dancing, it starts singing, as if suddenly the sun has risen and the dark night is no more, and the birds are singing and the lotuses are opening, and the whole earth is awakened.

Exactly like that, when you hear the truth really, totally, something immediately awakens in you. Truth has that immense impact. Hence Buddha says: Right listening, right effort . . .

You can make effort to the extreme, and then you will miss. You can make too much effort and you will miss. Or you can make too little effort and you will miss. You can become enlightened only when the effort is exactly balanced, in equilibrium.

Buddha's word is *samyaktva*. It is difficult to translate. Only one of the meanings has been translated: rightness. Another meaning is equilibrium. And it has a few other qualities too. The third meaning is equanimity. The fourth meaning is: looking at things with a similar eye, with no judgment; looking at things equally, without any *a priori* judgment, conclusion; looking at things with no conclusion at all—because if you already have a conclusion you can't look at the thing as it is, your conclusion will interfere. But the most important meaning is rightness.

Right effort means neither leaning too much to the left nor leaning too much to the right. Right effort is exactly like walking on a tightrope. Have you seen the tightrope walker? He continuously balances himself between the right and the left. If he leans a little too much to the left he will fall, so he immediately balances himself by moving to the opposite side. But if he leans a little too much to the right he will fall again; then again he balances himself by moving to the left. He is continuously moving between right and left. Balance is not something static; it is a dynamic process.

Hence you cannot decide your character once and for all. And those who decide their character once and for all are dead people. They simply go on following a dead routine; they are not transformed by this dead routine.

Life is a continuous process, a movement; it is a river. You have to adjust yourself according to the situations, otherwise you remain fixed and life goes on changing all around. The only result will be a gap arising between you and your life—and that gap creates misery, sorrow.

You are always missing the train. Either you are too early or you are too late, but you are never at the exact time. Either you are running ahead or you are lagging behind. Either you are in the past or in the future. A few people live in their memories and a few people live in their imaginations. And to live rightly means to be in the present, to be exactly in the middle—in the middle between past and future, in the middle between imagination and memory, in the middle between that which is no more and that which is not yet. In that exact middleness is rightness: *samyaktva*.

THE BOOK OF THE BOOKS, Vol. VII

RISK Sannyas is the greatest risk possible because it is going into the uncharted without a map. It is entering into the mysterious, not knowing exactly where you are going. But some intuitive force pulls you, calls you; some unknown source of energy functions like a magnet. You cannot resist; you cannot avoid, you cannot escape. But it is a risk because all that you have known will be useless in this venture. All that you are familiar with will have to be dropped because it becomes an unnecessary burden on the journey. And the journey can be made only if you are very light, utterly unburdened with philosophies, theologies, ideologies, religions. You can only go into this unknown with a mind with no thoughts.

And that's the risk, because the mind is well-acquainted with thoughts; with thoughts the mind is efficient, skillful. Without thought the mind becomes just like a child's mind, innocent, ignorant. But the search for God needs you to be innocent and ignorant; the knowledgeable never reach. God is available only to the innocent, to those who are full of wonder but have no knowledge. Great questions arise in their hearts, but not a single answer is there.

THE IMPRISONED SPLENDOR

If you are alive you have to take risks. Life is a risk. Only death is secure, life is never secure—there is no security. The companies that are called Life Insurance should really be called Death Insurance; in life there can be no insurance. Life is alive only because there is risk, danger—that's why there is so much thrill.

You ask, *Is it good to take risks*?

If you want to be alive you have to take risks, and the more risks you take, the more alive you will be. So really you are asking "Is it good to be alive?" Rightly interpreted, your question will mean "Is it good to be alive?" . . .

A person who is continuously thinking whether there is any risk or not becomes so self-conscious that he never lives. He becomes rigid and dull and stupid—mediocre: forget all about risks. Life *is* a risk. The day you were born, one thing became certain: that you are going to die. Now what more risk can there be?

My mother's mother was a very old woman, and she was always afraid about me. I was continuously traveling in the train—fifteen days a month I was in the train. And she was always afraid, and she would say "There are so many accidents!" and every day she would look in the newspaper just to see whether there had been some train accident, some airplane had fallen or something. And she would collect all the cuttings, and whenever I would go she would show them to me. "Look! So many car accidents, so many airplanes, and so many trains burned, and so many people killed. What are you doing? Fifteen days on the trains, planes, cars! Stop this!"

So, one day, I said to her "Listen. If you are really interested in statistics then do you know that ninety-seven percent of people die in their beds? So should I stand outside the bed the whole night? It is risky, there is no other thing more risky than to be in the bed. Ninety-seven percent of people have to die in the bed! You are safer in an airplane—rarely does somebody die in an airplane, rarely in a train . . . "

She was very much puzzled. She said "It is true, but that cannot be done—it is impossible. Yes, that's true." Since then she stopped talking about accidents—she understood.

The day you were born you took the greatest risk that you could ever take. Now death is going to happen, death is bound to happen. The day you were born you already took one step into the grave. Now what greater risks can you take? Even if you go on avoiding risks, you will die, so why not take the risk and live really authentically? . . .

Death is going to take everything. Why be worried then? Rather then saving it for death to take away, share it—take risks. The miserly man is the stupid man; everything will be taken away. Don't' be so cautious.

Don't be so cautious; have the spirit of adventure. Yes, I know sometimes you may commit a mistake, but nothing is wrong in it. Sometimes you may go astray, but nothing is wrong it it. Those who can go astray, they can come back; but those who never go anywhere, they are dead.

Never commit the same mistake again and again, that's true—invent new mistakes every day. Be creative. Risk in new ways. And that's what sannyas is all about: to be risky, to live dangerously, to live without security and safety. To be tremendously in love with life is what sannyas is.

And don't postpone it, because all postponement is again being very cautious. Do it right now. If you have understood the thing, let it happen.

                    TAO: THE PATHLESS PATH. Vol. I

See also Growth, 1st Series

RITUALS   I am against rituals, but that does not mean that a religious person cannot go into a ritual. But when a religious person goes into a ritual, it is not a ritual at all. His heart is in it; then his words have wings.

So remember it: I am against the ritual when there is no heart in it. Then it is a ritual! But if there is a heart . . .

A famous story about Moses:

He was passing through a forest. He saw a man praying. But the man who was praying was saying such absurd things that he could not go further. He had to stop the man. What he was saying was profane, sacrilegious. He was saying to

God: "God, you must be feeling sometimes very alone—I can come and be always with you like a shadow. You can depend on me! You need not be alone. Why suffer loneliness when I am here? And I am not a useless person either—I can be of much use, I can be handy. I will give you a good bath. I can massage too. I am a shepherd. And I will take all the lice from your hair and your body . . . . "

Lice? Moses could not believe his ears: "What is he talking about?"

"And I will cook for you. And do you know what?— everybody likes what I cook. It is delicious. And I will prepare your bed and I will wash your clothes. And I can do a thousand and one things! And when you are ill I will take care of you. I will be a mother to you, a wife to you, a servant, a slave—I can be *all* kinds of things. Just give me a hint so I can come."

Moses stopped him and said, "Listen! What kind of prayer is this? What are you doing? To whom are you talking? Lice in God's hair? He needs a bath? And you are saying 'I will rub your body and make it absolutely clean'? Stop this nonsense. This is not prayer. God will be offended by you."

Looking at Moses, the man fell at his feet. He said, "I am sorry. I am an illiterate, ignorant man. I don't know how to pray. Please, *you* teach me!"

So Moses taught him the right way to pray, and he was very happy because he had put a man on the right track. Happy, puffed up in his ego, Moses went away.

And when he was alone in the forest, a very thundering voice came from the sky and said, "Moses, I have sent you into the world to bring people to me, to bridge people with me, but not to take my lovers away from me. And that's exactly what you have done. That man is one of the *most* intimate to me. Go back! Apologize. Take your prayer back! You have destroyed the whole beauty of his dialogue. He is sincere. He is loving. His love is true. Whatsoever he was saying, he was saying from his heart. It was not a ritual. Now what you have given to him is just a ritual. He will repeat it but it will be only on the lips; it will not be out of his being."

I am not against prayer, I am against the ritualistic prayer—

because it is *not* prayer, that's why I am against it. Don't learn
empty gestures. Let your gestures be alive, spontaneous.
Otherwise, deep down you know that this is a ritual, deep
down you know that this is just a formality you are perform-
ing. And if that is your feeling inside, what is the point
of going into it? . . .

I am against rituals because they have killed the spirit of
religion in the world. But I am not saying don't pray, but
let the prayer arise. Let it be of your own. Let it be of your
own feeling. Don't repeat it parrot-like.

I am not against rules, but the rules should arise out of
your understanding. They should not be imposed from the
outside. I am not against discipline! But discipline should
not be slavery. All true discipline is self-discipline. And self-
discipline is never against freedom—in fact, it is the ladder
to freedom. Only disciplined people become free, but their
discipline is not obedience to others: their discipline is
obedience to their own inner voice. And they are ready to
risk anything for it.

Let your own awareness decide your lifestyle, life-pattern.
Don't allow anybody else to decide it. That is a sin: to allow
anybody else to decide it. Why is it a sin?—because you will
never be in it. It will remain superficial, it will be hypocrisy.
                              THE PERFECT MASTER, Vol. II

See also Robopathology

RIVER The first thing my own father taught me—and the
only thing that he ever taught me—was a love for the small
river that flows by the side of my town. He taught me just
this—swimming in the river. That's all he ever taught me,
but I am tremendously grateful to him because that brought
so many changes in my life. Exactly like Siddhartha, I fell
in love with the river. Whenever I think of my birthplace
I don't remember anything except the river.

The day my father died I only remembered the first day
he brought me to the river bank to teach me swimming.
My whole childhood was spent in a close love affair with
the river. It was my daily routine to be with the river for
five to eight hours at least. From three o'clock in the morning I would be with the river; the sky would be full of stars

and the stars reflecting in the river. And it is a beautiful river; its water is so sweet that people have named it Shakkar— *shakkar* means sugar. It is a beautiful phenomenon.

I have seen it in the darkness of the night with the stars, dancing its course towards the ocean. I have seen it with the early rising sun. I have seen it in the full moon. I have seen it with the sunset. I have seen it sitting by its bank alone or with friends, playing on the flute, dancing on its bank, meditating on its bank, rowing a boat in it or swimming across it. In the rains, in the winter, in the summer . . .

I can understand Herman Hesse's Siddhartha and his experience with the river. It happened with me: so much transpired, because slowly slowly the whole existence became a river to me. It lost its solidity; it became liquid, fluid.

And I am immensely grateful to my father. He never taught me mathematics, language, grammar, geography, history. He was never much concerned about my education. He had ten children . . . and I have seen it happen many times: people would ask, "In what class is your son studying?" and he would have to ask somebody because he would not know. He was never concerned with any other education. The only education that he gave to me was a communion with the river. He himself was in deep love with the river.

Whenever you are in love with flowing things, moving things, you have a different vision of life. The modern man lives with asphalt roads, cement concrete buildings. These are nouns, remember, these are not verbs. The skyscrapers don't go on growing; the road remains the same whether it is night or day, whether it is a full-moon night or a night absolutely dark, full of stars. It doesn't matter to the asphalt road, it does not matter to the cement concrete buildings.

Man has created a world of nouns and he has become encaged in his own world, and he has forgotten the world of the trees, the world of the rivers, the world of the mountains and the stars. *There* they don't know of any noun, they have not heard about nouns; they know only verbs. Everything is a process.

God is not a thing but a process.

ROBOPATHOLOGY   "Robopath" is a beautiful word. Sufis have always talked about this pathology. They have called it by many names. For example, they say that man is a machine. Gurdjieff introduced this Sufi idea into the western consciousness. Sufis say that man is asleep. Sufis say that man is dead. Sufis say that man is not yet. Sufis say that man only believes that he is but that belief is a kind of dream . . .

A few things . . . A robopath is a person whose pathology entails robot-like behavior and existence. He is man only for the name's sake. He could have been a computer. He may be. A robopath is a human who functions insensitively, mechanically—in short, in a dead way. A robopath is an automation. His existential state is not even inhuman. He is not human, certainly, he is not even inhuman—because to be inhuman first you have to be human. His existential state can only be described as the Sufis describe it—they call it "a-human". It has no human value, neither this way nor that. He is neither human nor inhuman, he is a-human.

These are the characteristics of this disease. Ponder over them—because they are your characteristics, everybody's. Until you become enlightened these characteristics will follow you like a shadow. We can define enlightenment as getting out of robopathology, becoming consciousness for the first time, dropping the mechanical, becoming a witness, awareness, awakenedness.

The first characteristic is sleep. You will find the robopath always asleep. He walks but he walks in sleep. He talks but he talks in sleep. He does many things, he has become perfectly efficient in doing the ordinary things of life. But watch yourself and watch people. You go on doing the same thing again and again. By and by there is no need to be alert about those things, you can simply do them. You need not be there.

When you first start learning to drive you have to be there for a few days. That's why it is so troublesome to learn anything— because to learn anything you will have to come out of your sleep a little bit at least. Otherwise how will you learn?

Robopaths are never interested in new things. Once they have learned a few things they go on moving in that vicious circle. Every morning is the same, every evening is the same.

Every time they eat or they talk or they make love, it is the same. They are not needed there at all. They don't do anything through consciousness, they go on making empty gestures. That's why there is so much boredom in life. How can you remain thrilled by constantly repeating the old? This is the first characteristic—sleep.

The second characteristic is dreaming—part of sleep. A robopath continuously dreams—not only in the night, even in the day. He has daydreams, reveries. Even while he is doing something, deep inside he is dreaming. You can find that any time. Close your eyes any time and look inside and you will find a dream unfolding. It is constantly there. It is like the stars—in the day they don't disappear, they only become invisible because the light of the sun is too bright. But the stars are there, the full sky is there as it is in the night—exactly as it is in the night. When the sun is gone you will see those stars appearing again. They have not gone anywhere, they were there just waiting for the sun to go.

In the night you start seeing dreams. Those dreams don't disappear in the day. Because you become involved in a thousand and one things in daily routine life, they go on lurking deep in the unconscious. You can find them any moment. Close your eyes, wait a single moment, and the dream is there. Sleep is constantly there. Your eyes are full of sleep and your mind is full of dreaming.

And the third characteristic is ritualism. A robopath remains in rituals, he never does anything through his heart. He will say "hello" because he has to say it or because he has always been saying it. His "hello" will not have any heart in it. He will kiss his wife but it will be just repeating an empty gesture. There is no kiss in his kiss. He will embrace somebody but only bones will touch and skin will touch—he will remain as far away as ever. He is not there. You can be certain about one thing—he is not there.

But robopaths are great ritualists. They depend on ritual. They do everything as it should be done . . .

Robopaths live a life of formality. Even their so-called intimate and emotional behavior is ritualistic and programmed. Their activities are all pre-packaged. They never do anything on the spur of the moment. Coming home they think about what they are going to say to their wife. Going to the office they prepare what they are going to say to the boss. They are always rehearsing. It is always a rehearsal. They are always getting ready. And naturally, when you are too prepared, you miss the moment . . .

A robopath is very dogmatic. He is always pretending to be certain about everything. He cannot allow doubt. Doubt creates trembling. He believes, he never suspects—because if you doubt then you have to enquire. And who knows where your doubt will lead? That's why you see so many believers on the earth and no religion at all . . .

A robopath is always past-oriented or future-oriented. He is never in the present. The past is good because you cannot do anything with the past. The past is finished and complete. The robopath feels very at ease with the past. The past is dead, things have happened, now there is no way to change and alter them.

With the past the robopath feels in tune, with the future he can desire and hope—but with the present he is very uneasy, with the present he is very restless. The present brings problems . . .

The present does not listen to you. It has its own being. That's why the robopath goes on avoiding the present. And the best way to avoid the present is either to remain past-oriented or to become future-oriented . . .

The robopath lives in image involvement. He is always concerned about how his image is, what people are thinking about him—whether they think him good, saintly, this and that. He is not really worried about transforming his life. If people believe in stupid things he will follow them . . .

A robopath is always a perfectionist. He is never satisfied. He will always be finding faults. He will try to be as faultless as possible and he will look always at others' faults. Now, if you want to be faultless you cannot be original. With the original comes the error. If you want to do something new you have to accept that sometimes you may commit mistakes. If you want to be faultless you have to have a very small routine repeated so many times that it has become absolutely rigid and you can do it perfectly.

That's why many people live at the minimum, they cannot go to the maximum. With the minimum they can remain perfect but the maximum is a danger—error may enter in. People live a very limited kind of life. They choose a small life and life has to be multi-dimensional, only then is it rich.

A robopath is really poor. He may have as much wealth as one can have, but he is poor. His life is one-dimensional. He always lives to the minimum, close to the minimum. Do as few things as possible because then you remain more perfect. If you do many more things, naturally you can't be perfect . . .

A robopath is necessarily anti-joy, anti-life. Not only is he anti-joy, he is a joy-killer. If somebody else is celebrating he will look with the eyes of condemnation . . .

The robopath has no compassion. He is hard. He is hard on himself, he is hard on others. And sometimes when robopathology goes to its very extreme he not only lacks compassion, he becomes a-compassionate. That value simply disappears. He is neither compassionate nor not compassionate—that value simply does not exist for him He only does his role—properly of course; he follows orders—blindly, of course. His great value is efficiency . . .

Robopaths are self-righteous. They always feel holier-than-thou. Their whole effort is how to look holier than others, how to be at the top. Their ego is very subtle. These people become saints, monks, mahatmas, and all kinds of neuroses are born in them. These people become politicians, puritans, moralists. They are ready to throw the whole world into hell. These are the people who have invented hell.

And the last thing that a robopath is, is alienated. The robopath is alienated from self, from other selves, and from nature. "He is alienated from self in the sense that his ego is only a function of ritualistic demands. It has no intrinsic self-definition." He does not know who he is, he knows only what others say about him. So he is alienated from himself. He has never encountered himself. He has never looked into his own being. He has always been looking into other people's eyes—looking for his image, for how he looks in other people's eyes. He has never come home. He is alienated from himself . . .

This is the robopathology that man has lived up to now, and man can go on living in it.

You can jump out of it. That jump makes you religious. That jump brings you to understanding, that jump makes you wise, that jump makes you enlightened.

SUFIS: THE PEOPLE OF THE PATH, Vol. I

ROLES A sannyasin has to learn pure acting. He has to look at the world as a great drama. A thousand and one plays are going on and you have to participate in many games. You are constantly moving form one stage to another: from the house to the office, from the office to the church, from the church to the club, and so on, so forth. They are all different stages, different sets, and you have to play different roles. But they are all roles—don't take them seriously.

There is no need to renounce them. To renounce them means you have taken them seriously.

That's why I say never to renounce anything. Live your role, enjoy it, it is fun, but take it lightly, take it easily. It is not worth worrying about. So whatsoever role you have to play in a certain circumstance, play to your utmost ability, play it totally, but once it is finished, whether you have succeeded or failed is irrelevant. Don't look back, go ahead: there are other plays you have to play. Failure or success are unimportant. What is important is the awareness that everything is a game.

When your whole life becomes full of this awareness you are freed, then nothing binds you. Then you are no more tethered to anything, then you don't have any chains around your hands, then you are no more imprisoned by anything. You use masks but you know that that is not your original face. And you can remove the mask, because now you know it is a mask—it can be removed, it is removable. And now you can know your original face too.

The man who is aware that life is a game comes to know his original face. And to know one's original face is to know all that is worth knowing, because that is the face of God. That is the face of truth. That is the face of love. That is the face of freedom.

EIGHTY-FOUR THOUSAND POEMS

ROOTS Love is the ancientmost religion, the original

religion; all the other religions are offshoots. Love is the root; all other religions are like leaves or at the most, small branches. Even the greatest religions—Christianity, Hinduism, Islam, Buddhism—are big branches, but they are visible. You can see the churches and you can see the temples and you can read the scriptures.

Love has no temple and love has no scripture. It is like the roots hidden underneath: it is underground, but it is the nourishment. Without it the whole tree will die. It is love that goes on creating more and more leaves, more foliage, more flowers, more fruits. Love is the original religion.

My effort here is to introduce you to the original. You are all clinging to the branches. Branches are beautiful but they are not the source. A Buddha, a Jesus, a Zarathustra, goes to the very roots; it is from there that he experiences God. And the only way to experience God is to go to the roots of life, of existence.

Find the roots, be more loving and you will enter into the invisible temple. You will be able to read scriptures in silence and sermons in the stones.

SCRIPTURES IN SILENCE AND SERMONS IN STONE

ROUTINE People have fixed habits. Even while making love they always make it in the same position—"the missionary posture". Find out new ways of feeling.

Each experience has to be created with great sensitivity. When you make love to a woman or a man, make it a great celebration. And each time bring some new creativity into it. Sometimes have a dance before you make love. Sometimes pray before you make love. Sometimes go running into the forest, then make love. Sometimes go swimming and then make love. Then each love experience will create more and more sensitivity in you and love will never become dull and boring.

Find out new ways to explore the other. Don't get fixed in routines. All routines are anti-life: routines are in the service of death. And you can always invent—there is no limit to inventions. Sometimes a small change, and you will be tremendously benefited. You always eat at the table;

sometimes just go on the lawn, sit on the lawn and eat there. And you will be tremendously surprised: it is a totally different experience. The smell of the freshly-cut grass, the birds hopping around and singing, and the fresh air, and the sun-rays, and the feel of the wet grass underneath. It cannot be the same experience as when you sit on a chair and eat at your table; it is a totally different experience: all the ingredients are different.

Try sometimes just eating naked, and you will be surprised. Just a small change—nothing much, you are sitting naked—but you will have a totally different experience, because something new has been added to it. If you eat with a spoon and fork, eat sometimes with bare hands, and you will have a different experience; your touch will bring some new warmth to the food. A spoon is a dead thing: when you eat with a spoon or a fork, you are far away. That same fear of touching anything—even food cannot be touched. You will miss the texture, the touch, the feel of it. The food has as much feel as it has taste.

Many experiments have been done in the West on the fact that when we are enjoying anything, there are many things we are not aware of which contribute to the experience. For example, just close your eyes and close your nose and then eat an onion. Tell somebody to give it to you when you don't know what he is giving—whether he is giving you an onion or an apple. And it will be difficult for you to make out the difference if the nose is completely closed and the eyes are closed, blindfolded. It will be impossible for you to decide whether it is an onion or apple, because the taste is not only the taste, fifty percent of it comes from the nose. And much comes from the eyes. It is not just taste; all the senses contribute. When you eat with your hands, your touch is contributing. It will be more tasty. It will be more human, more natural.

Find out new ways in everything. Let that be one of your *sadhanas*.

Tantra says: If you can go on finding new ways every day, your life will remain a thrill, an adventure. You will never be bored.

RUIN There are three ways to be ruined in this world: first is by sex, second is by gambling, and the third is by politics. Sex is the most fun, gambling is the most exciting, and politics is the surest.

THE GOOSE IS OUT

RULES See Society

RULING One can rule others or one can rule oneself. To rule others is a poor substitute, because the real ruler is one who rules himself. Because it is arduous to rule oneself, people have chosen the cheaper thing; the cheaper thing is to rule others. The lowest thing in the world is power politics; and by power politics I mean every effort in which you are trying to possess, to dominate, to rule the other. The highest thing in the world is religion; and by religion I mean the effort to rule oneself, to become a master of oneself.

If you rule others you remain a slave. Your being a ruler is only a facade; deep down you are a slave, maybe a slave of your own slaves. Ruling others does not bring freedom. But when one is able to rule oneself, when one is centered, rooted in one's own being—when one is not dominated by desires, dreams, thoughts, when one is not just a crowd of many, many minds inside but has become a master who can direct his body, mind, soul, into a particular rhythm, in a particular harmony, who can start moving as a togetherness, not like a multiplicity, not like a crowd, but like a unity, who has created inside a cosmos instead of a chaos—then one has become a real king. And that's what sannyas is all about.

The kingdom is within and the king is asleep: the king has to be awakened!

YOU AIN'T SEEN NOTHIN' YET

RUMORS People believe in rumors very easily. If somebody says something ugly, derogatory, about a person, you immediately believe it. But if somebody praises him, you don't believe, you ask for proofs. You never ask for proofs about derogatory remarks and rumors, you are very willing to believe them for the simple reason that you *want* to

believe that "Everybody is far worse then I am." That's the
only way to feel good, a little bit good, about yourself.
COME, COME, YET AGAIN COME

RUNNING   Any action in which you can be total becomes
meditation, and running is so beautiful that you can be
totally lost in it. And you are in contact with all the
elements—the sun, the air, the earth, the sky; you are in contact with existence. When you are running your breathing
naturally goes very deep and it starts massaging the *hara*
center . . . which is in fact the center from where meditative
energy is released. It is just below the navel, two inches
below the navel. When breathing goes deep it massages that
center, makes it alive. And when you are running, you are
throwing all carbon dioxide out of your lungs. Carbon
dioxide makes people dull, dead, frozen, blocked. Carbon
dioxide is good for trees and very bad for man. We are in
mutual agreement with the trees: they inhale carbon dioxide
and exhale oxygen; we inhale oxygen and exhale carbon
dioxide. That's why as there are becoming less and less trees
on the earth, man is becoming less and less alive, because
the partner is dying.

That's the whole message of ecology: we are together! You
breathe out, the tree breathes in; the tree breathes out, you
breathe in. The tree purifies you through oxygen, you
nourish the tree through carbon dioxide.

When you are running, the whole carbon dioxide is
thrown out and your lungs are full or oxygen. When they
are full of oxygen they purify the blood, they purify the
whole system. That's what purity is; it has nothing to do
with morality. Purity has something to do with biology, it
is a biological concept. When your blood is pure and is not
hampered by poisons and used garbage—it is red and alive,
full of joy and each drop of blood is dancing in you—you
are in the right mood to catch meditation. Then there is no
need to *do* it—it happens!

Running against the wind is a perfect situation. It is a dance
of the elements. And while running you cannot think: if you
are thinking, then you are not running rightly. When you
are running totally, thinking stops. You become too earthbound, the head no more functions. The body is in such

an activity that there is no energy left for the head to go on and on; the thinking stops.

And in those moments of non-thinking, your existence is pure, you simply are, you don't know who. You don't know if you are Indian, German, English, Christian, Mohammedan—you don't know who you are. All is forgotten, you are unburdened of the head . . . you are again an animal! In that moment—when you are again an animal—there is a possibility to contact God.

This is my message—that before a man can contact God he will have to become an animal, never before it . . . because man is a false entity, not authentic at all. Before we can rise high and reach the ultimate we will have to become authentic, as authentic as animals. Through running that authenticity happens . . . It is perfectly good, and now it will be coming more and more now that you know what meditation is. And both these things will help each other: in meditation you will again and again come to those moments which come in running, and in running you will come again and again to those moment which come in meditation. By and by both methods will become one. Then there will be no need to do them separately: you can run and meditate, you can meditate and run.

Sometimes try one technique . . . Just lying on the bed, imagine that you are running. Just imagine the whole scene: the trees and the wind and the sun and the whole beach and the salty air. Imagine everything, visualize it, make it as colorful as possible.

Remember any morning that you liked the most—when you were running on some beach or in some forest. Let it fill you completely . . . even the smell of the trees, the pine trees, or the smell of the beach. Anything that you have liked very much, let it be there as if it is almost real; then start running in imagination—you will find that your breathing is changing. Go on running . . . and you can do this for miles. There is no end to it, you can do it for hours.

And you will be surprised that even doing this on the bed, you will attain to those moments again when suddenly the meditation is there.

So if some day you cannot run for some reason—you are ill, or the situation does not allow, or the city is not worth running in, you cannot run—you can do this and you will attain to the same moments.

THIS IS IT!

S

SACRAMENT I say something to you—it can have two types of possibilities within you. One is that it may remain in the mind: you may become more knowledgeable, you may become a rabbi, a pundit, a scholar. That was not meant to be; you have misunderstood. Let it move deep down in the valley of your body. Let it become your blood, let it circulate, let it become your bones, let it become your breathing, let it become your very marrow so that you can live it. It becomes your life. Not that it adds to your information; it adds to your *being*. Let me be a part of your being, not part of your knowledge. Eat me, drink me, absorb me, digest me.

And Jesus says, *This is my body, which is given for you: this do in remembrance of me*—and continue to do it in remembrance of me. Continue to absorb me deep in your being.

Likewise also the cup after supper, saying: This cup is the new testament in my blood, which is shed for you. And the same he did with the wine, the red wine. He said, *This cup is the new testament in my blood . . .*

You have heard about testaments, verbal testaments, but in blood? You have heard about testaments written in ink, but in blood? What does Jesus mean? He means: Unless I become your life, like your blood, futile was my being with you, futile was your being with me. Fruitless. It was a wastage. Let me become your life. Let me come deep in you so that I am no more separate, so that I become your very heart and I can beat within you.

Unless a Master becomes your very heart, you are not yet a disciple. You may be a student, but not a disciple. You may be learning through him but you are not gaining being. That last night, Jesus did not say much, but whatsoever he said had tremendous meaning in it. Much more must have happened in silence. Just his presence, and the very closeness of death and crucifixion—much must have happened, much must have been communicated through silence . . .

On that last meeting with the disciples this is all that was said, but there was much which was said without saying; the *very* presence was communicated. In fact, the last day with the disciples was the greatest day. That day, seeing that death was coming, they could not postpone, they could not say, "Tomorrow". There was no tomorrow now; the Master would be gone. Now there is no future to postpone until. They had to be there with Jesus that night, all together. They didn't ask anything, because when death is coming nearer, how can you ask? That will be profane, sacrilegious. They were silent. In silence they must have eaten and drunk. The bread became Jesus, the wine become his blood.

That night Jesus transferred himself to them. The same that happened to Mahakashyap and Buddha with the flower, happened with Jesus and the disciples with the bread and wine. And remember, a flower is something not of the world. Buddha gave the flower; a flower is almost other-worldly. Jesus gave bread and wine; he is very earthly, earth-based. Bread and wine is something to eat. A flower you cannot eat, you can appreciate. A flower you cannot drink. It remains far away; there is a distance.

But bread will become your body. And wine?—the drunkenness that is the basic teaching of Jesus: Be drunk with God. Bread and wine, such small, ordinary, everyday things; he made them sacred on that night. He transformed the very earth into paradise. "In remembrance," says Jesus, "do it." And since that day, wherever a real Christian has existed—Christians are many, almost half of the earth, but I am not talking about those, but wherever a *real* Christian has existed—every day, whenever he has eaten or drunk, it is Jesus that he is eating, it is Jesus that he is drinking. Every small, ordinary thing has become a sacrament.

COME FOLLOW ME, Vol. IV

SACRED   Nothing in the world is more sacred than tears of love and joy. Such tears, so pure, are not of this world.

Though part of the body, they express something which is not.

A CUP OF TEA

Yes is life-giving. And yes has not to be partial; it has to be total. Yes has not to be something *against* the no, otherwise it will be partial. Yes has to be so huge that it contains the no in itself. And when the yes is so huge, so enormous, so infinite, that it is capable of containing its opposite, then it becomes a sacred yes.

Sannyas is a sacred yes to life and all that is contained in life. And to live with this yes needs courage! To live with this yes means that one is ready to dissolve into the ocean. But the moment the dewdrop drops into the ocean it also becomes the ocean . . .

Go beyond no, try to reach to the ultimate yes. That is prayer and that is true religion.

THE SACRED YES

SACRIFICE   To be religious means to live a life full of love, joy, innocence, freedom, individuality, to the extent that even if life has to be sacrificed for the higher values of freedom, love, truth, then one sacrifices it joyously. It is worth it! Freedom cannot be sacrificed, bliss cannot be sacrificed, love cannot be sacrificed, and life is significant only if these things are flowering, blossoming. The moment these things are sacrificed there is no point in living. Then life is simply vegetating.

Socrates was given the option that if he stopped talking to people about his philosophy of truth, then he could be released from the court and he could save his life. He laughed and he simply rejected the very idea. What he said is something worth remembering. He said: "To say the truth, to live the truth, is my life! If I cannot say the truth, if I cannot live the truth, then for what am I supposed to live?"

A life is life only when there is something higher in it—higher than life itself. Remember, only that which is higher than life brings significance to life, brings meaning to life. If life has nothing higher than itself then it is empty, utterly futile; then it is absurd.

I am giving you something to live for and something to die for! And the greatest joy in life is to have something to die for. Only when you have something to die for do you have something to live for.

THE WILD GEESE AND THE WATER

A single moment of passionate love, of passionate living, of passionate stillness, is more valuable than the whole of eternity. It is not a question of survival, it is really a question of how to live this moment. The idea of survival makes tomorrow more important than today, the idea of survival makes it easier for you to sacrifice today for tomorrow. And tomorrow never comes: whenever it comes, it is today. And your mind is programmed to sacrifice today for tomorrow, so you go on sacrificing your whole life.

Parents sacrifice their lives for their children. The children again in turn will sacrifice their lives for their children, and so on and so forth. And nobody will ever live.

I am against the very idea of sacrifice. Never sacrifice! Live this moment; live it totally, intensely, passionately. And then a miracle happens: if parents have lived their life beautifully, if they are fulfilled, their very fulfillment creates the space for their children to live, to live in the right way. And by the right way I don't mean the moral way, by the right way I mean the total way. To live partially is to live wrongly, to live totally is to live rightly.

If children are brought up by parents who have been living their lives afire, aflame, who have been celebrating their moments, these children will learn how to celebrate, how to live joyously, how to live affirmatively, how to live saying yes to existence. A deep yes will arise in their hearts: it will be triggered by their parents. And the parents were not sacrificing, not at all, and so the children will not learn the suicidal idea of sacrifice.

If parents are sacrificing for their children, then sooner or later, when the parents are old, they will demand sacrifice from the children. They will say, "We sacrificed so much for you, now you sacrifice for us."

The country demands sacrifice from the people who live in it, the church demands sacrifice, everybody demands sacrifice. Just look around you: they all are standing around you, asking for sacrifice. And they teach you that to sacrifice is moral.

To sacrifice is immoral! Whether you sacrifice for the country or for the religion or for the children, it is immoral. It is immoral because it does not allow you to live your life. You become sad, you become frustrated, and then in return you start coercing others to sacrifice for you. Then the whole life of the whole world becomes simply crippled and paralyzed . . .

I teach you a kind of self-love. You are not created to sacrifice yourself for somebody else, you are not created to serve others. You have been taught this because those others want you to serve them, to sacrifice. And because they want you to serve them, they have to serve you; because they want you to sacrifice yourself for them, they have to sacrifice themselves for you. So we are at each other's throats continuously, demanding sacrifice.

The whole idea has to be dropped. You are created to live and celebrate, just as others are being created to live and celebrate. God is not a murderer; he demands no sacrifice from you. He demands that you bloom and flower.

Only when you have flowered you will be accepted. And the way to flower is the way of acceptance. Don't resist, don't rage against existence: relax, surrender, go with the flow.

UNIO MYSTICA, Vol. II

SADNESS Sadness is also good. One has to learn that everything is good.

Goodness is not a quality of anything, it is just your approach, and how you look at it. Sadness is also good because it gives you a depth which no happiness can ever give. Happiness remains shallow, superficial. Sadness goes to the very depths of your being, reaches to the very center, penetrates you to the very heart.

God comes to you in everything, in different forms and different ways. Sometimes he comes as sadness to give you depth. Sometimes he comes as happiness to create ripples of laughter on your surface. Sometimes he comes as life, sometimes as death, but only he is coming through different forms.

Multi are his forms, many are his ways, and millions are his faces. One has to learn to recognize him in whatsoever form he comes. He will try to deceive you but you are not to be deceived. When he comes as sadness, remember that is also his image. Maybe this is needed right now.

There was one Sufi mystic, Bayazid, who used to pray to God every day, expressing thanks and gratitude. Sometimes there was nothing to be thankful for.

One time he and his disciples were hungry for three days. They were being hunted from one town to another because the Mohammedans were against them. But again, that evening, Bayazid thanked God.

One disciple said, "This is too much. We cannot tolerate it! For what are you thanking God?" Bayazid had been saying, "You are so good, my Lord. Whatsoever we need, you always give us." The disciple said, "Now it is going too far. For three days we have been hungry and have been thrown out of every village, and people have been out to kill us. And you are saying, 'Whatsoever is needed, you always give us!' Now what has he given us for these three days?"

Bayazid laughed and said, "He has given us three days' poverty, and hunger and people who are after our lives. Whatsoever is needed, he always gives. This is needed. This must be needed because he knows better than we."

This is the religious attitude. The religious attitude is very alchemical—it transforms everything. The baser metal is immediately transformed into gold once you have the religious outlook. The religious outlook is the philosopher's stone. You touch anything and immediately it becomes gold.

So touch your sadness with a religious, grateful heart, and suddenly you will see that even sadness has a beauty to it. A silence will immediately settle around you and you will feel thankful that he has given sadness to you. He always gives in the right moment whatsoever was needed. You may not understand. Sometimes you may even misunderstand, but that doesn't make any difference.

BELOVED OF MY HEART

Real love always brings sadness. It is inevitable—because love creates a space which opens new doors to your being. Love brings a twilight situation.

In the moment of love you can see what is unreal and what is real. In the moment of love you can see what is meaningless, what is meaningful, and at the same time you see you are rooted in the meaningless—hence sadness. In the moment of love you become aware of your ultimate potential, you become aware of the farthest peak, but you are not there—hence sadness.

You see a vision but it is a vision, and within a moment it will be gone. It is as if God has spoken to you in a dream and when you are awake you miss it. You know something has happened but it has not become a reality. It was just a passing breeze.

If love does not create sadness then know well it is not love. Love is bound to create sadness—the greater the love, the greater will be the sadness in the wake of it.

Love opens the door to God. Two hearts come close, very, very close, but in that very closeness they can see the separation—that is the sadness. When you are far away you cannot see it so clearly. You know you are separate but when you desire to be one with somebody and you long for it and there is great passion for it and you come close and you come close and then comes a moment when you are very, very close but beyond which you cannot go, you are stuck—suddenly you become sad. The goal is so close by and yet it is beyond reach . . .

If you want it to become an eternal reality for you then love itself is not enough—then prayer will be needed. Love makes you aware of this need—and unless you start moving in prayer, love will create more and more sadness . . .

Then what to do? Let your sadness in love become a pilgrimage into prayer. Let this experience of sadness become a great meditation in depth. First you have to dissolve the ego in your own inner being; you cannot dissolve it in anybody else. It will come back. Only for a moment you can create a state of forgetfulness . . .

But forgetfulness is not a dissolution. You are not dissolved. You are there, waiting. Once the drug has worn off, the ego will grab you again. The ego has to be dissolved, not forgotten. That's the sadness of love: the ego is only forgotten and that too for a moment. Then it comes back.

And comes back with vengeance. Hence you will find lovers fighting continuously. The ego becomes even more solid, crystallized . . .

A few things more . . . The sadness that love brings is very potential, it is very deep, it is very healthy, it is helpful. It will lead you to God. So don't take it negatively, use it. It is great blessing, that sadness felt in love. It simply shows that your aspiration is beyond the capacity of love, your aspiration is for the ultimate. Love can only give you a momentary satisfaction but not an eternal contentment. Feel grateful that love gave you that one momentary satisfaction and feel grateful that love made you aware of a tremendous sadness inside you . . .

So, it is a blessing that you have felt sadness while in those beautiful moments of love. Take the hint. Understand the message. Your unconscious has given you the message to now turn inwards. The beloved resides in you; the beloved is not outside. The beloved resides in your very heart. No other love and no other beloved is going to satisfy except God—hence the sadness.

SUFIS: THE PEOPLE OF THE PATH, Vol. I

You have to allow it and go deeply into it. Don't label it as sadness. That labeling will prevent you from going deeper into it, because in calling it sadness you have already condemned it, and when we condemn something we cannot go deep into it. We have already shrunk back, we have already decided that this is not something good. So don't label it, don't give it a name at all, and you will be surprised: it is a beautiful space, just your interpretation is wrong. It is a beautiful space. It is an overflowing emotion, and it is good. It will relax you and it will take many things off your heart which are burdening it. Those tears are part of an unburdening, and if you don't call it sadness, soon you will learn what it is: it is a new kind of silence that you have not known before.

It looks sad because there is no excitement in it, and that's what we call sadness. When there is some excitement we are happy and we think things are happening. When nothing is happening and the excitement is not there and we are not occupied, we think we are sad. That's how we have experienced sadness.

Now this is a totally new phenomenon. Something is happening but it is not an excitement, it is not feverish. It is not a kind of occupation. Something is happening, and it is so new that you cannot categorize it. So don't categorize at all; just watch what it is and go into it.

If in reading my books it comes, close the book. Let tears flow, enjoy, help them, and whatsoever is happening, receive it as a gift from God. And you will be surprised: it will give you such depth and such perception as you have not ever known before. It will keep your eyes so clean, so clear—and not only the physical eyes but the spiritual eyes too—that you will start seeing deeply into things. Things will become transparent to you, people will become transparent. And soon you will see this is not sadness but silence.

Silence and sadness have one thing in common, that's why the misunderstanding arises; that common thing is depth. The depth that happens in sadness, happens in silence, but sadness is a negative state and silence is a positive state; that is the difference, and that is a great difference.

TURN ON, TUNE IN AND DROP THE LOT

SAGE   See Sophist

SAINTS The saints that I criticize are not saints of love. They are all anti-love, anti-life, they are not life-affirmative. I don't condemn them because they are *saints,* I condemn them because they are anti-life. If somebody is full of life's joy and love for life then there is real saintliness.

Real saintliness cannot be against love and against life. It can't be against this celebration that goes on and on. Real saintliness will be a participation in existence as it is. The real sage or saint will not choose, he will accept whatsoever is given. The body is given, he will accept it. The world is given, he will accept it, and he will accept it in immense gratitude because it is God's gift.

So I am against the so-called saints—I am trying to create real saints. And unless we can create real people the world is doomed. Religion has been condemnatory too long. It has crippled, paralyzed people's lives. I want religion to give you freedom, not paralysis . . . a capacity to dance, to be fluid, to be liquid, a capacity to love, to relate, to communicate, not just to become a monk and close into yourself.

Saints are pinned butterflies. Sinners are alive—a snake resting on the rock in the afternoon sun. Sinners sometimes can become saints, but then their sainthood has a totally different quality to it. They cannot belong to any church, they cannot belong to any sect. They cannot belong—how can a saint belong? The saint is like a fragrance, free, moving in the winds—he cannot belong. Jesus never belonged to anybody. That's why Jews were angry with him—they wanted him to belong.

Real saints will not be recognized as saints, no church will sanctify them as saints. And the saints that are sanctified by the church are really bogus, mumbo-jumbo, false, artificial, synthetic, plastic saints. Yes, they don't laugh, that's true. But Jesus is not that kind of saint. He laughs, he drinks, he eats well, he loves. He was a true man of the earth, very earthly, rooted in the earth.

And the earth is not against the sky. Observe the trees—the tree can go higher in the sky only if it goes deeper in the earth. And so is the rule, so is the law. A man who is deeply rooted in the earth can go deeply in God—not otherwise. A man who can laugh and enjoy and be merry, can pray. His roots in the earth will give him enough nourishment to pray. He will be grateful—only then he can pray.

God is significant only when it comes out of your gratefulness.

THIS VERY BODY THE BUDDHA

SALVATION   Salvation is not something that man can do; it can only descend as a grace, it can only come as a gift. Salvation is so vast and man is so small that it is not possible for man to manage it. The more man tries to manage it, the more entangled he becomes in new kinds of chains, in new imprisonments. He moves from one cell of the prison into another cell, that's all.

To be really free, to be totally free, to be absolutely free, can only be a gift from God . . .

Then what should *we* do? We cannot attain salvation on our own, but still something is expected of us. We should become receivers—not doers, but receivers. We should be on the receiving end. And that's what love is, to be receptive. Man can be loving, and then God descends as salvation. In the womb of love, the child of ultimate freedom is conceived. Man has to become a womb, a receptable.

All that is needed on our part is to drop all armor, to drop all defences, to open all the doors and all the windows so that the wind can come, the rain can come and the sun can come.

WON'T YOU JOIN THE DANCE?

Buddha says: "I can only point the way. You will have to make all the effort. I cannot make it for you. I cannot be your salvation."

Look at the beauty of this man! He says: "I cannot be your salvation. If it was possible for me to be your salvation, then I would have done it already. I would not even have asked your permission!"

Christians go on saying that Jesus is the salvation. But that is nonsense, because if Jesus is the salvation then why is the world still in misery? Jesus has happened! He would have solved everybody's problems. He has not solved anybody's problems—not even those of the Christians. He cannot—nobody can do it. And it is good that nobody can do it because if others could do it then they could undo it too. And if your freedom can be given by others it won't be much of a freedom, it will be another kind of bondage.

Freedom has to be achieved by your own efforts. Nobody can give it to you, hence nobody can take it away from you. It is absolutely yours.

THE BOOK OF THE BOOKS, Vol. VII

SAMADHI *Samadhi* one enters only once and then one never comes out of it. There is no way out. There is no exit, there is only entrance. I have entered *samadhi*. Now wherever I am, whatsoever I am doing, it is all happening in *samadhi*. Now there is no way to come out of it. *Samadhi* is not a state, it is not a mood in which you go and then you can come out. *Samadhi* is your very being. Now where can I leave my being? It is my very nature. Now where can I leave my nature. I am it!

GUIDA SPIRITUALE

See also Satori

SANNYAS Sannyas is a crazy way of living life. The ordinary way is very sane, mathematical, calculated, cautious. The way of sannyas is non-calculative, beyond mathematics, beyond cunningness, cleverness. It is not cautious at all; it is knowingly moving into danger . . .

Sannyas is a way to live your life in total danger. What do I mean when I say sannyas is living dangerously? It means living moment to moment without a past. The past makes your life convenient, comfortable, because the past is known; you are familiar with it, you are very efficient with it. But life is never past, it is always present. The past is that which is no more and life is that which is. Life is always now, here, and all your knowledge comes from the past. Trying to live the present through the past is the way of the coward; it is the calculated way. People call it sanity, but it is very superficial and never adequate. There is no rapport with the present . . .

You cannot dance—you are chained to the past, you are imprisoned in the past.

Sannyas means escaping from that prison. The prison may be of Hinduism or Mohammedanism or Christianity or Judaism or Jainism—it does not matter what the name of the prison is . . .

Sannyas is rebellion against all slavery; it is living life in absolute freedom. To live life in absolute freedom without traditions, without conventions, without religions, without philosophies, without ideologies—political, social and others—to live unburdened is sannyas. But it will look crazy to the whole world. Freedom *looks* crazy because everybody is living an imprisoned life . . .

Sannyas is an escape from the prison—Catholic or communist, it does not matter; it is an escape into the open.

To live moment to moment is a crazy way, a poetic way, the way of the lover. People are living lives of prose—clear-cut but mundane, superficial . . .

The prose style of life is the ordinary lifestyle; the poetic style of life is sannyas. It is bound to be a little bit crazy—all poets are crazy, all painters are crazy, all dancers are crazy, all musicians are crazy. All that is great on this earth has something of madness in it.

Zorba the Greek says to his boss, "Boss, everything is right in you, only one thing is missing—a little bit of madness!"

And I agree with Zorba. Sannyas gives you a little bit of madness, but that little bit of madness brings rainbows to your life . . .

Sannyas is a risk! . . . The person who cannot risk deals with life in a businesslike way. He tries to cheat life, exploit life. He tries to give less and get more, because that is the way of profit.

The sannyasin does not care at all about getting anything back from life; he simply gives in sheer trust—and he receives a millionfold. But that's another matter; that is not his consideration at all . . .

Sannyas is hope—hope against all hope. People have lost all hope; they are living hopelessly . . .

The way of sannyas is the way of tremendous hope, trust. Life is basically good, beautiful, divine, so if we are missing then something is wrong with us, not with life itself . . .

Sannyas is not a way of doing anything, it is a way of being. It changes your inner world and, of course, your outer world changes with it. But that is secondary. It changes your center, it changes your awareness, and *then* your behavior, your actions. Whatsoever you do has a new quality to it, a grace that descends from the beyond, a song said or unsaid, sung or unsung, but it is there within your heart—a dance, the quality of dance to your feet.

Hence, I say it is a crazy way of living, but that's the only way to live rightly. A poetic way, the way of the lover—but only love knows. Logic is blind, love has eyes. Only love can see the ultimate truth that surrounds you within and without.

COME, COME, YET AGAIN COME

Sannyas is a rebellion against both the past and the future. Man has either lived in the past or in the future, but never in the present. And the present is the only reality there is; nothing else exists. Existence knows only one time, that is now, and one space, that is here. But mind either lives in the past, which is no more, or in the future, which is not yet. Mind exists in the non-existential, hence mind never comes across reality; it cannot by its very functioning.

Sannyas is a rebellion against mind itself. It is a way of life in which mind is not the master—no-mind is the master and mind functions only as a servant. Mind is actually a mechanism; it is good as a beautiful device of nature, but the moment the servant becomes the master there is danger, great danger. Then your life is bound to be a mess, a chaos. The servant is blind, unintelligent, unaware. To live according to the mind is not to live at all; it is sheer stupidity. Mind is never original, never intelligent; it is always repetitive, it is always borrowed, it is always mechanical—hence stupid, hence unintelligent.

Sannyas is a tremendous jump into reality, an escape to reality from the unreal.

THE WILD GEESE AND THE WATER

To be a sannyasin means not to be bothered about questions and answers. The whole process of sannyas is getting rid of the mind. Mind consists of questions and answers: the moment you get rid of the mind, then only consciousness is left in its purity, not even a ripple. The lake is so silent, so unperturbed, so still, it starts reflecting the stars, the clouds, the moon, the trees, the flowers, the birds on the wing.

There is a Zen saying that the birds have no desire to be reflected in the lake, the lake has no desire to reflect the birds, but it still happens. The birds are reflected, the lake reflects, although the desire exists neither on the part of the birds nor on the part of the lake. In this desirelessness everything happens, nothing is done.

And a sannyasin has to relax into that total state of let-go when everything happens and nothing is done. Much happens, miracles happen. But don't ask me what to do, ask me only one thing: "How to get out of the old rut of the mind?" And it consists of questions and answers; it is a question-and-answer game.

Slip out of the mind like a snake slips out of the old skin. The mind is always old, it belongs to the past; it is not in the present, it has no future. Mind *means* the past, the dead. Mind is like the rear-view mirror in a car. If you go on looking in the rear-view mirror continuously you are bound for a great disaster, because the car has to go ahead and you will be looking in the rear-view mirror at the road that you have already passed, at the dust you have raised on the road. That is not where you are going, and where you are going you are not looking at. The disaster is absolutely certain.

And this is happening in everybody's life. You go reading the Vedas; that is looking in the rear-view mirror. Five thousand years have passed, and still you go on looking at the Vedas, you go on reading the Bible, you go on reciting the Koran, you go on discussing Kanad, Kapil, Aristotle, Plato, Confucius, Mo Tzu, but all this is a sheer wastage of time.

Look at the present. *This* very moment God is within you and without you. And if you can live this God in total serenity, in total attunement, at-one-ment, you will have known the ecstasy that I am talking about, the bliss, the benediction.

COME, COME, YET AGAIN COME

The work consists of two things: I have to help people to become sannyasins—seeing their possibilities, potentialities, hoping for them; but when I see that a person is impossible, that the more I give to him the less he receives, the more I give to him the more closed he becomes—as if he is obliging me . . . When this feeling becomes settled—and it is not that I take a hasty decision about it, I give all the opportunities and occasions for the person; but if it is impossible, then it is impossible—then I withdraw myself from his being. Once I have withdrawn, sooner or later he will have to drop sannyas.

It functions both ways. The moment you take sannyas, you think *you* are taking sannyas. In the majority of cases I have chosen you—that's why you have taken sannyas. Otherwise you would not have been able to take such a risk. And it also works the second way: when you drop sannyas,

I have chosen you and I help you to drop it, because left to yourself you may go on postponing for your whole life. When you take sannyas, then you postpone for a long, long time. When you want to drop it, then too you postpone for a long, long time. You cannot do anything immediately. You cannot live the moment in its totality.

And this too I have felt: once you have left sannyas there is a possibility you may come back—because then you will miss me, and then you will understand what was being showered on you. Then you will miss the nourishment, then you will miss the contact. When you are getting it you start taking it for granted. Sometimes it is good to take it away so real thirst and an appetite arises in you and you start seeing.

But next time, when you come for sannyas, it is not going to be that easy. I will not initiate you so easily. Then you will have to earn it. Once you drop sannyas, coming back is going to be difficult. Then you will have to earn it. Once you drop sannyas, coming back is going to be difficult. I will create all kinds of barriers. Unless you transcend those barriers you will not be accepted again.

That too is to help you, because there are people who can enjoy things only if they are difficult. If things are very simple and easy they cannot enjoy them. They need long, hard, arduous ways.

Sannyas is a simple phenomenon because the whole foundation of it is to relax and live in Tao, relax and let God take care of you.

THE SECRET OF SECRETS, Vol. II

Sannyas is to give you a sense of direction, a togetherness, a rootedness, an awareness of what you are and what you can be. It is immensely significant to remember that sannyas is not a formality. It is not just a formal thing like being a Christian—you were born in a Christian home—or a formal thing like being a Hindu.

Sannyas is exactly like when Jesus was on the earth and a few people started walking with him, started moving into danger with him, or when Buddha was on the earth and a few people gathered together around him and risked all! The same drama is being played here again.

You are fortunate to become part of it. Feel blessed! And then slowly slowly you will start remembering what the meaning is of being appointed by God, what the meaning is of every man bringing a message into the world. No man comes empty-handed but very few people ever deliver the message. Those who do are the Buddhas, the awakened ones.

My effort here is to make thousands of Buddhas. Less than that won't do.

EIGHTY-FOUR THOUSAND POEMS

SANNYASIN It is very difficult to define a sannyasin, and more so if you are going to define *my* sannyasins.

Sannyas is basically a rebellion about all structures, hence the difficulty to define. Sannyas is a way of living life unstructuredly. Sannyas is to have a character which is characterless. By "characterless" I mean you don't depend anymore on the past. Character means the past, the way you have lived in the past, the way you have become habituated to living—all your habits and conditionings and beliefs and your experiences—that's what your character is. A sannyasin is one who no longer lives in the past or through the past; who lives in the moment, hence, is unpredictable.

A man of character is predictable; a sannyasin is unpredictable because a sannyasin is freedom.

A sannyasin is not only free, he *is* freedom. It is living rebellion. But still, I will try: a few hints can be given, not exact definitions, a few indications, fingers pointing to the moon. Don't get caught with the fingers. The fingers don't define the moon, they only indicate. The fingers have nothing to do with the moon. They may be long, they may be short, they may be artistic, they may be ugly, they may be white, they may be black, they may be healthy, they may be ill—that doesn't matter. They simply indicate. Forget the finger and look at the moon.

What I am going to give is not a definition; that is not possible in this case. And in fact, definition is never possible about anything that is alive. Definition is possible only about something which is dead, which grows no more, which blooms no more, which has no more possibility, potentiality, which is exhausted and spent. Then definition is possible.

You can define a dead man, you cannot define an alive man.

Life basically means that the new is still possible. So these are not definitions.

The old sannyasin had a definition, very clear-cut. That's why he is dead. I call my sannyas "neo-sannyas" for this particular reason: my sannyas is an opening, a journey, a dance, a love affair with the unknown, a romance with existence itself, a search for an orgasmic relationship with the whole. And everything else has failed in the world. Everything that was defined, that was clear-cut, that was logical, has failed. Religions have failed, politics have failed, ideologies have failed—and they were very clear-cut. They were blueprints for the future of man. They have all failed. All programs have failed. Sannyas is not a program anymore. It is exploration, not a program.

When you become a sannyasin I initiate you into freedom, and into nothing else. It is *great* responsibility to be free, because you have nothing to lean upon except your own inner being, your own consciousness. You have nothing as a prop, as a support. I take all your props and supports away; I leave you alone, I leave you utterly alone. In that aloneness . . . the flower of sannyas. That aloneness blooms on its own accord into the flower of sannyas.

Sannyas is characterless. It has no morality; it is not immoral, it is amoral. Or, it has a higher morality that never comes from the outside, but comes from within. It does not allow any imposition from the outside, because all impositions from the outside convert you into serfs, into slaves. And my effort is to give you dignity, glory. My effort here is to give you splendor.

All other efforts have failed. It was inevitable, because the failure was built-in. They were all structure-oriented, and every kind of structure becomes heavy on the heart of man, sooner or later. Every structure becomes a prison, and one day or other you have to rebel against it. Have you not observed it down through history?—each revolution in its own turn becomes repressive. In Russia it happened, in China it happened. After every revolution, the revolutionary becomes anti-revolutionary. Once he comes into power he has his own structure to impose upon the society. And once he starts imposing his structure, slavery changes into a new kind of slavery, but never into freedom. All revolutions have failed.

This is not revolution. This is rebellion. Revolution is social, collective; rebellion is individual. We are not interested in giving any structure to the society. Enough of the structures! Let all structures go. We want individuals in the world, moving freely, moving consciously, of course. And their responsibility comes through their own consciousness. They behave rightly not because they are trying to follow certain commandments; they behave rightly, they behave *accurately,* because they care. Do you know?—this word "accurate" comes from care? When you care about something you are accurate. If you care about somebody, you are accurate in your relationship.

A sannyasin is one who cares about himself, and naturally cares about everybody else—because you cannot be happy alone. You can only be happy in a happy world, in a happy climate. If everybody is crying and weeping and is in misery, it is very very difficult for you to be happy. So one who cares about happiness—about his own happiness—becomes careful about everybody else's happiness, because happiness happens only in a happy climate.

But this care is not because of any dogma. It is there because of love. And the first love, naturally, is the love for yourself. Then other loves follow.

Other efforts have failed because they were mind-oriented. They were based in the thinking process, they were conclusions of the mind. Sannyas is not a conclusion of the mind. It is rooted in joy, not in thought. It is rooted in celebration, not in thinking. It is rooted in that awareness where thoughts are not found. It is not a choice: it is not a choice between two thoughts, it is the dropping of all thought. It is living out of nothingness . . .

Each sannyasin will be a totally unique person. I am not interested in the society. I am not interested in the collectivity. My interest is absolutely in the individual, in *you!* . . .

Sannyas is just a beginning, a seed of a totally different kind of world where people are free to be themselves, where people are not constrained, crippled, paralyzed, where people are not repressed, made to feel guilty, where joy is accepted, where cheerfulness is the rule, where seriousness has disappeared, where a non-serious sincerity, a playfulness has entered. These can be the indications, the fingers pointing to the moon.

First: an openness to experience.

People are ordinarily closed; they are not open to experience. Before they experience anything they already take prejudices about it. They don't want to experiment, they don't want to explore. This is sheer stupidity . . .

So the first quality of a sannyasin is an openness to experience. He will not decide before he has experienced. He will *never* decide before he has experienced. He will not have any belief systems. He will not say, "This is so because Buddha says it." He will not say, "This is so because it is written in the Vedas." He will say, "I am ready to go into it and see whether it is so or not."

Buddha's departing message to his disciples was this: "Remember . . ." And this he was repeating for his whole life, again and again; the last message also was this— "Remember, don't believe in anything because I have said it. Never believe anything unless you have experienced it."

A sannyasin will not carry many beliefs; in fact, none. He will carry only his own experiences. And the beauty of experience is that the experience is always open, because further exploration is possible. And belief is always closed; it comes to a full point. Belief is always finished. Experience is never finished, it remains unfinished. While you are living how can your experience be finished? Your experience is growing, it is changing, it is moving. It is continuously moving from the known into the unknown and from the unknown to the unknowable. And remember, experience has a beauty because it is unfinished.

Some of the greatest songs are those which are unfinished. Some of the greatest books are those which are unfinished. Some of the greatest music is that which is unfinished. The unfinished has a beauty . . .

Experience always remains open—that means unfinished. Belief is always complete and finished. The first quality is an openness to experience . . .

The second quality is existential living. He does not live out of ideas: that one should be like this, one should be like that, one should behave in this way, one should not behave in this way. He does not live out of ideas, he is responsive to existence. He responds with his total heart to whatsoever is the case. His being is herenow. Spontaneity, simplicity, naturalness—these are his qualities.

He does not live a ready-made life. He does not carry maps—how to live, how not to live. He allows life; wherever it leads he goes with it.

A sannyasin is not a swimmer, and he does not try to go upstream. He goes with the whole, he flows with the stream. He flows so totally with the stream that by and by he is no longer separate from the stream, he becomes the stream. That is the beginning of Buddha's sannyas too—one who has entered the stream, one who has come to relax in existence. He does not carry valuations, he's not judgmental.

Existential living means each moment has to decide on its own. Life is atomic! You don't decide beforehand, you don't rehearse, you don't prepare how to live. Each moment comes, brings a situation; you are there to respond to it—you respond.

The third quality of a sannyasin is a trust in one's own organism. People trust others, the sannyasin trusts his own organism. Body, mind, soul, all are included. If he feels like loving, he flows in love. If he does not feel like loving he says "Sorry"—but he never pretends . . .

A sannyasin is one who trusts in his organism, and that trust helps him to relax into his being, and helps him to relax into the totality of existence. It brings a general acceptance of oneself and others. It gives a kind of rootedness, centering. And then there is great strength and power, because you are centered in your own body, in your own being. You have roots in the soil . . .

The fourth is a sense of freedom.

The sannyasin is not only free, he is freedom. He always lives in a free way. Freedom does not mean licentiousness. Licentiousness is not freedom, licentiousness is just a reaction against slavery; so you move to the other extreme. Freedom is not the other extreme, it is not reaction. Freedom is an insight: "I have to be free, if I have to be at all. There is no other way to be. If I am too possessed by the church, by Hinduism, by Christianity, by Mohammedanism, then

I cannot be. Then they will go on creating boundaries around me. They go on forcing me into myself like a crippled being. I have to be free. I have to take this risk of being free. I have to take this danger."

Freedom is not very convenient, is not very comfortable. It is risky. A sannyasin takes that risk. It does not mean that he goes on fighting with each and everybody. It does not mean that when the law says keep to the right or keep to the left, he goes against it, no. He does not bother about trivia. If the law says keep to the left, he keeps to the left—because it is not a slavery. But about important, essential things . . . If the father says, "Get married to this woman because she is rich and much money will be coming," he will say, "No. How can I marry a woman when I am not in love with her? This will be disrespectful to the woman." If the father says, "Go to the church every Sunday because you are born in a Christian home," he will say, "I will go to the church if I *feel*, I will not go because you say. Birth is accidental; it does not matter much. The church is not very essential. If I feel like it, I will go." I'm not saying don't go to church, but go only when your feeling has arisen for it. Then there will be a communion. Otherwise, no need to go.

About essential things the sannyasin will always keep his freedom intact. And because he respects freedom, he will respect others' freedom too. He will never interfere with anybody's freedom, whosoever that other is. If your wife has fallen in love with somebody you feel hurt, you will cry tears of sadness, but that is your problem. You will not interfere with her. You will not say, "Stop it, because I am suffering!" You will say, "This is your freedom. If I suffer, that is my problem. I have to tackle it, I have to face it. If I feel jealous, I have to get rid of my jealousy. But you go on your own. Although it hurts me, although I would have liked that you had not gone with anybody, that is *my* problem. I cannot trespass on your freedom."

Love respects so much that it gives freedom. And if love is not giving freedom it is not love, it is something else.

A sannyasin is immensely respectful about his own freedom, very careful about his own freedom, and so is he about others' freedom too.

This sense of freedom gives him an individuality. He is not just a part of the mass mind. He has a certain uniqueness—his way of life, his style, his climate, his individuality. He exists in his own way, he loves his own song. He has a sense of identity: he knows who he is, he goes on deepening his feeling for who he is, and he never compromises. Independence, rebellion—remember, not revolution but rebellion—that is the quality of a sannyasin. And there is a great difference . . .

A sannyasin is rebellious. By rebellion I mean his vision is utterly different. He does not function in the same logic, in the same structure, in the same pattern. He is not against the pattern—because if you are against a certain pattern you will have to create another pattern to fight with it. And patterns are all alike. A sannyasin is one who has simply slipped out. He's not against the pattern, he has understood the stupidity of all patterns. He has looked into the foolishness of all patterns and he has slipped out. He is rebellious.

The fifth is creativity. The old sannyas was very uncreative. It was thought that somebody becomes a sannyasin and goes to a Himalayan cave and sits there, and that was perfectly all right. Nothing more was needed. You can go and see Jaina monks: they are sitting in their temples, doing nothing—absolutely uncreative, dull and stupid looking, with no flame of intelligence at all. And people are worshipping and touching their feet. Ask, "Why are you touching the feet?" and they say, "This man has renounced the world"—as if renouncing the world is a value in itself. "What has he done?" and they will say, "He has fasted. He fasts for months together"—as if not eating is a value in itself.

But don't ask what he has painted, what beauty he has created in the world, what poem he has composed, what song he has brought into existence, what music, what dance, what invention? "What is his creation?" and they will say, "What are you talking about? He is a sannyasin! He simply sits in the temple and allows people to touch his feet, that's all." And there are so many people sitting like this in India.

My conception of a sannyasin is that his energy will be creative, that he will bring a little more beauty into the world, that he will bring a little more joy into the world, that he will find new ways to get into dance, singing, music, that he will bring some beautiful poems. He will create something, he will not be uncreative. The days of uncreative sannyas are over. The new sannyasin can exist only if he is creative.

He should contribute something. Remaining uncreative is almost a sin, because you exist and you don't contribute. You eat, you occupy space, and you don't contribute anything. My sannyasins have to be creators. And when you are in deep creativity, you are close to God. That's what prayer really is, that's what meditation is. God is the creator, and if you are not creators you will be far away from God. God knows only one language, the language of creativity. That's why when you compose music, when you are utterly lost in it, something of the divine starts filtering out of your being. That is the joy of creativity, that's the ecstasy—*svaha!*

The sixth is a sense of humor, laughter, playfulness, nonserious sincerity. The old sannyas was unlaughing, dead, dull. The new sannyasin has to bring more and more laughter to his being. He has to be a laughing sannyasin, because your laughter can create situations for others also to relax. The temple should be full of joy and laughter and dance. It should not be like a Christian church. The church looks so cemetery-like. And with the cross there it seems to be almost a worship of death . . . a little morbid. You cannot laugh in a church. A belly-laugh would not be allowed; people will think you are crazy or something. When people enter into a church they become serious, stiff, long-faced.

To me, laughter is a religious quality, *very* essential. It has to be part of the inner world of a sannyasin—a sense of humor.

The seventh is meditativeness, aloneness, mystical peak experiences that happen when you are alone, when you are absolutely alone inside yourself. Sannyas makes you alone; not lonely, but alone; not solitary, but it gives you a solitude. You can be happy alone, you are no longer dependent on others. You can sit alone in your room and you can be *utterly* happy. There is no need to go to a club, there is no need to always have friends around you, there is no need to go to a movie. You can close your eyes and you can fall into inner blissfulness: that's what meditativeness is all about.

And the eighth is love, relatedness, relationship. Remember, you can relate only when you have learned how to be alone, never before it. Only two individuals can relate. Only two freedoms can come close and embrace each other. Only two nothingnesses can penetrate into each other and melt into each other. If you are not capable of being alone, your relationship is false. It is just a trick to avoid your loneliness, nothing else. And that's what millions of people are doing. Their love is nothing but their incapacity to be alone. So they move with somebody, they hold hands, they pretend that they love, but deep down the only problem is that they cannot be alone. So they need somebody to hang around, they need somebody to hold onto, they need somebody to lean upon. And the others are also using them in the same way, because the other can also not be alone, is incapable. The other also finds you instrumental as a help to escape from himself.

So two persons that you say are in love are more or less in hate with themselves. And because of that hate, they are escaping. The other helps them to escape, so they become dependent on the other, they become addicted to the other. You cannot live without your wife, you cannot live without your husband because you are addicted. But a sannyasin is one . . . That's why I say the seventh quality is aloneness, and the eighth quality is love-relationship.

And these are the two possibilities: you can be happy alone and you can be happy together too. These are two kinds of ecstasies possible for humanity. You can move into *samadhi* when alone and you can move into *samadhi* when together with somebody, in deep love.

And there are two kinds of people: the extroverts will find it easier to have their peak through the other, and the introverts will find it easier to have their greatest peak while alone. But the other is not antagonistic; they can both move together. One will be bigger, and that will be the decisive factor in whether you are an introvert or an extrovert. The path of Buddha is the path of the introvert; it talks only about meditation. The path of Christ is extrovert; it talks about love.

My sannyasin has to be a synthesis of both. An emphasis will be there. Somebody will be emphatically more in tune with himself than with others, and somebody will be just the opposite—more in tune with somebody else. But there is no need to get hooked in one kind of experience. Both experiences can remain available.

And the ninth is transcendence, Tao—not ego: no-mind, nobodiness, nothingness, in tune with the whole.

That is the whole message of *Prajnaparamita Sutra,* The Heart Sutra: *Gate, gate, paragate*—Gone, gone, gone beyond; *parasamgate, bodhisvaha*—gone altogether beyond. What ecstasy! Alleluia!

Trancendence is the last and the highest quality of a sannyasin.

But these are only indications, these are not definitions. Take them in a very liquid way. Don't start taking what I have said in a rigid way—very liquid, in a vague kind of vision, in a twilight vision—not like when there is a full sun in the sky. Then things are very defined. In a twilight, when the sun has gone down and the night has not yet descended, it is both, just in the middle, the interval. In that kind of way, take whatsoever I have said to you. Remain liquid, flowing.

Never create any rigidity around you. Never become definable.

THE HEART SUTRA

SANSKRIT   Sanskrit is the oldest language on the earth. The very word *sanskrit* means transformed, adorned, crowned, decorated, refined—but remember the word "transformed". The language itself was transformed because so many people attained to the ultimate, and because they were using the language something of their joy penetrated into it, something of their poetry entered into the very cells, the very fiber of the language. Even the language became transformed, illuminated. It was bound to happen—just as it is happening today in the West: languages are becoming more and more scientific, accurate, mathematical, precise. They have to be because science is giving them its color, its shape, its form. If science is growing, then of course the language in which the science is expressed will have to be scientific.

The same happened five thousand years ago in India with Sanskrit; so many people became enlightened and they were all speaking Sanskrit; their enlightenment entered into it with all its music, with all its poetry, with all its celebration. Sanskrit became luminous. Sanskrit is the most poetic and musical language in existence.

A poetic language is just the opposite of a scientific language. In scientific language every word has to be very precise in meaning; it has to have only one meaning. In a poetic language the word has to be liquid, flowing, dynamic, not static, allowing many meanings, many possibilities. The word has not to be precise at all; the more imprecise it is the better, because then it will be able to express all kinds of nuances.

Hence the Sanskrit *sutras* can be defined in many ways, can be commented upon in many ways—they allow much playfulness. For example, there are eight hundred roots in Sanskrit and out of those eight hundred roots thousands of words have been derived, just as out of one root a tree grows and many branches and thousands of leaves and hundreds of flowers. Each single root becomes a vast tree with great foliage . . .

The Sanskrit language is called *devavani*—the divine language. And it certainly is—divine in the sense that it is the most poetic and the most musical language. Each word has a music around it, a certain aroma.

How did it happen? It happened because so many people used it who were full of inner harmony. Of course those words became luminous: they were used by people who were enlightened. Something of their light filtered through to the words, reached the words; something of their silence entered the very grammar, the very language they were using.

The script in which Sanskrit is written is called *devanagari; devanagari* means "dwelling-place of the gods", and so certainly it is. Each word has become divine, just because it has been used by people who had known God or godliness.

I AM THAT

SATISFACTION There is a great difference between satisfaction and contentment; not only is there a difference, in fact they are opposite to each other . . .

Satisfaction is pseudo. It is just an effort to cover up your wounds. The wounds are not healed; they are there, but only covered. And they go on growing, they go on becoming bigger, they go on collecting more pus; they can become cancerous.

Contentment is healed wounds. One has become whole. It is authentic. Satisfaction is only a consolation: because we cannot create bliss we are miserable, so we create many methods to console ourselves. Contentment is not a consolation, it is bliss itself.

Once your bliss starts functioning, contentment follows it like shadow. So I don't teach contentment, I teach bliss. For centuries the other religions have been teaching contentment; but if you try to be contented it will be only satisfaction, a consolation, a false coin. That's why this pseudo humanity has come into being.

I start with bliss. The old religious approach was to start with contentment. And they used to say—and it has been said in many scriptures of the world—that the contented person is blissful. I say just the opposite is true: the blissful person is contented. And one who is not blissful, his contentment is bogus.

So start by being blissful.

THE OLD POND—PLOP!

SATORI   There is a difference between *satori* and *samadhi*.

Satori means only a glimpse, a faraway glimpse. *Satori* is a Japanese word, very beautiful, untranslatable, but it can be described. It is like on an open day when there are no clouds you can see in the sun the Himalayan peaks, the virgin snow on the peaks shining like silver or gold, from thousands of miles away. You are seeing the truth, but the distance between you and the truth is there—you are not *it.* This is *satori.* Seeing the truth but not being it is *satori.*

Then there is the Sanskrit word *samadhi,* which is also untranslatable. *Samadhi* means *being* the truth; where the knower and the known become one, where the experienced and the experiencer are one. It is no more a question of an open, unclouded day, it is no more a question of the sunlit peaks rising high in the sky. *You are it!*—not even the distance of a single inch.

Chuang Tzu says: Even the distance of a hair is enough,

and heaven and earth fall apart. Just the distance of a hair—
not much at all, almost negligible—but it is enough to
separate earth from heaven. When even that much difference
is not there, one is enlightened.

THEOLOGIA MYSTICA

From the outside sometimes a *satori* looks like epilepsy;
from the outside the symptoms are almost the same. Even
up to now doctors suspect that Ramakrishna used to have
epileptic fits. Even about Ramakrishna they suspected
epilepsy because from the outside the symptoms are the
same. It is a particular kind of *satori*—what we call in India
bhaw samadhi; it is an emotional *satori.*

There are two types of *satoris*—one that happens through
the intellect . . . Then one remains alert—not only alert: one
becomes *tremendously* alert. That's what happened in Zen
satoris. The whole approach is through the intellect—through
the koan, the intellectual puzzle and thinking and meditation. They are all bringing a focal point where the mind
comes to the most intense of tensions, beyond which there
is no more to go. It comes like a peak, like a sexual peak,
and then from there everything explodes. But the person
remains very very conscious—in fact more conscious than
ever. It is a flash of consciousness—that is Zen *satori.* But
they are not aware of another kind of *satori,* because Zen
is half of the path . . . what in India we call *gyana yoga*—the
path of knowing. Zen is that.

There is another path—the other half, the other aspect of
reality—*bhakta yoga,* the path of devotion. On the path of
devotion, when a *satori* happens it happens though the heart
and not through the intellect. It happens through the emotions, and when it happens through the emotions one goes
unconscious—it is a flash of unconsciousness. Both are
satoris—one happens from the head center, another happens
from the heart center—but this *satori* is not so much known
in the West.

FAR BEYOND THE STARS

"Getting it" means coming to know that there is nothing
to get. "Getting it" means getting rid of all greed, of all ambition, of all goals. The day you get that the way things are
is the perfect way, you have attained. The day you recognize

the fact that things cannot be better than this, suddenly you have exploded into a new light, into a new being, into a new consciousness. "Getting it" is getting that there is nowhere to get to. Then one lives moment to moment. This is *samadhi*.

But many times you get it and it gets lost. You get it again and again you lose it. Then it is a mini-*satori*. Mini-*satori* means a glimpse. The possibility is you may lose it . . .

A mini-*satori* is a guarded statement about *satori*. It means that you can lose it. If you are very alert it can turn into a *satori*. A *satori* is an experience which has become established and there is no way to lose it. A mini-*satori* is an experience which has come just like a glimpse, like a breeze. Suddenly you see that all perception is available. The aperture opens. But it closes like a camera. Before a *satori* many mini-*satoris* happen, it depends—sometimes thousands of mini-*satoris*, sometimes hundreds, sometimes a few, sometimes one. It depends on the person. Sometimes the first *satori* can become the *satori*, there is no need for it to be a mini—it depends on you.

But whenever it happens to any of you I am going to call it mini for a certain reason. The reason is I want to make you alert so that you don't lose it. It can become a *satori* but if I call it a *satori* immediately you will lose it and it can become a mini. You follow me? I call it mini so that it can become a *satori*. Sometimes you will think that Bhagwan is being very miserly. Why does he call it mini? Why can he not call it *satori*? It is a very guarded statement—I have to protect you against you in many ways. Even if it is a satori I will call it mini—remember. In fact, "mini" is my invention; the Zen people don't call any *satori* mini.

I call it mini and the reason is very, very meaningful. I want you to be very, very alert and careful. A man who attains to a mini-*satori* has become pregnant. Now he should be as careful as a pregnant woman. He is carrying something valuable in him. There is every possibility of miscarriage. To avoid miscarriage I call it mini-*satori*. If I say it is *satori* you can become too confident, you can become too egoistic. And in that very confidence and egotism it is lost.

A mini-*satori* is a glimpse. It will depend on you. If you

nourish it, nurture it, protect it, if you care about it, it can grow into a *satori*. But it is a very soft and tender and fragile sprout. It can be destroyed very easily. Any accident can undo it. Remember, all that is great is fragile. The lower existence is more hard, the higher existence is more soft. A rock is hard, a rose flower is soft. The rock will be there if you don't even care about it but a rose flower needs great care. Uncared for there is every possibility that it will disappear. A *satori* is a rose flower.

And the day the glimpse happens you have to be very, very responsible from that moment. You are answerable. Then you owe something. The existence has given you something, you are not to throw it away. It can be thrown away very easily. It is very difficult to get it, it is very easy to lose it. That's how higher things are. They are so subtle. Hence I call it mini.

And sometimes hundreds of mini-*satoris* happen. Only by and by do you become alert and the thing gets established in you. A mini-*satori* is a vision; with a *satori* the vision has become your very style.

And then what is a *samadhi*? A *satori* is when you have become full of light inside you but still there is a separation between you and the whole. A *satori* is a person becoming enlightened; a *samadhi* is when the whole existence has become enlightened through the person. Now the person is no more separate. That is the meaning of the very strange statement of Buddha that the day he became enlightened the whole existence became enlightened. It is very strange because we know that we have not become enlightened yet and he says that the whole existence became enlightened that day. He is right. As far as he is concerned, the whole existence did become enlightened that day. And I repeat it again: the day I became enlightened the whole existence became enlightened.

Samadhi means that you are no more an individual. *Satori* gives you great individuality. Now listen to it . . . Before *satori* you are a person, not an individual. "Person" comes from a root which means *persona,* a mask. Before *satori* you are just a person, a personality, but not an individuality.

And in fact, a person is never a person, a person is many persons—because you can't keep only one mask, you have to keep many masks. In different situations you need different faces. With your wife you need a different face, with your mistress you have a different face, with your servant another, with your boss another. You have to go on changing your faces. You have many personalities. Personality is never singular, it is always plural. You are a crowd. When you are a person you are a crowd, you are many. *Satori* makes you one. By and by it brings unity in your being. Those many faces disappear, the original face appears—individuality. The word "individuality" means indivisible—that which cannot be divided. Undivided you become.

Satori makes you individual and *samadhi* makes you universal. Then you are no longer individual either. First you were not an individual because you were a crowd, now again you are not an individual because you are the whole. There are the three stages: personality, individuality, universality.

A mini-*satori* is a glimpse of your unity for a moment and then you lose the glimpse and again you are many. Yes, the original face appears as if in a dream. You see it, you recognize it, yes, it is there, you feel happy, you feel tremendously blessed—and suddenly it is gone, it was a vision. Again you fall back to your old pattern. The old gestalt again gathers around you. You will carry the memory, you will carry the fragrance, you will remember it—but it is not a reality any longer, it is just part of your memory.

When *satori* has become established then it never leaves you, it is always there; just like your shadow it follows you. Then you have become an individual. Then the individuality has also to be lost. Become one from many and then become zero from one. This is the whole mathematics of spirituality—from many to one and from one to nothingness.

Plotinus says about his own *samadhi*—he is one of the most important mystics in the West, can be compared to a Buddha—"There were not two; beholder was one with beheld; it was not a vision compassed but a unity apprehended. One has become unity, nothing within him or without inducing any diversity. No movement now. All being calmed, one turns neither to this nor to that, not even to the without or to the within. Utterly resting one has become the very rest."

The Plotinian rest is no other than *samadhi* itself. One has become the rest. Ordinarily, when you are a person, you are in tremendous unrest. Restlessness is what you are. When you come to *satori* you have become very, very restful. You are and you are rested, deeply rested. In *samadhi* you have disappeared, there is only rest, nobody resting . . . eternal rest.

ZEN: THE PATH OF PARADOX, Vol. I

SATSANG The Master is a presence; the Master is not a doer. The real Master never does a thing but his presence functions as a catalytic agent. Much happens through his non-doing. That is the paradox of the existence of a Master: without doing, much happens. So the whole thing depends really on the disciple: if he is receptive things start happening; if he is not receptive nothing happens. When nothing happens he throws the responsibility on the Master. The Master cannot do anything against you. In fact he cannot do anything because it is not a question of doing at all; it is simply a question of receiving, of taking it in.

That is the meaning of *satsang*: to be in the presence of a Master, in a loving communion. It is a very special word—it cannot be translated into any western language, because nothing like this has ever happened there; it is uniquely eastern. In fact, the relationship between a disciple and a Master is an eastern phenemenon, a contribution of the East to the world of consciousness.

In the West, at the most, the teacher and the student exist. The teacher teaches, the student learns. The Master is not a teacher; the Master simply imparts, shares, and the disciple imbibes, drinks. It is on a totally different plane. The student and the teacher communicate; the communication is verbal. It is a dialogue, it is transmitting some information. The teacher knows and the student does not know; he collects information, he becomes more knowledgeable. It is a transfer of knowledge.

Between a Master and a disciple the question is not of knowledge but of *being*. Not that the Master knows more than the disciple—sometimes it happens that the disciple may know more, but knowledge it not the question at all. The Master *is* more than the disciple, not that he knows more. He has more being, he has more soul. It is not a question of his memory, that he has more information fed in his memory cells, no. It is a question of his existence; he has a totally different kind of existence—integrated, centered, rooted. The teacher has knowledge, the Master knows. Knowledge means about and about.

The Master has perception, his own experience. He does not know *about* God—he *knows* God, he *is* God! When you know about, you remain different from the knowledge, separate from the knowledge. When you *know* God then the knower and the known become one. The Master is divine. He has not known God as a separate entity; he has recognized God as his own innermost core . . . not as the known, but as the knower, as a witness of all. He has being. Being cannot be learned. Knowledge can be learned; being has only to be drunk.

That is *satsang;* the disciple drinks. The Master is like alcohol; the disciple becomes more and more drunk, more and more drunk. The disciple slowly slowly abandons himself completely; he forgets all about himself. In that forgetfulness he remembers for the first time who he is, because that which was forgotten was only the personality, and now arises the essence, the soul, the being.

In the East for thousands of years this special phenomenon has been in existence: the disciple sits by the side of the Master, just imbibing. Just being with him is enough—just to pulsate with him, vibrate with him, sway with him, just to have a dance with his being. This is not communication; this is communion. Sometimes silences may be used; they are also devices. But that which is important is something so mysterious that no word can contain it. The very look of the Master's eyes in your eyes, the very touch of his being, the very touch of his presence, is enough to stir something that is fast asleep in you. The Master awakes you. His only message—conveyed through words, through silences, through love—is simple and single: Wake up!

GOD'S GOT A THING ABOUT YOU

So while you are here with me, let it be your deepest meditation. I speak to you—not that there is something to be told to you. It is just a device. It is just a device so you

can be close to me; it is just a device so you can be engaged
in listening and your being can be in deeper contact with
me. You have learned the ways of language; it is very difficult for you to sit silently with me. If you sit silently you
will be far away, you will be lost in your thoughts. There
will be a great distance between me and you. I have tried
that.

I used to sit silently with people, but I found they were
far away, thousands of miles away in their thoughts. They
look physically just close; spiritually they are not there at
all: somebody is moving into his past, somebody has already
moved into some imagination in the future. I used to look
into them and I found they were not there, they were somewhere else. Only their bodies were there—empty shells,
hollow. Their minds were not there. And if your mind is
not there it is very difficult for your soul to be there.

I talk to you so your mind becomes engaged in my
thoughts. While you are engaged in my thoughts, at least
you will be able to avoid *your* thoughts. You will be closer
to me—closer than you can be while you are thinking your
thoughts. At least my thoughts are mine: they come from
a deep emptiness, they carry the flavor, they have a subtle
vibe in them. While engaged with me in a verbal communication, listening to me attentively, your mind becomes
engaged, and your mind cannot go to the past and cannot
go to the future. It has to be here, it has something to do
here. While the mind is engaged in my words, I can communicate on a different level too; your being is close to me.
And just being close is enough.

That's the meaning of *satsang*: just to be close to someone
who has disappeared, just to be close to someone who is
no more, just to be close to someone who is just a tremendous nothingness.

Coming closer to this nothingness, you will also start
disappearing and melting. It is natural. There will be a few
moments when you suddenly disappear. Those are the
moments when you have tasted something of me. When
you disappear, when you are completely lost, when the mind
has simply stopped functioning—you are just a pure
attention—then you and I are not two. Then there is no

I-thou relationship. Then only one exists in which the I and the thou both have dissolved. Then we overlap each other: then your center is my center and my center is your center.

The more these moments come to you, the more you will produce the highest possibility . . . your destiny . . .

You ask, *Do Buddhas mind being gazed on for more than three seconds at a time?* They cannot mind because they don't have any mind. In fact if you don't gaze at them, they feel sorry for you. If you look here and there and don't look directly to them, they feel sorry for you. You are thirsty and pure water is available, but you go on looking sideways. You don't look straight, you don't look direct, you don't look immediate. You will miss. Look at me, not only looking— because eyes can absorb the subtlest vibe. It is a way of eating.

Eat me, be cannibals.

And remember, what I am saying is not important at all. What I am being here is important. So don't be lost in my words: they are just toys to play with. Listen to my being, to my presence.

THE DISCIPLINE OF TRANSCENDENCE, Vol. IV

SCHMUCK "Schmuck" is a Yiddish word, a very beautiful word. It has two meanings, and very relevant meanings. One meaning is "the idiot"; another meaning, in the beginning looks very far-fetched, means the male genital organ. But in a way both meanings are very deeply related. Idiots live only as sexual beings—they don't know any other life. So "schmuck" is beautiful. If a person has known only sex as life, he is stupid, he is an idiot.

A SUDDEN CLASH OF THUNDER

SCHOLARS Two large rats walked into a movie house one day and walked straight to the projection room. Once inside they ate the entire reel of film. After eating, one rat looked at the other and asked, "Did you like the movie?"

To which the other replied, "No, I liked the book better."

These are the scholars—the rats! They go on eating words, they go on accumulating words. They can have mountains of words and they become very articulate about words. They can deceive others; that is not so bad because they can deceive only people who are already deceived: you cannot do much more harm to them. But by deceiving others, slowly slowly they become deceived themselves, and that is the greatest problem.

Ninety-nine percent of so-called religious people—saints, mahatmas—are just scholars. As far as *words* are concerned they are very clever, but if you look deep into their eyes you will find just the same stupid human beings. Nothing has changed.

ZEN: THE SPECIAL TRANSMISSION

SCHOOL, MYSTERY Real work can be done only in a mystery school. It is hidden, it is underground. It is *not* public and it cannot be public.

In the middle ages the mystics disappeared behind the garb of alchemy; they had to disappear because of the Christians. The Christians were destroying all kinds of sources which were in any way in conflict with Christian ideology. They were not allowing anybody to practice anything else; even to talk about anything else was not permitted: "Christianity and only Christianity is the way."

The mystic had to disappear. They created a beautiful deception: they created the idea of alchemy. They started saying, "We are alchemists; we have nothing to do with spirituality. All that is rot. We are seeking and searching for the secret of immortal life, of eternal youth. We are trying to find ways and means to transform base metals into gold." And just to deceive the public they made chemistry labs. If you had entered into an alchemist's world, you would have encountered jars and medicines and herbs and test tubes . . . and you would have seen a kind of lab where much chemical work was going on. But this was only a facade; this was not the real work—the real work was happening somewhere else deep down in the school.

The real work was to create integral, crystallized human beings, to create wakefulness. The real work was meditation, but Christianity does not allow meditation. It says prayer is enough. It does not allow inward search. It says worshipping God is enough, going every Sunday to the church is enough, reading the Bible is enough. It has given you toys—and that's how it has happened in other countries too.

In India too the mystics have lived in disguise . . .

And that's what is going to happen in the new phase of my work. My commune will become hidden, underground. It will have a facade on the outside: the weavers and the carpenters and the potters . . . That will be the facade. People who will come as visitors, we will have the beautiful showroom for them; they can purchase things. They can see the creativity of the sannyasins: paintings, books, woodwork . . . They can be shown around a beautiful lake, swimming pools, a five-star hotel for them, but they will not know what is really happening. That which will be happening will be almost all underground. It has to be underground, otherwise it cannot happen.

I have a few secrets to impart to you, and I would not like to die before I have imparted them to you—because I don't know anybody else now alive in the world who can do that work. I have secrets from Taoism, secrets from Tantra, secrets from Yoga, secrets from Sufis, secrets from Zen people . . . I have lived in almost all the traditions of the world; I have been a wanderer in many lives. I have gathered much honey from many flowers.

And now the time, sooner or later, will come when I will have to depart—and I will not be able to enter again in the body. This is going to be my last life.

All the honey that I have gathered I would like to share with you, so that you can share it with others, so that it does not disappear from the earth.

This is going to be a very secret work. Hence, I cannot speak about it. I think I have already spoken too much! I should not have said even this.

The work will be only for those who are utterly devoted. Right now, we have a big press office to make as many people as possible aware of the phenomenon that is happening here. But in the new commune the real work will simply disappear from the world's eyes. The press office will function—it will function for other purposes. People will go on coming, because from the visitors we have to choose, we have to invite people who can be participants, who can dissolve in the commune. But the real work is going to be absolutely secret. It is going to be only between me and you.

And there will not be much talk between me and you either. More and more I will become silent, because the real communion is through energy, not through words. As you will be getting ready to receive the energy in silence, I will become more and more silent. But I am keeping a great treasure for you. Be receptive . . .

And as my work goes underground and becomes more secret and more mysterious, more and more rumors and gossip about it are bound to spread all over the world. People become suspicious of anything secret. And because they cannot find any clue, they start inventing their own ideas about what is happening there. So be ready for that too.

But don't be worried about it. It is going to be a mystery school—such schools existed when Zarathustra was alive; he created such a school. Many such schools existed in Egypt, India, Tibet. When Pythagoras came and visited this country he noted the fact of the mystery schools. He was initiated into many mystery schools in Egypt and in India. Jesus was trained by the Essenes, a very secret mystery school.

All that is beautiful and all that is great in human history has happened only through a few people who put their energies together for the inner exploration.

My commune is going to be a mystery school for inner exploration. It is the greatest adventure there is, and the greatest dance too.

THE BOOK OF THE BOOKS, Vol. II

SCIENCE Action means that which is external to you, meditation means that which is internal to you. Action is outer, meditation is inner. Action is extroversion, meditation is introversion. Action is an objective approach; science is rooted in it, hence science insists on experimentation. And because science insists on action, experiment, it destroys all that is more than the external—it denies it. It simply denies the world of interiority, the world of subjectivity. It is so absurd that science accepts the other without accepting the inner. How can the outer exist at all without the inner? It is nonsensical.

If there is a coin it is bound to have two aspects; you cannot find a coin which has only one aspect to it, only a one-sided coin; it is impossible. Howsoever thick you make it it will always have two sides to it; you cannot make it so thick that it has only one side.

But science goes on insisting on this foolishness: that the external is true and the internal is false. It believes in matter, but it does not believe in consciousness. It says matter has validity, and science asks for objective validity. Of course the world of subjectivity cannot have an objective validity—it is so obvious. The very asking is wrong. The inner cannot come and manifest itself as the outer, but science is blind about it. And those who believe in science say that consciousness is illusory.

Karl Marx, who thinks he is creating a scientific communism, says that consciousness is an epiphenomenon, a byproduct of matter. It does not exist in its own right; it is just a combination of material elements, chemistry, physics. It is just a combination, nothing more than that. When a person dies the elements start falling apart and then there is no consciousness left. Hence there is no immortality, no soul. Man becomes just a machine with a wrong notion that it has a soul. Man is not a he or she but only an it.

This scientific approach has colored even the world of psychology. In fact, ninety percent of psychologists should *not* use the word "psychology" at all; it is just wrong for them to use the word because they deny the psyche, and still they go on using the word "psychology".

Ninety percent of psychologists belong to the school called Behaviorism—Pavlov, Skinner, Delgado and others. They say man is nothing but his behavior; there is nobody inside him. The inside exists not; whatsoever man is, he is on the outside. Hence he can be studied just like any other object, he can be studied like any other machine . . .

They are falling into a blinding darkness by only following the outer, the extrovert, the objective. They are losing all sense of the inner. They will exist like robots . . .

Meditation alone again leads to an extreme. Meditation

means the internal, the subjective; it means introversion. And obviously the introverts start denying all external reality. They start saying it is *maya,* it is illusion.

Karl Marx says the inner is illusory, an epiphenomenon. And Shankara and Berkeley, they say the external is illusory, the internal is the only truth. Both are incapable of accepting the totality. They choose, they are not choiceless people.

Religion is born out of choiceless awareness. The first, who has chosen action alone, becomes a scientist. The second, who has chosen meditation alone, becomes a philosopher. But both miss the whole . . .

In the past this has been the case: either a person lived in the world . . . then he was very active but his action was superficial because there was no meditation in him, no depth, no inner world. He was just his behavior; he was just his outer garb, his periphery. Naturally he created a super-ficial world with no depth, with no height; he created a very poor world.

And then there was the other extremist who escaped from the world. Seeing its superficiality, seeing its peripheralness, he renounced it. Of course he started going deeper into himself, but his going deeper into himself became uncre-ative. He had a depth, but that depth remained unexpressed. He was silent, but there was no song in it. And when a silence is without a song it is dead; it has depth but no manifestation.

You may be a great painter but unless you paint, what is the point of being a great painter? You may be a great poet but unless you sing, what is the point of your being a great poet?

So on the one hand there were people who had chosen action, the world—the extroverts; and on the other hand were the introverts who had chosen their own being. Both were lopsided . . .

Life has to be total, not lopsided.

I AM THAT

I am not against science, I am not anti-science at all. I would like the world to have more and more of science, so that man can become available for something higher, for something which a poor man cannot afford.

Religion is the ultimate in luxury. The poor man has to think about bread and butter; he cannot even manage that. He has to think about a shelter, clothes, children, medicine, and he cannot manage these small things. His whole life is burdened by trivia; he has no space, no time to devote to God. And even if he goes to the temple or to the church, he goes to ask only for material things. His prayer is not true prayer: it is not that of gratitude; it is a demand, a desire. He wants this, he wants that—and we cannot condemn him, he has to be forgiven. The needs are there and he is constantly under a weight. How can he find a few hours just to sit silently doing nothing? The mind goes on thinking; he has to think about the tomorrow . . .

I would like the world to be richer than it is. I don't believe in poverty and I don't believe that poverty has anything to do with spirituality. Down the ages it has been told that poverty is something spiritual; it was just a consolation . . .

To me, spirituality has a totally different dimension. It is the ultimate luxury—when you have all and suddenly you see that although you have all, deep inside there is a vacuum which has to be filled, an emptiness which has to be transformed into a plenitude . . . One becomes aware of the inner emptiness only when one has everything on the outside. Science can do that miracle. I love science, because it can create the possibility for religion to happen . . .

I would like this earth to be a paradise—and it cannot happen without science. So how can I be anti-science?

I am not anti-science, but science is not all. Science can create only the circumference; the center has to be that of religion. Science is exterior, religion is interior. And I would like men to be rich on both sides: the exterior should be rich and the interior should be rich. Science cannot make you rich in your inner world; that can be done only by religion.

If science goes on saying there is no inner world, then I am certainly against such statements—but that is not being against science, just against these particular statements. These statements are stupid, because the people who are making these statements have not known anything of the inner.

Karl Marx says religion is the opium of the people—and

he has not experienced any meditation. His whole life was wasted in the British Museum, thinking, reading, collecting notes, preparing for his great work, *Das Kapital*. And he was so much into trying to gain more and more knowledge that it happened many times that he would faint in the British Museum! He would have to be carried unconscious to his home. And it was almost an everyday thing that he would have to be forced to leave the museum because it had to close some time, it could not remain open twenty-four hours a day.

Marx had never heard about meditation; he knew only thinking and thinking. But still in a way he is right, because the old religiousness has served as a kind of opium. It has helped poor people to remain poor, it has helped them to remain contented as they are, hoping for the best in the next life. In that way he is right. But he is not right if we take into consideration a Buddha, a Zarathustra, a Lao Tzu— then he is not right. And these are the really religious people, not the masses; the masses know nothing of religion.

I would like you to be enriched by Newton, Edison, Eddington, Rutherford, Einstein, and I would like you also to be enriched by Buddha, Krishna, Christ and Mohammed, so that you become rich in both your dimensions: the outer and the inner. Science is good as far as it goes, but it does not go far enough—and it cannot. I am not saying that it *can* go and it does not go, no—it cannot go into the interiority of your being. The very methodology of science prevents it from going in. It can only go outwards, it can study only objectively; it cannot go into the subjectivity itself. That is the function of religion.

The society needs science, the society needs religion. And if you ask me what should be the first priority, science should be the first priority—because first the outer, the circumference, then the inner, because the inner is more subtle, more delicate.

Science can create the space for real religion to exist on the earth.

THE BOOK OF THE BOOKS, Vol. IV

SCREAM, PRIMAL   See Trauma, birth, 3rd Series

SCREAMING And you have been screaming your whole life—whether you scream or not is not the point—you have been screaming your whole life. You have not done anything else up to now. Sometimes loudly, sometimes silently, but you have been screaming. That's how I see people—screaming people, their heart is screaming, their being is screaming. But that will not help. You can scream but that will not help.

Try to understand rather than screaming. Try to see what I am telling you. And what I am telling you is not a theory—it is a fact. And I am saying it because I have known it that way. If it can happen to me that there is no problem, why cannot it happen to you? Take the challenge of it! I am just as ordinary a man as you are; I don't claim any extraordinary miraculous powers.

I am very ordinary, just as you are. The only difference between me and you is you don't say okay to yourself and I have said an absolute okay to myself—that is the only difference. You are continuously trying to improve yourself and I am not trying to improve myself. I have said: Incompletion is the way life is. You are trying to become perfect and I have accepted my imperfections. That is the only difference.

So I don't have any problems. When you accept your imperfection, from where can the problem come? When whatsoever happens you say, "It is okay," then from *where* can the problem come? When you accept limitations, then from where can the problem come? The problem arises out of your non-acceptance. You cannot accept the way you are, so the problem will always be there. Can you imagine yourself some day accepting, totally accepting the way you are? If you can imagine, then why don't you do it right now? Why wait? For whom? For what?

I have accepted the way I am, and that very moment all problems disappeared. That very moment all worries disappeared. Not that I became perfect, but I started enjoying my imperfections. Nobody ever becomes perfect—because to become perfect means to become absolutely dead. Perfection is not possible because life goes on and on and on—there is no end to it.

So the *only* way to get out of these so-called problems is to accept your life as you find it right this moment, and live it, enjoy, delight in it. The next moment will be of more joy because it will come out of this moment; and the next to that will be of even more joy, because, by and by, you will become more and more joyous. Not that you will become more joyous through improvement, but by living the moment.

But you will remain imperfect. You will always have limitations, and you will always have situations where, if you want to create problems, you can immediately create. If you don't want to create problems, there is no need to create. You can scream but that won't help. That's what you have been doing—that has not helped.

Even primal therapy has not proved of much help. It allows people to scream—yes, it feels a little good—it is a tantrum therapy. It allows you to vomit. It feels a little good because you feel a little unloaded, unburdened, but then within a few days that euphoria disappears; again you are the same, again accumulating. Again go to the primal therapy—you will feel good for a few days . . . again the same.

Unless you understand that one has to *stop* creating problems, you will go on creating problems. You can go into an encounter group, you can do primal therapy, you can do thousands of other groups, and after each group you will feel tremendously beautiful, because you have dropped something that was on your head—but you have not dropped the *mechanism* that creates it. You have dropped something which you were having, but you have not dropped the very factory that goes on creating it.

THE TANTRA VISION, Vol. I

No, don't be worried about screaming—not at all. It is natural. Just one thing you have to remember—balance it by loving.

There are moments when one wants to scream—and the children understand that, because they themselves scream. That is really their language. If you are feeling boiling within and you don't scream, the child feels disturbed very much at what is happening, because it is beyond him to understand. He can feel . . . Your very vibe is screaming and you are not screaming; you are even smiling, controlling. The child is disturbed very much by that because he feels the mother is cheating—and they never forgive cheating. They are always ready to accept truth.

If you feel like screaming, you feel like screaming. What can you do? All that you can do is going to be a sort of repression. You can repress it, you can hold it in, but it will come out in indirect ways. And children cannot understand those indirect ways—they are not yet civilized. They don't know the language of repression. When they have done something wrong, they can understand that they are being beaten, but they cannot understand when they are doing something wrong and they have been caught and you smile. This simply puzzles them. It is so unnatural; they cannot believe it. The mother must be faking it, because they cannot do it, so how can you? And of course they are closer to nature than you and they understand nature more than you.

Screaming was very irrational, but natural. You will find some unnatural but rational excuse—that he has not done his homework or his clothes are dirty or he has not taken a shower today. Now you are angry but your anger is cold. You may get rid of it; that too will be ugly. It is just like eating cold food—it takes long to digest; it becomes heavy on the stomach.

You have to be in a natural, flowing relationship. Don't listen to what psychologists go on talking about—fifty percent of it is almost rubbish. They have destroyed many beautiful things in the world.

Listen to nature. You are a mother so you know. No cat goes and consults any manual on how to catch rats. She simply jumps and catches. She is a cat—that's enough! No certificate is needed, no counselors are needed. You are a mother—finished! Your mother nature will take care. Just be natural, and always balance. If you are natural it will balance itself. And I am saying it only so you don't forget it. Otherwise there is a possibility that you can scream and be natural and you may not love them.

DANCE YOUR WAY TO GOD

See also Motherhood, 2nd Series

SCRIPTURES A scientist cannot be a Hindu or a Mohammedan or a Christian; if he is then he is not scientific. At least in his scientific endeavor he should put aside all his prejudices.

If Galileo remains a Christian, then he cannot discover the truth that the sun does not move around the earth. If Copernicus remains a Christian even while he is doing his scientific research, then he cannot go beyond the Bible. And the Bible is many thousands of years old; it contains the science of those days. It is very primitive; it is bound to be so.

All religious scriptures contain certain facts which they should not contain. They are not religious facts; they are concerned with the objective world. But in the old days everything was compiled in religious scriptures—they were the only scriptures. Religious scriptures have functioned in the world for thousands of years as encyclopædias: everything that was known, was discovered, was theorized, was collected in them.

The Vedas in India are called *samhitas; samhitas* means a compilation, a collection. Their function was exactly that of the Encyclopedia Britannica. All kinds of things are compiled in them: the literature of those days, the science of those days, the geography, the history, the art; everything that it was possible to know was compiled. As man has progressed, everything has become more and more specialized . . .

About the outside world we have become a little more mature; we are ready to drop any belief. If a certain fact is discovered which goes against our older theories, we discard the older theories in favor of the new discovery. But the same is not true about the inner; to the inner we have a very deep clinging.

TAO: THE GOLDEN GATE, Vol. II

Scriptures *are* beautiful, but beautiful only for those who can understand them; you can only *mis*understand them. I am not against the scriptures—how can I be? I am speaking on one of the scriptures: the Dhammapada, Buddha's sayings. I have spoken on Jesus' sayings. I have spoken on Mahavira, on Krishna. I have spoken on the Upanishads. I have spoken on the Tao Te Ching. I have spoken on almost all of the beautiful scriptures of the world. How can I be *against* them and how can I think they are useless?— although I insist that you don't depend on them, for they are of no use.

Then what is their use? Their use is a totally different thing. When you become more meditative, the deeper you go into meditation, the greater will be your capacity and clarity to understand the scriptures. Scriptures will become witnesses to you, that you are on the right track. And when you attain to your innermost core, when you realize your being, then you will know what Jesus means by "the kingdom of God", then you will know what Buddha means by *nirvana,* then you will known what the Upanishads mean by "truth"—not before that.

Right now, if you read the Bible or the Koran or the Gita, you will interpret them according to your unconscious state, according to your non-meditative state. You will misinterpret, you will misunderstand. You are not in a right shape. You are upside-down, you are topsy-turvy. You are a confusion, a chaos. You are a crowd, you are not yet an individual. You don't have a center at all. So how are you going to understand Jesus or Buddha or Krishna?

Remember one very fundamental thing: you can understand Jesus only if you have tasted something of Christ-consciousness in you; otherwise there is no way. You can have glimpses of Buddha only when you have attained something of Buddhahood, some texture, some taste, some fragrance. When you have entered into the country of the Buddha and the Buddhas, then you will be able to see the meaning.

Otherwise, words are there, but who will put meaning into those words? *You* will put meaning into those words. You will be reading Krishna but you will not really be reading Krishna—you will be reading yourself *through* Krishna. Words will be Krishna's, meanings will be yours—and it is the *meaning* that is significant, not the word.

THE BOOK OF THE BOOKS, Vol. IX

I enjoy reading books, but I read the Bible, the Gita, the Koran just as one reads novels; they are ancient, beautiful stories. Krishnamurti says he never reads any scripture; he reads only detective stories. I read the scripture, but I read in the scripture just the detective story and nothing else. And I would suggest to Krishnamurti that it would be good if he should look into the Bible; you cannot find a more beautiful story—full of suspense. Everything is there: love, life, murder; everything is there. It is very sensational.

Scriptures, to me, have nothing special. Scriptures are as sacred as the trees and the rocks and the stars—or as secular. I don't make a distinction so I am not very serious about scriptures. The only thing I am serious about is jokes. So when I quote the scripture I quote from memory, when I quote a joke I have it written here in front of me. I never want to make any mistake about the joke—I am really serious. About everything else I am absolutely non-serious.

So it is very obvious. Listening to me you must have mis-understood it, that my emphasis is not on what the scrip-tures say—that is not the point; my emphasis is on what I am saying. If you go to a Christian priest, he quotes the scripture, his emphasis is on the scripture. He is very literal, he has to be—he himself is secondary, the scripture is primary. He is a witness to the scripture. With me it is just the opposite; the scripture is just a witness to me. What-soever I have to say, only that have I to say. If I feel the scripture can be a witness to it, I use it.

And I go on playing with the scripture, sometimes in one way, sometimes in another. Remember always, I am not try-ing to prove the scripture—that the scripture is right—I am simply using it as an illustration. It is secondary, you can forget about it; nothing will be lost. Whatsoever I am saying is direct. Just to help you, because you are not capable of listening to the direct truth, you need a few witnesses. So Jesus, Krishna and Buddha and Lao Tzu and Lieh Tzu— they are just witnesses to me. I am not to adjust with them, they have to adjust with me.

And this should always be so: the dead should exist and adjust with the living and for the living. Why should the living adjust with the dead? Lieh Tzu has to adjust with me, because only in adjusting with me can Lieh Tzu again have a little life. Jesus has to adjust with me, I am not to adjust with Jesus. The past has to adjust with the present, not other-wise. So I go on playing . . .

These are all just stories to me and, deep down, this is the approach: the whole of life is a fiction, it is *maya,* it is a dream. Jesus and Buddha and Krishna and I and you are parts of a big dream—God is dreaming. Don't be too serious about it.

TAO: THE PATHLESS PATH, Vol. I

How have you come here to me? From different corners of the world you have traveled, sometimes not even exactly clear as to why; but something has been pulling you, some unknown force has moved your heart, something has been felt by the deepest core of your being. Sometimes you have come even against yourself. Your mind was saying, "Don't go! There is no need to go anywhere." Still you have come. You must have smelled a perfume—a perfume which has nothing to do with the visible. It is an invisible phenomenon.

Many many more people will be coming soon. The fragrance is reaching them, is bound to reach. Anybody anywhere who is really in search of truth is bound to come. It is irresistible, it has to happen. That's how it has been happening all along, down the ages. Thousands of people traveled to Buddha, thousands of people traveled to Mahavira, to Lao Tzu, to Zarathustra—for *no* reason at all, because whatsoever they were saying was available in the scriptures.

What I am saying here you can read in the Bhagavad Gita, in the Bible, in the Koran, in the Dhammapada, what I am saying you can find easily in the Upanishads, in the Tao Te Ching—but you will not find the fragrance. Those are flowers—old, dead, dried up. You can keep a rose flower in your Bible; soon it will dry, the fragrance will be gone, it will be only a corpse, a remembrance of the real flower. So are the scriptures. They have to be made alive again by another Buddha, otherwise they cannot breathe.

That's why I am speaking on the Dhammapada, on the Gita, on the Bible—to let them breathe again. I can breathe life into them. I can share my fragrance with them, I can pour my fragrance into them. Hence, the Christian who is really a Christian, not just by social conditioning but because of a great love for Christ, he will find Christ alive again in my words. Or if somebody is a Buddhist he will find in my words Buddha speaking again—in twentieth century language, with twentieth century people . . .

That's my whole effort here: to make you contemporaries of Jesus, of Buddha, of Zarathustra, of Lao Tzu. If you can be contemporaries of those awakened souls, what is the point of remaining contemporaries to your ordinary world and its ordinary citizens, the so-called human beings, who have nothing of humanity in them, who have not yet become beings, who are just hollow, empty, meaningless? What is the point of living in the neighborhood of empty cells when you can be a neighbor of Gautam the Buddha?

Yes, that is possible—it is possible by transcending time and space. And in meditation you transcend both. In meditation you don't know where you are, you don't know the time, you don't know the space. In meditation, time and space both disappear—you simply are.

That moment, when you simply are, Buddha is just by your side; you are surrounded by Buddhas of all ages. You will be living for the first time, a life worth living, a life of significance: when you can hold hands with Buddhas and Krishnas, when you can dance with Krishna and sing with Meera and sit with Kabir. It is possible! Because only the flowers have disappeared, but the fragrance is eternal—it cannot disappear.

And then all the scriptures become alive for you. Then reading the Bible, you are not just reading a book—then Moses speaks to you, Abraham speaks to you, Jesus speaks to you, *face to face!*

THE BOOK OF THE BOOKS, Vol. II

Everybody's life contains a scripture, a bible. The outside Bible is not the real bible. The word "Bible" means the book of the books. It is not the book of books, the book of books is within you; it cannot be outside.

The outside Bible may have a few reflections of the inner, but they are only reflections. The moon reflected in the waters of the lake is not the real moon—don't be deceived by it. Although it is a reflection of the real moon, so it has a certain resemblance to reality, don't be deceived by it and don't jump into the lake to find it, otherwise you may get drowned. And you are not going to find the moon in the lake; you will get into unnecessary trouble.

People have jumped into lakes. Into the Bibles, into the Vedas, into the Gitas, into the Korans, they have jumped. These are just lakes, beautiful lakes, certainly, and capable of reflecting something of the real. But a reflection is a reflection. The face in the mirror is not your real face. Don't go on searching in the mirror for your real face. You will not find it there—the mirror is empty. So is the lake, so are all the scriptures—empty. They are beautiful words but empty.

Unless you find the inner scripture that is within you, you will not be able to understand the outer Bibles, Korans and Vedas. Once you have found the inner then there is a possibility; then doors open up, then suddenly there is a great opening. Whatsoever was closed and hidden becomes available, slowly the curtain is removed. You can see that which is. And once you have found it inside you will find it in the words of Jesus, in the words of Buddhas, very easily.

The man who knows the real moon is bound to know the moon in the lake. He will understand and he may even rejoice because he is not deceived; he knows perfectly well it is a reflection but a beautiful reflection. Sometimes when the lake is utterly calm and quiet, when there is no disturbance on its surface, it becomes a mirror of tremendous beauty. One can enjoy the scriptures, but not before realizing the inner truth.

JUST THE TIP OF THE ICEBERG

SEARCH The beginning of the pilgrimage starts with searching, seeking, inquiring; there is no other way to begin. Unless you inquire what is the meaning of life, unless you go in search of the essential core of existence, you will never move, you will not even take the first step. Hence the search has to begin, but if you continue searching for ever and ever, if your search never comes to an end, you will remain in the mind. It is the mind which searches.

Search is also a subtle desire. Even the inquiry to know is ambitious. The very desire to achieve something—money, power, prestige, meditation, God, whatsoever it is—any desire, any ambition leads you into the future; it distracts you from the present. And the present is the only reality, the only truth there is.

The person who never begins the search will remain unconscious; the person who always remains in the search will go crazy. The search has to begin so that you become a little more alert, a little more observant, vigilant, aware, and then the search has to be dropped so that you become silent, so that the mind disappears, so that the future evaporates and you are simply herenow, neither seeking nor searching. In that stillness of no-search, truth is found.

COME, COME, YET AGAIN COME

It is not only man who is in search of God, God is in search of man. If only man were in search there would be no possibility of ever finding God because man's capabilities are very tiny. It is just like dewdrops in search of the ocean: it may get lost anywhere. There are deserts and deserts to cross and the journey is long, arduous, and the address of the ocean is not known, nor is the direction. Neither does there exist any map.

Yes, sometimes there are guides—Buddhas, Christs—but the way they have reached the ultimate can't be your way. They moved from a different point, from a different angle, from a different space. Each individual has to find his own way. And the way is not ready-made, it is not like a superhighway already there that you just have to walk on. It is by moving towards God that you create the way, the way is created by you. It is like a footpath in the jungle of life: there is no direction, no map; no guide can hold your hand. Yes, they can indicate a few things, they can give you a few hints which will be helpful on the way, but they cannot give you the exact map—that is impossible.

So if man were alone in his search for God it would be impossible. But it has happened to many people for the simple reason that God is also searching for them, he is also groping for them. Once you start groping then your hands are going to meet somewhere. It is not only that the dewdrop is moving towards the ocean, the ocean is also rushing towards the dewdrop. The dewdrop may not be able to cross the deserts but the ocean can.

To know this, to trust that God loves you, is a great foundation. Then the whole of your life can be built accordingly, then your life can become a temple—but the right foundation is needed. Never forget for a moment that God is searching for you, that he is calling you, that he is calling everybody, that he is searching for everybody.

Jesus says: Just as the shepherd goes back into the forest to look for lost sheep . . . That is his way of saying that God also comes to seek and search for those who are lost. God is a shepherd, and when the shepherd finds the lost sheep he carries the sheep on his shoulders. He is not angry; on the contrary he is immensely loving because one who was lost is found.

So no one need lose heart, no one need lose hope. God *is* searching, calling, coming to you in many many ways— you just have to start looking for him also, then the meeting is inevitable.

EVEN BEING GAWD AIN'T A BED OF ROSES

SECRET All that is beautiful is inner, and the inner means privacy. Have you watched women making love? They always close their eyes. They know something. A man goes on making love with open eyes, he remains a watcher also. He is not completely in the act, he is not totally in it. He remains a voyeur, as if somebody else is making love and he is watching, as if the lovemaking is going on on a TV screen or in a movie. But a woman knows better because she is more delicately tuned to the inner. She always closes her eyes. Then love has a totally different fragrance . . .

Just like seeds need darkness and privacy in the earth, all relationships which are deep and intimate remain inner. They need privacy, they need a place where only two exist. Then a moment comes when even the two dissolve and only one exists.

Two lovers deeply in tune with each other dissolve. Only one exists. They breathe together, they are together; a togetherness exists. This would not be possible if observers were there. They would never be able to let go if others were watching. The very eyes of others would become the barrier. So all that is beautiful, all that is deep, happens in darkness.

In ordinary human relationships, privacy is needed. And

when you ask about the relationship of a Master and disciple, even more privacy is needed because it is a transmission of the highest energy possible to man. It is the highest peak of love, where one man pours himself into another and the other becomes a receptive womb. Even a slight disturbance—somebody watching—will be enough of a barrier.

Secrecy has its own reason to be there. Remember that, and always remember that you will behave very foolishly in life if you become completely public. It will be as if somebody has turned his pockets inside-out. That will be your shape—like pockets turned inside-out. Nothing is wrong in being outward, but remember that is only part of life. It should not become the whole.

I am not saying to move in darkness forever. Light has its own beauty and its own reason. If the seed remains in the dark forever and ever, and never comes up to receive the sun in the morning, it will be dead. It has to go into darkness to sprout, to gather strength, to become vital, to be reborn, and then it has to come out and face the world and light and the storm and the rains. It has to accept the challenge of the outside.

But that challenge can only be accepted if you are deeply rooted within. I am not saying to become escapists, I am not saying to close your eyes, move within and never come out. I am simply saying: go in so that you can come out with energy, with love, with compassion. Go in so that when you come out you are not a beggar, but a king; go in so that when you come out you have something to share—the flowers, the leaves.

Go in so that your coming out becomes richer and is not impoverished. And always remember that whenever you feel exhausted, the source of energy is within. Close your eyes and go in.

Make outer relationships; make inner relationships also. Of course there are bound to be outer relationships—you move in the world, business relationships will be there—but they should not be all. They have their part to play, but there must be something absolutely secret and private, something that you can call your own . . .

Life arises from that inner source and spreads into the sky

outside. There has to be a balance—I am always for balance. So I will not say, like Mahatma Gandhi, that your life should be an open book—no. A few chapters open, okay. And a few chapters completely closed, completely a mystery. If you are just an open book you will be a prostitute, you will just be standing in the marketplace naked, with just the radio on. No, that won't do.

If the whole book is open, you will just be the day with no night, just the summer with no winter. Then where will you rest and where will you center yourself and where will you take refuge? Where will you move when the world is too much with you? Where will you go to pray and meditate? No, half and half is perfect. Let half of your book be open—open to everybody, available to everybody—and let the other half of your book be so secret that only rare guests are allowed there.

Only rarely is somebody allowed to move within your temple. That is how it should be. If the crowd is coming in and going out, then the temple is no longer a temple. It may be a waiting room in an airport, but it cannot be a temple. Only rarely, very rarely, do you allow somebody to enter your self. That is what love is.

COME FOLLOW ME, Vol. I

Love is the secret, the secret of all secrets, the golden key, the master key, that opens all the locks of all the mysteries. Love, and love for no other reason but just for the sheer joy of it. Don't try to find out reasons to love, because then love becomes shallow. When love is for no reason at all it has tremendous depth. Love unconditionally. The moment you make a condition love becomes a bargain, mundane; without any condition, it is sacred.

Love to give, not to get. Much comes; but that is another matter. Your whole approach should be that of giving; and the more you give, the more you have to give; the more you pour yourself, the more you are overwhelmed from some unknown sources. Once that is known you have come to know the secret of love.

YOU AIN'T SEEN NOTHIN' YET

The most secret teaching that I want to give my sannyasins is how to create the possibility of meeting the inner woman

and man. When the inner woman and man meet you attain
to an orgasm which never ends. That moment one comes
to know oneself as divine. In that bliss, one knows one's
dignity. Before that we can believe that there is God, but
a belief is only a belief, it does not make any difference in
your being. It remains superficial. Unless something becomes
your own experience, it is not of any value. My whole
emphasis is on existential, experiential.

Religion has to be really a science of the within. And to
be a sannyasin is not a formal thing—it is entering into a
mystery school, it is entering into some secrets which cannot be made available to the common masses. In the first
place, they will not understand them; in the second place,
they will distort them; in the third place, they will harm
themselves by these great secrets because anything that is
very powerful is dangerous in the hands of those who are
childish. It is giving a sword to a small child: there is every
possibility that he will harm either himself or somebody else.

There are secrets which can be given only to those who
are ready to receive. Sannyas simply means that you are
showering your readiness, that you will not resist, that you
will put aside all your prejudices, that from this moment
you will be ready to hear what I am saying—and not only
to hear, but to go into experimentation. It is a great exploration, the greatest adventure there is.

THE RAINBOW BRIDGE

SECT   My sannyasin is not getting involved in a sect; this
is not a sect because we don't have *any* ideology. I don't
preach any ideology. Even atheists are here and they are
sannyasins and they don't believe in God. And I don't make
it a basic requirement. There are no basic requirements, except your longing for the truth—but that is not a thing that
makes you sectarian. In fact, the enquiry for truth, the longing for truth, makes you absolutely non-sectarian.

And a religious person is non-sectarian. He is simply
religious—not Christian, not Hindu. He cannot afford to be
a Hindu or a Christian. How can he afford to be so limited?
He cannot afford to get involved in prejudices; he cannot
believe in conclusions already arrived at by others. He is
on his own journey: he wants to know truth with his own

eyes, he wants to hear God with his own ears, he wants to feel life and existence with his own heart. His search is individual.

Sannyasins are not part of a sect. This is a meeting of individuals; we have met because we are on the same journey. There is no ideology binding my sannyasins to each other; it is just because of the same enquiry for truth that accidentally we have met on the same road. We are fellow travelers. Nothing binds one sannyasin to another sannyasin; there is no bondage of belief, tradition, scripture. And in fact sannyasins are not connected with each other at all directly—their connection is with me.

One sannyasin is connected with me, another sannyasin is connected with me, hence they are connected with each other—via me. There is no other organization. I am functioning only as a center and they are all connected with me, hence they *feel* connected with each other.

                              THE BOOK OF THE BOOKS, Vol. III

SECURITY See Insecurity, 2nd Series

SEEDS Once a farmer asked Buddha: "Why don't you do something? I cultivate the land, I create something; you simply sit under the tree with closed eyes, doing nothing. I have been watching you—people come to you, you talk to them or sometimes they sit silently by your side. Why don't you *do* something?"

The poor farmer was naturally curious; he had been watching Buddha sitting under a tree just by the side of his farm, with people coming, going, and no visible work happening.

Buddha said, "Can't you see that I am also a farmer? Can't you recognize me?—although my farm is of a different quality, on a different plane? I grow the crop of bliss, I sow the seeds of bliss. The people who come around and sit silently, or to whom I sometimes talk—they are my work. I am sowing seeds: seeds in people's consciousness, seeds of bliss. In the right season they will bloom. And look into my eyes: I have bloomed, I have cultivated my inner soil, my soul; now it is full of flowers!"

And it is said that the farmer recognized him. He looked

into Buddha's eyes, surrendered to Buddha, become a sannyasin. He said, "Then I have been wasting my life unnecessarily. You are the true farmer; I am the false one."

THE IMPRISONED SPLENDOR

SEEING Very few people are capable of seeing that which is. Before it reaches their being it is distorted. The mind plays all kinds of tricks. First it prevents the major part ... almost ninety-eight percent of reality is debarred, the mind only allows two percent to enter in. Only that which fits with the mind is allowed. Only that which strengthens the mind and the ego is allowed, and then too the mind colors it, it gives it artificial flavors; it makes it adjust totally to itself. Hence it becomes an accumulation for the mind but not a revelation for the soul. Otherwise each moment is a revelation, and at each moment reality is available in its totality. But *we* are not available to reality.

All concepts, all philosophies, religions, theologies, ideologies are barriers. And the real has to pass through so many barriers that by the time it reaches you it is no more the same.

To be a sannyasin means removing all spectacles, removing everything that can distort, that can project; letting your eyes be naked. Being with a Master means being with naked eyes, a naked soul, with nothing to hide, with nothing to cover. When the disciple is totally nude before the Master, only then something of immense value and beauty transpires. It is a love affair. The greatest love affair that can happen on earth happens between the disciple and the Master.

EVEN BEIN' GAWD AIN'T A BED OF ROSES

SEEKING One has to work on oneself, but only in a negative way. One cannot work upon oneself in a positive way, because it is not a question of creating something but a question of discovering something which is already there.

When you paint, it is a positive act—you are creating the painting—but when you dig a well it is a negative act. The water is already there; you have only to remove a few layers of earth, stones, rocks. The moment you have removed them, the water becomes available. The water is there, *you* are here, and between the two there is a barrier: the barrier has to be removed. That's what I mean by negative work.

Man already has got whatsoever he is seeking and searching for. The truth is there, the bliss is there, the love is there—in one word, God is there. God is not a person, God is only the totality of all the values which are beyond mind. But the *mind* is the barrier, and you have to dig a well. You have to remove a few layers of thoughts, memories, desires, fantasies, dreams. The moment you have opened a door in the mind to the beyond, all that you always wanted becomes available.

The moment Gautam the Buddha became enlightened he laughed, and he said to nobody in particular—he said to himself—"This is ridiculous! I have been searching for it for thousands of lives, and it has been lying deep down within myself."

The sought is the seeker. Hence the Upanishads say the method to find it is *neti neti*. *Neti neti* means "neither this nor that"; it is a process of elimination. You go on negating, eliminating. Finally, when there is nothing to be eliminated, nothing to be negated, when you have totally emptied yourself, it is found.

PHILOSOPHIA ULTIMA

We are wanderers, strangers, outsiders—man as such is an outsider. Do whatsoever, but you can never become an insider in this world because this world is unreal. You cannot become part of it because you come from reality. Man is a spirit and the world is material. We can go on playing the game, but we remain outsiders. We can try to forget ourselves, we can create a sort of oblivion, but it is just a trick; it doesn't help. We are strangers. This fact has to be realized. And that is the meaning of us being a discontinuity.

When we are in God, we are a continuity. When we are in the world, we are a discontinuity. We are uprooted from our soil . . . we are no more that which we could be. We are no more in the space that is ours—we are somewhere else. Hence everybody is seeking and searching—and every search is in vain, because if we search outside, we search in the world. And if we want to search inside, all search has to stop . . .

Seeking means separation. Seeking means suffering. You can go on seeking, and it is all in vain. It is doomed from the very beginning, because deep inside you is the one you are seeking. The sought has become the seeker—that is the discontinuity. And when all seeking drops, withers away, and you have no more hopes, then suddenly you are there where you always wanted to be. Then suddenly you are centered.

Seeking leads you astray. And the more you seek, the more frustrated you feel. The more frustrated you feel, the more you seek. It becomes a vicious circle, self-supporting . . . goes on and on. There is no end to it—it can continue for eternity. One has to understand the very fallacy of search.

Seek and you will never find. Do not seek and it is there.

But it is very difficult to stop searching and seeking. It is very difficult to drop hope, because then it seems as if the whole thing is futile. If there is no hope, why should one live? For what? Where is the meaning? The meaning is herenow—it is not in the seeking. But the mind goes on saying that if you don't seek, if you don't make the effort, if you don't go for it, it is not going to happen . . .

The mind is nothing but hope and desire and passion for the future. The mind is a disease, a fever, a feverish state. You will have to understand it: the problem is the mind. And once you understand how it functions, how it projects a desire into the future and then starts rushing towards it . . . And it goes on projecting like an horizon. It goes rushing. It gives activity to you but no happiness; it keeps you occupied. But it is a slow suicide and nothing else.

So I would like you to ponder over the very mechanism of seeking, the mind, the process of the mind. Once you start looking at the mind and how it functions, then the whole game becomes clear. Then one day in that very clarity, the mind disappears as if it had never existed. It disappears like a dream—and suddenly you are continuous again.

This mind creates a barrier: it always divides, separates—so seeking is separation. The more you seek, the more separated you become. Even if you are seeking unity, that seeking will separate you. And seeking is suffering because the more you seek, the more frustrated you feel.

The real religion starts the day one comes to understand

that this mind is the root cause of separation. God is herenow. It is already the case. You are not to achieve it and you are not to produce it; it has not to be manufactured. It is already the case . . . it has already happened. He is and he has always been, and he will always be.

THE GREAT NOTHING

SELF People have only egos. The ego is a substitute self. Because we are not aware of the true self, we create the ego; it is a make-believe. Because we cannot live without the center we have to invent a false center.

There are two possibilities: either know the true center or create a false center. The society helps the false center because the false person can easily be dominated—not only can he be easily dominated: he *seeks* domination. He is constantly in search of somebody to dominate him. Without being dominated he does not feel good, because only when he is dominated does he have a certain feeling of "I am". When he is fulfilling somebody's order, he feels "I have some worth." His worth, his life, all are borrowed. He has no meaning in his life on his own; somebody else has to give meaning to him.

He becomes part of a church, then he feels good: he is a Christian, and Christianity gives him at least a false feeling of meaning. Or he becomes a communist and the great crowd of communists helps him to feel that he is doing something important. He cannot stand alone; and that is the whole strategy of the society: it does not allow you to stand on your own. It cripples you, from the very beginning it makes you dependent on crutches. And the best way to do it is not to allow you to become aware of your true self.

Instead of the true self it simply gives you a toy called the ego. It supports the ego tremendously; the society praises the ego, nourishes it. If you follow the dictates of the society in every possible way you will be respected, and respectability is nothing but a food for the ego. If you don't follow the dictates of the society you will be disrespected. That is punishing your ego, keeping it starved; and it is very difficult to live without a center, so one is ready to fulfill all kinds of demands—rational, irrational.

My effort here is to help you to drop this false entity called the ego. Dropping it is half of the work, and the other half is easier: to make you aware of your true self. Once the false is seen as false, it is not very difficult to see the true as true . . .

The ego is a created thing, hence it has to die. The true self was before you were born and will be there after you are gone, dead. The true self does not exist only between birth and death. On the contrary, birth and death are just episodes in the long, eternal journey of the true self. And this is not the only birth; many have happened before and many may happen afterwards.

The moment one becomes aware of one's true center, one becomes aware of eternity, and to know eternity is to know God. Hence, the true self is the door to God.

TURN ON, TUNE IN AND DROP THE LOT

SELF-ACCEPTANCE   The problem is that you don't accept yourself. You can call it compulsion or can call it something else—but you don't accept yourself as you are. You want to improve yourself—and there is the core of the problem.

Improvement is not possible. Improvement is a very false notion. It has never happened . . . it cannot happen. By the nature of things it is not possible. Nobody ever improves, because everybody is already that which one can be, so one has to relax and accept it. If that is your pattern, then that is you.

Once you accept it, things will start changing. And I don't say they will improve—I say they will start changing. Change is a totally neutral concept. In improvement there is greed, in improvement there is ego. In change . . . It is just like summer changes, and then it rains, and rains change and it is winter, and seasons change—but there is no improvement.

The whole western mind is basically caught up with the concept of progress. Evolution is there, but there is no progress. Evolution is also not a right word, because that too gives an idea as if something is evolving into a higher state. Nothing is going anywhere—everything is where it is.

In the East we have the concept of circular motion . . . circular change. The wheel is the eastern symbol. That wheel is on the Indian flag. It is a Buddhist concept—very meaningful. In the West you have a linear concept of life—in a line: evolution, progress, improvement. Things are getting better! Nothing is getting better, nothing is getting worse; things are as they are. Things have always been the way they are, and they are going to be the way they are. You can get very much worked up and worried if you carry this concept of progress.

So on the social level in the West, there is the concept of a social progress, and on the individual level, improvement—how to improve yourself. In fact in the American book market so many books are available on how to improve yourself and how to succeed and how to be this and that, that one is simply surprised. In the whole of the East, for five thousand years we have not created a single book on how to succeed and how to improve, and how to win friends and influence people. We have not written a single book! We think that the whole existence is circular.

You are not caught in anything, because the very idea that you are separate from this pattern is wrong. You *are* this pattern! You are this that you want to get free of.

You are creating a difficult thing which cannot be done. How can you be free from yourself? It is you! It is as if a rose wants not to grow any more roses, and the rose bush comes to me and says, "Bhagwan, I am caught up in a compulsion—I always grow roses!" Mm? What nonsense! It is not a compulsion—it is the way you are.

So I will say to the rose bush, "With my blessings, go on growing bigger roses—as many as you can grow—and forget all this nonsense! You are not caught up in anything. This is *you.*"

Once you realize this fact, and the idea to improve and become better is dropped, suddenly you are free. To me, to become absolutely free of improvement, to be totally free of all nonsense—of growth, improvement, going somewhere, reaching high altitudes, *siddhis* and powers, and occult and esoteric things—is to become enlightened. Once you are finished with all that nonsense—it is ridiculous—and once you say, "This is what I am—if I am a rose bush, I am to be a rose bush, so why not be happily a rose bush? Why become sad? And why become neurotic and go to a psychiatrist's couch? I am a rose bush. God intends me to be a rose bush, so I will be a rose bush. Now I will happily be a rose bush"—there is no problem, because there is no division.

My suggestion is: simply be yourself. Don't bring in any categories, values. Once you see the fact that this is what you are, suddenly all problems disappear. Problems are created, manufactured, homemade. You weave and spin them. If this is the way things have been happening, this is the way they are going to happen; simply let them happen.

BLESSED ARE THE IGNORANT

SELF-DISCIPLINE   If you become aware that you are going to die, then immediately you start rethinking about life. Then you would like the death to be absorbed in life.

When death is absorbed in life *yam* is born: a life of discipline. Then you live but you always live with the remembrance of death. You move but you always know that you are moving towards death. You enjoy but you always know that this is not going to last forever. Death becomes your shadow, part of your being, part of your perspective. You have absorbed death . . . now self-discipline will be possible. Now you will think, "How to live?"—that not only does life become a crescendo of bliss, but death becomes the highest, because death is the climax of life.

To live in such a way that you become capable of living totally and you become capable of dying totally, that's the whole meaning of self-discipline. Self-discipline is not a suppression; it is to live a directed life, a life with the sense of direction. It is to live a life fully alert and aware of death. Then your river of life has both the banks, life and death, and the river of consciousness flows between these two. Anybody who is trying to live life, denying death its part, is trying to move along one bank; his river of consciousness cannot be total. He will lack something; something very beautiful he will lack. His life will be superficial—there will be no depth in it. Without death there is no depth.

YOGA: THE ALPHA AND THE OMEGA, Vol. V

SELFISHNESS   I teach you to be really selfish so that you can be altruistic. There is no contradiction between being selfish and being altruistic: being selfish is the very source of being altruistic. But you have been told just the opposite up to now, you have been taught the contrary: that if you want to be altruistic, if you want to love others, *don't* love yourself—*hate* yourself in fact. If you want to respect others, don't respect yourself. Humiliate yourself in every possible way, condemn yourself in every possible way.

And what has happened out of such teaching?—nobody loves anybody. The person who condemns himself cannot love anybody. If you cannot love even yourself—because you are the closest person to yourself—if your love cannot even reach to the closest point, it is impossible for you to reach towards the stars. You cannot love anything—you can pretend. And that's what humanity has become: a community of pretenders, hypocrites.

Please try to understand what I mean by being selfish. First you have to love yourself, know yourself, *be* yourself. Out of that you will radiate love, understanding, tenderness, care for others. Out of meditation arises true compassion, but meditation is a selfish phenomenon. Meditation means just enjoying yourself and your aloneness, forgetting the whole world and just enjoying yourself. It is a selfish phenomenon, but out of this selfishness arises great altruism.

And then there is no bragging about it; you don't become egoistic. You don't serve people; you don't make them feel obliged to you. You simply enjoy sharing your love, your joy.
GUIDA SPIRITUALE

SELF-KNOWLEDGE Man has two worlds available to him, the outer and the inner, but the inner is so obvious that one tends to forget all about it. The obvious is almost always forgotten because we take it for granted. The outer is not so obvious, it is not so easy, hence we become interested in the outer. We are always interested in the unfamiliar, and the outer is unfamiliar. And that's the first wrong step. Once you become interested in the outer there is no end to it.

Man has reached Everest, the South Pole, the North Pole, the moon, and now they are striving to reach Mars and nobody is bothered about the purpose. And man has not even made an intensive effort to know himself. We know more about the moon than we know about our own being—this is sheer stupidity.

I am not against knowing about the world but the first and the foremost thing in life is our own center. Self-knowledge should be our first priority, and once we have known ourselves then we can enquire about the whole world. Religion comes first, science can only be secondary . . .

Religion is no longer important, and that is the fall of humanity. That's why there is so much darkness and gloom and misery settling in people's hearts. They are accepting life as a tragedy—meaningless, futile—a tale told by an idiot, with no significance; it is no more a song. And the reason is that we are not at all interested in the inner.

Sannyas means initiation into your own interiority. You have gone too far away from yourself, you have to be brought back home. Sannyas is a homecoming—and the method is meditation.

Just as mind is the method to go out, meditation is the method to come in. It is the same energy, the same door: on one side of the door you have the label "entrance", on the other side "exit". It is the same door; when it opens outwards it becomes mind, when it opens inwards it becomes meditation. It is the same energy. And my whole work here is to help your energy take a one-hundred-and-eighty degree turn.

Once you can see just a glimpse of your being and its grandeur and its splendor, then the whole outside world simply becomes insignificant, it loses all value and you are for the first time really born. The journey towards home has started. And when you reach the center of your being you reach God because God is nothing but your innermost center.

On the circumference we are different people but at the center we are one, at the center we all meet. The farther away we go from the center, the farther away we go from each other. The distance between persons become wider and wider as we go farther away from the center; as you come closer, you start coming closer to people also. Hence love is a natural byproduct of meditativeness because you start feeling a new kind of closeness with people, with trees, with rocks, with stars—with everything that is. And when you are at the center suddenly you know that there is only one— we are all part of one organic unity—and that's the meaning of God.

GOING ALL THE WAY

SELF-LUMINOUS Wisdom is self-luminous. Knowledge is not self-luminous, knowledge needs supports.

Many times I receive letters from professors, academicians and pundits, saying, "In your books why don't you give footnotes or an appendix, so one can know from where these quotations have been taken and on what authority?"

What I am saying is self-luminous. It needs no footnotes, it needs no appendixes. It needs no support: I am enough unto myself. What I am saying is being said on my own authority. I am not trying to prove any hypothesis by supporting it with many arguments, by collecting data in support of it.

The Upanishads don't have any footnotes, the Koran is unaware of footnotes. Buddha has not given any sources— from where and on what authority he is speaking.

Whenever truth arrives it is self-luminous. It is the untruth that needs proofs, remember. It is the doubt inside you that collects proofs. Your statement is not a statement which can stand on its own; it needs props.

Knowledge gathers much information, data and argument. Wisdom is simply there: nude, innocent, available to those, all those who are ready to drink it.

In those moments of self-luminous wisdom there is the distinct realization that objects as such are never really directly related to or known, but rather it is only the knowledge of objects, as it takes place in consciousness, that is ever experienced or known. Therefore, all objects are essentially only objectifications of, and reducible to, pure consciousness, the one and only reality. In other words, what is known is not essentially different from the knower, so that one realizes that the world is essentially the knower himself or pure consciousness, and so all is *one*.

When you are in that state of wisdom—self-luminous, silent, utterly relaxed, absolutely at home—this realization arises that consciousness is all, because whatsoever is known is known through consciousness. Whatsoever is known is nothing but a reflection in consciousness, whatsoever is known is nothing but a formation in consciousness. All forms arise in the ocean of consciousness and disappear. But the consciousness remains, abides, it is eternal.

UNIO MYSTICA, Vol. I

SELF-NATURE Thomas a Kempis has written one of the most famous Christian treatises, *Imitation of Christ*. The very title is ugly. As far as imitation is concerned it can create only pseudo people, hypocrites. About that Friedrich Nietzsche is far closer to the truth than a Kempis. Nietzsche says the only Christian died on the cross two thousand years ago. He says the *only* Christian—and he is right. Nobody else can be a Jesus. Nobody else was before, nobody else will be again. And that is beautiful, that each individual has such uniqueness. Nobody else has to be imitated by you.

That is the meaning of self-nature. Bliss is your nature, intelligence is your nature. Meditation is only a way to discover it, to uncover it. Once you have found it you become free from all imposed patterns—Christian, Hindu, Mohammedan. You become free from all ideologies, you start living moment to moment, responding to the challenges of life according to *your* light. And then there is no repentance, no guilt, then whatsoever you do is right. Not that you are following a certain pattern which says, "This is right and this is wrong." You are not following those Ten Commandments. You are simply following your own consciousness, your own awareness.

So I give you the eleventh commandment, the only commandment really: your consciousness. Be a light unto yourself.

NO MAN IS AN ISLAND

SELF-REALIZATION The moment you realize, there is no self. The self exists only for the unrealized; for the realized, the self disappears. There is pure emptiness, just nothingness, no "I", no shadow of "I", no "I-amness". Hence what self? Self is only a religious term for the same game

called the ego. It is the same number; it differs not in any
way.

Self means "I am separate from the whole," and the realized
one knows he is *not* separate from the whole. He cannot
have a self; he can only have a no-self. *Anatta,* that's what
Buddha calls it—no-self.

It is a very paradoxical phenomenon. To realize who you
are is to realize that you are not! If you want to be, never
try to realize, because in the very process of realization the
ego disappears. And the self is only another name for the
ego. There is nothing like *self*-realization. Yes, there is realization, but the realization always makes you absolutely clear
that the self has never existed in the first place and it is not
there; it has never been there.

GUIDA SPIRITUALE

SENSATIONS   We live for sensations, we hanker for sensations. We go on seeking newer and newer sensations; our
whole life is an effort to obtain new sensations. But what
happens? The more you seek sensations, the less sensitive
you become. Sensitivity is lost.

It looks paradoxical. In sensations, sensitivity is lost. Then
you ask for more sensations and the "more" kills your sensitivity more. Then you ask for even more, and finally a
moment comes when all your senses have become dull and
dead. Man has never before been so ill and dead as he is
today. He was always more alive before, because there were
not so many possibilities to fulfill so many sensations. But
now science, progress, civilization, education, have created
so many opportuntities to move further and further into the
world of sensation. Ultimately, you turn into a dead person; your sensitivity is lost. Taste more foods—stronger
tastes, stronger foods, and your taste will be lost. If you move
around the world and go on seeing more and more beautiful
things, you will become blind: the sensitivity of your eyes
will be lost.

Change your love object every day—your girlfriend or
boyfriend, your wife or husband. If you change them every
day, your sensitivity to love will die. You are moving in
dangerous terrain. You will never move in depth; you will

only be moving on the surface, the periphery. The more things you experience, the less your capacity to experience becomes. And then in the end, when everything around you has gone dead, you ask for the divine, you ask for bliss, you ask for truth. A dead man cannot experience the divine. To experience the divine you need total sensitivity; you need aliveness. Remember, only the similar can bring out the similar.

If you want the divine—"the divine" means the most alive, the ever-alive, ever-young, ever-green—if you want to meet the divine, you will have to be more alive. How to do it? *Kill out all desires for sensation.* Don't seek sensation; seek sensitivity, become more sensitive.

The two are different. If you ask for sensations, you will ask for things; you will accumulate things. But if you ask for sensitivity, the whole world has to be done on your senses, not on things. You are not to accumulate things. You have to deepen your feelings, your heart, your eyes, your ears, your nose. Every sense should be deepened in such a way that it becomes capable of feeling the subtle.

We cannot even feel the gross, and we must become capable of feeling the subtle. The world appears to be gross only because we cannot feel the subtle. The invisible is hidden in the visible. Look at these trees. You look at the gross: the body of the tree. You never look, you never feel, the life within. The growth! The tree itself is not growing; the tree is just a body. Something else—the invisible—is growing in it. And because of it, the tree grows. The inner is growing and, because of it, the outer is growing. But you look only at the tree, so only the outer is seen.

Look around you. Look into your friend's eyes. You only look at the eyes, not at the one who sees through them. Touch your friend's body. You touch only the gross; you never feel the subtle within. Only the body, the external, is felt; because your eyes, your senses, have become so dull that they cannot feel the inner, the invisible.

More sensitivity is needed. Ask for less sensations and grow in sensitivity. When you touch, become the touch. When you see, become the eyes. When you hear, your whole consciousness must come to the ears. Listening to a song, or listening to the birds, *become* the ears. Forget everything else so it is as if you are only the ears. Come to the ears with your total being. Then, your ears will become more sensitive.

When you are looking at something—a flower or a beautiful face or the stars—become the eyes. Forget everything else, as if the whole rest of your body has gone out of existence and your consciousness has become just eyes. Then your eyes will be able to look more deeply, and you will become capable of looking at the invisible also. The invisible can also be seen, but you need more penetrating eyes to see it.

Kill out all desire for sensation, and grow in sensitivity. Think about the world less and about your senses more. Purify them. When you don't ask for sensations, they become purified. When you ask for more and more sensations, you are killing your senses.

The man who finds the divine is the man whose senses are totally alive, to their maximum capacity. Then it is not only that you can see the divine. You can taste the divine, you can smell the divine. The divine can enter in you through any of the senses. Only when the divine enters you from all the senses does the ultimate realization happen.

THE NEW ALCHEMY: TO TURN YOU ON

SENSE, INNER A boy was constantly scratching his head. His father looked at him one day and said, "Son, why are you always scratching your head?"

"Well," the boy responded, "I guess because I am the only one who knows it itches."

This is the inner sense. Only you know. Nobody else can know. It cannot be observed from the outside. When you have a headache, only you know. You cannot prove it. You cannot put it on the table to be inspected by everybody, dissected, analyzed.

In fact, the inner sense is so inner that you cannot even prove that it exists. That's why science goes on denying it, but the denial is inhuman. Even the scientist knows that when he feels love, he has an inner feeling. Something *is* there! And it is not a thing, and it is not an object; and it is not possible to put it before others. And *still* it is.

Inner sense has its own validity. But because of the scientific training, people have lost trust in their inner sense. They depend on others. You depend so much that if somebody says, "You are looking very happy," you start feeling happy. If twenty people decide to make you unhappy, they can make you unhappy. They just have to repeat the whole day whenever you come across them, they have to say to you that, "You are looking very unhappy, very sad. What is the matter? Somebody died or something?" And you will start suspecting: so many people are saying that are you unhappy, you must be.

You depend on people's opinions. You have depended on people's opinions *so* much that you have lost all track of inner sense. This inner sense has to be rediscovered, because all that is beautiful and all that is good and all that is divine can only be felt by the inner sense.

Stop being influenced by people's opinions. Rather, start looking in . . . allow your inner sense to say things to you. Trust it. If you trust it, it will grow. If you trust it you will feed it, it will become stronger . . .

It is through the inner sense that God is known.

There are six senses: five are outer; they tell you about the world. I say something about the light; without eyes you will not know light. Ears say something about the sound; without ears you will not know anything about the sound. There is a sixth sense, the inner sense, that shows and tells you something about yourself and the ultimate source of things. That sense has to be discovered.

Meditation is nothing but the discovery of the inner sense.
                              THE PERFECT MASTER, Vol. II

SENSES Never for a single moment think that your physical senses are as they should be—they are not. They have been trained. You see things if your society allows you to see them. You hear things if your society allows you to hear them. You touch things if your society allows you to touch things.

Man has lost many of his senses—for example, smell. Man

has almost lost smell. Just see a dog and his capacity to smell—how sensitive is his nose! Man seems to be very poor. What has happened to man's nose? Why can't he smell so deeply as a dog or a horse? The horse can smell for miles. The dog has an immense memory of smells. Man has no memory. Something is blocking the nose.

Those who have been working deep into these layers say that it is because of the repression of sex that smell is lost. Physically man is as sensitive as any other animal, but psychologically his nose has been corrupted. Smell is one of the most sexual doors into your body. It is through smell that animals start feeling whether a male is in tune with the female or not. The smell is a subtle hint. When the female is ready to make love to the male she releases a certain kind of smell. Only through that smell does the male understand that he is acceptable. If that smell is not released by the feminine sexual organism, the male moves away; he is not accepted.

Man has destroyed smell because it will be difficult to create a so-called cultured society if your sense of smell remains natural. You are moving on the road and a woman starts smelling and gives you a hint of acceptance. She is somebody else's wife; her husband is with her. The signal is there that you are acceptable. What will you do? It will be awkward, embarrassing . . .

You don't see people eye to eye; or, if you do see them, it is only for a few seconds. You don't see people really; you go on avoiding. If you see, it is thought to be offensive. Just remember, do you really see people? Or do you go on avoiding their eyes?—because if you don't avoid them then you may be able to see a few things which the person is not willing to show. It is not good manners to see something that he is not willing to show, so it is better to avoid. We listen to the words, we don't see the face—because many times the words and the face are contradictory. A man is saying one thing and he is showing another. Gradually we have completely lost the sense of seeing the face, the eyes, the gestures. We only listen to the words. Just watch this and you will be surprised how people go on saying one thing and showing another. And nobody detects it because you have been trained not to look directly into the face. Or, even if you look, the look is not that of awareness, not that of attention. It is empty; it is almost as if you are not looking.

We hear sounds by choice. We don't hear all kinds of sounds. We choose. Whatsoever is useful we hear. And to different societies and different countries, different things are valuable. A man who lives in a primitive world, in a forest, in a jungle, has a different kind of receptivity for sounds. He has to be continuously alert and aware of the animals. His life is in danger. You need not be alert. You live in a cultured world where animals don't exist any more and there is no fear. Your survival is not at stake. Your ears don't function perfectly because there is no need . . .

People don't touch each other, they don't hold hands, they don't hug each other. And when you hold somebody's hand, you feel embarrassed, he feels embarrassed. Even if you hug somebody, it feels as if something wrong is happening. And you are in a hurry to get away from the other's body, because the other's body can open you. The warmth of the other's body can open you. Even children are not allowed to hug their parents. There is great fear.

And all fear is basically, deep down, rooted in the fear of sex. There is a taboo against sex. A mother cannot hug her son because the son may get sexually aroused—that is the fear. A father cannot hug his daughter. He is afraid he may get physically aroused. Warmth has its own way of working. Nothing is wrong in being physically aroused or sexually aroused. It is simply a sign that one is alive, that one is immensely alive. But the fear, the sex taboo, says keep away, keep a distance . . .

That is the whole effort of yoga: to make your body alive, sensitive, young again, to give your senses their maximum functioning. Then one functions with no taboos around; then lucidity, grace, beauty flow. Warmth arises again, openness—and growth happens. One is constantly new, young, and one is always on an adventure. The body becomes orgasmic. Joy surrounds you.

Through joy the first corruption disappears. Hence my insistence to be joyous, to be celebrating, to enjoy life, to accept the body—not only to accept it, but to feel grateful that God has given you such a beautiful body, such a sensitive body, with so many doors to relate to reality: eyes and ears and nose and touch. Open all these windows and let life's breezes flow in, let life's sun shine in. Learn to be more sensitive. Use every opportunity to be sensitive so that that first filter is dropped.

If you are sitting on the grass, don't go on pulling it up and destroying it. I had to stop sitting on the lawn—I used to give *darshan* on the lawn—because people would go on destroying the grass, they would go on pulling up the grass. I had to stop it. People are so violent, so unconsciously violent, they don't know what they are doing. And they were told again and again, but within minutes they would forget. They were so restless, they didn't know what they were doing. The grass was available to their restlessness so they would start pulling it up and destroying it.

When you are sitting on the grass, close your eyes, become the grass—be grassy. Feel that you are the grass, feel the greenness of the grass, feel the wetness of the grass. Feel the subtle smell that goes on being released by the grass. Feel the dewdrops on the grass—that they are on you. Feel the sunrays playing on the grass. For a moment be lost into it and you will have a new sense of your body. And do it in all kinds of situations: in a river, in a swimming pool, lying on the beach in the sunrays, looking at the moon in the night, lying down with closed eyes on the sand and feeling the sand. Millions of opportunities are there to make your body alive again. And only you can do it. Society has done its work of corruption, you will have to undo it.

And once you start hearing, seeing, touching, smelling through joy, then you hear the reality, then you see the reality, then you smell the reality.

SUFIS: THE PEOPLE OF THE PATH, Vol. II

SENSITIVITY A real painting is not just the sum total of the colors, it is more—and that "more" is the meaning. A real life is not the sum total of what you do; unless there is something more to it, you live an inauthentic life. That "more" is God. That poetry is God, that music is God, that surrounds you and floods you.

People come to me and ask "Where is God?" It is not a question of asking "Where"; God is a meaning, not a person. I cannot indicate "There—go there, and you will find

him." God has no address, God cannot be located, it is a
meaning. You have to create meaning in your life, then God
is. God has to be created.

And the beginning of creating God is to start becoming
more and more sensitive to the existence that surrounds you.
The trees, the rocks, the stars, the earth—you are surrounded
by great poetry. But you remain separate, hence you go on
missing it.

UNIO MYSTICA, Vol. II

SENSUOUSNESS   To be sensuous means to become aware
of the circumference, and to be spiritual means to become
aware of the center. Sensuousness is the beginning of
spirituality.

Become more and more sensuous: that is the way of being
alive . . .

Yes, when you are sensuous God is available. All the
mysteries are close by, because that is the only way to know
the mysterious.

Sensuousness means you are open, your doors are open,
you are ready to throb with existence. If a bird starts singing, the sensuous person immediately feels the song echoed
in his deepest core of being. The non-sensuous person does
not hear it at all, or maybe it is just a noise somewhere. It
does not penetrate his heart. A cuckoo starts calling—a sensuous person starts feeling as if the cuckoo is not calling
from some faraway mango grove, but from deep down within
his own soul. It becomes his own call, it becomes his own
longing for the divine, his own longing for the beloved. In
that moment the observer and the observed are one. Seeing
a beautiful flower bloom, the sensuous person blooms with
it, becomes a flower with it.

The sensuous person is liquid, flowing, fluid. Each experience, and he becomes it. Seeing a sunset, he is the sunset.
Seeing a night, a dark night, a beautiful silent darkness, he
becomes the darkness. In the morning he becomes the light.

He is *all* that life is. He tastes life from every nook and
corner. Hence he becomes rich; this is real richness. Listening to music, he is music, listening to the sound of water
he becomes that sound. And when the wind passes through
a bamboo grove, and the cracking bamboos . . . he is not

far away from them. He is amidst them, one of them—he
is a bamboo . . .

To be sensuous is to be available to the mysteries of life.
Become more and more sensuous, and drop all condemnation. Let your body become just a door. All your senses
should become clear doors with no hindrances, so when
you hear you become the music, and when you see you
become the light, when you touch you become that which
you have touched.

THE SECRET OF SECRETS, Vol. II

SEPARATENESS Man can live either by his own will or
as part of God's will. The first is the way of the ignorant
person, and because of that the ignorant person suffers. His
whole effort is futile because he is trying to do something
which is impossible. We are part of the whole, we cannot
exist as separate entities, not even for a single moment.

We can *believe* that we exist as separate entities, but that
is only belief, not reality. And whenever belief goes against
reality it creates suffering because you live according to
something which is not the case; you start going wrong.
When you live according to the real there is no misery; bliss
is the outcome.

The man who understands drops his ego for the simple
reason that it is only a false notion. There is no way to mate-
rialize it; it will remain false. And to spin and weave your
life around something false is a sheer wastage of energy . . .
but that's what millions of people go on doing, hence they
suffer. The suffering is caused because without understanding the reality they go on trying to do something against
it. They are trying to go against the current. Their whole
energy becomes a constant fight—and they are bound to lose,
because how can the part win against the whole? It is like
a leaf fighting with the tree itself.

If the leaf has consciousness it *may* start thinking it is separate, that it has nothing to do with the tree, that it will have
its own way. And then immediately there will be trouble,
there will be conflict. It will become more and more
alienated from its own sources of energy. The tree is its
mother, and the tree is not only a tree, it is rooted in the
earth; it represents the whole earth. It breathes the air, it

represents the whole atmosphere. It is connected with the
sun and with the farthest star. To fight with the tree is to
fight with the universe. Just a poor, tiny leaf trying to fight
with the universe—the whole idea is stupid. But that's what
man goes on doing: he goes on pushing the river.

Sannyas means dropping the fight with the river, going
with the river, allowing the river to take you, learning the
art of let-go. Those two small, simple words "let", "go", define
the very spirit of sannyas. Then one can say, "Let thy kingdom come, thy will be done." Then one withdraws one's
will, and the moment you withdraw your will your life
becomes immensely rich. Suddenly the whole is with you,
and we can be victorious only when the whole is with us.
THE GOLDEN WIND

SERIOUSNESS   Those who take life seriously become pathological, because life is not a serious phenomenon, it is all
playfulness, from the top to the bottom. It is a song to be
sung, a dance to be danced, a love to be lived—but with
utter playfulness. The moment you become serious you
become blocked, the flow stops; you are cut off from the
universal energy. You cannot dance when you are serious
because seriousness is basically sadness. Seriousness is also
calculation, business: one is always looking for the motive—
why? One is always asking "Why do it? What am I going
to gain out of it? What will the profit be?" These are
businesslike attitudes. They are good in the marketplace but
they are absolutely wrong when you start moving inwards.
The more you move inwards, the more life appears as fun,
as tremendous fun. A sense of humor is needed and a sense
of playfulness.

In the past just the opposite has been the case: the saints
have been very sad and very serious, as if life was a burden,
a heavy burden; they were carrying mountains on their
heads. They were not free like children, playing for no reason
at all, playing just for the playing itself, playing for play's
sake . . . no idea of gaining anything out of it . . .

Let this be my message for you, let this be the foundation
of your sannyas: playfulness has to be the color you dye
your whole being in, let it vibrate through each fiber and

cell of your being. And whenever you find yourself serious, drop seriousness immediately. Don't allow it to remain with you for long because the longer it is there, the deeper its roots start reaching into you. Drop it immediately! Our roots have go into a totally different direction; the direction is playfulness. That has to be your dimension.

The West has not understood the idea of playfulness, *leela*, much. The western God is too serious, very angry; he makes much fuss about small things. Adam and Eve had just play-fully eaten from the Tree of Knowledge and this old guy made so much fuss! He cannot allow such small playful things—he becomes mad! He drives them out of heaven, closes the door and Christians say that now the door is being guarded with naked swords so that Adam and Eve cannot enter again easily.

This attitude of the Christian and the Jewish God seems to be very old-fashioned; it does not have any ingredient of love in it. The father has to be more loving and the ultimate father has to be an ultimate source of love. He can-not forgive just a small act of disobedience—what kind of father is he? And not only do Adam and Eve have to suffer, since then humanity has been suffering. Because *they* com-mitted the sin, we have to suffer; we are their inheritors so we are in sin. This whole approach is psychologically neurotic.

God is love, compassion. The East never thinks of God as so serious, but playful! Hence the Christians can never understand the eastern idea of God. In fact they cannot even conceive it, and they become very angry when they come to know the eastern idea of God. The eastern idea of God is not that of a creator but that of a flute player, a dancer, a singer. He has created the world out of the sheer joy of creating. It is like a child painting, with no idea of what he is doing—just throwing colors on the canvas. Something evolves out of it but there is no preplanned motivation. That is the eastern idea of God: God is playing; he has energies— what to do with those energies?

The ancient eastern parable says that God was alone and he got fed up with his aloneness, he was too bored with his aloneness. This seems to be very human. He wanted to create something to play with so that he could have some company, and of course he created a beautiful woman. The western God first creates a man; the eastern God first creates a woman. That seems to be more psychological. If God is male then the western God looks homosexual! This seems to be very natural, that God creates a woman just to have company! And he immediately falls in love with the woman.

Now that is inconceivable with the western approach. Christian missionaries have been condemning it like anything because they say that woman is his daughter! Yes, legally . . . because he has created her he is the father and the woman is the daughter. But the eastern God doesn't care—he falls in love with the woman. And the play starts: the woman starts escaping, as every woman is bound to do, and God follows . . . and the hide-and-seek . . .

The story is beautiful. The woman hides in many places. The woman becomes a cow and God becomes a bull! That's how the whole creation comes into life. The woman goes on hiding in new forms; that's how *all* female forms are created—and God goes on searching for her. Whatsoever form she takes, he takes the same form—of course he is male so he takes the male form. This is how existence goes on spreading—the play still continues. This seems to be more poetic; less legal but more human. And there is no question of sin anywhere! In the East there exists no idea of original sin.

To be a sannyasin means to start looking at life in a new way. It is a play. Play it as skillfully as possible but don't get serious about it. When it is a play, whether you succeed or fail makes no difference. All that is needed is that one plays it totally—success and failure are just immaterial.

Each moment of play is joy. Who cares about the ultimate result? In fact there is no ultimate result. All results are immediate, intrinsic to the moment.

EVEN BEIN' GAWD AIN'T A BED OF ROSES

SERVICE The Christian idea of service is that service has to be first then ecstasy follows. The eastern idea is just the reverse: ecstasy has to come first, then service follows. If service comes first it will be just a duty—imposed, cultivated, practiced; it is impossible for ecstasy to arise out of it. It will create only a hypocrite, and that's what the Chrisitian missionary has become in the world.

Service is something outer, something you do for others, but how can you love others if you have not even arrived at your own center? That love will be only lip service. You can force yourself into many kinds of services but there will be greed behind it: greed to go to heaven, greed to be known as virtuous, greed to become famous as a public servant, but deep down it will be greed. Out of this kind of service nobody has ever known ecstasy.

Ecstasy has to come first, and then service flows out of it of its own accord. When you have something to give, only then can you give. When love is overflowing in you it can be shared, and then there is no greed in it. In fact you are not obliging anybody; on the contrary, you feel obliged because they allowed you to serve them. You feel grateful because they did not reject your love. They could have, but they accepted it, they welcomed it.

And you don't ask for anything out of the service. Now service is a joy in itself. You don't ask for any virtue, you don't ask for any account of it in the bank of God, you don't ask for paradise for it; its value is intrinsic. In fact it is a byproduct of your joy. It is just like a shadow: you move— your shadow moves with you.

HALLELUJAH!

Service is nothing but a way of prayer—a very substantial way, a very potential way of prayer. If you serve, you are doing prayer. And if you pray, in a subtle way you are doing service. Both are complementaries; never divide them. Humanity has divided them and has suffered much for it.

If you serve without prayer, then service remains just on the periphery. If you pray without service, your prayer becomes isolated from life. You become like an island. If you pray and serve, and you serve in such a way that it is a way of prayer, and you pray in such a way that it is a way of service, then you are not isolated, and you are not on the periphery. You remain on the center, and yet one with the whole.

Service means feeling one with the whole, feeling one with the other. It means a point where I and thou disappears.

And when you are no more there, the whole starts functioning through you. And that's the real therapy.

NOTHING TO LOSE BUT YOUR HEAD

There are millions of Christian missionaries serving poor people for wrong reasons. Their reason for serving poor people is because this is the way to attain to heaven. This is greed, this is not service! And on the surface they are good people, nice people, very helpful people, doing good works in every possible way, but deep down their desire is nothing but a great greed, a greed projected towards the other world. They are so greedy—more greedy than the ordinary people, because the ordinary people are satisfied with a little bit of money, a good house, a garden, a car, this and that; a little prestige, power, becoming a prime minister or a president, and they are perfectly happy, satisfied. But these people are not satisfied with such small things—"mundane", "momentary"; they condemn all these things. They want eternal peace, they want eternal bliss, they want the eternal company of God.

And there is going to be great competition, because God must be surrounded by a great crowd of saints. Who is going to be close to God? In fact, this is what Jesus' disciples asked him. The last night before he departed from his disciples, this was the question uppermost in their minds.

I always feel sorry for Jesus: he was not so fortunate as Buddha, as Mahavira, as Lao Tzu, as far as disciples are concerned. He had a very poor lot!

Jesus was going to be crucified tomorrow. He has told them that this is the last night and that he will be caught; he predicts it. And do you know what they are asking? They are not concerned about Jesus' crucifixion: how to protect him, how to save him, or what can be done now; they are not worried about that. They ask him, "Lord, tomorrow you are leaving us. Just one question before you go: let it be settled. Of course, we know you will be on the right hand side of God in heaven, but who will be next to you? Who amongst us will be the one blessed to be next to you?"

This is pure greed! This is spiritual politics—more ugly than ordinary politics, because ordinary politics is gross and you can see it immediately when it is there, but this type of politics is very subtle and very difficult to see.

Serve, if service is your response out of no-mind. Don't desire anything out of it. Do it for the sheer joy of doing it.

That's what I am trying to create here. You are all involved in all kinds of work in this commune, and this is only the beginning, just the seed of the commune; soon it will grow into a big tree. But the basic foundation is being laid. You are all working, but it is not service because of some greed. You are not here to attain anything in the other world. I am teaching you how to enjoy each moment for its own sake; the joy is intrinsic.

THE WHITE LOTUS

SEX I am not teaching sex to you. If I have to talk once in a while about sex that is because of your Christian, Hindu, Mohammedan repressive traditions. I am not responsible for it, *they* are responsible for it. They have made man's life so paralyzed, so crippled and their whole strategy has depended upon repressing the energy called sex.

And remember, you have only one energy: you don't have many energies, only one energy. At the lowest it is called sex energy. You go on refining it, you go on transforming it through meditation, through the alchmey of meditation, and the same energy starts moving upwards. It becomes love, it becomes prayer. It is the same energy, just refined states of it. Sex is crude, raw, just like a diamond found in the mines. It has to be cut, polished; much work is needed. Then it will be possible to recognize that it is a diamond . . .

Sex is raw energy. It has to be transformed, and through transformation there is transcendence. Rather than transforming it, religions have been repressing it. And if you repress it the natural outcome is a perverted human being. He becomes obsessed with sex . . .

And sex is one of the most important phenomena, in fact *the* most important phenomenon of your life. But from our very childhood we are being deceived, we are told lies about sex. And the day we start discovering the facts of life, great guilt arises—as if we are doing something criminal. The criminal thing has been done to you by your parents, by your priests, by your politicians, by your pedagogues. They have created such a conditioning in you that you cannot discover the facticity of your life and its implications. They have falsified you, they have betrayed your trust . . .

Children are bound to discover the reality. How long can you hide it from them? There is no need to hide anything: everything should be explained. When the child is enquiring it should be explained as it is. There is no need to start a child's mind with lies. Don't stuff their minds with lies, because how long can you go hiding the facts? They will manifest themselves and then the child will be in a real fix, in a real difficulty. He will be divided, he will be split. His conditioning will say, "This is wrong," and life will say, "Go ahead." His biology will say one thing and his psychology will say another thing. You have created a schizophrenic condition in him . . .

Religions have created a strange situation. They have created your obsessiveness with sex and then they make you feel responsible for it. They are guilty of creating guilt in people, but they make *you* feel guilty . . .

Sex is a natural phenomenon; there is no need to be worried about it. And sometimes I have to talk about it; it is because of these religions. Once man is freed from religious exploitation and religious conventions, traditions, which are *very* oppressive, there will be no need to talk about sex. Then we can move into more intricate, scientific ways to transform it into higher forms of energy.

Sex is the lowest center of your existence and *samadhi* the highest, the seventh center. It is a ladder of seven rungs. And sex energy has to be moved rung by rung to the seventh where it opens up like a one-thousand-petalled-lotus. One becomes a Buddha only when sex is transformed.

ZEN: THE SPECIAL TRANSMISSION

Sex is such a significant phenomenon because it is the source of all life. It is so significant that if you repress it you will repress many other things. For example, the person who is sexually repressed will become uncreative, because creativity itself is a kind of sexual activity.

In *my* observation, if a person is totally creative he will transcend sex without repressing it, because his own energy will become creative. He will not need to go into sex—not that he will prevent himself—the very need will disappear. He now has a far higher bliss happening to him; the lower is bound to disappear when you have the higher in your hands.

Try to understand my arithmetic: never drop the lower, try to attain to the higher. When the higher is there, the lower is bound to disappear of its own accord. And when the lower disappears into the higher, then life becomes more beautiful, more healthy, more whole.

A real poet while producing, creating, composing, forgets all about sex. A real sculptor absorbed in his work, forgets all about sex. Even if a naked woman passes by he will not look at her, his concentration in his own creativity is so total. A real dancer disappears in his dance—his ego, his sex, all are dissolved into his dance.

But if sex is repressed, then just the contrary will be the result; your creativity will be repressed and creativity repressed means many things. Its implications are very great, because it has a multi-dimensionality to it. If your creativity is repressed, your science and the scientific endeavor will disappear . . .

If your sex life is flowing joyously you have tremendous interest in everything you are doing . . .

According to me, sex is the seed—the pleasure. If sex is allowed natural growth, respected, valued, then a transformation happens, a metamorphosis happens. Sex starts growing into the foliage of art, music, poetry, dance and a thousand other creative dimensions. Sex is only a seed, or the roots, but if supported, nourished, watered, taken care of, then many branches grow, much foliage comes, many green leaves moving in all directions, dancing in the wind, in the rain, in the sun . . . This is what the world of art is, the world of aesthetics. And if you allow the world of aesthetics to reach its highest peak, then flowers come.

Sex is pleasure, the lowest; art is happiness. Sex is animal, art is human. Sex is biological; the second step, higher than sex, is love. The man who has accepted sex respectfully, lovingly, will be able to transform it into love. And on the foliage, on the branches of love, the flowers of bliss happen. That is the highest stage; that is spirituality, true religion.

THE WILD GEESE AND THE WATER

Sex has four stages; those stages have to be understood . . . Not to understand those four stages is dangerous and the whole tradition has been keeping you unaware of those four stages.

The first stage is autosexual.

When the child is born he is a narcissist. He loves his body tremendously, and it is beautiful: he knows only his body. Just sucking his own thumb, and he is in such euphoria. You see the child sucking his own thumb—what euphoria is on his face, just playing with his own body, trying to take his toe into his mouth, making a circle of the energy. When the child takes his toe into the mouth a circle is created and the energy starts moving in a circle. The light circulates naturally in the child and he enjoys, because when the light circulates there is great joy inside.

The child plays with his own sexual organs not knowing they are sexual organs. He has not yet been conditioned; he knows his body as one whole. And certainly, the sexual organs are the most sensitive part of the body. He utterly enjoys touching them, playing with them.

And here is where the society, the poisonous society, enters into the psyche of the child: "Don't touch!" "Don't" is the first dirty, four-letter word. And out of this one four-letter word, then many more come: can't, won't—these are all four-letter words. Once the child is told: "Don't!" and the angry parent, mother or father, and those eyes . . . And the child's hand is taken away from his genital organs, which are naturally very enjoyable. He really enjoys it, and he is not being sexual or anything. It is just the most sensitive part of his body, the most alive part of his body, that's all.

But our conditioned minds . . . He is touching a sexual organ; that is bad, we take his hand away. We create guilt in the child.

Now we have started destroying his natural sexuality. Now we have started poisoning the original source of his joy, of his being. Now we are creating hypocrisy in him; he will become a diplomat. When the parents are there he will not play with his sexual organs. Now the first lie has entered; he cannot be true. Now he knows that if he is true to himself, if he respects himself, if he respects his own joy, if he respects his own instinct, then the parents are angry. And he is helpless against them, he is dependent on them, his survival is with them. If they renounce him, he will be dead; so the question is of choosing whether you want to live. The condition is that if you want to live you have to be against yourself, and the child has to yield . . .

And the natural outcome of this stupidity that has been perpetually practiced on humanity is that first the child is no more a natural being, hypocrisy has entered. He has to hide something from the parents or he has to feel guilty.

This is the autosexual state: many people remain stuck there. That's why so much masturbation continues all over the world. It is a natural state. It would have passed on its own, it was a growing phase, but the parents disturbed the energy's growing phase.

The child becomes stuck: he wants to play with his genital organs and he cannot. Repressing, repressing, one day it is too much and he is possessed by the sexual energy. And once he has started masturbating, it may become a habit, a mechanical habit, and then he will never move to the second stage.

And the people who are responsible are the parents, the priest, the politicians—the whole social mind that has existed up to now.

Now this man may remain stuck at this stage, which is very childish. He will never attain to full grown-up sexuality. He will never come to know the blissfulness that can come only to a grown-up sexual being. And the irony is that these are the same people who condemn masturbation and make much fuss about it. And they make such statements which are very dangerous: they have been telling people that if you masturbate you will go blind, if you masturbate you will become a zombie, if you masturbate you will never be intelligent, you will remain stupid. Now all the scientific findings are agreed upon one point: that masturbation never harms anybody. But these suggestions harm. Now this is an absolute agreement: there are no two opinions about it. All the psychological researches agree that masturbation never harms anybody, it is a natural outlet of energy. But these ideas—that you will go blind—may make it dangerous to your eyes, because again and again you will think that you will go blind, that you will go blind, that you will go blind . . . So many people are using glasses, and the reason may not be in the eyes; the reason may be just somewhere else. So many millions of people are stupid and the reason may not be that they are stupid—because no child is born stupid, all children are born intelligent. The reason may be somewhere else: in these techniques. You will remain ill, you will lose self-confidence. And so many people are afraid, trembling continuously, have no trust, no self-confidence, are continuously afraid, because they know what they have been doing.

Now thousands of letters come to me: "We are caught up in this trap; how can we come out of it?

And let me repeat: masturbation has never harmed anybody. But the moment when a person masturbates is a very sensitive and delicate moment; his whole being is open and flowing. In that moment if some suggestion is dropped in his mind—and he himself will drop the suggestion, "Now what if I go mad? if I go blind? if I remain always stupid? "— these constant auto-hypnotic suggestions are the cause of a thousand and one illnesses, of a thousand and one psychological problems, perversions.

Who is responsible for this?

And people who come to me come with all these perversions.

And I try to help them, and many are helped and many grow beyond it. But the society thinks I am teaching people perversions. This is just unbelievable. I am helping you to grow beyond your perversions; the society has given you perversions. You live in a perverted society!

If the child is allowed the natural phase of autosexuality, he moves on his own to the second phase, the homosexual— but very few people move to the second phase. The majority remain with the first phase. Even while making love to a woman or a man you may not be doing anything else but just a mutual masturbation. Because very few people attain to orgasmic states, very few people come to the glimpses that are bound to be there if your sexuality is mature. Very few people come to know about God through their lovemaking, which is a natural phenomenon. In lovemaking, meditation happens naturally.

But it doesn't happen, and the reason is that millions, the majority, are stuck at the first stage. Even if they have got married and they have children, their lovemaking is not more than mutual masturbation. It is not real lovemaking.

Lovemaking is an art; it needs great sensitivity, needs great awareness, meditativeness, it needs maturity.

The second phase is homosexual. Few people move to the second phase; it is a natural phase. The child loves his body. If the child is a boy, he loves a boy's body, his body. To jump to a woman's body, to a girl's body, would be too much of a big gap. Naturally, first he moves in love with other boys; or if the child is a girl, the first natural instinct is to love other girls because they have the same kind of body, the same kind of being. She can understand the girls better than the boys; boys are a world apart.

The homosexual phase is a natural phase. There society helps people to remain stuck again, because it creates barriers between man and woman, girls and boys. If those barriers are not there, then soon the homosexual phase fades away; the interest starts happening in the heterosex, the other sex. But for that, society does not give chances—a great China Wall exists between the boy and the girl. In the schools they have to sit apart or they have to be educated separately. In the colleges they have to live in separate hostels. Their meeting, their being together is not accepted . . .

You divide man and woman apart so much, you create watertight compartments. And when the man wants to love he cannot find the woman, and the woman wants to love and she cannot find the man. Then, whatsoever is . . . She starts falling in love with a woman, he starts falling in love with a man. And it is not satisfying either, but it is better than nothing. Nature has to find its way. If you don't allow the natural course, it will find some roundabout way. Otherwise homosexuality is a natural phase; it passes by itself.

And the third phase is heterosexual.

When a man is really out of autosex, homosex, then he

is capable and mature to fall in love with a woman—which is a totally different world, a different chemistry, a different psychology, a different spirituality. Then he is able to play with this different world, this different organism. They are poles apart, but when they come close—and there are moments when they are really close and overlapping—first glimpses, lightning glimpses of *samadhi* are attained.

Because it does not happen, many people think that I am just talking something like poetry. It is not poetry! I am not talking fiction, I am talking reality. What I am saying is an existential phenomenon, but the need is that the man and the woman must be mature. They must have gone beyond the first two stages; only then can this happen. And very rarely, very rarely, are there people who are mature men and mature women. So nothing happens; they make love, but that love is only superficial. Deep down they are auto-sexual, or, at the most, homosexual.

To love a woman or to love a man, a new kind of being is needed which can accept the polar opposite. And only with the polar opposite—just as with negative and positive electricity meeting, electricity is born, just like that—when life electricities meet, man and woman, *yin* and *yang,* Shiva and Shakti, when that meeting happens, that merger, that total oblivion, that drunkeness, they have disappeared as separate entities, separate egos. They are no longer separately there, therefore they are throbbing as one, two bodies in one soul. That is the first experience of no-mind, no-ego, no-time, and that is the first experience of *samadhi*.

Once this has been experienced, then a desire arises: how to attain this *samadhi* so that it can become a natural state of affairs and you need not depend on a woman, you need not depend on a man?—because dependence brings slavery. Only out of the experience of heterosexual orgasm does a person start searching for ways, means, and methods—Yoga, Tantra, Tao—so that he can attain the same state on his own or on her own.

And yes, it can be attained, because deep inside each man is a man and a woman—half comes from his father, half comes from his mother—and each woman is half woman, half man. So once you have known it happening through the outside woman, you will have the first glimpse that it can happen within too. The outer woman simply triggered it, the outer man simply acted as a catalytic agent; now you start meditating.

Then the fourth phase, the ultimate phase comes, which is *brahmacharya*, which is *real* celibacy; not the celibacy of the monks—that is not celibacy at all—but the celibacy of Buddhas. It is *brahmacharya*. Sex has disappeared; you don't need the outer woman, you don't need the outer man. Now your inner man and woman have fallen in a togetherness, and this togetherness is not momentary. This is real marriage; you are welded together. Now to be orgasmic is your natural state. A Buddha lives in orgasm continuously; he breathes in and out in orgasm.

These are the four stages of sex.

THE SECRET OF SECRETS, Vol. II

Sex is most foundational. Without sex there is no life. Life exists because of sex and life disappears with sex. That is why Buddha and Mahavira say that unless you go beyond sex you will be born again and again. You cannot go beyond life, because with the sexual desire inside you will be born again. So sex is not only giving birth to someone else; ultimately, it is giving birth to yourself also. It works in a double way. You reproduce someone through sex, but that is not so important—because of your sexual desire, *you* are reborn; you reproduce yourself again and again.

THE ULTIMATE ALCHEMY, Vol. II

A real sexual experience is also an experience of death. You die. That's why people are so afraid of sex, so afraid of women; I have not come across many people who are not afraid of women. Fear . . . Woman has given you birth, she must carry your death also.

Look at the Hindus' conception of Kali, mother Kali. She is both life and death, the giver and the taker, a beautiful woman, but black, black like death; a beautiful woman, but very dangerous. So dangerous that she is dancing on the body of her own husband, almost killing him. Shiva is lying there and she is dancing on his body, almost crushing him. And she wears a garland of skulls, and in one of her hands she has a cut head, freshly cut with blood dripping from it. In the West they cannot understand why a mother should be so dangerous, why a beautiful woman should be depicted in such a dangerous and terrible and horrible way. Hindus know better. They have penetrated the mystery of life better than anybody else. They know that sex and death are so close, so close that they are almost one. When the sex center starts throbbing and spreading its waves over your body, the death center also starts throbbing. That's why orgasm has become just a word. You don't achieve orgasm in sex. You cannot. Unless you accept death you cannot achieve orgasm, because orgasm means losing all control, orgasm means losing all mind, orgasm means the whole body, every fiber and every cell of the body throbs in ecstasy, the whole body celebrates in an unknown bliss; and the mind is no longer the controller and the manipulator.

Man can achieve only a local orgasm which is nothing but ejaculation, not an orgasm at all. Because if orgasm takes over then you are no longer there—you are possessesd by life and death both. Fear takes over. For thousands of years women have not achieved orgasm. Even now in India, I don't see that even two percent of women achieve orgasm. Only in the last few years has man become aware that women can also achieve orgasm—it has been a suppressed thing. Because if the woman achieves orgasm she will go so mad that she will become Kali. She will be so mad with ecstasy that she may start dancing on your chest and she will no longer be herself. She will be something else, a natural force, a whirlwind, a storm; she will laugh and cry and nobody knows what will happen; and the whole neighborhood will know that a woman has achieved an orgasm.

Sex is such a private affair. We have made it such a hidden and secretive thing, in darkness. The partners don't even see each other, and the woman has been trained to remain absolutely passive, non-moving, because of the fear that once she knows the beauty of going completely mad, then she will be uncontrollable. It will be impossible for any man to satisfy any woman because a woman can achieve multiple orgasms and a man can achieve only one. A woman can achieve within minutes at least six orgasms—six to sixty. It will be impossible for any man to satisfy a woman—she will go so mad because she is so natural that it is better to suppress her.

Sex has been suppressed as part of death. Only two things have been suppressed in the world: sex and death. It has been my observation that whenever a culture suppresses sex, it does not suppress death as much because there is no need—the suppression of sex will do; and whenever a culture suppresses death it does not bother to suppress sex, there is no need, because the suppression of death alone will do. If you suppress one, both are suppressed, because both are together—and both have to be freed. Then, you live tremendously, but you always live on the verge of death. You become a being, but you are always looking into the non-being, that is the beauty of it, and the horror also. In fact all natural, beautiful things are also terrible.

God is not only beautiful, God is also terrible. He is not only a mystery—he is not only *mysterium* he is also *tremendum;* he is not only life, he is also death. Once you suppress your own being or your non-being you drop the bridges; then you cannot reach into the existence. Be like the existence, only then the bridge is there; then you are connected and joined with it.

In the West, after Freud, they have allowed sex a little freedom, but now they have become more suppressive of death. In the West nobody talks about death. It is as if it doesn't happen. Professionals even exist who work on the dead body so that it appears alive—it is painted, colored. If a woman dies her face is painted, lipstick is used, beautiful clothes, a beautiful coffin, and she is carried as if she has gone into deep sleep, not death.

This is the fear of death. You don't want to look into the face of it.

TAO: THE THREE TREASURES, Vol. I

Sex should be more fun than such a serious affair as it has been made in the past. It should be like a game, a play: two persons playing with each other's bodily energies. If they both are happy, it should be nobody else's concern. They are not harming anybody; they are simply rejoicing in each other's energy. It is a dance of two energies together. It should not be a concern of the society at all. Unless somebody interferes in somebody else's life—imposes himself, forces somebody, is violent, violates somebody's life, then only should society come in. Otherwise there is no problem; it should not be any concern at all.

The future will have a totally different vision of sex. It will be more fun, more joy, more friendship, more a play than a serious affair as it has been in the past. It has destroyed people's lives, has burdened them so much—unnecessarily! It has created so much jealousy, possessiveness, domination, nagging, quarrelling, fighting, condemnation—for *no* reason at all.

Sexuality is a simple, biological phenomenon. It should not be given so much importance. Its only significance is that the energy can be transformed into higher planes; it can become more and more spiritual. And the way to make it more spiritual is to make it a less serious affair.

AH, THIS!

Meditation means catching the orgasmic reality of sex in the present, not somewhere else but now and here. When you are deeply involved in sex you have to be very very alert so that you don't miss the orgasmic moment and you can see through it. It becomes transparent, it brings the world of the beyond to you.

For the first time you become aware that sex contains something which is non-sexual. In fact that's the *real* center of the whole sexuality. To miss it is to miss all. Just as the body contains the soul and matter contains the spirit, sex contains something which is not sex—that is love. And once you have become aware of it you can start growing more and more towards it, you can start changing more and more energy towards it. You will know the knack of it. Just by becoming aware of what it is, you will know how to create more and more energy, moving in that direction you know how to create that space more and more.

Soon one can create it without any sex at all, without any need of the other. That is the day of great celebration in life, when you can be orgasmic without any need, without any dependence on the other. Then love becomes a pure fragrance. Then it is not even a flower but an invisible fragrance. That fragrance is the goal, the goal of life, and unless one attains it one remains unfulfilled. Unless one attains it one remains just a seed which does contain the fragrance, but first it has to become a tree and then it has to bloom and only then can the fragrance be released.

You cannot find it by cutting the seed. You will simply destroy the seed and you will not find anything, no fragrance. It is there, but unmanifest. Sex contains love in an unmanifest form. It has to be manifested, and the more manifest it becomes, less and less does sex remain in your life. A moment comes when your life is pure love. Then even if you are in a sexual relationship it is not sexual. It may appear to others as a sexual relationship but it is not.

This has to be your meditation: you have to attain to that fragrance called love, called God. God is another name for love.

Love is liberation. To live without love is to live in bondage—the bondage of the body, the bondage of the physical, the bondage of the gross. The seed is in a bondage; the fragrance is free, the fragrance is freedom.

DANCE TIL THE STARS
COME DOWN FROM THE RAFTERS

See also Tantra
        Transcendence

SEX, FREE   My effort here is to make this commune sexually free, and when I say "sexually free" it has two meanings. In the beginning people will be easily available to each other, and in the end the very availability will make their minds transcend sex. And that is happening every day. Hundreds of sannyasins write to me asking: "What has happened? When we had just arrived we were so full of sex, and now all that has disappeared; there seems to be no desire for it. Even if we are interested in somebody it is more like friendship than any sexual relationship. We love to be together, but there is no need to jump into bed immediately."

In fact, there are many sannyasins writing to me that sex has so completely disappeared that for months or for years they have been celibate. And you go and ask a Catholic monk or a Hindu sannyasin: they are *trying* to be celibate but their minds are full of sex. And we are *not* trying to be celibate here, but celibacy is happening. Whatsoever is easily available becomes automatically uninteresting.

COME, COME, YET AGAIN COME

SEXUALITY When I use the word "sexuality" I don't just mean genitality. The genital is only one very, very tiny experience and expression of the sexual. The sexual is a very great thing. By sexual I mean whenever your body is alive, sensuous, throbbing, pulsating—then you are in a sexual state. It may not have anything to do with the genital. For example, when you are dancing you are sexual; a dancer is sexual, the dance energy is sexual energy. It is not genital, you may not be thinking at all about sex, you may have completely forgotten all about sex; in fact, when you forget everything about sex and you are dissolved into any deep participation with your total body, it is sexuality. You may be swimming or running—running in the morning.

For ten years I used to run eight miles every morning and eight miles every evening—from 1947 to 1957. It was a regular thing. And I came to experience many, many things through running. At sixteen miles per day I would have encircled the world seven times in those ten years. After you run the second or third mile a moment comes when things start flowing and you are no longer in the head, you become your body, you are the body. You start functioning as an alive being—as trees function, as animals function. You become a tiger or a peacock or a wolf. You forget all head. The university is forgotten, the degrees are forgotten, you don't know a thing, you simply are.

In fact, by and by, after three or four miles, you cannot conceive of yourself as a head. Totality arises. Plato is forgotten, Freud has disappeared, all divisions disappear—because they were on the surface—and deep down your unity starts asserting itself.

Running against the wind in the early morning when things are fresh and the whole existence is a new joy, is bathed in a new delight of the new day, and everything is fresh and young, the past has disappeared, everything has come out of deep rest in the night, everything is innocent, primitive—suddenly even the runner disappears. There is only running. There is no body running, there is only running. And by and by you see that a dance arises with the wind, with the sky, with the sun rays coming, with the trees, with the earth. You are dancing. You start feeling the pulse of the universe. That is sexual. Swimming in a river is sexual. Copulating is not the only sexual thing; anything where your body pulsates totally with no inhibitions is sexual.

So when I used the word "sexual" I mean this experience of totality. Genitality is only one of the functions of sexuality. It has become too important because we have forgotten the total function of sexuality. In fact, your so called mahatmas have made you very, very genital. The whole blame falls on your saints and mahatmas—they are the culprits, the criminals. They have never told you what real sexualilty is.

By and by sexuality has become confined to the genitals; it has become local, it is no longer total. Local genitality is ugly because at the most it can give you relief; it can never give you orgasm. Ejaculation is not orgasm, all ejaculations are not orgasmic and each orgasm is not a peak experience. Ejaculation is genital, orgasm is sexual, and a peak experience is spiritual. When sexuality is confined to the genitals you have only relief; you simply lose energy, you don't gain anything. It is simply stupid. It is just like the relief that comes out of a good sneeze, not more than that.

It has no orgasm because your total body does not pulsate. You are not in a dance, you don't particpate with your whole, it is not holy. It is very partial and the partial can never be orgasmic because orgasm is possible only when the total organism is involved. When you pulsate from your toe to your head, when every fiber of your being pulsates, when all cells of your body dance, when there is a great orchestra inside you, when everything is dancing—then there is orgasm. But every orgasm is not a peak experience either. When you are pulsating totally inside, it is an orgasm. When your totality participates with the totality of existence it is a peak experience. And people have decided on ejaculation, they have forgotten orgasm and they have completely forgotten the peak experience. They don't know what it is.

And because they cannot attain the higher, they are confined to the lower. When you can attain the higher, when you can attain the better, naturally the lower starts disappearing on its own accord. If you understand me . . . sex will be transformed, but not sexuality. You will become more sexual. As sex disappears you will become more sexual. Where will sex go? It will become your sexuality. You will become more sensuous. You will live with more intensity, with more flame; you will live like a great wave. These tiny waves will disappear. You will become a storm, you will become a great wind that can shake the trees and the mountains. You will be a tide, a flood. Your candle will burn at both ends together, simultaneously.

And in that moment—even if you are allowed to live for only one moment, that's more than enough—you have the taste of eternity.

ZEN: THE PATH OF PARADOX, Vol. I

This is the first thing to be understood if you ever want any transformation of sex energy. The first thing is: don't deny it, don't reject it, don't repress it. Don't be too greedy about it, don't think that this is all—this is not. There is much more to life. And sex is beautiful, yet there is still much more to life. Sex is only the foundation, it is not the whole temple.

Repressed, it becomes sexuality. Fantasized, it becomes sexuality. One is an eastern way of tranforming sex into pathology, the other is the western way . . .

From sexuality come back to the sex center. From sex to love there is a direct route; they are bridged. In fact nothing needs to be done. Just live your sex moments with utter joy, silence, peacefulness, with celebration. Live your sex moments meditatively, and meditation transforms sex into love.

Not only does sex become love: one day it becomes prayer, worship. It goes higher and higher. The highest form is prayer, the lowest form is sex. Between the two is love, love is the bridge. And sexuality is abnormal, it is pathological, it is ill. So whether you have chosen a path of being pathological like the eastern people or like the western people, it doesn't matter.

Accept your life as it is, and let the acceptance be as total as possible. When you don't fight with yourself your energy starts falling into a subtle harmony. And that harmony brings you to love. And when the harmony becomes more and more refined, it brings you to prayer.

And unless sex has become prayer, remember, the goal has not been achieved.

UNIO MYSTICA, Vol. I

It is not accidental that husbands and wives continuously quarrel and are angry with each other. It is simply because of their sexuality—they are each other's sexual object, and wherever there is sexuality there is anger. Anger is like smoke. Logicians say, "Wherever there is smoke there is fire." You can say, "Wherever there is anger there is sexuality." When anger disappears, that means sexuality has disappeared.

The disappearance of anger happens only, is possible only, when the root is no more there. You cannot drop your anger, you will have to go to the very roots. Trying to drop your anger will only create new kinds of anger. You will repress it on one side, it will come from another side.

It is because of this well-known fact that for centuries no country has allowed its army people to have a free sexuality, because if soldiers are allowed to have the freedom of their sexuality, if their sex is not obstructed, then they lose destructiveness, then they lose anger, then they are no more angry.

Their sex has to be obstructed in many ways. They have to be deprived of their wives, they have to be kept away from their wives. Not only that: they have to be allowed to see all kinds of pornographic films, all kinds of pornographic magazines, they have to be allowed to come in contact with actresses. When two countries are at war, actresses go to meet and visit the soldiers to encourage them. And what is their encouragement? The encouragement is this: what when an actress comes, a Sophia Loren comes, all the soliders become sexually aroused. Of course, they cannot do anything about it; that aroused energy turns into anger, it becomes rage. Then they start destroying the enemy, then they are madly destructive. If they are allowed to have their wives with them at the front, their girlfriends, then they will lose interest in war . . .

And have you watched? It always happens whenever an army conquers a country; the first victims are the women of that country; they are raped immediately. Can you not see the relationship? Were the soldiers fighting for the women? Why do soldiers, the moment they enter a city as conquerors, immediately start raping around as if they were just waiting for the opportunity? There was no opportunity available; now it is available. The first thing is: rape the women. And the second thing is: rob people of their money. The first comes out of anger and the second comes out of greed, but the cause of both lies in the first. Repressed sex will create anger and greed.

You will be surprised to know that any religion that has been teaching its followers some kind of repression has always helped its followers to become rich. In India, Jainas have become very rich; they are the most repressive people. And something of significance has to be understood about their psychology. Their religion says: Repress sex; *brachmacharya,* celibacy, is their goal. And the second thing: Don't be violent; so anger is not allowed. Sex is not allowed, anger is not allowed. Now where is the energy to go? Now only the third possibility is left—greed. So all the Jainas have become the greediest people in this country. They are a small community, a very small community—in such a big, vast country they are nothing—but still they are very powerful because they have all the money. You will not come across a single Jaina beggar, nothing like it exists. They are not poor people, they cannot be poor; their religion has made it absolutely certain for them that they will be rich. Sex has to be repressed and anger has to be repressed. Now only one outlet is left—greed.

TAO: THE GOLDEN GATE, Vol. II

SHARING Love is innocent when there is no motive in it.

Love is innocent when it is nothing but a sharing of your energy.

You have too much, so you share . . . you want to share.

And whosoever shares with you, you feel grateful to him or her, because you were like a cloud—too full of rainwater—and somebody helped you to unburden. Or you were like a flower, full of fragrance, and the wind came and unloaded you. Or you had a song to sing, and somebody listened attentively . . . so attentively that he allowed you space to sing it. So to whomsoever helps you to overflow in love, feel grateful.

When love is not motivated, it is prayer.

BLESSED ARE THE IGNORANT

What am I doing here?—I am simply sharing my under-standing. That is my happiness: to share it. It is your happi-ness whether you take it or not—that is irrelevant to me. Even if you are not here, even if nobody is here, even if I am sitting alone, I will be still sharing my happiness with the trees and the rocks. In fact, to say that I am sharing it is not right. It is being shared. To say that *I* am sharing it, makes it wrong—as if I am doing something to share it. No, it is being shared.

A flower has bloomed and the perfume is spreading. Not that the flower is sharing it; the flower cannot help but share. The fragrance is on the wings, moving, going far away. Whether somebody will be able to fill his being with that fragrance or not is not a question for the flower. It has flowered, and that's all. The flower is happy that it has bloomed. The flower is happy because it is fulfilled, and fulfillment spreads a fragrance all around.

It is just like when you kindle a lamp and the light spreads. Not that the lamp is trying to share its light—what else can it do? It has to be so. Not that the light is waiting for some-body to come and enjoy it. If nobody comes, it is all the same. If many come, that too is the same.

I am not sharing, in a way; rather, I am being shared.

Ordinarily you think you breathe. When you become awake someday, you will see: you are breathed, you are not breathing. Ordinarily, you think that you are. When you be-come aware, you will say: "God is."

And don't call it work. I'm not doing anything. At the most, you can call it play, but don't call it work. Playing.

THE TRUE SAGE

SHORE, OTHER   "The other shore" is a beautiful metaphor, but let me remind you: *this* is the other shore, *this is that.* You are not going to change the shore, you are simply going to change your consciousness. The change has not to happen in the outside—not that you take a boat, a ferry, and you go to the other shore. That will be a change in the outer circumstances. No, you drop the mind and you become con-sciousness, and the other shore has arrived. You have not moved even a single inch, you may not have done *anything* at all—you may have been simply sitting with closed eyes.

That's what Buddha was doing when he reached the other shore. In Bodh Gaya he was sitting underneath a tree by the side of the river Niranjana. It was early morning, a beautiful, silent morning, and he opened his eyes. The last star was disappearing from the sky; he saw the last star disappearing, and something inside, in him, also disappeared . . . the last trace of the ego. The sky became empty, *he* became empty, and these two emptinesses met, merged, melted into each other. The sky entered into him, he entered the sky.

On the visible side, on the outside, nothing was changed; everything was exactly the same. The Niranjana continued to flow, the birds must have continued to sing, not even a leaf had fallen from the tree, nothing had changed . . . and all had changed. Now Buddha is no more a mind: he has become meditation. He is no more in thoughts: he has become a pure witness, a *sakshin*.

This is the other shore I am talking about.

THE BOOK OF THE BOOKS, Vol. IV

SHOULD   There should be no "should". Once the "should" enters life you are already poisoned. There should be no goal. There should be no right and wrong. This is the only sin: to think in terms of division, values, condemnation, appreciation.

THE TRUE SAGE

SHRINK   The word exactly describes what the psychotherapists are doing—they shrink people. They shrink people from persons into patients. That's their work. They reduce.

When you go to a psychotherapist, you go as a person, with dignity. They reduce you immediately to labels: you are a schizophrenic, paranoid, neurotic. Immediately you are reduced! You are no more the same person with the dignity. A label has been put on you. You are a disease! You have to be treated.

By reducing you to a patient, the psychotherapist has become much bigger. The more he reduces you to smallness, the bigger he feels.

This is an old trip, only the names have changed. In the past it was the priest, now it is the psychotherapist. In the past, the priest was shrinking you—trying to create the guilt feeling, trying to create the feeling that you are wrong somehow, that you need to be changed, that you are not acceptable as you are, that you are getting ready for hell.

The whole effort of the priest was to reduce you to criminals, sinners. The priest was creating a kind of guilt-feeling in you. Now the work has been taken up by the psychotherapist. The psychotherapist is the priest of the new age. He reduces you, he does not enhance you. He does not give you splendor, respect for your being. On the contrary, he makes you feel worthless.

And that's why we are trying to create a new kind of therapy here—in which you are not reduced to diseases, but enhanced, expanded. The psychotherapist is not there to label you as ill, but is there only to help you to know that you are not ill, that who says that you are ill? that you are carrying wrong notions about yourself. Who has told you that you are worthless? You are immensely valuable.

That is my whole effort here: to help you expand.

The psychotherapist said the priest and the so-called gurus, they have *all* been doing the same thing to people: they have been shrinking them. They have reduced humanity to worms, crawling on the earth, ugly, afraid of seeing their own faces in the mirror, afraid to look into their own beings, because there is nothing but all that is wrong. Wounds and pus.

Here the effort is to create a totally different kind of therapy, true to the very meaning of the word. The meaning of the word "therapy" is that which heals. And what heals? Love heals. Love is therapy. Nothing else is therapy. Not psychoanalysis, not analytical psychology. Only love heals. Healing is a function of love. But love expands your consciousness. It allows you to go higher and higher and touch the stars. It makes you feel respected. It makes you feel that you are needed in existence, that without you there will be something missing in existence, there will be a hole without you, unfulfillable. You are a must. This existence cannot be the same without you. You are not just an accident. You are essentially needed.

Let me remind you of Zusya again: Zusya is one of the most beautiful Masters—you can call him the perfect Master. One day he was caught praying in the synagogue. Why

caught? Because the people felt very offended. He was saying
to God, "Listen, I need you, so *you* need me. Without you
I will be nothing. And I say to you: without me *you* will
be nothing. I am me because of you; you are you because
of me."

They people were offended. They said, "What are you saying Zusya? Have you gone mad?"

He had not gone mad. This is the way one should have
a dialogue with God. This is not ego! Not at all. This is a
simple fact. Even a small leaf of grass is as valuable as any
star. There is no hierarchy in existence, nobody is lower
and nobody is higher. We are *all* joined into one organic
unity.

This is real therapy. Therapy when it is real will be nothing
but love. Therapy when real will help you to regain your
confidence, will help you to bloom.

The word "buddha" comes from a root *bodha*. In the
ancient days, the word *bodha* was used for the opening up
of a bud. It comes from the world of flowers; then it was
taken over. *Bodha* means originally opening up of a bud and
becoming a flower. Then it was taken in a metaphoric sense:
when a man opens up, blooms, releases fragrance and color
and dances in the sky, he becomes a Buddha—he has opened
up.

Real therapy does not shrink you: it opens you up. It
makes all that is yours available to you. It gives you your
lost treasure. But as far as the modern psychotherapy is
concerned, people are right in calling psychotherapists
shrinks—they are.

                              THE PERFECT MASTER, Vol. I

SHYNESS Shyness is always a byproduct of a very very
subtle ego. Shyness is never the problem; it is a symptom—
that you have a very subtle ego. So with the familiar it is
okay; with the unfamiliar there is danger. With the familiar
you are skillful—the ego knows what to do and how to
remain in power. With the unfamiliar, with the unknown,
the ego is at a loss because it has no skills for the unknown.
So it shrinks, withdraws, and that shrinking feeling is called
shyness. Shyness is always part of ego. The more egoistic
a person is, the more shy, because he cannot open himself

to new situations, because new situations may prove him to be a fool. The new situations may embarrass you, the new situations may take away the very ground from underneath you.

So shyness is never really a problem—it is just a symptom. But down the ages it has been thought to be a good quality because it protects the ego. We think a shy person is a good person, he is non-aggressive; he is not! His aggression is very subtle. So he keeps aloof, he always keeps at a distance. That distance is just a strategy: if things become too much he can always escape. He never gets involved, he remains on the periphery and pretends, "I am shy, that's why I am not getting into the crowd, not getting into people, not communicating with new people, not relating—because I am shy." That shyness is just an explanation, a blanket explanation. It covers many things, but basically and centrally it covers the ego.

Women have been more shy than men because they are very egoistic. But down the ages they have been praised for their shyness, particularly in the East, very much. A shy woman is thought to be a real woman, Mm? She is always looking down, hiding, always withdrawing, never taking any initiative. To the eastern woman, the western woman looks a little unsophisticated, vulgar, seems to be too masculine because she is not shy. But the eastern woman is very egoistic. Her shyness is just a facade, a beautiful mask.

So don't think that shyness is the problem—it is not. If you really want to look into the problem, look into the ego and you will find it there, the source is there. And once you understand the right cause, things can change easily. One can go on fighting with the symptom and nothing will be changed.

THE MADMAN'S GUIDE TO ENLIGHTENMENT

SIDDHA   See Rajneeshism

SIGNIFICANCE   In dictionaries "significance" and "meaning" are synonymous, but in existence they are not synonymous, they are antonyms. Meaning is of the mind, and significance is a natural phenomenon. It cannot be proved, it can only be felt—it is a heart thing. When you feel that the rose is beautiful it is not a head thing, so you cannot prove it. When you say, "This woman is beautiful," you cannot prove it. "This man is beautiful," you cannot prove it.

Because you cannot prove it—it is not of the mind, it is a feeling—your heart starts throbbing faster . . .

When your heart feels thrilled, it is a totally different dimension, it is the dimension of significance . . .

Mind is the most impotent thing in the world. It can make machines, it can create technology, it can do much scientific work, but it cannot create poetry, it cannot create love, it cannot give you significance. That is not the work of the mind. For that a totally different center exists in you—the heart and the opening of the heart. When the heart lotus opens the whole of life is significant.

THE WILD GEESE AND THE WATER

SILENCE   Silence is the explosion of intelligence. Silence means: inside you, you are just spaciousness, uncluttered spaciousness. Silence means you have put aside the whole furniture of the mind—the thoughts, the desires, the memories, the fantasies, the dreams—all you have pushed aside. You are just looking into existence directly, immediately. You are in contact with existence without anything in between you and existence. That is silence . . .

And when you can experience it happening here—you can hear the silence. And when you hear it, there is immediate understanding. Understanding comes like a shadow following silence.

To understand words and to hear words is very simple. Anybody can do it: just a little education about language is needed, nothing much. But a tremendous transformation is needed to hear silence and to understand silence. Silence is the basic requirement for understanding God, the basic requirement to know truth . . .

Being here with me, being a sannyasin, can be defined very simply as learning to be silent—sitting in silence with me. I am using so many words for the simple reason that words can give you the gaps . . . .

My words keep you awake, and just between the words I give you gaps. And those are the real, essential things. Waiting for another word, you have to listen to silence . . .

This whole situation is being used to hand over to you a few pieces of silence. It will look very strange to the newcomers that I am talking just to make you able to hear silence and to understand silence. But that has always been the way of the Buddhas.

THE WILD GEESE AND THE WATER

Silence means the path of *via negativa*. Bliss is very affirmative; it is *via positiva*. It affirms that the whole existence is divine, hence rejoice. It says *yes* to all that is. It does not renounce, it does not eliminate, it does not negate. It learns to enjoy, to experience, to sing, to dance, to celebrate. It is the way of a beautiful garden path. Many flowers bloom, birds sing.

But the path of silence is just the opposite of it: it is like a beautiful desert. Remember, the desert has its own beauty, not only gardens are beautiful. They have their beauty, but the desert has also its own beauty: the immensity of it, the unboundedness of it, the silence of it, the undisturbed, virgin peace that prevails in a desert—that has its own beauty. Beauty is found not only in one color and one size; it comes in all shapes, all sizes, all colors. There have been people who have loved deserts more than gardens . . .

A desert you can go on and on seeing; it ends nowhere. All the horizons are available. Its vastness and its profound silence have their own song, unheard, unspoken. The same is true about the path of silence.

GUIDA SPIRITUALE

And after these ten days of silence, it is exactly the right moment to bring Buddha back, to make him alive again amongst you, to let him move amongst you, to let the winds of Buddha pass through you. Yes, he can be called back again, because nobody ever disappears. Buddha is no more an embodied person; certainly he does not exist as an individual anywhere—but his essence, his soul, is part of the cosmic soul now.

If many many people with deep longing, with immense longing, with prayerful hearts, desire, passionately desire, then the soul that has disappeared into the cosmic soul can again become manifest in millions of ways.

No true Master ever dies, cannot die. Death does not

appear for the Masters, does not exist for them. Hence they are Masters. They have known the eternity of life. They have seen that the body disappears but that the body is not all: the body is only the periphery, the body is only the garments. The body is the house, the abode, but the guest never disappears. The guest only moves from one abode to another. One day, ultimately, the guest starts living under the sky, with no shelter . . . but the guest continues. Only bodies, houses, come and go, are born and then die. But there is an inner continuum, an inner continuity—that is eternal, timeless, deathless.

Whenever you can love a Master—a Master like Jesus, Buddha, Zarathustra, Lao Tzu—if your passion is total, immediately you are bridged.

My talking on Buddha is not just a commentary: it is creating a bridge. Buddha is one of the most important Masters who has ever existed on the earth—incomparable, unique. And if you can have a taste of his being, you will be infinitely benefited, blessed.

I am immensely glad, because after these ten days of silence I can say to you that many of you are now ready to commune with me in silence. That is the ultimate in communication. Words are inadequate, words say but only partially. Silence communes totally.

Words are becoming more and more difficult for me. They are becoming more and more of an effort. I have to say something so I go on saying something to you. But I would like you to get ready as soon as possible so that we can simply sit in silence . . . listening to the birds and their songs . . . or listening just to your own heartbeat . . . just being here, doing nothing . . .

Get ready as soon as possible, because I am may stop speaking any day. And let the news be spread to all the nooks and corners of the world: those who want to understand me only through the words, they should come soon, because I may stop speaking any day. Unpredictably, any day, it may happen—it may happen even in the middle of a sentence. Then I am not going to complete the sentence! Then it will hang forever and forever . . . incomplete.

THE BOOK OF THE BOOKS, Vol. I

There are two kinds of silences: one is that which you cultivate, the other is that which arrives. Your cultivated silence is nothing but repressed noise. You can sit silently, and if you sit long and you continue to practice for months and years together, slowly slowly you will become capable of repressing all noise inside. But still you will be sitting on a volcano—it can erupt any moment, any small excuse will do. This is not real silence, this is just imposed silence.

This is what is happening all around the world. The people who try to meditate, the people who try to become silent, are only imposing a silence upon themselves. It can be imposed. You can have a layer of silence around yourself, but that is just deceiving yourself and nothing else. That layer is not going to help.

Unless silence arises from your very being, is not imposed from without or the within but comes just the other way round—it comes, wells up from the within towards the without, rises from the center towards the circumference . . . That is a totally different phenomenon.

THE SECRET OF SECRETS, Vol. II

Once George Gurdjieff did a great experiment with a few of his disciples in a faraway part of Russia, near Tiflis. For three months all the disciples had to remain absolutely silent. Not only were they not to speak with each other, they were not even to recognize each other. Thirty disciples were living in one house, but each disciple had to live as if he were alone. In fact in each room there were at least six, seven disciples, sharing, but each disciple had to exist as if he were alone. That was the condition. Within three days twenty-seven disciples were thrown out—out of thirty! Only three remained to the very end. And the last day of the three month's experiment, Gurdjieff took them out in the garden, he sat with them, and suddenly all three become very surprised because he was not speaking and yet they heard him speaking. It was absolutely unbelievable. He was just sitting in front of them completely silent and they heard his voice so clearly . . .

That was the last day, they were allowed to speak now, so all three spoke almost simultaneously: "What are you doing? You are completely silent but we hear your voice coming from somewhere within our own being!"

Gurdjieff said, "Out of three months silence, it has become possible now, I can speak as your own self; your surrender has been total. In fact, today you have become a disciple. Now you are no more, hence I need not speak from the outside."

The outer Master becomes the inner to the true disciple. It is a great experience, but all depends on trust, surrender and such a total love that it knows no quarrelling, knows no argument, knows no doubt . . . It is difficult, but worth achieving; there is nothing else which is more valuable.

That utter silence, no noise of the mind and no center of the ego, that egoless, mindless consciousness, makes one a true disciple. And it is the greatest achievement in life, because God is available only to the true disciple.

THE RAINBOW BRIDGE

I am silent all the way, all the time. Even while I am speaking I am silent because speaking does not disturb my silence. If by speaking, the silence is disturbed, it is not worth. My silence is big enough. It can contain words, it can contain speaking. My silence is big enough; it is not disturbed by anything. My silence is not afraid of words.

You have seen people who are silent, then they don't speak. Their silence seems to be against speech—and a silence which is against speech is still part of speech. It is absence: it is not presence.

Absence of speech is not my silence! My silence is a presence. It can speak to you, it can sing to you. My silence has tremendous energy. It is not a vacuum; it is a fulfillment.

YOGA: THE ALPHA AND THE OMEGA, Vol. VII

Silence has three gates to pass. One is the most peripheral: speaking. Speak only telegraphically. Speak the essential and you will be surprised that almost ninety percent of your talking is useless; only ten percent will do. And you will also be surprised—that ten percent will become more effective because that ninety percent, that unnecessary burden, is no more there.

Words become more pregnant when you don't go round-about, when you go directly. And if one has to be telegraphic, one has to go directly. That's why you can write a long letter but it doesn't have that effect—a small telegram is more effective . . .

All the great scriptures of the world are telegraphic. That is the meaning of the sanskrit word *sutra*—just a hint has been given but very pregnant. This is the first step: be telegraphic, speak the essential. And then the second step. Think only the essential and you will be surprised. Ninety-nine percent is unessential; only one percent maybe is essential. That too I say maybe, perhaps; otherwise it is all holy cow dung.

So drop thinking unnecessarily about unnecessary things . . .

So drop useless thinking and you will be saving so much energy that the third step can be taken. The third step is the most subtle: feel only the essential. And if you come to the essential then there is only love. Anger, greed, lust—all these things are non-essential. They are parasites, they are exploiting you. When you come to the essential only love remains. And when your heart is only full of love you can enter into the very center of silence.

These three things have to be passed: the outer part of the mind—talking; the inner part of the mind—thinking; and the innermost part of the mind—feeling. And when you have passed all these three then there is silence. And that silence is the door to the divine.

THE SOUND OF ONE HAND CLAPPING

No! Nowhere to go. One has to find God in people, and in ordinary life. The mind is always tempted to go away, to escape, but escapism never helps, and it never makes one so rich—it makes one poor. In India many escapists are there, sitting in their Himalayan caves and just vegetating. You will not see anything in them . . . just sitting there! No worries, certainly; silence all around—but it is not the real silence. It is the silence of the cemetery . . . it is the silence of death.

I teach the silence of life, the silence which is throbbing, alive, pulsating . . . the silence which, when it is pulsating, is positive, affirmative. It is a joy. It is not just absence of worry—it is presence of ecstasy. One can easily escape, and one can attain to a certain silence—it will be just an absence of tension. It is nothing much.

The real silence has to be in the marketplace, in the crowd. When you are alone in the crowd, you have known what aloneness is. When the crowd cannot disturb your solitude, then it is yours—otherwise the solitude is of the Himalayas, not yours. When nothing disturbs you, when nothing distracts you, then you are centered.

It is easy to find a place where there is no objective disturbance, so of course you are not disturbed; but it is just the objective circumstances that are missing—you have not changed. After thirty years of living in the Himalayas, when a monk comes back to the world he again finds himself the same person. Again he gets disturbed—even more so—because in those thirty years of silence he has become very very delicate. Just a small thing and he is disturbed so much. He has lost in fact, rather than gaining anything.

So I am for life, all for life. Be in the world, help people, serve people, and pray towards that service. Let that be your meditation, and sooner or later you will find that you have become silent. Objective circumstances have not changed at all—you have changed. The subject has changed—the subjectivity is new . . . And it is going to happen.

My whole effort in introducing a new concept of sannyas, is to bring to the world that which for centuries we have been thinking can only be gained in the monastery, in the cave, away from the world. Because of that idea, humanity became divided into two parts—the worldly and the other-worldly, the religious and the irreligious. And of course, if silence can only be attained in the loneliness of the Himalayas and the Alps, then the whole world cannot go there. If the whole world goes there then there will be no silence either. Only a few people can escape. So the whole world will never become religious that way. That's how the world is not religious. I would like to change this whole idea.

You can become silent, you can become prayerful, meditative—in the world. Then the whole world can become religious. And this has been observed—that if in a village of one thousand people, even ten people start meditating, the whole quality of consciousness of that village changes. Because those five, ten persons are not isolated. They are not sitting in caves—they are living in the world. They create a certain vibe, they create certain ripples of peace around them. Those ten persons moving in the village of one thousand people come in contact with almost everybody. They go on infecting people. The whole quality of the village will change. Just ten people . . . that means one percent.

If one percent of human beings are changed towards, turned on, to meditation, we will be able to change the whole world consciousness . . . just one percent. And a totally new consciousness can come into being. The world needs it now—it has never been in so much need. It is really passing through a tremendous crisis. It has never been so; there have been crises before, but never of such proportion. So work hard!

BLESSED ARE THE IGNORANT

Learn silence. And at least with your friends, with your lovers, with your family . . . And this is your family, the orange family. Here, sit in silence sometimes. Don't go on gossiping, don't go on talking. Stop talking and not only on the outside—stop the inner talk. Be in an interval. Just sit there, doing nothing, just being presences to each other. And soon you will start finding a new way to communicate. And that is the right way.

It is said about Mahavira—a strange story but beautiful and meaningful—that when he became enlightened he remained silent. It created many problems, because he had attained and it was his duty to share it. When you have attained you have to share it. It is intrinsic to attainment to share. That's why Buddha has spoken, and Christ and Lao Tzu. Mahavira kept silent, he found another way. Maybe that is why his religion never became a world religion. His followers remain very few—even now there are only thirty *lakh* Jainas. That is nothing—after two thousand five hundred years, only thirty *lakhs*. That means if Mahavira had converted only thirty couples, that would have done—that many people would have been Jainas. He could not convert many people. And the reason? He wanted to commune through silence, he remained quiet. And the way that he found was strange but beautiful. It could not prove very effective, because it is very difficult to speak through silence in this mad world. He failed, but the experiment was worth trying.

What did he do? He prepared a few people for silence, to understand him in silence. He would sit silently, and only those few people who had learned how to listen to his silence would understand what he meant. And they would tell it to people. But then again the problem arose. He would not speak—he was a strange man, he thought it a kind of betrayal to speak. Because whatsoever you say is going to be misunderstood—then you become the cause of misunderstanding. Whatsoever you say will be only half true, because the whole truth cannot be reduced to words. So you will be destroying truth. And he was not the man to do that, he kept quiet. Just a few disciples who had learned how to commune with him in silence would sit silently there, listen to his silence—would feel what he wants, what he feels, what he knows, and would go to people and tell them.

But that doesn't help. Now these people who told others were misunderstood. So what is the point? He could have told it himself—there would have been less misunderstanding, because the power of Mahavira would have been there. Now, Mahavira gives to other people and those people are not so enlightened, not so conscious. They go to people and they relay and broadcast Mahavira's message. Much more misunderstanding will be there. And of course they could not convert many people, they had their limitations. But he tried—a great experiment.

I would also like to try it—but not only for a few people. I would like to create a great mass of people for silence. And it's that for which I am working slowly slowly. Once you are ready, thousands of people ready for silence, then I can really say that which cannot be said through words.

Buddha gave Mahakashyap his flower and said, "I am giving to you that which I could not give to others. I am giving you that which can only be given in silence." I would like thousands of Mahakashyaps to receive that flower. One is not enough.

THIS VERY BODY THE BUDDHA

SIMPLICITY A simple thing is indivisible; you cannot analyze it, you cannot dissect it. It is simply there; it is impossible to understand it.

That's why all that is simple eludes knowledge. God is simple, that's why science cannot know him. Love is simple, that's why science can have no idea what it is. Whenever you come across a simple thing you have to drop the effort to understand it; only then can you understand it. A totally new kind of understanding will be needed—an understanding of the heart, which does not analyze, which does not dissect.

TAKE IT EASY, Vol. II

Simplicity is to live without ideals. Ideals create complexity; ideals create division in you and hence complexity. The moment you are interested in becoming somebody else you become complex. To be contented with yourself as you are is simplicity. The future brings complexity; when you are utterly in the present you are simple.

Simplicity does not mean a life of poverty. That is utterly stupid because the person who imposes a life of poverty on himself is not simple at all. He is a hypocrite. The need to impose poverty means, deep down, he hankers for the diametrically opposite; otherwise why should there be any need to impose it? You impose a certain character upon yourself because you are just the opposite of it . . .

Simplicity means to be just yourself, whosoever you are, in tremendous acceptance, with no goal, with no ideal. All ideals are crap—scrap all of them.

It needs guts to be simple. It needs guts because you will be in constant rebellion. It needs guts because you will *never* be adjusted to the so-called, rotten society that exists around you. You will constantly be an outsider. But you will be simple, and simplicity has beauty. You will be utterly in harmony with yourself. There will be no conflict within you, there will be no split within you.

The ideal brings the split. The bigger the ideal, the bigger is going to be the split . . .

Simplicity is not an ideal; you cannot impose simplicity on yourself. That's why I never say that people like Mahatma Gandhi are simple. They are not, they cannot be. Simplicity is their ideal, they are trying to attain it. Simplicity is a goal far away in the future, distant, and they are striving, they are straining, they are in great effort. How can you create simplicity out of effort? Simplicity simply means that which is. Out of effort you are trying to improve upon existence. Existence is perfect as it is, it needs no improvement . . .

Simplicity simply means living moment to moment spontaneously, not according to some philosophy, not according to Jainism, Buddhism, Hinduism, not according to any philosophy. Whenever you live according to a philosophy you have betrayed yourself, you are an enemy to yourself. Simplicity means to be in deep friendship with oneself, to live your life with no idea interfering.

It needs guts, certainly, because you will be living constantly in insecurity. The man who lives with ideals is secure. He is predictable; that is his security. He knows what he is going to do tomorrow. He knows, if a certain situation arises, this is the way he will react to it. He is always certain. The man who is simple knows nothing about tomorrow, knows nothing about the next moment, because he is not going to act out of his past. He will respond out of his present awareness . . .

The simple man will be simple. He will live moment to moment with no idea how to live; he will not have any philosophy of life. He will trust in his intelligence. What is the need of having a philosophy? Why should one have a philosophy?—so that it can guide you. It means if you are stupid you need a philosophy of life so that it can guide you. If you are intelligent you don't need any philosophy of life. Intelligence is enough unto itself, a light unto itself . . .

Life is insecure. The security is only an illusion that we create around ourselves, a cozy illusion. And because of this cozy illusion we kill our intelligence. The man who wants to live simply will have to live in insecurity, will have to accept the fact that nothing is secure and certain, that we are on an unknown journey, that nobody can be certain where we are going and nobody can be certain from where we are coming.

In fact, except for the stupid people nobody has illusions of certainty. The more intelligent you are, the more uncertain you are. The more intelligent you are, the more hesitant—

because life is vast. Life is immense, immeasurable, mysterious. How can you be certain?

Living in uncertainity, living in insecurity, is simplicity.
THE SECRET

SIN The original Hebrew word for sin is very beautiful. By translating it as "sin" Christians have missed the very message of Jesus. The original Hebrew word for sin is so totally different from your idea of sin that it will be a surprise to you. The root word means "forgetfulness"; it has nothing to do with what you are doing. The whole thing is whether you are doing it with conscious being or out of unconsciousness. Are you doing it with a self-remembering or have you completely forgotten yourself?

Any action coming out of unconsciousness is sin. The action may look virtuous, but it cannot be. You may create a beautiful facade, a character, a certain virtuousness; you may speak the truth, you may avoid lies; you may try to be moral, and so on and so forth, but if all this is coming from unconsciousness it is all sin.
COME, COME, YET AGAIN COME

Martin Luther has said a tremendously significant thing. He says *"pecca fortiter:* sin boldly." It is strange. The statement seems to be unbelievable—a man like Luther saying "sin boldly". But the meaning is really worth pondering over. He is saying: Love permeates the whole of existence, so don't be afraid. Even if you are in sin, be boldly in it, because existence is always ready to forgive, is forgiving. Love always is forgiving. He does not mean that you should go and sin. He is simply saying: Your greatest sin is nothing compared to the forgiveness that goes on flowing from existence towards you.

Just the other day, somebody asked me, *I am a great sinner. Can I also realize God?*

You cannot be that great a sinner. You cannot be so fallen that God's hand cannot reach you, you cannot be so weighted and burdened by sin that God cannot uplift you. The gravitation of sin cannot be more than the grace of God.

This is one of the fundamentals of Sufism, that God is unconditionally forgiving—he has to be, because his nature is love. Love is his reality. It is not that love forgives: love is forgiveness. There is no question of forgiving you. The question arises only if God has already become angry with you. Only then does the question of forgiving arise.

But God cannot be angry with you. You are the way he has made you, you are not your own creation. How can he be angry with you? That would amount to being angry with himself; that would be self-condemnation.

But you start thinking about small things as if you are doing great sins. The ego always loves to do great things. Even if you are doing something wrong, you want to pretend that this is the greatest wrong that has ever been done or will ever be done. You want it to be unique, incomparable; you want it to be on the top. The ego always feels good if something great is being done. It may be a sin—that doesn't matter.

What great sin can you commit? All our sins are nothing but small things: we are small, our sins cannot be great. Our hands are small: whatsoever we do is going to remain small, because it will have our signature on it.

Your life, virtuous or wicked, is not going to be a barrier or a bridge—because you are already bridged, and there is no way of disconnecting yourself from God. And it is not a question that when you sin, God forgives you. He is forgiveness: he is continuously flowing in tremendous love towards you.

His love is like a flood, your sins are like straw: the flood will take them away. And the flood does not come to take your sins away; it is already there. To understand this, to see the point of it, is a great relief, as if a mountain suddenly disappears off your chest. You become light, weightless. And only in that weightlessness can you worship.

The sinner cannot worship, he is continuously frightened. Fear cannot create prayer. Prayer created by fear remains political, a strategy of the mind to persuade God; it is a kind of bribery. Real prayer arises out of understanding, out of love.

Luther is really right when he says "*Pecca fortiter:* sin boldly". Whatsoever you are doing, do it boldly. You belong to God and God belongs to you. This is your home. Don't live like a stranger, don't be here like a guest: you are part of the host. Live without fear.

UNIO MYSTICA, Vol. II

Just the other night I was reading about an Indian mystic who was invited into a Christian church. After the talk, the Christian priest shouted loudly to the congregation. "All you sinners! Now kneel down and pray! Kneel down in prayer!"

They all knelt down except the mystic, the Hindu mystic. The priest looked at him, and said, "Aren't you going to participate with us in prayer?"

He said, "I was going to participate, but I am not a sinner. And I don't see that anybody else here is a sinner. I was going to participate in the prayer, but now you have made it impossible for me. I cannot kneel down. I am not a sinner. God is within me. I cannot be that disrespectful to God. I can pray only because God is within me. And I am not praying for anything. My prayer is my thankfulness, my gratitude, for all that he has already given me; my thankfulness that he has chosen me as his abode, that he has honored me, that I am part of him, that he belongs to me. I am ready to pray, I am ready to kneel down, but not as a sinner, because that is not true."

You have been taught that you are sinners, that unless Jesus saves you, you are bound to go to hell. You have been condemned so much that when this eastern message bursts forth in your being, you start doubting: "This is not possible. I? And I have never left home? Maybe it is true about Buddha, maybe it is true about Jesus, but I?—I am a sinner."

Nobody is a sinner. Even while you are in the darkest hole of your life, you are still divine. You cannot lose your divinity, there is no way to lose it. It is your very being. It is the stuff you are made of.

THE DIAMOND SUTRA

See also Habits, 1st Series
        Mischief, 2nd Series

SIN, ORIGINAL Knowledgeable people never know God. In fact they cannot know God. Sinners can know, but not knowledgeable people. Hence I love the Biblical story that the original sin was eating the fruit from the Tree of Knowledge. It is really of great insight, but Christians have completely missed it. It fell into the wrong hands. If it had been in the hands of Zen Masters they would have made something beautiful out of it.

That is the original sin—because knowledge fills one, feeds the ego. One has to be innocent; one has to function from the state of not-knowing. One has to feel that "I know nothing"—only then can one feel wonder and awe. And to stand in awe and wonder is to face God, is to encounter God, is to be ready for God.

NO MAN IS AN ISLAND

SINCERITY   Sincerity means to live according to your own light. Hence the first requirement of being sincere is to be meditative. The first thing is not to be moral, is not to be good, is not be virtuous: the most important thing is to be meditative—so that you can find a little light within yourself and then start living according to that light. And as you live it grows and it gives you a deep integrity. Because it comes from your own innermost being there is no division.

When somebody says to you, "Do it, it *should* be done," naturally it creates a division in you. You don't want to do it, you wanted to do something else, but somebody—the parents, the politicians, the priests, those who are in power—they want you to follow a certain route. You never wanted to follow it so you will follow it unwillingly. Your *heart* will not be in it, you will not be committed to it, you will not have any involvement with it. You will go through it like a slave. It is not *your* choice, it is not of your freedom . . .

Sincerity means not living a double life—and almost everybody is living a double life. He says one thing, he thinks something else. He never says that which he thinks, he says that which is convenient and comfortable, he says that which will be approved, accepted, he says that which is expected by others. Now what he says and what he thinks become two different worlds. He says one thing, he goes on doing something else, and then naturally he has to hide it. He cannot expose himself because then the contradiction will be found, then he will be in trouble. He talks about beautiful things and lives an ugly life.

This is what, up to now, humanity has done to itself. It has been a very nightmarish past . . .

And everybody is guilty, and the priests want you to be guilty because the more guilty you are, the more you are in the hands of the priests. You have to go to them to get rid of your guilt. You have to go to the Ganges to take a bath, you have to go to Mecca, to Kaaba, so that you can get rid of your guilt. You have to go to the Catholic priest to confess so that you can get rid of the guilt. You have to do fasting and other kinds of penances and other kinds of austerities so that you can punish yourself. These are all punishments! But how can you be happy? How can you be cheerful and blissful? How can you rejoice in a life in which you are constantly feeling guilty and punishing yourself, condemning yourself?

And if you choose *not* to follow your inner voice and you follow the dictates of others—what they call morality, etiquette, civilization, culture—then too that inner voice will start nagging you, it will continuously nag you. It will say you are being untrue to your nature. And if you feel that you are being untrue to your nature then your morality cannot be a rejoicing; it will be only an empty gesture.

This is what has happened to man: man has become schizophrenic.

My effort here is to help you to become one. That's why I don't teach *any* morality, *any* character. All that I teach is meditation so that you can hear your inner voice more clearly and follow it, whatsoever the cost, because if you follow your inner voice without feeling guilty, immense is going to be your reward, and looking backwards you will find that the cost was nothing. It looked very big in the beginning, but when you have arrived at the point where sincerity becomes natural, spontaneous, when there is no division any more, no split in you any more, then you will see a celebration is happening and the cost that you have paid is nothing compared to it . . .

Sincerity is the fragrance of meditation.

I AM THAT

SKY Sky is very symbolic in eastern mysticism . . . the greatest symbol there is. It means many things. One: it is always present, yet absent. It is present everywhere yet absent. Its very way of presence is being absent. It exists by not being. That's how God exists. That's why you cannot show where God is; that's why you cannot pinpoint him. He is everywhere and nowhere . . . and that is the quality of the sky too. It is not just an accident that whenever people pray they look at the sky. Unknowingly, they raise their eyes to the sky, because God is like the sky: present and yet utterly absent.

The sky contains all, and nothing contains the sky. God contains all, and nothing contains God. The sky penetrates everything and yet never interferes. It is a miracle! It penetrates without trespassing. It is so non-violent. It accepts all: the sinner and the saint, the good and the bad, the beautiful and the ugly. It makes no distinctions: it has no likes, no dislikes. It has no mind. It is simply open and available to all, whosoever wants to partake of it. It makes no conditions. It is unconditionally everybody's: man and woman, animals, birds, trees, rocks, stars and sun. It is available to all. It protects but it never patronizes. It surrounds you within and without . . . without ever touching you. And these are the qualities of God.

Black clouds come and go and the sky makes space available for them. White clouds come and go and the sky makes space for them with no distinction; it is choiceless. The acceptance is total; Buddha calls it *tathata*. The sky exists in a state of *tathata,* suchness: whatsoever is the case is good. Clouds come and go; the sky remains, it abides. It is eternal, it is timeless. It is always the same. It is the ancientmost and yet as fresh as the dewdrops; it never becomes old.

So meditate on the sky, and whenever you have time just lie down on the ground, look at the sky. Let that be your contemplation. If you want to pray, pray to the sky. If you want to meditate, meditate on the sky . . . sometimes with open eyes, sometimes with closed eyes, because the sky is within too. As it is big without, within it is the same.

We are just standing on the threshold of the inner sky

and the outer sky, and they are exactly proportionate. As the outside sky is infinite, so is the inner sky. We are just standing on the threshold. Either way you can be dissolved, and these are the two ways to dissolve.

You asked what prayer and what meditation is. If you dissolve in the outside sky, then it is prayer. If you dissolve into the inside sky, then it is meditation. But finally it comes to the same: you are dissolved. And these two skies are not two; they are two only because you are. You are the dividing line. When you disappear, the dividing line disappears. The in is out and out is in.

ONLY LOSERS CAN WIN IN THIS GAME

SLAVERY The religions, particularly the organized religions, have always given three qualities to God. He is omnipotent—absolutely powerful; omniscient—knowing absolutely everything that is, that has been, that will be; and he is omnipresent—he is everywhere present, there is not a place where he is not present. The organized religion depends very much on these qualities. Why?—because people can be enslaved only if God is the suprememost power.

In fact, people are always seeking somebody who is more powerful than themselves so that they can throw all the responsibilties on his shoulders. God has to be omnipotent; there can be nobody more powerful than him. He is pure power. That is the strategy of the priest to enslave people. If he is power, pure power, the highest power, the omnipotent power, then of course all you have to do is just be a slave. Trying to escape from him is futile, trying to be independent is futile, trying for freedom is futile. It is better to serve him, to be just a servant.

You cannot escape from him because he is omnipresent; wherever you go you will find him. He is always watching, he is always looking at you. It is not only that he watches your acts, he watches even your thoughts, so even in thinking you are not free, you are not left alone; there is no privacy. If God is omnipresent then there is no privacy at all. Then you are never alone, he is always there. This is to create fear. You cannot do anything without him knowing it. In fact, before you have done it he knows it.

He is also omniscient: he knows all—past, present, future. So not only does he know your past, not only the present, but also the future. What are you going to do? You are absolutely caught, absolutely imprisoned. You cannot escape from God . . .

My own observation is that each child is born *very* intelligent, but our whole conditioning hitherto has been such that his intelligence starts gathering dust. And we *allow* it to gather dust: his sharpness is lost, his sword becomes rusty, and that's what we want. We don't want him to have a sharp intelligence because then he will ask questions—and there are no answers with the parents, with the priests, with the politicians. They don't have any answers. They have power—they can punish you for asking an embarrassing question. They don't allow you to ask questions; your function is to fulfill the order, to do and not to ask why. The whole of humanity has been reduced to slavery.

This is the real spiritual slavery! Political slavery is nothing compared to it. Regimes change—a capitalist country can become communist, a socialist country can become fascist, a Hindu country can be ruled by the Christians or Mohammedans, a Mohammedan country can be ruled by the Christians—it does not matter all; the spiritual slavery continues. It depends on the idea that God is omnipotent, omniscient, omnipresent: you cannot escape him, you cannot deceive him. It is really ugly, the very idea that he is always watching you, that you are never left alone.

THEOLOGIA MYSTICA

SLEEP Buddha's chief disciple was Ananda, who lived with him for forty years and served him with great love. He used to watch him in every possible way, because he was continuously following him like a shadow, and each of his movements was beautiful, was a grace. He was also watching him when he was asleep, because he used to sleep in the same room if the Master needed him in the night; he used to watch him while he was asleep. Awake or asleep, his grace was the same, his beauty was the same, his silence was the same.

One day he asked Buddha, "I should not ask such a

question—it looks so stupid—but I cannot contain my
curiosity. You sleep, but I have watched you for hours.
Sometimes in the middle of the night I wake up and watch
you, sometimes just before you get up early in the morning
I watch you, but my experience has been such that it seems
to me that you are still awake even while asleep. You look
so alive, so fresh! And one thing more—you never change
your posture. You go to sleep and you wake up in the same
posture. What is the secret of it?"

Buddha said, "There is no secret in it. Once you are awake
you are awake! The *body* goes to sleep; whether it is day
or night makes no difference, the inner flame goes on burning. The body goes to sleep because the body gets tired, and
now there is no mind any more so no question of the mind
arises at all."

There are only two things. In the *un*enlightened person
there are three things: the body, the mind, the soul. And
because of the mind he cannot see the soul. The mind is
a turmoil, a chaos; it is all smoke, it is all clouds. The
enlightened has no mind; there is only silence. So he has
the body and he has the soul. The body tires, needs rest,
but the soul is never tired, needs no rest; it is always awake.
The body is always asleep and the soul is always awake.
The nature of the body is to be unconscious and the nature
of the soul is to be conscious. These are intrinsic qualities.
Once the mind is no more there, then even in your sleep
only the body sleeps, not you.

I AM THAT

The very line from where you drop into sleep is the line
where you can enter into the unconscious.

You can try this. You have been sleeping every day, but
you have not encountered sleep yet. You have not seen it—
what it is, how it comes, how you drop into it. You have
not known anything about it. You have been dropping into
it daily, coming out of it, but you have not felt the moment
when sleep comes on the mind—what happens. So try this,
and with three months' effort, suddenly, one day, you will
enter sleep knowingly: drop on your bed, close your eyes,
and then remember, remember that sleep is coming and,
"I am to remain awake when the sleep comes." It is very

arduous, but it happens. One day it will not happen, one week it will not happen. Persist every day, constantly remembering that sleep is coming and, "I am not to allow it without knowing. I must be aware when sleep enters. I must go on feeling how sleep takes over, what it is."

And one day, suddenly, sleep is there and you are still awake. That very moment you become aware of your unconscious also. And once you become aware of your unconscious you will never be asleep again in the old way. Sleep will be there, but you will be awake simultaneously. A center in you will go on knowing. All around will be sleep, and a center will go on knowing. When this center knows, dreams become impossible. And when dreams become impossible, daydreams also become impossible. Then you are asleep in a different sense, and then you will be awake in the morning in a different sense. That different quality comes by the encounter.

THE ULTIMATE ALCHEMY, Vol. I

Sleep is a great spiritual activity—don't be worried! It is far better than your waking hours; waking hours are more worldly than sleeping hours. Sometimes in sleep your mind completely stops, there are not even dreams, and you are very close to home.

Patanjali says that *sushupti,* the dreamless state of sleep, is almost *samadhi*—almost. Just a little thing is missing, awareness—that's all. If you add awareness, it is *samadhi.* Everything is ready: the mind has stopped, dreams have gone, thoughts are no more there, the whole body-being is relaxed. You are ready, just a little ray of awareness . . .

So don't be worried about sleep—enjoy it! Sleep is divine, more divine than any other time in twenty-four hours. So accept it, otherwise that will create a tension in you . . .

If one falls asleep meditating, the meditation goes on resounding down into the layers of one's unconscious. If doing prayer you fall asleep, the prayer continues in a subtle way.

Have you ever watched one thing?—whatsoever is your last thought in the night will be your first thought in the morning. Watch it—the last, the very last, when you enter into sleep. You are standing just on the threshold—the last thought will always be the first thought when you again stand on the threshold and you are coming out of sleep.

That's why all the religions have insisted on one praying before one goes to sleep, so the last thought remains of prayer, the last thought remains of God, and it goes and sinks into one's heart. The whole night it remains like an aroma around you—it fills your inner space, and in the morning when you awake, again it is there.

Eight hours of sleep can be used as meditation. Now modern man has not much time, but these eight hours of sleep can be converted into meditation. So don't be worried about it. My whole approach is that everything can be used and should be used—even sleep!

FOR MADMEN ONLY

Man as he is is utterly unconscious. He is nothing but his habits, the sum total of his habits. Man is a robot. Man is not yet man: unless consciousness enters into your being, you will remain a machine.

That's why the Sufis say man is a machine. It is from the Sufis that Gurdjieff introduced the idea to the West that man is a machine. It is very rarely that you are conscious. In your whole seventy years' life, if you live the ordinary so-called life—healthy and whole within and without, with no pain of growth, with no pain within you of a growing pearl of exceeding beauty—then you will not know even seven moments of awareness in your whole life.

And even if you know those seven moments or less, they will be only accidental. For example, you may know a moment of awareness if somebody suddenly comes and puts a revolver on your heart. In that moment, your thinking, your habitual thinking, stops. For a moment you become aware, because it is so dangerous, you cannot remain ordinarily asleep.

In some dangerous situation you become aware. Otherwise you remain fast asleep. You are perfectly skillful at doing your things mechanically.

Just stand by the side of the road and watch people, and you will be able to see that they are all walking in their sleep. All are sleepwalkers, somnambulists. And so are you.

UNIO MYSTICA, Vol. I

When one becomes aware of how unconscious one is, one

always has been, one feels very sad, one feels in great turmoil. One cannot believe that "This is the way I have existed up to now!" One feels absurd, ridiculous . . .

If you look back, it is all night—and of course you can only look back because of what your mind contains, your past memories. You cannot look ahead, you cannot understand what is going to happen the next moment, but I can see it. That's the function of the Master: to help the disciple to remain aware not only of the past but of the future possibility.

The disciple can only see the past, the Master can also see the future. The disciple can see only his stupidity, the Master can also see your Buddhahood, your awakenedness. It is a moment of transformation, a transitory period, a bridge. Don't look at the back—forget all that night and the darkness and sleepiness. You are finished with it—finished in the sense that the first ray of light has come in. It is because of that ray of light that you are becoming aware of your sleep, of your darkness. Now help—pour all your energy into that ray of light. Make it as powerful as possible. Concentratedly become one with it. Get rooted in it. Risk everything for its growth. And then the day is not far away—it is very close by, it is just by the corner.

THE WILD GEESE AND THE WATER

SMELL My own understanding is that Buddha's sense of smell is far deeper than yours. Your sense of smell is repressed, very much repressed. For centuries you have been repressing sex, and the sense of smell is very much connected with your sexuality. You have been repressing your sense of smell. You use so many perfumes just to hide the smell of your sexuality.

Otherwise, when a woman is having her period she smells differently; you can smell that she is having her period. When a woman is sexually aroused she starts smelling differently; you can know just by her smell that she is sexually aroused. And the same is true about man: sexually aroused, his body starts smelling differently because there are great chemical changes happening inside him. They affect his body, his perspiration, his breathing, his blood.

Man has been so much afraid of his sexuality: somebody

may become aware, somebody may note what is happening to him. He has used clothes to hide his body, he has used perfumes to hide his natural smells. He has tried in every possible way to appear *as* non-sexual as possible. And we have had to repress our noses very much.

You know the animals: they know through their noses whether the female is willing or not. Just the smell is enough to know whether the female is saying yes. Unless the smell says the female is saying yes, the male won't approach the female; that is aggression, that is rape.

No animal ever rapes, remember, except man. Man is the only rapist animal in the world. I am not including the animals which live in the zoos, because they have become more like human beings; living in the company of human beings they have been distorted. Otherwise no animal rapes. Love happens only when both the parties are absolutely willing.

But man has lost his sensitivity for smell. It is because of so-called religious teachings for centuries . . .

My understanding is that Buddha's sense of smell is far more clear than yours because there is no repression in him. His eyes see better than you can see because his eyes are not clouded by any prejudice, by any *a priori* conceptions. He hears perfectly well because his ears are not full of noise, his mind is silent.

When the mind is utterly silent you are capable of listening. Then you are capable of listening to the song of the birds, a distant call of the cuckoo. Then you are able to listen even to the silence. Just now, listen to the silence . . . not only sound but soundlessness can be listened to. But you have to be noiseless.

And you can start smelling people—not only their sexuality: you can start smelling their anger, because anger also changes their body chemistry. You can start smelling their greed, their jealousy, their hatred. You can start smelling all kinds of emotions. The moment a person comes to you, if your mind is silent and your senses are clear, unclouded, without any fog, you can smell everything that the man is carrying. He may be smiling on the surface, but deep down you can tell that he is angry, a hypocrite. Try smelling people, their greed, their anger, their cruelty. And if you can learn to smell cruelty, anger, greed, slowly slowly you will be able to smell more subtle things: their compassion, their love, their prayer. Yes, even their meditativeness, their silence has its own fragrance. When a person is full of greed, he stinks of greed; when a person is full of silence, he exudes something of the beyond, something of the unknown.

Buddha is not saying destroy your senses. He is saying master your senses, become more aware of your senses. Bring awareness to your senses so that they become more sensitive. They are doors, windows, bridges to existence.

THE BOOK OF THE BOOKS, Vol. X

See also Perfume, 2nd Series

SMOKING   People smoke only when they are very tense. When they are not tense they don't tend to smoke. When they are tense they smoke. If you don't smoke your tension goes on accumulating, which is far more dangerous than smoking. Smoking is just stupid, not dangerous. Maybe you will live one or two years less—so what? What are you going to do even if you live two, three years more? If you have not done anything in seventy years, what are you going to do in those extra years? You will go on doing the same nonsense, you will be living the same misery. So that is not the point . . .

But people try to control it. If they succeed they become egoistic, which is far more dangerous. If they fail they feel guilty, they feel depressed, which is far more dangerous. If they fail they become condemnatory towards themselves, they lose respect for themselves. And the moment you lose respect for yourself, remember, you are losing your trust in life. You will be living now just at the minimum, your life will not have the dance, it will not have the quality of celebration; it will be only a dragging.

ZEN: ZEST, ZIP, ZAP AND ZING

I am not against smoking. I don't smoke myself because now there is so much smoke in the air that one need not bother carrying a clay pipe or a waterpipe in one's hand; just ordinary air is enough—it is so polluted.

In fact, ecologists say that it is a wonder how man is surviving because just fifty years ago scientists used to think that if air became as polluted as it has become today in New York, in Bombay, in Calcutta, in London, then people will die. But man has a tremendous capacity to adjust to *any* situation. Where so many cars are moving and trains are moving and planes are moving and there are factories and so much smoke, there is no need to carry a private pipe anymore; you simply breathe air and you are smoking!

I am a lazy person; Gurdjieff was not a lazy person, that's why he used to carry his beautiful waterpipe. And in Baal Shem's days the air was not so polluted. If you wanted some smoke to go in your lungs you had to make private arrangements! Now it is universal.

And I am not against it because at the most it can kill you a little earlier. So what? If you don't live eighty years and only live seventy-eight, does it matter? In fact, the world is so overcrowded that everybody will be happy that you are gone. Do you know how much we celebrate when somebody goes? We don't celebrate anything like that! A little space is created.

So you can smoke as much as you want. Health is merely the slowest possible rate at which one can die.

You can go a little quicker! And in these days of speed when everything is going faster and faster, this is old-fashioned just to go on dying in a healthy way, to go on lingering and lingering. Health is the longest route! But finally, you have to reach the grave, and when shortcuts are available the wise people always choose the shortcuts. So don't be worried.

WALKING IN ZEN, SITTING IN ZEN

The most important thing is not to stop smoking; the most important thing is to watch why you smoke in the first place. If you don't understand the cause of it, and if the cause is not removed, you can stop smoking but then you will start chewing gum because the basic cause is there and you will have to do something. If you don't start chewing gum then you may start talking too much.

I don't smoke! . . . If any day I have to stop talking I may have to start smoking! You will do something . . .

Smoking is keeping many people from many things which will be far more dangerous. Your hand is engaged, your mouth is engaged, your mind is engaged. And you are not harming anybody in particular, only harming yourself. That is your birthright, that is your freedom. Otherwise you will do something.

Have you watched? Whenever you feel nervous, tense, you start smoking. It helps you to cool down, to relax a little bit; otherwise life will become too much. When you are not feeling nervous, when you are enjoying, when you are relaxed, you don't remember smoking. Hours may pass and you may not smoke—for the simple reason that there is no cause. Otherwise you become afraid you may do something wrong; better keep yourself engaged.

My suggestion is: first go deep down into your smoking habit. Meditate over it, why in the first place you smoke. It may take a few months for you to go into it, and the deeper you go the more you will be freed of it. Don't stop smoking. If it disappears through your understanding that is a totally different matter. If it disappears because you went to the root cause of it and you saw the point . . .

For example, it may be that your mother's breast was taken away from you earlier than *you* wanted and smoking is just a substitute. To many people I have suggested—and it has been of help—to smokers I say, "If you really want to stop smoking, then start sucking your thumb." They say, "But that will look very stupid!" That is true . . . smoking looks as if you are doing something great! You are the doing the same thing, in fact a little more harmful. Just sucking on your thumb is not harmful at all, but smoking is harmful. But because everybody is smoking and it is an accepted thing and it seems to be a very grown-up thing . . . Small children want to grow up, if not for anything else then just for being allowed to smoke. Seeing grown-up people smoking they feel very inferior—they are not allowed. They are told, "You are too small, wait a little. This is something which only grown-up people can do." It symbolizes a grown-up person. And if you are smoking really costly cigarettes, costly cigars, rare, exotic, and then it shows your success, it shows that you have arrived, it gives you dignity.

Go deep into it. It may be that your mother's breast was taken away too early. Then my suggestion is: in the night before you go to bed have a bottle with a rubber nipple fixed to it and suck it. Every night before you go to sleep become a child again. Go on sucking it. Fill the bottle with warm milk. That's what the smoking is doing; the warm smoke going in and out symbolizes the milk of the mother. You will have to go deep into the causes.

One of the great things in life is that if you understand the root cause of something you can overcome it without any trouble, without any will power. If you use will power to stop it you will find some substitute—you will have to find some substitute. Maybe you are not allowed to speak; in the office the boss won't allow you, in the home the wife won't allow you. She goes on talking, she gives you no time to talk. And you are also afraid—if you talk you get into trouble; whatsoever you say is wrong. And the wife jumps upon it, takes the clue from that and starts nagging you. So in the home you have to hide behind a newspaper. Whether you read the newspaper or not is not the point, but you have to hide behind the newspaper. You have to look engaged, occupied, so you need not talk and you need not hear what the wife goes on saying.

Women all over the world, except in a few countries in the West, don't smoke, for the simple reason that they talk too much. Their lips have so much exercise that there is no need! In a few countries in the West they have started smoking and the reason is the Women's Lib movement. They have to compete with men in everything; whether it is sense or nonsense it doesn't matter. I am very much afraid they may start pissing standing any day, because they are equal to men! However stupid it is, they will do it.

Go into the cause of it, and if you can find the cause it will simply melt away. But don't stop it by force—let it go of its own accord, through watchfulness, through awareness.

So I will not say stop smoking or stop anything. But I will suggest always: watch, meditate, be aware, go into the roots. This is a fundamental law of life: if you can understand the root of something it disappears, it evaporates. Unless you understand the root it will continue in one form or another.

THE BOOK OF THE BOOKS, Vol. IX

Do one thing: don't stop smoking right now—because that will not help and you will again smoke. Do one thing:

breathing. Whenever you have an urge to smoke, make it a point that first you have to breathe deeply for five minutes. Start by exhaling: exhale deeply. Inhale deeply, exhale deeply, but the emphasis should be on exhalation more than on inhalation, Mm? The whole air has to be thrown out. Just squeeze the whole system so all the air is out. Do this for five minutes before each cigarette . . .

You have to pay the price for each cigarette, Mm?—that is five minutes of deep breathing. If after that five minutes the desire, the urge disappears, there is no need to smoke; if the urge remains, you can smoke. And this will help— this will help in many ways . . .

Firstly, out of one hundred times, seventy-five times, the desire will disappear. Good breathing will give you such a good feeling that you will not feel like smoking. You will feel so happy and so full of vitality, you will not feel like smoking.

In fact breathing does just the opposite, because through breathing you take in more oxygen. The system functions on a higher plane, on a higher altitude with more oxygen, and you feel more vital. The blood circulates better, the blood is purified better. The whole system functions at the maximum. With smoking you go on dumping carbon dioxide inside the system: the system falls to the minimum. It is just the opposite.

And once you are enjoying five minutes' breathing you will not feel the urge. That urge always comes when you are not enjoying life; if you are enjoying something you can forget cigarettes. If you are looking at a movie and you are really into it, you will not smoke. If you are listening to music and you are really into it you will forget. In anything in which you get involved and in which you are happy you will not smoke. You will smoke only when you are not feeling in tune so you want something to do—smoking.

> THE NO BOOK
> (NO BUDDHA, NO TEACHING, NO DISCIPLINE)

SNAKE You must have seen the symbol—a very ancient symbol and very significant too—of a snake eating its own tail. Many ancient mystery schools used that symbol; it is certainly very indicative. The snake eating its own tail means a one-hundred-and-eighty-degree turn. The snake is turned upon itself, the consciousness has recoiled upon itself.

And in almost all the cultures of the world the snake has represented wisdom. Jesus says: "Be ye as wise as a snake." And in the East the snake, the serpent, has symbolized the inner energy of man, *kundalini;* hence it is called serpent power. The energy is coiled at the lowest center of your being; when it uncoils, the snake starts rising upwards. It simply represents that there is something in the snake which can be used as a metaphor.

The snake can catch hold of its own tail; the dog cannot do it. Dogs try—you must have seen dogs trying—and the more they try, the more crazy they go, because the tail goes on jumping with them. They think it is something separate. They try to catch hold of it, and when they cannot catch hold of it . . . of course they try desperately, but the more they try the more they are at a loss. Only the snake can do it, no other animal.

The same happens in enlightenment: your energy starts moving upon itself, it becomes a circle.

I AM THAT

SOCIALISM I am not for socialism, because to me freedom is the ultimate value; nothing is higher than that. And socialism is basically against freedom—it has to be, it is inevitable, because the very effort of socialism is to bring something unnatural into existence.

Men are not equal, they are unique. How can they be equal? Not all are poets and not all are painters. Every person has unique talents in him. There are people who can create music and there are people who can create money. Man needs absolute freedom to be himself.

Socialism is dictatorship of the state; it is a forced economic structure. It tries to equalize people who are not equal; it cuts them down to the same size, and they have different sizes. Naturally, a few people, a very few people it will fit, but for the majority it will be a crippling phenomenon, paralyzing, destructive.

I appreciate freedom in every sphere of life so that everybody is allowed to be *himself.* The society is not the end but only a means; the end is the individual. The individual has a greater value than the social organization. The society exists for the individual, not vice versa. Hence I believe in *laissez-faire*.

Capitalism is the most natural economic structure; it has not been forced, it has grown. It has not been imposed, it has come on its own. Certainly I would like poverty to be eradicated from the world—it is ugly—but socialism cannot do it. It has failed in Russia, in China; in every country it has failed to eradicate poverty. Yes, it has succeeded in one thing: it has made everybody equally poor; it has distributed poverty.

And man is so foolish that if everybody else is also as poor as you are you feel more at ease; you don't feel jealous. The whole idea of socialism has arisen out of jealousy. It has nothing to do with understanding man, his psychology, his growth, his ultimate flowering; it is rooted in jealousy. A few people become rich; those few people are the targets of everybody else's jealousy—they have to be pulled down. Not that *you* will become richer by pulling them down; you may become even more poor than before because those few people know how to create money and if they are destroyed you will lose all capacity to create richness.

That's what has happened in Russia: the rich people have disappeared, but that has not made the whole society rich; everybody has become equally poor. Of course people feel happier in that way because there is nobody who is richer than them. Everybody is equally poor, all are beggars; it feels good. If somebody is rising higher than you, your ego is hurt.

People *talk* about equality, but something fundamental has to be understood: men are *not* psychologically equal. What can be done about it? Albert Einstein is not equal to any Tom, Harry, Dick—he is not! You can sooner or later start trying to equalize people as far as intelligence is concerned, but Shakespeare, Milton, Shelley are *not* equal to other people; they have a dimension of their own.

About one thing I agree: that there should be freedom for everybody, and *equal* freedom for everybody, to be himself. To put it more precisely: freedom means that everybody is free to be unequal! Equality and freedom cannot go together, they cannot coexist. If you choose equality, freedom has to be sacrificed and with freedom all is sacrificed. Religion is sacrificed; genius, the very possibility of genius, is sacrificed; man's higher qualities are sacrificed. Everybody has to fit with the lowest denominator, only then can you be equal . . .

And *my* observation is that every individual is born with some specific talent, some genius specific to himself. He may not be a poet like Shelley or Rabindranath, he may not be a painter like Picasso or Nandalal, he may not be a musician like Beethoven or Ravi Shankar, but he must have something. That something has to be discovered. He has to be helped so that he can discover what he has brought to the world as a gift from God.

Nobody comes without a gift; everybody brings a certain potential. But the idea of equality is dangerous, because the rose has to be the rose and the marigold has to be the marigold and the lotus has to be the lotus. If you start trying to make them equal then you will destroy all; the roses, the lotuses, the marigolds, all will be destroyed. You can succeed in creating plastic flowers which will be exactly equal to each other, but they will be dead.

And that is what is going to happen if socialism becomes our way of life in the whole world: man will be reduced to a commodity, he will be reduced to a machine. Machines are equal. You can have millions of Ford cars exactly equal to each other. They go on coming through the assembly line, absolutely the same as one another. But man is not a machine, and to reduce man to being a machine will be destroying humanity on earth . . .

The idea of equality is absolutely unpsychological. I can accept it only in one sense: that everybody *should* be given equal opportunity to be himself—and that means to be unequal. You have to understand this paradox: everybody has to be given equal opportunity and freedom to be himself, and that simply means everybody has to be given equality to be unequal.

I AM THAT

SOCIETY What is happening here is not a movement: it a mutation. It has no concern with the society: its whole concern is with the individual. It is a revolution in the true sense of the word.

There is no idea of changing the society or the world, because there is no society at all. Only individuals exist— society is an illusion. And because we believe in society, all the revolutions have failed. The belief that the society exists has sabotaged all efforts to change man—because the belief is rooted in illusion . . .

You ask me: *What does your movement signify about the condition of society?*

It simply signifies that the society is rotten, that the society is ill, that there is no possibility of reforming the society. Because if this society is reformed it will be simply a modified form of the same rottenness—maybe a little bit better decorated, better painted, but it will be the same disease. In five thousand years' history, many times society has been reformed. And nothing basically ever changes; it remains the same in every form. It is the same illness, the same ugliness, the same sickness that continues.

Enough is enough!

Those who are intelligent have become aware that all revolutions have failed—all social revolutions have failed. And we have not listened yet to Buddhas who have been telling of a totally different revolution: the revolution in the heart of the individual—because the individual is substantial, real. Society is only a relationship.

For example, we are sitting here, two thousand people. You can think of it as a society, as a community. But what is society? What is community? There are two thousand individuals sitting here. You will never come across society anywhere; you will never meet the community. Whenever you come across anything, you will come across the real individual.

Society is only a word—and a very dangerous word. And man is very very efficient at inventing dangerous words. For example, "humanity". Now, I have never seen humanity; I have only seen human beings. Humanity is just an abstraction. But there are people who love humanity. You cannot hug humanity, you cannot kiss humanity. But that becomes a very very subtle camouflage. In the name of humanity you can go on hating human beings—because you love humanity; there is no need to love human beings because you love humanity.

And if the need arises, you can sacrifice all human beings for your love of humanity. That has been done again and again: people love nations, and people kill people in the name of "nation". In the name of "motherland", "father-land"—stupid words—but in the name of "motherland" thousands of people can be killed very easily.

The real is sacrificed on the altar of the abstract.

PHILOSOPHIA PERENNIS, Vol. II

I know bureaucracy is there but it has to be there because people are absolutely irresponsible. There is no way to sud-denly drop the bureaucracy and the court and the law and the policeman. There is no way because you will not be able to live for a single moment. It is a necessary evil. One just has to learn to live with people who are not alert, who are fast asleep; they are snoring. It may be disturbing to you, but nothing can be done about it.

At the most, the one thing you can do is not to enforce the same stupid behavior that has been forced on you by society. Don't force it on anybody else. You may have your wife someday, your children someday, but don't force it on them, on your friends. That's all you can do. But you have to live in society and you have to follow the rules.

Man is born in the society, he lives in the society. He is a social animal. You are born of two persons' love affair. Society was there even in your birth. Your mother was following a certain rule, your father was following a certain rule; husbands and wives and this and that. Because they followed certain rules, they brought you up, otherwise they would have thrown you into the river. Why bother? Who are you? Why should you disturb their life and become a burden on them? They followed a rule that children have to be looked after.

So the game has to be understood and if you want to play the game, you have to follow the rules. If you don't want to follow the rules, don't follow the game. It is simple. And you will unnecessarily create trouble. Now if you don't have a passport the police will catch you. If you don't have the right papers, you will be thrown out of the country. So how is it bringing you freedom? It will destroy all your freedom, so don't do that.

This type of idea arises many times because there are
stupid rules, but that's how things are. We have such a small
life that we cannot hope to change the whole society. So
it is better to be wise and to simply follow the rules. You
will be freer if you follow the rules. If you follow the rules
perfectly, you will be completely free. The moment you
break a rule, you are caught.

So a wise man simply follows the rules. Be a Roman when
you are in Rome and just follow the rules. You will fit there
and nobody will create any trouble for you. They can create
trouble because the power belongs to them. You are a tiny
individual. What can you do? There is no point in fighting
because you are fighting against a brick wall. You will hurt
your own head.

That's where the hippie attitude is wrong. They are perfect
in their insight that these rules are just bogus, but they don't
understand that they are needed. The bigger the group, the
more rules are needed. When you are alone, no rules are
needed. When two are there, a few rules; three are there,
more; four, more. And the world is populating itself so fast
that more and more rules will be needed. Otherwise there
will be chaos and madness.

So don't just condemn things. Try to understand. There
are many evils which are needed; they are necessary. The
choice is not between right and wrong. In real life the choice
is always between a bigger evil and a lesser evil, a bigger
wrong and a lesser wrong. The choice is not between right
and wrong, otherwise it would have been very easy. The
choice is of the lesser evil.

Just think of a society where no passport is needed, no
documents are needed, no papers are needed. We could not
have electricity. We could not sit here so silently. A mob
would come and start dancing and we would not be able
to talk. Somebody comes and starts living in your house.
You cannot say "Get out!" because there are no papers; the
house belongs to nobody. Then you cannot even keep your
shirt on your body. Anyone who has more power will take
it away.

Just conceive of a society existing even for twenty-four
hours without any rules and regulations. Within twenty-four
hours the whole civilization will go to dust. There will be

murders and robberies and nobody will be able to even sleep because when you want to go to sleep a mob comes inside the room and they want to play cards or drink there, and who are you to prevent it? Somebody takes your wife or your girlfriend and you cannot do anything. Even for twenty-four hours without those stupid rules, society cannot exist.

There is a possibility—but that is simply a possibility; it is not going to ever happen—that in some future time there will be a society of enlightened people. Then there will be no rules because they will be so responsible. But that you cannot in fact even hope for. It is a utopia.

This word "utopia" is beautiful. It means "that which never happens". The very word means "that which never happens". It is just a dream.

A ROSE IS A ROSE IS A ROSE

Man is being hypnotized from the very moment he is born. He is being hypnotized to believe that the society exists in his favor, for his good. That is utterly wrong . . .

The society is interested only in your body—your body can be put to use—your soul is dangerous.

A man of soul is always dangerous because a man of soul is a free man. He cannot be reduced to slavery. A man who has an immortal soul in him has a deeper commitment to existence itself, to God himself. He does not care a bit about the man-made structures of society, civilization and culture; these are prison cells for him. He does not exist as a Christian or a Hindu or a Mohammedan. He cannot be part of a crowd. He exists as an individual.

The body is part of the crowd, your soul is not. Your soul is deeply individual. Its flavor is that of freedom.

But your soul cannot be put to any use in the marketplace. The society needs only your body. And it is very dangerous for the society if you start striving for the soul, because then your interest changes. You turn from being an extrovert into an introvert; you start moving inwards. The society is outside, the society wants you to remain an extrovert, interested in money, power, prestige, and all that, so your energy goes on moving outwards. If you start moving inwards, that means you have become a dropout, you are no part of the game that is being played on the outside. You don't belong to it. You start diving deep within your own being. And there is the source of immortality.

The society prevents you from going inwards. And the best way is to give you a false idea that you are going inwards . . .

When you go to a church you are not going inwards. When you go to the temple you are not going inwards. But the society has hypnotized you to believe that "If you want to go inwards, go to the church." But the church is as much outside as anything else. The society has hypnotized you to believe that "If you want to go inwards, you go to the priest." And the priest is an agent of the state and the society. The priest has always been against the mystics, because if you go to a mystic you will start moving inwards.

A mystic lives in a totally different way. His energy moves in a different gestalt: his river moves inwards. So one who comes to a mystic, will start moving inwards naturally, simply, spontaneously. That is the whole purpose of being with a Master, with a mystic.

THE SECRET OF SECRETS, Vol. II

SOLAR PLEXUS   Man has lost contact with the solar plexus because of the fear of sex, because of the repression of sex, because of life-negation.

The solar plexus is the center of life and death both. That's why Japanese call it *hara; hara* means death. And the Indians call it *manipura. Manipura* means the diamond, the most precious diamond, because life comes from there. In the solar plexus is your seed. It is the first thing that is created in the womb of the mother; then everything else grows around it.

In the solar plexus your father's seed and your mother's seed are both present. The life cell from the father and the life cell from the mother create your solar plexus. That is your first blueprint; from there everything grows and it remains the center forever and ever. You can forget about it, you can become oblivious of it, you can repress, you can start hanging in the head but it remains in the center. You just become less and less alive. The farther away you go, the less and less alive you become and the farther you are from the solar plexus. You live more on the periphery; you lose centering, you lose grounding. It is very alive. Start living more and more.

That is the primitive mind, the most primal mind. The Primal therapists are not yet aware that the primal scream comes from the solar plexus. It is the first mind. Then the second mind arises—the heart, feeling. Then the third mind arises—the head, thinking.

Solar plexus is being, heart is feeling, head is thinking. Thinking is the farthest, feeling is just in the middle; that's why when you feel you are more alive, just a little more alive than when you think. Thoughts are dead things: they are corpses; they don't breathe. Feelings breathe, feelings have a pulsation but nothing to be compared with the first, primal mind. If you reach the solar plexus and be there and live from there, you will have a totally different kind of life— the real life.

The few moments you feel that you are real are the moments when you are at the solar plexus. That's why sometimes people seek danger, they go mountain climbing, because when danger is very real you simply go into the solar plexus. That's why whenever you are in a shock your solar plexus has the first pulsation. In a shock you cannot think, you cannot feel: you can only be.

If you are driving and suddenly you feel an accident is going to happen, your solar plexus is hit. That's the reason why people like speed in driving, and the speedier your car becomes, the more alive you feel, thrilled. You are coming closer to the solar plexus. That's why there is such attraction in war. People go to the cinema to see a murder story. It is creating a situation in which you can feel your solar plexus again. People read detective novels and when the story really comes to its peak they cannot think, they cannot feel: they are!

Try to understand it. All meditations lead to it. It is your *elan vital,* it is the source of your vitality. Go into it, and you can go easily, that's why I am saying to go into it. Whenever you are sitting silently, be there. Forget the head, forget the heart, forget the body: just be a throb behind the navel.

If you go deeper into it, it will become possible for you

to understand the real concept of trinity—because your father is there, your mother is there. If you are also there, the trinity arises. That is the basic idea of the trinity—not God and the Son and the Holy Ghost. If you are there, then the trinity, a triangle. The father and mother are already there. If you are also there then the Christ is born, the Son is born. And when the Son is born there is real unity.

Two cannot meet: the third is needed to bridge the two. So your father and mother are there, consummated but not consumed, in a kind of union but not yet a unity. The feminine and the masculine are there but still not bridged, and that is the whole conflict—that he is two, dual. He is bound to be two: something has been given by the father and something has been given by the mother. They are both there, flowing together like two currents but still there is a subtle separation.

If your presence reaches there, if you become more and more aware of it, your very awareness will become the catalytic agent: the two will disappear and there will be oneness. That oneness is called "Christ consciousness".

THE OPEN SECRET

SOLITUDE   The solitary person is in a negative space. He is feeling lonely, he is hankering for the other. He is in a deep sadness because he does not know how to be with himself, he does not know how to enjoy himself, he does not know how to celebrate himself. All that he knows is relationship, so whenever he is in relationship he feels at ease. Whenever he is with somebody he can forget himself. To be with somebody is something like alcohol, it is an intoxicant. It is simply drowning yourself, your worries, anxieties, your very existence in the other. And the other is doing the same with you. That's what people call relationship. Each is using the other as a means to avoid himself.

Solitude is totally different. It is not loneliness, it is aloneness. It is not negative, it is utterly positive. It is not the experience that the other is absent but the experience that "I am present". It is so overwhelming an experience of one's own presence that everything else fades from the mind and one starts feeling ecstatic. The sheer joy of breathing, the sheer joy of being, the sheer joy of participating in existence is enough. It is a wonder to be, the wonder of wonders.

Bliss makes real solitude. Then solitude becomes a temple, bliss becomes the deity in it. And that's what meditation is all about: the art of changing loneliness into aloneness, the alchemy of changing solitariness into solitude.

DANCE TIL THE STARS
COME DOWN FROM THE RAFTERS

Bliss is found in solitude, but not an extrovert solitude. You can go to the mountains—the beauty of the mountains will enchant you, the silence of the mountains will enthrall you—but within a few days you will be bored because your mind will go on, round and round in circles, in the old circles. The old gibberish will continue; in fact it will be more than ever before because there is nothing else to do. The mind becomes too occupied with imagination, hallucination, dreaming, and the silence outside becomes a contrast. And the mind becomes afraid of the silence outside also, so it starts working too much just to keep itself occupied. Hence mountains can't help, woods can't help.

Down through the ages many people have gone to the woods, to the desert, to the mountains, to find solitude, but it has never been found there; they have only become dull and dead. And one can mistake dullness for silence. They have not gone beyond the mind; in fact they have fallen below it. They have become more like animals than like gods. Yes, there is a certain beauty, an innocence, in being an animal, but it is below humanity. It has something of the child but it has no maturity in it; it is more ignorance than innocence.

And a man who has lived long in the mountains becomes more and more ignorant of the world, becomes more and more a part of the physical environment, but does not gain maturity, richness, does not become more conscious; in fact he becomes more lazy, lousy, relapses into a kind of sleepy existence. He becomes a sleepwalker, because the challenges are missing which keep oneself alert and awake.

So I am not in favor of people going to the mountains in search of solitude. The solitude has to be found inwardly.

It is not an extrovert journey, it is introversion; it has to be found in your very subjectivity. It is not an object, something outside; it is your very being. The deeper you go into yourself, the deeper you are going into the real woods, the real deserts, into the real mountains. And if you have found solitude within yourself then it makes no difference: you can be in the marketplace and you will be silent, and you can be in the mountains and you will be silent. Then the outer makes no difference at all, the outer becomes irrelevant.

And to make the outer irrelevant is the basic approach of my sannyas. Hence one has not to escape from it, it has to be made irrelevant. One has to *live* in it and yet be not part of it. And the moment you know the beauty of your aloneness, the beauty that exists when you are utterly oblivious to the whole world, when there is no interference, no distraction, when you are simply resting in yourself—that's what meditation is, resting in yourself; that is the best definition of meditation possible, resting, relaxing into one's own being—then bliss arises naturally, as a byproduct. Bliss can never be the goal; it is a byproduct of solitude.

THE IMPRISONED SPLENDOR

SONG   We know songs which are composed of words, but they are not real songs. There are songs which are composed of silence and they are the real songs. Once you have heard the song of silence then all the great poets just look childish. Then Shakespeares and Miltons and Byrons simply fade away; they are just playing with toys.

In India—and I think it is only in India that it is so—we have two words for a poet. One is *kavi,* which can be exactly translated as "a poet". The other is *rishi,* which is untranslatable. A poet means one who composes songs with words and a *rishi* is a poet who has heard the song of silence. And it is the *rishi* who has really known the harmony of existence, who has seen the beauty of that which is. And not only has he seen it—because the only way to see it is to become it— he has become it, it is his own heartbeat.

You have to go deep within yourself to hear the song of silence. You have to leave all words far away, far behind. The greatest barrier is that of words. You can enter Russia because they have only an iron wall; and China is even easier—they have only a bamboo wall. But the real problem arises when you try to enter yourself. And the wall is very delicate. It is not made of steel, it is not even made of bricks; it is only made of words, but a thick jungle of words—Christian, Hindu, Mohammedan—millions of words. And when you start penetrating yourself you go on finding words and words and words.

The meditator has to go on peeling himself like an onion. Peel one layer, another layer comes up, but go on peeling till you come to the point where nothing is left in your hand. So go on peeling within yourself; when nothing is left, that nothing is the song of silence.

Once heard it transforms your life. You go beyond time, you become deathless. All fear disappears and there is only freedom. All misery disappears and there is only rejoicing and celebration.

THE GOLDEN WIND

SONG, SACRED   There is a difference between an ordinary song and a sacred song. The difference is not of words, the difference is not of composition; the difference is somewhere within you, not in the song itself. One can sing a film song in a sacred way, then it becomes a *bhajan*. And one can sing a so-called sacred song in such a stupid way that it becomes very mundane.

My emphasis is always on you, not what you do but what you are. From you comes the quality. You are the source, the song becomes what you are . . .

For a song to be sacred two things are needed. One is silence in your heart. That is not possible without meditation. And the second is blissfulness. Silence alone won't do. It may be there but it will not explode into songs. When silence and bliss meet then there is *bhajan,* the sacred song. The meeting point of silence and bliss creates a miracle; your song has something of your silence and something of your bliss together. Then whatsoever you sing . . . you may simply utter nonsense words but they will have a sacred quality.

A Christian sect uses a certain beautiful method—I like it. It is one of the secrets that has been followed by many

mystics down the ages. It is called glossolalia. One simply
relaxes, becomes silent, and then whatsoever comes one
allows it—gibberish, nonsense words, sounds. One has not
to prevent anything, one has to enjoy whatsoever is coming. The word "gibberish" comes from a great mystic's name;
his name was Jabar, a Sufi mystic.

You ask him a very rational question and he will utter
some absurd words or meaningless sounds; you cannot
figure out what he is saying, what he means. But you can
see his joy and you can see his silence. That is his message.
Whatsoever the question, that is his answer. It is from Jabar
that the English word "gibberish" has arisen. Gibberish is
called glossolalia, a divine language, by this certain sect of
Christians.

You are not speaking, something is speaking through you.
You are simply silent, then an urge arises in you to shout—
you shout. An urge arises in you to jump and you jump,
and you jog and you dance. You simply follow the inner
feeling, and then it is *bhajan,* then it is sacred.

> I'M NOT AS THUNK AS YOU DRINK I AM

SOPHIST *Sophos* is a beautiful word—the sage. Remember,
the sage does not mean the saint. The saint is against the
sinner; it has a polar opposite to it. The saint is one who
is not a sinner; he has chosen to be virtuous, against vice.
The sinner is one who has chosen vice against virtue. They
are polarities like negative and positive. The saint cannot
exist without the sinner; the sinner cannot exist without the
saint—they are partners, they can only co-exist. A world
without saints will be a world without sinners too. If you
really want sinners to disappear from the world, let the saints
disappear first—and immediately there will be no sinner ...

The sage is a tremendously beautiful phenomenon,
because of his wholeness. The sage is a perfect circle. He
contains all, he rejects nothing. That was the idea of *sophos;*
it was a beautiful word. But it fell from its reputation.

It fell because it is a dangerous word too: it can easily be
used by the cunning people. Because the sage is whole, he
is both, now the sinner can use it. He can say, "I am both.
I don't choose—whatsoever is the case ..." Now the sinner

can pretend to be a sage. He can say, "Because it is so, this moment I am like this. This is happening—what can I do? I have dropped choosing. I have accepted life in its totality."

Now the sage is a totally different phenomenon from this cunning person. This cunning person used the word and the word became associated with this cunning mind. It became a camouflage for doing whatsoever you want to do. Deep down there is choice, but you can pretend on the surface that you are not a chooser, and you live in choiceless awareness. It is a very subtle cunningness.

So the word *sophos* fell from its pedestal and became "sophist". The word "sophist" is ugly—it means a pretender. It means one who is pretending to be a sage and is not, one who is pretending to be a sage and is not even a saint. He is simply a sinner but has found a beautiful rationalization for remaining a sinner.

PHILOSOPHIA PERENNIS, Vol. I

SORROW Sorrow arises out of clinging to momentary things which you cannot make permanent. It is not in the nature of things. It is against the universal law, it is against Dharma, it is against Tao. You cannot win. If you fight with the universal law you are fighting a losing battle; you will simply waste your energies. And what is going to happen is bound to happen; nothing can be done about it.

All that you can do is to go with your consciousness. You can change your vision. You can see things in a different light, in a different context, in a new space, but you cannot change things. If you think of the world as very real you will suffer. If you see the world as a strange dream you will not suffer. If you think in terms of static entities you will suffer. If you think in terms of nouns you will suffer. But if you think in terms of verbs you will not suffer.

Nouns don't exist; they exist only in language. In reality there are no nouns. Everything is a verb because everything is changing and everything is in a process. It is never static, it is always dynamic.

The second thing Buddha says is:

Existence is sorrow.

To be is sorrow. The ego is sorrow.

The first thing he says is: See the world as dream, fluctuating, changing, moment-to-moment new. Enjoy it, enjoy its newness, enjoy all the surprises that it brings. It is beautiful that it is changing; there is nothing wrong with it. Just don't cling to it. Why do you cling? You cling because you have another fallacy: that *you* are.

The first fallacy is that things are static, and then the second fallacy is that *you* are, that you have a static ego. They both go together. If you want to cling, you need a clinger. If you have no need to cling, there is no need for a clinger. Go deep into it. If you don't need to cling, the ego is not needed at all; it will be pointless. In fact, it cannot exist without clinging.

The dancer can exist only if he dances. If the dance disappears, where is the dancer? The singer exists only in singing. The walker exists only in walking. So is the ego: the ego exists only in clinging, in possessing things, in dominating things. When there is no domination, no desire to dominate, no desire to cling, no desire to possess, the ego starts evaporating. On the outside you stop clinging and on the inside a new clarity starts arising. The ego, with all its smoke, disappears. The ego, with all its clouds, disappears. It can't exist because it cannot be nourished anymore. For it to exist it has to cling. It has to create "my" and "mine" in every possible and impossible thing.

The ego says, "This is *my* country," as if you had brought it with your birth, as if the earth were really divided into countries. The earth is undivided, it is one. But the ego says, "This is *my* country—and not only is this my country, this is the greatest country in the world. This is the holiest land . . ."

Anything and everything will be claimed by the ego. And "ours is always better," whatsoever it is. The ego exists only through such claims. The "I" exists only as an island in the ocean of "my" and "mine". If you stop claiming things as "my" and "mine", the ego will disappear of its own accord.

Neither the wife is yours nor the husband nor the children. All belong to the whole. Your claim is foolish. We come empty-handed into the world and we go empty-handed from the world. But nobody wants to know the truth—it hurts.

"Empty-handed we come and empty-handed we go?" One starts feeling shaky, one starts feeling scared. One wants to be full, not empty. It is better to be full of anything—any garbage—than to be empty. Emptiness looks like death, and we don't want the truth. Our whole effort is to live in convenience, even if that convenience is based on illusions.

"I demand an explanation, and I want the truth!" shouted the irate husband upon discovering his wife in bed with his best friend.

"Make up your mind, George," she calmly replied. "You can't have both."

Either you can have the explanation or the truth. And people are more interested in the explanation than in the truth. Hence so many philosophies. They are all explanations— explanations to explain *away* things, not to give you the truth; explanations to create great smoke so that you need not see the truth. And Buddha's insistence is: *See* it, because without seeing it you can't go above sorrow.

THE BOOK OF THE BOOKS, Vol. VIII

SOUL "Psyche" means soul. The word "psychology" comes from the same root although psychology is not yet a science of the soul. The name is false.

The East has psychology, the West has not yet evolved it. Whatsoever is known as psychology in the West is very rudimentary, primitive, because it believes in the body. The major part of the so-called psychologies is behavioristic; they only believe in the physiology, the biology, the chemistry. They don't even believe in mind, they believe only in the behavior—that which can be observed, experimented with.

The other half believes in the mind. It is a little better than the behaviorists, the Skinners and Pavlovs—it is better than those people—but even the other half does not go beyond the mind.

Mind means a byproduct: it is born with the body and dies with the body; it is a time phenomenon. The eastern approach is *really* psychology because it believes in the soul which is not born with the birth and does not die with the death, which is beyond birth and death.

Soul means that which is eternal in you, that which is not

of time, but transcendental to time. The West has yet to enter into it. And unless western psychology starts seeking and searching for the soul it will remain a very ordinary thing with much jargon. But nothing really significant has come out of it. It has created a great system but the essential core is missing.

"Psyche" is a beautiful world, the most significant word in any language, because it indicates something in you which is beyond you. You are not the body, not the mind either: you are the witness of it all. Unless one starts growing more and more in witnessing one will not know that one is a soul.

You become aware of your eyes only when you see; if you keep your eyes closed you will forget all about them. If a child is never allowed to use his legs he will not be able to walk and he will forget all about his legs. If, from the very beginning, a bird is not allowed to rise on his wings he will not know that he has wings. It is by using a certain faculty that we become aware of it. By seeing we become aware that we have eyes, by hearing we become aware that we have ears, by smelling we become aware that we have a nose. Exactly like that, by witnessing one becomes aware that one has a soul. Witnessing is the function of the soul.

That has been the search in the East: how to become a witness of all, just a watcher, a pure watcher, with no identification. You are just looking at the body and the mind and all their functions and their activities and movements, but you are simply a watcher standing by the side of the road—the traffic goes on. You are neither the car moving, nor the truck, nor the bus, nor the people, nor the buffaloes nor the cows—nobody. You are simply the watcher standing by the side of the road.

That's what meditation is: to see your body-and-mind complex without getting identified with it. Then suddenly a new center starts integrating in you. By using it you create it, by using it more, you intensify it. And soon a totally different phenomenon is experienced: the existence of the soul. Then you know that birth was not your beginning, you existed before—and then death is not going to be the end, you will exist afterwards.

To be aware of this, that one is eternal, is to be aware that one is God or part of God. That's my whole work here: to make you aware that you are gods, goddesses, that you are eternal beings. With the experience of eternity bliss arises, fear disappears; love arises, hate disappears; light arises, darkness disappears!

SCRIPTURES IN SILENCE AND SERMONS IN STONE

SOUL, DARK NIGHT   When the mind starts disappearing there comes a gap, an interval. Before something beyond the mind descends, there is a gap. The old is gone and the new has not come, hence the desert-like feeling.

The Christian mystics have the right name for it—they call it "the dark night of the soul". One feels completely dried up, empty—and negatively empty. The emptiness has the quality of darkness, not of luminosity—no greenery anywhere, not even an oasis, not even on the faraway horizon. This desert has to be passed through.

Many people become afraid and they escape back into their world of illusions. This is a natural outcome, because all the greenery that has existed before was illusory, was just hallucinatory. You created it—it was not there.

Now the dreams have disappeared, and the empty screen . . . You have been sitting in a movie house, and on the empty screen there have been many many things— beautiful flowers and mountains and rivers and the ocean and people and everything was populated—and suddenly the projector has stopped: the screen is empty.

It is empty because whatsoever you were seeing just a moment before was just illusory . . . it was *maya*. Many people become afraid and they start the projector again—again they populate the world with their own fantasies.

This is the time when courage is needed. This is the time when a person really becomes a sannyasin. So let this desert be. You have to pass through it, and the deeper your acceptance the sooner it will disappear. Sometimes it can disappear in a single moment, it depends on the intensity of the acceptance.

It you accept, you say, "It is okay. I will live with the empty screen but I am not going to create any illusion any more. All those love affairs, relationships, all those desires and greeds and all ambitions—I am not going to bring them again. If it is desert, so let it be; I am ready to live with this desert."

Once you are totally ready, suddenly you will see that the desert is also disappearing. Just as the greenery has disappeared, the desert is also disappearing. The pictures disappeared, now the screen has disappeared, and then for the first time you become aware of the reality—which is tremendously beautiful. It is very colorful . . . it is luminous.

So these are the two things: first the movie has to start, then the screen has to disappear. Then you face the reality, the real world as it is. But to become capable of that, this is the price one has to pay.

Christian mystics have said that there are three stages of inner growth. The first they call *via purgativa*. One has to become completely pure, pure of all illusions—that is purgation.

The second stage they call *via illuminativa*. When one has become completely pure of illusions, the second stage will come—a great light will descend. Life will become glorious. One will feel very very fulfilled, very close to home.

And then the third stage they call *via unitiva*. One becomes one with the reality. There there is no-one as the seer and nothing as the seen.

In the first stage there is no light and it is very painful— purgation. Many many cherished dreams are being broken. It is painful, it hurts, and one feels dried up, because all that one was thinking was juice was nothing but dream.

In the second stage one feels very happy but still something is missing. One is happy but one has not become happiness yet. One is luminous but one has not become luminosity yet. Yes, a light has come, but it is separate from you—duality still exists.

In the third stage, *via unitiva,* one becomes one with existence. Only then is the journey complete . . . the pilgrimage is over.

WHAT IS, IS, WHAT AIN'T, AIN'T

SOULMATE   It is certainly almost impossible to find the soulmate—even if all facilities are available. The earth is big, millions and millions of people; and life is very short—how are you going to find your soulmate? And remember, even if all the facilities are available . . . right now, no facilities are available. It becomes even more impossible when facilities are not available, when you are prevented in every way from finding the soulmate. But even if you are helped, educated in how to find the soulmate, then too it will be difficult to find them in a small seventy years' life. It rarely happens; it is a rare phenomenon.

Man has seven centers. The lowest is the sex center and the highest is the *samadhi* center, and between these two there are five more centers. It is a ladder. When all the seven centers of a man are in tune and harmony with all the seven centers of a woman, then you have found the soulmate. It has happened only once in a while—with Krishna and Radha, with Shiva and Shakti. It could have also happened with Majnu and Laila if they had been allowed to meet—but the society hindered them.

And remember: Krishna and Radha were not allowed by the society either; it was not a legal marriage, it was illegal. Radha was not Krishna's wife but just a girlfriend. And with Shiva and Shakti, the parents were very much against Shakti getting married to Shiva. He looked a very strange man—he was. It was against the parental advice that Shakti jumped into a love affair with Shiva.

But only once in a while has this happened, and this seems to be natural. Whenever it happens, absolute oneness is felt—unity, not union. Two persons utterly disappear into each other; there is not even a small, thin screen dividing them; there is no division at all. It is *unio mystica.* Two persons function as if they are one person; two bodies, but one soul. It is absolute harmony. It is love at its peak. No meditation is needed—this love is enough.

You must have seen Shiva temples in India; you must have seen the *shivalinga. Shivalinga* simply represents the orgasmic state of these two lovers. *Shivalinga* simply represents Shiva as masculine energy; and just below *shivalinga*—the phallic symbol—is the symbol of Shakti: *yoni. Shivalinga* and Shakti's *yoni* are meeting; they have become one, they have disappeared into each other. They have lost all personality. That's why it is the only image in the world which has no face.

Just pure energy is symbolized by *linga* and *yoni,* by the male sexual organ and the female sexual organ. Simply energy is represented—creative energy, vital energy; energy out of which the whole of life flows. Neither does Shakti have any face nor does Shiva have any face; those faces are no more meaningful, the personalities have disappeared. It is a meeting of pure energy, and only pure energies can dissolve into each other—because if you have a solid personality it will obstruct dissolution. Only pure energies, liquid, can enter into each other and become one. If you put two rocks together, they may be together but they cannot become one. But if you pour water into water, it becomes one.

At this highest peak where all the seven centers meet, persons disappear, only energies remain, a play of energy, a play of consciousness. And the joy is constant, it is orgasmic. It is a spiritual communion. No meditation is needed for such a couple—because for such a couple love is meditation enough. It is a mystic phenomenon, it is transcendental. But it is very rare. Amongst millions and millions of people, once it will happen. It will be almost a chance meeting . . .

Tantra is the science of transforming ordinary lovers into soulmates. And that is the grandeur of Tantra. It can transform the whole earth; it can transform each couple into soulmates. It has not yet been used; it is one of the greatest treasures that is lying there, unused. The day humanity uses it, a new love will surround the earth; the earth will become aglow with a new love. Only the new man can use it—*Homo novus* can use it.

That's why I herald the new man. Only the new man can use it because only the new man will accept his body in its totality. The old man never accepted his body. He was always fighting with his body, quarrelling with his body, trying to destroy his body. The old man was suicidal; the old man was schizophrenic.

The new man will have a wholeness to him. He will not be suicidal. He will be so tremendously in love with life that he will want to come back again and again and again. Only the new man can transform these life-energy centers.

That's what I am trying to do here. It is offending the whole country—not only the whole country but the whole world,

because they have never heard anything like this. This is
a great experiment. On the success of this experiment much
will depend.

If we can help people to grow into such depths of love
that each couple becomes a Krishna-Radha, that each couple
becomes a Shiva and Shakti, just think of the world, how
beautiful it can become. The paradise will become pale
before it. This very earth can be the paradise.

But the science is subtle, and only those who are really
ready to understand without prejudices can understand it.
And the work is very delicate, mysterious. Outsiders will
never be able to understand what is going on; they are bound
to misunderstand it.

It is just the same: if you take outsiders to some scientific
lab where they are researching atomic energy, do you think
the outsiders will be able to understand anything at all? This
is a far deeper experiment! Because to work on atomic
energy is to work on matter, and to work on human energy,
love energy, is to work on consciousness. It needs very
perceptive people to see it.

But this is what my intention is in creating a commune,
a Buddhafield—where I can transform each couple into
Krishna-Radha, where each couple can have that joy, that
cosmic joy, that cosmic orgasm, that total ecstasy, when all
the seven centers of man and woman meet and mingle and
disappear into each other.

PHILOSOPHIA PERENNIS, Vol. I

SOUND   The mystics have found—and it is one of the
ancientmost discoveries, at least ten thousand years old—
that life, that the whole of existence, is made of sound, of
subtle vibrations of sound.

Modern physics discovered it too from a very different
route; because of their different routes their definitions are
a little bit different. But anybody who has some perception,
who can think in both ways—scientifically and mystically—
can see the unity, can see that they are talking about the
same thing in different languages, different jargon.

Modern physics says that the world, existence, consists
of electricity. The whole existence is nothing but electricity.
The whole existence is nothing but electrical vibration.

And if you ask them what sound is, they will say it is nothing but a certain kind of vibration in the electric energy. If you ask the mystics what electricity is, they say it is a certain form of sound vibrations—and then things become very clear.

The mystics discovered sound first, hence they define electricity by sound. In the East there has been a certain melody called *deepak rag,* a light melody. It is said that there have been singers . . . And it seems to be almost an historical fact, not just a mythology, because there are so many records about it and very recent records—five hundred years old.

In the great emperor Akbar's court there was a musician, Tansen, who was expert in that melody. It is a certain music that can help the unlit lamp to become lit. The musician simply plays on his sitar, surrounded by unlit lamps and by and by they start becoming suddenly aflame. It is possible because a sound can hit the air in a certain way so that it can create heat—that's a known phenomenon. Sound can create heat. If it can create heat it can create fire; if it can create fire it can create electricity; and vice versa is also true.

The mystics and the physicists have traveled towards the same destination from different angles.

IS THE GRASS REALLY GREENER ON THE OTHER SIDE OF THE FENCE?

When you become absolutely silent in meditation, a subtle humming sound is heard within one's own being. It does not come from the outside; it comes from one's own innermost core.

In the East we have called it *omkar;* the sound *aum* comes closest to it—it is just approximate, remember, not exact. But if you go into an empty temple and you just chant *"Aum, aum, aum . . ."* and you go on chanting, and then you stop suddenly, because the temple is empty it will go on resounding. That resounding comes very close to the innermost sound. And once this soundless sound, as it is called, this inner melody of your being is heard, bliss explodes, your whole life becomes harmonious. Then suddenly everything fits, then it is no more a problem. Life for the first time is not a problem, not a riddle to be solved but a mystery to be lived.

But the sound is so subtle that unless your mind is completely empty you cannot hear it. The mind makes so much noise you cannot hear the still, small voice within yourself; hence meditation is the door to reach to the inner music. And the person who hears the inner music becomes capable of hearing the celestial music of the spheres. He has learned the first lesson; now he can hear it all around, in the stars, in the trees, in the wind passing through the pine trees, in the sound of the running water.

That music has to be heard. Hearing it, one's life becomes sheer beauty, bliss, benediction.

THE OLD POND—PLOP!

And deep within there is a music which is not created by anybody, which is not created by hands, which is not produced on any instrument. There is a special name for it; it is called *anahad*. When you play on a guitar it is called *ahad*, because you strike on the strings with your fingers. *Ahad* means striking. It is created out of conflict, there is a little aggression in it, there is struggle. The musician is struggling to create music on the instrument, there is a kind of fight. But in the innermost recess of your being there is neither instrument nor musician, but music is there, without the musician and without the instrument.

Zen people call it "the sound of one hand clapping". The Christian mystics call it "the soundless sound". It is a silence and yet it is musical silence.

Again, these words of T. S. Eliot will be significant:

*At the still point of the turning world. Neither flesh
    nor fleshless;*
*Neither from nor towards; at the still point where the
    dance is.*
*But neither arrest nor movement. And do not call
    it fixity,*
*Where past and future are gathered . . . Except for the
    still point,*
There would be no dance, and there is only the dance.

The still point . . . There is a point within you where nothing ever moves—no movement from or to, no stirring, no sound created by any instrument. Nobody is there, just stillness, but that stillness is the dance and that stillness is the music. It is called *anahad . . . is ghat antar anahad garje, isee men uthat fuhara . . .* And the moment you have heard that music, a great fountain bursts forth, of joy, of bliss. You become a rejoicing, you become a dance yourself, you become a song yourself. Then your life is religious—not like the so-called saints, sad, serious and ugly. The really religious person is one whose inner wells have started flowing, who has become a fountain of joy, of song and dance and celebration.

THE GUEST

SPACE   You are there, I am here: just between the two, something transpires—between my nothingness and your beingness something transpires which has nothing to do with me and which has nothing to do with you. Just an empty valley, and you sing a song, and the valley repeats, and the valley resounds it.

So it will make no difference whether you are here or in the West. If you feel any difference that will be because of you, not because of me. When you are close to me you feel more open. Just your idea, that because you are here, you feel more open. Then you go to the West, just your idea— that now you are too far away, how can you be open—you become closed. Just drop that idea, and wherever you are I am available; because this availability is not personal, so it is not a question of time and space. Go to the West, go to the farthest end of the earth, but remain in the same attitude.

Many of you will be going. Every morning, eight o'clock, Indian time, just come as you come here, sit as you sit here, wait as you wait here, and immediately you will start feeling your thoughts are being answered. And it will be an even more beautiful experience than being close to me because then there will be nothing physical. It will be totally tran-scendental; it will be the purest possible. And then if you can do that, space disappears. Between a Master and a disci-ple there is no space.

And then another miracle is possible: then one day you can drop time also. Because someday I will leave this body; I will not be here. If you have not transcended time before I leave my body then I will become unavailable to you. Not that I will be unavailable, I will remain available, but just your idea that now I am dead so how can you relate to me . . . you will become closed.

It is your idea. Drop that idea of time and space. So first try eight o'clock in the morning, Indian Standard Time, wherever you are, and then drop that Indian Standard Time also. Then try any time. First drop space, then drop time. And you will be so ecstatic to find that I am available wherever you are. Then there is no question.

Buddha died. Many started crying and weeping, but there were a few who just sat there. Manjushree was there, one of his great disciples. He was sitting under the tree; he remained the same. He heard, as if nothing has happened. It was one of the greatest events in the history of the world. Rarely a Buddha is born, so there is no question of Buddha dying; rarely it happens. Somebody came to Manjushree and he said, "What are you doing? Are you shocked so much that you cannot move? Buddha is dead!" Manjushree laughed and he said, "Before he died I dropped time and space. He will remain available to me wherever he is, so don't bring such absurd news to me." He never followed, he never went to see the dead body. He is quite at ease, relaxed. He knows that that availability was not confined to time or to space.

Buddha has remained available to those who are available to him. I will remain available to you if you are available to me, so learn how to be available to me.

YOGA: THE ALPHA AND THE OMEGA, Vol. VII

Allow her as much space as possible. This is one of the fundamental problems of love. Every lover has to learn it, nobody knows it by birth. It only comes slowly slowly and through much pain, but the sooner it comes, the better— that each person needs his or her own space, that we should not interfere in that space. To interfere is very natural for lovers, because they start taking the other for granted. They start thinking that they are no more separate. They don't think of "I" and "thou"; they start thinking of "we". You are that too, but only once in a while. "We" is a rare phenomenon. Once, for a few moments, lovers come to that point where the word is meaningful, where you can say "we", when "I" and "thou" disappear into each other, where boundaries overlap. But these are rare moments; they should not be taken for granted. You cannot remain "we" twenty-four hours a day, but that's what every lover demands—and that creates unnecessary misery.

When you come close once in a while you become one, but those are rare moments, precious, to be cherished, and you cannot make them a twenty-four hour thing. If you try, you will destroy them; then the whole beauty will be lost. When that moment is gone, it is gone; you are again "I" and "thou".

You have your space, she has her space. And one has to be respectful now, that the other's space should not be in any way interfered with; it should not be trespassed. If you trespass it, you hurt the other; you start destroying the other's individuality. And because the other loves you, she or he will go on tolerating it. But toleration is one thing; it is not something very beautiful. If the other is only tolerating it, then sooner or later the other will take revenge. The other cannot forgive you and it goes on accumulating—one day, another day, another day . . . You have interfered with a thousand and one things, then they all pile up, and then one day they explode.

That's why lovers go on fighting. That fight is because of this constant interference. And when you interfere in her being, she tries to interfere in your being, and nobody feels good about it.

DON'T LOOK BEFORE YOU LEAP

Only a meditator can transform solitariness into solitude. Then when he is totally alone he is not lonely, not at all. He is full of his own being, overflowing; in fact more overflowing than ever, because others are there they encroach on your space. In life it is really a continuous struggle to keep your space intact. Everybody is treading on everybody else's space, nobody is respectful of anybody's space.

This is one of the greatest problems humanity is facing today, because the earth has become too overcrowded and people are really suffering from an immense confinement. The crowd is coming closer and closer; you are in a crowd everywhere and everybody is interfering with your space. Your privacy is lost—and when privacy is lost all is lost.

The people who have been studying animals have come to know that there is a territorial imperative. For example, if you see a monkey and you start moving slowly towards the monkey, up to a certain point he will not take any notice of you, but only up to a certain point. Beyond that he will immediately start getting angry—maybe at ten feet, twenty feet. You will be surprised that every monkey behaves in the same way, they always get angry at the same distance. It is as if the monkey has a certain sense of territory and he wants nobody to come into his space.

In zoos animals go berserk, mad. Only in zoos do animals go mad, not in the woods—never. Nobody has heard of any lion going mad in the jungle or any elephant going mad in the jungle. But in a circus they do, in a zoo they do because they are confined. If you go to the zoo you will see the lion continuously walking around the cage, confined, enraged, angry because his space has been taken away—and in the jungle he has a vast space. And all animals respect each other's space, none of them interferes in the other's realm. The moment you enter their space you are in danger; if you don't enter their space there is no danger to you. The snake will not bite you if you don't enter his space.

Now they have measured how much space every animal has got for himself. But man has no sense of that; he has completely forgotten the language, he does not know it, he has lost the very sense. And that's why humanity is almost in a state of insanity. It needs methods to create space again.

Meditation is a method to create your own space. If it is not available on the outside than create it inside. Perhaps it is no more available on the outside, perhaps it will never be available on the outside again; on this earth it does not seem to be possible. Then find space within. That's the whole alchemy of meditation, finding space within. Then even in the crowd you remain in solitude because now you know how to create an inner space.

You remain centered. Nobody can interfere with your inner space. People can interfere with your outer space; the wife can interfere, the husband can interfere, the children can interfere—everybody. And it is so crowded that they are not at fault. There is no more space left on the outside.

Meditation becomes something of absolute value when society is so overcrowded. Meditation has never been of such importance before. Only few very intelligent people—a Buddha, a Jesus, a Zarathustra—had the sense to create some inner space. The other people lived outside, there was enough space outside; there was no reason to find it inside.

But now, everybody has to become a Buddha in some way or other, otherwise life will not have any meaning, it will not have any salt, it will not have any taste at all.

So by becoming a sannyasin you will be working in the inner world to create a space there. An infinite space can be created there because you can throw out all the junk that is inside. You can throw the thoughts, the desires, the memories, the past, the future, the dreams, the imagination. You can go on throwing all this junk and you can create great space. That's what meditation is all about: throwing out all the contents that we are carrying inside so the room is empty, so that you can feel yourself surrounded by infinite vastness. And that vastness is divine. That is solitude.

JUST THE TIP OF THE ICEBERG

SPECIAL   You are special, you are unique—God never creates anything less than that.

Everyone is unique, utterly unique. There has been no person like you before, and there will never be a person like you again. God has taken this form for the first time and the last time, so there is no need to try to become special, you already are. If you are trying to be special you will become ordinary. Your very effort is rooted in misunderstanding. It will create confusion, because when you try to become special you have taken one thing for granted—that you are not special. You have become ordinary already. You have missed the point.

Now, once you have taken it for granted that you are ordinary, how can you become special? You will try this way and that, and you will remain ordinary, because your base, your foundation is wrong. Yes, you can go to the dressmaker and can find more sophisticated dresses, you can have your hairstyle done again, you can use cosmetics; you can learn a few things and become more knowledgeable, you can paint and start thinking that you are a painter; you can do a few things, you can become famous or notorious, but deep down you will know that you are ordinary. All these things are on the outside. How can you transform your ordinary soul into an extraordinary soul? There is no way.

And God has not given any way because he never makes ordinary souls, so he could not think about your problem. He has given you a special, extraordinary soul. He has never given it to anybody. This is just made for you.

What I would like to say to you is, recognize your specialness. There is no need to get it, it is already there—recognize it. Go into your self and feel it. Nobody's thumbprint is like yours—not even the thumbprint. Nobody's eyes are like yours; nobody's sound is like yours; nobody's flavor is like yours. You are absolutely exceptional. There is not a double of you anywhere. Even two twins are different—howsoever alike they look, they are different. They go different ways, they grow different ways, they attain to different kinds of individualities.

This recognition is needed.

You ask: *How can I stop wanting to be special?*

Just listen to the fact. Just go into your being and see, and the effort to be special will disappear. When you know that you are special, the effort will disappear. If you want me to give you some technique so that you can stop being special, then that technique will disturb. Again you are trying to do something, again you are trying to become something. First you were trying to become special, now you are trying not to become special. But trying . . . trying . . . improving in some way or other, but never accepting the you that you are.

I SAY UNTO YOU, Vol. II

Everyone deep in their heart knows that he is special. This is a joke God plays on people. When he makes a new man, and pushes him down towards the earth, he whispers in his ear, "You are special. You are incomparable, you are just unique!"

But this he goes on doing to everybody and everybody

goes on carrying it deep in the heart, although people don't say it as loudly as you are doing it, because people are afraid others may feel offended. And nobody is going to be convinced, so what is the point of saying it? If you tell somebody, "I am special," you cannot convince him because he himself knows that he is special. How can you convince anybody? Yes, maybe sometimes somebody may be convinced, at least pretend to be convinced—if he has some work with you, as a bribe, he may say, "Yes, you are special, you are great." But deep down he knows business is business.

A braggart is telling a friend about his three cars, etc., etc. When he also mentions that he has two kept mistresses in New York, but that he has made his ravishingly beautiful and terribly passionate private secretary pregnant, and must therefore take his gorgeous blond stenographer with him on his business trip to Rio de Janeiro to see the Carnival, the listener suddenly begins to pant, grabs at his own necktie, and has a heart attack.
The braggart interrupts his tale, gets water, pats the victim on the back, etc., etc., and he asks solicitously what the matter is, "Can I help it?" the man gasps. "I am allergic to bullshit."

It is better to keep such bullshit hidden deep down inside yourself, because people are allergic . . .
If you think you are special then you are bound to create misery for yourself. If you think you are higher than others, holier than others, wiser than others, then you will attain to a very very strong ego. And the ego is poison, pure poison. And the more egoistic you become, the more it hurts, because it is a wound. And the more egoistic you become, the more you become unbridged from life, you feel separate from life, you are no more in the flow of existence, you have become a rock in the river. You have become ice-cold; you have lost all warmth, all love. A special person cannot love, because where are you going to find another special person?
Your life will become very difficult if you live with such ideas. And, yes, the ego is so tricky, so cunning, it can give you this new project: "You are so special, become just ordinary." But in your ordinariness you will know you are the

most extraordinarily ordinary man. Nobody is more ordinary
than you! It will be the same game, camouflaged.

That's what so-called humble people go on doing. They
say, "I am the most humble man. I am just the dust on your
feet." But they don't mean it! Don't say, "Yes, I know you
are," otherwise they will never be able to forgive you. They
are waiting for you to say, "You are the most humble man
I have ever seen, you are the most pious man I have ever
seen." Then they will be satisfied, contented. It is ego hiding
behind humbleness.

You cannot drop the ego this way.

You ask: *I feel that I am a very very special person. I am
so special that I want just to be ordinary. Please can you say
something about this?*

No one is special, or everyone is special. No one is ordinary, or everyone is ordinary. Whatsoever you think about
yourself, please think the same about everyone else, and the
problem will be solved. You can choose. If you want the
word "special", you can think you are special, but then everybody is special—not only people, but trees, birds, animals,
rocks—the whole existence is special. Because you come out
of this existence and you will dissolve into this existence.
But if you love the word "ordinary"—which is a beautiful
word, more relaxed—then know that everybody is ordinary,
then the whole existence is ordinary.

One thing to be remembered: whatsoever you think about
yourself, think the same for everybody else and the ego will
disappear. The ego is the illusion that is created by thinking
about yourself in one way and others in another. It is double
thinking. If you drop double thinking, ego dies of its own
accord.

THE BOOK OF THE BOOKS, Vol. I

SPECTATOR Man has become a spectator, somehow he
has become only an observer. He does not participate in
the celebration. That is because of the mind. The mind is
an observer, a spectator, it avoids participation. It would like
to see a movie on love but it would not like to fall in love
itself because that is dangerous. It would love to read a book
like *Siddhartha* or *The Prophet,* but it would not like to

become Siddhartha—that is dangerous. It always keeps aloof. It wants to see everything on the TV screen—there is no danger.

Meditation means participation in the celebration of existence. Don't be just a spectator, participate in the mystery of life. Dance it, sing it, feel it, be it.

THE MIRACLE!

SPEED I can understand your desire, I can understand your thirst, your longing for it. But nothing can be done fast. There is no shortcut. Shortcuts are promised only by the false teachers. There is no shortcut. Growth is arduous and nothing can be done faster than you can absorb. There is a certain limit to your absorption, there is a certain limit to your intelligence. Once you have absorbed something your capacities become bigger, then something more is possible. When you have absorbed that, then your capabilities become still bigger, and something can be done again. And that's how it goes. Growth is slow.

Growth is not like seasonal flowers. Growth is slow. It is like great trees that take hundreds of years to grow. But then they can have a dialogue with the stars. Seasonal flowers are only there for a few weeks. They come fast, they go fast. They are like dreams, they are not really real. They only pretend to be here. Be a real cedar of Lebanon. It takes time, it is hard. When you start rising towards the sky and the clouds and the moon and the stars, it is hard. It is hard because you have to grow roots, deep roots into the earth. The tree grows in the same proportion—if it has to grow a hundred feet into the sky, it has to grow a hundred feet underneath the earth. Those roots take time.

You don't see the roots. Roots are not visible. When you come to a Master, the Master sees your roots. He sees how many roots you have. If you suddenly grow too fast and the roots are not ready to hold you that big, you will fall down, you will topple down. You will not be able to grow at all. And once you have fallen down it is very difficult to get rooted again.

So no Master can help you faster.

This speed mania has to be stopped. There is no need. Each step has to be enjoyed and celebrated . . .

Speed is unspiritual. The very idea of speed is unspiritual. Why not enjoy each moment of life? Then each moment becomes a goal itself. Then each moment is intrinsically valuable; it cannot be sacrificed for anything else. When you are going towards a goal you don't look by the side—the trees are standing there and are waiting for a little caress from you, and the birds have been singing for you. And you are hurrying. How can you look here and there? And a child was there smiling at you, and you missed. And a woman was crying, and you missed her tears. And a rose has flowered, and you were in such a hurry you could not see it.

Yes, you can go at jet speed. Where are you going? You will miss the whole pilgrimage. And if you miss the pilgrimage there is no goal, there is no other goal. Life is its own goal.

SUFIS: THE PEOPLE OF THE PATH, Vol. I

SPIRITUALISM
See Materialism, 2nd Series

SPIRITUALITY Religiousness means the circumference and spirituality means the center. Religiousness has something of spirituality, but only something—a vague radiation, something like a reflection in the lake of the starry night, of the full moon. Spirituality is the *real* thing, religiousness is just a byproduct.

And one of the greatest misfortunes that has happened to humanity is that people are being told to be religious not spiritual. Hence they start decorating your circumference, they cultivate character—character is your circumference. By painting your circumference the center is not changed, but if you change the center, the circumference automatically goes through a transformation.

Change the center, that is spirituality. Spirituality is an inner revolution. It certainly affects your behavior but only as a byproduct; because you are more alert, more aware, naturally your action is different. It has a different quality, ·

a different flavor, a different beauty, but not vice versa . . .

Spirituality belongs to your essential being and religiousness only to the outermost: actions, behavior, morality. Religiousness is formal; going to the church every Sunday is a social affair. And the church is nothing but a kind of club—a Rotary Club, a Lions' Club, and there are many clubs. The church is also a club but with religious pretensions.

The spiritual person belongs to no creed, to no dogma. He cannot belong to any church, Hindu, Christian, Mohammedan. It is impossible for him to belong to any. Spirituality is one, religions are many. My insistence here is on *inner* transformation. I don't teach you religion, I teach you spirituality . . .

Spirituality is rebellion, religiousness is orthodoxy. Spirituality is individuality, religiousness is just remaining part of the crowd psychology. Religiousness keeps you a sheep and spirituality is a lion's roar.

COME, COME, YET AGAIN COME

The world of spirituality is a subtle world; it is more like air than like earth. You can feel it but you cannot see it. You can breathe it and live on it but you cannot hold it in your fist. It is invisible.

THE BOOK OF THE BOOKS, Vol. III

SPONTANEITY Spontaneity simply means now there is nothing to hinder your self-nature from expressing itself. All the rocks have been removed, all the doors have been opened. Now your self-nature can sing its song, it can dance its dance . . .

Spontaneity has not to be created; if it is created it is not spontaneity. Then there is a contradiction: if it is cultivated then it is not spontaneous, obviously. A cultivated spontaneity cannot be true; it will be false, phony, pseudo, it will be only a mask. You may be simply acting, you will not be really spontaneous. And it cannot go very deep; it will remain only something painted from the outside. Just scratch the so-called cultivated, spontaneous person, and all his spontaneity will be gone. He was only acting, he was not really spontaneous.

Real spontaneity comes from the center; it is uncultivated,

that's why we call it spontaneity. There is no way to cultivate it, no way to create it, no need either. But if you want to become an actor, if you want to act, then it is a totally different matter—but remember: any real situation will immediately provoke your mind. It will come rushing towards the surface; all spontaneity will disappear . . .

So I will say the first thing to remember is: spontaneity has to be discovered—or, it will be better to say, rediscovered, because when you were a child you were spontaneous. You have lost it because so much has been cultivated—so many disciplines, so many moralities, virtues, characters. You have learned to play so many roles, that's why you have forgotten the language of being just yourself.

PHILOSOPHIA ULTIMA

The mind lives in past and future—God lives in the present; that's why the mind cannot have an encounter with God. It is impossible. Their dimensions are different; they don't criss-cross. The mind goes on living in the past and in the future—it always bypasses the present; and God is always now. Now is his other name. So only one who becomes spontaneous can have the taste of God.

To be spontaneous means not to live out of the past, not to live out of yesterday. To be spontaneous also means not to live for tomorrow either. When one lives utterly in the present moment, disconnected from the past and the future, one explodes into spontaneity and thousands of flowers bloom there. Life takes on a totally different dimension; it becomes vertical. It attains to height and depth—it is no more shallow. It is no more mundane—it becomes sacred.

And always remember that God is a taste. It is not something to think about—it is something to drink, something to eat, something to digest so it circulates in your blood, in your bones, so that it becomes your very marrow.

THE TONGUE-TIP TASTE OF TAO

STATUE   The image of Gautam the Buddha is exactly the image of meditation carved in marble. It represents something of the inner. The statues of Buddha were the first statues ever made in the world. They don't represent the physiology of Buddha, they have nothing to do with his body;

they represent in a symbolic way what happened to his interiority—the silence, the peace, the tranquility, the purity, the innocence, the state of no-mind.

If you observe the statue of Buddha you will see many things. One is, it is made of white marble. White represents all the colors, it is the synthesis of all the colors. It has the whole spectrum of the rainbow hidden behind it. It is the color of light and light can be divided into seven colors, or if those seven colors are re-synthesized you will have white.

So the first thing is the color white; it represents the synthesis. Life should be a totality, nothing should be rejected; everything should be absorbed, transformed. Everything has some significance, you only have to put it in the right place, in the right context. The color white is the orchestra of all the colors.

Many people have to work in an orchestra. They can work in discord; every player can go on his own way, then there will be only noise, insanity, chaos, ugliness. But they can all join together. They can create a rhythm in which they are all participants. Then the same energy that was turning into insanity becomes the peak of sanity, of health, of wholeness.

The second thing is that Buddha statues are carved out of marble. Marble is something of the earth but it is as if it does not belong to the earth, it is as if it is part of the beyond.

When you see the Taj Mahal on a full-moon night you will understand what I am saying. Then the Taj Mahal does not seem to be part of this world. Suddenly you are transported to a fairyland. It is so beautiful that it is almost unbelievable.

I lived in one place, Jabalpur, for twenty years. Near Jabalpur there is a miracle of nature. I don't think there exists anywhere in the world anything comparable to it—it is just unique: the river Narmada flows between two mountains of marble. For a river to flow between two mountains of marble for at least four or five miles is a rare thing. And on the full-moon night when you enter a boat inside that world, suddenly . . . another dimension of life. It is as if God is real and the world is unreal, as if dreams are real and matter is unreal.

I took one of my teachers of philosophy there. He was a lover of nature so I invited him and took him; he was an old man. I took him to the marble rocks. When he saw them he said "Take the boat very close. I want to touch them and feel whether they really exist or if you are playing a trick." He said to me "I have heard that you can hypnotize people. Don't do such tricks on an old man like me! And at least be respectful of me—I have been your teacher in the university. Take me very close." I took him very close to the mountains, he had to touch them to believe them! That was actually the case: unless you touch them you cannot believe it. It seems such a dreamland.

In the beginning the statues of Buddha were carved in pure white marble just to show that this earth can have something of the beyond. And the shape of the Buddha statue is so symmetrical that one can see the balance, that everything is balanced.

Buddha talked about meditation as the middle way, *majjhim nikaya*. Meditation is really the golden mean; it is neither leaning to the right too much nor to the left too much, remaining exactly in the middle of all the extremes of life. There is success and there is failure and there is richness and there is poverty, and one day you are full of life and one day life slips out of your hands. There is respect and there is insult. Life consists of polar opposites; the man of meditation walks exactly in the middle. Neither success excites him nor failure depresses him—he remains absolutely untouched. That is his symmetry, that is his balance—and that balance you will see in the statue of the Buddha.

In the statue Buddha's eyes are half-closed and half-open. The meditator should not completely close his eyes to the outer, because that too is our reality. And he should not open his eyes too much so that he has nothing left for the inner world. Half-closed eyes represent standing just in-between, available to both worlds, the objective and the subjective, with no division, with no judgment. The meditator will live in the world but will not be of the world . . .

Create a golden mean in your life. Create balance, symmetry; create a synthesis of all the conflicting elements within you so that they become pure white—the *summum bonum,* the highest combination of all the opposites—so that they can become a cosmos instead of a chaos. Then one becomes an image of meditation itself.

A sannyasin has to be an image, a living image of meditation in his moment-to-moment life. In his relationships with the world, with people, in his relationship with himself, while he is alone, when he is with people—in every kind of situation he has to remain still, silent, perceptive, clear, alert, aware. And then life becomes a celebration. So many flowers shower from the beyond that it is impossible to count them . . . as if the whole of infinity starts falling upon you.

Kabir has a very beautiful statement. He says, "When meditation happened for the first time I thought the dewdrop had slipped into the ocean. That was my first contact with meditation. It was as if the dewdrop had slipped into the ocean. But as I became more and more accustomed to the experience I had to change my statement. Finally I discovered that it is just vice versa: the ocean has slipped into the dewdrop."

Both are true. You can say the dewdrop has slipped into the ocean—that is the experience of the beginner; you can say the ocean has slipped into the dewdrop—that is the experience of the *siddha,* of one who has arrived.

But the beginning is the end, because the beginning contains the end. The first step is also the last step.

NIRVANA: NOW OR NEVER

See also Symbols

STEPS One should not think in terms of limits; one should get rid of all ideas of limitations. That's the whole process of sannyas. Knowing that "I am not the body," is the beginning of a great pilgrimage. Then knowing that "I am not the mind either," is a further step. Then finally knowing that "I am not even my feelings," is the last step.

With these three steps the journey is over because on the

fourth step you discover your being and that being is vast, infinite, as vast as the ocean, as vast as the sky. To experience it is to experience God. And to experience it is to experience bliss, ecstasy.

That is the only experience worth striving for.

NO MAN IS AN ISLAND

STOMACH The stomach has to change continuously with the mind. If you are angry, you have a certain type of stomach. If you are loving, you have a different type of stomach. When you are angry you can immediately feel a great tension in the stomach, hot, boiling. When you are loving, you can feel a certain relaxation in the stomach. When you are happy, you have a certain stomach, and when you are unhappy, you have a different stomach.

That's how people who are continuously in stress and tension, start having ulcers in the stomach. That simply says that a continuous strain in the mind creates wounds in the stomach. There is no other way for them unless they change their minds.

We have an expression—"I cannot stomach it." That's exactly the right expression. There are things you cannot stomach. Everything has to go into the stomach. Somebody insults you and you say, "I cannot stomach it. I cannot swallow it." But whatsoever you swallow goes into the stomach, and it will have its reaction.

When the mind starts changing, parallel to it, the stomach starts changing. This is my observation, that people who are doing meditation will have to come to a moment where their stomachs have to be readjusted.

That's why meditators came to believe in vegetarianism. That was not a philosophy. It had nothing to do with any philosophical attitude. Just through deep meditation they came to understand that they could not stomach many things. It was impossible.

Vegetarianism is nothing but a byproduct of deep meditation. If a person goes on meditating, by and by he will see that it has become impossible to eat meat. Not that somebody says not to; at least I don't. Whatsoever you feel like eating, eat. But if you go on in meditation one day you will simply not be able to stomach it; it will be nauseating.

The very idea to eat meat will be vomit-inducing and will not be tolerated by your stomach. Now you are feeling that you are in such a smooth world, so subtle and refined, that you cannot believe how you used to eat meat before. It looks impossible—and for what?

We can stomach meat and things like that because many animal instincts are there in the mind: anger, greed, hatred, violence. When those things disappear from the mind, then the parallel will disappear from the stomach.

THE CYPRESS IN THE COURTYARD

STRANGER   The man of meditation becomes a stranger in the world because everybody is living through the mind and he is living without the mind. He is moving with people who will not be able to understand his language. He will be able to understand their language because he has lived their way too. He has known both lives, life with the mind and life without the mind, hence he will be able to understand them but they will not be able to understand him. They are bound to crucify such a man, they will be afraid because he is an absolute stranger.

If you know only Chinese and you come to India where nobody knows Chinese you will not be such a stranger; at least you can manage through gestures. The basic gestures are the same. If you are thirsty you can make a gesture, if you are hungry you can make a gesture, if you want to sleep you can make a gesture. Slowly you can get people to understand you and you can understand them. A bridge is possible.

Even if some day man reaches a planet where he finds a totally different kind of people, there will still be a possibility to communicate. But when a Buddha or a Jesus or a Zarathustra walks on earth he is really an outsider. He cannot make any gestures because the thing he has come to know is inexpressible in any way, by any means; hence he looks very dangerous, so different—qualitatively different.

But these outsiders are the salt of the earth. There is some joy on earth, some song, some splendor because of these few outsiders. They have brought something of God into the world, something of the beyond to the earth. Of course they have suffered much; still they have given to the world that which is the greatest treasure . . .

Only a man of meditation can become a vehicle for joy, for bliss, for celebration. Meditation makes him a stranger in the world but at the same time, simultaneously makes him immensely blissful. Even if you take his life he loses nothing because he has attained to something which is far more than life itself; he has found eternal life.

I'M NOT AS THUNK AS YOU DRINK I AM

STRENGTH   There are two possibilities open to man: either he can move in search of manly strength or he can move in the search of womanly strength. The manly strength is gross, aggressive, violent; the feminine strength is subtle, non-aggressive, non-violent. Politics remains in the first, religion moves into the second.

To be strong is good, but in the feminine way. The rock is strong in the masculine way, the water is strong in the feminine way, and ultimately the water wins over the rock. Hence Lao Tzu says: My message is, follow the watercourse way. In the beginning the rock seems to be so unconquerable and the water so humble, so polite, so liquid. But in the end, the rock will be gone, it will turn into sand, and the water will still be there.

There is a strength in a big, strong cedar; that is manly strength. And there is also strength is the grass; that is feminine strength. When the strong wind comes the cedar will resist and the grass will bow down. The cedar can fall because of its resistance, and once it falls there is no way of getting up, but the grass will be back again when the wind is gone. The wind has not done any harm to it, on the contrary, it has been a blessing because it has taken all its dust.

Again, Lao Tzu says: Be like the grass—don't be like a proud cedar—bending, surrendering, liquid.

YOU AIN'T SEEN NOTHIN' YET

STRESS   A Canadian psychoanalyst, Doctor Hans Selye, has been working his whole life on only one problem—that is stress. And he has come to certain very profound conclusions. One is that stress is not always wrong; it can be used in beautiful ways. It is not necessarily negative, but if we think that it is negative, that it is not good, then we create problems. Stress in itself can be used as a stepping stone, it can become a creative force. But ordinarily we have been taught down the ages that stress is bad, that when you are in any kind of stress you become afraid. And your fear makes it even more stressful; the situation is not helped by it.

For example, there is some situation in the market and that is creating a stress. The moment you feel that there is some tension, some stress, you become afraid that this should not be so: "I have to relax." Now, trying to relax will not help, because you cannot relax; in fact, trying to relax will create a new kind of stress. The stress is there and you are trying to relax and you cannot, so you are complicating the problem.

When stress is there use it as creative energy. First, accept it; there is no need to fight with it. Accept it, it is perfectly okay. It simply says "The market is not going well, something is going wrong," Mm?—"You may be a loser". . . or something. Stress is simply an indication that the body is getting ready to fight with it. Now you try to relax or you take painkillers or you take tranquilizers; you are going against the body. The body is getting ready to fight a certain situation, a certain challenge that is there: enjoy the challenge!

Even if sometimes you can't sleep in the night there is no need to be worried. Work it out, use that energy that is coming up: walk up and down, go for a run, go for a long walk, plan what you want to do, what the mind wants to do. Rather than trying to go to sleep, which is not possible, use the situation in a creative way. It simply says that the body is ready to fight with the problem; this is no time to relax. Relaxation can be done later on.

In fact if you have lived your stress totally you will come to a relaxation automatically; you can go on only so far, then the body automatically relaxes. If you want to relax in the middle you create trouble; the body cannot relax in the middle. It is almost as if an Olympic runner is getting ready, just waiting for the whistle, the signal, and he will be off, he will go like the wind. He is full of stress; now that is not time to relax. If he takes a tranquilizer he will never be of any use in the race. Or if he relaxes there and tries to do TM he will lose all. He has to use his stress: the stress is boiling, it is gathering energy. He is becoming more and more vital and potential. Now he has to sit on this stress and use it as energy, as fuel.

Selye has given a new name for this kind of stress: he calls it *eustress*, like euphoria; it is a positive stress. When the runner has run he will fall into deep sleep; the problem is solved. Now there is no problem, the stress disappears of its own accord.

So try this too: when there is a stressful situation don't freak out, don't become afraid of it. Go into it, use it to fight with. A man has tremendous energy and the more you use it, the more you have of it . . .

When it comes and there is a situation, fight, do all that you can do, really go madly into it. Allow it, accept and welcome it. It is good, it prepares you to fight. And when you have worked it out, you will be surprised: great relaxation comes, and that relaxation is not created by you. Maybe for two, three days you cannot sleep and then for forty-eight hours you can't wake up and that is okay!

We go on carrying many wrong notions—for example, that every person has to sleep eight hours every day. It depends what the situation is. There are situations when no sleep is needed: your house is on fire, and you are trying to sleep. Now that is not possible and that should not be possible, otherwise who is going to put that fire out? And when the house is on fire, all other things are put aside; suddenly your body is ready to fight the fire. You will not feel sleepy. When the fire is gone and everything settled you may fall asleep for a long period, and that will do.

Everybody does not need the same length of sleep either. A few people can do with three hours, two hours, four hours, five hours, six, eight, ten, twelve. People differ, there is no norm. And about stress also people differ.

There are two kinds of people in the world: One can be called the racehorse type and the other is the turtle type. If the racehorse type is not allowed to go fast, to go into things with speed, there will be stress; he has to be given his pace. And you are a racehorse! So forget about relaxation and things like that; they are not for you. Those are

for turtles like me! Mm? So just be a racehorse, that is natural
for you, and don't think of the joys that turtles are enjoying; that is not for you. You have a different kind of joy.
If a turtle starts becoming a racehorse he will be in the same
trouble!

You can get out of the market. It is so easy; the mind says
"Get out of the market, forget about it. Just come and be
here in the ashram." But you will not feel good. You will
feel more stress arising because you will not feel your energy
is engaged, and I will have to make you a racehorse again
in something else . . .

So accept your nature. You are a fighter, a warrior; you
have to be that way, and that's your joy. Now, no need to
be afraid; go into it whole-heartedly. Fight with the market,
compete in the market, do all that you really want to do.
Don't be afraid of the consequences, accept the stress . . .
Once you accept the stress it will disappear. And not only
that, you will feel very happy because you have started using
it; it is a kind of energy.

Don't listen to people who say to relax; that is not for you.
Your relaxation will come only after you have earned it by
hard labor. One has to understand one's type. Once the type
is understood there is no problem; then one can follow a
clean-cut line. Stress is going to be your way of life.
DON'T BITE MY FINGER, LOOK WHERE I'M POINTING

See also Hypertension, 1st Series

STUDENT See Disciple, 1st Series

STUDY In India we have a word, *swasthya*. It can be translated as study, but it misses the whole point. In fact, *swasthya*
means self-study, studying the self. It is not a question of
reading scriptures, it is not a question of going more and
more into information. Rather it is a question of going more
and more inwards, into transformation.

And when Sufis say, "Study with us," they simply mean
"Be with us." Being with a Master is the study; just being
with the Master, *adab*, just being in the presence of the one
who knows, drinking his presence, savoring his being, tasting

him, digesting his energy. You will be surprised: if you come to a Sufi study circle, it has nothing to do with the study circles that exist in the West. In a western study circle you read a book, then questions are raised and then questions answered, and discussion follows.

In a Sufi study group no question is raised, no book is read. People sit silently for hours, and maybe somebody starts swaying. But the one thing to be remembered is: nobody has to do anything. If it happens it is good. Somebody sometimes starts saying something, but the rule has to be followed: nobody should try to say anything. If it happens on its own, if one finds that something needs to be said, on its own is ready to be said, is just on the tongue, wants to come out "in spite of me," then it's okay.

It is just like the Quaker prayer meeting. Quakers learned it from the Sufis. In the Middle Ages, Sufis penetrated deep into European countries. Quakers learned how to sit silently from the Sufis. The Quakers sit silently for hours, then somebody may stand up and may start saying something; but those statements are very inspired. They are not from the person himself—as if God has taken possession of him. He has become just a hollow bamboo, a flute, and some unknown energy has started singing through him.

The rule has to be followed. But in a Quaker group it is very difficult to follow the rule, because the basic thing is missing—the Master is missing.

In a Sufi group the Master is a must.

THE SECRET

SUBSTITUTES Knowledge never makes you blissful; on the contrary it makes you more and more miserable. And it can be easily observed, it is a factual phenomenon. As man has grown more and more in knowledge, he has become more and more miserable. Whenever a society is well-educated, people start feeling life is meaningless, people start feeling a kind of deep boredom.

Move to the primitive societies, go to the aboriginals who are still living as they were five thousand years ago and you will be surprised by one thing: they don't have anything to be blissful about but they are blissful. They don't have big airplanes and palaces and television sets, they have no technology, they are living in a primitive way, but one thing is very clear, very obvious, they are blissful—poor, but blissful. Why is it so?

Move to a very knowledgeable society where education has become available to almost one hundred percent of the people and you will be surprised: people look very miserable. They have lost something rather than gaining. In accumulating knowledge they have forgotten to move into the world of wisdom. They have made knowledge a substitute, and remember substitutes never fulfill.

You love a woman—that is a tremendously beautiful experience—but you can get a substitute with a prostitute. Now in America they have substitute wives. And psychologists are suggesting to people to go to a substitute just for a change because they are so bored with their wife, bored with their family. But a substitute wife is after all a substitute; it is a plastic flower. She does not love you, you don't love her. At the most it can be sexual, but it can't have intimacy; it can never be spiritual. You use the woman and the woman uses you. It is a monetary relationship; you are ready to pay, she is ready to sell.

Now there are male prostitutes also. Of course not in poor countries like India, but in England, in America you can find male prostitutes. These are the great things that are happening through Women's Liberation. If men can have women prostitutes, why cannot women enjoy male prostitutes?—equality after all is equality. So people can go to foolish extremes, absurd extremes.

But slowly slowly everything is becoming a substitute. The true thing goes on disappearing. Instead of the true thing some substitute takes its place because a substitute can be manufactured, it is easily available, sellable, marketable. The real thing is not sellable or marketable; you have to deserve it.

Knowledge is a substitute. You can go to any university, to any library, to any museum, and you can accumulate much knowledge, but for wisdom you cannot go anywhere. In fact you have to stop going, you have to be very still and silent. You have to dig deep within yourself, to the very rock-bottom of your being. It is arduous, but when you are absolutely silent, when all thoughts have disappeared, when your eyes are as clear as a mirror without any dust, you become capable of seeing that which is. That is wisdom.

And simultaneously, as wisdom happens your heart starts dancing. In fact for the first time you hear the *real* heart beat. For the first time you hear the song of the heart. For the first time your whole being—body, mind, heart, soul—are all dancing together and there is tremendous grace. My sannyasins have to achieve it. That's the only thing worth achieving, a blissful wisdom.

THE GOLDEN WIND

SUCCESS Never think of success. Success is a natural byproduct. If you work really sincerely upon yourself, success will follow you just as your shadow follows you. Success has not to be the goal. That's why Lu-tsu says, "Work quietly, silently, untroubled by any idea of success or failure."

And remember if you think too much of success you will constantly be thinking of failure too. They come together, they come in one package. Success and failure cannot be divided from each other. If you think of success, somewhere deep down there will be a fear also. Who knows whether you are going to make it or not? You may fail. Success takes you into the future, gives you a greed game, an ego projection, ambition, and the fear also gives you a shaking, a trembling—you may fail. The possibility of failure makes you waver. And with this wavering, with this greed, with this ambition, your work will not be quiet. Your work will become a turmoil; you will be working here and looking there. You will be walking on this road and looking somewhere faraway in the sky.

I have heard about a Greek astrologer who was studying stars, and one night, a very starry night, he fell into a well. Because he was watching the stars and moving about—and he was so concerned with the stars that he forgot where he was—he moved closer and closer to a well and fell into it. Some woman, an old woman who used to live nearby, rushed up, hearing the sound. She looked inside the well, brought a rope, and pulled the great astrologer out. The astrologer was very thankful. He said to the old woman, "You don't know me but I am the royal astrologer, specially appointed by the king. My fee is very large—only very rich people can afford to enquire about their future. But you have saved my life. You can come tomorrow to me and I will show you: I will read your hand, I will look into your birth chart and I will interpret your stars, and your whole future will be plainly clear to you." The old woman started laughing. She said, "Forget all about it. You cannot see even one step ahead, that there is a well. How can you predict my future? All bullshit!"

Don't look ahead too much, otherwise you will miss the immediate step. Success comes, Lu-tsu says, of its own accord. Leave it to itself. This existence is a very rewarding existence, nothing goes unrewarded.

That is the whole Indian philosophy of *karma:* nothing goes unrewarded or punished. If you do something wrong, punishment follows like a shadow. If you do something right, rewards are on the way. You need not bother about them, you need not think at all, not even an iota of your consciousness need be involved with them; they come— their coming is automatic.

When you move on the road do you look again and again for your shadow—whether it is following you or not? And if somebody looks back again and again to see whether the shadow is following or not, you will think that he is mad. The shadow follows; it is inevitable. So if your work is in the right direction, with the right effort, with the totality of your being, the reward follows automatically.

THE SECRET OF SECRETS, Vol. I

SUCHNESS First try to understand the word "suchness"; Buddha depends on that word very much. In Buddha's own language it is *tathata,* suchness. The whole Buddhist meditation consists of living in this word, living with this word so deeply that the word disappears and you become the suchness . . .

You eat in suchness, you sleep in suchness, you breathe in suchness, you love in suchness, you weep in suchness. It becomes your very style; you need not bother about it, you need not think about it, it is the way you are. That is what I mean by the word "imbibe". You imbibe it, you digest it, it flows in your blood, it goes deep in your bones, it reaches to the beat of your heart. You accept.

Remember, the word "accept" is not very good. It is loaded because of you, not because of the word—because you accept only when you feel helpless. You accept grudgingly, you accept half-heartedly. You accept only when you cannot do anything, but deep down you still wish; you would have been happy if it was otherwise. You accept like a beggar, not like a king—and the difference is great.

If the wife leaves or the husband leaves, finally you come to accept it. What can be done? You weep and cry and many nights you brood and worry, and many nightmares and suffering around you. Then what to do? Time heals, not understanding. Time—and remember, time is needed only because you are not understanding, otherwise instant healing happens. Time is needed because you are not understanding. So by and by—six months, eight months, a year—things become dim in the memory, they are lost, covered with much dust. And a gap of one year comes; by and by you forget.

When you really accept, in that attitude of suchness there is no grudge, you are not helpless. Simply you understand that this is the nature of things. For example, if I want to go out of this room, I will go out through the door, not through the wall, because to try and enter the wall will be just hitting my head against it, it is simply foolish. This is the nature of the wall: to hinder—so you don't try to pass through it. This is the nature of the door: that you can pass through it—because the door is empty, you can pass through it.

When a Buddha accepts, he accepts things like wall and door. He passes through the door, he says that is the only way. First you try to pass through the wall, and you wound yourself in many millions of ways. And when you cannot get out—crushed, defeated, depressed, fallen—then you crawl towards the door. You could have gone through the door in the first place. Why did you try and start fighting with the wall?

If you can look at things with a clarity, you simply don't

do things like trying to make a door out of a wall. If love disappears, it has disappeared; now if there is a wall, don't try to go through it. Now the door is no longer there, the heart is no longer there, the heart has opened to somebody else. And you are not alone here, there are others also.

The door is no more for you, it has become a wall. Don't try, and don't knock your head on it, you will be wounded unnecessarily. And when you are wounded, defeated, even the door will not be such a beautiful thing to pass through.

Simply look at things. If something is natural don't try to force any unnatural thing on it. Choose the door—be out of it. Every day you are doing the foolishness of passing through the wall. Then you become tense, and then you feel continuous confusion; anguish becomes your very life, the core of it—and then you ask for a meditation.

But why in the first place? Why not look at the facts as they are? Why can't you look at the facts? Because your wishes are there too much, you go on hoping against all hope. That's why you have become so hopeless a case.

Just look: whenever there is a situation don't desire anything because desire will lead you astray. Don't wish and don't imagine. Simply look at the fact with your total consciousness available and suddenly a door opens. And then you never move through the wall, you move through the door, unscratched—then you remain unloaded.

HSIN HSIN MING: THE BOOK OF NOTHING
(Original Title: NEITHER THIS NOR THAT)

SUFFERING Growth in itself has no suffering in it: suffering comes from your resistance towards growth. Suffering is created by you because you resist continuously, you don't allow it to happen. You are afraid to go totally with it; you go only half-heartedly. Hence the suffering because you become divided, you become split. A part of you cooperates and a part of you is against it, resists it. This conflict inside you creates suffering.

So drop the idea—many people have that idea that you have to suffer if you are to grow. It is sheer nonsense. If you cooperate totally there is no suffering at all. If you are in a let-go, instead of suffering you will rejoice. Every moment of it will be a moment of bliss and benediction.

So don't throw the responsibility on growth. Our mind is very tricky and cunning: it always throws the responsibility on somebody, on something; it never takes the responsibility on itself. *You* are the cause of suffering.

If you can remember three things . . . The first is: drop the past if you want to grow, because it is from the past that resistance arises. You are always judging from the past. The past is no more, it is absolutely irrelevant, but it goes on interfering. You go on judging; according to it you go on saying, "This is right and that is wrong," and all those ideas of right and wrong, all those judgments are coming from something which is dead. Your dead past remains so heavy on you that it does not allow you to move.

Drop the past completely and you will be surprised: much of the suffering has disappeared.

The second thing to remember is: don't create expectations for the future. If you are expecting then again you will create suffering, because things are not going to happen according to *you;* things are going to happen according to the whole. The wave, the small wave in the ocean, cannot be the deciding factor. The *ocean* decides; the wave has to be in a state of let-go. If the wave wants to go to the east, then there is going to be trouble, then there is going to be pain. If the winds are not going to the east, if the ocean is not willing, then what is the wave going to do? It will suffer. It will call it fate, it will call it circumstances, social conditions, the economic structure, the capitalist society, the bourgeois culture, the Freudian unconscious . . . and now you will call it growth pains. But you are simply shifting the responsibility.

The real thing is that you are suffering from your expectations. When they are not fulfilled—and they are never going to be fulfilled—frustration arises, failure arises, and you feel neglected, as if existence does not care for you.

Drop the expectations for the future. Remain open, remain available to whatsoever happens, but don't plan ahead. Don't make any psychological, fixed ideas about the future—that things should be like this—and more suffering will disappear. These two are the root causes of suffering.

And the third is: the Human Potential Movement lacks something essential. It tries to help you to grow, but it has not yet been able to create a meditative space in you. So there is constant struggle, effort, will, but no relaxation, no rest. Hence the third thing to be remembered and all suffering will disappear: create meditative energy, create a meditative space within you. Western methods lack that something very essential.

That's why here in my commune the effort is to use all the western methods side by side with all the eastern methods. This may be the only place in the whole world today where East and West are really meeting, and not meeting in a diplomatic way as they meet in the UN. Here they are really merging—not politically, not diplomatically, because a diplomatic meeting is not a meeting, it is only a facade, it is pseudo. It is a love meeting that is happening here. For the first time East and West are in a love affair . . .

My effort here is to create the first synthesis between extroversion and introversion and help man to become so capable of both, together, simultaneously, so easily able to move from extroversion to introversion and from introversion to extroversion that there is no need to divide man into such categories. Man can become so fluid.

It is as simple as when you come out of your house. You don't think that you are becoming extrovert coming out of your house. When you feel it is cold inside and outside there are no clouds and it is so sunny you come out, but you don't think at all. You don't decide that "Now I want to be an extrovert." Or when the sun becomes too hot and you start feeling the heat, you don't make a deliberate decision that "I should go in. Now I want to be an introvert." No, when the sun is too hot you simply move in! And when inside is cold you come out. Coming out of your house or going in to the house is not a problem at all, because you are free from the inner and the outer.

My effort here is to help you to be free from the inner and the outer, because you are neither the inner nor the outer—you are something transcendental to both. The inner and the outer are just parts of your personality; it is the house in which you live which has an outside and an inside. But your awareness has no inside and no outside.

So these three things to be remembered: drop the past, drop future expectations, and third, create a synthesis between extroversion and introversion . . . and all misery disappears.

It is not inevitable for a spiritual seeker to suffer. You suffer because you are not aware of your own responsibility. It is not because of growth that you suffer. You suffer because you are unconscious of your resistance, of your past-orientation, of your future expectations, and you are unconscious that you don't have any meditative space with you.

BOOK OF THE BOOKS, Vol. XI

It is a training, suffering is a training—because these is no possibility of becoming mature without suffering. It is like fire: the gold, to be pure, has to pass through it. If the gold says, "Why?" then the gold remains impure, worthless. Only by passing through the fire will all that is not gold be burned, and only the purest gold will remain. That's what liberation is all about: a maturity, a growth so ultimate that only the purity, only the innocence remains, and all that was useless has been burned.

There is no other way to realize it. There cannot be any other way to realize it. If you want to know what satiety is, you will have to know hunger. If you want to avoid hunger, you will avoid satiety also. If you want to know what deep quenching is, you have to know thirst, deep thirst. If you say, "I don't want to be thirsty," then you will miss that beautiful moment of deep quenching of the thirst. If you want to know what light is, you will have to pass through a dark night; the dark night prepares you to realize what light is. If you want to know what life is, you will have to pass through death; death creates the sensitivity in you to know life. They are not opposites; they are complementary.

There is nothing which is opposite in the world; everything is complementary. "This" world exists so that you can know "that" world; "this" exists to know "that". The material exists to know the spiritual; the hell exists to come to heaven. This is the purpose. And if you want to avoid one you avoid both, because they are two aspects of the same thing. Once you understand, there is no suffering: you know this is training, a discipline. Discipline is to be hard. It has to be hard because only then will real maturity come out of it.

Yoga says this world exists as a training school, a learning school—don't avoid it and don't try to escape from it. Rather live it, and live it so totally that you need not be forced again to live it. That's the meaning when we say that an enlightened person never comes back—there is no need. He has passed all the examination that life provides. He need not come back.

YOGA: THE ALPHA AND THE OMEGA, Vol. V

The basic thing is not to ask what to do so that suffering is not created. The basic thing is to know that you are the creator of your suffering. Next time whenever a real situation arises and you are in suffering, remember to find out whether you are the cause of it. And if you can find out that you are the cause of it, the suffering will disappear, and the same suffering will not appear again—impossible.

But don't deceive yourself. You can—that's why I say it. When you are suffering you can say, "Yes, I have created this suffering," but deep down you know that someone else has created it. Your wife has created it, your husband has created it, someone else has created it, and this is simply a consolation because you cannot do anything. You console yourself: "No one has created it, I have created it myself, and by and by I will stop it."

But knowledge is instant transformation; there is no "by and by". If you understand that you have created it, it will drop immediately. And it is not going to come up again. If it comes again, it means the understanding has not gone deep.

So there is no need to find out what to do, and how to stop. The only need is to go deep and to find out who is really the cause of it. If others are the cause then it cannot be stopped, because you cannot change the whole world. If you are the cause, only then can it be stopped.

That's why I insist that only religion can lead humanity towards non-suffering. Nothing else can lead, because everyone else believes that the suffering is caused by others; only religion says that suffering is caused by you. So religion makes you the master of your destiny. You are the cause of your suffering, hence you can be the cause of your bliss.

THE BOOK OF THE SECRETS, Vol. IV

SUFI Idries Shah has condemned the definition of "sufi" from *suf*—wool—on exactly the same grounds as I am approving of it. He says that Sufis are so alert about symbols how can they choose wool as their symbol? The wool represents the animal and Idries Shah says Sufis cannot choose the animal as a symbol. They are the people of God—why should they choose the animal? He seems very logical, and he may appeal to many people.

But on exactly the same grounds I approve the definition. To me, to be an animal means to be innocent, not to know morality, not to know immorality. To be an animal is not a condemnation. A saint is more like animals than like you, than like the so-called human beings. The human beings are not natural beings, they are very unnatural, artificial, plastic. Their whole life is a life of deception. If you touch somebody's face you will never touch his face, you touch only his mask. And remember, your hand is also not true. It has a glove on it. Even lovers don't touch each other; even in love you are not innocent; even in love you are not without masks. But when you want to love God you have to be without masks. You have to drop all deceptions. You have to be authentically whatsoever you are, to be choicelessly whatsoever you are. In that primal innocence God descends.

So the reasons Idries Shah finds to condemn the definition that Sufi comes from *suf* are exactly the reasons I approve it . . .

By asserting the symbol of the animal Sufis declare, "We are simple people. We don't know what is good and what is bad. We know only God, and whatsoever happens is his gift. We accept it. We are not doers on our own accord." This is the first meaning of the word Sufi.

There is another possibility: the word Sufi can be derived from *sufa*—purity, cleanliness, purification. That too is good. When you live a life of choicelessness a natural purity comes. But remember, this purity has nothing of morality in it. It does not mean pure in the sense of being good; it means pure in the sense of being divine, not in the sense of being good. Pure simply means pure of all ideas, good and bad both. Purity means transcendence. One has no idea at all, no prejudices. One trusts life so utterly that one need not have any ideas, one can live without ideas. When ideas are there in the mind they create impurity, they create wounds. When you are too full of ideas, you are too full of dirt. All ideas are dirty. Yes, even the idea of God is a dirty idea, because ideas are dirty.

For a Sufi, God is not an idea, it is his lived reality. It is not somewhere sitting on a throne high in the heavens, no—it is herenow, it is all over the place, it is everywhere. God is just a name for the totality of existence.

Purity means a contentless mind—so please don't be misguided by the word "purity". It does not mean a man who has a good character. It does not mean a man who behaves according to the Ten Commandments. It does not mean a man who is respected by the society as a good man.

A Sufi has never been respected by the society. A Sufi lives such a rebellious life that the society has almost always been murdering Sufis, crucifying them—because the Sufi makes you aware of your falsity. He becomes a constant sermon against your artificiality, against your ugliness, against your inner inhumanity to human beings, against your masks, against all that you are and represent. A Sufi becomes a constant pain in the neck to the so-called society and to the so-called respectable people.

I have heard . . . It happened that Abu Yasid, a Sufi mystic, was praying—these are parables, remember, they are not historical facts—and God spoke to Abu Yasid and said, "Yasid, now you have become one of my chosen people. Should I declare it to the world?" Abu Yasid laughed. He said, "Yes, you can—if you want me to be crucified. Declare. You declared about Al-Hillaj and what happened? They crucified him. Whenever you declare that somebody has attained, people crucify him immediately. They don't love you and they cannot tolerate your people. So if you want me to be crucified, declare." And it is said that God never declared about Abu Yasid. He kept quiet.

This has been the case.

Somebody asked Al-Hillaj Mansoor, the greatest mystic ever, "What is the ultimate in Sufi experience?" Al-Hillaj said, "Tomorrow, you will see what the ultimate in Sufi experience is." Nobody knew what was going to happen the next day. The man asked, "Why not today?" Al-Hillaj said, "You just wait. It is going to happen tomorrow—the ultimate." And the next day he was crucified. And when he was crucified he shouted loudly for his friend who had asked the question. He said, "Where are you hiding in the crowd? Now come on and see the ultimate in Sufism. This is what it is."

If you start living in God you become intolerable to the so-called society. The society lives in hypocrisy. It cannot tolerate truth. Truth has to be crucified. It can love the Church but it cannot love Christ. It can love the Vatican pope but it cannot love Jesus. When Jesus is gone then it is good—you can go on worshipping him. When Mansoor is gone you can go on talking about him. But when he is there he is a fire. Only those who are ready to be consummed by the fire will be ready to fall in love with Mansoor.

Sufa means purity; purity in the sense that there is no content in the mind any more. Mind has disappeared. There is no mind, no thinking, no thought. It is a state of *satori, samadhi.*

There is another possibility and that too is beautiful. And I accept all these possibilities. The third possibility is from another word, *sufia,* which means: chosen as a friend by God.

Sufis say that you cannot search for God unless he has already chosen you. How can you search for God if he has not already searched for you? All initiative is from the side of God. He is searching for you, he is desiring you, he goes on groping for you—"Where are you?" When he chooses somebody only then do you start choosing him. You may not know it—because when he chooses, how can you know?

The same is true about a Master. You think that you choose a Master? Nonsense, just nonsense! It is always the Master who chooses you. The very idea that you choose the Master is egoistic. How can you choose the Master? How will you know in the first place who the Master is? How will you decide? What criterions have you got? You cannot choose a Master, the Master chooses you.

SUFIS: THE PEOPLE OF THE PATH, Vol. I

The Sufi story is not a riddle, it is a parable. It is not a shock, it is not a sword; it is persuasion, it is seduction. It is the way of the lover. It is very gentle and soft and feminine.

Zen is very masculine, Sufism is feminine. The Zen story drives you mad: through creating a maddening state in the mind it helps you to go beyond it. It drives you crazy! The Sufi story intoxicates you slowly, slowly but inevitably.

The Sufi story has a poetry in it, a rhythm. The Sufi story has to be contemplated, not meditated upon. The Zen story has to be meditated upon. The Sufi story has to be imbibed, sipped like tea, enjoyed in a relaxed mood. The Zen story has to be penetrated with a very, very concentrated mind, in a very tense attitude, in intensity. You have to focus all your energies on the story. You have to forget the whole world; only that small absurd story exists. And you know it cannot be solved, and yet you have to put your whole energy into it. And all the time you know that this is absurd, it is not going to lead you anywhere, but the Master says, "Focus! Concentrate! Pay attention! Look into the riddle of the story!"

The Sufi story has to be listened to just like a story. Sufis are great storytellers. They will sip tea or coffee, they will sit together in a cozy place, warm. The story will start, and the Master will tell the story. And the story only gives glimpses, hints, but very potential, very penetrating. All that is needed on the part of the disciple is to listen, not attentively but sympathetically, with an open heart, not with any tension. The story has to be enjoyed. It reveals its mysteries when you are enjoying it.

THE WISDOM OF THE SANDS, Vol. I

Rumi says, "Hey! Drink this fine fiery wine, these needles of fire, and fall so drunk that you will not wake on the day of resurrection."

The way of the Sufi is the way of the drunkard, the dancer, who becomes almost intoxicated in his dancing, who is transported through his dance. He is inebriated; his dance is psychedelic.

It is said that Mohammed once said to Ali, "You are of me, and I am of you." When he heard this, Ali became ecstatic and involuntarily started dancing. What else can you do, when a man like Mohammed says to you, "You are of me, and I am of you?" How to receive this? Ali did well.

And remember, it is not anything that he did. It was involuntary. He started dancing; out of ecstasy the dance started flowing.

Another time, Mohammed said to Jafar, "You are like me in both looks and character." Here again, in *wajd,* Jafar started dancing. What else to do? When Mohammed must have looked into the eyes of Jafar, *wajd, samadhi,* was created, the transfer beyond the scriptures happened. How to receive this? How not to dance? It would have been impossible not to dance. Jafar danced.

It is said, "The enrapturing of the Sufi by God, or rather the "pull" of God, keeps the Sufis continually in spiritual, inner dance and movement . . ." It is not that the Sufi dances—God keeps dancing in him. What can he do?

"Whenever a wave of such divine rapture strikes the heart of the Sufi, it creates great waves in the lake of his inner being . . ." He is just a receptacle. To say that the Sufi is dancing is not right. The Sufi is being danced. He cannot help it, he is helpless. Something is pouring into him and it is too much; it starts overflowing in his dancing and singing.

"This, in turn, causes his body to move. Upon seeing such movement non-Sufis have often supposed that the Sufi is dancing. In reality, however, it is the waves of the ocean of God that are tossing and turning the anchorless vessel that is the heart of the Sufi."

On the surface, from the outside, the Sufi seems to be dancing. But he is not dancing, because there is no dancer. It is pure dance. God has taken possession of him. The Sufi is drunk, intoxicated. His state is that of non-being. He is anchorless. The waves of the ocean toss and turn. First his inner being is stirred, great joy arises there; and then it starts spreading towards his body . . .

The way of the Sufi is the way of dance, song, celebration.

THE SECRET

See also Hiding, 2nd Series

SUICIDE Each suicide has something unique about it—as each life has something unique about it. Your life is yours and your death is also going to be yours. Sometimes it is possible that your life may not be yours, but it is not possible that your death may not be yours.

Life can be anonymous. If you live with others, you can compromise too much, you can imitate—but death is always unique because death is alone. You die alone. There is no society. They don't exist in your death. The crowd, the mass is there when you are alive, but when you die you die absolutely alone, utterly alone.

Death has a quality.

So sometimes it happens that a man may commit suicide because he has become tired of the anonymous existence. He has become tired of all the compromises that one has to make in order to live. That's why van Gogh committed suicide—he was a rare man, one of the greatest painters ever. But he had to make compromises every moment of his life. He got tired of those compromises; he could no longer tolerate being part of the crowd mind. He killed himself in order to be himself. If he had been in the East there would have been another alternative: suicide or sannyas. These are the two alternatives which every man who has some sense of life, of individuality, has to choose between.

In the West nothing like sannyas has been in existence. If you become a Christian monk that is again a compromise; you still remain part of the society. Even if you go out of the society you remain part of it. The society goes on controlling you—it has a remote control system. It does not allow you to really go out of it. You remain a Christian, you remain a Catholic, even when you have moved to a monastery. It does not make much difference.

In the East, sannyas has a totally different flavor. The moment you become a sannyasin you are no longer a Hindu, you are no longer a Mohammedan, you are no longer a Christian. The moment you become a sannyasin, you drop out of all collectivities. You become yourself. You will be surprised to know that in the East people don't commit suicide as much as in the West. And the difference is big— too big to be just accidental. In the East we have created a creative kind of suicide, that is sannyas. You can still live, but you can live in your own way. Then the need for suicide disappears, or becomes very much less.

In the West it always has happened that the unique individuals have to commit suicide. The mediocre go on living, the unique have to commit suicide. A van Gogh, a Hemingway, a Mayakovski, a Nijinsky—these are unique individuals. Either they have to commit suicide or they have to go mad—the society drives them mad. The society puts so much pressure on them that either they have to yield to the society and become just anonymous, or they have to go mad, or they have to commit suicide. And all are destructive alternatives.

Nietzsche went mad; that was his way of committing suicide. Nijinsky committed suicide; that was his way of going mad. Nietzsche had the same quality as Buddha. Had he been in the East he would have become a Buddha, but the West does not give that alternative at all. He had to go mad. Van Gogh had a unique quality of tremendous intelligence, creativity. He could have moved on the path of sannyas and *samadhi,* but there was no door open. He got tired; just going on living a compromise was hurting too much. It was not worth it. One day he completed his painting— the painting that he had always wanted to do—and that day he felt, "Now there is no need to make any compromise with anybody for any reason. I have done my painting, I have done my best. It is time to disppear."

He had always wanted to paint a sunrise. He had painted sunrises for years, but still something was missing and lacking and he would paint again and again. The day his painting was complete and he was fulfilled and satisfied and contented that it had happened—that very moment it was absolutely clear to him that now there was no need—"I was only waiting for this painting. I am fulfilled in it, I have bloomed. Now why make compromises? For what? " He committed suicide.

He was not mad, he was simply not mediocre. His suicide was not a crime, his suicide was simply a condemnation of your so-called society which asks for so many compromises. Mediocre people are ready to compromise; they have nothing to lose. In fact they feel good being part of a crowd, of a mob, because in the crowd they need not think about themselves as mediocre; all are just like them. They can lose themselves in the crowd. They can lose themselves and forget themselves in the the mass mind, and in the mass mind they have no responsibility. They need not bother whether they are asleep or awakened.

But a man who has some soul in him will find it continuously heavy to go on degrading himself, to go on compromising for small ordinary trivia, meaningless things—for bread and butter, for a house, a shelter, for clothes . . .

But each suicide will have a different quality to it.

You ask why Hemingway committed suicide. Hemingway's suicide has another flavor, different from van Gogh's. Hemingway's whole search was the search for freedom. Birth happened; it was not your choice. You were thrown into life—as the existentialists say. You were thrown into it, it was not your choice. Nobody ever asked you whether you wanted to be born or not. So birth is not freedom. It has already happened.

The next most important thing is love, but that is also not possible to do. When it happens, it happens; you cannot manage it, you cannot will it. If you want to love a person just through will, it is impossible. It happens when it happens—suddenly you are in love. That's why we use the phrase "falling in love". You "fall" into it. But you cannot will it; it comes from the unknown. It is just like birth. It is as if God manages that you fall in love with this person; it is as if the decision comes from the blue. You are not the decisive factor, you are more like a victim. You cannot do anything against it. If it happens you have to go into it; if it does not happen you can do whatsoever you want and it will not happen. Nobody can produce love on order.

And the most important three things in life are birth, love, death. Death is the only thing that you can do something about—you can commit suicide.

Hemingway's search was for freedom. He wanted to do something that he had not done. He had not managed birth, he had not managed love, now there was only death. There was only one thing which if you wanted to do, you could do. It would be your act, an individual act, done by you.

Death has a mysterious quality about it; it is a very strange paradox. If you are standing by the side of a small baby, just born, and if somebody asks you to say something absolutely certain about the baby—the baby is in his crib, asleep, relaxing—what can you say absolutely certainly? You can say only one thing: that he will die.

That is a very strange thing to say. Anything else is uncertain. He may love, he may not love. He may succeed, he may fail. He may be a sinner, he may be a saint. All are "maybes", there is nothing certain about anything. It is not possible to predict anything. There is only one thing you can say—and it looks very absurd at the side of a baby who has just been born—only one thing is absolutely certain: that he will die. This prediction can be made, and your prediction is never going to be wrong.

So death has a certain quality of certainty about it—it is going to happen. And at the same time it has something absolutely uncertain about it too. One never knows when it is going to happen. There is certainty that it is going to happen and uncertainty about when it is going to happen. Both this certainty and uncertainty about death make it a mystery, a paradox. If you go on living, it will happen—but then again it will come from out of the blue. You will not be the decisive factor. Birth happened, love happened—was death also to happen? That made Hemingway uneasy. He wanted to do at least one thing in life to which he could have his own signature, about which he could say "This I did". That's why he committed suicide. Suicide was an exercise in freedom.

You cannot know anything about death unless you go into it. Hemingway's attitude was that if it is going to happen then why be dragged into it? Why not go into it on your own? It is going to happen. His whole life's concern was death, that's why he become so interested in bullfights. Death was very close by. He was constantly attracted by the theme of death—what it was. But you cannot know. Even if somebody is dying in front of you, you don't know anything about death. You simply know that the breathing has disappeared, that this man's eyes won't open again, that this man will never speak again, that his heart is no longer beating—that's all. But this is nothing. How can you know about death from these things? The mystery remains a mystery, you have not even touched it.

You can know it only by going into it. But if you are dragged into it there are more possibilities of your becoming unconscious—because you are being dragged into it. Almost always people die unconsciously. Before death happens they become so afraid, so very afraid, that a kind of coma surrounds them and protects them. It is a natural anesthetic. When you go for an operation, you need an anesthetic—and death is the greatest operation there is: the soul and body will be torn apart. So nature has some built-in mechanism—before you start dying you go into a coma; all consciousness disappears. In the first place your consciousness was not very much. Even while you were alive, it was just a tiny flicker. When the wind of death comes, that flicker is gone—there is complete darkness.

Hemingway wanted to go into death fully conscious. It was a conscious exercise in dying. But that is possible only through suicide or through *samadhi*. These are the only two possibilities. You can die consciously in only two ways. You can commit suicide; you can manage your own death. You can have your revolver ready, contemplate it, put it to your chest or your head, pull the trigger yourself consciously, see the explosion and see death. This is one possibility. It is a very destructive possibility.

Another possibility is to go more and more into meditation, to attain to a state of awareness that cannot be drowned by death. Then there is no need to commit suicide. Then whenever death comes, let it come. You will be dying fully alert, aware, watchful.

So it is suicide or sannyas, suicide or *samadhi* . . .

I'm not talking about all suicides—but you asked about these two. And there are as many as people commit suicide. But these two are very rare. These two are very potential. If Vincent van Gogh or Hemingway had been in the East or had had the eastern attitude, they would have flowered as great sannyasins.

SUFIS: THE PEOPLE OF THE PATH, Vol. II

There are people for whom ordinary death is unnatural; it won't fit with them. It will be simply like an accident that they died on their bed just by accident. It won't fit with them. There are people for whom it is natural to put their lives aside and take the jump and the plunge into the unknown. Because we cling too much to life, suicide looks like a sin.

It is our clinging—because we are clingers, and if somebody commits suicide we condemn. But it is not necessarily that it is bad. The person may have taken a plunge into the unknown. He has known life, he is finished with it, now he wants to know what death is—and he wants to know it very consciously.

In India there exists one of the most ancient religions, Jainism. That is the only religion in the world that allows suicide. It is very rare. It says that when a person, out of his meditation, comes to feel that now he has lived his life and there is no more to it so why go on repeating, he surrenders his life on his own.

That is the only religion. And I feel that sooner or later that is going to become part of every country and every constitution, because a man has a fundamental right to live and to die. Nobody should be allowed to prevent anybody. If somebody wants not to live, then who are others to force him to live? Then it is an imprisonment.

DANCE YOUR WAY TO GOD

I had a friend. He was in love with a woman and the woman rejected him. So, of course, being a poet, he thought of committing suicide. His family was very disturbed. They all tried to convince him; but the more they tried, the more he became convinced that he was going to commit suicide. This happens. Not knowing what to do, they locked his door. He started beating his head against the door. They became very much afraid. What to do?

Suddenly they remembered me and called me. I went there. He was beating his head against the door; he was really in a fury and completely determined. I went near the door and I said to him: "Why are you making so much show out of it? If you want to commit suicide, do it. But why so much noise? And why are you beating your head? Just by beating your head on the door you will not die. So, listen to me, come with me. We can go to the river; there is a beautiful point where I have always meditated. If ever I am to commit suicide, this is the place. You come with me, this is a good chance."

Because I was not saying anything against suicide, he calmed down. He was not hitting his head. He was really puzzled, because you never expect that your friend will help you to commit suicide. So I told him: "You open the door and don't make a fool of yourself, and don't help crowds to gather here. Why so much showmanship about it? You simply come with me and drown yourself in the river. There is a waterfall in the river and you will simply disappear . . ."

So he opened the door and he looked at me, he was very puzzled. I took his hand, brought him home. He said: "When are we going?" But he was a little afraid, now that I was ready I was dangerous. So I said: "This is a full-moon night and there is no hurry. When one wants to die, one should choose an auspicious moment. So we will go in the middle of the night, then the full moon will be just there and I can say goodbye and you can jump." He became more and more afraid. I was simply delaying the time.

We went to bed at ten o'clock. I fixed the alarm for twelve, and I told him that sometimes I didn't hear the alarm, so if he heard it first he should wake me. Immediately the alarm started he put it off. I waited for a few minutes then I said: "Why are you waiting? Wake me." He became suddenly angry and said: "Are you my friend, or my enemy? It seems you want to kill me." I said: "I'm not making any judgment on my own. If you want to die, I am a friend, I have to cooperate and help. If you don't want to die, that's your decision, so you tell me. I am neutral. The car is ready, I will drive you to the spot; the night is beautiful and the moon has come up. Now it is up to you." He said: "Take me to my home. I am not going to die. And who are you to force me to die?"

I was not forcing anybody—just a delayed moment and one comes to one's senses.

THE GRASS GROWS BY ITSELF

SUPERIOR *Satsang* means always choosing the company of the superior. The mind will help you to choose the company of the inferior. Be alert and avoid this, because with the inferior you will become inferior. More and more the ray of consciousness will be lost in darkness.

Always choose the superior, move towards the superior. But your ego will feel hurt. The ego has to be left. *Satsang* means living against the ego, transcending the ego, always seeking the superior. And you want to encounter God, and you are not happy in encountering Jesus and Buddha? How will it be possible then? Because God is the superiormost light, the climax of the whole existence, the flowering of all life. If you always choose the inferior, how can you really desire to enter into the kingdom of God? You are following a wrong path.

Remember this, and only one point has to be continuously kept in mind and that is: move in circles, with people, with friends, with books, always remembering that something superior is there, so that you can drop your ego; you can feel inferior and drop the ego. Always seek the superior. By and by, one step, another step . . . you will be able to encounter Jesus. And only if you can encounter Jesus will you be able to encounter God.

THE MUSTARD SEED

SUPERMAN   Man is really only a bridge; man has no being. Man is a becoming a process. He has to arrive; he is still on the way. Man has to surpass himself. He has to become a superman . . .

When you have arrived at your deepest depth, when there is nowhere to go anymore, when you have reached the core, the very center, then you are no more a man.

A Buddha is not a man; he is a superman. So is Jesus, so is Krishna, and so are all the awakened ones of the earth. And you have to become part of those chains of awakened people; you have to become part of the glory that belongs to an awakened one. Each of my sannyasins has to become a superman.

And a superman has nothing to do with race, blood. I am not using the word in the sense that Adolf Hitler used it. I am using it in a totally different sense: the ultimate state of your awakening. Then how can you be called just a human being? You have surpassed yourself, you have gone beyond. You have reached the other shore.

SNAP YOUR FINGERS, SLAP YOUR FACE AND WAKE UP!

SUPPRESSION   See Repression

SUPRARATIONAL   See Infrarational, 2nd Series

SURPRISE   The most surprising thing in life is that nobody seems to be surprised! People take life for granted. Otherwise everything is a mystery, everything is simply amazing! It is a miracle that a seed becomes a tree, that as the sun rises in the morning the birds start singing. It is a miracle! Each moment you come across miracles, and still you don't look surprised. This is the most surprising thing in life . . .

Only children don't take it for granted. That's why children have a beauty, a grace, an innocence. They are always living in wonder; everything brings awe. Collecting pebbles on the seashore or seashells . . . watch the children, with what joy they are running, with what joy they are collecting—just colored stones, as if they have found great diamonds, collecting flowers, wild flowers, and look into their eyes . . . or running after butterflies, watch them. Their whole being, each cell of their body is mystified. And that's the most important quality that makes life worth living.

The person who loses his quality to be surprised is dead. The moment your surprise is dead, *you* are dead. The moment your wonder is dead, *you* are dead. The moment you become incapable of feeling awe, you have gone impotent.

To be born with the gift of laughter and a sense that the world is mad is the quality that makes life worth living—not only worth living but worth living dancing, worth celebrating . . .

Bring your quality of being surprised back, as you had it in your childhood. Again look with those same innocent eyes. Dionysius calls it *agnosia,* a state of not-knowing, and the Upanishads call it *dhyana, samadhi,* a state of not-knowing. It is not ignorance.

Ignorance and knowledge belong to the same dimension: ignorance means less knowledge, knowledge means less ignorance; the difference is of degrees. *Agnosia, samadhi* is not ignorance; it is beyond ignorance and knowledge both. It is a pure state of wonder. When you are full of wonder, existence is full of God.

I AM THAT

SURRENDER   To enter into the unknowable is the greatest adventure, the greatest ecstasy, but one feels afraid; one feels that one is losing something. You can lose only that which you have not got. Let me repeat. You can lose only that which you have not got. You can never lose that which you have got; there is no way to lose it, that which you have got. If your knowledge has disappeared, that simply means it was not real knowing.

Now is the beginning—*ahato Brahma jigyasa*—now begins the enquiry into God.

Surrender is the quantum leap from mind to no-mind, from ego to egolessness. And in a single step the whole journey is contained. It is not a long journey from you to God, it is a single-step journey. It is not a gradual phenomenon; it is not that slowly slowly, gradually you come to the divine. It is a quantum leap! One moment you were in darkness and the next moment all is light. All that is needed is to put the ego aside . . .

And the moment you put the ego aside, the curtain disappears. God is not hidden, only your eyes are closed. Open your eyes!

Surrender means opening your eyes. Surrender means dropping a false idea that "I am separate from the whole". It is a false idea, so in fact you are not dropping anything. You are calculating wrongly: you are doing some arithmetic, two plus two is four, but you are putting five . . .

Ego is a hallucination. You are not separate from the whole—trying to be, of course, hence the whole misery. Trying to do something which is not possible, which is impossible, is bound to create misery. Misery is unnatural; it is your invention. Misery does not exist; it is your hallucination. It is a nightmare created by you. It is your great work!

Bliss is natural. Bliss is the very nature of the way things are. *Ais dhammo sanantano* says Buddha: bliss is the way things are. But you are trying to be something which is not possible; you are trying to be separate, you are trying to be an island, and you belong to the continent, the vast, infinite continent of God or godliness.

Surrender means seeing that "I am not separate"—just *seeing* that "I am not separate". Nothing is surrendered, nothing is dropped; just a nonsense idea, a dream is no more there because you are awake.

GUIDA SPIRITUALE

When you surrender your ego to the Master, the Master is only an excuse. You are really surrendering to God, not to the Master. In fact you are simply surrendering. It is not of any importance to whom: the question is not to whom, the question is that you are surrendering the ego. The moment the ego is surrendered there is a possibility of communion.

THEOLOGIA MYSTICA

When the disciple and the Master meet, merge, melt into each other, it is a love affair, it is a deep, orgasmic experience, far deeper than any love, because even lovers go on carrying their egos and egos are bound to clash, conflict. The Master and the disciple exist without egos. The Master's ego has evaporated—that's why he is a Master—and the disciple surrenders his ego to the Master.

And remember, by surrendering the ego the disciple is not surrendering anything in particular, because ego is just an idea and nothing else. It has no substance; it is made of the same stuff dreams are made of. When you surrender your dreams, what are you surrendering?

If you come to me and you say, "I offer all my dreams to you," *you* are offering, but I am not getting anything! And you may be thinking that you are offering great dreams of golden palaces and beautiful women and great treasures . . . you are offering great dreams, but I am not getting anything.

When you offer your ego to the Master you are offering something as far as you are concerned, because you think it is very substantial, significant. When *you* surrender you think it is you who are doing something great. As far as the Master is concerned he is simply laughing at the whole thing, because he knows what your ego is—just hot air! Nothing much to brag about.

But a device, a simple device, can help immensely. It is a device. The Master says, "Surrender the ego." When he says, "Surrender the ego," he is saying, "Give me that which you don't have at all but *you* believe that you have. Give me your belief—I am ready to take it. Let this excuse help you." You may gather courage to risk. Love encourages you to risk. In love you can go to any lengths. When you are

in love with the Master and he says, "Give me your ego,"
how can you say no?

To be with a Master means to be in a state of saying yes,
yes, and again yes! It is an absolute yes, an unconditional
yes. So when he says, "Give me your ego," you simply give
your ego to the Master. To you it is very important; to him
it has no meaning, no substance, no existence, but he accepts it.

The moment you drop your ego the meeting starts happening. Now two zeros start moving into each other. Two
lovers enter into each other's bodies; that is a physical phenomenon and the orgasm that happens is a physical thing.
The Master and the disciple are lovers on the spiritual plane:
two zeros, two egoless beings enter into each other. In that
merger something transpires. Not that the Master gives you
something, not that *you* take something, but because of the
meeting something happens, out of the meeting something
happens—something which is greater than the Master and
greater than the disciple, something more than the meeting
of these two, something transcendental.

I AM THAT

At the last moment Jesus says to God, "Have you forsaken
me?" And that shows that he was still living in the mind,
expecting, desiring, hoping—even from God. There were a
few expectations that at the last moment some miracle
would happen. Not only were the people who had gathered
there expecting a miracle—looking at the sky hoping that
a divine hand would appear and Jesus would be raised to
ultimate glory; that he would be saved at the last moment—
but Jesus himself was also waiting.

He says, "Have you forsaken me?" What does it mean?
It is a complaint, it is not a prayer. It is frustration, it is disappointment. And disppointment is possible only if there is
some deep desire, some longing to be fulfilled. God has failed
him—he has not come to his rescue. He was hoping.

And these are the signs of an unenlightened person. These
are symbolic of the ego, of the head, of the mind, of the
very process of the mind.

But he was a man of great intelligence too: immediately

he recognized: what he is saying is wrong, the very desire is wrong. One should not expect anything from the universe, one should not feel disappointed, one should not feel frustrated. This is not trust! This is not a love affair! This is not an absolute yes, it is a conditional yes: "You fulfill these conditions, then of course I will be grateful. But because the conditions have not been fulfilled I am angry." There is anger in his voice; there is anxiety, disappointment.

But he understood the point, and immediately he corrected it. A single moment . . . and he is no more Jesus, he becomes Christ. Suddenly he looks at the sky and says, "Forgive me! Let *thy* kingdom come, let *thy* will be done—not mine. Let *thy* will be done!"

This is surrender. He has dropped the mind, he has dropped the ego and all the expectations. "Let *thy* will be done." In this egoless state he became enlightened.

I AM THAT

I promise that you will be transformed, but your asking is not good. If you make it a condition, you are not surrendering. I promise—you will be transformed—but on your part, if you ask for the promise, you are not ready to surrender.

This is my promise: that you will be transformed. But don't make it a condition, because then there is no surrender. And if you are not surrendered, how can I transform you? So, please, forget my promise. It will happen, it is going to happen, but don't make it a condition. With a condition there is no surrender. Surrender is unconditional; it cannot be otherwise.

Even if I lead you to hell, be ready for it. Only then is heaven possible. Your readiness to move with me to the very hell—this readiness transforms you.

Really, your surrender transforms you; there is no need of me. I am just an excuse because you cannot surrender to a vacuum, to the emptiness. You can use me. But, really, there is no need for me. If you can simply surrender, without surrendering to anyone, then too it will happen. It happens through surrendering.

But it is difficult to surrender without surrendering to

anyone. Our whole mind, the whole working of our consciousness, makes it impossible for us to surrender to the empty sky. If I tell you to love, you will ask me, "Whom should I love?" Can you just love without loving anyone? It is difficult to conceive of how to love when there is no one to be loved. If you are alone on earth and there is no one except you, can you love? If you even try to imagine it, you will imagine loving some tree or loving some rock, but then again the someone else has entered. A "thou" is needed; you cannot love without a "thou". The "thou" may be a tree, the "thou" may be a flower, the "thou" may be a rock—it makes no difference.

If you can love, simply love, without there being any object of love, then you can also surrender without there being any object of surrender. But it is difficult, almost impossible to conceive of surrender just as an act within you, without there being anyone to surrender to.

You can surrender to me. But surrender means that you are not asking for anything. Everything will be given, but don't ask. Your asking becomes the barrier. Surrender means trust. Even if nothing happens you will wait; you will not lose trust. Even if nothing happens and your whole life is wasted you will wait. If you can wait in such a deep way, everything will happen this very moment. It can happen this very moment! There is no need to promise for the future; it can happen here and now.

But, surrender. And surrender without any condition, without asking for any promise. Your very asking will destroy the promise. I promise—but that promise is just a consequence, not a precondition. It will happen, because that's how the law of the universe works.

It is going to happen, but, please, you need not be concerned about the result. Just be concerned with the act of surrendering. Leave the result to the divine, to the eternal law, to the Tao.

THE NEW ALCHEMY: TO TURN YOU ON

Surrender is a light. Learn to open your eyes towards that light. Learn to say: *Buddham sharanam gachchhami, sangham sharanam gachchhami, dhammam sharanam gachchhami.*

Three surrenders: one surrender to the one who has become awakened, the second surrender to the company that lives in the company of the awakened—because the perfume of the awakened one starts filtering into the company, the blessed company that lives with the awakened one—and the third surrender to the law, the ultimate through which the sleepy one has become awakened and the other sleepy ones are becoming awakened.

These three surrenders and a single moment's reverence are more valuable than a hundred years of worship, than a thousand offerings . . .

By revering a Buddha, by respecting a Buddha, by trusting a Buddha, you are conquering life itself. And you will attain to beauty, strength and happiness. In that surrender you will become beautiful, because the ego is gone and the ego is ugly. And you will become strong, because the ego is gone—the ego is always weak and impotent. And you will become happy for the first time, because for the first time you have had a glimpse of truth, for the first time you have had a glimpse of your own being. The Buddha is a mirror: when you bow down you see your original face reflected in the Buddha.

Let your heart be full of the prayer: *Buddham sharanam gachchhami, sangham sharanam gachchhami, dhammam sharanam gachchhami.*

THE BOOK OF THE BOOKS, Vol. III

SURVIVAL Life is more than just to survive, but millions of people have decided just to survive and not to live. Their only value in life seems to be how to survive, how to survive for a long time. Survival has become their god, and because of it they have missed the whole opportunity of life. Because when survival becomes the goal you become afraid of living. Life is dangerous and one has to risk one's survival again and again; only then can one live.

If one is too interested and obsessed with survival then one tries to be secure, safe, and in being secure and safe one becomes dead. One loses aliveness. Then one lives only superficially, with no depth, with no height. One's life is very dull, flat, boring. There is no adventure, no exploration, and no surprises, no mysteries; and nothing is ever revealed to such a person. He remains closed to existence and existence remains closed to him. They never meet; there is no communion.

Being initiated into sannyas means that from this moment survival will not be the goal, but life, not security but life, not safety but life. And to live intensely and totally even for a single moment is more valuable than to survive for a hundred years. That is not life; that is vegetating.

So the real man knows no other goal than life itself. Living totally is his goal; living moment to moment, intensely, passionately, hot, that is his goal. Then each moment becomes so precious, such a gift. And only when you know those gifts can you be thankful to God, can you feel grateful, can prayer arise in you.

I see survival as one of the greatest calamities, the idea of survival and the obsession with it and the attachment with it. It is worthless, the whole is meaningless. We are not here just to survive and live long—one hundred years or one hundred and twenty years. We are here to live and to know life in its multi-dimensions, to know life in all its richness, in all its variety. And when a man lives multi-dimensionally, explores all possibilities available, never shrinks back from any challenge, goes, rushes into it, welcomes it, rises to the occasion, then life becomes aflame, life blooms. Life knows what spring is, and then the spring is something that follows you wherever you are; it becomes your very climate, your milieu.

THE SACRED YES

SUTRAS And in the East the great statements of the Masters have been called *sutras,* threads, for a certain reason. A man is born as a heap of flowers, just as a heap. Unless a thread is used and the thread runs through the flowers, the heap will remain a heap and will never become a garland.

And you can be offered to God only when you have become a garland. A heap is a chaos, a garland is a cosmos— although in the garland also you only see the flowers, the thread is invisible.

The sayings of the Masters are called *sutras,* threads, because they can make out of you a garland. And only when you are a garland can you become an offering to God, only when you have become a cosmos, a harmony, a song.

Right now you are just gibberish. You can write down . . .
sit in a room, close the doors and start writing on a piece
of paper whatsoever comes to your mind. Don't edit it, don't
delete anything, don't add anything because you are not
going to show it to anybody. Keep a matchbox by your side
so once you have written it you can burn it immediately,
so that you can be authentic. Just write whatsoever comes
to your mind and you will be surprised: just a ten minutes'
exercise and you will understand what I mean when I say
that you are just gibberish.

It is really a great revelation to see how your mind goes
on jumping from here to there, from one thing to another
thing, accidentally, for no reason at all. What nonsense
thoughts go on running inside you, with no relevance, no
consistency. Just a sheer wastage, a leakage of energy!

The sayings of the Buddhas are called *sutras*.

THE BOOK OF THE BOOKS, Vol. III

SWAMI I call my sannyasins Swami.

The word swami means the master. *Swa* means the center
of your being and swami means one who has found it.

Finding one's center is the beginning of a divine
dimension—then all is peace, then flowers of peace go blossoming, endlessly.

THE SOUND OF ONE HAND CLAPPING

See also Ma, 2nd Series

SWAN Have you seen swans leaving the lake? I am
reminded of Ramakrishna. His first *samadhi,* his first glimpse
of God, glimpse of truth or bliss, happened when he was
only thirteen years old. He was coming from his farm—he
was a farmer's son—he was coming back to his home. On
the way there was a lake. The rainy season was just to come,
the monsoons were approaching. The sky was becoming
cloudy, dark clouds, thunder, lightning, and Ramakrishna
was almost running because it seemed that it was going to
pour heavily. He was passing by the lake of the village;
because he was running he disturbed the swans in the lake
and they all flew up together.

The swan is one of the most beautiful birds, the whitest—

symbol of purity, innocence. A long arc of swans suddenly rose high against the backdrop of the black clouds. Ramakrishna was transported into another world. The vision was so beautiful, and the vision was such a message that he fell there on the bank of the lake in utter ecstasy. The joy was such that he could not contain it; he became almost unconscious as far as the outside was concerned.

Other farmers were returning home. Everybody was in a hurry; the clouds were there and it was going to rain and they wanted to reach home. They found Ramakrishna lying on the bank of the lake absolutely unconscious, but such joy was on his face, so radiant was his being that they all fell on their knees. The experience was so superb! It was something not of this world.

They carried Ramakrishna to his home. They worshipped Ramakrishna! When he came back he was asked, "What has happened?"

He said, "A message from the beyond: 'Ramakrishna, be a swan! Open your wings—the whole sky is yours. Don't be trapped by the lake and its comfort, security and safety.' I am no more the same person—I have been called. God has called me."

And from that day he was never the same person: something was triggered by the swans rising high in the sky.

Buddha says: Like swans, they rise and leave the lake. As if Buddha is predicting something about Ramakrishna! The distance is vast, twenty-five centuries, but the prediction is true. It is not only about Ramakrishna, it is about all those who are ever going to awaken, it is about all the Buddhas.

The swan has become a symbol in the East of the awakened one, hence the awakened one is called *paramahansa*. *Paramahansa* means the great swan.

THE BOOK OF THE BOOKS, Vol. III

SWEETNESS See Bitterness, 1st Series

SYMBOLS Yes, religion has nothing to do with symbols. Religion in its essence is absolutely pure, just an experience, a knowing. It has nothing to do with outside symbols. But that is not the question. That pure religion is not possible for you as you are; the way you are you will need symbols.

Once it happened, Joshu was sitting in front of his temple. A great Zen Master.

A seeker came and he asked Joshu, "Master, where is Buddha? Who is Buddha? What is this Buddhahood?"

Joshu looked into the eyes of the man and said, "You ask who is Buddha? Go inside the temple. He is there."

The man laughed and said, "There is only a stone statue. And I know and you know that a stone statue is not Buddha."

Joshu said, "Perfectly right. A stone statue is not Buddha."

Then the man said, "Then tell me, who is Buddha?"

Joshu looked again into his eyes and said, "Go into the temple, you will find the Buddha there."

Now this is very puzzling. The questioner is not yet able to understand the non-symbolic. Though intellectually he understands that the statue is just a stone statue and is not Buddha, it is only intellectual understanding.

If your lover gives you a small handkerchief, has it any more meaning than any other handkerchief of the same make, of the same value? If it is lost, tears may come to your eyes. Your mind is still symbolic, still lives in symbols. That handkerchief, a small, valueless handkerchief given by your lover or beloved, carries a certain meaning which nobody else can see. It is an ordinary handkerchief but to you it is very symbolic. It has a message, a love message. That handkerchief is worth a kingdom. It is no more a commodity in the marketplace, it is no more a part of the world of things—that handkerchief has a personality, almost a soul. Have you not watched this inside you?

If this is so, then symbols are still meaningful for you and you cannot just drop them unless the whole mind is dropped. It depends on you. If those symbols have a certain response in your heart they are alive.

When a Buddhist goes to the Buddhist temple and bows down before the stone statue of Buddha, if it is really a heartfelt prayer, if he is really bowing down in deep humbleness, then don't bother about the statue. The real thing is the humbleness, the desire, the love, the heartfelt urge. That stone statue is just instrumental.

If you go and you are not a Buddhist and you have no heart for Buddha, then, of course, it is a stone statue. A Buddhist has a love affair with Buddha. If you call that stone statue just stone, he will be hurt because he sees something more in it. That something more is in his eyes, certainly so, absolutely so—it is not there in the statue. But in front of the statue something responds in him, something starts singing in his heart. His heart beats faster, he feels transfigured. That transfiguration is meaningful. It does not matter if the statue is Buddha or not, it does not matter at all. But it helped . . .

Man is a symbolic creature, man lives in a world of symbols. Even science cannot do without symbols. Science, which is expected to be absolutely factual, cannot work without symbols. In fact, there is no possibility of growing without symbols. That's why animals are not growing; they cannot grow unless they move into the dimension of symbols. So everything is a symbol . . .

The whole human consciousness has grown out of symbolism. All our languages—the language of science, the language of religion, the language of poetry—are all symbols. Our whole life of love, relationship, is nothing but symbolism.

Unless you have come to a point where the whole mind disappears, symbols are meaningful. The questioner asks: *You talk about a living religion yet in some centers people kneel over the cast of your feet.* Those feet are irrelevant, their kneeling is relevant. Those feet are just symbolic, but their kneeling is real. That is not symbolic. They are affected by it . . .

Please tell me why we need your symbols. They are not you nor your teachings here. They are neither me nor my teachings but you cannot see me yet. Whatsoever you see is just a symbol—my body is just a symbol, it is not me; my photograph is a symbol, it is not me; whatsoever I am saying is symbolic, it is not me. And what I am saying is not my teaching because my teachings cannot be said. Nobody's—Buddha's nor Christ's—nobody's can be said. Whatsoever is being said is not the real thing. The real is elusive. Truth cannot be uttered.

But I have to talk to you to persuade you to become silent. This is a very absurd effort, but this is how it is! I have to seduce you towards silence through words. Words are just symbols; silence is . . . Remember, when I say silence, the word "silence" is not silence.

Yes, Joshu was right. The Buddha is in the temple.

The man said, "But there is no Buddha, there is only a stone statue. How can an enlightened man like you say that a stone statue is a Buddha?"

And Joshu said, "You are right. It is just a stone statue."

Then the man said, "Now tell me, where is Buddha?"

Joshu said, "Go into the temple, he is there."

If you have the eyes to see then you can see even in a stone. If you don't have the eyes to see you may come across Jesus and you may not recognize him. Many of you were there when Jesus was there, many of you were there when Buddha was there and you never recognized him. Many of you are here just in front of me and you may never recognize me. So the deepest question is of your recognition. If you can recognize something in a stone, if you can recognize something in a cast of my feet, yes, Buddha is there.

The whole thing is yours—your Buddha, your Christ, your me. Everything is yours, you are the only one. This is the beauty, the drama of life: you are the actor, you are the director, you are the audience, you are the storywriter, you are the play-back singer, you are all, alone . . .

Beware. Don't go on dropping symbols otherwise nothing will be left.

Yes, that is the highest peak; get ready for it. Symbols will help you to reach that highest peak but if you drop them right now you will never reach to that height. One has to move up a staircase. When one has reached the top one has to leave the staircase. But if you leave at the very beginning you will remain on the bottom floor.

Symbols are to be left only when you have come to see the non-symbolic, not before that. Otherwise you will remain very low—somewhere crawling on the earth.

Once you have symbolism it gives a vision to your life, a style. Then you are not haphazard, then you become an order, you are not a chaos. Then things start crystallizing inside you and everything starts gaining a significance—your life has a direction, you have a sense of direction.

"In the synagogue I heard men praying," said the puzzled young boy. "It must be awfully hard for God."

"Why?" asked the rabbi gently.

"The woodcutter was praying for cold weather."

"Naturally," said the rabbi. "He makes his living cutting wood for our stoves. The colder it is the more wood he sells."

"But the fruitseller prayed for mild weather."

"Well," said the rabbi, "he stores autumn fruit to sell in winter. Severe cold would freeze his stored fruit."

"The farmer prayed for rain and the brickmaker for dry weather. They are all godly men: how does God know how to answer all their prayers?"

"How is the weather now?" asked the rabbi.

"Dry and mild."

"And last week?"

"Let me see. On Monday and Tuesday it rained and on Thursday it was cold."

"See?" said the rabbi.

Once you have a symbol you can see. Then God is fulfilling everybody's needs: someday it is raining, someday it is dry, someday it is hot, someday it is cold—God is fulfilling everybody's desires.

But if you have the symbol of God then the whole thing is no longer disorderly. If you don't have that symbol then you are simply surprised: you find persons praying in the synagogue and everybody asking for different weather, and it looks almost foolish. And they all are good people, religious people—how is God going to fulfill them? In fact, if you don't have the symbol of God, those five prayers are chaotic, you cannot make any sense out of them. Once you have the symbol, that symbol crystallizes everything.

"See?" said the rabbi.

DANG DANG DOKO DANG

SYMPATHY In fact, people enjoy being sorry for others. They are always looking for situations where they can feel sorry for others—it is so ego-fulfilling. It is such a nourishment for the ego. If somebody's house is on fire you go with tears in your eyes and you show great sympathy, you show much concern, as if you are immensely pained. But deep down, if you watch, you will find a certain joy, a certain glee.

But people never look within themselves. It is bound to be there for two reasons: it is not *your* house which is on fire, "Thank God!"—that is the first thing. Secondly, you must be enjoying your tears, because when somebody builds a new house, a beautiful house, you feel jealous; great envy arises in you. You cannot enjoy, you cannot participate in his joy. You want to avoid—you don't even *look* at his house.

If you cannot participate in the joy of others, how can you feel sorry when they are in trouble? If you feel jealous when they are joyful, then you will feel joyful when they are in trouble. But you will not show it, you will show sympathy. "Sympathy" is not a good word.

There are a few words that are very ugly but which are now very respected: words like "duty", "service", "sympathy"—these are ugly words. A man who is fulfilling his duty is not a man of love. A man who is doing service knows nothing of love, because service is not done, it happens. And the man who sympathizes is certainly enjoying some kind of superiority: "I am not in that sorry state, the other is in the sorry state. I have the upper hand—I can feel sorry for him."

The lover never feels superior—the lover cannot feel superior, the lover cannot even *think* that he has obliged anybody. On the contrary, when somebody receives your love you feel obliged that your love was not rejected—it could have been rejected—that your love was respected, welcomed. You feel obliged, you feel thankful, you feel grateful.

ZEN: ZEST, ZIP, ZAP AND ZING

See also Empathy, 1st Series

SYNCHRONICITY   To be a Buddha means to be awakened to your inner light. How can you be awakened by following somebody? My sannyasins are not my followers, they are my friends, they are my lovers. They are not my followers! I am not giving you any instructions about how to live; I am not giving you any commandments about how to behave. I am not giving you any character to cultivate. I am simply sharing my insight—I am simply sharing with you what has happened to me. I am simply telling my story to you. And I am grateful that you are listening to it.

Just listen to it as totally as possible, and then something will start happening in you. It will not be caused by me: it will be a synchronicity. It will be acausal.

The law of synchronicity has to be understood. This is one of the greatest contributions of Carl Gustav Jung to modern humanity: the law of synchronicity . . .

The credit goes to Carl Gustav Jung. The law has been known down the ages, but nobody had named it exactly. He called it "the law of synchronicity". It suddenly happened to a scientist. A scientist a hundred years ago was staying in an old house. In that old house there were two old clocks on the same wall. He was surprised to see that they always kept exactly the same time, second to second: "Old clocks, and so perfect? Not even a single second's difference?"

Being a scientist he became curious. He put one clock five minutes back, and after twenty-four hours in the morning when he looked again, they were again keeping the same time. Now it was a great puzzle. He enquired . . . nobody had changed, nobody had touched anything. He tried again and again, and again and again they would come to the same rhythm. Then he tried to find out: "What is happening?— something strange. They are disconnected!"

Then he observed more minutely and he came to conclude: "The vibration of the one clock, which is more powerful, the bigger clock, goes through the wall—just the vibration—and keeps the other clock in tune." It is a subtle rhythm. Nothing is visible.

That was the beginning of a new phenomenon . . . then many many more things happened. And by the time Carl Gustav Jung started working on how things happen in consciousness, he came to conclude that the vibe of one heart, if it is powerful enough, can change the rhythm of another heart—just like the bigger clock was changing the smaller clock.

The vibe is invisible. There is not yet any way to measure, but it is there. It is not tangible, but it functions. It is not causal.

That's what happens in *satsang*—in communion with a Master. If you are with a Christ, he is a tremendous power— he is God! He is a window to God. God is flowing through him. If you come close to him—and that's what disciplehood is all about: to come close to a Master, to come close to a window from whom God is flowing—his power, his vibe, will set the rhythm of your heart. It is acausal, one of those mysterious intangibles, but it has been happening down the ages.

Have you watched it? Two lovers, if they are really lovers, and deep in intimacy, slowly slowly start looking alike— that is synchronicity. You can see it: real lovers, slowly slowly start looking like brother and sister. Something in them starts becoming synchronized, they start having the same rhythm . . .

Many people become puzzled . . . just a few nights ago, a couple came to me and the husband was very much puzzled. He said, "What is happening to us? We are no more husband and wife—all sex has disappeared, but still we feel a deep intimacy." And I told them, "Something immensely valuable is happening. You are becoming brother and sister. Your love is taking on a new dimension, a higher one—that of non-sexuality. It is becoming purer."

Hearing it, immediately everything became clear to him. They hugged each other, tears started flowing from their eyes. It was a beautiful scene to see—they understood it. Yes, it clicked. Yes, that's what is happening. They were worried because they came from the West—the East has always known it: that if love deepens it transforms the relationship; husbands and wives become brothers and sisters. And ultimately a moment comes when not even brothers and sisters . . . a kind of oneness arises, they become one.

This is synchronicity! And this is what happens between the Master and the disciple—on a far deeper level than any other love, on a far higher plane than any other intimacy. You need not imitate Buddha, you need not imitate me, you need not follow Christ or Krishna or Mohammed. If you are fortunate enough to be with an alive Master, just become vulnerable to him. Let intimacy happen, come closer and closer. Drop your defences and armors. And the powerful dynamo of the Master, his magnetic field, his Buddhafield, will transform you. And he will not even give you any commandment. And his transformation will not be something imposed on you but something stirred within you that will bring your own being alive.

THE FISH IN THE SEA IS NOT THIRSTY

SYNERGETIC See Androgyny, 1st Series

SYNTHESIS Life can be lived in two ways: either as calculation or as poetry. Man has two sides to his inner being: the calculative side that creates science, business, politics; and the non-calculative side, which creates poetry, sculpture, music. These two sides have not yet been bridged; they have separate existences. Because of this, man is immensely improverished, remains unnecesarily lopsided— they have to be bridged.

In scientific language it is said that your brain has two hemispheres. The left-side hemisphere calculates, is mathematical, is prose; and the right-side hemisphere of the brain is poetry, is love, is song. One side is logic, the other side is love. One side is syllogism, the other side is song. And they are not really bridged, hence man lives in a kind of split.

My effort here is to bridge these two hemispheres. Man should be as scientific as possible, as far as the objective is concerned, and as musical as possible as far as the world of relationship is concerned . . .

And if you can be as scientific as possible with objects, your life will be rich, affluent: if you can be as musical as possible, your life will have beauty. And there is a third dimension also, which is beyond the mind. These two belong to the mind: the scientist and the artist. There is a third dimension, invisible: the dimension of no-mind. That belongs to the mystic. That is available through meditation.

Hence, I say these three words have to be remembered— three M's, like three R's: mathematics, the lowest; music, just in the middle; and meditation, the highest. A perfect human being is scientific about objects, is aesthetic, musical, poetic, about persons, and is meditative about himself. Where all these three meet, great rejoicing happens.

This is the real trinity, *trimurti*. In the East, particularly in India, we worship a place where three rivers meet—we call it a *sangam*, the meeting place. And the greatest of all of them is Prayag where the Ganges and Jamuna and Saraswati meet. Now, you can see the Ganges and you can see Jamuna, but Saraswati is invisible—you cannot see it. It is a metaphor! It simply represents, symbolically, the inner meeting of the three. You can see mathematics, you can see music, but you cannot see meditation. You can see the scientist; his work is outside. You can see the artist; his work is also outside. But you cannot see the mystic; his work is subjective. That is *saraswati*—the invisible river.

You can become a sacred place, you can hallow this body and this earth; this very body the Buddha, this very earth the Lotus Paradise. This is my slogan for the sannyasins. A sannyasin has to be the ultimate synthesis of all that God is.

God is known only when you have come to this synthesis. Otherwise, you can believe in God, but you will not know. And belief is just hiding your ignorance. Knowing is transforming, only knowledge brings understanding. And knowledge is not information: knowledge is the synthesis, integration, of all your potential.

Where the scientist and the poet and the mystic meet and become one—when this great synthesis happens, when all the three faces of God are expressed in you—*you* become a God. Then you can declare "*Aham Brahmasmi! I am God!*" Then you can say to the winds and the moon and to the rains and to the sun "*Ana'l Haq! I am truth!*" Before that, you were only a seed.

When this synthesis happens, you have bloomed, blossomed—you have become the one-thousand-petalled lotus, the golden lotus, that never dies: *ais dhammo sanantano*. This is the inexhaustible law that all the Buddhas have been teaching down the ages.

                              THE BOOK OF THE BOOKS, Vol. II

See also Analysis, 1st Series
           Paths, 2nd Series

T

TABOOS   There have been only two taboos in the world: sex and death. It is very strange why sex and death have been the two taboos not to be talked about, to be avoided. They are deeply connected. Sex represents life because all life arises out of sex, and death represents the end. And both have been taboo—don't talk about sex and don't talk about death.

And there have been only two types of cultures in the world. One category consists of the cultures for whom sex is taboo. They can talk about death, in fact they talk too much about death. For example, in India, listen to the mahatmas, to the saints, and you will find it. Nobody talks about sex, everybody talks about death—to frighten you, to create fear in you, because out of fear you can be enslaved, out of fear you can be forced to bow down to some stupid idea of God, to some stupid idol of God . . .

In a society like India, death is not taboo. Indian scriptures are full of very detailed descriptions of death. They describe with gusto how ugly death is. They describe your body in such ugly, disgusting ways that you will be surprised at these people—why are they so interested, so obsessed with all that is disgusting and nauseating?—for the simple reason that they want you to become so afraid of life, so antagonistic to life, so negative to life . . . They destroy your love for life, your affirmation of life by talking about death, by making death as big as possible and as dark as possible, by depicting death in all the ugliest colors.

And then there are societies . . . For example, Christianity for centuries has been a society, a culture against sex; sex is the taboo. "Don't talk about sex." Hence the idea—a sheer nonsense idea—that Jesus is born of a virgin mother. They have to create this fiction because how can Jesus, a man of such purity, come out of sexuality? Such purity coming out of such impurity? Impossible, illogical! A lotus coming out of mud? Impossible! But, in fact, all lotuses come out of mud.

Jesus is born as naturally as you are born—he is not a freak! He is not abnormal. And this whole nonsense about the Holy Ghost, that the Holy Ghost makes Mary pregnant . . .

Sex is taboo for Christianity: "Don't talk about sex!"

Now, after Sigmund Freud, the first taboo is broken; sex is no more a taboo. We have shifted to another taboo; now death has become the taboo. Now don't talk about death. It seems as if man needs some taboo or other. The Victorian society was a society rooted in the taboo of sex. Now the modern society, western society, is rooted in the taboo of death. Don't talk about death at all, forget all about death as if it does not happen—at least it does not happen to you, at least it has not happened to you up to now, so why bother about it? Forget all about it.

When a man dies in the West now, there are experts to decorate the man. He may never have looked so beautiful as he looks after death—painted and his cheeks so red as if he had just come from a three months' vacation in Florida! And so healthy, as if he had just been exercising and were now doing *shravasan*—the death posture—not really dead. The pretension has to be created that he is not dead. And even on the gravestone it is written: "He is not dead, he is only asleep."

And in all the languages we say . . . whenever somebody dies nobody says that he is simply dead. We say, "He has gone to God. He has become beloved of God. God has chosen him and called him. He has gone to the other world. He has become heavenly . . ."

Once a man dies, nobody speaks against him, nobody says anything against him. He becomes suddenly a saint, suddenly great. His place will never be filled again, his place will always remain empty. The world will always miss him; he was so essential. And nobody had taken any notice while he was alive. These are tricks—tricks to keep death away, to shut the doors, to forget all about death.

A real humanity will not have any taboos: no taboo about sex, no taboo about death. Life should be lived in its totality, and death is part of life. One should live totally and one should die totally.

And that's my message to my sannyasins.

WALKING IN ZEN, SITTING IN ZEN

T'AI CHI *Chi* means energy. The whole concept is that solidity is false—just as in modern physics. These walls are not real—it is just pure energy, but the electrons are moving so fast, with such terrific speed that you cannot see the blades separately. So it gives a sense of solidarity. The same is true with your body. What modern physics has come to know right now, Taoists have known for thousands of years—that man is energy.

It is said about a T'ai Chi Master that he would tell his
disciples to attack him, and he would just sit in the middle.
Five or ten disciples would rush from every corner of the
room to attack him, but when they came near him, they
would feel as if he were a cloud; there was nothing solid . . .
as if you could pass through him and you would not be
obstructed by anything.

If you continue this idea that you are energy, it is possible to become just like a cloud with no boundaries, melting
and merging with existence. This anecdote is not just an
anecdote. With a man who has gone deep into T'ai Chi, it
is very easily possible that when you come across him, you
will not find any obstruction; you can simply go through
him. You cannot hurt him because he is not there to be hurt.
THE PASSION FOR THE IMPOSSIBLE

TALENT   And that's how I see every human being—as
having a deep skill to be divine. One may refine it or not:
one may become a great artist in it, or one may leave it
undeveloped and crude. It is like a rock, but a little work
and it can become a beautiful statue. That skill is everybody's
potentiality, but very few people develop it, and it cannot
be developed on its own.

Everybody is born with it, but millions of people never
use it, so the faculty goes on shrinking; it remains a seed
and never sprouts. Just a little work towards it and much
is the payoff, tremendous is the benefit. And there is no
greater skill than that. One may be a poet, but then there
are only a few seconds in the life of a poet which are
beautiful, otherwise he crawls on the earth like everybody
else. One can be a painter, but only for a few moments are
there—rare and far apart—where there are glimpses of the
unknown. They come and go; they don't last. The painter
is back on the earth again—and more miserable than ever.

That is the misery of great artists, because they have
something to compare. They have known a few moments
when they were no more of this earth. They have known
a few moments when they were part of the stars. They have
known a few moments when there was depth and height
and they were expansive . . . when everything was totally
different, was a benediction. Then they are thrown back

again and again. They don't know what to do. Back on earth they are more miserable, and the darkness is far darker.

When you know a few moments of happiness, your unhappiness becomes very very penetrating; you can compare. So all great artists have a few moments of what I call the divine. They live in misery, they live in a nightmare; they are almost on the verge of becoming mad.

So all other talents are just partial talents. There is only one talent which is total and whole—and that is the talent to become divine. And if you develop it a little, it remains with you. Then whatsoever you do it is there, silently, like a shadow surrounding you, engulfing you . . . like a glow following you. It becomes your golden aura . . .

THE PASSION FOR THE IMPOSSIBLE

TALKING If a person can remain silent for a few hours every day he will become aware of his whole phoniness, because he will see his real face again and again. If you continuously talk and continuously relate with people you forget your original face, because you have to wear masks continuously. For twenty-four hours you are talking, using words. And when you continuously use words, slowly slowly you start believing in those words, in the sound of those words.

Words have a hypnotic power. If you use a certain word again and again, it hypnotizes you. If you use the word "God" again and again, slowly slowly you start thinking that you know what you mean, that you know what God is. It is very dangerous to repeat words.

But people go on talking. They don't give any gap in which they can simply be silent and be. If you are silent for at least one hour every day, you will be aware continuously that your talk is nonsense. And then ninety-nine percent of your talk will start disappearing. What is the point of talking nonsense?

But why do people talk then? They talk just to hide themselves behind the noise. Whenever you are nervous you start talking.

Now it is a known fact: if people are forced to live in solitude, after three weeks they start talking to themselves.

They cannot *bear* silence, it becomes intolerable, so they start talking to themselves. They have to talk; words somehow keep them clinging to their personality. Once words disappear, they start falling into the impersonal. And they are very much afraid of the impersonal.

The impersonal is your reality. And you are afraid of the reality and you are clinging to the illusions that words create.

UNIO MYSTICA, Vol. I

People are continuously talking, particularly women—for the simple reason that man has taken every other avenue from them. They are left only with one thing—talking; they are not allowed anything else. Every other door has been closed, so their whole energy is turned into talking. They are talking because their minds are too noisy and they have to pour it out: it is a kind of catharsis. Even when you are eating you are talking. How can you taste food and how can you be sensitive to taste?

When you go into the garden you are talking. If you are not talking with somebody else you are in a constant dialogue with yourself. You divide yourself into many persons, you make a crowd inside yourself. You don't look at the flowers. You don't feel the fragrance, the joy of the birds, the celebration of the trees. You don't allow yourself any sensitivity, any opportunity to be more sensitive, to be more available to existence, to be more vulnerable.

Sensitivity means openness, vulnerability, availability.

THE BOOK OF THE BOOKS, Vol. X

TANTRA Tantra is an effort to make you more conscious. The very word "Tantra" means expansion of awareness. It comes from a Sanskrit root *tan*; *tan* means expansion. Tantra means expansion of consciousness—and the basic fact, and the most fundamental fact to be understood is that you are fast asleep, you have to be awakened . . .

To be in contact with someone who is already awake is a must. And to be together with those people who are all thinking to become awake is also a must. This is the meaning of a school method, a group method. Tantra is a group method. It says: Be together. Find out all the possibilities; so many people can be together and they can pool their energies. Somebody is very intelligent, and somebody is very loving. Both are half, but together they become more of a unity, more wholeness.

Man is half, woman is half. Except for Tantra, all the seekers have tried to do without the other. Man has tried alone, women have tried alone. Tantra says: Why not be together—join hands together? The woman is half, the man is half—together they are a greater energy, a more whole energy, a healthier energy. Join together. Let *yin* and *yang* function together. There will be more possibility of getting out of it.

Other methods use fight and conflict. Man starts fighting with women, starts escaping from women—rather than using the possibility of the help, he starts thinking of the woman as the enemy. Tantra says this is sheer foolishness; you are wasting your energy unnecessarily fighting with the woman —because there are greater things to be fought about! It is better to keep company with the woman; let her help you, and you help her. Go together as one unit and you have more chances to stand against the unconscious nature.

Use all possibilities; then only is there *some* chance that you can evolve into a conscious being, you can become a Buddha.

THE TANTRA VISION, Vol. I

So whenever Tantra says "sex-energy" it means the *elan-vital*, the life-energy itself. They are synonymous. Whatsoever we call sex is just one dimension of life-energy. There are other dimensions. And really it should be so. You see a seed sprouting, somewhere flowers are coming on a tree, the birds are singing—the whole phenomenon is sexual. It is life manifesting itself in many ways. When the bird is singing it is a sexual call, an invitation. When the flower is attracting butterflies and bees it is an invitation, because the bees and butterflies will carry the seeds of reproduction. Stars are moving in space . . . No one has yet worked on it but it is one of the oldest Tantra concepts that there are male planets and female planets—otherwise there would be no movement. It must be so because the polarity is needed, the opposite is needed to create magnetism, to create attraction. Planets must be male and female. Everything must be divided into these two polarities. And life is a rhythm between these two opposites. Repulsion and attraction, coming nearer and going far . . . these are the rhythms.

Tantra uses the word "sex" wherever the opposites meet. It is a sexual phenomenon. And how to make your inner opposites meet is the whole purpose of meditation.

THE BOOK OF THE SECRETS, Vol. V

Man is bisexual—every man, every woman. Half of you is male and half of you is female. If you are a woman, then the female part is dominant and the male part is hidden behind it. And vice versa. Once you have become aware of this, then some new work starts: your inner woman and inner man can have a meeting. And that meeting can remain absolute; there is no need to come back from the peak. But the first vision comes from the outer woman or man.

Hence Tantra uses the outer woman, the outer man, as part of the inner work. Once you have become aware that you have a woman inside you or a man inside you, then the work takes a totally new quality, it starts moving into a new dimension. Now the meeting has to happen inside: you have to allow your woman and man to meet within.

In India we have had that concept for at least five thousand years. You may have seen the statues of Shiva as *ardhanarishwar*: half man, half woman. That is the picture of everybody's being, inner being. You must have seen the *shivalinga*: it symbolizes the male. But the *shivalinga* is placed in the female sexual organ; it is not alone, they are together. That again represents the inner duality, the inner polarity. But the polarity can meet and merge.

With the outer, the merger will be only for the moment. And then will come great frustration and great misery; and the higher the moment, the deeper will be the darkness that follows it. But the meeting can happen within.

First learn that the peak is possible, and then feel grateful to the woman or the man who has given you the peak. Tantra worships the woman as a goddess and the man as a god. Any woman who helps you attain to this vision is a goddess, any man that helps you attain to this vision is a god. Love becomes sacred, because it gives you the first glimpses of the divine. Then the inner work starts. You have worked without, now you have to work within.

Tantra has two phases, two stages: the outer, the extrovert Tantra, and the inner, the introvert Tantra. The beginning always has to be from without, because that is where we are. And we have to start from the place where we are, and then move inwards.

When the inner man and woman have met and melted, and when you are no longer divided inside, you have become one—integrated, crystallized, *one*—you have attained. This is enlightenment.

THE BOOK OF WISDOM, Vol. II

I will give you a simple method . . .

While making love, three things have to be remembered. One is: before you make love, meditate. Never make love without meditating, otherwise the love will remain sexual. Before you meet the woman you should rise higher in your consciousness because then the meeting will happen on a higher plane. For at least forty minutes sit looking at the wall with just a very dim light on so that it gives a mysteriousness.

Sit silently and don't move the body; remain like a statue. Then when you make love, the body will move, so give it another extreme of first being unmoving so the body gathers momentum to move deeply. Then the urge becomes so vibrating that the whole body, every fiber is ready to have a movement. Then only Tantric orgasm is possible. You can have some music on . . . classical music will do; something that gives a very subtle rhythm to the body.

Make the breathing as slow as possible because when you make love the breathing will go deep and fast. So just go on slowing down, but don't force it, otherwise it will go fast. Simply suggest that it slows down.

Both meditate together and when you are both feeling meditative, that is the moment to love. Then you will never feel tension and energy will be flowing. If you are not feeling meditative, don't make love. If meditation is not happening that day, forget all about love.

People do simply the opposite. Almost always couples fight before they make love. They become angry, nag each other and bring all sorts of conflict—and then they make love. They fall very low in their consciousness, so of course love cannot be very satisfying. It will be frustrating and you will feel a tension.

The second thing is: when you are making love, before you start, worship the partner and let the partner worship you. So after meditation, worship. Face each other totally naked and worship each other, because Tantra cannot be between man and woman. It can only be between a god and a goddess. It is a gesture, but very significant. The whole attitude has to become sublime so that you disappear. Touch each other's feet, put garlands of flowers there.

The man becomes transformed into Shiva and the woman is transformed into Shakti. Now your humanity is irrelevant, your form is irrelevant, your name is irrelevant; you are just pure energy. Worship brings that energy into focus. And don't pretend. The worship has to be true. It cannot be just a ritual, otherwise you will miss. Tantra is not a ritual. There is much ritual in it, but Tantra is not ritual.

You can repeat the ritual. You can bow down to her feet and touch them; that won't help. Let it be a deeply meaningful gesture. Really look at her. She is no more your wife, no more your girlfriend, no more woman, no more body, but a configuration of energy. Let her first become divine, then make love to her. Then love will change its quality. It will become divine. That's the whole methodology of Tantra.

Then in the third step you make love. But let your making love be more like a happening than like a making. The English expression "making love" is ugly. How can you *make* love? It is not something like doing; it is not an action. It is a state. You can be in it but you cannot make it. You can move in it but you cannot do it. You can be loving but you cannot manipulate it. The whole western mind tries to manipulate everything.

Even if the western mind comes to find God someday God will be in trouble. They will harness him in some way or other, manipulate him. They will put him to some use, some utilitarian purpose. Even love has become a sort of doing. No.

When you make love, be possessed. Move slowly, touch each other's bodies; play with each other's bodies. The body is like a musical instrument. Don't be in a hurry. Let things grow. If you move slowly, suddenly both your energies will rise together, as if something has possessed you. It will happen instantly and simultaneously together. Then only Tantra is possible. Move now into love . . .

Just feel energy descending on you and let that energy have its movement. Sometimes you will start shrieking, shriek. Sometimes you will start saying things, say. Sometimes only moans will be coming out, or some *mudras*, gestures; allow them. It is going to be a maddening thing, but one has to allow it. And don't be afraid, because it is through your allowing that it is happening. The moment you want to stop it, it stops, so you are never beyond control.

And when gods make love it is almost wild. There are no rules, no regulations. One moves just on the spur of the moment. Nothing is taboo . . . nothing is inhibited. Whatsoever happens in that moment is beautiful and holy; whatsoever, I say, unconditionally. If you bring your mind into it you will destroy it completely. If you suddenly feel like sucking her finger and you say "What nonsense!" then you have brought in the mind. You may feel like sucking her breast; nothing wrong in it.

Nobody knows what is going to happen. You are simply left in the divine vortex. It will take you, and it will take you wherever it wants. You are simply available, ready to move with it. You don't direct it . . . you have simply become vehicles. Let energies meet in their own ways. The man should be dropped out of it—just pure energy. You will not be making love only through the genital organs; you will be making love through your whole body.

That's the meaning of *shivalingam*: no face, no hands, no feet—just the phallic symbol. When Shiva made love he became just the phallus—the whole of his body. It is very beautiful . . . no face, nothing. Everything has disappeared.

It is not that you are using your sexual organs only; the sex has spread all over. Your head is as much a part of it as your feet. You have become a phallus. You are no more man; you are just energy. She is also no more a woman; just energy, a vulva. It is a very wild thing.

If you meditate before and then worship each other, there is no danger; everything will move rightly. You will attain to a peak of orgasm that you have never known. Sometimes you will achieve it: a very great orgasm in which the whole body throbs and pulsates. By and by you reach a climax; again you come down. It will cleanse your whole being, the whole system. Sometimes there will be no ejaculation but orgasm will be there.

There are two types of orgasm: the peak orgasm and the valley orgasm. In the peak orgasm you will have an ejaculation and she will have also an ejaculation of some subtle energies. In the valley orgasm you will not have any ejaculation. It will be a passive orgasm . . . very silent, very subtle. The throb will be there but almost imperceptible. In the peak orgasm you will feel very very blissful. In the valley orgasm you will feel very very peaceful. And both are needed; both are two aspects of Tantra. Every peak has its valley and every valley has its peak. A peak cannot exist without the valley or vice versa.

And when it has happened and you have both achieved to a deep orgasm, don't pull yourself out of her. After the orgasm, remain inside her and rest for a few moments. That rest is very very deep. Afer an orgasm a rest is like a valley. You have reached to the very peak and now you have come back to the valley. It is very cool and shady and you rest.

And really much happens after the orgasm . . . the merging, the melting. Bodies are tired, exhausted, spent. The mind is shocked. It is almost like an electric shock.

When you come out of your love state, again pray together; end with a prayer. The difference is that when you meditate, you meditate separately and she meditates separately, because meditation cannot be done together. Meditation is a lonely effort. It is not a relationship. So you may be meditating together but still you meditate alone; you are alone and she is alone.

Then you worship each other. That's again different. The other becomes the object of worship. Then you make love and you are completely lost. You are not yourself, she is not herself. Nobody knows who is who. All is lost in a whirlpool of energy. The polarity of man and woman is no more a polarity; boundaries merge, mingle. Sometimes you will feel like a woman and she will feel like a man. Sometimes she comes on top of you. Sometimes you become passive and she becomes active and the role changes. It is a great drama of energies. All is lost, abandoned. Then you come out of the innermost experience, pray together. That's the fourth thing.

Just thank God. And never complain. Whatsoever happens is right. Don't say, "This has not happened. This should have happened." Who are we? He knows better. So just thank him, whatsoever happens; thank him with deep gratefulness. Bow down and put your head on the earth and remain there for a few moments in deep gratefulness.

Meditation is alone. In worship, the other is important, and in prayer you both pray to God. So these three things have to be involved. They will create the ecology in which Tantra happens. And once a week will do.

If you are moving in Tantra then no other love should be allowed, otherwise it dissipates energy. But whenever you want to make love, make sure you have enough time. It should not be done in a hurry. It should not be like work. It is a game, play, and these energies are so subtle that if you are in a hurry, nothing happens.

Tantra is not a fragment. You cannot practice it unless you create the situation. It is like a flower.

You have to sow the seed and take care of the plant and water it every day. You look to whether the sun is reaching it or not. You cannot bring the flower, but you can create the situation in which one day the flower comes and the bud opens.

So these three things are sowing the seed, caring for the plant, watering it and being continuously concerned about it; being careful, protecting it. Then one day suddenly—the flower of Tantra. It will happen.

BELOVED OF MY HEART

TAO   Tao is another name for God, far more beautiful than God because God, the word "God", has been exploited too much by the priests. They have exploited in the name of

God for so long that even the word has become contaminated—it has become disgusting. Any man of intelligence is bound to avoid it because it reminds him of all the nonsense that has happened on the earth down the ages in the name of God, in the name of religion. More mischief has happened in the name of God than in any other name.

Tao in that sense is tremendously beautiful. You cannot worship Tao because Tao does not give you the idea of a person. It is simply a principle, not a person. You cannot worship a principle—you cannot pray to Tao. It will look ridiculous, it will be utterly absurd, praying to a principle. You don't pray to gravitation, you cannot pray to the theory of relativity.

Tao simply means the ultimate principle that binds the whole existence together. The existence is not a chaos, that much is certain; it is a cosmos. There is immense order in it, intrinsic order in it, and the name of that order is Tao. Tao simply means the harmony of the whole. No temples have been built for Tao; no statues, no prayers, no priests, no rituals—that's the beauty of it. Hence I don't call it a doctrine, nor do I call it a religion, it is a pure insight. You can call it *Dharma*; that is Buddha's word for Tao. The word in English that comes closer or closest to Tao is "Nature" with a capital N.

TAO: THE GOLDEN GATE, Vol. I

TAROT See Astrology, 1st Series

TEA You might have heard about Bodhidharma, one of the greatest Masters of meditation in the whole history of humankind. A very beautiful story is reported about him. He was concentrating on something—something outward. His eyes would blink and the concentration would be lost, so he tore his eyelids. This is a beautiful story: he tore his eyelids, threw them away and concentrated. After a few weeks, he saw some plants growing on the spot where he had thrown his eyelids. This anecdote happened on a mountain in China, and the mountain's name is "Tah" or "Ta". Hence the name "tea". Those plants which were growing became tea, and that is why tea helps you to be awake.

When your eyes are blinking and you are falling down into sleep, take a cup of tea. Those are Bodhidharma's eyelids. That is why Zen monks consider tea to be sacred. Tea is not any ordinary thing. It is sacred—Bodhidharma's eyelids. In Japan they have tea ceremonies, and every house has a tearoom, and the tea is served with religious ceremony; it is sacred. Tea has to be taken in a very meditative mood.

Japan has created beautiful ceremonies around tea drinking. They will enter the tearoom as if they are entering a temple. Then the tea will be made, and everyone will sit silently listening to the samovar bubbling. There is the steaming, the noise, and everyone just listening. It is no ordinary thing—Bodhidharma's eyelids. And because Bodhidharma was trying to be awake with open eyes, tea helps. Because the story happened on the mountain of "Tah", it is called tea. Whether true or untrue, this anecdote is beautiful.

If you are concentrating outwardly, then non-blinking eyes will be needed, as if you have no more eyelids. That is the meaning of throwing the eyelids. You have only eyes without eyelids to close them. Concentrate until the point dissolves: it dissolves! If you persist, if you insist and do not allow the mind to move, the point dissolves. And when the point dissolves, if you were concentrated on the point and there was only this point for you in the world, if the whole world had dissolved already, if only this point remained and now the point also dissolves, then the consciousness cannot move anywhere; there is no object to move to. All the dimensions are closed. The mind is thrown to itself, the consciousness is thrown to itself, and you enter the center.

THE BOOK OF THE SECRETS, Vol. I

TEACHER The teacher is one who teaches borrowed knowledge. He knows nothing, he has not experienced anything—it has not happened to him—but he has heard it, read it. He is skillful in transmitting it verbally, intellectually; he is capable of communication.

The perfect teacher is one who knows this: that he does not know. The teacher forgets it, tends to forget it. He starts believing in whatsoever he is teaching others. He is not only a deceiver, he is also deceived. He starts living in a deep auto-hypnotic sleep. First he convinces others, and when others are convinced, seeing their conviction he becomes convinced himself . . .

The teacher becomes auto-hypnotized. The great teacher is one who teaches, but knowing that "It is not my own." Not only does he know it, he makes it clear to everybody that "I am just an interpreter, a commentator," that "I have studied, I am a scholar, a professor, I am teaching things about which I have no experience of my own," and who is capable of so much awareness that he never becomes deceived. Even though others start believing in him, he never believes in himself unless he starts experiencing.

THEOLOGIA MYSTICA

My whole teaching can be condensed into these two words: *Be yourself.*

GUIDA SPIRITUALE

I was also a teacher for many years . . . but a different kind of teacher. My children were absolutely free to do whatsoever they wanted to do. If they shouted, I would join them! Why should I be just standing there? Then they would become silent because . . . that is they could not believe what was happening! If they laughed, I would laugh. I would tell them so many jokes that they would say, "Stop, sir! Our bellies will burst. You make us laugh so much that we start crying!"

I was turned out from one college because so many students who were not my students would come to attend my class . . . but my doors were open. It was a crowded class, and students from other classes would come. The principal was of course angry and the other professors were angry and they said, "This is not right. Our classes are empty and they make so much noise! It is such a celebration— what is going on? And why do you allow people who are not your students?"

Just be here and just look into *your* problems, into your expectations, into your ego trips, into your obsessions and into the ideas that have been put into your mind, for which you have been conditioned.

Once they are dropped one cannot find a better job than being a teacher. Otherwise it is very ugly: if you cannot drop these things I will tell you to get out of it, to do something else that you can love and with which you are not angry. But first we will try—if you can drop these things . . . and these can be dropped. I can see that you are a perfect person—you can see things clearly; you just have not been courageous enough to drop them.

Once you see that the children are victims of the society, the family, the teachers, you will love them; you will feel much compassion for them: you will be for them and with them! You will become part of them, and once you are part of them you will see how much they can love you. Nobody has *really* been there to whom they can show their love and their respect, and they have great reverence in their minds, in their hearts, but nobody seems to be worthy.

Your old teacher has to go, and that old teacher is not good—it is making you disturbed and it is making those children also worried because when a teacher is angry, students cannot feel good. They also feel guilty that they are making you angry, that they are doing something wrong, that they are should not be doing such things.

You are creating the guilt feelings in them: you are getting angry and they are becoming guilty, and this is how all neuroses arise. Our schools, our colleges, our universities, are breeding grounds for neuroses.

But I will make you a different kind of teacher, Mm?

FAR BEYOND THE STARS

The mind plays so many games, and the ultimate game is the game of becoming a teacher. It is difficult, arduous, to transform yourself; it is very easy to teach others. It is difficult to be a disciple, it is very easy to be a teacher—because the disciple has to surrender and the teacher can keep all his ego. In fact, he can have more ego because so many people are surrendering to him.

Unless he has become established in the way—that means he has attained to love and to watchfulness—unless he has come to that clarity of consciousness which makes one a Buddha, he should not teach.

First establish yourself in the way.
Then teach.
And so defeat sorrow.

Otherwise this happens: listening to a Buddha, his beautiful teachings, you become so full of the teachings that a great desire arises to teach others. You forget completely that first you have to practice before you can preach. That's how it is happening all over the world.

Once I was taken to a Christian college, one of the biggest in India, where they create missionaries, ministers, priests, et cetera. I was a little puzzled: how can you create priests, ministers, missionaries in a college? That is impossible! The principal was very much interested in me; he invited me. He said, "Come and see!"

It was a six-year course, and I looked around the college, a big campus—seven hundred people were getting ready to become priests, preachers, teachers—I looked around, I went into many classes, and what I saw was really hilarious. It was so ridiculous!

In one class the teacher was telling the students, "When you give this sermon, this is how you have to stand, and when you come to this point, this is how you have to raise your hand, these are the gestures you make, this is how you have to close your eyes—as if you have gone into a deep, deep meditation . . ." As if—don't forget the "as if"! They were learning like actors!

In Poona there is a film institute where they prepare actors; that I can understand—acting can be taught. Even there I have never heard that film institutes have created great actors, but one can understand that acting can be taught, even though great actors have not been created by film institutes. Even there it fails.

Actors are also born like poets, because acting is poetry, it is art; you have to have an inborn spirit. Not everybody can be an actor, because one has to get so much involved in the act, so deeply involved, that one forgets that one is separate. One has to lose one's identity in the acting, one has to become one's part; one has to forget everything about oneself. This is no ordinary feat.

One can think that acting can be taught—but how can you teach people to become Masters?

Taking leave of the principal I told him one story: "I have heard—it must have happened in some college like yours—the teacher was telling the students, 'When you talk about paradise, heaven, smile a heavenly smile, your eyes full of joy and light, and look upwards towards heaven. And for a moment become silent and just let people see how joyous, full of light and joy you are.'

"A student raised his hand and he said, 'That's right, but when we are talking about hell, what to do?'

"The teacher said, 'Then just as you are will do—just stand as you are. You need not do anything else, just be yourself, that's all, and that will show them what hell is.'"

Teaching people to become Masters is such an absurdity. Jesus did not learn in any college. It is fortunate that such colleges did not exist in those days, otherwise they may have destroyed Jesus. Buddha never went to any religious institution to learn. Religion has to be lived, because that is the only way to learn it.

THE BOOK OF THE BOOKS, Vol. V

See also Rajneeshism
          Education, 1st Series

TEARS People have almost lost the dimension of tears. They allow tears only when they are very much in deep pain or suffering. They have forgotten that tears can also be of happiness, tremendous delight, or celebration.

Tears have nothing to do with suffering or happiness. Tears have something to do with anything that is too much inside and wants to overflow. It may be happiness, it may be unhappiness. Anything that is too intensely there, unbearably there, overflows; the cup is too full. The tears come out of too-muchness. So enjoy them.

The whole world has to learn again the beauty of crying and weeping and tears, because if you cannot celebrate through tears it means you never overflow with happiness. It means you only overflow when you suffer, when you are in deep pain. The logic is simple. It means that you have lost the dimension of happiness—being so happy that you come to a point where the cup is overflowing.

ABOVE ALL, DON'T WOBBLE

The heart is frozen . . . and the tears are the beginning of its melting. The more you allow tears, the more the heart will melt. And because you have never really cried in your life, the heart has forgotten how to melt. But it is beginning to. It is again getting the spark . . . it is sprouting.

So don't be worried about why you are crying—sometimes for sadness, good, sometimes in joy, good. Sometimes even if there is a mixed feeling—on the one hand it is sad and on another hand it is delightful—don't be worried about it. Just go on pouring yourself out in your tears.

Tears are one of the most beautiful things. They unburden you and they cleanse your vision . . . not only the physical vision. They cleanse the physical vision—tears are basically meant to clear the dust from the eyes—but spiritually also they cleanse the vision. The capacity to see becomes clearer, innocent, and the heart starts melting.

Tears are the language of the heart. Just as thoughts are the language of the mind, tears are the language of the heart. Tears are the poetry of the heart. It doesn't matter whether you are crying in sadness or happiness. What matters is that you are crying, that you are totally in it. And don't hold them! Don't hesitate, don't feel embarassed, don't feel shy. Become like a small child. Don't judge, and soon they will be coming like a flood. And with their coming your heart will start functioning again. It will start getting warmth, it will become alive. And in the shadow, love will grow.

ONLY LOSERS CAN WIN IN THIS GAME

The tears are the greatest possible prayer. Don't be worried about analyzing them, don't try to interpret them; they are beyond interpretation and beyond analysis. Words will not be adequate to say anything about the tears. Tears come from a deeper source than words. And if tears are coming, all that is needed is not to think about them but to allow them, to give them an intensity, to give them a kind of totality. You will understand those tears only when you are not hesitant about going into them, when you are not somehow holding yourself back. Go into them utterly. Become tears, and when tears come, enjoy. You are overflowing. Thinking of love, if tears don't come—then you were not thinking about love. Thinking of God, if tears don't come then your thinking is futile, impotent. Listening to me, if your heart does not start overflowing with tears, then you were listening only through the head—which is not listening. You have been hearing but

not listening. When you listen, the heart will start dancing.
And the heart has only one way to express itself, and that
way is the way of tears.

Meditate on these lines by an anonymous poet:

Sing until your breath crackles to the last.
Note what is caught upon the passing wind.
Laugh until the pains squeeze authority into chaotic
    blasts, and then into puny puffs.
Cry until the peak of your tears, like the pure tips
    of a wave before it folds into the gulping sea.
Ah, but love when your heart beats the beat of nights
    full of daffodils,
For then you are.

If you can allow your tears totally, then you are.

My message is of laughter and tears. It looks contradictory
but it is not. Deep down in your being laughter and tears
are joined together, they are part of one energy. If you laugh
long, tears will come. If you go on crying, you will suddenly
see the change—one moment a sudden change—and the
laughter has entered into you. See this polarity. Go into tears
as deeply as possible until tears become laughter. Then you
have really gone into the very end; from that end, the wheel
moves. When you are laughing, laugh so deeply and so
totally, so wildly, that laughter turns into tears and your eyes
start raining. Then you will know that all paradoxes are only
on the surface—deep down they are one, laughter and tears
are one. And when your prayer is of laughter and tears, it
is a true prayer.

                    THE WISDOM OF THE SANDS, Vol. I

TECHNIQUE   There are just two or three things I would
like to say before you start your work.

One is: bring more love into it. The techniques are
beautiful, but love is lacking. Whenever you just become
technique-oriented, then by and by you forget that love is
the greatest technique. All else is secondary—can be helpful,
but cannot replace love.

So don't be just technical, otherwise you will help a little
but not enough, and you will not be able to help to the very
end. Sooner or later a technique comes to an end, but love

never does. Each technique should become a vehicle of love, so that when the technique ends, love takes over. And one never comes to the point where one can say that now the journey is finished and there is nothing left.

When you work on people, don't work on them as if they are means. Each individual is an end. The technique exists for the individual—the sabbath is for man, not man for the sabbath. Always remember this, because the mind tends to forget. It is very technical and does not believe in love.

So help people, but remain alert to give them as much care and love as possible. You will see that the same methods used in the West—which work up to a certain limit and then stop—don't stop anywhere; they go on and on. So make it a very loving process. You follow me?

And the second thing: always start with a prayer and always end with a prayer. In the beginning you pray with the idea of asking for help. In the end it is a thank you. Always ask for divine help, because man is helpless: and if you remember this, you will never condemn one who fails. Whenever you work with techniques, the fallacy is possible that you start thinking that man is enough. You forget God, you forget the whole.

In Yoga they simply dropped the concept of God. Only once in Patanjali's *sutras* is God mentioned—and that too is a technique: that if you surrender to God—not that God exists, no; he is just an excuse for surrender—it will be helpful. Yoga is completely godless. The word "yoga" means technique, and technique always feels that man is sufficient unto himself and that there is no need to ask for help from beyond.

So make it a point that you start with a prayer together, the teacher and the taught both. The teacher should never feel that he is special. He should always feel that both are part of an ongoing process of growth; that he is also going to learn much, not only teach. Don't become teachers, just remain helpers, fellow travelers; don't become "holier than thou"—and then you will be very very deeply helpful. All Upanishads in India start by a prayer which is done by the teacher and the taught together. They pray that they should not go astray; they, the teacher and the taught, the Master and the disciple, should not go astray.

And the third thing: always try to see that if some technique is not working on someone, then don't go on forcing it, because all techniques are not for everybody. So give them a try, and if one is not working, then there is no need to create the feeling that the person is lacking; just say that this technique does not suit you, but there is nothing wrong in that.

Never create the feeling of failure, remember, because by and by the person can start becoming a failure. He begins to feel that nothing is going to happen; that this is not for him, it is only for very special and rare people, and he is an ordinary person. Once this happens, a great rock has fallen on his being. And many of the teachers in the world go on doing that. Rather than helping people, they hinder. So don't condemn anybody, otherwise you will be closing their whole possibility of growth.

If in your three days' work you can give only this much to a person—that he comes out more confident; more confident about himself, more certain of his step, his growth, more confident that it is going to happen—you have given him something beautiful, a treasure: you have succeeded.

But always remember that if he leaves the group feeling he has been a failure, then you have betrayed that person, you have harmed him and put him back. These three things . . .

HAMMER ON THE ROCK

TECHNOLOGY   The first and most fundamental thing to be remembered is that enlightenment can never have a technology. By its very nature it is impossible. But the West is obsessed with technology, so whatsoever comes into the hands of the West, it starts reducing it into a technology. Technology is an obsession. For the outside world, science is a valid approach, but partial, not total; not the only approach, but only one of the approaches. Poetry is as valid as science.

Science is knowledge without love, and that is the danger in it. Because it is knowledge without love, it is always in the service of death and never in the service of life. Hence, the whole progress of science is leading man towards a global suicide. One day when man has committed suicide—

the Third World War—cockroaches will think, "We are the most fit to survive." Some Darwin, some cockroach-Darwin, will prove, "We are the fittest because we have survived; the survival of the fittest."

Man has committed suicide; he has destroyed himself. Knowledge without love is dangerous, because in its very root is poison.

Love keeps balance, never allows knowledge to go too far, so it never becomes destructive. Science is knowledge without love; that is its danger. But it is one of the valid approaches: the object, the material, can be known without love—there is no need. But life is not only matter. Life is suffused with something tremendously transcendental. That transcendental is missed. And then science, by and by, automatically turns into a technology. It becomes mechanical. More and more it becomes a means to exploit nature, to manipulate nature. The very beginning of science has been with that idea: how to conquer nature. That's a foolish idea.

We are not separate from nature: how can we conquer it? We *are* nature, so who is going to conquer whom? It is absurd. With that absurdity, science has destroyed much: the whole nature is destroyed, the climate is poisoned, the air, the water, the seas, everything polluted. The whole harmony is dying, the ecology is being continuously destroyed. Please remember—that is enough, more than enough.

Don't turn science inwards. If the application of scientific methodology has been so devastating for outer nature, it is going to be more devastating to the inner nature—because you are moving towards the more subtle. Even for the outside nature, a different kind of knowledge is needed which is rooted in love; but for the innermost core of your being, the subtlest, the transcendental, knowledge is not needed at all. Innocence is needed. Innocence with love—then you will know the inside, then you will know the interior of your being, the subjectivity.

But the West is obsessed with technology. It seems technology has succeeded in nature: we have become more powerful. We have *not* become more powerful! The whole idea is just fallacious; we have not become more powerful. We are becoming weaker every day because the natural resources are being exhausted. Sooner or later the earth will be empty, it will not grow anything. We are not becoming powerful, we are becoming weaker and weaker and weaker every day. We are on the deathbed. Humanity cannot survive, the way it has been behaving with nature, for more than fifty years, sixty years, or, at the most, one hundred years—which is nothing. If the Third World War does not happen, then we will be committing a slow suicide. Within a hundred years, we will be gone. Not even a trace will be left.

And man will not be the first to disappear. Many other animals, very strong animals, have disappeared from the earth. They used to roam the earth, they were the kings of the earth, bigger that the elephant. They are no longer anywhere. They were thinking they had become very powerful. They were very huge, with tremendous energy, but then the earth could not supply food for them. They had to die.

The same is happening with man: man thinks he is becoming more and more powerful, he can reach to the moon; but he is destroying the earth. He is destroying the whole possibility of future life. Slowly, humanity is disappearing. Please, don't turn your technology towards the inner; you have done enough harm. Enlightenment cannot be reduced to a technology.

So the first thing: the inner journey is of innocence, not of knowledge; certainly not of science, *absolutely* not of technology. It is more of love, innocence, silence. Meditation is not a technique really. Because you cannot understand anything other than technique, I have to talk in terms of technique. Otherwise, meditation is not a technique at all. Meditation is nothing that you do. Meditation is something that you fall into, just like love. Meditation is something in which you can be, but you cannot do it. Doing ceases.

How can there be a technology for non-doing? Technology is relevant with doing; you have to do something. Meditation is not something that you do. It is only when your doer has gone and you are totally relaxed, not doing anything, in a deep let-go, rest . . . there is meditation. Then meditation flowers. It is the flowering of your being. It has nothing to do with becoming. It is not an achievement, it is not an improvement; it is just being that which you already are. What technique is needed?

People are foolish; that's why techniques have to be talked about. If you understand, nothing is needed. Just being silent and just being yourself, not moving in any direction, not moving at all, and you will see the benediction, the meditation. When this meditation has become such a spontaneous flow that you need not even sit for it in a certain posture, that you need not find a small corner in the house where nobody disturbs you, when in the marketplace it is always there, even when you are asleep it is there, you go on feeling it, it goes on like breathing, or the beating of the heart, that's what Kabir calls *sahaj samadhi,* spontaneous ecstasy. It needs no technique. It needs only spontaneity, it needs only naturalness, it needs only simplicity.

So I say to to you: Blessed are the ignorant, for theirs is the kingdom of God. Become innocent and become ignorant. Don't remain knowledgeable . . .

You ask, *Many people in the West are engaged in the creation of a science of technology of enlightenment.* Those people are criminals. They are dangerous people; avoid them. Just these same people were engaged in creating technology two hundred years ago. They have destroyed nature, now they are turning towards consciousness. They will destroy that too.

Now there is a movement all over the world to protect the ecology of nature, the "naturality" of nature. But it is too late really. Now nothing can be done, nothing much can be done. And these people who propagate in favor of ecology appear to be eco-nuts, another species of Jehovah's Witnesses—fanatics, desperately fighting something which seems impossible.

Before the plague of technology turns to human consciousness, stop it. Stop it in the seed.

And you say, *The need is certainly there.* It is not, certainly not. There is no need. *But how do you see the possibility?* There is no possibility either. But man is dangerous: the more impossible a thing, the more he becomes attracted and challenged. That's what Edmund Hillary said when he reached to the top of Everest. Somebody asked him, "Why did you try at all? What is the point? Why?" Edmund Hillary said, "I had to, because Everest is there. Because it is there, I had to. It stands like a challenge." Anything unconquerable is a challenge to man's ego.

There is no possibility; naturally, it will never happen—but that very impossibility can become a challenge to these mad, obsessed people who want to reduce everything into technique. They cannot create a technology of enlightenment. That is not possible at all, in the very reality. But they can create a technology which can manipulate the mind, and even deceive people, and create an illusion of enlightenment.

That's what is happening with drugs: drugs have become a technology of enlightenment. And the guru of drugs, Ginsberg, goes on talking as if all the mystics of the world were saying the same things, were trying to give you the same vision as LSD can give, or psilocybin, or marijuana. It is nonsense. No drug can lead you to enlightenment, but drugs can create an illusion of enlightenment.

Is it irresponsible to engage in its creation without having reached the state of enlightenment?

Only people who have not known enlightenment can try it. Those who have known cannot even think of the possibility.

THE PATH OF LOVE

TELEVISION In fact, before TV happened, down the centuries, people had never looked into a source of light for five hours continuously. Now the scientists say that the whole nervous system changes because of those five hours of looking directly into the source of light. The TV goes on throwing strong rays on your eyes. It has never happened before. Five hours is too much. Scientists say if you sit near a color TV, four feet away, you will get cancer, you will suffer from many diseases which your parents had not known, ever. The eyes are eighty percent of your life. Five hours of just strong light rays reaching into your head—your sleep will be disturbed. If America suffers from insomnia, it is natural. The TV is one of the basic causes.

Ordinarily man has lived with light, natural light. In a

primitive society, the sun rises, people rise, and the sun sets and people go to sleep. A natural rhythm with light. Now we are living too much with the light; the eyes are not made for that much light. The inner nervous system is disturbed; it becomes too loaded.

And a thousand and one things will happen. In America a new phenomenon is happening. Many places it has happened, and people have become really worried about it, what to do? In one place a woman was murdered, and twenty persons were standing there, almost paralyzed, not doing anything. A psychological investigation was done. What is the matter? Twenty young, healthy people standing there, and a woman was killed just in front of them and they didn't do anything—they didn't even shout, they didn't call the police. What happened? And you will be surprised. The finding is that it is because these twenty people have lived on TV for too long.

On the TV screen murder happens so many times. What do you do? You don't do anything; you remain glued to your chair. They have become accustomed to it. It was another TV scene. They have lost track of reality. The TV has become more real. For five hours you are not with anything else—and a continuous bombardment of light, and strong light, and things are moving in your head. You become a watcher. They were standing there just glued to their spots, paralyzed —just watching. They could not do anything, because they are no more doers.

THE FIRST PRINCIPLE

TEMPLES All the temples are false, all the mosques are false, all the churches are false. I am not condemning—I am stating a fact, because they are creations of imagination. And I don't say destroy them. I say enjoy them! But don't think enjoyment is leading you towards the ultimate. Enjoy them! It is a good game, nothing is wrong with it. People are going to the movies, people are going to dancehalls. Why should they not be allowed to enjoy a religious fantasy? In their temples, in their mosques, in their *gurudwaras,* they should be allowed—they are free! And it is better to have a religious fantasy than not to have anything. *But* don't think that you are realizing the Brahman there. You cannot. It is not there, so you cannot do anything. *You* can enjoy yourself. You can enjoy your fantasy, your dreamworld.

If this is understood, then temples can exist. They are beautiful, artistic creations, but don't be lost in them. Go there, but don't be lost there. And go on remembering that whatsoever is worshipped by the people is not the real Brahman, because the real Brahman is hidden in the worshipper.

THE SUPREME DOCTRINE

You are not to go to any temple or church: wherever you are, you are surrounded by your own contentment, and that is the temple.

The word "temple" comes from a root *tem; tem* means to cut off. The temple is the place that cuts you off from the world. Now the outer temple cannot do that. It is part of the world; how can it cut you off from the world? It is part of the establishment, it is part of the status quo; how can it cut you off from the world?

Something totally different is needed. One needs to create a temple around oneself. It is made of contentment, that is the stuff that the real temple is made of; and when you are surrounded by a vibe, an aura of contentment, you are cut off from the world, you are no more part of it. You are here and yet not here: you walk on earth but your feet no more touch the earth. That is really to be in a temple. One becomes a temple oneself. Contentment is a miracle, it is a magic key.

Be contented with whatsoever life has given to you, feel utterly grateful. Even sometimes when you think that something is wrong, know perfectly well that the whole knows better than you. Don't disturb your contentment for small things, because nothing is more valuable than contentment. Once it is crystallized in you, you have arrived; you have arrived home! You have penetrated the source of your being.

TURN ON, TUNE IN AND DROP THE LOT

You are gods in disguise.

And when I said this is a Sufi assembly, I literally meant it. See this silence, this grace, this benediction that is showering on you? See this stillness? See this *faqr*? In this moment there is no ego in you, but only a pure silence. The personality has disappeared, there is only presence, and the light rises to the highest heavens. Wherever the wild ones meet, wherever there is simplicity and love, and wherever there is prayer, *zikr,* remembrance of God, this miracle happens. You may not be able to see it. It is happening. You will have to become tuned to this miracle that is happening here.

I am not just teaching you about God. I am not interested in giving you knowledge about God. I am sharing my God with you; it is a sharing. I want to challenge your God which is asleep in you. And that is the work Sufis have been doing down the ages: provoking the potential into the actual.

Khwajah Esmat Bokhari says:

> *This is no Kaaba*
> *for idiots to circle*
> *nor a mosque*
> *for the impolite to clamor in.*
> *This is a temple of total ruin.*
> *Inside are the drunk, from pre-eternity*
> *to the Judgment Day,*
> *gone from themselves.*

The Sufis call their assemblies "temples of total ruin"—*kharabat*—because you have to die, you have to disappear. When Sufis really meet, there is nobody to meet. The Sufi assembly is utterly empty of persons. Only God is. It is a *kharabat,* a temple of ruin. Very revolutionary words of Bokhari: "This is no Kaaba for idiots to circle."

I also say the same about this assembly: This is no Kaaba for idiots to circle—hence idiots are very much angry with me—"nor a mosque for the impolite to clamor in." This is not a place for the mob and the crowd. This is a place only for the chosen ones, only for those who are ready to die in their love, only for those who are ready to risk all in their search for God.

This is a temple of total ruin—*kharabat.*

THE SECRET

Temples don't exist on the outside. One has to become a temple and the only way to become a temple is to create in your interiority an immense gratitude for all that is happening to you—and it is incalculable, immeasurable. But certainly one has to be courageous for it—courageous, because the whole crowd is complaining. It is always asking for more. It needs guts to say, "I don't ask for more, that in fact, whatsoever is given to me is more than I could have asked for in the first place." And from that very moment a transformation starts happening. Your life becomes more and more attuned to the existence; it becomes more and more a dance.

And that has to be the flavor of my sannyasins—a deep inner contentment and on the outside the manifestation of that contentment, in celebration, in celebrating the day-to-day life, the moment-to-moment life, the ordinary life.

Once you are ready to celebrate the ordinary life, it is no more ordinary at all.

THE SOUND OF ONE HAND CLAPPING

TEMPTATION What temptations are there? Life is so simple! But you can label things as temptations, then they become temptations . . .

For example, I was born in a Jaina family . . . Up to my eighteenth year I had not tasted the poor tomatoes, because Jainas are absolutely vegetarian and the poor tomato has the color of meat—just the color! . . .

When I was eighteen years old, I went for a picnic with a few of my Hindu friends. I was the only Jaina and they were all Hindus. And up to that time I had not eaten in the night either, because Jainas don't eat in the night—that is a great sin because in the night a mosquito may fall in your food, some insect may crawl in, and unknowingly you may eat something live. That will drag you to hell . . .

So I had not eaten in the night and I had not tasted tomatoes up to my eighteenth year. They were great temptations. I had seen tomatoes in the market, and they were really tempting . . . Potatoes are also not allowed in Jaina families because they grow beneath the ground, and anything that grows in darkness is dangerous to eat because it will bring darkness to your soul . . .

I was feeling hungry—the journey, the traveling, and the mountains' fresh air. I was feeling hungry and the night was coming closer, and I was feeling afraid also: "What is going to happen? If they cook food in the night, then I will have to sleep without food." And my stomach was hurting.

Then they started cooking food. And great temptations: tomatoes, potatoes, and the beautiful smell of the food. I was wavering between temptation and virtue . . .

And they all tried to persuade me: "There is nobody else here, and we are not going to tell your family either. Nobody will ever come to know that you have eaten in the night, that you have eaten tomatoes or potatoes."

Reluctantly, hesitatingly, I agreed. But I could not sleep until I vomited in the middle of the night. Nobody else vomited—they were all fast asleep and snoring—only I vomited. It was my psychology, because I was suffering from the idea that I had committed a sin. It was not tomatoes that I vomited, it was my attitude. And that day it became clear, absolutely clear, that you can live totally only if you drop all attitudes. Otherwise you will live partially, and to live partially is not to live at all.

THE GOOSE IS OUT

TEN COMMANDMENTS You ask for my Ten Commandments.

This is very difficult because I am against any sort of commandment. Yet just for the fun of it I set down what follows:

1. Obey no orders except those from within.
2. The only God is life itself.
3. Truth is within, do not look for it elsewhere.
4. Love is prayer.
5. Emptiness is the door to truth, it is the means, the end and the achievement.
6. Life is here and now.
7. Live *fully awake*.
8. Do not swim, float.
9. Die each moment so that you are renewed each moment.
10. Stop seeking. That which is, is: *stop and see*.

A CUP OF TEA

TENDERNESS It is tenderness that makes you vulnerable, that makes you open, that makes you sensitive to the mysterious that surrounds us. People who are not tender, who are hard like rock, go on missing life. Life passes by; it cannot penetrate them; they are impenetrable.

One should be like a rose flower, very tender; then one comes to know the mysterious and the miraculous. Life is full of surprises, but only for those who have a tender heart.

But we all have been brought up in such a way that we become hard, because we have been told that life is a struggle, it is a conflict; it is a constant struggle for survival so one has to be hard. If you are not hard you will not be able to compete. And that is true: you will not be able to compete. But competition leads nowhere. It is a sheer wastage. One should live a non-competitive life, then only does one know what God is.

Jesus says: "Those who are the last in this world will be the first in my kingdom of God." Now he is teaching non-competitiveness. "Those who are the last in this world will be the first in my kingdom of God." But remember, don't be the last in order to be the first, otherwise you miss the whole point. Enjoy being the last. And to be the first in the kingdom of God is a consequence, it is not a goal.

Life is such a joy for those who are tender, soft, loving, compassionate, sensitive. That life itself is proof. In thousands of ways it proves that God is. But to the hard, to the rocklike person, there is no proof for God. God cannot be proved for him because he has no sensitivity to feel. He has lost all feeling. He lives only in the thinking. He has lost his heart, he is just a head. And the head is just rubbish! Be a heart. Even if you have to lose the head, lose the head— it is worth it. It is beautiful to be headless but it is ugly to be heartless.

My sannyasins have to be heartful and headless. That is the very definition of my sannyas.

EIGHTY-FOUR THOUSAND POEMS

TENSION   There is a beautiful story in Buddha's life: .

A great prince became initiated, became a sannyasin of Buddha. He had lived in great luxury his whole life, he had been a great sitarist, his name was known all over the country as that of a great musician. But he became impressed by Buddha's inner music— maybe his insight into music had helped him to understand Buddha.

When Buddha was visiting his capital he heard him for the first time, fell in love at first sight, renounced his kingdom. Even Buddha wanted him not to do such a great act so impulsively. He told him, "Wait. Think. I will be here for four months"— because during the whole rainy season Buddha never used to move; in the rainy season he would remain in one place. "So I am going to be here: there is no hurry. You think over it. Four months time and then you can take sannyas, you can become an initiate."

But the young man said, "The decision has happened; there is nothing more to think about it. It is now or never! And who knows about tomorrow? And you have been always saying, 'Live in the present,' so why are you telling me to wait for four months? I may die, you may die, something may happen. Who knows about the future? I don't want to wait even a single day!"

His insistence was such that Buddha had to concede; he was initiated. Buddha was a little uncertain about him, whether he would be able to live this life of a beggar. Buddha had known it from his own experience; he himself was a great prince once. He knew what it was to be in luxury, what it was to live in comfort, and what it was to be a beggar on the street. It was a great, arduous phenomenon, but Buddha had taken time. It took him six years to become enlightened, and slowly slowly he had become accustomed to being without shelter, sometimes without food, without friends, enemies all over for no reason at all, because he was not hurting anybody. But people are so stupid, they live in such lies, that whenever they see a man of truth they are wounded of their own accord—they feel hurt, insulted.

Buddha knew the whole thing was going to be too much for this young man. He felt sorry for him, but he initiated him. And he was surprised and all the other sannyasins were surprised, because the man simply moved to the other extreme. All Buddhist monks used to eat only once a day; that new monk, the ex-prince, started eating only once in two days. All Buddhists monks used to sleep under trees; he would sleep under the open sky. The monks used to walk on the roads; he would not walk on the roads but always on the sides where there were thorns, stones. He was a beautiful man; within months his body became black. He was very healthy; he became ill, he became lean and thin. His feet became wounded.

Many sannyasins came to Buddha and said, "Something has to be done. That man has gone to the opposite extreme: he is torturing himself! He has become self-destructive."

Buddha went to him one night and asked him, "Shrona"— Shrona was his name—"can I ask you a question?"

He said, "Of course, my Lord. You can ask any question. I am your disciple. I am here to tell you whatsoever you want to know about me."

Buddha said, "I have heard that when you were a prince you were a great musician, you used to play the sitar."

He said, "Yes, but that is finished. I have completely forgotten about it. But that is true, I used to play the sitar. That was my hobby, my only hobby. I used to practice at least eight hours per day and I had become famous all over the country for that."

Buddha said, "I have to ask one question. If the strings of your sitar are too tight, what will happen?"

He said, "What will happen? It is simple! You cannot play upon it—they will be broken."

Buddha said, "Another question: if they are too loose, what will happen?"

Shrona said, "That too is simple. If they are too loose no music will be produced on them because there will be no tension."

Buddha said, "You are an intelligent person—I need not say anything more to you. Remember, life is also a musical instrument. It needs a certain tension, but only a certain tension. Less than that and your life is too loose and there is no music. If the tension is too much you start breaking down, you start going mad. Remember it. First you lived a very loose life and you missed the inner music; now you are living a very tight, uptight life—you are still missing the music. Is there not a way to adjust the strings of the sitar in such a way that they are exactly in the middle, neither loose nor tight, with just the right amount of tension, so that music can arise?"

He said, "Yes, there is a way."

Buddha said, "That is what my teaching is: be exactly in

the middle between the two poles. The tension has not to disappear completely, otherwise you will be dead; the tension has not to become too much, otherwise you will go mad."

And that's what has happened in the whole world. The East has become too loose, hence there is death, starvation. And the West has become too tight, hence there is madness, neurosis. The West is breaking down under its weight. The East has become so lazy and lousy out of its looseness.

A certain tension is needed, but there is a state of tension which is also a state of equilibrium. And that is the whole art of Tao. The equilibrating pulse of the mystical life, the secret . . .

TAO: THE GOLDEN GATE, Vol. I

The inner can flower only when there are no outer tensions, when you are not going anywhere, just resting—then the inner flowers.

THE EMPTY BOAT

See also Hypertension, 1st Series
     Stress

THEOLOGY Theology is a perverse discipline: it is masochistic. It is a subtle way of torturing yourself, but very subtle. In fact, nobody has ever said that it is a hidden form of masochism, self-torture and perversion, but I would like to make it clear to you that the theology of all the religions is basically stupid. It talks about things it knows not. It talks about things which cannot be talked about. It goes on moving in a vicious circle of contradictions—because religion is silence and theology is nothing but words . . .

It is a kind of insanity. It is a kind of chess with words. You can become very proficient at playing with words, but howsoever proficient you are, anybody who has a little intelligence can see the utter nonsense of it. And the libraries of the world are full of all these theological treatises— although nobody reads them, fortunately. They are written by theologians for other theologians. Nobody else reads them.

"Don't you find writing a thankless job?" a great theologian was once asked.

He said, "On the contrary, everything I write is returned to me with thanks."

THEOLOGIA MYSTICA

Religions are all based on theologies, and the very word "theology" is a contradiction in terms. *Theo* means God, *logy* means logic—logic about God. In fact, there is no logic about God; there is love but no logic. You can approach the phenomenon God or godliness through the heart, through love, but not through logic.

By following a tradition or religion, what are you doing? Your approach is bound to be through the head. Following is always from the head: you are convinced logically, hence you follow, but it is not a love affair.

A love affair is possible only when you find a living Master. You cannot fall in love with Jesus now, you cannot fall in love with Buddha now; they are no more there. Those dewdrops have disappeared into the ocean. You can fall in love only with a living Master. Buddha must have been very beautiful, but love can happen only between two living hearts.

I AM THAT

Even in scientific work the real insights have not happened through thinking. They have all been intuitive, they have not been of the intellect. All the great scientists are convinced of the fact that it was not their effort that made them discover new ways of life, new secrets of nature, but something of the beyond, something very mysterious. It was not *their* work; at the most they were only vehicles. Hence I am not in favor of making you great thinkers. In fact, you are already great thinkers: everybody is a great thinker. So much traffic goes on in the mind. You are continuously thinking, day in, day out—your whole life you are thinking—to what purpose, to what conclusion?

And I am more against theology than any other kind of thinking because that is the ultimate stupidity. *Theo* means god, *logia* means logic: logic about God; that is a contradiction in terms. There is no logic about God—love, yes, logic, no, a thousand times no. Yes, there can be love for God, but not logic. And if you come through logic to love, your love is also false, pseudo, plastic, synthetic.

Love happens; it is not an argument. Then how does it happen? It does not happen through thinking, it happens through glimpses into no-thought, by entering into the intervals between two thoughts. Those are the windows, windows to the divine. I am against theology.

THE BOOK OF THE BOOKS, Vol. VIII

THERAPY In this commune there are at least fifty therapy groups running, for a certain reason. It is just to balance the thousands of years of repression—it is just to balance. It is just to bring into light all that you have repressed as Christians, Hindus, Mohammedans, Jainas, Buddhists. It is just to undo the centuries old harm that has been done to you.

But remember, these groups are not the end: they only prepare you for meditation. They are not the goal; they are just simple means to undo the wrong of the past. Once you have thrown out of your system all that you have been repressing all along, I have to lead you into watchfulness. Now it will be easier to watch.

THE BOOK OF THE BOOKS, Vol. I

The therapist may be suffering from the same pathology as the patient, he may have the same problems. But he is an expert, a knowledgeable person. He knows more than the patient. He is not more than the patient, he *knows* more than the patient. He can be helpful.

He is like a plumber. The plumber knows more than you about your bathroom but that doesn't mean that he is more than you. When something is wrong—the heater is not functioning and the water is not flowing—you call the plumber. He knows more. He will be helpful. He is an expert.

The therapist is a plumber of the mind. Something is blocked—he knows. He will help you. I have many plumbers around here and they do good work, they really know what they are doing—but remember, a plumber is a plumber.

A Master is not a plumber. A Master is not quantitatively different from you, he is qualitatively different from you. Sometimes it can happen that the disciple knows more than the Master. It is possible, there is no problem in it, but the disciple is not more than the Master. And that is the difference.

The Master has being. He has arrived. He has no problems. His problems have disappeared—because *he* has disappeared the basic problem has disappeared. The problem-creator has disappeared. He has no problems. When you relate to a Master you are relating to a person who has no problems. He is utterly quiet. There is absolute silence. No question, no problem, nothing to be solved, nowhere to go, nothing to do . . . all has already happened. There is no more to happen. Happening has disappeared. He simply is. It is a pure is-ness, a pure existence.

A therapist is a man just like you, but he has a certain expertise. He can help you so far . . .

A therapist can go so far, but don't push him too much. Take his help. He knows much more about how the human mind functions, how man behaves, than you know. He has studied it. He can be helpful. If your mind is not functioning well he can put things right. He can make you readjusted.

A Master does not readjust your mind, he helps you to dissolve it. He is not concerned in adjusting you to the society, adjusting you to particular norms, standards, principles; he is not concerned with adjusting you at all—because this society is sick. It is as sick as it can be. To adjust you to this society is to adjust you to great sickness. This society is mad, it is neurotic. And all your psychotherapists are in the service of this neurotic society. When somebody starts going beyond the limits of the commonly accepted neurosis the psychotherapist has to be brought in—you are going too far. Come back. He helps you to come back to the accepted boundaries. He makes you a normal abnormal, that's all. He is in the service of the society.

SUFIS: THE PEOPLE OF THE PATH, Vol. I

Now modern psychology is by and by turning from individual therapy to group therapy, and the only reason for it is this: that it is very difficult for the psychoanalyst to convince the patient, person to person, about what he is doing to himself. About the patient, about his complexes, about his rationalizations, repressions, about his deceptions, stupidities; it is very difficult to convince him person to person. But in a group it becomes easier because the whole group can see the foolishness, the obviousness of it—that he is clinging to something and unnecessarily becoming miserable. The whole group can see it, and the understanding of the whole group functions more tremendously and deeply than the understanding of one person can function on you. That's why group therapy is growing, individual therapy is disappearing.

Group therapy has a tremendous advantage. Twenty persons working in a group: nineteen persons become alert that you are doing something which you don't want to do and to which you are still clinging . . .

In a group, if you work for a longer time, by and by you have to become aware that the whole group is seeing that you are doing something foolish, stupid, contrary to your own wishes—against your own fulfillment, against your own growth. You are clinging to a disease and you go on saying, "I want to get rid of it."

Almost everybody knows where you are going wrong—except you. Everybody knows that you are an egoist—except you. Only you think you are a humble man, a simple man. Everybody knows your complexity. Everybody knows your double bind. Everybody knows your madness except you. You go on defending it. And because of politeness, etiquette, formalities, in the society nobody will tell you. Hence, the group is helpful—because it is not going to be polite. It is going to be truthful. And when so many people say that this is your problem, and pinpoint it and finger it, and put their fingers on your wound and it hurts . . . It is very difficult to make you alert, individual to individual, because you can think this man may be wrong, but twenty persons? The possibility of twenty persons being wrong is less, and you have to fall back on yourself and see the point of it.

That's why Buddha created a great *sangha,* a great order of monks—ten thousand monks. It was the first experiment of group therapy. It was a great experiment.

That's what I am doing. Sixteen thousand sannyasins—one of the greatest experiments in therapy. A community, a commune, in which you have to become aware because, otherwise, you will not be part of this commune, where everybody is understanding and seeing your error and showing it to you. Because sannyasins are not meant to be polite or formal. None of that rubbish. A sannyasin is here to transform himself and become a situation for others' transformation.

See, whenever somebody points at some fault about you, don't get angry. That is not going to help you. Don't get mad. That is not going to help you. Try to see the point. Maybe the other is true; and there is more possibility for the other to be true because he is so detached from you, he is so far away from you. He is not involved in you. Always listen to people, what they are saying about you. Ninety-nine percent they will be right; there is only one percent possibility they may be wrong. Otherwise they are not wrong. How can they be wrong, because they have a detached view of you.

That's why a Master is needed: to show you your wounds. And it is possible only if you are in deep respect and trust. If you get angry and you start fighting, then there is no trust and no respect. If you are here to defend your illnesses and diseases, then it is not for you—don't be here. What is the point of wasting your time here?

If I say that you are a coward and you cannot see the point, rather you have to fight and prove to me that you are not, then, simply there is no point of being here. The relationship is finished with me. Now I cannot be helpful to you. When I say something to you, you have to look into the fact. Why should I call you a coward? There is no investment with you, and I have not invested anything in your cowardness. I simply say so because of compassion, because I see the illness is there. And unless you know it, unless it is diagnosed, how are you going to get rid of it?

If the doctor puts his hand on your pulse and says that you have fever and you jump on him and start fighting, "What are you saying? How can I ever have any fever? No, you are wrong, I am perfectly healthy," then why in the first place had you gone to the doctor? Just to get a certificate of health?

You are here—remember it—you are here not to get recognition for your illnesses and certificates that they don't exist. You are here to be diagnosed, dissected—destroyed—so that your real nature can arise, bloom. But if you are defending, then it is for you to defend. It is none of my business; defend it. But then you will suffer.

YOGA: THE ALPHA AND THE OMEGA, Vol. IX

Therapy is basically a function of love, and love flows only when there is no ego. You can help the other only to the extent that you are non-egoistic. The moment the ego enters, the other becomes defensive. The ego is aggressive; it creates an automatic urge in the other to be defensive. Love is non-aggressive. It helps the other to remain vulnerable, open, non-defensive. Hence, without love there is no therapy.

Therapy is a function of love. So with ego, you can't help. You may even destroy the other. In the name of help you may hinder his growth. But western psychology is caught up in a mess.

The first thing: western psychology still thinks in terms of a healthy ego. And ego can never be healthy. It is a contradiction in terms. Ego as such is ill. Ego can never be healthy. Ego is always leading you towards more and more illness. But western psychology thinks—the whole western mind has been—that people are suffering from weak egos. People are not suffering from weak egos; people are suffering from too much of egoism.

But if the society is male-mind-oriented, aggression-oriented, the only desire of the society is how to conquer all, then naturally you have to drop all that is feminine in you, you have to drop half of your being into oblivion—and you have to live with the other half. The other half can never be healthy because health comes through wholeness. The feminine has to be accepted . . . the feminine is ego-lessness, the feminine is receptivity, the feminine is love.

A really healthy person is one who is utterly balanced between the male and the female. In fact, he is one whose maleness has been cut, destroyed by his femaleness, who has transcended both, who is neither male nor female—who simply is. You cannot categorize him. This man is whole, and this man is healthy. And to such a man, in the East, we have always looked as the Master.

In the East we have not created anything parallel to the psychotherapist. The East has created the Master, the West has created the psychotherapist. When people are mentally disturbed, they go to the psychiatrist in the West; in the East, they go to a Master. The Master's function is totally different. He does not help you to attain to a stronger ego. In fact, he makes you feel the ego that you have is already too much. Drop it! Let it go!

Once the ego is dropped, suddenly you are one and whole and flowing. And there is no block and no hindrance . . .

In the East our approach is that the therapist has not to work at all. The therapist becomes just a vehicle for God's energy. He has just to be available like a hollow bamboo so God can pass through him. The healer has to become just a passage.

The patient is a man—in eastern eyes—who has lost his contact with God. He has become too egoistic and he has lost his contact with God. He has created such a China Wall around himself that he no more knows what God is, he no more knows what the totality is. He's utterly disconnected from the roots, from the very source of life. That's why he is ill—mentally, physically or any other way. Illness means that he has lost track of the source. The healer, the therapist in the East, is expected to connect him to the source again. He has lost the source, but you have the connection still.

You hold the hand of the person. He is hidden behind a wall. Let him be hiding behind the wall. Even if you can hold his hand through a hole in the wall . . . if he can trust you—he cannot trust a God, he does not know what God means. That word has become meaningless to him. But he can trust the therapist, he can hold the hand of the therapist. The therapist is empty, just in tune with God, and the energy starts flowing. And that energy is so vital, so rejuvenating, that sooner or later it destroys those China Walls around the patient, he has a glimpse of egolessness. That glimpse makes him healthy and whole, nothing else makes him healthy and whole.

So if the therapist himself is an egoist, then it is impossible. Both are prisoners. Their prisons are different, but they cannot be of much help.

My whole approach about therapy is that the therapist has to become instrumental to God. I'm not saying don't know the knowhow. Know the knowhow!—but make that knowhow available to God. Let him use it. Learn psychotherapy, learn all kinds of therapies. Know whatsoever is possible to know, but don't cling to it. Put it there, let God be available through you. Let God through all your knowhow, let God flow through all your knowhow. Let him be the source of healing and therapy. That's what love is.

Love relaxes the other. Love gives trust to the other. Love showers on the other, heads his wounds.

ZEN: THE PATH OF THE PARADOX, Vol. III

THINKING Be less a thinker and more an experiencer. That's my fundamental message: be existential. Intellect can go round and round but it never reaches the real thing. It cannot, it's not possible for it. Truth has to be found in a state of no-mind, so the whole work here consists in putting the mind aside, in living beyond mind, in just living and rejoicing in living without thinking about it . . .

Truth is within you, just be silent and know it. It is a question of being silent and knowing. Thinking keeps you occupied, so much so that you cannot know that truth is already inside you, that it is already the case.

IS THE GRASS REALLY GREENER ON THE OTHER SIDE OF THE FENCE?

You may not have observed: whenever you think, what happens? Whenever you think, you are closed. All that is present drops. You move on a dream-path in your mind. One word creates another, one thought creates another, and you go on moving. The more you move in thinking, the further away you go from existence. Thinking is a way to go away. It is a dreamway; it is dreaming in concepts. Come back to the earth. Religion is very earthly in this sense; not worldly but very earthly, substantial. Come back to existence.

Life's problems can be solved only when you become deeply rooted in existence. Flying in thoughts you move away from the roots, and the further away you are, the less is the possibility of solving anything. Rather, you will confuse everything, and everything will become more entangled. And the more entangled, the more you will think, and the further away you will move. Beware of thinking!

THE BOOK OF THE SECRETS, Vol. IV

Consciousness and bliss are two aspects of one phenomenon: from one side it is consciousness, from the other side it is bliss. And exactly in the same way unconsciousness and misery are related, they are aspects of one phenomenon —from one side unconsciousness, from another side, misery. It is impossible to be conscious and miserable, just as it is impossible to be unconscious and blissful. Seek one and the other follows; there is no need to seek both.

And to you my suggestion is: seek consciousness, because that will be easier for you. Your involvement is with intelligence. Your involvement is not with feeling; your involvement is with thinking. You think too much.

The thinking person can easily become conscious; the feeling person can easily become blissful. So for the feeling person the journey starts by being blissful; for the thinking type the journey starts by being conscious.

So transform your energy that is involved in thinking into consciousness. Rather than becoming identified with the thoughts that come to you, watch them; don't become identified. Just see them as a procession . . . separate from you. They *are* separate. You are always a witness. Don't get lost in the crowd of the thoughts. Remain aloof, standing by the side of the road, let the traffic pass, and slowly slowly become more and more detached, distant. The more detached you are, the more distant you are. Soon you will see that thoughts are still coming but the old rush is no more there. Thoughts are still coming but their grip over you is lessening. They are still coming but they look pale, ill, not so healthy and strong as they used to be, because their health depends on your identification with them.

When you become identified with thought, the thought becomes very strong. It is your energy that the thought lives on. A thought is a parasite: it exploits you, can possess your whole being. The more detached, the more observing you are, the more you will see that thoughts are faraway, distant noises. Slowly slowly they lose all meaning, and the day they lose all meaning they disappear. When you don't give them any importance they disappear. They come only because they are welcomed guests. When they become unwelcome, ignored, they stop coming. And the day that the no-thought moves in the mind, the whole energy is available to be conscious; and then consciousness rises in a vertical direction.

Thoughts move horizontally: one thought followed by another, followed by another. They move horizontally. Consciousness moves vertically: it goes higher and higher and higher. Thoughts move like a river . . . consciousness rises like a tree . . . but it can rise only if the energy is no more involved in thoughts.

So this is your work: you have to become more alert, conscious, aware of your thinking process, detached and distant. And as you become distant you will start feeling a great blissfulness arising in you for no reason at all. Just in the same gap that was occupied by thoughts, bliss arises. In the same emptiness in which thoughts were continuously gathering and crowding, bliss arises.

Nature abhors vacuum—it is true for the outer nature, it is also true for the inner nature. When you create an emptiness in your mind, immediately something that has always been there inside you, waiting for some space to spread, starts spreading. And that phenomenon is bliss.

HALLELUJAH!

THIRST Truth is possible only if one has a total thirst for it. It is not a question of intellectual enquiry: it is a question of life and death. It is just like a man lost in the desert is thirsty. It is not an intellectual question for him: it is his life and death question. And his whole being is thirsty; it is not only the mind, each cell of his body is thirsty.

When truth is enquired after with such tremendous energy, with such intense passion, with such heat, it is not far away. That very heat burns the barrier between you and reality; that very passion proves to be a fire. In the fire the ego is reduced to ashes; and the moment the ego disappears, God is, truth is.

TURN ON, TUNE IN AND DROP THE LOT

TIME In Sanskrit we have the same word for both time and death. We call death *kal* and time also *kal*. Sanskrit may be the only language in the whole world which has the same name for time and death. That's why it can be said truthfully that Sanskrit is the only language transformed by the insight

of the seers; all other languages have remained ordinary.
For ten thousand years thousands of people in the East have
become enlightened, and they have changed the very structure of the Sanskrit language . . .

Now to call time and death by the same name is a great
insight. It is not a question of knowing linguistics, it is a
question of experiencing something tremendously valuable.
Time and death *are* the same; to live in time means to live
in death. And the moment time disappears, death disappears.
So when you are utterly silent, when no thought moves in
your mind, time disappears; you cannot have any idea what
time it is. And the moment time disappears and the clock
of your mind stops, suddenly you enter the world of the
timeless, the eternal world, the world of the absolute.

Jesus is asked by a seeker . . . it is not reported in the New
Testament, but it is part of the Sufi tradition. A seeker asks
Jesus: "What will be the most significant thing in your
kingdom of God?" And the answer is amazing. Jesus says:
"There shall be time no longer. That will be the most significant thing in my kingdom of God—there shall be time no
longer. There will be no past, no future; there will be only
the present."

And let me tell you that the present is not part of time.
Of course ordinarily in the schools, colleges and the universities you have been told and taught and your dictionaries
go on saying again and again that time has three tenses: past,
present, and future. That is absolutely wrong—wrong according to those who know. Past and future are in time, but
the present is not in time; the present belongs to eternity.
Past and future belong to *this*—the world of the relative,
change. Between the two penetrates the beyond, the
transcendental, and that is the present. *Now* is part of
eternity.

If you live in time, death is bound to happen. In fact, to
say "bound to happen" is not right—it is already happening. The moment a child is born he starts dying. It takes
seventy, eighty years to die, that's another matter. He dies,
slowly, miserly, in installments, a little bit every day, every
hour. He goes on dying, dying, dying . . . then the process
is complete after seventy years or eighty years. When you
say that somebody has died today, don't be misguided by

your statement: he has been dying for eighty years, today the process is complete . . .

If you use the methods of meditation you will leave the mind behind, and mind is the source of both time and death. Mind is time, mind is death. One aspect of mind is time, another aspect of mind is death. Through meditation, through *watching* the mind, you can leave death behind.

But this is only a negative process; the Upanishads call it *neti neti*—neither this nor that—the process of eliminating: "I am not this—the body, the mind. Then who am I?" First eliminate the non-essential, put it aside, and go on eliminating all that is non-essential until only the essential is left. And what is the essential? How will you decide that only the essential is left? When there is nothing left to be denied, nothing left to be eliminated . . . go on emptying your house, throw all the furniture out. When there is nothing left to be thrown out, then a great revelation happens: you gain immortality, the absolute arises in you in all its beauty and splendor, in all its ecstasy.

I AM THAT

Time means mind. When the mind stops, time stops. You may have sometimes felt it. When there is no thought in your mind, is there any time left? The procession of thoughts creates time.

This is the most fundamental insight of Albert Einstein's Theory of Relativity: that time is a flexible phenomenon, it depends on your moods. If you are happy time goes by fast, if you are miserable time slows down. If you are sitting by the side of a dying man the night seems to be almost unending—it seems as if the morning is not going to happen at all. And if you are sitting by the side of a woman or a man you love, then it seems time has got wings; it is flying. Hours pass like minutes, days pass like hours, months pass like days.

As far as the clock is concerned it makes no difference whether you are joyous, sad, happy or miserable. The clock moves unconcerned with you.

So there are two things to be remembered: clock time is one thing, totally separate from psychological time; psychological time is within you.

Einstein was not a meditator, otherwise his Theory of Relativity would have reached a higher peak. He only says: When you are joyous time goes fast, when you are miserable time slows down. A great insight, but had he been a meditator the world would have been immensely enriched because then he would have said one thing more: If you are absolutely without mind, just pure consciousness, time stops completely, disappears, leaving no trace behind.

THEOLOGIA MYSTICA

TIME, KILLING   I had been traveling for twenty years all over this country and I was puzzled. Just if the train is one hour late, everybody is so angry and condemning the government and the society and everything. Why can't you rest? If the train is one hour late it is a great opportunity. One hour is yours!—you can rest. You have at least one excuse: "The train is late, what to do? So I rested, relaxed." But no, they cannot; they become more and more boiled up. They start spitting fire.

And these same people when they reach home will sit before the idiot box—TV—for five hours. The average American is doing that for five hours per day. There is a great danger for America through this idiot box. If you look at an idiot box for five hours it has a hypnotic effect—you are bound to become idiotic! And only an idiot can look at a box for five hours. And they are glued to their chairs; they cannot get up. I have heard they will take their food just sitting before the TV. Not only that—they will even make love just before the TV so they can do both things, making love and watching the TV, because something may be missed.

Now these idiots are in the majority. And they will play cards and if you ask why they will say, "Killing time". One minute the train is late and they are angry, and then what do they do with the saved time? They kill it! Going to the movie, killing time . . . sometimes going to see the same picture again! Stupidity seems to be infinite . . .

Killing time, saving time, killing time, saving time . . . The whole life is gone! And you come empty-handed into the world and you go empty-handed.

GUIDA SPIRITUALE

TIMES The times of confusion and chaos are the greatest times to live in. When the society is static there is not much to live for, to live with. When a society is secure and there is no confusion and there is no chaos, then people live a dull, drab, dragging life—comfortable, convenient, stable, but not alive.

It is only in times of chaos and confusion that great things happen, because people are loose. They are loose, uprooted: they can search for new soils, they can search for new lands, they can search for new countries, they can search for new continents of being.

This is one of the greatest moments in the history of human consciousness. It has never been so; this is a crescendo.

Buddha said—and he seems to have detected it rightly—that after each twenty-five centuries there comes a moment of great turmoil and chaos. And that is the time when the greatest number of people become enlightened.

Now twenty-five centuries have passed since Buddha. Again you are coming closer and closer to a moment where the past will lose all meaning. When the past loses all meaning, you are free, you are untethered from the past: you can use this freedom to grow tremendously, to grow to undreamed-of heights.

But you can destroy yourself too. If you are not intelligent, the confusion, the chaos, will destroy you. Millions will be destroyed—because of their unintelligence, not because of the chaos. They will be destroyed because they will not be able to find a secure and comfortable and convenient life, as was possible in the past. They will not be able to find where they belong. They will have to live from their own sources; they will have to be individuals, they will have to be rebels.

The society is disappearing, the family is disappearing; now it is very difficult. Unless you are capable of being an individual it is going to be difficult to live. Only individuals will survive.

Now people who have become too accustomed to slavery, accustomed to being commanded, accustomed to being ordered by somebody else—people who have become too much accustomed to father-figures—they will be in a state of insanity. But that is their fault, it is not the fault of the times. The times are beautiful, because the times of chaos are the times of revolution.

It is possible now to get out of the wheel of life and death more easily than it has been possible for twenty-five centuries since Buddha. In Buddha's time, many people became enlightened; the society was in a turmoil. Again it is happening. Great times are ahead—prepare for them.

And that's what I am trying to do here. Orthodox people cannot understand what is happening here; they have no eyes to see it and no heart to feel it. They only have old rotten values, and they go on judging me according to those values. Those values are out of date. I am creating new people, I am creating new values, I am creating a new future. They live in the past; they cannot understand the future that I am trying to bring here to the earth.

My sannyasins don't belong to the past, they don't represent any tradition. They belong to the future: they belong to something that is going to happen and has not yet happened. Hence there are no criterions—they cannot be judged easily, and they will be misunderstood.

I am going to be misunderstood, because people have their values, and those values come from the past. And I am trying to create a space for the future to happen.

UNIO MYSTICA, Vol. II

See also Cycles, 1st Series

TODAY See also Yesterday

TOMORROW There is not much time, you don't have much time. Don't postpone: this is the moment. Don't say "Tomorrow"—tomorrow is a mirage. Be alert now, be awake now, this moment, and there is serenity and there is calmness. And suddenly one is relaxed, and the source is contacted and one has arrived home.

This is the home for which you have been searching for so many lives. But your very methodology of search has been wrong. You made it a goal. And it is not a goal, it is the source.

God is not where we are going. God is from where we

are coming. God is not there, God is here. God is not then, God is now.

UNIO MYSTICA, Vol. I

TOTALITY The time for totality is now and the space for totality is here.

And remember this distinction: society wants you to become perfectionists—never total; they never talk about totality. They talk about perfection. Perfection is in the future; it is a goal.

Totality can be herenow—it is not a goal at all. It is a tremendous conversion, a great radical revolution—not future-oriented at all, just a great understanding. You can be total this moment, because there is no other requirement for it except the very decision that one wants to be total, that's all—no other requirements.

Just sitting in front of me, this moment can be total . . . *is* total. There is no going anywhere, one is just here.

The idea of perfection is a neurotic idea—it drives you crazy. And it is never fulfilled—it cannot be fulfilled. I am against perfection and I am all for totality.

Totality means each moment lived without any past and without any future . . . each moment lived unconnected with the past and unconnected with the future . . . each moment lived atomically . . . each moment lived in such a way as if this is the first and the last . . . as if there was no time before and there is going to be no time after.

For example, if this moment you become aware that you are going to die in the next moment, this moment will be total because there will be no future. And if, in the same way, there is no past, your whole energy dances herenow . . . then you vibrate. Because there is nowhere to go in the past or in the future, you don't spread out. A great intensity arises—you become an intense flame.

Rosa Luxemberg has said that a man lives only in such moments when his torch of life burns from both ends. So when you burn so intensely from both ends that you are not saving yourself for the future, that you are ready to lose all and all—because who knows, next moment may never come—then there is a *metanoia*, there is a conversion, a transformation, a mutation. Then suddenly that very intensity of energy becomes aflame, and the very quantity of the energy becomes a qualitative change . . .

So remember it: love is the door towards totality—the only door left, the only door that has survived, which has not yet been completely destroyed. So love, and let love be your religion, your meditation.

WHAT IS, IS, WHAT AIN'T, AIN'T

Just be total, and you will never be extreme. Ordinarily, if you think about it, it appears that if you become total you will become extreme—because you don't know what totality is. Totality always happens in the middle. It is a phenomenon of the middle, because totality is balance.

YOGA: THE ALPHA AND THE OMEGA, Vol. VI

Just look at a child of three and you will see what liveliness should be, how joyous he is and how sensitive to everything that goes on happening around him, how alert, watchful; nothing misses his eye. And how intense in everything: if he is angry, he is just anger, pure anger. It is beautiful to see a child in anger, because old people are always half-hearted: even if they are angry they are not totally in it, they are holding back. They don't love totally, they are not angry totally; they don't do anything in totality, they are always calculating. Their life has become lukewarm. It never comes to that intensity of one hundred degrees where things evaporate, where something happens, where revolution becomes possible.

But a child always lives at one hundred degrees—whatsoever he does. If he hates you he hates you totally, if he loves you he loves you totally; and in a single moment he can change. He is so quick, he does not take time, he does not brood over it. Just one moment before, he was sitting in your lap and telling how much he loves you. And then something happens—you say something and something goes wrong between you and him—and he jumps out of your lap and says "I never want to see you again." And see in his eyes the totality of it!

And because it is total it does not leave a trace behind. That's the beauty of totality: it does not accumulate psychological memory. Psychological memory is created only by partial living. Then everything that you have lived only in part hangs around you, the hangover continues for your whole life. And thousands of things are there, hanging unfinished.

That's the whole theory of karma: unfinished jobs, unfinished actions go on waiting to be finished, to be completed, and they go on goading you: "Complete me", because every action wants to be fulfilled.

But if you live totally, intensely, then you are free of it; you have lived the moment and it is finished. You don't look back and you don't look ahead, you simply remain herenow; there is no past, no future. That's what I mean by celebration. In a real moment of celebration only the present exists. And to be in the present is to be a sannyasin, and to be in the present is to be blissful.

THE GOLDEN WIND

See also Perfection, 2nd Series
        Permanence, 2nd Series

TOUCH   When somebody takes your hand with great love and care in his hand, have you watched one thing happen? Your hand becomes alive immediately; your whole consciousness becomes focused on the hand. Just a moment before you were not aware of the hand. Now somebody has taken your hand with great love and you have become aware of your hand. Your hand throbs with a new life! It pulsates with something which was not there just a moment before. Just a moment before you were completely oblivious of its existence. Now it is there so much! Your whole body has disappeared; only the hand is there.

When somebody hugs you your whole body becomes alive. Those people are very poor who have never been hugged; they are living in a dead body. Nobody made their body alive, hence so much hankering to be touched, the need to get some warmth.

People are living at a distance. Even if people are standing close by they keep a certain distance. The body becomes alive when love touches it and the soul becomes alive when love moves it. One comes to one's total expression only in the moments of love.

THE SACRED YES

TOURIST *Bhagwan, I am a tourist. I am here only for one day. Can I also receive your grace?*

Tom, so you have come! I was always waiting. Where are Dick and Harry? And you are from California—of course, you can't be from anywhere else. Californialand consists only of tourists!

"Tourist" is a new species: they are not ordinary human beings. That is a new development, a breakthrough—or a breakdown. A tourist is a strange kind of person: he is always rushing to nowhere, he does not know why—from one place to another place. When he is in Kabul he thinks of Poona, when he is in Poona he thinks of Goa, when he is in Goa he thinks of Kathmandu. He is never where he is, he is somewhere else; he is all over the place except the place where he is. He is never at home. You will never find him in his own home; he has always gone somewhere else, he is always dreaming of other places.

The tourist goes on missing everything; he is in such a rush that he can't see anything. To see things you have to be a little more relaxed, a little more restful. But the tourist is always on the go. He will take his breakfast in New York, his lunch in London, and he will suffer indigestion in Poona.

He carries a camera, inevitably, because he cannot see anything right now, so he goes on taking photographs. Later on he makes albums—he is a bum and makes albums! And then later on, when it is all over, he looks at the Himalayan peaks, at the Goa beach—and when he was there he was not there! The camera was doing his work. He need not be there; in fact, why does he bother at all? He can purchase these photographs anywhere and better photographs than he can take because he is amateurish; professionals are always taking photographs. He can get beautiful albums and sitting at home he can look at them. But now the problem is that he cannot sit down.

It is one of the qualities that a few people are completely losing: they cannot sit. They have to do something, they have to go somewhere, and they have to go fast. They don't want to lose any time—and they are losing their whole lives in not losing time! They will not appreciate anything because appreciation needs intimacy.

If you want to appreciate a flower you have to sit by the side of the flower, you have to meditate, you have to allow the flower to have its say. You have to experience the joy, the dance of the flower in the sun, in the wind, in the rain. You have to see all the moods of the flower in the morning, in the afternoon, in the hot sun, in the evening, in the full moon. You have to see all the moods of the flower. You have to become acquainted, you have to create a friendship. You have to say hello to the flower; you have to get into a dialogue, an existential dialogue. Then only can the flower reveal its secrets to you.

But the tourist is pathological. Why is he rushing?—for the simple reason that he does not know what to do with himself if he is left alone, if he is not to go anywhere, if he has just to sit silently. He does not know what to do with himself. He feels awkward, embarrassed; he has to do something.

Man has become a doer. He has lost the quality of being a witness, a watcher.

THE BOOK OF THE BOOKS, Vol. XII

TRADITION   What can you do by following a tradition? You will become an imitator. A tradition means something of the past, and enlightenment has to happen right now! A tradition may be very ancient—the more ancient it is, the more dead.

A tradition is nothing but footprints of the enlightened people on the sands of time, but those footprints are not enlightened. You can follow those footprints very religiously and they will not lead you anywhere, because each person is unique. If you remember the uniqueness of the person then no following is going to help you, because there cannot be a fixed routine.

That's the difference between science and religion: science depends on tradition. Without a Newton, without an Edison, there would have been no possibility for Albert Einstein to have existed at all. He needs a certain tradition; only on that tradition on the shoulders of the past giants in the world of science, can he stand. Of course when you stand on the shoulders of somebody else you can look a little farther than the person on whose shoulders you are standing, but that person is needed there.

Science is a tradition, but religion is not a tradition; it is an individual experience, utterly individual. Once something is known in the world of science it need not be discovered again, it will be foolish to discover it again. You need not discover the theory of gravitation—Newton has done it. You need not go and sit in a garden and watch an apple fall and then conclude that there must be some force in the earth that pulls it downwards; it will be simply foolish. Newton has done it; now it is part of the human tradition. It can be taught to any person who has a little bit of intelligence; even schoolchildren know about it.

But in religion you have to discover again and again. No discovery becomes a heritage in religion. Buddha discovered, but that does not mean you can simply follow the Buddha. Buddha was unique, you are unique in your own right, so how Buddha entered into truth is not going to help you. You are a different kind of house; the doors may be in different directions. If you simply follow Buddha blindly, that very following will be misleading.

Traditions cannot be followed. You can understand them and understanding can be of immense help, but following and understanding are totally different things.

I AM THAT

Truth is not a tradition. It cannot be, because truth is never old. It is eternally new, it is eternally fresh, as fresh as the dewdrops in the morning or the stars in the night.

The claim of tradition is basically anti-truth. The word "tradition" comes from a root tradere. It means "handed to someone by somebody else, transferred". From tradere also comes the word "trade". Truth cannot be transferred from one person to another person. It is impossible to transfer it. It is not a thing, hence it is not transferable. It cannot be traded, nobody can give it, nobody can take it. It arises in each individual's own being, it is a flowering of your own heart.

UNIO MYSTICA, Vol. II

TRAINING, MILITARY In the university it was compulsory to have a certain military training. I refused. I said, "I am not that stupid! Some fool tells me, 'Right turn! Left turn!' Why? I don't have any need to turn right or left. I refuse on the grounds that this is stupid! And unless I am proved wrong I am not going to participate."

My vice-chancellor said, "You do one thing. We can free you only on grounds of health; there is no other possibility. And I will tell the university doctor to give you a certificate saying that your health does not permit you to participate in the military training."

I said, "Do whatsoever you want to do, but I am not going to participate and if you make trouble for me, I will create much trouble for you. I am going to convince others."

He knew me . . . He said, "Don't worry. Don't you go to the doctor, I will manage it. I will get the certificate from the doctor and I will do everything that is needed. You are freed, but don't say it to anybody. I can understand your point—you are right."

People can see, but still this goes on and on for the simple reason that so much energy is boiling within, and it has to be thrown out somewhere. Now, a stupid game, a silly game like football, and thousands of people get so excited . . .

TAO: THE GOLDEN GATE, Vol. II

TRAINS So there is no need to look back, there is no need to think about the past, no need to think about the future. Live in the present but live in such a way—silently, peacefully—that nothing disturbs your center. It is just as the noise of this train passing by is there but at the very center of your being there is no noise. In fact this noise of the train can enhance your inner silence, it can become a background, a backdrop for it.

I traveled for twenty years continuously in the trains all over India and I know how beautiful it is and how silent

it is. So whenever I was not traveling I used to miss my
trains—all the noise and all the hustle and bustle of the plat-
forms . . . But if you know how to remain silent inside it
all enhances, it becomes a contrast.

Life should be taken as a contrast—and then nothing is
wrong. A sannyasin has to remember only one thing, not
to get disturbed at the center; whatsoever happens on the
circumference is okay. If that much is possible then you are
free from all, you know the taste of freedom. And the taste
of freedom is the taste of God too.

GOING ALL THE WAY

TRANSCENDENCE Transcendence precisely defines meditation. One has to transcend three things and then the
fourth is achieved. The fourth is our true nature. Gurdjieff
used to call his way the fourth way and in the East we have
called the ultimate state of being *turiya,* the fourth.

We have to transcend the body—that is our outermost circumference. We have to become aware that we *are* in the
body but we are not it. The body is beautiful, one has to
take care of it, one has to be very loving to the body. It is
serving you beautifully. One has not to be antagonistic to it.

The religions have been teaching people to be antagonistic
to their body, to torture it—they call it asceticism. That is
sheer stupidity! And they think that by torturing the body
they will be able to transcend it. They are utterly wrong.

The only way to transcend is awareness, not torture. There
is no question of torturing. You don't torture your house;
you know that you are *not* it, it is your house. Just awareness
is needed. There is no need to go on a fast, there is no need
to stand on your head, there is no need to contort your body
in a thousand and one postures. Just watching, becoming
aware, is enough. And the same is the key for the other two
transcendences.

The second is, you have to transcend the mind—that is
a second concentric circle, closer to your being than the
body. The body is the gross, the mind is the subtle, and then
there is a third, the subtlest: your heart—the world of your
feelings, emotions, moods. But the key is the same.

Start with the body because the body is the most easily
observable thing. It is an object. Thoughts are also objects

but they are more invisible. Once you have become aware of the body you will be able to watch your thoughts too. Once you have become aware of your thoughts you will be able to watch your moods too, but they are the subtlest; so only at the third stage that awareness has to be tried. Once one becomes aware of all these three concentric circles around your center the fourth happens of its own accord. Suddenly you know who you are—not verbally, you don't get an answer, you cannot tell anybody—but you know. You know in the same way you know when you have a headache. You know in the same way as you know when you are hungry or thirsty. You know in the same way you know that you have fallen in love.

You cannot prove it, there is no way to prove it, but you know. And that knowing is self-evident; you cannot suspect it, it is indubitable. When one has come to the fourth, one has transcended the world.

I don't teach renunciation of the world. I teach transcendence of the world—and this is the way.

THE OLD POND—PLOP!

Transcendence means the disappearance of the need for the other, the disappearance of the desire to get lost into a woman or into a man. And this is possible only if you have understood. And understanding comes only through experience. So I don't say drop out of your relationships, rather, become more meditative in your relationships.

Making love, let it be a meditation too. And you will be surprised: if while making love you also move in a meditative state you will have great insights into what is happening, and the whole urge called sex will become conscious. And once it has become conscious it can disappear.

And it disappears on its own; you need not cultivate, you need not practice anything for it. When it goes on its own it is beautiful. Yes, sex disappears—one transcends it—but not by fighting with it.

This is true, and because of this truth much misunderstanding has happened in the world. Sex disappeared in Buddha's life, sex disappeared in Christ's life. People have seen sex disappearing, and people have seen that when sex disappears there is great splendor. Something of the sky dances on the earth. The beyond reaches to the earth. The mundane becomes suffused with the sacred. And because people have seen these things, great desire has arisen in them too to transcend sex. But then the whole thing goes wrong: they start fighting it.

It is a secret science, and if you don't move rightly, everything will go wrong . . .

The first and the most significant thing is that when you are going into a deep orgasm, when the climax is happening, there is great joy because in that moment sex disappears. Sex brings you to the orgasmic state, and once its purpose is fulfilled, sex disappears. In the orgasmic state there is no sexuality left in you. You are simply throbbing and there is no desire. You are utterly herenow, there is no future, no fantasy, no imagination, nothing. And when the orgasm happens, the man is alone—the woman may be there but he is not aware of the woman. And the woman is alone— the man is there but she is not aware of the man.

Orgasm is individual: it is happening inside the man, it is happening inside the woman. The other has triggered it, but then the function of the other is finished; you are no more interested in the other. In deep orgasm you are simply inside yourself. There is no sex in it, hence the bliss. And after a good orgasm, for hours you will feel very very blissful. And for hours you will not think of sex again. The desire has left you. What has happened?

If you are feeling blissful, the desire cannot be there. If the desire is there, bliss cannot be there. Desire and bliss are never together.

And if you meditate deeply while making love, you will become aware that time disappears. At the peak there is no time, suddenly you are herenow. Only then do you know the meaning of here and now, otherwise you are in the past or in the future. And when time disappears, mind disappears, because mind is another aspect of time, another name for time. Mind is past plus future. When there is no time there is no mind. Just think: no mind, no time, no sexual desire—and there is great bliss.

But people miss it because they are not alert about it. People go into love-making unconsciously, mechanically.

Go consciously, mindfully, remembering what is happening, watching, remaining a witness, and that will release understanding in you. That will release awareness in you. And awareness is transcendence. Awareness is freedom.

THE SECRET OF SECRETS, Vol. I

TRANSCENDENTAL MEDITATION   In Sanskrit we have two words for sleep; one is *nidra. Nidra* means ordinary sleep, natural sleep; every night you go into it. The other word is *tandra; tandra* means deliberately created sleep. It can be translated as "hypnosis". Hypnosis also means sleep, but a different quality is attached to hypnosis: it is deliberate, it is created, it is not natural.

What do you do in hypnosis? You repeat certain things. For example, you repeat, "I am falling into deep sleep. My body is becoming numb and I am falling into deep sleep." You go on repeating, repeating, repeating, concentratedly repeating, and the idea slowly slowly sinks from the conscious mind into the unconscious, and the moment it reaches the unconscious you fall into deep sleep. It is a created thing.

The same happens with Transcendental Meditation and other methods which are nothing but chanting of mantras. *Any* kind of repetition can create *tandra,* hypnosis. And of course, afterwards when you are back you will feel very good, a certain well-being will be there, but this is not the realization of the ultimate truth. This is good for health purposes . . .

That's why I call the Transcendental Meditation of Maharishi Mahesh Yogi a non-medicinal tranquilizer. It is good for people who are suffering from sleeplessness, who cannot fall asleep easily—it is good. Perhaps that's why in America it has so many followers, because America is the country which suffers most from sleeplessness, from such a restlessness that it does not allow them to fall into sleep; they go on tossing and turning. But any kind of repetition, remember . . .

You can create your own, there is no need to ask anybody—it is such a simple thing, it can easily be done. Your own name you can repeat and that will do. There is nothing special in Sanskrit words or Arabic words—*anything* will do, just go on repeating it.

But this creates only suspension of awareness, because repetition creates boredom and boredom creates sleep. If you are continuously naggng yourself . . . that's what Transcendental Meditation is—nagging yourself. Just go on torturing yourself with a mantra, go on chanting, don't listen to yourself. The mind will say, "I am bored with it! I am fed up with it!" But don't be worried, go on and on. Then there is only one escape left for the mind: to fall asleep, to get rid of you and your mantra and your Maharishi! So it falls into sleep.

PHILOSOPHIA ULTIMA

Transcendental Meditation and methods such as it have become more important in the West for the simple reason that the West is losing the art of how to fall asleep. People are suffering from sleeplessness more and more; they have to depend on tranquilizers. Transcendental Meditation is a non-medicinal tranquilizer. And nothing is wrong if you know that you are using it as a tranquilizer, but if you think that you are doing something religious then you are stupid. If you think this is going to lead you to meditation you are a fool, an utter fool, just a simpleton.

It is not going to take you into meditation because meditation means awareness. It is taking you towards just the opposite of awareness: it is taking you towards sleep. I am not against sleep—a good sleep is a healthy thing. And I prescribe TM for all those who suffer from sleeplessness, from insomnia. It is perfectly good, but remember that a good sleep has nothing spiritual about it. It is good for the body, it is good for the mind too, but it has nothing to do with the spiritual dimension. The spiritual dimension opens up only when you are awake, fully awake. And the only way to be awake is to drop all sleep and all dreaming.

GUIDA SPIRITUALE

TRANSFORMATION The greatest desire in the world is that of inner transformation. The desire for money is nothing, the desire for more power, prestige, is nothing. The greatest desire is the so-called spiritual desire. And once you are caught in that desire you will remain miserable forever.

Transformation is possible, but not by desiring it. Transformation is possible only by relaxing into that which is, whatsoever is. Unconditionally accepting yourself brings transformation.

UNIO MYSTICA, Vol. I

TRANSMISSION *Bhagwan, why is it that the ultimate secret is usually transmitted to only one in many traditions?*

It is not transmitted to only one. It is transmitted to many, but only one is authorized to transmit it further. Buddha transmitted his knowing to thousands, but he gave his authority to Mahakashyap because he was the most capable of being a Master. It is not so difficult to become enlightened, but to become a Master is very difficult. There are many enlightened persons, but not all enlightened persons are Masters.

When you become enlightened, it is your own thing, but to be a Master you need some art to convey it to others. And it is the *most* difficult art because something has to be conveyed which cannot be conveyed, something has to be transmitted which is not transmittable, something has to be said which cannot be said in language. So only a very highly qualified artist can be appointed to transmit it . . .

It is not that enlightenment and the secret keys of its knowledge are delivered to only one. They are delivered to many, but only to one as a Master who will be capable of delivering the key on further.

THE SUPREME DOCTRINE

TRAUMA, BIRTH Aloneness is absolute . . .

But you forget. And you forget because of the birth trauma. When the child is born he remembers—he remembers perfectly all that has happened in the past life; he knows it. But the birth trauma is such, the pain of being born is such . . . He lived in the womb comfortably for nine months—never again will you be in such comfort, not even an emperor can be in such comfort.

You were floating in warm liquid. And all needs were

fulfilled, and you had no responsibility, no worry. You were just fast asleep and dreaming, dreaming sweet things. You were completely protected, secure. Everything was happening of its own accord; not a single effort was needed on your part.

And suddenly one day after nine months, all that world is destroyed. You are uprooted. You were grounded in the womb, you were connected with the mother; you are disconnected. And you have to pass through the birth canal, which is a very narrow canal.

The child feels immense pain. The pain is such that he becomes unconscious. That is a built-in mechanism in the mind—whenever something becomes unbearable, the mind simply turns you off so that you need not feel it. In fact, to call any pain unbearable is existentially wrong, because whenever pain becomes unbearable you become unconscious. So you have never known unbearable pain—if you know it, and you are conscious, it is still bearable. Once it reaches to the point where it becomes unbearable, immediately the whole mechanism for consciousness is turned off. You fall into a coma—a natural anesthesia.

So each child passing through the birth canal falls into a coma, and that disrupts his memory. And again he starts fooling around in the same old way, thinking that he is doing something new.

Nobody is doing anything new. All that you are doing now you have done so many times, so many *million* times. It is nothing new. This anger, this greed, this sex, this ambition, this possessiveness—you have done it all millions of times. But because of the birth trauma there has been a discontinuity, a gap. And because of that gap your past is no more available to you.

Through deep primal scream the past can become available. If you can move backwards into the birth trauma you can remember your past lives. But you will have to move deep into the birth trauma. And once you have reached back into the womb-state of your consciousness, suddenly you will see your whole autobiography. And it is long. It is tedious—it is nothing but anguish, failure and frustration.

TAKE IT EASY, Vol. II

TREES Once a scientist was staying with me. I love my garden to be a jungle, so I had a beautiful jungle around my house. The scientist said to me, "Are you aware of what you are doing? If you allow these trees to grow so close to the house they will run over the house. These are dangerous things. There is a constant fight between man and trees. If you don't keep them away, within years their roots will enter into your walls and they will destroy your house." He said, "I hate trees."

That has been the attitude of man: destroy. If you take that attitude then everything becomes inimical—even poor trees, innocent trees. And there is some fact to it, so you can base your reasoning on it. Yes, it is true that if trees are left to grow completely in freedom then they will run over your towns and your houses. That's true, it is factual. But to base your whole life on that small fact and make it a philosophy, is wrong.

The other thing is as much a fact as this—we exist with the trees. Destroy all the trees and you will die. You breathe oxygen in, trees exhale oxygen. You exhale carbon dioxide, trees inhale carbon dioxide. So when you are surrounded by trees you are more alive. It is not just poetry. When you go into a jungle and a great jubilation comes to your heart, you suddenly feel more alive—as if the greenery makes you also green. It is not just poetry, it is pure science. It is because there is more oxygen, more life throbbing all around, more vitality. And when you breathe that oxygen in, your blood is purified; you can throw the toxins out more easily and you live at the maximum.

So there is a partnership with the trees: they take your poison in and purify it and create oxygen for you; you take oxygen in, you use the oxygen and throw the carbon dioxide outside. Trees use carbon dioxide as their food. So there is an absolute partnership. Man cannot live without trees and trees cannot live without man.

Animals are needed for trees and trees are needed for animals. They are not separate; they are part of one rhythm. This too is a fact. And life should not avoid this. One has to understand the totality of it; and one has to live in such a way that no one fact becomes, or pretends to become, the whole. There is no need to destroy. There is no need to fight. That is the approach of Tao, the approach of Sufism, Zen.

There is a famous Zen story . . .

A king told his carpenter that he would like a certain table. The old man said, "I am very old and my son is not yet ready. He is learning by and by. But I will try. I will do my best. Give me time."

For three days the old man disappeared in the forest. After three days he came back.

The king asked, "It takes three days to bring a little wood for the table?"

The old carpenter said, "Sometimes it takes three days, sometimes three months. And sometimes you may not find wood for three years. It is a difficult art."

The king was puzzled. He said, "Explain it. What do you mean? Explain in detail."

And the man said, "First I have to go on a fast—because only when I am on a fast does my mind by and by slow down. When my mind slows down, all thoughts disappear, all aggression disappears. When I am no longer violent, then there is pure compassion and love—a different vibe. When I feel that vibe of no-mind, then I go into the forest, because only through that vibe can I find the right tree. With aggression, how can you find the right tree? And I have to ask the trees themselves whether one of them is willing to become a table. I go, I look around, and when I feel that this tree is willing . . . That willingness can be felt only when I have no mind. So there is fasting, meditating—and when I become absolutely empty, I simply roam around with the trees to have a feel. When I feel that this tree fits, I sit by its side and ask its permission—'I am going to cut a branch from you. Are you willing?' If the tree says yes wholeheartedly only then do I cut—otherwise who am I to cut its branch?"

Now this is a totally different approach. There is no fight between the man and the tree, there is a friendship. The man tries to fall *en rapport* with the trees, and he asks their permission. This is absurd for a western mind. The western mind says, "What nonsense are you talking about? Asking a tree? Have you gone crazy? And how can you the tree say yes or no?" But now even western science is gradually becoming aware that the tree can say yes or no. Now sophisticated instruments exist that can detect the moods of a tree—whether the tree is willing, whether the tree is unwilling, whether the tree is happy or unhappy. Now subtle instruments have been developed—just like a cardiogram. You can have a cardiogram of the tree. Electronic instruments can detect the moods of the tree.

When a woodcutter comes around the tree the tree is shaken with fear, is sad, is afraid, clings to her life. No Taoist will cut a tree in that state, no, not at all. If the tree is not willing, then who are we? When the tree on its own is ready to share, then only can it be cut.

Now this table will have a different quality to it. It has been a gift from the tree; it has not been taken away. The tree has not been robbed, it has not been conquered. It will not be difficult to understand that this table will have a different vibe to it. It will have something sacred about it. If you put this table in your room you will create a certain kind of space around the table which will not be possible with other tables. It will be there befriending you because you befriended it. It will be there as part of your family, not as a limb cut from an enemy.

The western mind has been too aggressive against itself and against nature. It has created schizophrenia against people, it has created politics, war, and it has created the ecological crisis.

But things have gone now to the extreme. Either man has to turn back and drop the western aggressive attitude or man has to get ready to say goodbye to this planet. This planet cannot tolerate man any more; it has already tolerated him for long enough.

SUFIS: THE PEOPLE OF THE PATH, Vol. II

TRINITY The Upanishads talk about two trinities. One is called *satyam shivam sunderam*. *Satyam* means truth; *shivam* means good, virtue, goodness; *sunderam* means beauty . . .

And they also talk of another trinity: *satchitanand—sat, chit, anand. Sat* means being, *chit* means consciousness, *anand* means bliss . . .

These two trinities are far more beautiful, far more

meaningful that the Christian trinity of God the father and
Christ the son and the holy ghost. Compared to these two
trinities the Christian trinity looks very immature, childish.
Sometimes even children have more insight than the Christian trinity demonstrates.

When Sigmund Freud said that God the father is nothing
but the deep desire of an immature person to cling to the
father, the idea of a father, it is a father-fixation, he was right.
But he had never heard about *satyam shivam sunderam* or
satchitanand. He would not have been able to say anything
derogatory about these ultimate visions.

The Christian trinity is certainly very childish, and I say
to you, sometimes even children are far more intelligent.

A small child was asking another child, his friend . . . they
were learning the alphabet and the first child asked the
second, "Why is it so that b always comes before c?"

And the other child said, "Obviously, you can see only
if you are. First you have to *be* and then only you can *see*!
That's why c comes after b. How can it come before?"

Now even these two children are far more developed, far
more perceptive than the Christian trinity. Father, son, holy
ghost—what nonsense are they talking about?

I AM THAT

TRUST Trust is a mystery—that is the first thing to be
understood about trust. Hence it cannot be explained. I can
give you a few indications of it, just fingers pointing to the
moon, a few hints, but it cannot be described or defined.

It is the highest form of love, it is the essential core of
love. Love itself is a mystery and indefinable, but love is
like a circumference and trust is its very center, its soul. Love
is like a temple and trust is the innermost shrine in the temple where God is situated.

Ordinarily people think that trust means faith; that is
wrong. Trust does not mean faith. Faith is emotional, sentimental. Faith creates fanatics. Hindus, Mohammedans,
Christians, these are the people who have faith. Trust creates
only a quality of religiousness. Trust never makes anybody
a Hindu or a Mohammedan or a Christian. Faith is
borrowed—borrowed from the parents, from the society in
which you are born. Faith is accidental. You live in faith

out of fear or out of greed, but not out of love. Trust is out of love . . .

Faith is egoistic, hence it is fanatic. Faith is borrowed, hence it is ugly. Faith is a bondage because you have been forced into it by subtle strategies. It is not trust. Trust is a totally different phenomenon, with a different flavor. It is your own growth that brings you to trust; it is your own experience, it is your own knowing. Faith happens through conditioning and trust happens through unconditioning. One has to drop faith before one can attain to trust.

And the second thing to remember: trust is not belief either. Belief is again a trick of the mind to repress doubt. Man is born with many doubts, millions of doubts, and it is natural, it is a gift of God. Doubt is a gift of God, but it creates trouble for you. If you start doubting . . .

Doubt is a sword: it cuts all beliefs, but it is a dangerous path. The path to truth is bound to be dangerous because truth is the ultimate peak. The higher you move towards Everest, the more you are entering into a dangerous arena. A single wrong step and you will be lost forever . . .

If you doubt and go on doubting, a moment comes when all that you have ever believed, disappears, evaporates. It is almost a state of madness. One can fall any moment into the abyss that surrounds you. If one falls, it is a breakdown. If one keeps alert and aware, watchful, cautious, then it is a breakthrough.

Trust is the ultimate breakthrough: it helps you to know the truth on your own. And truth liberates only when it is *yours*; somebody else's truth cannot liberate anybody. It creates bondage and nothing else.

GUIDA SPIRITUALE

Be intelligent. This is your life—don't be guided by stupid people; be guided by your own intelligence. Just look into me, just feel me, and you will find the same person that you have been seeing in Christ. The only difference will be of the form, of the body, of the words; otherwise there is no difference.

I am not a missionary! I don't represent anybody—I simply represent myself. Jesus never represented anybody; he simply represented himself. A missionary represents somebody else. His knowing is not his own, it depends on the scriptures. I am my own authority, I am my own scriptures—read me! And while I am available, don't be distracted by such foolish people. They are simply foolish.

And remember only one thing: it is not a question of whether you trust in me or not—I am not saying to trust in *me,* I am only saying trust. If you cannot trust in me, trust in somebody else, but *trust.* If you cannot trust in an alive person, then trust in a dead person, but trust. Trust will help, it will help your Christ-consciousness. It will make you luminous, capable of seeing, capable of understanding that which is.

And don't listen to people who have some investment—Christian missionaries, others. They are all politicians in the garb of religion.

Pour your energy into trust and don't pour your energy into doubt; pour your energy into trust and don't pour your energy into hate. Soon you will be able to understand. And only your understanding will help. Don't try to find substitutes for it.

Mm? You opened the Bible and you found the sentence that there will come a very wise and strong man who will take people astray. Now you became afraid that the Bible might be talking about me. Open the Bible tonight and you will find something else. Go on opening it every night and then you will see it is just coincidence.

It is just like you go to the railway station and you stand on the weighing machine: the ticket comes showing your weight and also something about your character. Then weigh yourself again: another ticket comes and it also shows something about your character which may be even contradictory to the first. Weigh yourself again, just go on weighing yourself, and you will be surprised—after reading ten tickets you seem to be the whole world. All kinds of characters are yours. This is how people go on consulting the I-Ching. It is just your imagination, nothing else. But these are unintelligent ways. The intelligent way is only one and that is experiential, existential.

THE NINETY-NINE NAMES OF NOTHINGNESS

There is a famous Sufi story: a man has just got married

and is coming home with his wife. They are crossing a lake in a boat, and suddenly a storm arises. The man is a warrior, but the woman becomes very afraid. It seems that life is finished: the boat is small and the storm is really huge, and at any moment they are going to be drowned. But the man sits silently, calm and quiet, as if nothing is happening.

The woman is trembling and she says, "Are you not afraid? This may be our last moment of life! It doesn't seem that we will be able to reach the other shore. Only some miracle can save us, otherwise death is certain. Are you not afraid? Are you mad or something? Are you a stone or something?"

The man laughs and takes the sword out of its sheath. The woman is even more puzzled about what he is doing. He brings the naked sword close to the woman's neck, so close that just a small gap is there, it is almost touching her neck. He says, "Are you afraid?" She starts giggling and laughing and she says, "Why should I be afraid? If the sword is in *your* hands, why should I be afraid? I know you love me."

He puts the sword back and he says, "This is my answer. I know God loves, and the sword is in his hands, the storm is in his hands, so whatsoever is going to happen is going to be good. If we survive, good; if we don't survive, good, because everything is in his hands and he cannot do anything wrong."

This is the trust that a sannyasin needs to imbibe. Such tremendous trust is capable of transforming your whole life.

THE RAINBOW BRIDGE

TRUTH Zen says there is no teaching, truth cannot be taught. Nobody can give you the truth; truth has to be discovered within your own soul. It cannot be borrowed from the scriptures. It is not possible even to communicate it, it is inexpressible; by its very nature, intrinsically, it is indefinable. Truth happens to you in wordless silence, in deep, deep meditation. When there is no thought, no desire, no ambition, in that state of no-mind truth descends in you—or ascends in you. As far as the dimension of truth is concerned both are the same, because in the world of the innermost subjectivity height and depth mean the same. It is one dimension: the vertical dimension.

Mind moves horizontally, no-mind exists vertically. The

moment the mind ceases to function—that's what meditation is all about: cessation of the mind, total cessation of
the mind—your consciousness becomes vertical, depth and
height are yours.

So you can say truth descends, as many mystics like Patanjali, Badnarayana, Kapil and Kanad have said. It is
avataran—coming from the heights to you. Hence whenever
a person becomes self-realized he is called an *avatara*.
Avatara means truth has descended in him; the word *avatara*
simply means descending from the above, from the beyond.

But the other expression is as valid. Adinatha, Neminatha,
Mahavira, Gautam Buddha, these mystics have said that
truth does not come from the beyond, it arises from the
deepest source of your being. It is not something coming
down but something rising up, welling up.

Both expressions are valid to me, two ways of saying the
same thing: that the dimension is vertical. Either you can
talk in terms of height or in terms of depth. But truth never
comes from the outside, so nobody can teach you . . .

Zen says truth cannot be communicated, hence it can only
happen in a Master-disciple relationship. It cannot be taught
so there is no question of a relationship between teacher
and taught—there is no teaching so there is no teacher and
no taught. But it is a transmission. Transmission means heart
to heart: teaching means head to head.

I AM THAT

I don't know anything about the coming Masters in the
world, and I will *not* make you beware of the coming
Masters. I would like you to enjoy all the Masters you will
find in the future. Don't miss a single opportunity. Enjoy
the truth from whatsoever source it comes. The question
is of being with truth, not with me. If you are with truth
you are with me. Truth is nobody's possession; it is neither
mine nor Christ's nor Buddha's.

In Buddha's time Buddha was the most clear-cut expression of truth, that's why people were with him. In Jesus'
time a few people were with Jesus because they could see
something beautiful in him. And this has always been so.
If you are with me you are not with *me*—you are with truth.
Because you feel truth being imparted, communicated,

showered on you, that's why you are with me. So wherever you find truth in the future when I am not here, nourish yourself on it. Don't cling to persons. Persons are insignificant, truth is significant.

I AM THAT

Truth is beyond structure. It comes only when you are in an unstructured state of consciousness. It comes only when there is no expectation for it, not even preparation for it, because all preparation is expectation. Truth comes unawares, truth comes as a surprise. You cannot manage and manufacture it; it comes when it comes.

There is no way to truth. This is one of the most fundamental things to understand, that there are no ways to truth. All ways lead astray, because having a way means that you have already decided what truth is. You have decided the direction, the dimension, you have decided how to approach it, what discipline to follow, what doctrine to adopt. Wherever you reach will just be a projection of your own mind. Not that you will not reach anywhere; you will reach somewhere, but that will be just your own mind playing a game with itself. There is no way to truth, because the mind is the barrier and it is the mind that creates the ways. The mind has to go. The mind has to cease for truth to be. The mind is structure.

Truth is not a discipline either, because truth is freedom. Truth is a bird on the wing, not a bird in the cage. The cage may be of gold, may be studded with diamonds, but a cage is a cage and it cannot contain freedom. Truth can never become a prisoner, its intrinsic quality is freedom, so only those who are capable of being free attain to it.

U

UGLINESS   Ugliness has nothing to do with your body. The beauty or the ugliness of the body is very superficial; the real thing comes from within. If you can become beautiful within, you will become luminous. It has happened many times: even an ugly person, when he becomes meditative, starts looking beautiful.

This I have watched continuously, year in and year out. When people come here they have totally different faces. When they start meditating, when they start dancing, when they start singing, their faces relax. Their tensions drop. Their misery, which had become part of their face, slowly slowly wears off. They become relaxed like children. Their faces start gleaming with a new inner joy, they become luminous.

Physical beauty and ugliness is not very important. The real thing is the inner. I can teach you how to be beautiful from within, and that is real beauty. Once it is there, your physical form won't matter much. Your eyes will start shining with joy; your face will have a gleam, a glory. The form will become immaterial. When something starts flowing from within you, some grace, then the outer form is just put aside. Comparatively it loses all significance; don't be worried about it . . .

Meditate, love, dance, sing, celebrate here with me, and the ugliness will disappear. Bring something higher into yourself, and the lower will be forgotten, because it is all comparative, it is all relative. If you can bring something higher into yourself . . .

It is as if there is a small candle burning in the room: bring a bigger light into the room and the small candle simply loses all significance.

Bring the beauty of the within, which is easier. With the other beauty I cannot help much; I am not a plastic surgeon. You can find some plastic surgeon who can help you, but that will not help in any way. You may have a little longer nose, better shaped, but that will not help anything much. If you remain the same inside, your outer beauty will simply show your inner ugliness; it will become a contrast.

Bring some inner beauty.

That's what we are doing here. Sannyas is the science of bringing inner beauty, inner beatitude, inner benediction. Let God shower on you, and the body is completely forgotten. The body becomes compost and your whole life becomes a garden and great flowers, golden flowers, bloom in you.

UNIO MYSTICA, Vol. I

UNAWARENESS People are moving unconsciously, mechanically, unaware; they don't know what they are doing. How can they know what they are doing because they don't know who they are. If you don't know your being, you can't be aware of your doing; it is impossible. First, one has to be aware of the being—and that is growth. Growing inwards is growth, reaching inwards is growth.

UNIO MYSTICA, Vol. II

UNCLARITY Stop calling those moments, "moments of confusion". That is a condemnation, and that very condemnation creates the problem. There are moments of clarity, moments of unclarity, and both are good, both are needed. A few things grow through clarity and a few things grow only through unclarity. And you will be surprised to know that things that grow through clarity are not as valuable as the things that grow through unclarity. Unclarity is the mystery of life. Clarity is tiny; unclarity is infinite. Clarity is just like this small lighted place, unclarity is the whole cosmos and its darkness. Clarity is just like a clearing in a forest: you can manage a small clearing, but beyond that is the forest. And the real life is there in the forest. The child needs the womb to grow, because the womb is dark and mysterious. The seed needs the soil to grow: it has to go deep into the soil, it disappears into the darkness. Keep it in the light and it will never grow; the clarity will kill it.

Those moments that you call "moments of clarity" belong to your conscious mind, and those that you call "moments of confusion", and I am calling "moments of unclarity", belong to your unconscious, and the unconscious is vast. If you call it confusion, you are already against it; you have made a judgment. Use words very carefully; they mean much. Even meaningless words mean much, because they decide the trend, attitude, approach and vision. Just think: if you call it unclarity, you are not against it. You have not taken any standpoint, you are simply stating a fact. Call it confusion and you have already decided that this is something bad, a kind of illness, something that has to be got rid of; you have to be free of it. You have chosen!

And be careful about other words that we use, because those words carry the taboos and repressions of centuries. Confusion is a condemnatory word invented by the logical mind, and the logical mind is a very small, mediocre mind. The real belongs to the illogical. Love will come out of the illogical. Calculation is of logic, but love is not. Cleverness, cunningness is of logic, but tears and laughter are not of logic; they come from within, beyond.

Remain open to it. And be in deep acceptance, cherish it. When those moments of unclarity are there, enjoy them. They make life mysterious.

   THE SUN BEHIND THE SUN BEHIND THE SUN

UNCONSCIOUS, COLLECTIVE
See also Discovery, 1st Series
   Perversions, 2nd Series

UNCONSCIOUSNESS   See also Mechanicalness, 2nd Series
               Robopathology

UNDERSTANDING   Analysis always becomes an obstacle. There are a few processes which happen only if you don't understand them. If you understand them, the very understanding stops them, because understanding is of the mind and the happening, *all* happenings, are of the heart. Once the mind starts trying to understand—it dissects, analyzes, categorizes, conceptualizes—it disturbs the whole heart process.

For example, if you fall in love and you start trying to understand what love is, one thing is certain: the phenomenon that was happening will disappear. You may understand many things about love but love will disappear. You may understand its chemistry, its biology, its physiology—you will understand everything—and by the end of your life you will have become a very knowledgeable person about love, but one thing you will have missed: you will have missed love!

When love happens it is better not to try to understand it—let it happen. Live it, enjoy it, celebrate it, but don't try to understand it. These are things which grow in darkness, like the roots of a tree. You should not pull the tree up to see the roots, to see from where life is coming up, from where the juices are flowing. If you do that you have killed the tree. Enjoy the flowers but don't bring the roots to the light. In the sunlight they die. They cannot be exposed to sunlight; they need the dark womb of the soil. They *have* to remain hidden. They need intimacy, privacy. Make them public and you have killed them.

There are many things which can simply be killed by making them public. If you love a woman, just kiss her in the marketplace and something sacred has been destroyed. Something that was intimate and private and which could have grown in privacy, you have made public.

Have you seen *Playboy* pictures of naked women? How dead they look! If you look deep into their eyes they look as if they are made of stones, stony. Their faces are inhuman; they have become dehumanized. They have become a public thing. They are exposed to the cameras. Their body is no more a sacred phenomenon. It is not being shared in love—it has become a commodity; it is a thing. Something has died *All* those pornographic pictures are ugly: I have never come across a single pornographic picture which is beautiful. Roots have been brought to sunlight and something has died. Those women look as if they are without souls. The mystery is no more there.

So don't try to analyze these experiences that have started happening. Enjoy them, nourish them, feel grateful that God has become gracious towards you, that you are under the impact of grace, and many more things will happen. But never analyze.

If you are feeling happy, feel happy; don't start thinking "What is happiness?" otherwise you will destroy it.

DON'T LOOK BEFORE YOU LEAP

So if you depend only on intellectual understanding you may become more and more informed, knowledgeable; you will come to understand everything, and still you will remain the same. The transformation is not possible through intellect. The transformation is going to be of the total being. It is going to be orgasmic. Intellect is just a part of your total being, so you will have to understand in the heart also, as you understand in the head. Not only that; you will have to understand in your very bones, in the very guts, if you really want to understand.

When you understand intellectually you understand the logic of it, you understand the verbal coherency of it, the consistency of it. It appeals to you as a logical syllogism. But life is not logic. It is infinitely more than that. Not only is it not logical; it is very illogical, because logic thinks in terms of either/or—and life is paradoxical. Life is absurd. It is more like chaos than like a logical system . . . more poetic, less mathematical.

This is one of the problems for the modern mind—it is too much hung up in the head. And you have lost contact with the body, with the heart, with your real substantial being.

So you will have to do something, not just reading. Meditation, swimming, running, dancing, singing, weeping and laughing may be helpful—thinking alone won't help. Read a book, there is nothing wrong in it—but don't be confined to it. It can open a door but don't remain at the door. If you stand there, if you cling to the door, you will never enter the palace. And treasures are not there, nobody keeps treasures at the door. They are hidden deep in the innermost shrine of your being.

So meditate more, love more. Find moments when you are in the body and not in the head. Do something where you can be total. For example, if you are dancing you have to become total. A moment comes in whirling when only whirling remains, and your head completely disappears. It is good to read. If you are aware you can use that too, but use it as a means and don't make it an end . . .

Just try to understand from a different dimension, not from the intellect. Intellectual understanding is as if you are thirsty and you ask for water and I explain to you that water means H_2O. You understand perfectly, there is no problem, it is obvious. But that is not going to help your thirst, it is not going to quench it. H_2O won't help. You can write out the formula and you can remember it, but the formula is not going to quench the thirst. Thirst needs real water, and H_2O is just a parallel concept—it is not reality . . .

You need somebody to pull you down; you are going higher and higher. You are missing the roots in the earth.
ABOVE ALL, DON'T WOBBLE

Understanding is totally different from knowledge. Knowledge is borrowed, understanding is one's own. Knowledge comes from without, understanding wells up within. Knowledge is ugly, because it is secondhand. And knowledge can never become part of your being. It will remain alien, it will remain foreign, it cannot get roots into you. Understanding grows out of you, it is your own flowering. It is authentically yours, hence it has beauty, and it liberates.
THE SECRET OF SECRETS, Vol. II

Understanding is a second step. The first step is hearing. You don't hear me. You miss the first step, then the second is not possible.

While you are listening to me, a thousand and one thoughts are roaming in your mind. They keep you deaf. My words never reach you intact, in their purity. They are distorted, they are colored by your thoughts, by your prejudices, by your already-arrived-at conclusions. You listen to me through your knowledge—that's why you really *don't* listen. And whatsoever reaches you is something totally different than what was conveyed. I'm saying one thing, you go on hearing something else. Hence the misunderstanding. That's why you don't understand me. Otherwise I am using very simple words.

I'm not using any intellectual jargon. I'm using the day-to-day language, I never use big words. My words are simple, as simple as they can be. If you don't understand, that simply means that somehow you are inwardly deaf. A great clamor of words and thoughts and conclusions and theories and prejudices and knowledge and experience—the Hindu, the Mohammedan, the Christian, the Jew—they are all there inside. It is very difficult for me to find a way to you. It is almost impossible to reach you.

It is not a question of understanding. Understanding will flower of its own accord if you can do one thing: if you can *listen,* if you can allow me to reach you, if you can open your heart, if you are not deaf—then understanding is bound to happen. Truth heard is understood, is bound to be understood. Understanding needs no other effort, it simply needs an opening, a vulnerability. Just open a window to me, just a window will do, and I can steal into you. Just a window will do. If you cannot open the front door, don't be worried, the back door will do. But open some door to me, let me come in, and then it is impossible not to understand, it is impossible to misunderstand.

Truth has such clarity that once understood it transforms your life. Once heard, it is understood. Truth has a very simple process: once heard, it is understood; once understood, it transforms your life. If rightly heard you never ask how to understand. If rightly understood you never ask, "Now what should I do to transform my life according to it?" Truth transforms, truth liberates.

THE BOOK OF THE BOOKS, Vol. II

See also Misunderstanding, 2nd Series

UNEXPECTED There was a wrestler, the most famous wrestler in those parts, who was defeated. He was going to be the champion, the district champion of something, and he was defeated by a totally unknown man! The whole crowd laughed in ridicule, people enjoyed it like anything! And I was surprised, everybody was surprised; in a second everybody fell silent, because he also clapped and laughed . . . the man who had been defeated! He laughed so uproariously that the whole crowd fell silent in embarassment; what was the matter with this man? And when they fell silent he laughed even more.

Later on I went to him; he was staying just in front of my house in a temple. And I said, "This is strange—and I loved it! It was very unexpected!"

He said, "It was so unexpected, that's why I also laughed! It was really unexpected. I had never expected that I would be defeated by an ordinary man of whom nobody has ever heard! The whole thing was ridiculous, that's why I laughed!"

But I have never been able to forget his face, the way he laughed and the way he clapped and the way the whole crowd fell silent. This man defeated the whole crowd and their ridicule . . . he participated! But great courage is needed!

To me he was the winner, and I told him, "I am a small child and I cannot say much. But to me you are the winner and I will remember you." After twenty years I visited his town and he came to see me. He was a very old man now, and he said, "Do you remember me? I have not been able to forget your face either—a small child coming to me and saying, 'You are the real winner; the other is defeated. You have defeated the whole crowd.' I have not been able," he said, "to forget your face either."

FAR BEYOND THE STARS

UNHAPPINESS To be unhappy no intelligence is needed. Everybody is capable of being unhappy but happiness is very, very rare. Great talent is needed. Not only intellect, intelligence is needed. Only rarely does a Buddha, a Krishna, become happy. It is almost impossible to be happy.

So let us try to understand what unhappiness is. Unhappiness is the incapacity to understand life, the incapacity to understand oneself, the incapacity to create a harmony between you and the existence. Unhappiness is a discord between you and reality; something is in conflict between you and existence. Happiness is when nothing is in conflict—when you are together, and you are together with existence also. When there is a harmony, when everything is flowing without any conflict, smooth, relaxed, then you are happy. Happiness is possible only with great understanding, an understanding like the peaks of the Himalayas. Less than that won't do.

Anybody is capable of being unhappy any moment, that's how the whole world is so unhappy. To be happy you will have to create such a great understanding about you and about the existence in which you exist, that everything falls in line, in deep accord, in rhythm. And between your energy and the energy that surrounds you a dance happens and you start moving in step with life.

Happiness is when you disappear. Unhappiness is when you are too much. You are the discord, your absence will be the accord. Sometimes you have glimpses of happiness—when by some accident you are not there. Looking at nature, or looking at the stars, or holding the hand of your beloved, or making love . . . in some moments you are not there. If you are there, even then there will be no happiness. If you are making love to your beloved and it is really as you express it, a "making", then there will be no happiness.

Love cannot be made. You can be in it or not in it, but there is no way to make it. The English expression is ugly. To "make love" is absurd. How can you make it? If the maker is there, the doer is there, the technician goes on existing. And if you are following some techniques from Masters and Johnson or Vatasyayana or some other source, and you are not lost in it, happiness will not happen. When you are lost you don't know where you are going, you don't know what you are doing, you are possessed by the whole, the part does not exist separate from the whole . . . then there is an orgasmic experience. That is what happiness is.

DANG DANG DOKO DANG

UNION   The wall between you and the whole has to be removed, there is no separation. That state of non-separation, that state of *unio mystica* —the mystic union—is the ultimate expression of love. The lowest is the man/woman relationship and the ultimate, the highest, is the meeting of the meditator with the whole.

Hence I say the journey is from sex to superconsciousness.

THE FISH IN THE SEA IS NOT THIRSTY

UNIQUENESS   There is not anybody like you anywhere in the world—there has never been before and there will never be again. You are the only one! . . .

Each individual is unique; uniqueness is a gift from existence.

THE WILD GEESE AND THE WATER

UNIVERSITIES   In the western universities they have been teaching knowledge for centuries. Now in the East also, universities are teaching knowledge, because they are nothing but copies of the West. Basically, originally, eastern universities never taught knowledge. Nalanda and Taksha-shila, they were not teaching knowledge: they were teaching meditation. They were teaching a deep ignorance and a deep mystery around. Now there exists no eastern university. All the universities are western wherever they exist, whether in the East or the West. They go on stuffing the mind with knowledge.

So whenever a student comes back from a university he is a stuffed being. He has no soul; he has only knowledge. And then he creates problems. He will create them, because the university has given him only the ego—nothing else. He has not learned a single piece of humanity, humbleness. He has not touched a single point of non-ego. He has not looked from that window where life is mystery and he is ignorant—he has not looked from that window. He has been stuffed with knowledge. Knowledge gives him the feeling that he is very significant and very important because he *knows*. The ego is strengthened, then the ego creates every problem that is possible.

The ego creates politics, the ego creates ambition. The ego creates jealousy, the ego creates a constant struggle, violence, because the ego cannot be satisfied unless it reaches to the top. And everyone is trying to reach the top. A cut-throat competition arises in every arena of life—economics, politics, education, everywhere a cut-throat competition. No one is interested in himself. Everyone is interested in the ambition to reach to the top. And no one thinks where he is going when he is reaching to the top. What will you achieve just by reaching the top? Nothing is achieved. You simply waste your life.

Eastern universities were teaching a deep ignorance—the basic ignorance that man cannot penetrate the mystery, because the mystery is ultimate. It is *basic* to nature, and man is just part of that same mystery. When these two mysteries meet—the mystery within man and the mystery within existence—when these two mysteries meet, there is ecstasy. Life becomes beautiful. It becomes an eternal music. It becomes a dance. You can dance only if there is mystery. The dancing God is needed—a God who can dance. And existence is dancing all around. Look! This is not a theory. Look at existence! It is dancing all around. Every particle is dancing. Only you have become stuck to the ground. You cannot move, you cannot dance, because you know—your knowledge has become poison.

THE SUPREME DOCTRINE

UNKNOWABLE The Master is always pushing you into the unknown; he never leaves you for a single moment to settle in the known. The known has to be constantly renounced for the unknown. And finally, when you have become courageous enough to move from the known to the unknown without the Master's push, of your own accord, then he pushes you from the unknown to the unknowable.

These are the two steps of this eternal pilgrimage: from the known to the unknown and from the unknown to the unknowable. The moment you take the plunge into the unknowable you disappear. Then only God is or godliness is. The Master is found no more, the disciple is found no more, but godliness . . . just a fragrance, a fragrance which is of the beyond.

THE WILD GEESE AND THE WATER

These three words have to be remembered: the known, the knowable and the unknowable.

The known was unknown yesterday. The knowable is unknown today but tomorrow it may become knowable, known. Science believes in only two categories, the known and the unknown. But the unknown means the knowable; up to now we have not been able to know it but sooner or later we will know it. Hence science believes a moment will come in history, some time in the future, where there will be nothing left to know, when the whole unknown will have become known. But religion has a third category also, the unknowable, which always remains unknowable. It was unknowable yesterday, it is unknowable today, it will remain unknowable tomorrow.

Science thinks that existence can be demystified, religion knows it cannot be demystified because that unknowable will always remain a mystery. And that unknowable is called God, truth, *nirvana*—so many names have been given to it—Tao, Dhamma, Logos, but one quality is definitely there in all these words: it is unknowable, it is an absolute mystery.

You can enter into it, you can become part of it but you cannot know it.

You can live it but you cannot know it, you can taste it but you cannot say anything about it. You can feel it in your belly but you will be absolutely dumb. And that is the most precious experience. It is experienceable but not expressible. That's why it cannot become part of the known.

Many people have experienced it—Buddha experienced it, Lao Tzu experienced it, Patanjali experienced it, Kabir experienced it, but nobody has ever been able to say anything about it. All that they say is how to find it, but they never say anything about that which you are going to find.

Lao Tzu begins his book, *Tao Te Ching*: "Truth is that which cannot be expressed. Remember this," he says, "and then you can read my book. Don't forget it—because truth you will not find in the words. Perhaps one can find it in the gaps between the words or between the lines but not in the words, not in the lines themselves."

That is our search—the unknowable. And the only way to seek it is to dissolve into the whole just like a dewdrop dissolves into the ocean and becomes it.

> *IS THE GRASS REALLY GREENER*
> *ON THE OTHER SIDE OF THE FENCE?*

UNKNOWN   The unknown can never create any fear. How can you be afraid of the unknown? You don't know it, so you cannot be afraid of it. Fear is not of the unknown but of losing the known. We wrongly think that it is of the unknown—it is always of losing the known. The known is known; we have our comforts and securities and safeties and our involvement with the known, our investment with the known. And we are afraid of losing it, we are afraid of moving away from it. That is the fear—of losing the known. We call it fear of the unknown; that is not right.

The unknown can only excite you; the unknown can only challenge you. The unknown can only provoke and seduce you to a pilgrimage. It can call you forth, but it cannot make you afraid. It is always to do with the known, and the fear arises because you will have to lose it if you go into the unknown. Once you understand the problem rightly it is almost solved.

To understand a problem exactly is to solve it. And if you remain in a misunderstanding about the problem itself, then the solution is very far away. Then it is almost impossible, because you are moving in a wrong direction.

Now to say that "I am afraid of the unknown" is to create a false problem, and you will never be able to solve it. Change it! The problem is, the fear is, of losing the known. Once the problem is rightly pinpointed, things become simple.

Then the second thing to be asked is: what is there in the known that you are so much afraid of losing? What has it given to you? What has it made you? Search into it, and you will not find anything; it has not given you anything. Then why be afraid of losing that which has not given anything? It only promises but never fulfills any promise. It goes on postponing till death arrives.

The past has not given you anything. In fact it is good to get rid of it. It is good to learn the ways of the unknown, because the known is *known*. Even if it has given something to you and you cling to it, it will be only a repetition, and repetition can never satisfy. Each time it is repeated it gives you less and less and less. It follows the law of diminishing returns.

You saw a film; it was beautiful. You want to see it again; it will not be so beautiful now. It will be a repetition. It was really beautiful because it was unknown. The first time you saw it, it was not known. The beauty came out of the unknown. Now you want to see it again, you want to repeat— you have become greedy. It was such an ecstasy! You go to see it again. Now there is nothing because now it is known; the basic thing is missing. It was the unknown that had given it the ecstatic flavor. Now it is known so the ecstasy is not possible. If you see it a third time it will drive you crazy! A fourth, fifth, and sixth and seventh . . . and you will be in the mental hospital.

That's how people have gone mad—almost the whole humanity is mad—by repeating. The same thing, the same sex, repeating again and again in the hope that it will give

you again the first glimpse, the first joy. It cannot! That joy
was *because* of the unknown.

Once you understand that all bliss arises out of the
unknown, how can you be afraid of it? You will be enchanted by it! You will continuously search the unknown
and you will continuously go on dropping the known.

That's what I call a meditative mind: looking into things,
enquiring into the root causes, and then *following* your
understanding. If you watch deeply, this is a simple truth:
die every moment to the past so that every moment remains
new. With the new is life; with the old is death.
SNAP YOUR FINGERS, SLAP YOUR FACE AND WAKE UP!

UNMANIFEST   This fundamental has to be remembered:
the Upanishads say that the world is the manifest form of
God and God is the unmanifest form of the world, and every
manifest phenomenon has an unmanifest phenomenon inside it.

When you see a flower, the flower is only the manifest
form of something inside it, its essence, which is unmanifest,
which is its soul, its very being. You cannot catch hold of
it, you cannot find it by dissecting the flower. For that you
need a poetic approach, not the scientific approach. The
scientific approach analyzes; the poetic perspective is totally
different. Science will never find any beauty in the flower
because beauty belongs to the unmanifest form. Science will
dissect the manifest form and will find all kinds of
substances that the flower is made of but will miss its soul.

Each and everything has both, the body and the soul. The
body is the world and the soul is God, but the body is not
against the soul, the soul is not against God. The world
manifests God, expresses God. God is silence and the world
is the *song* of that silence. And the same is true about you.
Every person has both: the manifest, the bodymind structure, and the unmanifest, your consciousness.

Religion consists in discovering the unmanifest *in* the
manifest. It is not a question of escaping anywhere; it is exploring your innermost depths. It is exploring the silent
center, the center of the cyclone. It is not something that
has to be found somewhere else, in the Himalayas or in a

monastery. It is within *you!* You can discover it in the Himalayas, you can discover it in the marketplace.

I AM THAT

UNPREDICTABLE   Something about man remains unpredictable, and that unpredictable quality is his very essence. That's what makes him man; that is his freedom. He is not bound by the law of cause and effect; he functions under a totally different kind of law. He can behave in such a way that, seeing the situation, given the situation, would have been inconceivable to you. If you had predicted, your prediction would have been an absurdity. Man can function outside the law of cause and effect.

Then how to help man? Then how is a Master supposed to help others? He helps not by giving detailed information, instructions, he helps only by indicating. He hints, he does not guide.

THE BOOK OF THE BOOKS, Vol. VII

UNSANITY   This whole mind of communicating with people in an attempt to be verified by them simply shows a deep darkness inside. Otherwise, there is no need. And I am not saying that when a man becomes full of light, he stops communication, no. Only *he* can communicate, because he *has* something to communicate. What have you got to communicate? What is there that you can share with people? You are a beggar. You are begging.

When you want to be verified, validated, certified, you are begging. You are telling them, "Please say something good to me, something nice, so I can feel nice about myself. I am feeling very down, I am feeling very worthless—give me some worth! Make me feel significant." You are begging: it is not communication. Communication is possible only when a song has burst forth in your being, when a joy has arisen, when a bliss has been experienced—then you can share. Then not only communication, not only verbal communication, but on a far deeper level, communion also starts happening. But then you are not a beggar: you are an emperor.

Only Buddhas can commune and communicate. Others have nothing to say, nothing to give. In fact, what you are doing while you are talking with people . . . and people are continuously talking, chattering, if not actually, then in their minds, just as you say that deep in your mind also you are always talking with somebody, some imaginary person. You are saying something from your side, and you are also answering from the other side. A continuous chattering, a dialogue inside you.

This is a state of *unsanity*. I will not call it a state of insanity but unsanity. The whole of humanity exists in the state of unsanity. The insane person has gone beyond the normal boundary. The unsane person is also insane but within boundaries. He remains insane inside, but on the outside he goes on behaving in a sane way. So for him I have this word "unsanity".

Sanity happens only when you become so totally silent that all inner chattering disappears. When the mind is no more, you are sane. Mind is either unsane—that is normally insane—or insane—that means abnormally insane. No-mind is sanity. And in no-mind you understand, you realize not only your own being but the being, the very being of existence. Then you have something to share, to communicate, to commune, to dance, to celebrate.

Before that, it is a desperate effort to somehow collect an image of yourself from others' opinions. And your image will remain a mess, because you will be collecting opinions from so many sources, they will remain contradictory.

One person thinks you are ugly, hates you, dislikes you; another person thinks you are so beautiful, so graceful, that there is nobody who can be compared to you—you are incomparable. Now what are you going to do with these two opinions? You don't know who you are; now these two opinions are there—how can you judge which is right?

You would like the opinion to be right which says you are beautiful. You don't like the opinion which says that you are ugly, but it is not a question of liking or disliking. You cannot be deaf to the other opinion, that too is there. You can repress it in the unconscious, but it will remain there.

And you will be collecting opinions from your parents, from your family, from your neighborhood, from the people you work with, from the teachers, from the priests . . .

thousands of opinions clamoring inside you. And this is how you are going to create an image of yourself? It will be a mess. It will not have any face, any form; it will be a chaos. That's how everybody is: a chaos. No order is possible, because the very center is missing which can create the order.

That center I call awareness, meditation—*ais dhammo sanantano*—this is the inexhaustible law, that only those who become aware know who they are. And when they know, then nobody can shake their knowing. Nobody can! The whole world may say one thing, but if you *know,* if you have realized yourself, it doesn't matter.

THE BOOK OF THE BOOKS, Vol. II

UNWORTHINESS How can one feel worthy? You have not earned it. It has nothing to do with your effort, your doing, your practicing. It has simply come to you for no reason at all. Hence one feels dumb, lost, in such an awe that breathing stops, that the heart beats no more. The whole world stops.

Whenever it happens to anybody, the same is the experience—the feeling of great unworthiness. But it is beautiful! It will give you a depth in humbleness; slowly, slowly the ego will be eroded. And sooner or later you will find that with your effort, with your worth, only small things are possible. All great things *happen,* they cannot be done—and they happen for no reason at all, remember it.

The beauty of the sunset, the song of a bird, a small lonely flower, the moon . . . there is no reason for it at all. Nobody can answer why it is there: why the rose is so beautiful, and why this existence exists at all, and why the universe moves with such tremendous grace, harmony. There is no reason at all!

Hence I say it is a mystery, and it remains a mystery even for those who have gone deeply into it, who have become dissolved into it. It is never demystified.

But you are fortunate that those moments have started happening. Don't be shy to receive them, don't be embarrassed. It is natural in the beginning to feel unworthy. Slowly, slowly that grace will transform you. Those moments will come more and more; they will become natural. They will become a shadow to you: where you will be, they will be there. Waking, asleep, you will find that grace surrounding you. That grace will be without and within. That grace will become a luminous point within your heart, and the flame will go on burning.

But remember, don't become too much worried about your unworthiness. If you become too much worried about your unworthiness those moments will start disappearing, because your focus has changed. Rather than feeling unworthy and becoming focused on it, feel the compassion of God and become focused on it. Remember, these are two different gestalts; both are possible.

THE GUEST

UPANISHAD   The very word *upanishad* is of immense importance. The word *upanishad* is derived from the Sanskrit root *shad*; *shad* has many meanings and all are significant. The first meaning is "to sit".

The Zen people say:

Sitting silently, doing nothing,
The spring comes and the grass grows by itself.

That is the meaning of *shad*: just sitting silently in deep meditation; not only sitting physically but deep down sitting psychologically too. You can sit physically in a yoga posture, but the mind goes on running, chasing; then it is not *true* sitting. Yes, physically you look still, but psychologically you are running in all directions.

Shad means sitting physically and psychologically both, because body and mind are not two things, not two separate entities. Body and mind are one reality. We should not use the phrase "body *and* mind"; we should make one word, "bodymind". The body is the outer shell of the mind and the mind is the inner part of the body. Unless both are in a sitting posture, not running anywhere—into the past, into the future—not running anywhere, just being in the present, now and here . . . that is the meaning of *shad*; it is the very meaning of meditation.

It also means "to settle". You are always in chaos, in a state of turmoil, unsettled, always hesitating, confused, not knowing what to do, what not to do. There is no clarity inside—

so many clouds, so much smoke surrounds you. When all these clouds have disappeared, when all this chaos has disappeared, when there is no confusion at all, it is called settling.

When one is settled absolutely, clarity arises, a new perspective. One starts seeing what *is* the case. Eyes are no more covered by any smoke; for the first time you have eyes to see that which is.

The third meaning of *shad* is "to approach". *You* are confused, you are living in darkness, you don't know who you are, you don't know the meaning of your life, of your existence. You have to approach somebody who has arrived home, who has found the way. You have to approach a Buddha, an enlightened Master—a Lao Tzu, a Zarathustra, a Jesus, a Mohammed. You have to approach somebody who is afire with God, aflame, who is radiating godliness, in whose presence you feel bathed, refreshed, in whose presence something starts falling from your heart—the whole burden of anguish, anxiety—and something starts welling up within you: a new joy, a new insight. Hence the meaning "to approach".

Upa-ni-shad is made of three words. *Shad* is to sit, to settle, to approach—to approach a Master, to sit by his side in a settled, silent state. And from the prefix *upa* which means near, close, in tune with, in harmony, in communion . . . When you are settled, sitting silently by the side of the Master, doing nothing, running nowhere, then a harmony arises between you and the Master, a closeness, an intimacy, a nearness, a possibility of communion, the meeting of the heart with the heart, the meeting of the being with the being, a merging, a communion. And *ni* means down, surrendered, in a state of prayer, in a state of egolessness.

This is the whole meaning of the word *upanishad*: sitting in a settled state, unconfused, clear, approaching the Master in egolessness, surrendered, in deep prayerfulness, openness, vulnerability, so that a communion becomes possible.

This is *upanishad*—what is happening right now between you and me. This sitting silently, in a deep, loving, prayerful mood, listening to me not through the intellect but through the heart, drinking, not only listening—this communion is *upanishad!* We are living *upanishad,* and that is the only way to understand what the Upanishads are. It has to become an alive experience for you.

I AM THAT

The word *upanishad* means: sitting in deep communion with the Master . . .

That's the meaning of *upanishad,* a very strange meaning—sitting by the side of a Master, just sitting by the side of a Master . . . and then something transpires. Something like a flame jumps from the heart of the Master to the heart of the disciple.

The Master has come home, the Master has experienced the truth. The disciple is seeking, but the seeker has to be silent, utterly silent. It is not a question of asking questions, because the ultimate questions can neither be asked nor answered. They are only transmitted—without asking, without answering. That transmission beyond words is the meaning of the word *upanishad.*

PHILOSOPHIA ULTIMA

V

VACILLATION The mind is vacillation, the mind is either/or, the mind is always in that space of "to be or not to be". If you really want to grow, mature, if you really want to know what this life is all about, don't vacillate. Commit yourself, get involved. Get involved with life, get committed to life, don't remain a spectator. Don't go on thinking about whether to do something or not—"Should I do this or that?" You can go on vacillating your whole life, and the more you vacillate, the more trained you become in vacillation.

Life is for those who know how to commit themselves—how to say "yes" to something, how to say "no" to something, decisively, categorically. Once you have categorically said "yes" or "no" to something, then you can take a jump, then you can dive deep into the ocean.

People are just sitting on the fence. Millions of people are fence-sitters—this way or that, just waiting for the opportunity to come. And the opportunity will never come, because it has already come, it is there!

My own suggestion is that even if sometimes it happens that you get committed to the wrong thing, even then, it is good to commit yourself, because the day you know it is wrong, you can get out of it. At least you will have learned one thing, that it is wrong, and never to get into anything like that again. It is a great experience; it bring you closer to truth.

Why do people vacillate so much? Because from your very childhood you have been told not to commit any mistake. That is one of the greatest teachings of all the societies all over the world—and it is very dangerous, very harmful. Teach children to commit as many mistakes as possible, with only one condition: don't commit the same mistake again, that's all. And they will grow, and they will experience more and more, and they will not vacillate. Otherwise there is a trembling: time is passing by, out of your hands, and you are vacillating.

I see many people standing on the shore vacillating—whether to take the jump or not? Here, it happens every day.

Just a few days ago, a young man came to see me. For three years he has been vacillating about whether to take sannyas or not! I said "Decide yes or no, and be finished with it! And I am not saying decide yes, I am only saying *decide*. No is as good as yes. But wasting three years? If you had taken sannyas three years ago," I told him, "by this time you would have known whether it is worth it or not: at least one thing would have been decided. Vacillating for three years, nothing has been decided. You are in the same space, and three years have gone by."

THE BOOK OF WISDOM, Vol. II

VALLEYS There was a great Sufi Master—one of the greatest in all the ages—Al-Ghazzali. He says: "On the path of human growth from man to God—from man the potential to man the actual, from possibility to reality—there are

seven valleys." These seven valleys are of immense importance. Try to understand them because you will have to pass
through those seven valleys. Everybody has to pass through
those seven valleys.

If you understand rightly what to do with a valley you
will be able to go beyond it, and you will attain to a peak—
because each valley is surrounded by mountains. If you can
pass through the valley, if you don't get entangled in the
valley, if you don't get lost in the valley, if you don't become
too attached to the valley, if you remain aloof, detached,
a witness, and if you keep on remembering that this is not
your home, that you are a stranger here, and you go on
remembering that the peak has to be reached, and you don't
forget the peak—you will reach to the peak. With each valley
crossed there is great celebration.

But after each valley you have to enter another valley. This
goes on. There are seven valleys. Once you have reached
the seventh then there are no more. Then man has attained
to his being, he is no longer paradoxical. There is no tension, no anguish. This is what in the East we have called
Buddhahood . . .

And each valley has its own allurements. It is very, very
possible that you may get attached to something and you
will not be able to leave the valley. You have to leave it if
you want to enter the second valley. And after each valley
there is a peak, a great mountain peak. After each valley
there is jubilation and the jubilation goes on becoming more
and more intense. And then finally, in the seventh valley,
you attain to the cosmic orgasm—you disperse. Then only
God is . . .

The first valley . . . The first valley is called the valley of
knowledge.

Naturally, knowledge has to be the first because man starts
by knowing. No other animal has knowledge; only man
knows, only man collects knowledge. Only man writes,
reads, talks. Only man has language, scriptures, theories. So
knowledge has to be the first valley . . .

Knowledge is a double-arrowed phenomenon. One arrow
points to the known, another arrow points to the knower.
If you start looking to the knower you cannot be lost, you
will be able to transcend the valley . . .

The second valley is called the valley of repentance . . .

When you start looking at who you are, naturally great repentance arises. Because of all that you have done wrong, all that you have done and should not have done, you start feeling repentance. So a great peak comes with consciousness—but suddenly, with consciousness, conscience arises. Remember, the conscience that you have is not the true conscience. It is a pseudo-coin; it is given by the society . . . This borrowed conscience does not help, it simply burdens you. With the first valley crossed, your own conscience arises. Now you know exactly what is wrong and it becomes impossible to do otherwise . . .

The third valley is called the valley of stumbling blocks.

Once the conscience has arisen you will now be able to see how many blocks exist. You have eyes to see how many hindrances there are. There are walls upon walls. There are doors too but they are few and far between. You will be able to see all the stumbling blocks . . .

So the first is the tempting world; the second is people—attachments to people . . . The third Al-Ghazzali calls Satan, and the fourth, the ego . . .

The negative part is to start fighting with these stumbling blocks. If you start fighting, you will be lost in the valley. There is no need to fight. Don't create enmity. Just understanding is enough.

Fighting means repression. You can repress the ego, you can repress your attachment to people, you can repress your lust for things, and you can repress your Satan, your mind, but the repressed will remain, and you will not be able to enter into the fourth valley.

Only those who have no repressions enter the fourth valley . . .

Entry into the unconscious happens in the fourth valley . . .

The valley of tribulations is the entry into the unconscious. It is the entry into what Christian mystics have called "the dark night of the soul". It is the entry into the mad world that you are hiding behind yourself. It is very weird, it is very bizarre. Up to the third a man can proceed without a Master, but not beyond the third. Up to the third one can go on one's own. With the fourth a Master is a must . . .

The Master starts teaching you about trust and surrender from the very beginning so that by and by it becomes your climate—because it will be needed when you enter into the fourth valley . . .

The fifth valley . . . the thundering valley.

In the fifth valley you enter death. In the fourth you entered sleep, darkness; in the fifth you enter death. Or, if you like to use modern terminology for it: in the fourth you enter the personal unconscious; in the fifth you enter the collective unconscious. Great fear arises because you are losing your individuality . . .

With entry into death, entry into the collective unconscious, great fear arises, great anguish is felt—the greatest anguish that you will ever feel—because there comes the question: to be or not to be? You are disappearing; your whole being will hanker to be. You would like to go back to the fourth. It was dark, but at least it was good—you were there. Now, the darkness has become more dense. Not only that, you are disappearing into it. Soon not even a trace will be left of you . . .

Then comes the sixth valley—the abysmal valley . . .

Death happens, one disappears. This is what Christians call crucifixion. Nothingness has arrived; one is just an empty sky. Hindus call it *samadhi*, Zen people call it *satori* . . .

And then comes the seventh valley, which is the last, the ultimate—the valley of hymns, the valley of celebration.

Rebirth, resurrection, happens in the seventh valley. That is the meaning of the Christian idea of resurrection—that Christ is reborn, reborn in the body of glory, reborn in the body of light, reborn in the body divine. Now there is no positive, no negative. Now there is no duality. One is *one*. Unity has arisen—what Hindus call *adwaita*. The dual has disappeared. One has come home.

The valley of the hymns . . . Al-Ghazzali has given it a beautiful name. Now there is nothing left—just a song, a song of celebration, praise of God, utter joy. This is what I call the ultimate orgasm.

If I were going to name this valley I would call it the valley of total orgasm. Only celebration is left. One has flowered, bloomed. The fragrance is released. Now there is nowhere to go. Man has become that for which he was seeking, searching, struggling.

SUFIS: THE PEOPLE OF THE PATH, Vol. II

VALUE   Lieh Tzu said:
> *"Value is not the name for it."*

It is so invaluable that you can only call it invaluable. Value is not the name for it: value means commodity, value means that which can be defined in terms of human use, that which can become a means and is not an end. The end cannot be valuable in the ordinary sense of the term. For example, if somebody asks you, "You love, but what is the value of love?" What will you say? You will say, "Value is not the name for it." Love is not a value in the same sense that a car has value, a house has value. Money has value, health has value, but love? Love is the ultimate, the end. You love for love's own sake. It is not a means to anything else, it is its own end. Its value is intrinsic, its value is in life itself; it is not outgoing.

If somebody asks, "What is the value of life?" certainly you will say, "Value is not the name for it."

"Why are you living?" You will say, "Because I enjoy being alive."

"But what is the value?" "Value . . . there is none."

All that is ultimate is valueness in the ordinary sense of the word, but because of the ultimate, everything else is valuable. So value is not the name for it, although all values exist because of it.

You go to the office, you work—it is valuable: you will get one thousand rupees per month. And then you come and give one thousand rupees to your wife because you love the woman. You work for her, you work for your children— you love them. Love has no value. Your work has value, but finally all that has value comes at the feet of that which is valueless, or invaluable.

Remember, the goal cannot have any value. That's why Taoists say that life has no purpose. It shocks people.

One day a man came to me and he said, "What is the purpose of life?"

And I said, "There is no purpose. Life simply is."

He was not satisfied. He said, "I have come from very far." He had come from Nepal, and he said, "I am an old man, a retired professor. Don't send me away empty-handed. I have come to ask only one thing: What is the purpose of life?"

And I said, "If I can send you away empty-handed then your journey has been purposeful, because to be empty-handed is the goal."

He said, "Don't talk in puzzles. Just tell me, in clear-cut language, what is the purpose of life?"

Now he could not understand that he was asking an absurd question. Life cannot have any purpose, because if life has any purpose then something will become more valuable than life, and again the question will arise: What is the purpose of that? If we say, "Life is to attain truth," then truth becomes the real purpose. But then what is the purpose of truth? If we say, "Life is to seek God," then the question arises: What is the purpose of God? Or of achieving God? Or of realizing God? In the end you have to drop the word "purpose", finally you have to drop it.

Yes, value is not the name for it, purpose is not the name for it; and if you understand this insight, great light will arise in you. Life has no purpose and no value. Love has no purpose and no value. God has no purpose and no value. Truth has no purpose and no value. That means God, life, truth, love, are just four names for the same thing. They are not different, because there can be only one thing which has not any purpose—everything else has purpose because of it. It is the topmost, the very peak.

TAO: THE PATHLESS PATH, Vol. I

VEGETARIANISM Pythagoras' contribution to western philosphy is immense. It is incalculable. For the first time he introduced vegetarianism to the West. The idea of vegetarianism is of immense value; it is based on great reverence for life.

The modern mind can understand it far better now we know that all forms of life are interrelated, interdependent. Man is not an island: man exists in an infinite web of millions of forms of life and existence. We exist in a chain, we are not separate. And to destroy other animals is not only ugly, unaesthetic, inhuman—it is also unscientific. We are destroying our own foundation.

Life exists as one organic unity. Man can exist only as part of this orchestra. Just think of man without birds and without animals and without fish—that life will be very very boring; it will lose all complexity, variety, richness, color. The forests will be utterly empty, the cuckoo will not call, and the birds will not fly, and the water will look very sad without the fish.

Life in its infinite forms exists as one organic unity. We are part of it: the part should feel reverence for the whole. That is the idea of vegetarianism. It simply means: don't destroy life. It simply means: life is God—avoid destroying it, otherwise you will be destroying the very ecology.

And it has something very scientific behind it. It was not an accident that all the religions that were born in India are basically vegetarian, and all the religions that were born outside India are non-vegetarian. But the highest peaks of religious consciousness were known in India and nowhere else.

Vegetarianism functioned as a purification. When you eat animals you are more under the law of necessity. You are heavy, you gravitate more towards the earth. When you are a vegetarian you are light and you are more under the law of grace, under the law of power, and you start gravitating towards the sky.

Your food is not just food: it is you. What you eat, you become. If you eat something which is fundamentally based on murder, on violence, you cannot rise above the law of necessity. You will remain more or less an animal. The human is born when you start moving above the animals, when you start doing something to yourself which no animal can do.

Vegetarianism is a conscious effort, a deliberate effort, to get out of the heaviness that keeps you tethered to the earth so that you can fly—so that the flight from the alone to the alone becomes possible.

The lighter the food, the deeper goes the meditation. The grosser the food, then meditation becomes more and more difficult. I am not saying that meditation is impossible for a non-vegetarian—it is not impossible, but it is unnecessarily difficult.

It is like a man who is going to climb a mountain, and he goes on carrying many rocks. It is possible that even when you are carrying rocks you *may* reach to the mountain peak, but it creates unnecessary trouble. You could have thrown those rocks, you could have unburdened yourself, and the climb would have been easier, far more pleasant.

The intelligent person will not carry rocks when he is going to the mountain, will not carry anything unnecessary. And the higher he moves, the lighter and lighter he will become. Even if he is carrying something, he will drop it.

When Edmund Hillary and Tenzing reached Everest for the first time, they had to drop everything on the way—because the higher they moved, the more difficult it was to carry anything. Even very essential things were dropped. Just to carry yourself is more than enough.

Vegetarianism is of immense help. It changes your chemistry. When you eat and live on animals . . . The first thing: whenever an animal is killed the animal is angry, afraid—naturally. When you kill an animal . . . just think of yourself being killed. What will be the state of your consciousness? What will be your psychology? All kinds of poisons will be released in your body, because when you are angry a certain kind of poison is released into your blood. When you are afraid, again a certain other kind of poison is released into your blood. And when you are being killed, that is the utmost in fear, anger. All the glands in your body release all their poison.

And man goes on living on that poisoned meat. If it keeps you angry, violent, aggressive, it is not strange; it is natural. Whenever you live on killing, you don't have any respect for life; you are inimical to life. And the person who is inimical to life cannot move into prayer—because prayer means reverence for life.

And one who is inimical to God's creatures cannot be very friendly towards God either. If you destroy Picasso's paintings, you cannot be very respectful towards Picasso—it is impossible. All the creatures belong to God. God lives in them, God breathes in them, they are *his* manifestation, just as you are. They are brothers and sisters.

When you see an animal if the idea of brotherhood does not arise in you, you don't know what prayer is, you will never know what prayer is. And the very idea that just for food, just for taste, you can destroy life, is so ugly. It is impossible to believe that man goes on doing it.

Pythagoras was the first to introduce vegetarianism to the West. It is of profound depth for man to learn how to live in friendship with creatures. That becomes the foundation. And only on that foundation can you base your prayer, your meditativeness. You can watch it in yourself: when you eat meat, meditation will be found to be more and more difficult.

Buddha was born in a non-vegetarian family. He was a *kshatriya*—belonged to the warrior race—but the experience of meditation slowly slowly transformed him into a vegetarian. It was his inner understanding: whenever he ate meat, meditation was more difficult; whenever he avoided meat, meditation was easier. It was just a simple observation.

You will be suprised to know that the greatest vegetarians in the world have been Jainas—but all their twenty-four Masters were born into families of non-vegetarians. They were all warriors; they were brought up as fighters. All the twenty-four Masters of the Jainas were *kshatriyas*.

What happened? Why did these people who were brought up, conditioned from the very beginning to eat meat, create one day the greatest movement in the world for vegetarianism? Just because of their experiments with meditation.

It is an unavoidable fact that if you want to meditate, if you want to become thoughtless, if you want to become light—so light that the earth cannot pull you downwards, so light that the sky becomes available to you—then you have to move from non-vegetarian conditioning to the freedom of vegetarianism.

Vegetarianism has nothing to do with religion: it is something basically scientific. It has nothing to do with morality, but it has much to do with aesthetics. It is unbelievable that a man of sensitivity, awareness, understanding, love, can eat meat. And if he can eat meat then something is missing—he is still unconscious somewhere of what he is doing, unconscious of the implications of his acts.

But Pythagoras was not heard, not believed—on the contrary, he was ridiculed, persecuted. And he had brought one of the greatest treasures from the East to the West. He had brought a great experiment—if he had been heard, the West would have been a totally different world.

The problem that has arisen today, that we have destroyed nature, would never have arisen. If Pythagoras had become the foundation for the western consciousness, there would not have been these great world wars. He would have changed the whole course of history. He tried hard, he did whatsoever *he* could—it is not his fault. But people are blind, people are deaf; they can't hear a thing, they can't understand a thing. And they are not ready to change their habits.

People live in their habits, mechanically they live. And he had brought a message of becoming aware. Great meditative energy would have been released in the West. It would have become impossible to produce Adolf Hitlers and Mussolinis and Stalins. It would have been a totally different world. But still the same old habit persists.

We cannot change human consciousness unless we start by changing the human body. When you eat meat you are absorbing the animal in you—and the animal has to be transcended. Avoid! If you really want to go higher and higher, if you really want to go to the sunlit peaks of your consciousness, if you really want to know God, then you will have to change in every possible way.

You will have to look all around your life, you will have to observe each small habit in detail—because sometimes a very small thing can change your whole life. Sometimes it may be a very simple thing, and it can change your life *so* totally that it looks almost unbelievable.

Try vegetarianism and you will be surprised: meditation becomes far easier. Love becomes more subtle, loses its grossness—becomes more sensitive but less sensuous, becomes more prayerful and less sexual. And your body also starts taking on a different vibe. You become more graceful, softer, more feminine, less aggressive, more receptive.

Vegetarianism is an alchemical change in you. It creates the space in which the baser metal can be transformed into gold.

PHILOSOPHIA PERENNIS, Vol. II

VERBS   My suggestion to all of my sannyasins is don't trust in nouns, trust in verbs. Become a verb rather than becoming a noun. Rather than love, think of loving. Rather than being, think of becoming. Rather than of a flower, think of flowering. Always think in terms of verbs and you will never be frustrated. Your life will become a constant growth from one peak to another peak, and those peaks go on becoming higher and higher.

THE GOLDEN WIND

VERTICAL Time consists of two tenses, not three. The present is not part of time; the past is time, the future is time. The present is the penetration of the beyond into the world of time.

You can think of time as a horizontal line. A is followed by b, b is followed by c, c is followed by d, and so on and so forth: it is a linear progression. Existence is not horizontal, existence is vertical. Existence does not move in a line— from a to b, from b to c—existence moves in intensity: from a to deeper a, from the deeper a to an even deeper a. It is diving into the moment.

Time conceived of as past and future is the language of the mind—and the mind can only create problems, it knows no solutions. All the problems that humanity is burdened with are the mind's inventions. Existence is a mystery, not a problem. It has not to be solved, it has to be lived.

THE GOOSE IS OUT

VICIOUS But I tell you that only man is violent. You may not understand other animals: they may have killed more that they could eat—that only shows they are not doing right arithmetic, that's all. They might have killed more than they could eat; that simply shows they don't know how to calculate beforehand. But it is not a sport. They are not doing it just for their enjoyment, no.

And the ants walking on your body when you are meditating are not vicious, they don't know at all that you are meditating, they don't know at all that you are. They may be on their own business—ants are very businesslike— they may be on their own trip, you are just in their way, that's all. In fact, you are disturbing them, not they you. You are just sitting there like a rock—you think you are

meditating—and you are disturbing their whole route. Ants
are great followers of their leaders—the leader has gone one
way, so all the ants are going that way. They are always very
controlled, they are like the army. So they have to pass you.

You think that they are in the way, you think that they
are disturbing you; they think that you are just in their way,
disturbing them. No, they are not vicious. Nobody is vicious
except man, nobody can be, because to be vicious, one has
to think about the future, much thinking capacity is needed.
To be vicious, one has to calculate about the future. To be
vicious, one has to think very, very much about the past—
past experiences, possibilities, impossibilities—and the
future. One has to be cunning, clever. To be vicious, one
has to be a disciple of Machiavelli or Chankya. Machiavelli
says in his *Prince* that before somebody attacks you, you
should attack him, because that is the only defense. Even
if the other has not attacked you yet, you have to suspect,
and before he attacks, you attack first, because that is the
only great defense. If you attack first there is more possibility
of winning; if he attacks first there is less possibility of winning . . .

Man is vicious because only man can be Machiavellian.
Other animals are simple, very simple, and when you think
that they are doing something viciously, you are wrong. You
think that mosquitoes are disturbing your meditation—they
don't know. They don't know you at all, you are just food
for them, and they are seeing their food, a simple thing . . .

When you go to a tree, to an apple tree or to any other
fruit tree and you take the fruit from the tree, have you ever
thought that you are vicious to the tree? No, the idea never
comes. The same is being done by the mosquito to you and
mosquitoes are very impartial—even to a Buddha they will
do the same.

They did. I was staying in Sarnath once, the place where
Buddha gave his first sermon. Buddha moved around only
a small part of India, the Bihar, so in forty years of wandering he passed through every village many times, but to Sarnath he never came again. He visited it only once, the first
time, and he never came again.

So I asked the Buddhist *bhikkhu* who was head of the

Sarnath temple, what the matter was. "Why did Buddha never come again?" He brooded and he said, "Maybe mosquitoes . . ." Sarnath has the biggest mosquitoes in India.

Mosquitoes are impartial. They don't bother whether you are a Buddha or not; whether you are meditating or murdering someone they are in search of their food. And as you are in search of your food and you never feel that you are vicious, why should they be thought of as vicious? Nobody is vicious. Even the germs that can kill you, they too are not vicious, they are in search of their food. Even the germs that create a cancer in your body that will certainly kill you, that no medicine can help—even they are not vicious, they are not Machiavellian, they are not politicians. They are simple people, just in search of food and they are very happy that they have found a home within you. They are not doing any harm to you knowingly because they cannot do anything knowingly. They are enjoying life as you are enjoying life.

Once you understand this . . . I don't mean that you just sit naked and become food for them, that is not my meaning. You protect yourself, but don't think them vicious. You protect yourself. If the tree could have protected herself she would have protected herself against you. You protect yourself. Even the mosquito protects itself, even the mosquitoes are not vicious. You should sit naked and allow them on you because they are in search of food? Then you are moving to the other extreme, to another foolishness.

You protect yourself, everybody protects. Even the mosquito will protect himself—but don't think that they are vicious, because the idea that life around you is vicious is very dangerous.

That idea will harm you more than all the animals and all the mosquitoes and all the ants combined, because that idea will give you a feeling of separateness from life, that idea will give you an enmity towards life, that idea will never allow you to surrender to the whole.

TAO: THE THREE TREASURES, Vol. II

VICTORY If you surrender to existence you are victorious: immediately you are the crowned one—that is the meaning of the word "christ". But Christ was crucified. His crucifixion was really his crowning ceremony. For those who understand, for those who have eyes to see, his crucifixion is a crowning ceremony because at the last moment on the cross he surrendered totally. He said: "Thy kingdom come, they will be done." That was his last prayer. That is surrender.

To have one's own will is egoistic; to allow God's will to happen to you is surrender. To be with God and in God is to be victorious; there can be no other victory greater than this.

A sannyasin has to live this paradox: the paradox of surrendering and realizing victory.

SCRIPTURES IN SILENCE AND SERMONS IN STONE

It is always truth that wins. Untruth promises but cannot fulfill its promises. Lies are very very alluring but ultimately they are going to ditch you into failure, frustration. They can't lead you to victory. How can the false ever be victorious?—it is impossible. Only the true can be. And without victory life is meaningless. Without victory you are an unlit lamp, an empty house. Victory brings light, victory brings joy; victory brings meaning and significance. Victory brings many flowers; it is victory that becomes a spring to the soul. But always remember that untruth may win small battles— for the moment it may seem that you are winning with untruth—but it never wins the war. The ultimate victory is always of truth.

In India they have an ancient saying, *Satyameva jayate*: Truth is always victorious. This is the trust of a sannyasin, that truth is always victorious. Be true to yourself and to the world. Don't be phony, don't be pseudo, don't pretend. Let things be as they are. Don't hide—be authentic.

SCRIPTURES IN SILENCE AND SERMONS IN STONE

In Japan, when wrestlers fight, this is a ritual—that first they will bow down to each other. It is very symbolic.

The Zen explanation is that whether you are defeated or you become victorious does not matter, and you both need each other, you both depend on each other. If you are defeated and the other has become victorious, the other has to bow down to you because without you he could not have been victorious. His victory depends on your defeat so he is dependent on *you*—he has to be thankful. He cannot take it that this is *his* victory, he cannot be victorious alone; without you he will be nowhere, so he has to thank you and feel grateful. So even victory does not create an ego-trip. And if you are defeated and you know this is just a game, nothing serious to be worried about—no problem arises.

In Mexico thay have been studying some school children. The ancient tradition in Mexico is that the father has to give rewards, toys, things, to every child irrespective of their success or failure in life. One child has come first in the class, he gets a reward, and the one who has failed also gets one. And there is no difference—it is irrelevant. That's tremendous insight: it doesn't matter whether you fail or you succeed—all is a game; you are rewarded all the same.

And the psychologists who have been studying this have come to feel that the Mexican children are more at ease with life—unworried, non-tense, more relaxed. The civilized child becomes very very tense from the very beginning—five years old, six years old—and he carries the whole burden of the earth. He is so tense and so worried and afraid about whether he is going to make it or not.

You have destroyed his childhood and you are creating the poison of ambition. You are making things very serious: if he comes first it is something great, if he comes second he has not been up to the mark, and he will carry the inferiority complex, and when the child comes home as a failure nobody even looks at him, everybody's eyes are condemning. We make things unnecessarily serious.

Life should be taken as an acting.

FAR BEYOND THE STARS

VIOLENCE We have worked for thousands of years to make the earth a big madhouse, and we have succeeded, unfortunately . . . There is violence everywhere for the simple reason that we have, in subtle ways, not allowed people's energies to be creative, and whenever creative energies are prevented they become destructive.

Violence is not the real problem. The real problem is how to help people to be creative. A creative person cannot be violent because his energies are moving in the direction of God. We call God the creator. Whenever you are creating something you participate in God's being. You cannot be violent, you cannot be destructive; it is impossible.

But for thousands of years we have destroyed every possible door to creativity. Instead of helping people to be creative we train them to be destructive. The warrior, the soldier, we have respected too much. In fact, the warrior is someone who should be condemned, not respected—he is destructive. The soldier should not be respected.

We need sannyasins, not soldiers. We need lovers, not fighters. But love is condemned and violence is praised . . .

It is easier to fight with a person and decide who is right. "Might is right." That rule still remains—the rule of the jungle.

We call man civilized? He has yet to be civilized. Civilization is only an idea which has not yet been realized. Man is just superficially civilized, not even skin-deep. Just scratch a little and you will find the animal coming out—a ferocious animal, far more ferocious than any wild animals, because wild animals, howsoever wild they are, don't carry bombs—atom bombs, hydrogen bombs. Compared to man and his violence all animals are left far behind.

And in the past this has been the rule. The Buddhas are exceptions.

GUIDA SPIRITUALE

War gives a chance for man to become animal; hence war has great attraction. In three thousand years' history man has fought five thousand wars—continuously, somewhere or other, the war continues. Not even a single day passes when man is not killing other men. Why such tremendous joy in destruction, in killing? The reason is deep down in the psychology of man.

The moment you kill, suddenly you are one; you become the animal again, the duality disappears. Hence, in murder, in suicide, there is a tremendous magnetic force. Man cannot be persuaded yet to be non-violent. Violence erupts. Names change, slogans change, but the violence remains the same. It may be in the name of religion, in the name of political ideology, or any absurd thing—a football match is enough for people to get violent, a cricket match is enough.

People are so much interested in violence that if they cannot do it themselves—because it is risky and they think of the consequences—they find vicarious ways to be violent. In a movie, or on the TV, violence is a must; without violence, nobody is going to see the film. Seeing violence and blood, suddenly you are reminded of your animal past; you forget your present, you completely forget your future—you become your past. You become identified; what is happening on the screen somehow becomes your own life. You are no more a spectator—in those moments you become a participant, you fall *en rapport*.

Violence has great attraction. Sexuality has great attraction, because it is only in sexual moments that you can become one; otherwise you remain two, divided, and the anxiety and the anguish persist. Violence, sex, drugs, they all help you, at least for the time being, temporarily, to fall back, to become an animal. But this cannot become a permanent state of affairs.

One fundamental law has to be understood: nothing can go backwards. At the most you can pretend, at the most you can deceive, but nothing can go backwards because time does not move backwards. Time always goes ahead. You cannot reduce a young man to a child, and you cannot reduce an old man to a young man—it is impossible. The tree cannot be reduced back to the original seed—it is imposssible.

Evolution goes on and on and there is no way to prevent it or force it backwards. Hence all efforts of men to become animals and find peace are doomed to fail. You can be drunk through alcohol or through other drugs—marijuana, LSD—you can be completely drowned. For the moment all the worries disappear, for the moment you are no more part of a problematic existence, for the moment you move in a totally different dimension—but for the moment only.

Tomorrow morning you will be back, and when you are back the world is going to be more ugly than it ever was before, and life is going to be more of a problem than it ever was before. Because while you were intoxicated, unconscious, asleep in the drug, the problems were growing. The problems were becoming more and more complicated.

While you were thinking that you had gone beyond the problems, the problems were taking root more in your being, in your unconscious.

Tomorrow again you will be back in the same world—it will look more ugly compared to the peace that you had attained by reduction, by intoxication, by forgetfulness. Compared to that peace, the world will look even more dangerous, more complex, more scary. And then the only way is: go on increasing the doses of your drug. But that too does not help for long. And this is no way to get out of the dilemma. The dilemma remains, persists.

The only way is to grow towards the divine, the only way is forwards. The only way is to become that which is your potential—the only way is to transform the potential into the actual.

THE FISH IN THE SEA IS NOT THIRSTY

Violence is never part of nature. Nobody is born violent; one learns it. One is infected by a violent society, by violence all around and one becomes violent. Otherwise every child is born absolutely non-violent.

There is no violence in your being itself. It is conditioned by situations. One has to defend oneself against so many things and offense is the best method of defending. When a person has to defend himself so many times, he becomes offensive, he becomes violent, because it is better to hit first than to wait for somebody to hit you and then reply. The one who hits first has more chances of winning . . .

Hence people become violent. Very soon they come to understand it—that they will be crushed. The only way to survive is to fight, and once you learn this trick, by and by your whole nature becomes poisoned by it. But it is nothing natural, so it can be dropped. It will go; nothing to worry about.

A ROSE IS A ROSE IS A ROSE

And violence *is* there. It is not around you; it is around everybody. Man has lived very violently; he has not lost his inner animality. Man is still wild inside; only on the surface does he look civilized. So violence is everywhere, the whole of life is full of violence. And where you don't see violence that is just a facade. If you go deep into it you will find violence there too. Even behind the name of love there is violence, so what to say about other things? But this is how life is!

And you have to learn to live without violence in such a violent world. It is difficult to live sanely in an insane world but that is the only life there is and one has to find one's way to live through it. All that we can do is to never become violent against violence, because that is not going to help. Have deep compassion. If one has to suffer, one should suffer through compassion. And people who are violent are completely unaware; they don't know what they are doing. That's what Jesus has to say to the people; it is his last message to the world. He asks God to forgive these people because they don't know what they are doing.

So one can pray, one can love and one can have compassion, but the violence is there. And you cannot change it because the world is so big; how can you change it? One has to accept it. And one can go on doing whatsoever one can do on one's own—a little bit, whatsoever one can spread. Spread your love. The world is like a desert but even if you can sow a single seed and only two flowers come to it, even that is something. In this vast desert land if two flowers or even a single flower comes up, that too is good.

So don't be too concerned about it. Just be concerned about one thing: how you can love people who are violent and how to live in a world which is not sane at all. Find ways. And this is the whole effort here—through meditation, prayer, groups. These are ways to seek and search for some secrets so that you can go unscratched, uncontaminated by people's violence. But it is possible. The world will remain violent, you can become non-violent . . . and that is all that can be done. So don't be worried about it.

THE OPEN SECRET

VIPASSANA Buddha brings a totally new vision of meditation to the world. Before Buddha, meditation was something that you had to do once or twice a day, one hour in the morning, one hour in the evening, and that was all. Buddha gave a totally new interpretation to the whole process of meditation. He said: This kind of meditation that you do one hour in the morning, one hour in the evening, you may do five times or four times a day, is not of much value. Meditation cannot be something that you can do *apart* from life just for one hour or fifteen minutes. Meditation has to become something synonymous with your life; it has to be like breathing. You cannot breathe one hour in the morning and one hour in the evening, otherwise the evening will never come. It has to be something like breathing: even while you are asleep the breathing continues. You may fall into a coma, but the breathing continues.

Buddha says meditation should become such a *constant* phenomenon; only then can it transform you. And he evolved a new technique of meditation.

His greatest contribution to the world is *vipassana;* no other teacher has given such a great gift to the world. Jesus is beautiful, Mahavira is beautiful, Lao Tzu is beautiful, Zarathustra is beautiful, but their contribution, compared to Buddha, is nothing. Even if they are all put together, then too Buddha's contribution is greater because he gave such a scientific method—simple yet so penetrating that you are in tune with it, it becomes a constant factor in your life.

Then you need not do it; you have to do it only in the beginning. Once you have learned the knack of it, it remains with you; you need not do it. Then whatsoever you are doing, it is there. It becomes a backdrop to your life, a background to your life. You are walking, but you walk meditatively. You are eating, but you eat meditatively. You are sleeping, but you sleep meditatively. Remember, even the quality of sleep of a meditator is different from the quality of sleep of a non-meditator. Everything becomes different because a new factor has entered which changes the whole gestalt.

Vipassana simply means watching your breath, looking at your breath. It is not like *yoga pranayama:* it is not changing your breath to a certain rhythm—deep breathing, fast breathing. No, it does not change your breathing at all; it has nothing to do with the breathing. Breathing has only to be used as a device to watch because it is a constant phenomenon in you. You can simply watch it, and it is the most subtle phenomenon. If you can watch your breath then it will be easy for you to watch your thoughts.

One thing immensely great that Buddha contributed was the discovery of the relationship between breath and thought. He was the first man in the whole history of humanity who made it absolutely clear that breathing and thinking are deeply related. Breathing is the bodily part of thinking and thinking is the psychological part of breathing. They are not separate, they are two aspects of the same coin. He is the first man who talks of bodymind as one unity. He talks for the first time about man as a psychosomatic phenomenon. He does not talk about body *and* mind, he talks about bodymind. They are not two, hence no "and" is needed to join them. They are already one—bodymind—not even a hyphen is needed; bodymind is one phenomenon. And each body process has its counterpart in your psychology and vice versa.

You can watch it, you can try an experiment. Just stop your breathing for a moment and you will be surprised: the moment you stop your breathing, your thinking stops. Or you can watch another thing: whenever your thinking is going too fast your breathing changes. For example, if you are full of sexual lust and your thinking is going too hot, your breathing will be different: it will not be rhythmic, it will lose its rhythm. It will be more chaotic, it will be unrhythmic.

When you are angry your breathing changes because your thinking has changed. When you are loving, your breathing changes because your thinking has changed. When you are peaceful, at ease, at home, relaxed, your breathing is different. When you are restless, worried, in turmoil, in anguish, your breathing is different. Just by watching your breath you can know what kind of state is happening in your mind.

Meditators come across a point: when the mind really completely ceases, breathing also ceases. And then great fear arises—don't be afraid. Many meditators have reported to me that "We became very much afraid, very much frightened, because suddenly we became aware that the breathing has stopped." Naturally, one thinks that when breathing stops death is close by. Breathing stops in death; breathing also stops in deep meditation. Hence deep meditation and death have one thing similar: in both the breathing stops. Therefore, if a man knows meditation he has also known death. That's why the meditator becomes free of the fear of death; he knows breathing can stop and still he is.

Breathing is not life; life is a far bigger phenomenon. Breathing is only a connection with the body. The connection can be cut; that does not mean that life has ended. Life is still there; life does not end just by the disappearance of breathing.

Buddha says: Watch your breathing; leave it normal, as it is. Sitting silently, watch your breath. The sitting posture will also be helpful; the Buddha posture, the lotus posture, is very helpful. When your spine is erect and you are sitting in a lotus posture, your legs crossed, your spine makes a ninety-degree angle with the gravitational forces. And when the ninety-degree angle with the gravitational forces is there, the body is at its best relaxed state. Let the spine be erect and the body loose, hanging on the spine—not tense. The body should be loose, relaxed, the spine erect, so gravitation has the *least* pull on you . . .

Hence this lotus posture is something valuable. It is not just a body phenomenon; it affects the mind. It changes the mind. Sit in a lotus posture—the whole point is that your spine should be erect and should make a ninety-degree angle with the earth. That is the point where you are capable of being the most intelligent, the most alert, the least sleepy.

And then watch your breath, the natural breath. You need not breathe deep, you don't change your breathing; you simply watch it as it is. But you will be surprised by one thing: the moment you start watching, it changes—because even the fact of *watching* is a change and the breathing is no more the same.

Slight changes in your consciousness immediately affect your breathing. You will be able to see it: whenever you watch you will see your breathing has become a little deeper. But if it becomes so of its own accord it is okay; you are not to do it by your will. Watching your breath, slowly slowly you will be surprised: that as your breath becomes calm and quiet your mind also becomes calm and quiet. And watching the breath will make you capable of watching the mind.

That is just the beginning, the first part of meditation, the physical part. And the second part is the psychological part.

Then you can watch more subtle things in your mind—thoughts, desires, memories.

And as you go deeper into watchfulness, a miracle starts happening: as you become watchful less and less traffic happens in the mind, more and more quiet, silence, more and more silent spaces, more and more gaps and intervals. Moments pass and you don't come across a single thought. Slowly slowly, minutes pass, hours pass . . .

And there is a certain arithmetic in it: if you can remain for forty-eight minutes absolutely empty, that very day you will become enlightened, that *very* moment you will become enlightened. But it is not a question of your effort; don't go on looking at the watch because each time you look, a thought has come. You have to again count from the very beginning; you are back to zero. There is no need for you to watch.

But this has been the experience in the East of all great meditators: that forty-eight minutes seems to be the ultimate point. If this much of a gap is possible, if for this much of a gap thinking stops and you remain alert, with no thought crossing your mind, you are capable of receiving God inside. You have become the host and the guest *immediately* comes.

THE BOOK OF THE BOOKS, Vol. XI

VIRGINITY Now "virgin birth" has nothing to do with biological virginity; that is utter nonsense. Jesus is not born of a biological virgin mother, but then what is meant by saying that Mary was virgin? "Virgin" simply means utterly pure, so pure that there is no sexuality in the mind. It is not a question of the body but a question of the mind—so pure that there is no idea of sexuality.

And at the deepest core everybody is a virgin. Virginity means purity of love. Jesus must have been born out of great love. Love is always virgin. Love transcends sex—that is the meaning of virginity.

But there are foolish people everywhere; they go on insisting that "No, he *was* born of a virgin mother." They make him a laughing stock. And because of *their* foolishness, a great parable, a great metaphor, loses all meaning.

A mother and her daughter came to the doctor's office. The mother asked the doctor to examine her daughter. "She has been having some strange symptoms and I am worried about her," the mother said.

The doctor examined the daughter carefully, then he announced, "Madam, I believe your daughter is pregnant."

The mother gasped. "That's nonsense!" she said. "Why, my little girl has nothing whatsoever to do with men." She turned to the girl, "You don't, do you, dear?"

"No, Mumsy," said the girl. "Why, you know that I have never so much as kissed a man."

The doctor looked from mother to daughter and back again, then silently he stood up and walked to the window. He stared out; he continued staring until the mother felt compelled to ask, "Doctor, is there something wrong out there?"

"No, madam," said the doctor. "It is just that the last time anything like this happened, a star appeared in the East—and I was looking to see if another one was going to show up."

Mary must have been in tremendous love; that's why she is virgin. Mary must have been so deep in love that sex was not the point at all.

Remember, you can make love to a woman without any love in your heart—then it is pure sexuality, animality; it is prostitution. You can make love to a woman with no idea of sex, then love is just a pure communication of two energies, a sharing, a dance, a celebration. No idea of sex in the mind and you can make love to a woman, and the woman can make love to you not thinking of sex at all. The whole point is where your mind is. If you are thinking of sex, if your mind is obsessed with sex, you simply want to use the woman, the woman simply wants to use you, it is ugly. It has no aesthetics in it, no poetry in it. There is nothing of the beyond in it—it is very muddy.

But the same act . . . Remember, the act will be the same when two lovers make love and when a man goes to a prostitute. Biologically the act is the same, but spiritually there is a tremendous difference. The man who goes to the prostitute is thinking only of sex, and the lover when he makes

love to the woman has no idea of sex. It is simply a communion, coming closer and closer. Then sex happens only
as a gesture of communion. It is virgin.

That's my idea of virginity. The lover always remains
virgin; the lover cannot lose his virginity. And Jesus, a man
like Jesus, can only come out of great love. But please try
to understand the language of the ancients. It is very simple
to misunderstand, because centuries have passed, words
have changed their meanings. And we have forgotten that
the old days were not days of scientific language but of poetic
language . . .

Poets also stumble upon the same truths, but when they
express them they are expressed in a different way. In fact,
poets always arrive before the scientists ever arrive, because
scientists move very cautiously and poets move in a drunken
way. Poets don't care about logic; poets don't move in a
logical, syllogistic way—they simply jump from one point
to another. And they are not afraid to be laughed at, and
they are not afraid even if people think they are mad. So
they always discover things before scientists discover
them—almost thousands of years before. Because the scientist moves so cautiously, so slowly, step by step . . . he has
to look into details; he has to prove something. The poet
has to prove nothing: he simply asserts. Nobody asks any
proof. Whatsoever happens in his intuition, he simply goes
on singing it. Nobody wants any consistency, nobody wants
any objective proof, nobody wants him to go and prove
it in a lab. Naturally he goes on saying things long before
the scientist comes to know about it.

These are poetic expressions. You will have to understand
the language of the poets . . .

Remember: scriptures talk about truth; they are not history
books. History books talk about facts. That's why in history
books you will find Alexander the Great and Ivan the Terrible and Adolf Hitler and all kinds of neurotics. But Buddha,
Mahavira, Jesus, they are not part of the history books. For
them we need a totally different approach. And it is good
they are not part of history books—they are *not* part of
history; they come from the beyond, they belong to the
beyond. They are only for those who are ready to rise and
soar to the beyond.

Meditate over this beautiful truth that Jesus is born of a virgin mother—but it is not a fact. It is certainly a truth: he is born of a mother who is utterly innocent. He is born of a mother who is in tremendous love—and love *is* virgin, and love is always virgin.

PHILOSOPHIA PERENNIS, Vol. II

VIRTUE   The real virtue has nothing to do with so-called morality. There is one very profound and pregnant statement of Socrates: he says "Knowledge is virtue." By knowledge he means wisdom, knowing, because his whole emphasis was "Know thyself". That's what I mean by being conscious, because it is only consciousness that makes you capable of knowing yourself. And the moment you have known yourself you cannot do anything harmful to anybody. It is simply impossible. You cannot be destructive.

It is like a man who has eyes: how can you think that he will try to pass through the wall? He has eyes so he knows where the door is—he will pass through the door. But the blind man can try. He will knock all around, and he can even try to get out through the wall or from the window. He does not know where the door is. He will ask others where the door is. But each moment you are in a different house—as far as life is concerned—and each moment the house is changing. Sometimes the door is on the right and sometimes it is cn the left, sometimes it is at the back and sometimes in the front—no directions from others can be of much help, because the door goes on changing.

You need your own eyes. Then there is no need to ask, then there is no need to think about the door; whenever you want to get out, you simply look and you know where the door is. That's what consciousness gives you: an insight, a new vision, a way of seeing, a new eye—in the East we call it the third eye. That is only a metaphor; but there are a few fools who try to dissect a dead body to find out where the third eye is. These fools can be great experts, scientists, but that does not make any difference. They have not understood the metaphor, they have not understood the poetry of the word. It is only an expression. The third eye does not exist in the physical body; it is only a way of saying that you have found how to see directly into reality, you have become conscious. And out of that consciousness is virtue.

And remember: if virtue is imposed from the outside then it is a regimentation. When it comes from the within it has an individuality. It is not like ready-made clothes; it is made for you, it is made by your consciousness. Its harmony is total with your being.

Now Moses wrote the Ten Commandments three thousand years ago, and there are fools who are still following them. They were perfectly good for Moses but they are not good for anybody else. They came out of his consciousness. That's the parable, that they came out of an encounter with God; that's an old way of saying that one has become so conscious that one knows what truth is, what God is. His experience of the ultimate truth gave birth to those Ten Commandments; they were only applicable to him—and to nobody else.

In India, Hindus have followed the rules and the discipline of Manu, who is even farther back than Moses—five thousand years old. They may have been perfectly good for many but they are not at all adequate for anybody else. And this is my insistence, that each person has to find his own religion, his own morality, his own virtue. Then your virtue has *your* signature. Then it is alive, breathing, and then you are doing it not for any other reason, but just because that's the right thing to do. Your very *heart* wants to do it. Then you are not asking for any rewards in heaven, you are not greedy for anything and you are not afraid of hell, of any punishment. You are doing exactly what your insight is telling you to do—whatsoever the result, whatsoever the ultimate consequence. Nobody of deep consciousness ever cares about the consequences. He acts immediately, responds to reality directly—and that's all. And he enjoys the moment when he acts with reality, with his total being. He enjoys that harmony, that meeting, that merger, that union.

THE OLD POND—PLOP!

There are small virtues which can be cultivated by us; that's what is taught by the society, that's what is taught by the family. They are small virtues: they only create a kind of character but they don't create consciousness. They help you to live in the society more comfortably than you could have lived without them. They function like a lubricating agent between you and other people. You are not constantly in fight with people; that is their purpose. You are not alone, you live with so many people; constant friction will destroy you. So the small virtues are just a kind of protection, they create an armor around you, they don't bring you into unnecessary conflict; but they have nothing to do with religion. Morality has nothing to do with religion, morality is a social phenomenon: religion is divine; it is not man-made, it is a revelation.

When you become alert about your own consciousness, of your own center, out of that alertness the great virtue flows. That virtue does not give you a character; it gives you a conscience. It does not give you a fixed pattern to follow; it simply gives you responsibility, ability to respond. It does not give you fixed rules; it simply gives you eyes to see the situation and to immediately act accordingly.

The smaller virtues give you fixed rules: they tell you what to do, what not to do, they tell you what is right and what is wrong. The great virtue never tells you what you should do and what you should not do; it simply tells you "Be aware". And then whatsoever you do is going to be good. Good is a byproduct of awareness and evil is a byproduct of unawareness.

Smaller virtues there are many . . . In the Buddhist scriptures where very minute details are given, thirty-three thousand have been counted: do this, don't do that—small details, thirty-three thousand. Even to remember them is difficult but a Buddhist monk is expected to fulfill those thirty-three thousand virtues. They are all small, mundane, trivial.

I give you only one virtue—it takes care of all: that is awareness. Be alert, act out of awareness, don't act out of unawareness. A single virtue fulfills all those thirty-three thousand virtues, and more. It cuts the very root of immorality. It cuts the very root of all that is evil. Rather than cutting the branches and the leaves, it is better to cut the very root in a single blow.

TURN ON, TUNE IN AND DROP THE LOT

VISION A blind man looks at the sun. The sun is there, but the blind man cannot see because he has no sight, he has no eyes. If he attains to sight he will have the vision of the sun. Sight has to happen inside, and the vision will be outside.

You have to search for eyes, you have to become a seer. You have to drop your blindness. You have to drop all kinds of buffers that are covering your eyes. You have to become open: that is the meaning of attaining to sight, or insight. Insight is far better because it emphasizes the "in". Sight happens in—that is the meaning of insight. You open up, you hear, you see, you are capable of receiving, and then all that is already present there—the primordial sound of *omkar*, the celestial music that surrounds you . . . and you have not heard it yet, because you don't have ears to hear it, you don't have that sensitive ear. You can hear only noises, you can't hear music. If you train, if you cultivate the ear, slowly, slowly, your ear becomes more and more meditative, silent, receptive, passive. It comes to a state that Taoists call *wu-wei*, no action—just utterly silent with no stirring of its own—because if you are having some stirring of your own, you will miss that which is there. When your eyes are just empty, you have insight. Eyes full of thoughts, prejudices, concepts, beliefs, can't see. They go on seeing that which they believe, they don't see that which is. Hence you have to de-nude yourself utterly from all beliefs—Christian, Hindu, Mohammedan—you have to drop all kinds of philosophies. When your eyes are utterly naked—you don't have any kind of belief inside you, you don't know what is what, you simply don't know at all; you know only one thing, that you don't know, that you are innocent—in that innocence you have insight. And then whatsoever you see through that insight is called vision.

It is called vision to show a difference from dreams. The vision is *really* there. The dream also looks there but is not really there. The dream is projected by you, the vision is part of reality. In dream, you have worked upon reality; in vision, reality works upon you. In dream you are active, you are doing something—projecting. In vision you are *wu-wei*, inactive, passive. You allow the reality to work upon you.

In a dream you are a great doer; the dream is your doing. In vision you are a non-doer, a receptive end, a womb, open, waiting, ready to receive, welcoming. You are in a kind of let-go. And when you are in a kind of let-go, reality happens to you because you don't hinder it. It is continuously trying to happen to you but you go on hindering it.

God comes to you in millions of ways. But you have a certain idea of God, and God has no obligation to fulfill your idea. He goes on coming in his own ways and you go on waiting according to your belief. Hence, you go on missing.

For example, Christians will go on missing Christ because they are waiting for the *same* Christ. Not that Christ has not been happening in the world—it happened in Kabir, it happened in Mohammed, it happened in Nanak, it happened in *many* more people. But Christians are waiting for the *same* Christ that they have some ideas about. They are waiting for the second coming of Christ. It is not going to happen, ever. They are waiting in vain. Christ goes on coming, but never again the same way. Because for Christ to come in the same way, the whole existence will have to be in the same situation—and that is not going to happen ever again. Just think . . . *exactly* in the same situation: each stone in the same place as it was, and each man with the same shape as he had. Now how is this possible? Pontius Pilate is no more Governor General, he writes no more rules. That world of the Jews, that mythological world of their dreams, is no more valid. Things have changed . . .

Now the world has changed utterly. Christ cannot come the way he came that time. He can come in that way only if the world again repeats *exactly* the same situation, and that is impossible. The world is never again the same. It is a flux, things go on moving. And Christians go on waiting for Christ, and Hindus are waiting for Krishna. For five thousand years they have waited, because Krishna had said, "When there is trouble, and the dark night, and religion will be uprooted, and there will be atheism in the world, and when my people will be oppressed and will be in misery, I will come. I promise." And they are waiting. Now what more misery does India need for him to come? Can you think of any country being more miserable than India is?

If he can't come now then there is no hope, because more misery is not possible. But he is not coming, and Hindus go on waiting and they go on looking at the sky.

He *has* been coming, but God cannot come according to *your* belief. You have to be in a state of receptivity. You have to drop all beliefs; then suddenly, the vision! When the insight is ready, the vision happens. Vision is not a dream, it is reality, it is so.

Christians are dreaming. Hindus are dreaming. These are different kinds of dreamers. They go on dreaming that things will again be the same. They go on dreaming about the past. They go on projecting the past in their minds again and again. They go on playing the same game that they have become very skillful in playing, and they *don't* see that the reality has changed and their game is simply absurd.

Vision is not your dream. Vision is when all dreams have disappeared and you don't have a dreaming mind; then what happens is a vision. But for that, insight is needed. You have to learn how to see, and you have to learn how to be, and you have to learn how to hear, and you have to learn how to touch. You have to learn how to smell, how to taste. And then you will be surprised—God comes through all the senses.

Be more sensitive—less of belief, less of the head, and more of sensitivity. Be more sensuous, alive in your senses, and then suddenly one day you will see: it is not simply the light that is coming to you, it is God in the form of light; and it is not the tree that is standing there in front of you, but God; not the rock, but God; not the woman that you have fallen in love with, but a god; not the man, but God. When the insight becomes clear, unclouded, suddenly you start seeing that everywhere God is, because all is God.

THE WISDOM OF THE SANDS, Vol. II

The higher your consciousness, the greater your vision; the lower your consciousness, the smaller your vision. Go and stand on the street under a tree and look: you have a vision—you can see to the nearest corner of this road, then there is a turning and the vision stops. Climb the tree and have a look from the tree—then you have a greater vision. Move in an airplane—then you have a bird's-eye view of the whole city. Go higher and greater becomes the vision; go lower, smaller is the vision. There are rungs in the ladder of consciousness. If you are at the peak of your consciousness, look from there: eternity is revealed.

THE MUSTARD SEED

VOICE, INNER There are many people here who go on listening to inner voices. These inner voices are just crap. These are just fragments of your mind; they have no value at all. And sometimes you may think that you are listening to some inner guide or you are listening to some master from the beyond—Master K.H., or some spirit, some Tibetan spirit—and you can go on imagining these things. And you will be simply befooling yourself.

These are all your fragments. And if you go on following them you will go crazy—because one part will pull you to the north, another part to the south. You will start falling apart. Remember, this is neurosis—you have to learn to watch all these voices. Don't trust any. Only trust silence. Don't trust any voice, because all voices are from the mind. And you don't have one mind, you have many. That fallacy persists—we think we have only one mind. That is wrong.

You have many minds. In the morning, one mind is on top. By noon, another mind is on top. By the evening, a third mind—and you have many. Gurdjieff used to say that you have many selves, Mahavira has said that man is polypsychic. You are a crowd! If you go on listening to these voices and following them you will be simply destroying your whole life.

THE REVOLUTION

Find out the witness. Only then will you find out the inner voice.

The inner voice will direct you. Its directions will be absolutely different from what society says—absolutely different. But for the first time you will become religious, not simply moral. You will be moral in a much deeper sense. Morality will not be a duty, it will not be something imposed upon you. It will not be a burden; it will be spontaneous. You will be good, naturally good. You will not become a thief—not because society says, "Don't be a thief," but because you cannot be. You will not kill because it is impossible. You love life so much now that violence becomes impossible. It is not a moral code; it is an inner direction.

You affirm life, you revere life. A deep reverence comes to you, and through that reverence everything follows. That is what Jesus says, "Find out the kingdom of God first, and then everything will follow." Find out the inner voice, and then everything will follow.

THE NEW ALCHEMY: TO TURN YOU ON

Emptiness has its own voice. Literally, it is not a voice; it is an urge. It is not a sound, it is silence. Nobody says something to do; you simply feel like doing. Listening to the inner voice means leaving everything to the inner emptiness. Then it guides you. You always move right if you move empty. If you have the inner emptiness nothing will be wrong, nothing can go wrong. In emptiness nothing ever goes wrong—that is the very criterion of being right, always right. Yes, emptiness has its own voice, silence has its own music, no-movement has its own dance; but you will have to reach to it.

I'm not saying listen to the mind. In fact mind is not yours. When I say, "Listen to your voice," I mean drop all that society has given to you—your mind is given by the society. Your mind is not yours. It is a society, a conditioning; it is social. Emptiness is yours; mind is not yours. Mind is Hindu, Mohammedan, Christian; mind is communist, anti-commnunist, capitalist. Emptiness is none, nobody; it is *sunya*. In that *sunya*, nothingness, is the virginity of your being. Listen to it.

When I say listen to it, I don't mean there is somebody speaking to you. When I say listen to it I mean be available to it, give your ears and your being to it; and it will guide you. And it never misguides anybody. Out of nothingness whatsoever comes is beautiful, is true, is good, is a benediction.

YOGA: THE ALPHA AND THE OMEGA, Vol. V

VOID

If one can realize the Tao unmistakably,
his mind will be like the great space . . .

Like sky, unbounded, open on all the sides, infinite. It will be vast, immeasurable. It will be void—it will be absolutely empty of all content. It will be just a mirror reflecting nothing, just a silent lake, absolutely silent and absolutely clear. In that clarity is Buddhahood, in that clarity is awakening. That clarity is awakening . . .

There is nothing left. There is no question of this and that, so one cannot have any doubt. It is unmistakably so. There is only void, vast clarity and infinite sky. And all is silent: all duality gone, the knower gone, the known gone, the seer gone, the observer gone, the observed gone, the objective, the subjective . . . all are gone. There is only a pure clarity, a silent witnessing.

ZEN: THE SPECIAL TRANSMISSION

VOW Life is never changed by vows, life is changed by awareness. Never take a vow; the vow simply means that you are forcing something upon yourself. Try to understand. When there is understanding there is no need to take a vow; your understanding is enough. You see something is wrong and it drops.

Seeing is enough, understanding is enough; no other discipline is needed. Whenever you need some other discipline it means your understanding is lacking, something is missing in your understanding.

I AM THAT

VULNERABILITY And bliss is a rain shower. When it really happens it is almost like rain showering. When it happens one is soaked with it, bathed in it. And all that is needed for it to happen is just vulnerability; nothing else is required. One should not protect against it, that's all.

There is no need to seek God. If we don't protect ourselves against him, he is ready to seek us any moment. The problem is not how to seek God—the problem is how not to protect ourselves against him.

In trust one starts becoming vulnerable. In trust one becomes insecure and does not cling to securities.

It is better to die with God than to live alone.

It is better to be lost with the unknown than to remain

with the known. Because the known has nothing in it—it is already known. That which is known is already finished. It is going to be just a repetition, a boring circle. With the unknown is life—the known is dead—but with the unknown is insecurity. With the unknown comes trembling because one is not aware of where one is going and what is going to happen . . . because things become unpredictable, and one is no more capable of controlling and manipulating. Hence we protect and always keep to the safer side. That's how we go on missing.

God is dangerous, and people who keep themselves to the safer side always miss. Only daredevils reach that which is called God.

So become more vulnerable, Mm? Drop more and more armors from around you. There is nothing to fear, because all that is, is going to disappear. The body will be gone . . . the mind will be gone. The money will be gone, the life will be gone. All is going to go, so what is the point of becoming afraid? It is okay; if it is going to go, it is going to go. One relaxes . . . one is not disturbed. And one does not make any arrangements to protect.

In that unprotected state of mind, God penetrates. In that helpless state, God becomes your help. When you are losing all ground, he becomes your very ground.

Blessed are those who are helpless. Blessed are those who don't have ground to stand on, because for them only God can become the ground. Cursed are those who have safety, protection, security, insurance, because they will not know what God is, and without knowing God, life remains unknown.

THE BUDDHA DISEASE

WAITING Waiting has to be pure. Enjoy waiting for itself, for its own sake. Don't you see the beauty of just waiting— the purity of it, the benediction of it, the innocence of it—

just waiting, not even capable of answering for what? See the point of it: pure waiting, not knowing what is going to happen. If you know what is going to happen that will be supplied by your past, it will be a continuity with the past; it will not be new. Maybe modified, but it will be again the same thing, it will be a repetition. How can you know what is going to happen? You have not known it before so how can you even imagine it?

Finding that there is no way to imagine the future, no way to imagine the unknown, the known ceases, all ideas in the mind disappear—ideas about God, ideas about *samadhi,* enlightenment. All disappears; in that disappearance is enlightenment. Never think for a single moment that your idea of enlightenment is going to be fulfilled. How can you have any idea of enlightenment? And whatsoever idea you have is going to be wrong.

When enlightenment happens you will be surprised. You had read all the scriptures, and it wasn't mentioned anywhere. It can't be mentioned. You will be surprised. You have been hearing me year in, year out, and I had never mentioned it. I am trying, but it can't be done in the very nature of the case. I am trying to do it in a thousand and one ways, but they are only indications . . . But when you arrive at the reality of it, when it explodes in you, then you will know that no Buddha has ever been able to say it. And then you will know that nobody is ever going to say it. It has remained unuttered.

And it is good that it has remained unuttered; otherwise it would never be a new phenomenon to anybody. Millions of Buddhas have happened and they have talked about it and talked about it; you already know about it—and then it happens. It may be just something known, then it will not be a breakthrough, it will not be a discontinuity, it can't be utterly new and radical.

It *is* utterly new and utterly radical.

So waiting has to be with no idea for what. A real waiter can not answer the question for what he is waiting; he can only shrug his shoulders, he can say "I don't know." But one thing is certain: that waiting is infinitely beautiful, waiting is infinitely joyous. When the whole turmoil disappears and it is all silence, it has beauty of its own . . .

Waiting allows the whole to take possession. You disappear, the whole appears. Waiting is vacating for the truth to be. It is void, voidness—empty of all that we have known, experienced, believed—and then from nowhere, or everywhere, comes the feeling of being lifted up. Gratitude arises naturally and spontaneously as when we receive a loving gift. Thinking stops, thanking begins. This is prayer. It has nothing to do with your silly ideas of God, and prayer, and all that. This is prayer: when you are waiting, waiting, waiting, empty. And there is nothing to do, there is no way to do; you cannot get occupied. When you are just silent, utterly silent—a kind of absence—one is lifted up; the whole takes you. In that lifting up arise gratitude and prayer . . .

Waiting is simply waiting; not waiting for somebody, not waiting for something to happen. How can you wait for something you don't know? And all that you will think should happen will be wrong, because it will come out of your past, and your past has been nothing but darkness, your past has been nothing but ignorance. Negative thinking cannot do anything—not even thinking about what is going to happen.

This state, this silence, this utter purity, is the death and the resurrection.

Waiting has no object, and that's what meditation is. Let me define meditation: meditation is waiting without prospect, waiting for waiting's sake. And truth is always there, pulsating at the core of being. Waiting allows it to bloom. Waiting helps you to melt. Waiting helps the innermost to express itself. Waiting releases the song that you are, the celebration that you are.

THE SUN RISES IN THE EVENING

WAKE It is only a question of remembering that you *can* wake up. Nothing else is needed, no other effort, no method, no technique, no path. Just a remembrance that "This is my dream." A remembrance that "I have decided to dream it—and the moment I decide not to dream it, I will be awake." Once your cooperation is withdrawn, the dream is nullified.

If you are living in misery, you are creating it. And nobody else can take it away from you unless *you* decide not to create it any more. Your hell is your work. All that you

are is your self-creation. In a single moment, you can awake.
                                        TAKE IT EASY, Vol. II

WANDERER   When you travel, you travel with a goal in
the mind. When you travel, you are not interested in traveling itself; your whole focus is on the goal and you miss all
that is along the way.

A wanderer is one who is not going anywhere in particular . . . who is simply enjoying the wandering. North is good,
south is also good. If he reaches east, good; if he reaches
west, good. Wherever he reaches he will enjoy. The whole
earth is his; the whole existence is his. He is not going
anywhere. He has no mind to go anywhere, so wherever
he is, he is totally there.

When you have a mind to go somewhere you cannot be
totally in places where you don't want to be. You have
already moved in the mind, in your imagination. Physically
you may exist here but in the mind you have already reached
where your goal is. The mind always hovers around the goal.
When there is no goal the mind has no place to abide in.

So in the east the wanderer has been one of the most
important devices of sannyas. Buddhists call the wanderer
parivraqika —one who goes from one place to another. Not
that he has to go anywhere; he just enjoys being anywhere,
all over the place. He never stays in one place long. He never
burdens any place long. He does not make a house
anywhere. The tent is his house, so he can fix it anywhere
and it becomes his house. He can unfix it any moment and
it is on his shoulders. He is a vagabond.

This wandering by and by relaxes one totally in the
moment. Then you can enjoy all along, whatsoever is
there—the moon, the trees, the birds, the people, strangers,
unknown places.

                DON'T JUST DO SOMETHING, SIT THERE

WAR   Man has lived under the calamity of war too long.
We have to destroy all gods of war; instead we have to create
a temple of love. We *should* kill all gods of war, because
only through their death—the god of war dead, all gods of
war dead—will the god of love be born.

War exists, not because there are warring groups outside

in the world; fundamentally war exists because man is in conflict. The root of war is within; on the outside you only see the branches and the foliage of it. After each ten years, humanity needs a great world war. In ten years' time, man accumulates so much rage, madness, insanity inside him that it has to erupt.

Unless we transform the very script of man, unless we give him a totally new program of living and being, we can go on talking about peace but we will go on preparing for war. That's what we have been doing for thousands of years: talking about peace and creating war. The absurdity is that even in the name of peace we have been fighting; the greatest wars have been fought in the name of peace. This has been a sheerly destructive past. With the same energy, man could have created paradise on earth; and all that we have done is to create a hell instead. But it is not a question of changing the political ideologies of the world, it is not a question of teaching people to be brotherly, because these things have been done and they have all failed.

Something more basic is wrong. Man is split, and the same people who talk about peace are the cause of the split. They have divided man into good and bad, the lower and the higher, the earthly and the divine, the material and the spiritual. They have created a rift inside the human soul, and there is a constant war inside. Everybody is fighting with themselves, and when it becomes too much they start fighting with somebody else.

That's why in times of war, people look happier. Their faces shine with enthusiasm, their step has a dance to it. They are thrilled because at least for a few days they will not need to fight with themselves; they have found a scapegoat outside. It may be the fascist, it may be the communist, it may be the Mohammedan, it may be the Christian—it doesn't matter, but somebody is there outside. It is an escape from the inner fight; in a very sick way it is relaxing. But one cannot go on warring continuously; sooner or later man has to turn inwards again. The politician creates war without, and the priest creates war within. This is the longest and the greatest conspiracy against humanity.

My vision of a sannyasin is that of an integrated soul. The

body is respected, not denied; it is loved, praised, one feels grateful for it. Matter is not condemned, it is enjoyed; it is part of our spiritual growth. There is no duality: it is a dialectics of growth. This is how we move on two feet, the bird flies on two wings. Matter and spirit, body and soul, lower and higher, are two wings.

What I am trying to bring here is something utterly new, something that has never existed before on the earth: a man who is at ease with both the worlds, this and that; a man who is as worldly as one can be and as other-worldly as one can be; a man who is a great synthesis; a man who is not schizophrenic, a man who is whole and holy. That's what my sannyas is all about.

WON'T YOU JOIN THE DANCE?

War is the greatest thing that man has remained involved with. Destruction seems to be very very attractive; killing and murder seems to be the goal of the human mind. In three thousand years, man has fought five thousand wars. Vietnam is nothing new, it is as ancient as man. It is not something that is happening today, it has been always there—because man is ill.

And you ask me, *How much inner peace is appropriate . . . ?* As much as you can manage—the more you have, the better. Because only pools of peace will destroy the compulsive attraction towards violence. Only pools of peace all over the world, many many Buddhas, will be able to create a new vibe, a new wave, a new consciousness, in which war becomes impossible—in which all energy moves in a creative way, all energy moves towards love.

So don't say . . . I understand the logic of it. The logic is, if man becomes very peaceful then he will not bother about Vietnam. I understand what you mean by your question. You mean, if people become very silent and very peaceful they won't care what is happening in the world around them, they will become indifferent. So how much peace is appropriate?—that's why you ask the question.

But try to understand. The war is not the disease itself. Peace is missing in the heart—hence the war exists. The war is a consequence: more peace, less war. If peace becomes predominant, war will disappear.

War cannot disappear by the efforts of people who call themselves pacifists. War cannot disappear because of Bertrand Russell. War cannot disappear because there are people who are against war—no. The people who are against war will create another war. You can see, if you have observed a pacifist protest, you can see how war-like they are—shouting, screaming, protesting . . . You can see in their faces they are dangerous people. They may call themselves pacifists, but they don't know what peace means. They are very argumentative, arrogant, ready to fight.

It almost always happens that a peace protest becomes a battlefield between the police and the pacifists. The pacifist is not really the man of peace. He is against war. He is so much against war that he will be ready to go to war if that is needed. The cause changes, the war continues.

A man of peace is not a pacifist, a man of peace is simply a pool of silence. He pulsates a new kind of energy into the world, he sings a new song. He lives in a totally new way—his very way of life is that of grace, that of prayer, that of compassion. Whomsoever he touches, he creates more love-energy.

The man of peace is creative. He is not against war, because to be against anything is to be at war. He is not against war, he simply understands why war exists. And out of that understanding he becomes peaceful.

Only when there are many people who are pools of peace, silence, understanding, will the war disappear.

ZEN: THE PATH OF PARADOX, Vol. II

WARMTH   There is no other prayer. If one can be lovingly warm the prayer has happened. To live a cold life is to live without prayer, and many people, millions of people, are living cold lives, frozen, ice cold. That's why there are so many lonely people in the world. They themselves are lonely and they create loneliness for others. And they could easily have been warm, because to remain warm is very natural to life. Life is warmth: death is cold. They have died before dying, they have not lived.

Warmth is the language of life. The more you allow warmth to flow from you towards others, the richer the life you have. And love is the secret of remaining warm, so love as deeply as possible and love as many people as possible. And not only people—love existence as such. It is really very strange to see people passing through the trees without any warmth for them, looking at the stars with dead, cold, ice-cold eyes, talking to people with no warmth in their words and no warmth in their hearts, holding hands, but dead and dull. There is no wonder why they are in such suffering. And it is *their* decision.

The decision has a reason in it: there is a fear in being loving—you may get involved, you may get caught, you may become committed. And people are afraid of getting involved, people are afraid of getting committed, so they are escaping from all commitments. But to live a life of no commitment is escapist. Then your life will never have any splendor to it; it needs the challenge of commitment, involvement. One needs to be involved in as many things as possible: in art, in poetry, in music, in people, in dance, in as many things as possible. The more you are involved, the more you *are,* the more being you have.

HALLELUJAH!

WATCHING The real silence happens when you start watching the noise of your mind.

There is a constant traffic in the mind—thoughts, memories, imagination, thousands of desires. It is always a crowd moving in all directions. If you can stand by the side of the road and just watch, without any evaluation, judgment, without condemning something or appreciating something— just sitting on the bank of the river, watching the flow of the river, unconcerned, detached, just being a pure witness, then the miracle happens.

THE SOUND OF ONE HAND CLAPPING

Be aware of the body and its action. Walking, walk with alertness; don't walk like a robot, like a machine. When thinking, watch what thoughts are moving. Just go on seeing what desires are spinning and weaving their nets around you. Just go on watching. Go on watching how subtle dreams are moving like an undercurrent deep down in your unconscious. Watch your feelings, moods, how they suddenly arise as if from nowhere; just a moment before you were so full of joy and now you are so sad. Just watch how it happens, see the bridge . . . how joy becomes sadness, how sadness becomes joy.

I am not saying to do anything. Meditation is not a doing at all, it is pure awareness. But a miracle happens, the greatest miracle in life. If you go on watching, tremendous and incredible things start happening. Your body becomes graceful, your body is no more restless, tense; your body starts becoming light, unburdened; you can see great weights, mountainous weights falling from your body. Your body starts becoming pure of all kinds of toxins and poisons. You will see your mind is no more as active as before; its activity starts becoming less and less and gaps arise, gaps in which there are no thoughts. Those gaps are the most beautiful experiences because through those gaps you start seeing things as they are without an interference of the mind.

Slowly slowly your moods start disappearing. You are no more very joyous and no more very sad. The difference between joy and sadness starts becoming less. Soon a moment of equilibrium is reached when you are neither sad nor joyous. And that is the moment when bliss is felt. That tranquility, that silence, that balance, is bliss.

There are no more peaks and no more valleys, no more dark nights and no more moon nights, all those polarities disappear. You start becoming settled exactly in the middle. And all these miracles go on becoming deeper and deeper, and ultimately when your body is in total balance, your mind is absolutely silent and your heart is no more full of desires, a quantum leap happens in you: suddenly you become aware of the fourth—of which you have never been aware before. And that is you, the fourth. You can call it the soul, the self, God or whatsoever you want to call it, that is up to you; any name will do because it has no name of its own.

Lao Tzu says, "Because it has no name I have chosen to call it Tao." You can choose anything—xyz, but to attain it is the ultimate goal of life. And in that moment all is light—your inner eye has opened. It is only through that inner eye and that light that one becomes aware of the truth of existence, and that truth liberates.

THE MIRACLE!

WATER In all the primitive tribes water symbolizes life. Life is based on water: the human body is eighty-five percent water. And life depends—the life of animals and the trees and man and birds—all life depends on water. So water was one of the basic elements to be worshipped. Just as the sun was worshipped by all primitive people, water was also worshipped; both were respected as gods. And it is significant as a metaphor also.

Water represents a few things. One: it has no form, yet it can take any form, it is capable of adjusting into any form. You pour it into a pot, it takes the form of the pot; you pour it into a glass, it takes the form of the glass. It is infinitely adjustable. That's its beauty: it knows no rigidity. And man should be so unrigid, unfrozen, like water, not like ice.

Water is always moving towards the sea. Wherever it is, its movement is always towards the sea, towards the infinite. Man should be like water, always moving towards God. Water remains pure if it moves and flows; it becomes impure, stagnant, if it becomes dormant. So should be man and his consciousness always flowing, moving, never becoming stuck anywhere.

It is by getting stuck that man becomes dirty, impure. If the flow remains and one is ready to move from one moment to another moment without any hang-ups, without carrying the load of the past, one remains innocent, pure.

THE RAINBOW BRIDGE

WAVES See Ocean, 2nd Series

WAY There is no way leading to it; all ways are misleading. A way as such is going to mislead, because a way means you are going farther away from yourself—a way always takes you away. There is no way to come to yourself—you are already there! There is no need to come. Simply stop these fantasies of going somewhere, of becoming spiritual, of becoming religious, of attaining enlightenment, *nirvana,* *samadhi*—simply stop all this nonsense. Just rest within your being, at home, at ease, relaxed . . . and *this* very moment, now and here, you are enlightened!

PHILOSOPHIA ULTIMA

WEAKNESS   Relax—that's my whole teaching. Relax into your being, whoever you are. Don't impose any ideals. Don't drive yourself crazy; there is no need. Be!—drop becoming. We are not going anywhere, we are just being here. And this moment is so beautiful, is such a benediction. Don't bring any future into it, otherwise you will destroy it. Future is poisonous. Relax and enjoy. If I can help you to relax and enjoy, my work is done. If I can help you to drop your ideals, ideas about how you should be and how you should not be, if I can take away all the commandments that have been given to you, then my work is done. And when you are without any commandments, and when you live on the spur of the moment—natural, spontaneous, simple, ordinary— there is great celebration, you have arrived home.

Now don't bring it again . . . *"Must I be strong and coura- geous?"*

For what?

In fact it is weakness that wants to be strong. Try to under- stand it; it is a little bit complex but let us go into it. It is weakness that wants to be strong, it is inferiority that wants to be superior, it is ignorance that wants to be knowledgeable—so that it can hide in knowledge, so that you can hide in your so-called power, your weakness. Out of inferiority comes the desire to be superior. That is the whole substratum of the politics in the world, power-politics. It is only inferior people who become politicians: a power urge, because they know they are inferior. If they don't become the president of a country or the prime minister of a country, they cannot prove themselves to others. In themselves they feel weak; they drive themselves to power.

But how, by becoming a president, can you be powerful? Deep down you will know that your weakness is there. In fact, it will be felt more, even more than before, because now there will be a contrast. On the outside there will be power, and in the inside there will be weakness—more clear, like a silver lining in a black cloud. That's what happens: inside you feel poor and you start grabbing, you become greedy, you start possessing things, and you go on and on and on, and there is no end to it. And your whole life is wasted in things, in accumulation.

But the more you accumulate, the more penetratingly you feel the inner poverty. Against the riches, it can be seen very easily. When you see this—that weakness tries to become strong—it is absurd. How can weakness become strong? Seeing it, you don't want to become strong. And when you don't want to become strong, the weakness cannot stay in you. It can stay only with the idea of strength—they are together, like negative-positive poles of electricity. They exist together. If you drop this ambition to be strong, one day suddenly you will find weakness has also disappeared. It cannot keep hold in you. If you drop the idea of being rich, how can you go on thinking yourself poor? How will you compare, and how will you judge that you are poor? Against what? There will be no possibility to measure your poverty.

Dropping the idea of richness, of being rich, one day poverty disappears.

When you don't hanker for knowledge and you drop knowledgeability, how can you remain ignorant? When knowledge disappears, in the wake of it, like its shadow, ignorance disappears. Then a man is wise. Wisdom is not knowledge. Wisdom is the absence of both knowledge and ignorance.

There are three possibilities: you can be ignorant, you can be ignorant and knowledgeable, and you can be without ignorance and knowledge. The third possibility is what wisdom is. That's what Buddha call *prajnaparamita* —the wisdom beyond, the transcendental wisdom. It is not knowledge.

First, drop this desire for strength, and watch. One day you will be surprised, you will start dancing, the weakness has disappeared. They are two aspects of the same coin, they live together, they go together. Once you have penetrated to this fact in your being, there is a great transformation.

THE HEART SUTRA

WEST   See East/West, 1st Series

WHEEL   See Chakras, 1st Series
                Dhamma, Wheel of, 1st Series
                Relativity

WHIRLING   Rumi does not mean anything, it is a name of a place; because he came from Rum he was called Rumi. His message is love, and he belongs to the highest categories of the Buddhas. He was the man who invented a new method of meditation, whirling.

There have been hundreds of devices; Rumi has also contributed one special device. He became enlightened not by sitting silently like a Buddha, he became enlightened by dancing. And his dance is a special kind of dance. You turn round and round, as if you are just a wheel moving faster and faster; you are both the axle and the wheel. Small children enjoy it very much. Almost all over the world parents have to stop their children from doing it because they are afraid they may get dizzy, but they don't know that the children are enjoying something very special.

When a small child goes on whirling he loses the sense of being a body, he starts hovering above his body, he can see his own body turning—and that is the miracle of the method. But we are stopped by our parents very early.

Jalaluddin introduced that method. He himself became enlightened by thirty-six hours of continuous whirling; day in, day out he went on and on. He was riding on a cloud, he could not stop till he fell down. But when he opened his eyes and got up he was a totally new man, the old was gone. People had gathered to watch him, thousands of people—he was a well-known mystic. What had happened to him? Had he gone crazy or something? And he had told his disciples that he should not be disturbed.

For thirty-six hours he danced and danced. The dancer disappeared in the dance, there was only dance and no dancer—the ego died. And he could see his own body from the higher plane dancing somewhere on the earth. He became a watcher on the hill, the body was in the deep dark valley. And that's how he introduced the method to his disciples.

His message was love and dance. Love the whole existence

so you can dance, and dance to abandon so that you can love.

I'M NOT AS THUNK AS YOU DRINK I AM

WHOLE Man exists as an ego, that's why he feels continuously afraid, unprotected, insecure. The moment you drop your ego the whole existence becomes your protection, your security.

You cannot be more wise than the whole. The part cannot be bigger than the whole. Whatsoever we can think is bound to be small, tiny; it comes out of a tiny mind. Its vision is small, its capacity to see is limited. But we depend on this small capacity, we depend on our blindness, and then we suffer. The mind is very short-sighted. It is because of the egoistic approach that people live in misery, anxiety, anguish, suffering; they create their own hell.

Sannyas means a radical change, dropping the ego and relaxing with the whole—because the whole is wiser than the part—trusting the whole. The whole is our source, we have come from it, we are in it even at this moment. Just as the fish is in the ocean, we are in God. We are born in God, we live in God and we will disappear in God; hence the whole effort to fight with the universe is idiotic.

The sannyasin relaxes, he becomes a let-go. He allows the whole to possess him, to direct him, to guide him. He surrenders himself totally so the whole can possess him without any hindrance from his side, without any resistance from his side—and then he is protected.

God is a wise protector. It is up to us to live in insecurity or to live in the ultimate security. To be in the ego is to live in insecurity; to be egoless is to live in ultimate security. Then all is good because you don't have any expectations, you don't have any private goal. You are simply one with the whole so wherever it is going you are going; you need not worry. Then you become just like a small child who is holding the hand of his father.

The father may be worried, the father may have got lost in the forest, but the child is not worried. He knows his father is with him, his hand is in his father's hand—that's enough. The child is enjoying while the father is worrying;

the child is enjoying the butterflies and the birds and the flowers. He can enjoy them because of his trust. He has no worry, no anxiety.

To relax with the whole is the beginning of a joyous life. It is the beginning of an authentic ceremony. Then each moment is so full of juice and ecstasy that one can become drunk. And the person who relaxes with the whole becomes drunk with the divine. His joy knows no limits, his bliss is infinite.

GOING ALL THE WAY

WHOLENESS Love is the feminine part in you and awareness is the masculine part in you. And they both have to meet and merge into each other. If one only knows how to love and is not aware, one remains half. If one knows how to be aware and does not know how to love, again one remains half. And to be half is to be in misery. Hence the so-called worldly man is in misery and the man who lives in the monastery is in misery. They have chosen different kinds of miseries—that is true—but misery is misery. From what end you progress towards it makes no difference.

There is only one bliss in the world, and that bliss comes by becoming whole. And this is the most fundamental thing in becoming whole: your man and your woman inside must fall in love and disappear into each other. Then one is integrated, one is one. Otherwise one is many, otherwise one is poly-psychic, and to be poly-psychic is to be neurotic. To be poly-psychic means that one has many minds, one is a crowd—a thousand and one voices, and each dragging one in its own direction. One's life remains just a constant struggle . . . for no purpose. One rushes into one direction and then into another and then into another. This goes on and on and then one falls into the grave. From the cradle to the grave one rushes, runs too much, but reaches nowhere.

To become one is to arrive. And it is easier to choose one of the two; that's why people have chosen one. The worldly people have chosen love, the other-worldly people have chosen awareness. It is easy to choose one—it seems simple, less complicated, but then your being remains poor too.

Richness is always complex. One need not be afraid of complexity; one should be afraid only of a crowd. Complexity is perfectly good if it is centered in oneness, if it is a harmony.

If you listen to people's hearts they are like single notes—repeating the same. Very rarely do you find a man who is an orchestra.

HALLELUJAH!

I teach the individual, I teach the unique individual. Respect yourself, love yourself, because there has never been a person like you and there will never be again. God never repeats. You are utterly unique, incomparably unique. You need not be like somebody else, you need not be an imitator, you have to be authentically yourself, your own being. You have to do your own thing.

The moment you start accepting and respecting yourself you start becoming whole. Then there is nothing to divide you, then there is nothing to create the split . . .

I teach you a new man, a new humanity, which will not think of the future and which will not live with shoulds and oughts, and which will not deny any natural instinct—which will accept its body, which will accept all that is given by God with deep gratitude.

Your body is your temple, it is sacred. Your body is not your enemy. It is not irreligious to love your body, to take care of your body—it is religious. It is irreligious to torture your body and destroy it. The religious person will love his body because it is the temple where God lives.

You and your body are not really two, but manifestations of one. Your soul is your invisible body, and your body is your visible soul. I teach this unity. And with this, man becomes whole. And I teach you joy, not sadness. I teach you playfulness, not seriousness. I teach you love and laughter, because to me there is nothing more sacred than love and laughter, and there is nothing more prayerful than playfulness.

I don't teach you renunciation, as it has been taught down the ages. I teach you to rejoice, rejoice and rejoice again! Rejoicing should be the essential core of my sannyasins.

Yes, my approach to life is holistic, because to me to be whole is to be holy.

THE BOOK OF WISDOM, Vol. II

WHY? There is a beautiful story by Turgenev:

In a village there was a poor man who was thought to be an idiot. The whole village laughed at him. Even as he said something very serious they would laugh, they would find something idiotic in it. It was a determined thing that the idiot could not say anything meaningful.

The idiot was getting tired of it.

A mystic was passing by. The idiot went to the mystic, fell at his feet and said, "Save me, the whole village thinks I am an idiot! How should I get rid of this idea that surrounds me? And everybody goes on and on hammering the same idea on me."

The mystic said, "It is very simple. You do one thing: for seven days don't make any statement on your own part, so nobody will say, 'This is idiotic'. Instead, you start asking others 'Why?'—whatsoever they say. Somebody said, 'Look, the rose flower is so beautiful.' Ask 'Why? Prove it. How can you prove that this rose flower is beautiful? What grounds have you got?' And that will make him feel foolish, because nobody can prove it. Somebody said, 'Tonight is beautiful, the full moon . . . ' Immediately ask, don't miss any opportunity, 'Why? What grounds have you got?' For seven days don't make any statement so nobody can ask *you* why . . . "

For seven days the idiot did the same thing. The whole village was very much puzzled—he made everybody feel idiotic. Naturally, they all started thinking he had become wise. After seven days he came to the mystic, immensely happy. He said, "It was a great trick. I was not thinking that much was going to happen out of it, but now the whole village worships me."

THE WILD GEESE AND THE WATER

Philosophers are the most miserable men. They go on asking, "Why this? Why that?" Their constant "Why?" is an inner disease. Look at it in this way: only when something goes wrong do you ask why. When everything is okay, you never ask why. You ask why there is misery; you never ask why there is bliss. You ask why there is death; you never ask why there is love. When there is love, there is no question about it. You accept it totally. When there is hate, the question arises. When you are in bliss, no questioning, no inquiry, no philosophy arises out of it. When you are in anguish, suffering, you ask, "Why this suffering? Why I am suffering? Why is the whole world suffering?" Only when something goes wrong does the question arise. When everything is okay, there is no questioning. You accept existence in its totality.

So remember this: if you have a "Why?" you need meditation, because without meditation the "Why?" will not disappear.

And the answer comes only to those who have stopped questioning. The answer can only be understood by those who are not in the mood to question. A questioning mind is not in the mood to hear. It goes on questioning. Questions are created in the mind just like leaves grow on a tree. If your mind is ill, questions will come out of it. Only if your mind has disappeared, and inner wholeness and health has been gained, will questions stop.

And when there is no question, you have got the ultimate answer. That ultimate answer is not in words. It is existential. You live it; you become it.

THE NEW ALCHEMY: TO TURN YOU ON

"Why?" is a wrong question to ask. Things simply are. There is no why to them. The question why, once accepted, will lead you farther and farther into philosophy, and philosophy is a wasteland. You will not find any oasis there, it is desert. Ask the question "Why?" and you have started moving in a wrong direction; you will never come home.

Existence is, there is no why to it. That's what we mean when we say it is a mystery, because there is no why to it. In fact it should not be there and it is. There seems to be no need for it to be there, no reason for it to be there, and it is there. "Why?" is a mind question.

And now you can be in a very great puzzle, because the

mind is asking a question about itself: "Why is the mind?" The question comes from the mind, and the mind is capable of turning each answer into a new question. You will be moving in a vicious circle. To ask the question "why?" is to fall into the trap of the mind. You will have to see to it. The question "why?" has to be dropped; that's the meaning of trust.

THE WISDOM OF THE SANDS, Vol. II

Bhagwan, why am I here?

This is a very philosophical question.

There is a story about two big beefy American football players in philosophy class, sitting their final examination. The exam question was just one word: "Why?"

All the students began writing madly, filling exam book after book. The football players looked at each other and shrugged. The first wrote two words on his exam paper: "Why not?" and left the room. The second fellow wrote one word: "Because", and left with his friend.

Not knowing what to do, the professor gave the first fellow the grade of A, and the second fellow the grade of A minus.

This is really a philosophical question: *Why am I here?* I don't know. Why not? Or—because.

THE BOOK OF WISDOM, Vol. II

WIFE *Bhagwan, what are the essential things to keep one's wife happy?*

I don't know much about wives. I am an unmarried man; you are asking a wrong person this question. But I have been observing many wives and many husbands. So this is not my *experience* —just my opinion!

There are two things necessary to keep one's wife happy. First: let her think she is having her own way. And second: let her have it.

THE BOOK OF BOOKS, Vol. X

Bhagwan, I am bored with my husband. I have tried everything, but nothing seems to work. Have you any suggestions?

Not many, just one. Write a letter to five of your friends like this:

Hello there!

This letter was started by a woman like yourself, in hopes of bringing relief to a tired and discontented wife.

Unlike most chain letters, this one does not cost anything, just send a copy of this letter to five of your friends who are equally tired. Then bundle up your husband and send him to the woman at the top of the list and add your name to the bottom of the list.

When your name comes to the top of the list you will receive 16,478 men and some of them are bound to be a hell of a lot better than the one you already have.

Do not break the chain . . . have faith!

One woman broke the chain and got her own son-of-a-bitch back.

At the date of writing this letter, another friend of mine received 183 men. They buried her yesterday . . . but it took three undertakers thirty-six hours to get the smile off her face.

THE BOOK OF THE BOOKS, Vol. IX

WILDNESS First: what is wrong in being wild? I don't see anything wrong in being wild. To be too much civilized may be dangerous—a little wildness is good. And in a better world, with more understanding about human nature, we will keep a balance between civilization and wildness.

We have become very lopsided: we have become just civilized. When you become too much civilized you become plastic. The wild rose flower has a beauty—may not be so permanent as the plastic flower, by the evening it may be gone, gone forever, it blooms only for the moment, but still it is alive. Look at the wild animals—they have something—don't you feel jealous? Don't you feel a radiance, an aliveness, God, more solidly present in them than in you?

So first, I don't see anything wrong in being wild. If your wildness is not destructive to anybody, it is perfectly religious. If your wildness is just your expression of your freedom and it is not an interference with anybody else's freedom, if it is not a trespass on anybody else's life, liberty, it is perfectly good.

In a *right* world people should be allowed all kinds of wildness, with only one condition: that their wildness should not be violent to anybody else. They should be given total freedom. Civilization only has to be negative, it should not be positive. The function of the police and the state has to be negative, it should not be positive. It should not tell you what you should do, it should only tell you what you should not do, that's all. Because we live in a society you cannot be absolutely wild, there are other people. You have to be careful about them too. They are careful about you, they are making compromises for your happiness, you have to make a few compromises for their happiness. But that's all.

The society, the state, the law, should be negative. They should only pinpoint a few things: that which interferes with other people's lives and happiness should not be done. And everything else should be left open.

Second thing: Eros is the root of all that is beautiful in the world. The flowers bloom because of eros, and the cuckoos cry because of eros, and the birds dance and sing because of eros. And all that is great and all that is beautiful is because of eros—even *samadhi* is the ultimate flowering of the energy called eros. God is very erotic. You can see it all around, no proof is needed. The whole existence is erotic.

And the day man started thinking against eros, man started falling into a kind of abnormality. Since then man has not been normal. And because eros has been crushed, repressed, man has become more and more destructive—because creation comes out of eros. Children are born out of eros, so are paintings, so are songs, so is *samadhi!*

Once you are repressive towards eros, afraid of eros, once you don't worship the god of eros, then what are you going to do? All creativity is closed, you become destructive— then wars, violence, aggression, competition, money-mania, power-politics—they all arise. Man has suffered much because of this stupid attitude about eros. It has given all kinds of perversions.

Somebody is after money. Can't you see the perversion?— money has become the god. He does not love a woman, he loves money instead. Somebody loves his car, and somebody loves power, respectability. These are perversions of eros, and these are the really dangerous people. They should not be there. Genghis Khan and Tamerlaine and Alexander and Adolf Hitler and Stalin and Mao—these are the really dangerous people. These are the people who are destructive. Their joy is destruction. And whenever creative energy is not allowed to have its own say, it turns sour, it becomes bitter, it becomes poisonous.

Man has not suffered from eros, no, not at all. Man has suffered from anti-eros. When you are anti-eros, *thanatos* — death—becomes your god. Death is worshipped. Money is dead, so is politics, so is ego—all dead things become very, very important. And you worship these dead idols.

You ask me: *If man's erotic instincts were liberated, would they not run wild?*

Maybe, if they were immediately given total freedom, for the time being they may run wild. But that will be only transitory—and the reason is not in eros. The reason will be because for centuries it has been repressed. It is as if a person has been starved for many years. Then you suddenly give him all freedom—you give him the key to the kitchen. Yes, he is going to be wild for a little while, but what is wrong in it? For a few days he is going to eat too much, but only for a few days. He will become obsessively attached to food. He will drink, eat and dream and desire only food and food—only food will float in his mind. But the reason is not hunger: the reason is that you have been starving him.

Yes, that's right. And the priests and the popes and the *shankaracharyas,* they go on saying that eros cannot be given freedom, otherwise people will become just wild. But the reason is not in eros, the reason is in the popes. They are the sole cause. They have starved humanity for so long, they have crippled humanity for so long—and there is a reason why they have crippled the human eros.

If you want to make human beings slaves, the only way is to destroy their eros. A man whose eros is fully alive is a master. A man whose eros is fully flowering does not bother about anything. He will not be ready to go to any war, to any foolish Vietnam or Korea or anywhere. A man who is really in love with love and enjoying it will not bother about becoming the president or the prime minister of a country. The man who is really living his eros will not even go to the church or to temple, because he has found the real temple of God. Love is his prayer. Then where will these priests be, and the politicians, and the warmongers, and the people who depend on your obstacles? Your energies have to be destroyed, you have to be set in such a way that you start moving in wrong directions. And a person whose eros has been killed becomes very weak.

That's what you do. Have you not seen a bull and an ox? What is the difference? The erotic freedom of the bull has been destroyed, he becomes an ox. An ox is a poor specimen. A bull is something alive, something divine. In India we worship the bull as divine. He is the bodyguard of Shiva—the bull. Not an ox, remember. An ox would have been far better, more manageable—but the bull . . . Why? The bull is so erotic, such a perfect eros; and such beauty exists with the bull. And look at an ox pulling a bullock-cart—a slave. If you want people to be slaves, destroy their eros, pervert their erotic instinct. That's why it has been done up to now.

In the future, eros has to become the religion. Love should be the worship, and the only god that can really be God is eros—because eros is creativity, and we call God the creator.

What is happening to the modern man? What has happened in the past too?

You can only be happy when your eros is fulfilled . . .

And the last thing I would like to tell you: It is only through eros that eros is transcended, never otherwise. It is only through eros that one day you transcend it. Anything that has been lived *totally* is always transcended. Hang-ups simply mean that you have not lived something totally. So people who have not lived their eros, have been afraid, will remain confined to it. Their sex will become cerebral. It may disappear from their bodies but it will remain in their heads—which is not the right place for it!

People who have lived their sexual lives naturally, with no inhibition and no taboo, one day come to a point where it simply disappears—not through fight, but through understanding. A transcendence comes, and that is *brahmacharya*.

Brahmancharya is the ultimate fragrance of eros. It is *not* against eros; it is the ultimate fragrance of eros. It is the subtlest eros. One is so much in tune with one's erotic energy that the man does not need the woman and the woman does not need the man. One is so enough unto oneself, one has discovered one's own inner woman by and by. Looking into many other men's eyes, being with many men, going deep into their being, looking into their mirror, finding oneself, one has found one's inner man.

And remember, man is both woman and man; woman is both man and woman. We carry both inside. There comes a point where our inner woman and inner man meet. In Tantra we call it *yoga nadha*.

You must have seen a tremendously significant statue of Shiva, *ardharnarishwar*—half is man and half is woman. Shiva is depicted half as man and half as woman. That is the ultimate meeting, the real orgasm, the cosmic orgasm. When it has happened one becomes a *brahmacharin,* one attains to real celibacy. That is ultimate virginity: no need for the other; the need for the other has disappeared.

                   ZEN: THE PATH OF PARADOX, Vol. III

WILL   A man has to be a synthesis of will and surrender. A man has to grow his will power, his ego, first. My approach is: that if life is going to be for an average of seventy years, then thirty-five years, the beginning of life, should be devoted to strengthening the ego and will power. And one should listen to Nietzsche, and one should listen to Steiner, and one should listen to Freud—and the ego has to strengthened, made *very* integrated.

And after the thirty-fifth year one has to learn relaxing, dropping the ego, and becoming more and more surrendered to the divine. The West is the first part of life; the East is the second part of life. Life should start as western and should end as eastern. One should first go into the world; in the world, will will be needed. One should first go and fight and struggle, because struggle gives you sharpness, intelligence. But one should not continue fighting and fighting to the very end. Then what is the point?

First, sharpen your intelligence, know the ways of the world, wander all over the world, be a conqueror, and then . . . then move inwards. You have known the outside; now try to know the inner.

And to know the inner one has to relax. One has to forget anxiety, anguish, tension. One has to be non-competitive; will is not needed. To conquer the world will is needed; to conquer God will is not needed. To conquer God means to be conquered by God; to conquer God means to relax and surrender unto his feet.

Now this will seem very difficult, very illogical. I am an illogical person. My understanding is this: that only strong egos can surrender; weak egos cannot surrender.

Every day I come across weak egos. Whenever a weak ego comes, he hesitates: to surrender or not to surrender, to take sannyas or not to take sannyas. And why is he afraid? He is afraid because he knows he has a very weak ego; if he surrenders he is gone. He will not be able to stand. He is afraid of his inner weakness. He pretends on the outside, but he knows his inner reality—that he is ready. So he becomes defensive; he defends.

Whenever a person of strong ego comes he says, "Okay, let us see. Let us try this too." He knows, he is confident enough that even if he goes into some unknown path, he can still protect himself. And if he decides to come back, he can come back; he has enough trust, enough self-confidence. He has enough will.

Remember, surrender is the last and the greatest act of will. Surrender is not a cheap and easy thing. It is not something that because you cannot stand you surrender; because you were already falling you say, "Okay, I surrender"— because you were not able to stand on your feet.

Surrender is not impotence. Surrender is not out of impotence, it is out of trememdous power.

You have lived the ways of the will and you have found nothing. You have looked into all the possibilities of the ego and you have only suffered; it simply hurts. Then you decide, "Now let us try the ultimate: dropping of the ego."

To drop the ego you will need a great will—otherwise it is not easy to drop the ego. It is the greatest act in the world, the last. Only very courageous people can do it. You will be surprised: in India all the great saviors, *avataras,* are warriors. This is not coincidental. Krishna, Rama—both belonged to the warrior race, *kshatriya.* Buddha, Mahavira, the twenty-four *teerthankaras* of the Jainas, all are *kshatriyas.* This has to be not only a coincidence. Why have all these great people come from the warriors, and why do they talk about surender? And they say, "Surrender is the way." They had the will to surrender.

A *brahmin* has not yet come to the state of a Buddha or Mahavira. Why?—the *brahmin* has no will. He has thought, from the beginning, of surrender. He has not arrived to a will that he can surrender.

Or take it from a different angle: a poor man wants to renounce—what will he renounce, what has he got to renounce? What does his renunciation mean? When a Rockefeller decides to renounce his renunciation will mean something. It carries weight, he has something to renounce.

A beggar declares, "I have renounced the world"; people will laugh. In the first place, you had nothing to renounce. A king renounces, then the renunciation is meaningful: this man has known what will is—and knowing it well, he has understood that it cannot be the last thing in life. It is good for the beginning, good for the young people to play with as a toy, but for those who are becoming mature, useless, they have to drop it.

We give small children toys to play with. The day they become a little more mature, they throw the toys—and they start asking for the real thing. We give them a toy train and they say, "Forget about it." We give them a toy airplane and they say, "Throw it away. I want a real car, a real airplane. I want the real thing."

Ego can give you only toys to play with. But it is needed—otherwise you will never grow and will never become mature. One day you understand: "Now I need the real thing"—and the real thing is God. And for God to happen, you have to surrender . . .

Up to the age of thirty-five, move in the ways of the world, the ways of will. Strengthen your ego as much as you can with knowledge, with power, with money, with ambition.

Live it—because that is the only way to know it. Go into the deepest hell the world can make available to you, know it—because only by knowing one is liberated.

And then, suddenly a light will dawn on you. You will see the whole absurdity of it. And you start returning home; then you start returning towards the source. For thirty-five years go into the world, and then for the remaining part come back to yourself. First lose yourself so that you can gain. First sin so that you can become a saint. If you are a saint from the very beginning, your sainthood will not be of much value.

I am not against sin; I am not against anything. I say: Use everything, go into it. God has made this whole world available to you for a certain purpose: the purpose is learning. Sin is a lesson, is a must. If a child is a saint from the very childhood, is forced to be a saint, he will not have any spine. Let him first know what sin is. Let him himself become aware, and let him drop it on his own accord. Don't force him, don't discipline him. Give him freedom to move so one day he can see with his own eyes, feel with his own heart. And he can realize that Buddha is right, that Kabir is right, that Christ is right.

But this has to come from your own understanding— otherwise it is borrowed. And God never wants anybody second-hand. Be first-hand. Let your experience be original.

So this is what I am to say to you: will and surrender have to become part of your life, together—because you are man and woman together, and you are East and West together. The world is one, the earth is one village. All distinctions are just utilitarian, not real.

What is East and what is West? And what is surrender and what is will? They are both part of the one wave. They are not two, they are a quantum, one; two aspects of the one thing, one phenomenon.

So grow in will, and don't be afraid. Become a strong egoist, don't be afraid. Let it hurt, let it become a self-torture, let it become a cancer in your soul—then one day you drop it. And that dropping is out of your own feeling, your own experience. Then it is beautiful.

THE PATH OF LOVE

WIN How can you conquer this existence? It was there before you ever were, it will be there when you are gone. How can you win against this? And you are such a tiny part of it. The whole idea is absurd. A wave trying to win over the ocean, your hand trying to win over the whole body: the whole idea is absurd.

Relax, be in a let-go. Live with nature as an intrinsic part of it. Cooperate rather than conflict.

The very idea of survival of the fittest is utterly wrong. Survival in itself is not a value either. It is not a question of how long to survive; it is a question of how to live totally, deeply intensely, passionately. Then even a single moment of total life is more valuable than a long life of a hundred years.

UNIO MYSTICA, Vol. II

WINDOW See Master, 2nd Series
Worship

WISDOM Wisdom is a byproduct of meditation. It does not come through learning; on the contrary it comes through unlearning. Unlearn whatsoever you know. First become completely empty through unlearning, just a clean slate, and the suddenly a writing starts appearing on your clean slate. And the handwriting is not yours—it is God's! Suddenly from your own inner being you start having new insights, new visions.

EIGHTY-FOUR THOUSAND POEMS

Man can have knowledge but not wisdom. Man can achieve as much knowledge as he wants. It is easy, you just need a little mind effort, a little exertion. You can go on feeding your memory system. It is a computer; you can accumulate whole libraries. But wisdom is not something that you can accumulate because it does not happen through the mind at all. It happens through the heart, it happens through love, not through logic.

When the heart is open with love, with trust, when the heart is surrendered to the whole, then a new kind of insight arises in you, a clarity, a tremendously deep understanding of what life is all about, of who you are, of why this whole existence exists in the first place. All the secrets are revealed, but through love not through logic, through the heart not through the head. God has a direct connection with the heart, no connection with the head at all. So if one wants to approach God the way goes through the heart.

Once you have known wisdom through the heart then you can use your mind also as a good servant, then you can use even the knowledge accumulated by the mind in the service of wisdom—but not before you have known through the heart. Hence, rather than wasting time in accumulating unnecessary information—and people go on accumulating such stupid information, which is utterly ridiculous. If you look in the history books . . . children are forced to remember the names of stupid kings and queens and their birth dates and their death dates—and what do they have to do with this poor child?

Once a teacher asked a child "If Adam has never left the garden of Eden what would have happened?" The child said "One thing is certain: there would have been no history and no history class! It all began with Adam getting out of the garden of Eden."

It is rumored that the first words that Adam uttered when he was coming out of the gate . . . to Eve he said "We are passing through a great crisis." And since then we have always been passing through a great crisis! It is always a crisis. Not for a single moment have the crises stopped: one crisis after another crisis. And the poor children have to read history.

When I was a student in the school that was a constant problem for my teachers, because I would insist "What is the purpose? Why should I know about this man? Did he know anything about me? Then why should I bother?" My history teacher would simply close his eyes and sit silently— what to do? Many times he sent me to the principal saying "Please explain to the boy. He asks such questions that cannot be answered. And in a way he is right . . . " because what do I have to do with some Henry, some Edward? What do I have to do with these people? And still I am wondering because I have not come across any situation in which they were needed. And I don't think they will ever be needed. And all kinds of geographies . . .

Don't waste your time with information. All the universities are wasting peoples' lives. Almost ninety-nine percent that they teach is rubbish.

The one percent, it seems, enters the rubbish without their knowledge, otherwise they would stop that too. Somehow it gets mixed into the rubbish and enters the curriculums and the texts; otherwise it is all absurd . . .

Move your energy to the heart, be more loving and you are in for a great surprise. As your love grows, as your love petals open and your heart becomes a lotus, something tremendously beautiful starts descending on you—that is wisdom. And wisdom brings freedom.

Knowledge brings information, wisdom brings transformation.

THE GOLDEN WIND

The most fundamental question before Gautam the Buddha was "What is wisdom?" And the same is true for everyone. Down the ages the sages have been asking "What is wisdom?" If it can be answered by you, authentically rooted in your own experience, it brings a transformation of life.

You can repeat the definitions of wisdom given by others, but they won't help you. You will be repeating them without answering them, and that is one of the pitfalls to be avoided on the path. Never repeat what you have not experienced yourself. Avoid knowledge, only then can you grow in wisdom.

Knowledge is something borrowed from others, wisdom grows in you. Wisdom is inner, knowledge outer. Knowledge comes from the outside, clings to your surface, gives you great pride and keeps you closed, far, far away from understanding. Understanding cannot be studied; nobody can teach it to you. You have to be a light unto yourself. You have to seek and search within your own being, because it is already there at the very core. If you dive deep you will find it. You will have to learn how to dive deep within yourself—not in the scriptures but within your own existence.

The taste of your own experience is wisdom. Wisdom is an experience, not information.

THE BOOK OF THE BOOKS, Vol. V

WITHIN It is one of the greatest mysteries of life that we are born with perfect bliss in our being and we remain beggars because we never look into our own selves. We take it for granted, as if we already know all that is within. That is a great idiotic idea, but it prevails all over the world. We are ready to go to the moon to seek and search for bliss, but we are not ready to go inside ourselves for the simple reason that we already think without ever going in, "What is there inside?" We somehow go on carrying this notion, that we know ourselves. We don't know ourselves at all.

Socrates is right when he says: "Know thyself." In those two words the whole wisdom of the sages is condensed, because in knowing thyself all is known and all is fulfilled and all is achieved.

We are not to become perfect, we are born perfect. And we are not to invent bliss, we have only to discover it. Hence it is not such a difficult matter as people think; it is a very simple process of relaxing, resting, and slowly slowly getting centered.

The day you stumble upon your center, suddenly there is all light; you have found the switch. It is just like groping in a dark room: you go on groping and then you find the switch and it is all light. But one can sit in darkness for the whole night, crying and weeping just underneath the switch. And that's actually the situation; we are unnecessarily crying and weeping.

Hence those who have known have a very strange feeling about people. They feel great compassion and also great laughter because they can see the stupidity—that you have already got it but you are running hither and thither for no reason at all. And because of your running you go on missing. And they have great compassion also because you are suffering—that is true, although your suffering is simply foolish . . .

This absurd, ridiculous life-pattern has to be changed completely. Look within, and if you cannot find anything there, then look outside. But I say categorically that nobody who has looked within has ever missed it, so there is no reason for you to miss it. Nobody is an exception, it is an absolute law: one who goes within, finds it—finds the kingdom of God, the perfect bliss, the absolute truth. And with it comes freedom and great fragrance. Life becomes a dance, a poetry, a constant ecstasy; moment-to-moment it goes on growing.

One is bewildered at how much ecstasy is possible and "Can I contain any more?" But one can contain infinite ecstasy. And it goes on becoming more and more. Unbelievable it is, because you think "Now this is the limit, more is not possible," but next day you discover that there is still more possible, and you go on discovering. It never comes to an end. There is a beginning in this journey but no end.

THE GOLDEN WIND

WITNESSING Witnessing is the key of my sannyas, the master key. I don't give you any other discipline, because giving you any discipline will not help. Your unconsciousness will be there, and the discipline will only cover it. You can look like a saint but you will be as unconscious as before. Your saintliness will be as unconscious as your sinfulness was; there will be no qualitative difference in it.

So I am not interested in making saints out of you. I am not interested in helping you to drop your sins either. What I am interested in is: to make you aware. And the moment you start becoming aware of your actions, your thoughts your feelings . . . these are the three dimensions awareness has to be applied to. Walk, but *know* that you are walking. Remain alert to each gesture. Eat, but eat with awareness; don't just go on stuffing food inside. Think, but witness your thoughts, the process of thoughts, desires, dreams. Feel, but remain a little aware that these feelings, these moods are not you.

You are only pure awareness and nothing else. You are not the body, nor the mind, nor the heart. You are the fourth, and the fourth is the miracle. Once you have tasted the fourth, then wherever you are—*even* in hell—you will be in heaven.

THE WILD GEESE AND THE WATER

In witnessing, mind remains only as a biocomputer, a mechanism, but separate from you; you are no longer identified with it. When you want any memory you can use the mind just as you can put on your tape recorder. Mind is *really* a tape recorder. But it is not continuously on, not twenty-four hours on. When needed, the witness, the man of meditation, the man of awareness is capable of putting the mind on or off. He puts it on when there is some need.

If I am talking to you I have to put the mind on, otherwise language will not be possible. No-mind is silent, there is no language; only mind can supply the language. I have to use the mind to relate with your mind; that's the only way to relate with your mind, so I put it on. When I go back and sit in the car I put it off. Before Heeren turns the ignition on I turn *my* ignition off! In my room I don't need my mind. When Sheela comes with the letters or with some work I say to her, "Hello, Sheela." And inside I say, "Hello mind. Sheela has come!" Otherwise there is no need for the mind.

When you are witnessing, mind remains, but not constantly working; your identity is broken. You are the watcher, the mind is the watched. It is a beautiful mechanism, one of the most beautiful mechanisms that nature has given to you. So you can use it when needed for factual memory. for phone numbers, for addresses, for names, for faces. It is a good tool, but that's all it is.

COME, COME, YET AGAIN COME

Tantra says don't try to cut leaves—anger, greed, sex, don't bother about them; it is simply foolish. You just find the root and cut the root, and the tree will wither away by itself, of its own accord. The leaves will disappear, the branches will disappear—you simply cut the root.

Identification is the root and everything else is nothing but leaves. Being identified with greed, being identified with anger, being identified with sex, is the root. And remember, it is the same whether you are identified with greed, or sex, or even meditation. Love, *moksha,* God, it makes no difference, it is the same identification. Being identified is the root, and all else is just like leaves. Don't cut the leaves, leave them, nothing is wrong in them.

That's why Tantra does not believe in improving your character. It may give you a good shape—if you prune a tree you can make any shape out of it—but the tree remains the same. Character is just an outer shape—but you remain the same, no transmutation happens. Tantra goes deeper and says, "Cut the root!" That's why Tantra was misunderstood too much—because Tantra says, "If you are greedy be greedy; don't bother about greed. If you are sexual be sexual, don't bother about it at all." The society cannot tolerate such a teaching: What are these people saying? They will create chaos. They will destroy the whole order, but they have not understood that only Tantra can change the society, the man, the mind, nothing else; and only Tantra brings a real order, a natural order, a natural flowering of the inner discipline. But it is a very deep process—you have to cut the root.

Watch the greed, watch sex, watch anger, possessiveness, jealousy. One thing has to be remembered: don't get identified, simply watch; simply look, become a spectator. By and by, the quality of witnessing grows; you become able to see all the nuances of greed. It is very subtle. You become capable of seeing how subtly the ego functions, how subtle are its ways. It is not a gross thing; it is very subtle and delicate and deep-hidden.

The more you watch, the more your eyes become capable of seeing. The more perceptive they become, the more you see and the deeper you can move, and the more distance is created between you and whatsoever you do. Distance helps because without distance there can be no perception. How can you see a thing which is too close? If you are standing too close near a mirror, you cannot see your reflection. If your eyes are touching the mirror, how can you see? A distance is needed. And nothing can give you a distance except witnessing. You try it and see.

Move into sex; nothing is wrong in it, but remain a watcher. Watch all the movements of the body; watch the energy flowing in and out, watch how the energy is falling downwards; watch the orgasm, what is happening—how two bodies move in a rhythm; watch the heartbeat—faster and faster it goes, a moment comes when it is almost mad. Watch the warmth of the body, the blood circulates more, watch the breathing, it is going mad and chaotic. Watch the moment when a limit comes to your voluntariness and everything becomes involuntary. Watch the moment from where you could have come back, but beyond which there is no return. The body become so automatic that all control is lost. Just a moment before the ejaculation you lose all control, the body takes over.

Watch it: the voluntary processes, the non-voluntary process. The moment when you were in control and you could have come back, the return was possible, and the moment when you cannot come back, the return has become impossible—now the body has taken over completely, you are no more in control. Watch everything—and millions of things are there. Everything is so complex and nothing is as complex as sex, because the whole body-mind is involved—only the witness is not involved, only one thing remains always outside.

The witness is an outsider. By its very nature the witness can never become an insider. Find this witness and then you are standing on the top of the hill, and everything goes on in the valley and you are not concerned. You simply see; what is your concern? It is as if it is happening to somebody else. And the same with greed and the same with anger; everything is very complex. And you will enjoy it if you can watch—the negative, the positive, all the emotions. You simply remember one thing: that you have to be a watcher, then the identification is broken, then the root is cut. And once the root is cut, once you think you are not the doer, everything suddenly changes. And the change is sudden, there is no gradualness to it.

Cut the root of the tree and the leaves will wither,
cut the root of your mind and samsara falls.

The moment you cut the root of the mind, the identification with it, the *samsara* falls, the whole world falls like a house of cards. Just a small wind of awareness and the whole house falls. Suddenly you are here, but no longer in the world—you have transcended. You can live just the old way, doing the old things—but nothing is old, because you are no longer the old. You are a perfectly new being—this is rebirth. Hindus call it *dwij*, twice-born. A man who has attained to this is twice-born, this is a second birth—and this is the birth of the soul. This is what Jesus means by resurrection. Resurrection is not the rebirth of the body; it is a new birth of consciousness.

TANTRA: THE SUPREME UNDERSTANDING

WOMB   A Master is nothing but a womb: through him you are reborn. You die in him; you die with him. The Master is the cross and the resurrection. This is the meaning of Jesus' story: in him you die, and through him you are reborn. The Master is a womb.

One womb is the mother's womb; another womb is the Master's womb. The mother sends you into the world, the Master sends you beyond it. The Master is a mother.

YOGA: THE ALPHA AND THE OMEGA, Vol. VI

Some people never come out of the womb. Even when they are dying, their need for others' presence, their need for contact, relationship, continues. They have not come out of the womb. Physically they have come out many, many years before—the man may be eighty, ninety. Ninety years before, he had come out of the womb, but all these ninety years also he has been living in contact—seeking, always greedy for body contact. He has lived in a lost womb again and again in his dreams.

It is said that whenever a man falls in love with a woman—whatsoever he thinks, that is not the point—he is again falling in the womb. And maybe, it is almost certain—I say "maybe" because it is not yet a scientifically proved hypothesis—that the urge to enter the woman's body, the sexual urge, may be nothing but a substitute for entering the womb again. All sexuality may be a search how to enter the womb again. And in all the ways that man has invented to make his body comfortable, psychologists say he is trying to create a womb outside. Look at a comfortable room: if it is really comfortable it must have something in common with the womb—the warmth, the coziness, the silk, the velvet—the inner touch of the mother's skin. The pillows, the bed—everything gives you a feeling of comfort only when somehow it is related with the womb.

Now in the West they have made small tanks, womb-like. In those tanks lukewarm water is filled, exactly of the same temperature as the mother's womb. In deep darkness the man floats in the tank, absolutely comfortable—in darkness, just as in the womb. They call them meditation tanks. It helps: one feels very, very silent, and inner happiness arises—you have again become a child. A child in the womb floats in liquid of a certain temperature. The liquid has all the ingredients of the sea, the same salty water with the same ingredients. Because of that scientists have come to realize that man must have evolved from fishes—because still in the womb the atmosphere of the sea has to be maintained.

All comfort is, deep down, womb-like. And whenever you are lying with a woman, curled up, you feel good. Every man, howsoever old, becomes a child again; and every woman, howsoever young, becomes a mother again. Whenever they are in love the woman starts playing the role of the mother and the man starts playing the role of the baby. Even a young woman becomes a mother and an old man becomes a child.

In a yogi this urge disappears—and with this urge, he is really born. We in India have called him "twice-born", *dwij*. This is his second birth, the *real* birth. Now he is no longer in need of anybody; he has become a transcendental light. Now he can float above the earth; now he can fly in the sky. He is not earth-rooted now. He has become a flower— not a flower, because even a flower is earth-rooted . . . he has become the fragrance of the flower. Completely free. Moves into the sky with no roots in the earth. His desire to come in contact with others' bodies disappears.

YOGA: THE ALPHA AND THE OMEGA, Vol. VI

WOMEN   There is an old Sanskrit legend to the effect that, after making man, the Creator took the rotundity of the moon, the curves of the creeper, the lightness of leaves, the weeping of the clouds, the cruelty of the tiger, the soft flow of fire, the coldness of the snows, and the chattering of the jays, and made woman, and presented her to man.

After three days the man came and said to the Almighty, "This woman you have given me chatters constantly, never leaves me alone, requires much attention, takes all my time, cries about nothing and is always idle. I want you to take her back."

So the Almighty took her back. But pretty soon the man came again and said, "She used to dance and sing, and she looked at me out of the corner of her eye, and she loved to play; she clung to me when she was afraid, her laughter was like music, and she was beautiful to look upon. Give her back to me again."

So the Almighty gave her back to him again. But three days later he brought her back again and asked the Almighty to keep her. "No," said the Lord, "you will not live with her, and you cannot live without her. You have to get along the best you can."

THE BUDDHA DISEASE

To be male or to be female is more a question of psychology than of physiology. One may be a male physiologically and may not be a male psychologically, and vice versa. There are aggressive women—and, unfortunately, they are growing in the world—very aggressive women. The whole Women's Lib Movement is rooted in these aggressive women's minds. When a woman is aggressive she is not womanly.

Joan of Arc is not a woman and Jesus Christ is a woman. Psychologically Joan of Arc is a man; her approach is basically that of aggression. Jesus Christ is not aggressive at all. He says if somebody hits you on one cheek, give him the other cheek too. That is psychological non-aggressiveness. Jesus says, "Resist not evil." Even evil has not to be resisted! Non-resistance is the essence of feminine grace.

Remember that if a man is totally receptive, physically he remains a man but his interiority becomes more that of a womb. And only such men, whose interiority becomes feminine, are capable of receiving God. To be receptive, totally receptive, you will need to learn how to be a woman. Each seeker of truth has to learn to be a woman.

Science is male, religion is female. Science is an effort to conquer nature, religion is a let-go, dissolving oneself into nature. The woman knows how to melt, how to become one. And each seeker of truth has to know how to dissolve into nature, how to become one with nature, how to go with the flow, without resisting, without fighting. And then you will see: the proportion will always be the same.

Here also you will see that change happening. Many women have reported to me, complained, "What is happening to men here? They are becoming more and more feminine!" That is true—that is bound to happen. As you become more and more meditative, your energies become non-aggressive. Your violence disappears; love arises. You are no longer interested in dominating; instead you become more and more intrigued by the art of surrendering. That's what makes a feminine psychology.

To understand feminine psychology is to understand religious psychology. The effort has not been made yet, and whatsoever exists in the name of psychology is male psychology. That's why they go on studying rats, and through rats they go on concluding about man.

If you want to study the feminine psychology, then the best examples will be the mystics, the purest examples will be the mystics. Then you will have to learn about Basho, Rinzai, Buddha, Jesus, Lao Tzu. You will have to learn about these people, because only through *their* understanding will you be able to understand the peak, the crescendo of feminine expression.

Because the woman has been dominated for centuries, religion has disappeared from the earth. If religion comes back, the woman will again gain respect. And because the woman has been dominated and tortured and reduced into a nonentity she has become ugly. Whenever your nature is not allowed to go according to its inner needs it turns sour, it becomes poisoned, it becomes crippled, paralyzed, it becomes perverted.

The woman that you find in the world is not a true woman either because she has been corrupted for centuries. And when the woman is corrupted, man cannot remain natural either because, after all, the woman gives birth to the man. If she is not natural, her children will not be natural—she is going to mother the child, male or female—those children will naturally be affected by the mother.

Woman certainly needs a great liberation, but what is happening in the name of liberation is stupid. It is imitation, it is not liberation . . .

I would like the woman to become *really* a woman, because much depends on her. She is far more important than man because she carries in her womb both the woman and the man, and she mothers both the boy and the girl; she nourishes both. If she is poisoned then her milk is poisoned, then her ways of bringing up children are poisoned. If the woman is not free to really be a woman, man will never be free to really be a man either. The freedom of woman is a must for the freedom of man; it is more fundamental than man's freedom.

And if the woman is a slave—as she has been for centuries—she will make a slave of man too, in very subtle ways. Her way are subtle. She will not fight with you directly; her fight will be indirect—it will be feminine. She will cry and weep. She will not hit you, she will hit herself, and through hitting herself, through crying and weeping, through using these Gandhian methods, she will dominate you. Even the strongest man becomes henpecked. A very thin, weak woman can dominate a very strong man simply by using Gandhian methods. Gandhi is not the inventor of those methods; they have been used for centuries by women. He simply rediscovered them and used them politically. The woman has been using them for centuries, but only in a family context.

The woman needs total freedom so that she can give freedom to man too.

This is one of the fundamentals to be remembered: if you make somebody a slave you will be reduced to slavery ultimately, finally; you can't remain free. If you want to remain free, give freedom to others; that's the only way to be free.

THE BOOK OF THE BOOKS, Vol. VII

Nobody can befool a woman for the simple reason that she does not function through logic, she functions through love, through the heart. Her process is illogical; she simply jumps to conclusions. She cannot argue, but she immediately arrives at conclusions. Her process is like a quantum leap: she immediately understands, she can see through and through. The more you try to hide from her, the simpler it is for her to find it out.

Women are powerful people, not in the muscular sense but as far as their resistance is concerned, as far as their life energy is concerned, as far as their tolerance is concerned. And I am bound to be a little afraid because my whole work depends on them.

This is the first time that a commune is being run by women—for the first time in the whole history of man. I have given more power to women knowingly, because my understanding is that their functioning is graceful, insightful, loving, compassionate; it is not rude. And since I have made them the pillars of my temple, certainly I cannot speak against them!

So whatsoever I say about women, listen very cautiously!

They are in many ways more powerful than men. Modern research says that sexually they are more powerful. And if sexually they are more powerful as a corollary, remember, spiritually they are bound to be more powerful, because it is sex energy that becomes transformed into spiritual energy . . .

If a woman really goes into orgasmic joy she will start saying things which will not be meaningful. Sheer joy, utterances of joy, like "Alleluia!" It does mean anything; meaning is left far behind. It has tremendous intensity and passion in it.

Man became afraid because the whole neighborhood would know that you were making love to your woman and the police would come and dogs would start barking, and all kinds of things would happen! And people used to live in joint families. In one house there would be a hundred or more people—and one woman going into orgasmic joy would create such chaos.

And more difficulties were ahead . . . When a woman goes into orgasmic joy she has the capacity for multiple orgasms, which man is incapable of fulfilling. Man can have only one orgasm and the woman can have multiple orgasms—twelve, fifteen, twenty. Then how is the man going to satisfy her? Either he will feel defeated, ashamed, poor, humiliated, or he will have to call his friends! And that too is against his ego . . .

It is because of that fear that man has repressed all of woman's orgasmic capacities.

Millions of women have lived and died without knowing that they have the capacity to experience orgasm. And without knowing that you can have great orgasmic explosions you will not be able to understand anything of spirituality; it will be almost impossible for you. The woman is more powerful sexually. It is because of her greater power that she has been repressed. It is out of fear that man has repressed her.

You are right. I am a little afraid. Knowing perfectly well that I am doing something which has never been done before, I have to move very cautiously. It is a new experiment, but great possibilities will be released out of this experiment. If this experiment succeeds on a small scale it can succeed on a bigger scale too.

My own vision is that the coming age will be the age of the woman. Man has tried for five thousand years and has failed. Now a chance has to be given to the woman. Now she should be given the reins of all the powers. She should be given an opportunity to bring her feminine energies to function, to work. Man has utterly failed. In three thousand years, five thousand wars—this is man's record. Man has simply butchered, killed, murdered; he has lived as if only for war. There are a few days in between two wars which we call days of peace. They are not days of peace; they are only days of preparation for the new war, they are preparations for the new war. Yes, a few years are needed to prepare, and again war, again we go on killing each other. It is enough! Man has been given enough chances. Now feminine energies have to be released.

My commune is going to be rooted in feminine energy, in the energies of the mother. To me God is more a "she" than a "he", and "she" is better also because it includes "he". "He" is poorer; it can't include "she".

THE BOOK OF THE BOOKS, Vol. VII

There is a difference between the male mind and the female mind: their functioning is different. They are polar opposites, never forget that. Spiritually they are exactly the same, but physiologically they are poles apart; they function in different ways.

For example, man is more physical than woman, man is

more extrovert than woman. The woman is more psychological and more introvert. That's why there are so many magazines like *Playboy* with nude women on their covers and with pictures of nude women—and millions of copies are sold, and so much pornography exists all over the world. But it is all a male idea. The woman is not so interested in the nude man as the man is interested in the nude woman.

When a man and a woman are in a deep, loving embrace, the woman immediately closes her eyes. Kiss a woman, and she closes her eyes. But the man watches himself kissing the woman, watches the woman being kissed, watches her reactions, watches continuously whether she is getting an orgasm or not. He remains more or less an outsider, a spectator. He is more interested in watching than in *being* in it. The woman simply closes her eyes. She is less concerned with the man and what is happening to him; she is more concerned with her inner being, what is happening there. Hence women are not interested in pornography; their real interest is in their inner processes.

These differences are so great that they make for different lifestyles.

You are right: modern research has certainly found a very strange-looking fact. It is not really strange. Men are happier being married than not, because when they are not married they simply feel lonely. When they are married, even if the marriage is miserable, it is better than being lonely; at least there is something to keep you occupied. Misery also keeps you occupied. Man always wants to remain occupied with something on the outside so that he need not go in, so he can keep his eyes open.

The woman is not so interested in the outside, so when a woman is unmarried she feels more alone than lonely. And she can enjoy her aloneness better than a man because she is more inner-directed—she is more selfish, in a way. I am using the word with a very positive meaning: she is selfish, she is self-centered. The man is other-centered, he is constantly thinking of others.

The woman thinks more about herself; at the most she remains interested in the neighborhood—who is fooling around with whom. She is not much concerned about Vietnam or Iran. She simply feels a little puzzled about why men go on being so interested in Vietnam. What have you to do with Vietnam? It is so far away, why be bothered about it?

I have not come across a single woman who has asked me about proof for God. It is so far away! No woman has asked me: Does heaven really exist? Is hell a reality? She is not concerned about these things. She is more concerned with things that are close to her; she is more concerned with clothes than with God! And man thinks that all these feminine interests are stupid: when there are such great subjects, the woman is concerned about clothes! She will not discuss communism, and Karl Marx, Mao and Mahatma Gandhi; at the most she can listen to all these things out of politeness. Her interest is where you have got your *sari* from, the texture of your clothes and who is looking beautiful. She is concerned with that which is close; her concern is herself.

Hence she can remain alone in a more healthy way than man; he feels very lonely. If he can't get his morning newspaper he starts freaking out! He has to know about the whole world—what is happening. He can't be alone. Even in his aloneness he will create some imaginary beings—God, angels—and imaginary problems: how many angels can stand on the point of a needle? And he will be really into the problem; he will waste his whole life counting the angels and he will argue to no end! The woman simply laughs. The woman knows deep down that boys are just boys—let them talk nonsense! They call it philosophy, theology—they are very skillful in giving great names to stupid things!

That's why man will commit suicide if he is lonely. Marriage is a must for him; he needs a woman for many things. First: she gives him an earthing. The woman is very earthly, earthbound. In all the mythologies of the world she has been represented by the earth. The woman gives him roots into the earth; otherwise, without women, he is without earth, without roots, just hanging in the air. The woman gives him a nest, the woman becomes a home for him. Without the woman he is homeless, a vagabond, driftwood.

There is going to be conflict, there is going to be misery, there is going to be constant nagging—it is inevitable because they are such polar opposites; their interests never meet.

Hence the woman has to nag, otherwise the man will never fulfill *her* desires—and the man has to concede. Slowly slowly, if the man is intelligent enough, he becomes henpecked. Only very stupid and stubborn people never become henpecked. A little intelligence, and the man understands it: that it is better to listen to whatsoever she says and follow it, otherwise she will be after you twenty-four hours a day, she will not give you any rest. It is better to do whatsoever she is saying and be finished with it so you can read your newspaper!

All that nagging and all that misery can be tolerated because the woman fulfills a certain very deep need: she makes you earthbound and she takes care of your body. She is not much concerned about your soul—that she leaves for you to think about—but she nourishes your body. She nourishes, she cares, she loves; she makes you feel loved, needed; she gives you a deep contentment. Without her you simply don't know who you are. Without her you are always a lost child. She mothers you.

Hence it happens that married men are happier than unmarried men. It should not be so, because the unmarried man has no problems and the married man has problems, so logically it seems very strange that the married man should be happier than the unmarried one. But life does not follow logic; life has its own strange ways. The unmarried man is without roots, without nourishment, without warmth. He is cold, living in a cold world; he goes on shrinking and dying. The woman gives warmth, gives life, makes him feel at home, helps him to remain together. Without the woman he starts falling apart.

But the woman can be more happy alone than married, because she can make herself rooted without the man; the man is not such a great need for her. She can be more independent than the man—she *is* more independent.

Just because the woman is more independent, down the ages man has tried to make her dependent in other ways—economically, socially. Naturally, she is more independent, and that hurts the man and his ego. So he has tried to make her dependent in some way; artificial dependence has been created for her. Economically she has been paralyzed, she has to depend on the man. This is a consolation for the man:

if he depends on her, she also depends on him. It is a compensation and a consolation. Politically, socially, she has been thrown out of society; she has been forced to remain in the home so that man can feel, "Not only I am dependent, she is also dependent on me." This is a psychological strategy of the ego, of the male ego. Otherwise, if the woman is given total freedom—economic, social, political—man will look really poor compared to her.

In matriarchal societies man *is* poor. There are a few tribes still alive on the earth which are matriarchal, where the woman rules, and the women are stronger, more confident of themselves, and the men are weaklings.

Certainly, the woman is stronger than the man in many ways—she lives longer than man, five years longer than man. If the man's average age is seventy, then the woman's average age will be seventy-five. She lives five years longer than man. Why? She must have more resistance power. And after giving birth to ten, twelve children . . . Just think of a man giving birth to ten, twelve children—he would be finished long before! Just carry one child in your womb for nine months and you will commit suicide! Or if that is too difficult, just try to bring up a child—and you will either kill the child or you will commit suicide!

The woman has great resistance, great tolerance of things. The woman is more balanced: physiologically, chemically, she is more balanced. That's why she looks more beautiful: her beauty has roots in her physiological balance.

It is like this: if a person has two cells, one from the mother and one from the father, each cell consisting of twenty-four smaller cells, then the man has two cells, one consisting of twenty-four cells and the other of twenty-three, and the woman has two cells, each consisting of twenty-four cells equally. The woman is more balanced.

Man has an inner imbalance, hence he goes berserk more easily, he goes mad very easily. Any woman can drive any man mad, it is such a simple phenomenon! Women are less ill than men, men are more ill; they suffer from more illnesses. One hundred and fifteen boys are born for each hundred girls, and by the time they reach to a marriageable age fifteen boys have disappeared. The age of marriage finds one hundred girls to one hundred boys. Nature also gives birth to fifteen boys more knowing perfectly well that fifteen are going to die sooner or later, so that by the time the boys and girls come to a marriageable age the proportion will be the same.

Unmarried women are more at ease with themselves. If they were not prevented politically and economically they would like, they would *love,* to remain unmarried. Maybe that is one of the reasons why man has made them so helpless politically, socially and economically, so that they *have* to decide for marriage; otherwise many women would like to remain unmarried. Even if they would like to become mothers they would like to become mothers without marriage. Yes, there is a great need to be a mother in a woman, but there is no great need to be a wife.

Man's needs are more physiological; women's needs are more psychological. Hence in marriage the woman always feels as if she is exploited. And her feeling *is* true, because the man's interest is sexual and the woman's interest is far more total; it is not just sexual—sex may be a *part* in that totality. But man's interest is basically sexual; everything else is just decorative, it is not essential. He is continuously interested in sex, for the simple reason that their sexualities are very different.

Man has a local sexuality; his sex is confined to the genital organs, it is not spread all over his body. The woman is totally sexual, her whole body is sexual; it is not genital. Hence a woman needs a longer foreplay before she can really go into love-making. And the man is always in a hurry: his love is nothing but a hit-and-run affair! The woman is not even warmed up, and the man is dressing and going away; the man is finished! His sexuality is genital. The woman is more total; her whole body has a deep sexuality in it. Unless her whole body becomes involved she can't have an orgasmic experience. And if she can't have an orgasmic experience she becomes disinterested in sex. So wives are disinterested in sex. Man's whole interest is sex . . .

For men, sex is not a spiritual phenomenon but only a physiological release. For women it is a spiritual phenomenon, hence the woman always feels offended. Unless love happens as part of a great spiritual experience she is unable to cooperate in it. Yes, she can be a part of it in a cold way.

It is because of this situation that millions of women have completely forgotten what orgasm means; they have become frozen. It is due to man's non-understanding about the difference.

Each man and each woman needs a great education about it: that they are different, their physiologies are different, their psychologies are different. And they have to understand each other's psychology, each other's physiology. They have to be taught. Each university should help the students to understand each other's biology and spirituality. Nothing is being taught.

Sex is taboo—don't talk about it. People think as if we are born with all the knowledge needed. That is sheer nonsense! You may be able to produce children, that's possible, but that is not enough.

Sex has a far deeper significance. It is not only for reproduction, it has a multidimensional quality to it. It is also fun, it is play, it is prayer, it is meditation, it is religion, it is spirituality. Sex has the whole spectrum, it is the whole rainbow—all the colors from the lowest to the highest.

A great education is needed so that man can understand the woman and can help her to move towards orgasmic peaks, and the woman can understand the man and can help him.

THE BOOK OF THE BOOKS, Vol. VII

WOMEN, BEAUTIFUL   So, here are a few clues for you.

If you want a peaceful life, find a homely woman and your life will be peaceful—of course without joy. You can't have both together. It will be peaceful, completely peaceful, but there will be no ecstasy in it. It will be as if you are already dead; there will be no excitement. It will be flat, like a flat tire, stuck in one place . . .

The second is: take the risk, fall in love with a beautiful woman. There will be great excitement, ecstasy, but there will be trouble too. Heaven and hell come in the same package. You will have a few heavenly moments, but they are worth it—for all the hell that will follow, they are worth it. And they will teach you a lesson. That's how one finally becomes a Buddha. Without women there would have been no Buddhas; about that I am absolutely certain. There would have been no religion, no Buddhas, no Mahaviras. It is because of women.

Many women ask me the question, "Why haven't women become enlightened?" How can they become enlightened? Who will drive them to become enlightened? That is the point. They drive men to become enlightened. Finding no other way in life, he becomes enlightened. It is simple! I have not answered it yet, but today I thought better to say it and settle it forever. Never ask me again, "Why don't women become enlightened?" There is no need! Their function is to make people enlightened—to drive them crazy—so sooner or later they start meditating, sooner or later they want to be left alone. They are finished! Their dreams are shattered, they are disillusioned. It is the great work of woman; the whole credit goes to women.

Buddha, Mahavira, Lao Tzu and Chuang Tzu, they were possible only because the woman was continuously forcing them: Either become enlightened or go crazy! And they decided to become enlightened. They said, "It is better to become enlightened." It is good to pass through the experience.

So, choose a beautiful woman and fall wholeheartedly . . . don't hold anything back. The deeper you love, the sooner you will get free of it. The more passionately you go in, the more quickly you come out.

I AM THAT

WOMEN, ENLIGHTENED   A man has a need for love once in a while but the woman lives in love for twenty-four hours a day. The man has many other interests also; one of his interests is love. But the woman has no other interest, her whole interest is love. And out of that love other interests may grow but they are part of love, they are not competitors to love. Hence a man can always sacrifice love for his art, for his music, for his meditation, for religion—he can easily renounce love. It is only one of his interests, it is not his whole being. But a woman cannot do that.

It is because of this fact that you don't find so many women enlightened because nobody has worked out from the woman's side how to attain enlightenment. Enlightenment has remained basically a masculine interest. And of course when it is a masculine interest love has to be denied; love is an unnecessary distraction. So all the religions have been against love.

My effort here is multidimensional. I am trying to do many things here. Now is the time for love to find a way towards enlightenment so that women can also be Buddhas. It has not happened in the past.

You see Jesus and Mohammed and Mahavira and Chuang Tzu and Lieh Tzu and Zarathustra, but they are all men. And unless women start becoming enlightened humanity will remain lopsided, the balance will not there. And unless women become enlightened they cannot be really free, because enlightenment is the ultimate in freedom. The freedom of women cannot come through stupid movements like Women's Liberation. It can only come through a totally different approach: women should learn how to become enlightened. If we can create a few women Buddhas in the world the woman will be freed from all chains and fetters.

And there is no difficulty at all. In fact nobody has bothered about it, nobody has thought about it. Woman was never taken into consideration, she has been ignored. She has never been given the same status as man; she was thought to be just secondary. But because of this the whole of humanity has suffered.

Enlightenment is everybody's birthright.

Man can easily make an approach through meditation but the woman can more easily make an approach through love. Love is going to be her meditation. To be loving, totally loving, unconditionally loving—that is going to be her path towards light, towards godliness. And out of love the woman will have a new birth. She will become a child of light, a child of moonlight . . .

And you can see that thousands of women are gathered around me. It has never happened before. It has always been a male-dominated quest. For years even Buddha denied entry to women, he was against it. He was afraid, and I can understand his fear. His whole method was male-oriented, and he was afraid that if women were allowed to become initiates, sannyasins, then the males would find ways to be distracted. They might start falling in love and the whole method would be disturbed, the whole process would be disturbed.

Mahavira, another enlightened man of the same category as Buddha, who established Jainism, said that women can be enlightened only when they are born again as men. In this life when they are women all that they can do is to work to be born as men, only then is enlightenment possible— not through the body of a woman, first they have to attain the body of a man. And I can understand what he means by it. His method is such that there is no space, no place, for love in it.

Mary Magdalene loved Jesus more than any of his disciples did but she was not accepted as an apostle; those twelve fools became apostles! And they all escaped when Jesus was crucified. He was taken down from the cross by three women and all the apostles escaped. But still those three women are not respected. Even Jesus did not show any respect to women, even to his mother he did not show much respect.

Once his mother came to see him when he was talking to a crowd. The people said. "Your mother is waiting outside to see you," and he said, "Tell that woman that nobody is my father and nobody is my mother." *Tell that woman . . .* This is ugly, but this has been the approach of all the male-oriented methodologies.

My effort is to create a path for women also, because unless they are free religiously they will not be free in other ways. Religious freedom is the central core of all other freedoms. And even in the twentieth century there are religions that don't allow women in their temples, they don't allow women to be priests; no woman can be a pope.

This is ugly, unnecessarily violent. It is something of the rotten past, still a hangover of the past. It has to be completely finished.

As meditation can lead to enlightenment, love can lead to enlightenment. They are different paths but they reach the same peak.

I'M NOT AS THUNK AS YOU DRINK I AM

WOMEN, FEAR OF   So many women write to me: *Why in your commune are men so afraid of us?*

Man has always been afraid. This is nothing new. But one man was living with one woman; he was afraid but was able to manage somehow. Now here he sees women and women and women; he becomes really afraid. There are biological reasons for the fear.

Women are capable of multiple orgasms, man is not. Sexually man is very poor compared to women. No man is capable of satisfying any woman. If the woman is allowed freedom she will make anybody afraid, because she will make you feel very inferior. She is capable of multiple orgasms—within seconds she can have many orgasms—and you can have only one orgasm. And with one orgasm you are finished! She has not even started and you are finished—that is very embarrassing. Because of this fear man has repressed women all over the world.

It is not that man is stronger and that's why he has repressed women, no. It is out of fear.

Man has destroyed women's capacity for orgasm. For centuries man has said that orgasm is possible only for men, not for women. He has taught women to be absolutely unalive in a sexual relationship. He has told them, conditioned them, hypnotized them for centuries, that it is more womanlike, ladylike, to be just silent, unmoving. It is for the man to make all the movements, take all the initiative.

Hence man makes love, not the woman. The woman is just there, a silent partner. And the reason is his great fear, because if she becomes an active partner she will reduce the man to almost nothingness. If she becomes active, man is very much afraid—how is he going to satisfy her? All his manhood will be at stake. He will no more be capable of bragging that he is a man, something higher, superior. Sexually he is not; sexually he is very inferior. In a muscular way he may be stronger than the woman, but sexually he is not.

There are even countries in Africa where operations were done on small girls: their clitorises were cut when they were very small—a very painful operation—just to make sure that they don't have any idea of orgasm. In the Sudan you will not find a single woman who knows anything about orgasm, because their very mechanism for orgasm is damaged. Their vaginas are more like wounds than healthy organs. What fear!—to cut their clitorises. Then they will always be inferior . . .

In my commune it is a totally different phenomenon. Centuries-old taboos are broken, centuries-old inhibitions are thrown to the winds. I am all for freedom, particularly sexual freedom because all other freedoms are rooted in that. If a man or a woman is not orgasmic he is not alive, she is not alive—they are dead. They breathe, they eat, they walk, but that is not life. They only vegetate.

A scientist was doing an experiment on a certain species of fish. In the species the female fish, whenever approached by a male fish, starts moving away in a very coquettish way—alluring, enchanting, inviting, but she starts escaping; does not really escape but pretends that she is escaping. That excites the male; he starts running after her. The more he runs after her, the more excited he becomes, his passion is aroused. Then, of course in a very diplomatic way, the female fish allows him to make love.

One scientist, Lorenz, trained a female fish to do just the opposite: whenever she came across a male, to go, take the intiative, jump upon the male fish. And Lorenz was surprised: whenever this was done, the male fish was very very afraid. The male fish could not believe his own eyes: "What is happening!" And the male fish was unable to make love. A sudden impotence!

The mechanism works in a certain way: the female has to be seductive but unavailable—not *absolutely* unavailable, because that will destroy the whole game—just a pretension of unavailability. That excites the male energy. That makes the male more and more interested, obsessed. He is functioning at the optimum, and when he is functioning at the optimum he makes love easily—because the male mind, whether in men or mice, is the same, the male mind: it wants to conquer . . .

I am just like another Lorenz. This commune is a pond, and I am training female fish to embrace every male fish!

THE BOOK OF THE BOOKS, Vol. IX

WOMEN, MARRIED Millions of people, both men and women, are more interested in the married person. First, the unmarried person shows that nobody has yet desired him or her; the married person shows that somebody has desired him. And you are so imitative that you cannot even love on your own. You are such a slave that when somebody else is loving somebody, only then can you follow. But if the person is alone and nobody is in love with them then you are suspicious. Maybe the person is not of worth, otherwise why should he or she wait for you?

The married person has great attraction for the imitator.

Secondly, people love less—people, in fact, don't know what love is—they compete more. The married man . . . and you become interested. Or the married woman . . . and you become interested— because now there is a possibility to compete. The triangular fight is possible. The woman is not easily available. There is going to be struggle.

In fact, you are not interested in the woman, you are interested in the struggle. Now the woman is almost a commodity. You can fight for her and you can prove your mettle. You can displace the husband, and you will feel very good— an ego trip; it is not a love trip. But remember, once you succeed in disposing of the husband, you will not be interested in the woman any more. You want to prove yourself against the man: "Look, I have taken interest in the unmarried woman now." Again you will start looking for some fight somewhere: you will always make it a triangle. This is not love.

In the name of love there is jealousy, there is competition, there is aggression, there is violence. You want to prove yourself. You want to prove yourself against the man: "Look, I have taken away your woman." Once you have taken away the woman, you will not be interested in the woman at all, because she was not the desired thing; the desired thing was a sort of victory . . .

Another thing: the married woman is not easily available. That too creates desire. Easy availability kills desire. The more unapproachable, the more inaccessible the woman is, the more the desire; you can dream about her. And, in fact, there is not much possibility that it will ever become an actuality. There is every opportunity to be romantic about a married woman: you can play with your fantasy. It is not easy to make her available to you. You are not interested in unmarried women because they will not leave much chance for romance. If you are interested, they are ready. There is no space left. There is not that long, long waiting.

Many people are interested not in love but in waiting; they say that waiting is far more beautiful than love. In a way it is so, because while you are waiting you are simply projecting, you are dreaming. Of course, your dream is your dream and you can make it as beautiful as you want.

The real woman is going to shatter all your dreams. People are afraid of the real woman. And a married woman becomes more unreal than the real . . .

People fall in love with a married woman—this a halfway house, it is a trick. They can believe that they are in love and they can avoid it also.

Love creates great fear because love is a challenge, a great challenge. You have to grow. You cannot remain juvenile and immature. You will have to grapple with the realities of life. Your so-called great poets are almost always very childish immature people still living in the fairyland of childhood. They don't know what reality is; they don't allow the reality to penetrate into their dreams.

A woman is a sure destroyer of fictions. She is not fictitious, she is, in fact, a truth. So if you want to believe that you are in love and you still want to avoid love, it is good, safe, to fall in love with a married woman or a married man. This is very tricky, this is a deception, a self-deception.

Women are also afraid to fall in love with a free man, because with the free man or free woman there is involvement—a twenty-four hour involvement. With a married woman the involvement is not that big. You can have a few stolen kisses, you can meet her somewhere in a dark corner—always afraid that the husband may be coming, somebody may see. It is always half-hearted, it is always in a hurry, and you don't come to know the woman as she is in her twenty-four hour life. You come to know only her painted face, you come to know only her performance, not her truth.

When a woman comes out of her house ready to go shopping, she is not the same woman. She is almost a different person. Now she is a managed woman, now she is a performer. Women are great actresses. In the house they don't look so beautiful. Out of the house they suddenly become tremendously beautiful, joyful, cheerful, delighted. They again become small, giggling girls in love with life. Their faces are different, radiant. Their eyes are different; their makeup, their performance.

Seeing a woman on the beach, or in the shopping center, you are seeing a totally different kind of reality. To live with a woman twenty-four hours a day is very mundane—it has to be. But if you really love a woman, you would like to know her reality, not her fiction, because love can exist only with reality. And love is capable of knowing the reality and yet being able to love her, of knowing all the defects and yet being able to love her. Love is a tremendous strength.

When you are with a person twenty-four hours a day— man or woman—you come to know all the defects: all that is good, and all that is bad too; all that is beautiful, and all that is ugly too; all that is like light-rays, and all that is like dark night. You come to know the whole person. Love is strong enough to love the other, knowing all the defects, limitations, frailties that a human being is prone to.

But this fictitious love is not strong enough. It can only love a woman on the movie screen. It can only love a woman in a novel. It can only love a woman in poetry. It can only love the woman as a faraway, distant star. It can only love a woman who is not real.

Love is a totally different dimension. It is falling in love with reality. Yes, reality has defects, but those defects are challenges to growth. Each defect is a challenge to transcend it. And when two persons are really in love, they help each other to grow. They look into each other; they become mirrors to each other: they reflect each other. They help each other; they hold each other. In good times, in bad times, in moments of happiness, in moments of sadness they are together, they are involved— that's what involvement is all about.

If I am only with you when you are happy and I am not with you when you are unhappy this is not involvement, this is exploitation. If I am only with you when you are flowing, and I am not with you when you are not flowing—then I am not with you at all. Then I don't love you. I love only

myself and I love only my pleasure. "When you are plea-
surable, good; when you become painful I will throw you
away." This is not love, this is not involvement, this is not
commitment. This is not respect for the other person.

It is easy to love somebody else's wife because he has to
suffer the reality and you enjoy the fiction. It is a very good
division of labor. But this is inhuman. Human love is a great
encounter. And love is only if growth happens out of it,
otherwise what type of love is it?

Lovers are enhanced by each other—in every way. Lovers
reach to higher peaks of happiness when they are together,
and they also reach to the deeper depths of sadness when
they are together. Their range of happiness and sadness
becomes vast—that's what love is. Alone, if you cry and
weep, your tears don't have much depth. Have you watched
it? Alone, they are shallow. When you weep together with
somebody then there is a depth, a new dimension to your
tears. Alone you can laugh, but your laughter will be shallow.
In fact it will be something insane—only mad people laugh
alone. When you laugh with somebody there is a depth in
it, there is sanity in it. Alone, you can laugh, but the laughter
will not go very deep, cannot go. Together, it goes to the
very core of your being.

Two persons together, together in all the climates—day
and night, summer and winter—in all the moods, grow. The
tree needs all the climates and all the seasons. Yes, it needs
the burning-hot summer and it needs the ice-cold winter.
It needs the daylight, the sun showering on it, and it needs
the silence of night so it can close into itself and go into
deep sleep. It needs silent, cheerful, joyful days; it needs
gloomy, cloudy days too. It grows through all these
dialectics.

Love is a dialectic. Alone, you cannot grow. Remember
always that if you are in love then don't avoid commitment,
don't avoid involvement. Then go totally into it. Then don't
just stand on the periphery ready to escape if things get too
troublesome.

And love is a sacrifice too. You have to sacrifice much . . .
your ego. You have to sacrifice your ambition, you have to
sacrifice your privacy, you have to sacrifice your secrets;

you have to sacrifice many things. So just to be in a romantic love needs no sacrifice. But when there is no sacrifice there is no growth.

Love changes you almost utterly: it is a new birth. You are never the same person again as you were before you loved a woman or a man. You have passed through fire, you are purified. But courage is needed.

You ask me: *Why am I always interested in married women?*

Because you are not courageous. You want to avoid the involvement. You want it cheaply, you don't want to pay the price for it.

THE TANTRA VISION, Vol. II

WOMEN'S LIBERATION   There is a great attraction between man and woman for the simple reason that they are mysterious to each other. The same things creates conflict and the same thing creates attraction. The farther away they are, the greater the distance between them, the more the attraction between them.

In modern societies, in advanced countries particularly, the attraction is disappearing for the simple reason that men and women are coming so close to each other, they are almost similar. They dress alike, they both have started smoking, they both drink, they both behave in the same way, they both use the same language. The Liberation Movement has contributed much to this nonsense.

The Women's Liberation Movement is teaching women all over the world to be just like men—strong, rough, aggressive. They can be aggressive and they can be rough, but they will lose something immensely valuable: they will lose their feminineness. And the moment they become just like men they will not be mysteries anymore. This is something new happening in the world; it has never happened before.

The wise sages of the ancient days always made it clear to the old societies: make men and women as distinct as possible. Nature makes them distinct, but culture also should help them to be distinct. That does not mean that they are not equal; they are equal but they are different, they are unique. Equality need not mean similarity; equality should not be misunderstood as similarity. Similarity is not equality.

And if women start becoming like men they will never be equal to men, remember.

The Women's Liberation Movement is going to do some very deep harm to the women's cause in the world, and this will be the harm: they will become carbon copies of men, they will have a secondary kind of existence. They will not be real men because they cannot be naturally so aggressive. They can pretend, they can cultivate aggression, they can be rough, but that will be just a facade: deep down they will remain soft. And that will create a split in their being, that will create a schizophrenia in their being. They will suffer from a dual personality and they will lose their mysteriousness. They will argue with men with same logic, but they will be like men and they will become ugly. To be unnatural is to be ugly, to be natural is to be beautiful.

I would like them to be equal to men, but the idea of similarity should be dropped. In fact, they should become as dissimilar as possible; they should keep their uniqueness intact. They should become more and more feminine, then the mystery deepens. And that is the way of existence, the way of Tao.

TAO: THE GOLDEN GATE, Vol. I

WONDER   See Religion

WORDS   Words are very troublesome because words carry the past; they are made by the past, they are overburdened by the past. Any word is dangerous, because its meaning comes from the past. And for me the problem is: to use the words which come from the past—because there are no other words—but to give them such a twist and turn that they can give you a little insight into a new meaning. The words are old, the bottles are old, but the wine is new.

THE GOOSE IS OUT

Thousands of people have been burned by Christians. The people who talk about love, the people who talk about peace, the people who think that Jesus came into the world to give the message of love, brotherhood—they have killed more people that anybody else. And all their bloodshed was only a question of words—words became so important.

With foolish people it happens always: the reality fades away and words take its place. The word "God" becomes more important than the reality of God; the word "love" becomes more important than the phenomenon of love. Then they can kill each other for the word.

It is unbelievable that for thousands of years people have trusted in words so much—as if the word "fire" is fire, as if the word "water" is water! When you are thirsty, the word "water" is not going to help.

THEOLOGIA MYSTICA

The really significant things in life can never be said through words; only silence is capable of communion. Words are utilitarian—they belong to the marketplace—hence when you really want to say something of the heart you will always find it unsayable. Love cannot be uttered, gratitude cannot be spoken of, prayer is bound to be a deep silence inside you.

And this is of fundamental importance to understand because we are brought up through words, with the idea that everything can be said: we try to say it, and by saying those things which are not sayable we falsify them.

Lao Tzu says, "Tao cannot be said, The moment you say it you have already falsified it." Truth cannot be communicated—no word is adequate enough, big enough to contain it. It is so vast, vaster than the sky, and words are so tiny. They are good for day-to-day things, utilitarian ends, but as you start moving towards the non-utilitarian you start moving beyond words.

That's exactly what religion is: transcendence of words and transcendence of the world that belongs to words. The mind consists of words; the heart consists only of silence, profound silence, virgin silence, unbroken silence.

TAO: THE GOLDEN GATE, Vol. II

The Bible begins with a very strange statement: In the beginning was the word, and God was with the word, and God was the word. This beginning of the Bible has led the whole western mind in a wrong direction.

The word can never be the beginning because before the word can exist the sound is needed. To transform the sound into the word a mind is needed. The word can never be the beginning.

The sound of running water is not a word. The sound of wind passing through the pine trees is not a word. Word came much later on. Word came with man, not with existence. Word is a mind product. It is giving meaning to sound. Sound is there, then comes the mind; then mind interprets the sound and makes the word. The word is a human creation.

If I was to write the Bible again I would say in the beginning was "the sound of one hand clapping."

A soundless sound, the sound of silence itself. And I can say it authentically. Because if one goes within oneself one comes to the beginning of everything, because you contain both the beginning and the end, the seed and the flower.

First you have to drop the words. The moment you drop the words the mind becomes useless because its whole function is to interpret sounds into words, to create words out of sound. Hence there are so many languages in the world, thousands of languages. Because the interpretation of a certain sound is our interpretation. We can make any interpretation out of it. Different people, different tribes, different races have all heard the same sounds but they all have interpreted differently.

Once interpretation is dropped, once you are no more interested in the words, but you become interested in the sound, the whole function of the mind is taken away; the very earth below the mind is withdrawn. The mind flowers, and the death of the mind is the beginning of meditation. Then you are falling into sound first. Then as you go deeper into sound it becomes more and more silence. Of course that silence has a certain rhythm and music to it, but it is pure silence—no word, no mind, no interpretation. And this is the beginning. And remember, this is also the end. The source is always the goal. Only then is life complete. It becomes a perfect circle. When the source is reached again you have come home.

THE SOUND OF ONE HAND CLAPPING

WORD, SPOKEN The Masters have always believed in the spoken word; there are reasons for it. The Masters have never written books. The spoken word has an alive quality to it; the written word is dead, it is a corpse.

When I am speaking to you it is a totally different thing than when you read it in a book, because when you are reading in a book it is only a word; when you are listening to the Master it is more than the word. The presence of the Master is overpowering! Before the word reaches you, the Master has already reached; he is already overflooding you. Your heart is beating with the Master in the same rhythm. You are breathing in the same rhythm. There is a communion, an invisible link. The presence of the Master, his gestures, his eyes . . . the words spoken by him are ordinary words, but when spoken by a Master they carry something of the beyond; they carry some silence, some meditativeness, some of his experience, because they come from his innermost core.

It is like passing through a garden: even though you have not touched a single flower, when you reach home you can still feel the fragrance of the garden; your clothes have caught it, your hair has caught it. The pollen of the flowers was in the wind. You had not touched anything, but the fragrance was in the air; it has become a part of you . . .

All the Masters of all the ages have depended on the spoken word for the simple reason that the spoken word comes directly from their innermost core. It carries the fragrance of their inner world, the richness of their inner world, the beauty of their inner world. It is soaked with their inner being, it is full of their energy. By the time it is written it will not be the same thing.

The spoken word means a communion between the Master and the disciple. The written word is not a communion, it is a communication; anybody can read it. The student can read it, he need not be a disciple. The enemy can read it, he need not even be a student. Somebody can read it just to find faults in it, just to find something so that he can argue against it.

But with the spoken word it is totally different. Even if an opponent comes, the spoken word dances around him. There is every possibility that although he came with a conclusion, a fixed idea, his fixed idea may become a little bit loosened, he may become a little relaxed. He may start looking again before he makes any decision. He may start putting his *a priori* ideas aside. The rumors that he has heard can easily be put aside if he comes in contact with the spoken word.

I AM THAT

WORK   We never work as much as we can, we never work to the maximum potential. In fact, at the most, people work fifteen percent of their potential—and those are the very hard workers.

As I see it, you are not working more than seven or eight percent. The more you work, the more you are capable of working. The less you work, the less you become capable of working. Life has its own logic.

Jesus says, "If you have, more will be given to you. If you don't have, even that which you have will be taken away from you." If you work hard you will get more energy. If you don't work hard, if you don't work at all and you avoid it, even the energy that you have will disappear. So whatsoever you want to do, do it, and do it to the optimum. And soon you will see that more and more doors are opening, and more energy becomes available.

Always try to reach more than you can grasp; always try to reach beyond your grasp. That is how one grows.

HAMMER ON THE ROCK

Put your love into it, your whole awareness into it. Just don't do it for the money—do it for love also. Do it with care, and then there is no need for any other meditation: your work becomes your meditation.

If you can change your work into meditation, that's the best thing. Then meditation is never in conflict with your life. Whatsoever you do can become meditative. Meditation is not something separate; it is a part of life. It is just like breathing: just as you breathe in and out, you meditate also.

And it is simply a shift of emphasis; nothing much is to be done. Things that you have been doing carelessly, start doing carefully. Things that you have been doing for some result, for example, money . . . That's okay, but you can make it a plus phenomenon. Money is okay . . . One needs money, but it is not all. And just by the side if you can reap many

more pleasures, why miss them? They are just free of cost.
DANCE YOUR WAY TO GOD

Work is not work. And without work you will become more rotten, because what will you do? Your whole energy will become just a whirlpool inside and will create a thousand and one problems. Work is needed . . . it is a relaxation. You create energy by food, by sleep. Where to put that energy?

You have to be creative about it. And work is a very ugly word, and particularly in the West, it is very ugly. That has created a certain subconscious attitude. In primitive villages, work is taken to be almost a play, a game. Everything is thought to be a game.

In a primitive village, even now in India in remote parts, the villagers will get up at four or three o'clock in the morning and the whole village will start singing. They are getting ready for their day's work. From every hut song will arise, drums will beat and somebody will start playing on the flute. Then everybody will come out and move towards their fields to work, singing together in choruses. And it continues the whole day. The work seems to be joined with play. By the end of the day they come back, tired. It has been hard work under the hot sun. They will return to their villages and start dancing again into the night. They will go on dancing late, and then fall asleep under the trees. Again in the morning they are there singing. It is very difficult to decide what separates their work from their play; they overlap.

Once a man came to see me. He was a bus driver. Of course to drive a bus in a city like Bombay or Delhi where the whole traffic is neurotic, brings one to be continuously on the edge of a nervous breakdown. He was very nervous, shaking.

He told me, "I want to get rid of this work. It is too much! I cannot sleep—it gives me nightmares. And the whole day on the wheel in such neurotic traffic I cannot relax for a single moment."

I told him, "Try a meditation that I will give you, for seven days. Take this as a challenge—that these people are running into the middle of the road and doing everything in disorder. Take it that they are just creating a situation for you in which to test your skill. Take it as a play. Take it as a situation in which your energy is put to test, and your whole skill is to be judged."

This idea appealed to him and after seven days he came and said, "It has worked . . . tremendous! Now I am not worrying about the road; I am enjoying it! The more disorderly it is, the more I enjoy it. It is really beautiful how I can avoid all the problems of the traffic. When I come back home, I come almost as a victorious player; like somebody who has won a gold medal in the Olympics!"

Take work as a game and enjoy it. Everything is a challenge.

BELOVED OF MY HEART

You were made to work your way through this darkness of existence. This is a task to be done, this is a way of growth. To be here on the earth simply means that God has given an opportunity to you to grow. This earth is a challenge. Accept the challenge, encounter life: don't escape.

A few people escape in words, a few people escape into monasteries, a few people escape into politics, a few people escape into money—these are all escapes. A few become learned people, a few become rich, a few become very powerful in the world, a few become very respectable, moral and virtuous. But the real work is not done.

What is the real work? Sufis call only one thing real work, and that is self-remembrance.

Gurdjieff learned the word "work" from the Sufis. He used to call his teachings "the work". He also learned the word *zikr*, self-remembering, from the Sufis.

The work is to remember oneself. The only work worth doing is to remember oneself.

UNIO MYSTICA, Vol. I

Work is worship. Work is prayer.

While I am talking to you, it is a prayer to me, it is worship. You are my temples, my gods. Whatsoever I am saying, I am not saying just to teach something. Teaching is a byproduct, a consequence. Whatsoever I say to you is a prayer—it is love, it is care. I *care* about you; I care as much as a painter cares about his canvas.

Have you ever heard about Van Gogh being on a holiday? Have you ever heard about Picasso being on holiday?—yes, you must have heard. He used to go for many holidays, but always with his canvas and brush; on the holiday also he would be painting. It was not a holiday from painting.

When you love something, there is no holiday—and then *all* your days are holidays. Each day to me is a Sunday, full of light—that's why I call it Sunday. Each day to me is a Sunday because it is full of holiness.

THE DISCIPLINE OF TRANSCENDENCE, Vol. III

And, really, to say that I work is not good. This is the way I am. It is not a work; it is simply the way I am. It is happening. I cannot do otherwise. Once you allow your heart to throb with me, it starts working. In fact it is a question for you to decide. If you want me to work, simply allow. I am working already.

You may be twenty-five thousand all around the world—you can become twenty-five *lakhs*, that will not make any difference. My work remains the same. Even if the whole world is converted to sannyas, my work remains the same. It is just like a light burning in a room: one person enters—the light functions for one; then, ten persons enter into the room. Not that the light is more burdened—when there was nobody then too the light was burning, in absolute silence and loneliness. One entered: he could see. Now ten enter: they can see. Millions enter and they can see. The light is always burning there; when there is nobody, then too it burns.

If nobody is there I will go on functioning in the same way. It is not a question of numbers, and there is no secret to it. And, in fact, it is not a work. It is simply love. When you have attained to a state of love, you have attained to a state of light. It goes on burning. The flame is there; anybody who is ready to open his eyes can be benefited.

YOGA: THE ALPHA AND THE OMEGA, Vol. VI

Bhagwan, Is it really true that you never worked in your whole life?

It is really true. I am the original hippie! You may not know but I am the founder of the whole movement!

The shop-foreman, irritation showing plainly on his face, strode over to Sheldon, a hippie.

"Listen," he grated, "do me and everyone else in the shop a big favor and quit whistling while you work."

"Hey, man," retorted Sheldon defensively, "who is working?"

I have lived, I have not worked! And whatsoever I have done I have enjoyed it; it was not work, it was my joy, it was play. I loved it, that's why I did it. I was not doing any service to anybody, I was not working for any other motive, hence it was not work at all. It was my joy.

I am talking to you. It is not work, it is my joy. I enjoy— yakkety, yakkety, yakkety . . . this is not work! I simply love it. To call it work will not be right—it is fun!

Whatsoever I have done in my life, it has never been work. I have been simply whistling!

THE BOOK OF THE BOOKS, Vol. X

WORLD I declare to you that this is the only world there is, and this is the only life there is. Don't start thinking of some other life somewhere after death, beyond the seven skies, in heaven. Those are all just mind dreams, mind trips, new ways to fall asleep again.

Hence my insistence that no sannyasin has to leave the world, because leaving the world is part of a project, part of a dream of reaching to the other world. And because there is none, all your efforts will be in vain. You are not to go to the monasteries or to the Himalayas; you are not to escape from here. You have to become awakened here.

THE BOOK OF WISDOM, Vol. I

If you understand, if you become aware, if you become alert and you see into things, even that which you had always been thinking was real is no more real. Then all is a dream.

That is the meaning when Buddha says, "The world is a dream." He is not condemning it, remember. He is not saying "Renounce it"—how can you renounce a dream? He is not saying "Escape from it"—what is the point of escaping from a dream? He is simply saying, "Know it as it is . . ."

Buddha simply says: If you understand, you will not make

much fuss, that's all. You will pass through the world without making much fuss. That is real renunciation, that is sannyas—passing through the world without making much fuss, without taking it too seriously, without taking it so significantly. It is nothing—a tale told by an idiot, full of fury and noise, signifying nothing. Enjoy the story, but don't think that it is something serious.

TAKE IT EASY, Vol. II

WORRY If worries, anxieties, are there they go on dissipating our energy; and overflowing energy is needed to be drunk with God. Worries are leaks, holes, from where we go on dissipating.

Drop worrying. There is nothing to worry about; all is taken care of. Live with that trust. Existence loves you. No harm is going to happen, no harm can *ever* happen, because how can the whole do any harm to its own part? It is impossible. And if sometimes you feel that some harm is happening that must be some misinterpretation on your part; there must be some blessing in disguise.

Once this trust arises in a person he becomes religious. Then there is no need to worry, then there is no need to remain in a state of anxiety. Anxiety means "There is nobody to look after me. I have to carry the whole burden on my own shoulders. If I don't carry it then I am finished, and the whole existence is inimical." That's what creates anxiety: "Everybody is against me. Somehow, everybody is conspiring against me, everybody is at my throat. I have to protect myself. I have to be watchful, I have to plan, I have to move in such a way that I and not others prove the winner. Otherwise everybody is a competitor and they are bent upon defeating me."

This attitude creates anxiety, and this attitude is the attitude of a non-religious person. When I say a non-religious person I don't mean that he does not go to church, he does not read the Bible; that is not the point. He may read the Bible, he may go to church, but if he remains in anxiety he is not religious. And it is possible that he goes to church *only* because of his anxiety, out of his anxiety; he prays to God out of anxiety, he reads the Bible as a protection, as a security. But if anxiety is there a person is not religious.

He is pathological and his religion will be pathological.

The religious person knows nothing of anxiety; he changes the whole gestalt. He knows "I am part of this whole existence, and if trees are not worried and the birds are not going crazy and mad and the animals are utterly happy, why can't *I* be? I belong to this existence, I am an essential part of it." This trust, this understanding, this faith, and anxieties simply disappear, they are not found any more; you have stopped creating them, you have stopped secreting them. Then so much energy is preserved that it starts overflowing in a kind of festivity; it becomes a dance. It is so abundant, it is so exuberant, that life becomes a festival. Then a person is religious, then one is drunk with the divine.

TURN ON, TUNE IN AND DROP THE LOT

WORSHIP   The only way to worship God is to be a creator in some way, whatsoever you can create. You can create a garden, you can create a statue, you can paint, you can compose a song, you can play upon the guitar or the flute, or you can dance. Whatsoever you can contribute, be a creator. To be creative is the only real prayer; all other prayers are just empty rituals. If God is the creator, then the only way to know God is to be creative. That is the only way to participate with him, to be a participant in life, in his work, in his being.

Here my sannyasins are taught only one prayer: that of being creative.

GUIDA SPIRITUALE

Real worship consists of living. Real worship consists of small things. A religious man lives day to day, moment to moment. Cleaning the floor, and there is worship. Preparing food, and there is worship . . . Worship is a quality—it has nothing to do with the act itself, it is the attitude that you bring to the act. Recognize! See! And there is worship.

TAKE IT EASY, Vol. II

The living Master is a danger, but the dead Master is no more a danger. The living Master can wake you up; you cannot dodge him, he simply goes like an arrow into the heart. But a dead Master is a dead Master. He is just a memory, he is no longer there.

And now the disciples start worshipping him. Why? It is out of a feeling of guilt that they never heard him while he was alive. They feel guilty, they repent. Now they have to do something to get rid of the guilt. Worshipping is out of guilt, you will be surprised to know. You may not have thought that worship is guilt standing upside down.

The people crucified Jesus, and the same people started worshipping him. It is repentance. They started feeling a great pain, a great heaviness, a great anxiety. They had done something wrong; they had to compensate, they had to worship this man. They condemned him as a criminal and they worshipped him as God.

The same has been happening again and again. Worship comes out of guilt—one thing. Second: worship is a way to avoid the Master. By worshipping him you start feeling that you are doing whatsoever you can do. What more is there? You need not change, worship is enough. If the Master is alive and you only worship him and you don't change, he is going to hit you on the head.

The living Master, even if he allows you to worship him, allows you to worship him only so that you can come closer to him, that's all. He allows you to worship him so that you can come close and he can really destroy your ego. He wants you to become intimate with him. If this is the only way you know . . . And this is the only way you know, because you have always been worshipping Buddha, Krishna, Jesus, Mohammed. You have been worshipping, so when you come to a living Master, the first thing that you can do is worship him. He allows you to worship him so that you can come closer, so that you can be caught into his net.

But a dead Master is no longer there to do anything to you. Now you can start doing things to the Master—you can take revenge! You can make a stone or wooden statue of the Master and you can bow down to the statue that *you* have made. You are bowing down to yourself, to your own creation! It is like—and it will be far better . . . When you make a temple in your house it is better to fix up a big mirror and sit before the mirror and bow down to your own image—because the Master that you created is the Master that you create in your own image.

The Bible says: God created man in his own image. Maybe

in the beginning he did, but man has paid him out well, and in the same coin. Man has made God in his own image.

When you worship a Master you start creating a Master to your own idea—hence the myth springs up. The myth comes from your unconsciousness. The Master is physically dead, now you want him to be spiritually dead, too. The myth will do it: he will become spiritually dead, too. Your myth is a lie! And the more the Master becomes surrounded by myth and fictions, the more and more unreal he becomes.

That's why it is very difficult to believe that Jesus is a historical person—very difficult to believe. It is because of the mythology that has been created around him: he walks on water, he turns water into wine, out of a few loaves he makes enough bread for thousands of people to eat.

The people who created these myths are really getting rid of the reality of the Master. Although he is dead, a certain impact of the Master still continues that has to be effaced. The myth will do the work. Death has destroyed his body, myth will destroy his spirituality. He will become just a mythological figure, utterly impotent, useless.

The myth is a process in which you change the Master's historical reality into a fiction. Jesus as a historical person may be embarrassing. Jesus as a myth is beautiful—because a myth is created by you, according to your expectations.

No living Master ever fulfills anybody's expectations; he lives his own life. Whether you accept him or you reject him makes no difference. You can kill him, you can worship him, it makes no difference. He goes on living in his own way, he goes on doing his own thing. He cannot be forced to fulfill your requirements of him.

THE WHITE LOTUS

I am here, available, with open hands—look into me! I am just a window. Jesus is a window, Buddha is a window. And about windows one thing has to be remembered: when they are gone—when Jesus is gone—people think the window is very valuable, so they frame it with gold, stud it with diamonds and pearls and emeralds. By and by they completely forget that this is a window—you have to *look through it*. It is a medium, not an object of worship. And then there are so many diamonds and so much gold and so much silver that accumulate on the window that you cannot see beyond it. It becomes an altar, it becomes an object of worship; but it was just a passage to see through, it was a medium.

Jesus is a medium, I am a medium. Those who are intelligent will see through me and will find God. Those who are unintelligent will wait. When I am gone and when the window is framed in gold, studded with diamonds and is no more a window, they will worship me.

THE NINETY-NINE NAMES OF NOTHINGNESS

And by "worship" is meant wonder, awe, love. By "worship" is not meant any formal worship: going to a temple and worshipping a statue—that is not meant. Worship is a new vision, a new insight into reality.

When the child looks at the sun rising, look into his eyes: that is worship—he is so mystified, in such awe. When the child looks at the starry night, look into his eyes: those stars reflected in his eyes, that is worship.

The child knows what worship is. We have forgotten, because we have forgotten the language of wonder. We have become too knowledgeable: when the sun rises, we know what it is. Nobody really knows, but we have been to school, to college, to university, so we have become knowledgeable. When a flower blooms, we know what the name of the flower is, what species it belongs to, and from what country it comes. But all these things are meaningless, irrelevant.

Something wonderful is happening: the flower has opened, the fragrance is released. The flower is utterly beautiful, alive, and you simply label it. You say "This is a rose"—and you think you have known it just by giving it a name? You have missed. You have demystified the flower, and hence you have missed the wonder of it. Otherwise, each flower will give a thrill to your heart, each star will give it a new beat and each bird will start singing within you.

Life is so psychedelic, it is such a splendor. To feel the wonder of it, to feel the awe, is worship. And then in some unknown moment you may bow down to existence. You may kneel down on the earth, or you may fall on the sand, in great prayer, in great love, as if the earth is your mother—it is: the existence is your mother—and great love will upsurge in you. That upsurging love is worship.

UNIO MYSTICA, Vol. II

WOUNDS Wounds heal only when they are open— wounds never heal when they are protected, defended. It is painful to have an open wound but that's the only way it heals. So don't try to close it again. Remain vulnerable, Mm?—let the wind and the sun rays touch it, play with it. Yes, many times it will hurt, but remember only one thing: this time let it hurt but don't create a wall to protect it. Those walls ultimately become our imprisonment.

FAR BEYOND THE STARS

Mind is a hoarder of bitterness. It collects wounds, hurts, insults. It goes on sulking over them for years.

Psychologists are very aware of the fact that something said when you were only four years old may have hurt you so much that it is still there like a wound, still oozing pus. You don't allow it to be healed. You go on fingering the wound so you make it hurt again and again, again and again you create it, never giving it an opportunity to be healed by itself. If we look at our mind, it is nothing but wounds and wounds. Hence life becomes a hell; we collect only thorns.

A man may have been loving to you for years, he may have been compassionate, kind and everything, and he says just one thing which hurts you, and years of love and friendship disappear. That one thing becomes important, weighs more than all that he has done. You will forget all his love and his friendship and all his sacrifices for you. You will remember that one thing—and you would like to take revenge.

This is the way of the mind. Mind functions in a very ugly way. It has no grace. Go beyond the mind and you go beyond all bitterness. And the more you surpass the mind, the more your life becomes sweet, as sweet as honey.

Meditation is sweet, mind is bitter. Move from mind to meditation. Surpass mind. Don't be controlled and dominated by the mind: be a master. Then mind is perfectly good, then you can use it. Once you know what meditation is, once you know how you can be without the mind, you can use the mind and mind cannot use you. That is the moment when the gestalt changes inside, when the rebellion happens, when the fragrance is released.

IF YOU CHOOSE TO BE WITH ME
YOU MUST RISK FINDING YOURSELF

WRONG Freedom basically means, intrinsically means that you are capable of both: either choosing the right or the wrong.

And the danger is—and hence the fear—that the wrong is always easier to do. The wrong is a downhill task and the right is an uphill task. Going uphill is difficult, arduous; and the higher you go, the more arduous it becomes. But going downhill is very easy; you need not do anything, gravitation does everything for you. You can just roll like a rock from the hilltop and the rock will reach to the very bottom; nothing has to be done. But if you want to rise in consciousness, if you want to rise in the world of beauty, truth, bliss, then you are longing for the highest peaks possible and that certainly is difficult . . .

Freedom gives you the opportunity either to fall below the animals or to rise above the angels. Freedom is a ladder: one side of the ladder reaches hell, the other side touches heaven. It is the *same* ladder; the choice is yours, the direction has to be chosen by you.

PHILOSOPHIA ULTIMA

Y

YES This simple word "yes" contains all the religions of the world. It contains trust, it contains love, it contains surrender. It contains all the prayers that have ever been done, are being done, and will ever be done. If you can say yes with the totality of your heart, you have said all that can be said. To say yes to existence is to be religious, to say no is to be irreligious.

That's my definition of the atheist and the theist. The atheist is not one who denies God, and the theist is not one who believes in God—not necessarily so, because we have seen great theists who never believed in any God. We have known Buddha, Mahavira, Adinath: we have known tremendously enlightened people who never talked about God. But they also talked about yes; they *had* to talk about yes.

God can be dropped as an unnecessary hypothesis, but yes cannot be dropped. Yes is the very spirit of God. And yes can exist without God, but God cannot exist without yes. God is only the body, yes is the soul.

There are people who believe in God and yet I will call them atheists, because their belief has no yes behind it. Their belief is bogus, their belief is formal; their belief is given by others, it is borrowed. Their parents, priests and teachers have taught them that God is; they have made them so much afraid that they cannot even question the existence of God. And they have given them promises of great things if they believe in God: there will be great rewards in heaven if you believe, and great punishments in hell if you don't believe.

Fear and greed have been exploited. The priest has behaved with you almost like the psychologist behaves with the rats upon which he goes on experimenting. The rats in psychological experiments are controlled by punishment and reward: reward them, and they start learning the thing for which they are rewarded; punish them, and they start unlearning the thing for which they are punished . . .

Theists, atheists, both are victims. The really religious person has nothing to do with the Bible or the Koran or the Bhagavad Gita. The really religious person has a deep communion with existence. He can say yes to a rose flower, he can say yes to the stars, he can say yes to people, he can say yes to his own being, to his own desires. He can say yes to whatsoever life brings to him; he is a yea-sayer.

And in this yea-saying is contained the essential prayer.

The last words of Jesus on earth were: "Thy kingdom come, thy will be done. Amen."

Do you know this word "amen", what it means? It simply means "Yes, Lord, yes. Let thy will be done. Don't listen to what I say, I am ignorant. Don't listen to what I desire; my desires are stupid—bound to be so. Go on doing whatsoever you feel right—go on doing in spite of me." That is the meaning of the word "amen".

Mohammedans also end their prayer with *amin*—it is the same word.

Your question is tremendously significant. First, it is not a question, hence it is significant. It is a declaration, it is a dedication, it is surrender, it is trust.

You say: *Beloved Bhagwan, YES!*

This is the beginning of real sannyas. If you can say yes with totality, with no strings attached to it, with no conditions, with no desire for any reward, if you can simply enjoy saying yes, if it is your dance, your song, then it is prayer. And all prayers reach God—whether God is mentioned or not, whether you believe in God or not. All prayers reach God. To reach him, a prayer has only to be an authentic prayer.

But I would like to tell you that your yes should not only be a prayer. It should become your very lifestyle, it should become your flavor, your fragrance.

Down the ages, religions have been teaching people life-negation, life-condemnation. Down the ages, religions have been telling you that you are sinners, that your bodies are the houses of sin, that you have to destroy your life in order to praise the Lord, that you have to renounce the world to be able to be accepted by the Lord. This is all holy cow dung, utter nonsense.

Life-affirmation, not life-negation, is religion—because God *is* life, and there is no other God. God is the green of the trees and the red of the trees and the gold of the trees. God is all over the place: only God is. To deny life means to deny God, to condemn life means to condemn God, to renounce life means you are thinking yourself wiser than God.

God has given you this life, this tremendously valuable gift, and you cannot even appreciate it. You cannot welcome it, you cannot feel any gratitude for it. On the contrary, you are complaining and complaining and complaining. Your heart is full of grudges, not gratitude.

But this is what you have been taught by the priests down the ages. Priests have lived on it; this has been their basic strategy to exploit people.

If life is lived in its totality, the priest is not needed at all. If you are already okay as you are, if life is beautiful as it is, what is the need for a priest? What is the need of a mediator between you and God? You are directly in contact with God: you are living in God, breathing in God, God is pulsating in you. The priest will be utterly useless, and so will be all his mumbo-jumbo, his religion and scriptures. He can be significant only if he can create a rift between you and God. First the rift has to be created, then he can come and can tell you, "Now I am here, I can bridge the rift." But first the rift has to be there, only then can it be bridged.

And of course, you have to pay for it. When the priest does such great work bridging the rift, you have to pay for it. And in fact deep down, he is not interested in bridging it. He will only pretend that he is bridging it; the rift will remain. In fact he will make it more and more unbridgeable: the more unbridgeable it is, the more important he is. His importance consists in denying life, destroying life, making you renounce it.

I teach you a tremendous total yes to life. I teach you not renunciation but rejoicing. Rejoice! Rejoice! Again and again, I say rejoice!—because in your rejoicing you will come closest to God.

THE BOOK OF WISDOM, Vol. I

See also No, 2nd Series

YESTERDAY Yesterday is no more . . . Only today is—

and even that has passed. Only this moment is . . .

Yesterday, you heard me. Be finished with it. There is no more yesterday, but the mind carries it. If you really heard me yesterday, you will not carry it, for if you carry it, how can you hear me today? The smoke of yesterday will be a disturbance. There will be that smoke and you will only hear me through yesterday and you will miss.

Yesterday should be dropped so you can be here and now . . .

A carried past creates problems. The problem is not what I said yesterday or what I am saying today, the problem is that you carry yesterdays and miss today . . .

There is no past, no future. Only this moment is.

ROOTS AND WINGS

YIN/YANG Existence is made of two energies. On the surface they are polar opposites; deep down they are not opposites but complementaries. One can call them *yin-yang* or negative-positive or Shiva and Shakti or male and female. In fact *yin* and *yang* imply *all* possible opposites, with the underlying meaning that opposites are not opposites but complementaries.

The moment it happens that the opposites meet within you, that *yin* becomes *yang, yang* becomes *yin,* that the male and female inside you meet and merge into one—or in modern psychological jargon the conscious and unconscious meet and merge into one—for the first time you experience your organic wholeness . . .

Yin and *yang* divided, we are very small; *yin* and *yang* together and we contain the whole universe. The art of meditation is to help the man and the woman within you meet and merge and become one.

When man meets even with his outer woman, for a single moment a different quality comes to his being. Just for a split second when you are at the climax of your orgasmic joy, when you are not separate from the woman and the woman is not separate from you, then you are not there, she is not there; suddenly a duality has disappeared and in that disappearance of duality you have the first glimpse of what unity can be.

The ultimate secrets of meditation have been discovered

through this orgasmic joy. The whole tradition of Tantra is a proof of it. But the meeting with the outer woman or outer man can only be momentary. The same can happen inside you.

One of the greatest contributions of Carl Gustav Jung to modern psychology is that he accepted this ancient Taoist idea that, inside, man has both the male part and the female part. And the same is the case with the woman, she has both. But they are separate; a very subtle wall keeps them separate inside you. The wall is really subtle. It is just like a Japanese paper curtain, it can easily be removed. And once it is removed the whole is experienced.

To remain clinging to the part is misery, to allow the whole to happen is bliss.

JUST THE TIP OF THE ICEBERG

YOGA By "yoga" I mean exactly the literal translation: union, communion. When you are painting or playing music or dancing or singing, then you are in a state of yoga.

In *my* commune, this is going to be the yoga: you have to create. And the more you create, the more you become capable of creating. The more you create, the more sharpened is your intelligence. The more you create, the more you become available to infinite sources of creativity—that is God. The more you create, the more you become a vehicle for the magic to flow through you.

Yes, by "God" I mean the magic that surrounds you. Can't you feel the magic that surrounds you every moment—*this* very moment? The birds making sounds . . . the trees utterly silent, in a state of meditation . . . and you all here together with me, from faraway countries . . . a silence pervading. You are utterly tuned with me, breathing with me, your hearts beating with my heart. Can't you see the magic of the now, of the here, and the beauty of it and the benediction? This is God!

THE BOOK OF THE BOOKS, Vol. IV

First, yoga is not a religion—remember that. Yoga is not Hindu, it is not Mohammedan. Yoga is a pure science just like mathematics, physics or chemistry. Physics is not Christian, physics is not Buddhist. Even if Christians have discovered the laws of physics, physics is not Christian. It is just accidental that Christians have come to discover the laws of physics. Physics remains just a science and yoga is just a science. It is just an accident that Hindus discovered it. It is not Hindu. It is a pure mathematics of the inner being . . .

Yoga is pure science, and Patanjali is the greatest name as far as the world of yoga is concerned. This man is rare. There is no other name comparable to Patanjali. For the first time in the history of humanity, religion was brought to the state of a science: he made religion a science of bare laws. No belief is needed.

So-called religions need beliefs. There is no other difference between one religion and another: the difference is only of beliefs. A Mohammedan has certain beliefs, a Hindu certain others, a Christian certain others. The difference is of beliefs. Yoga has nothing to say as far as belief is concerned; yoga doesn't tell you to believe in anything. Yoga says to experience. Experiment and experience are both the same, only their directions are different. Experiment means something you do outwardly; experience means something you do inwardly. Experience is an inner experiment . . .

Belief is easy because you are not really required to do anything. It is just a superficial dressing—a decoration—something which you can put aside any moment you like. Yoga is not belief. That is why it is difficult, arduous, and sometimes it seems impossible. It is an existential approach. You will come to the truth not through belief, but through your own experience, through your own realization. That means you will have to be totally changed. Your viewpoints, your way of life, your mind, your psyche will have to be completely shattered as they are. Something new has to be created. Only with that new will you come into contact with the reality.

So yoga is both a death and a new life. As you are you will have to die, and unless you die the new cannot be born. The new is hidden in you. You are just a seed for it, and the seed must fall down, become absorbed by the earth. The seed must die; only then will the new arise out of you. Your death will become your new life. Yoga is both a death and a new birth. Unless you are ready to die, you cannot be reborn. So it is not a question of changing beliefs.

Yoga is not a philosophy. I say it is not a religion; I say it is not a philosophy. It is not something you can think about. It is something you will have to be; thinking won't do. Thinking goes on in your head. It is not really deep in the roots of your being; it is not your totality. It is just a part, a functional part, and it can be trained. You can argue logically, you can think rationally, but your heart will remain just the same. Your heart is your deepest center and your head is just a branch. You can be without the head, but you cannot be without the heart. Your head is not basic.

Yoga is concerned with your total being, with your roots. It is not philisophical. So with Patanjali we will not be thinking, speculating. With Patanjali we will be trying to know the ultimate laws of being, the laws of its transformation, the laws of how to die and how to be reborn again, the laws of a new order of being. That is why I call yoga a science.

Patanjali is rare. He is an enlightened person like Buddha, like Krishna, like Christ, like Mahavira, Mohammed, Zarathustra, but he is different in one way. Buddha, Krishna, Mahavira, Zarathustra, Mohammed, none of them have a scientific attitude. They are great founders of religions. They have changed the whole pattern of the human mind and its structure, but their approaches are not scientific.

Patanjali is like an Einstein in the world of Buddhas. He is a phenomenon. He could easily have been a Nobel Prize winner like an Einstein or Bohr or Max Planck or Heisenberg. He has the same attitude, the same approach as that of a rigorous scientific mind. He is not a poet; Krishna is a poet. He is not a moralist; Mahavira is a moralist. Patanjali is basically a scientist thinking in terms of laws. He has come to deduce the absolute laws of the human being, the ultimate working structure of the human mind and of reality.

If you follow Patanjali, you will come to know that he is as exact as any mathematical formula. Simply do what he says and the result will happen. The result is bound to happen; it is just like two plus two equals four. It is just like when you heat water up to one hundred degrees and it evaporates. No belief is needed; you simply do it and know. It is something to be done and known. That is why I say that there is no comparison. On this earth, there has never existed another man like Patanjali.

You can find poetry in Buddha's utterances; it is bound to be there. Many times while Buddha is expressing himself, he becomes poetic. The realm of ecstasy, the realm of ultimate knowing, is so beautiful, the temptation to become poetic is such, the beauty is such, the benediction is such, the bliss is such, that one starts talking in poetic language.

But Patanjali resists that. It is very difficult. No one else has been able to resist. Jesus, Krishna, Buddha—they all became poetic. When the splendor, the beauty, explodes within you, you will start dancing, you will start singing. In that state you are just like a lover who has fallen in love with the whole universe.

Patanjali resists that. He will not use poetry; he will not even use a single poetic symbol. He will not do anything with poetry; he will not talk in terms of beauty. He will talk in terms of mathematics. He will be exact, and he will give you maxims. Those maxims are just indications of what is to be done. He will not explode into ecstasy; he will not try to say things which cannot be said; he will not try the impossible. He will just put down the foundation, and if you follow the foundation you will reach the peak which is beyond. He is a rigorous mathematician—remember this.

YOGA: THE ALPHA AND THE OMEGA, Vol. I

YOU Remember: God created you. You cannot be unnecessary, you cannot be accidental. And God has created you as so unique, so individual, that there is no other "you" like you. You are the only one! He has never created a person like you before, and will never create another person exactly like you. See how much respect he has paid to you.

God is not like an assembly line that Ford cars go on coming out of—the same Ford cars, millions of Ford cars, all alike. God is a creator, not an assembly line. Each individual has been made not according to a mold, not according to a certain fixed pattern—each individual has been paid *individual* attention. He has painted you individually, he has cut you in certain way, given you a certain shape, a certain being. You are unique, you are original, you are not a copy.

He treasures you more . . .

And certainly you are his creation—if you are lost, it is his loss.

He treasures you more than you do yourself.

And that's a very obvious fact. People don't love themselves, they don't respect themselves. On the contrary, they condemn themselves. You are all self-condemners. That's what you have been brought by the priests, again and again, everywhere in the world: you have been conditioned to condemn yourself. And you go on condemning yourself. You don't think yourself of any worth. And this is one of the barriers, greatest barriers.

Love yourself, respect yourself, and you will be giving respect to God—because to respect the painting is to respect the painter, and to love the poetry is to love the poet. And you are the poetry and you are the painting. You are the music created by him. You are the visible proof that God is; the creation is the visible proof that the creator is. Love the creation, relish it, celebrate it; this is the only way to celebrate God. And you are the closest creation.

UNIO MYSTICA, Vol. I

YOUTHFULNESS Sannyas is initiation into spring; hence I have chosen the orange color. That is the color of spring in the East, the color of flowers. Green is the color of the trees and the shades of red are the colors of flowers. The goddess of spring, Kveta, is also the goddess of youth, youthfulness, and all the pleasures that youthfulness brings to you.

To be a sannyasin means to remain young forever. The body will become old but you can remain young always because consciousness knows no aging; it never grows old, it is always young, always fresh. All that is needed is a constant cleaning, a constant awareness so that the past does not become accumulated, so that the dust of experience does not gather on the mirror of consciousness. Then it always remains youthful. A Buddha dies young; although he is old in body, eighty-two years, he dies young. Mahavira dies young, although he is old physically. But physical age means nothing. Your body is part of time but your consciousness is beyond time; it is part of eternity. And to enjoy eternity is the real pleasure. All other pleasures are only reflections, faraway echoes of the reality.

The real pleasure is to be in deep silence, still, rooted in your own being—that is the deepest pleasure. It is incomparable. Nothing can be higher and nothing can be deeper than that, because it is God itself. When you are rooted in your being, totally at home and relaxed, a great bliss arises in you.

SCRIPTURES IN SILENCE AND SERMONS IN STONE

Z

ZEN Zen is not a religion, not a dogma, not a creed. Zen is not even a quest, an inquiry; it is non-philosophical. The fundamental of the Zen approach is that all is as it should be, nothing is missing. This very moment everything is perfect. The goal is not somewhere else, it is here, it is now. Tomorrows don't exist. This very moment is the only reality.

When you enter into the world of Zen there is no-mind. Zen is equivalent to no-mind. It is not freedom of the mind, it is freedom *from* the mind, and there is a lot of difference, an unbridgeable difference. The mind is not free, you are free of the mind. The mind is no longer there, free or unfree, the mind has simply ceased. You have gone through a new door which was always available to you, but you had never knocked on it—the door of being, the door of eternity.

Zen, the very word Zen comes from the Sanskrit word dhyana. Dhyana means meditation, but the word meditation does not carry its total significance. Meditation again gives you the feeling that mind is doing something: mind meditation, concentrating, contemplating—but mind is there. Dhyana simply means a state of no-mind, no concentration, no contemplation, no meditation, in fact—but just a silence, a deep, profound silence where all thoughts have disappeared; where there is no ripple in the lake of consciousness; where the consciousness is functioning just like a mirror reflecting all that is—the stars, the trees, the birds, the people, all that is—simply reflecting it without any distortion, without any interpretation, without bringing in your prejudices. That's what your mind is: your prejudices, your ideologies, your dogmas, your habits.

But when people who are accustomed to continuous thinking, logical reasoning, start studying Zen, they take a false step from the very beginning. Zen cannot be studied; it has to be lived, it has to be imbibed—imbibed from a living Master. It is a transmission beyond words.

THE GOOSE IS OUT

Zen says: Zen is like looking for the spectacles that are sitting on your nose already.

Sometimes it happens to people when they are in a hurry—they have to catch a train or something—and they start looking for their spectacles. And they are looking through the spectacles themselves. The spectacles are sitting on their noses. But they are in such a hurry they have forgotten.

Zen says: Buddhahood is not somewhere far away. You are just sitting on top of it. *You are it!* So there is *no* need to go anywhere; you just have to become a little alert about who you are. *It has already happened!* Nothing has to be achieved, nothing has to be practiced! Only one thing: you have to become a little more alert about who you are.

Zen teaches, therefore, not by words. Zen teaches, therefore, not by goals. Zen teaches by direct pointing. It hits you directly. It creates a situation. It creates a device.

A man came to a Zen Master and asked, "I would like to become a Buddha." And the Master hit him hard.

The man was puzzled. He went out and asked some old disciple, "What kind of man is this? I asked such a simple question and he got so angry. He hit me hard! My cheek is still burning. Is it wrong to ask how to become a Buddha? This man seems to be very cruel and violent!"

And the disciple laughed. He said, "You don't understand

his compassion. It is out of his compassion that he has hit you hard. And he is old, ninety years old; just think of his hand—it will be burning more than your cheek! You are young. Think of his compassion, you fool! Go back!"

But the man asked, "But what is the message in it?"

And the disciple said, "The message is simple. If a Buddha comes and asks how to become a Buddha, what else is there to do? You can hit him and make him aware that you *are* it. What nonsense are you talking about!"

If a rose bush starts trying to become a rose bush, it will go mad. It is *already* the rose bush. You may have forgotten. Zen says you are in a state of slumber, you have forgotten who you are, that's all. Nothing has to be done, just a remembrance. That's what Nanak calls *surati,* Kabir calls *surati*— just a remembrance. You have only to *remember who you are!*

So Zen teaches not by words, not by scriptures, not by theories, but by direct pointing, by engaging us in a game in which the only answer is a new level of consciousness.
        ZEN: THE PATH OF PARADOX, Vol. III

I had a gardener once—an old man, but *really* a gardener, utterly absorbed. I had chosen him only because he was so meditative in his work. He would not see day, he would not see night. Even sometimes in the middle of the night I saw him with the plants. He was not paid that much for that work, but he was around his plants continuously. He had great compassion. Just his work was such an absorption for him. Compassion arose. He had no other life. He was not concerned with anything, he was not interested in anything. His whole world was his plants. The plants were the only people he lived with.

Even weeds he would not throw away. Weeds! He would pluck the weeds—but very carefully, very lovingly. They are plants too. And he would put those weeds around rose bushes, underneath, close to the roots of the rose bushes.

I asked him, "What are you doing?"

He said, "Weeds carry great energy. There is no need to throw them, and they are people too. They have to be taken out, otherwise my roses will be spoiled. I have to take them, but I give them beautiful goodbyes. This is their graveyard. And I put them close to the roots of the roses. They will become roses sooner or later. They become manure. I transform them. I don't kill them."

That's art, that's skill. That's what Zen is. Zen doesn't say to you, "Fight with your sex, fight with your passion and lust!" It says: "There is no need to fight, create the bridge." And the lust becomes love, passion becomes compassion. It is desire itself, freed from objects, that becomes desirelessness.

> *This very world, the lotus land.*
> *This very body, the Buddha.*

Zen does not solve the problems, it dissolves them.
                    ZEN: THE PATH OF PARADOX, Vol. III

I love the statement that the "man of Zen walks in Zen and sits in Zen" for the simple reason that meditation cannot be just a part of your life. You cannot make a fragment of your life meditative; it is not possible to be meditative for one hour and then non-meditative for twenty-three hours. It is absolutely impossible. If you are doing that, that means your meditation is false.

Meditation can either be a twenty-four-hour affair or it cannot be at all. It is like breathing; you cannot breathe for one hour and then put it aside for twenty-three hours, otherwise you will be dead. You have to go on breathing. Even while you are asleep you have to go on breathing. Even in a deep coma you have to go on breathing.

Meditation is the breath of your soul. Just as breathing is the life of the body, meditation is the life of the soul.

The people who are not aware of meditation are spiritually dead.
                    WALKING IN ZEN, SITTING IN ZEN

ZERO   Jews, even today, whenever they write "god" never write G-O-D because that is a crime; they always write G-D. They drop the O so that we know that whatsoever we utter is incomplete. The O is missing—the most central part is missing. The O is also the symbol for zero—and zero is the essential core of existence—nothingness, *shunya*. It is beautiful the way the Jews write "God," G-D; the O is missing because that is the true God. But when you take the O separately it is nothing but zero. It simply represents nothingness.

These are ways of saying that God is absolute nothingness. You cannot worship God. All that you can do is: *you* can become nothing. That is true worship, that is prayer.

That is what I teach you here: to be nobodies, to be nothingness. Sannyas can be defined as a way of life which believes only in nothingness. To live as a zero, that's what sannyas is all about.

THEOLOGIA MYSTICA

One can have a new being, a new life, but one has to be ready to get rid of all that is old, to be utterly empty of the old, to be just a zero, nobody, a nothingness. Only out of that nothingness does the new begin.

The new is not the modified old, it is discontinuous with the old. So it is not a renovation of the old; the old simply dies without leaving any trace behind. And then the miracle happens: the new sprouts up. The grave of the old is the womb for the new.

And sannyas is nothing but a process of emptying you of all that you have been up to now so that you can have a new beginning, a fresh beginning; only then can misery disappear, only then is bliss possible.

The story of Jesus being crucified and then after three days resurrecting is beautiful. Christians have not been able to make much use of its symbolism: crucifixion means death and resurrection means birth. But for three days he was neither alive nor dead, for three days he was in a state of being a zero. And those three represent the three stages of the mystics: getting rid of the body, getting rid of the mind, getting rid of the heart; and then is the rebirth—the being is discovered.

*IS THE GRASS REALLY GREENER
ON THE OTHER SIDE OF THE FENCE?*

INDEX
The Third Series from R to Z

BOOKS PUBLISHED BY
RAJNEESH FOUNDATION
INTERNATIONAL

BOOKS PUBLISHED BY
RAJNEESH FOUNDATION
INTERNATIONAL

For a complete catalog of all the books published by
Rajneesh Foundation International, contact:

> Rajneesh Foundation International
> P.O. Box 9
> Rajneeshpuram, Oregon 97741 USA
> (503) 489-3462

THE BAULS

The Beloved (2 volumes)

BUDDHA

The Book of the Books (volume 1 & 2)
the Dhammapada

The Diamond Sutra
the Vajrachchedika Prajnaparamita Sutra

The Discipline of Transcendence (4 volumes)
the Sutra of 42 Chapters

The Heart Sutra
the Prajnaparamita Hridayam Sutra

BUDDHIST MASTERS

The Book of Wisdom (volume 1)
Atisha's Seven Points of Mind Training

The White Lotus
the sayings of Bodhidharma

HASIDISM

The Art of Dying

The True Sage

JESUS

Come Follow Me (4 volumes)
the sayings of Jesus

I Say Unto You (2 volumes)
the sayings of Jesus

KABIR

The Divine Melody

Ecstasy: The Forgotten Language

The Fish in the Sea is Not Thirsty

The Guest

The Path of Love

The Revolution

RESPONSES TO QUESTIONS

Be Still and Know

From Sex to Superconsciousness

The Goose is Out

My Way: The Way of the White Clouds

Walking in Zen, Sitting in Zen

Walk Without Feet, Fly Without Wings
and Think Without Mind

Zen: Zest, Zip, Zap and Zing

SUFISM

Just Like That

The Perfect Master (2 volumes)

The Secret

Sufis: The People of the Path (2 volumes)

Unio Mystica (2 volumes)
the Hadiqa of Hakim Sanai

Until You Die

The Wisdom of the Sands (2 volumes)

TANTRA

The Book of the Secrets (volumes 4 & 5)
Vigyana Bhairava Tantra

Tantra, Spirituality & Sex
Excerpts from The Book of the Secrets

The Tantra Vision (2 volumes)
the Royal Song of Saraha

TAO

The Empty Boat
the stories of Chuang Tzu

The Secret of Secrets (2 volumes)
the Secret of the Golden Flower

Tao: The Golden Gate (volume 1)

Tao: The Pathless Path (2 volumes)
the stories of Lieh Tzu

Tao: The Three Treasures (4 volumes)
the Tao Te Ching of Lao Tzu

When The Shoe Fits
the stories of Chuang Tzu

THE UPANISHADS

The Ultimate Alchemy (2 volumes)
Atma Pooja Upanishad

Vedanta: Seven Steps to Samadhi
Akshya Upanishad

Philosophia Ultima
Mandukya Upanishad

WESTERN MYSTICS

The Hidden Harmony
the fragments of Heraclitus

The New Alchemy: To Turn You On
Mabel Collins' Light on the Path

INITIATION TALKS
between Master disciple

Hammer On The Rock
(December 10, 1975 - January 15, 1976)

Above All Don't Wobble
(January 16 - February 12, 1976)

Nothing To Lose But Your Head
(February 13 - March 12, 1976)

Be Realistic: Plan For a Miracle
(March 13 - April 6, 1976)

Get Out of Your Own Way
(April 7 - May 2, 1976)

Beloved of My Heart
(May 3 - 28, 1976)

The Cypress in the Courtyard
(May 29 - June 27, 1976)

A Rose is a Rose is a Rose
(June 28 - July 27, 1976)

Dance Your Way to God
(July 28 - August 20, 1976)

The Passion for the Impossible
(August 21 - September 18, 1976)

The Great Nothing
(September 19 - October 11, 1976)

God is Not for Sale
(October 12 - November 7, 1976)

The Shadow of the Whip
(November 8 - December 3, 1976)

Blessed are the Ignorant
(December 4 - 31, 1976)

The Buddha Disease
(January 1977)

What Is, Is, What Ain't, Ain't
(February 1977)

The Zero Experience
(March 1977)

For Madmen Only (Price of Admission: Your Mind)
(April 1977)

This Is It
(May 1977)

The Further Shore
(June 1977)

Far Beyond the Stars
(July 1977)

The No Book (No Buddha, No Teaching, No
Discipline)
(August 1977)

Don't Just Do Something, Sit There
(September 1977)

Only Losers Can Win in this Game
(October 1977)

The Open Secret
(November 1977)

The Open Door
(December 1977)

The Sun Behind the Sun Behind the Sun
(January 1978)

Believing the Impossible Before Breakfast
(February 1978)

Don't Bite My Finger, Look Where I am Pointing
(March 1978)

Let Go!
(April 1978)

The Ninety-Nine Names of Nothingness
(May 1978)

The Madman's Guide to Enlightenment
(June 1978)

Don't Look Before You Leap
(July 1978)

Hallelujah!
(August 1978)

God's Got a Thing About You
(September 1978)

The Tongue-Tip Taste of Tao
(October 1978)

The Sacred Yes
(November 1978)

Turn On, Tune In, and Drop the Lot
(December 1978)

Zorba the Buddha
(January 1979)

Won't You Join the Dance?
(February 1979)

You Ain't Seen Nothin' Yet
(March 1979)

The Sound of One Hand Clapping
(March 1981)

OTHER TITLES

The Book
an introduction to the teachings of
  Bhagwan Shree Rajneesh
  Series I from A to H
  Series II from I to Q
  Series III from R to Z

A Cup of Tea
letters to disciples

The Orange Book
the meditation techniques of
  Bhagwan Shree Rajneesh

Rajneeshism
an introduction to Bhagwan Shree Rajneesh and His
  religion

The Sound of Running Water
a photobiography of
  Bhagwan Shree Rajneesh and His work

BOOKS FROM OTHER PUBLISHERS

ENGLISH EDITIONS
UNITED KINGDOM

The Art of Dying
(Sheldon Press)

The Book of the Secrets (volume 1)
(Thames & Hudson)

Dimensions Beyond the Known
(Sheldon Press)

The Hidden Harmony
(Sheldon Press)

Meditation: The Art of Ecstasy
(Sheldon Press)

The Mustard Seed
(Sheldon Press)

Neither This Nor That
(Sheldon Press)

No Water, No Moon
(Sheldon Press)

Roots and Wings
(Routledge & Kegan Paul)

Straight to Freedom (Original title:
Until You Die)
(Sheldon Press)

The Supreme Doctrine
(Routledge & Kegan Paul)

The Supreme Understanding (Original title:
Tantra: The Supreme Understanding)
(Sheldon Press)

Tao: The Three Treasures (volume 1)
(Wildwood House)

UNITED STATES OF AMERICA

The Book of the Secrets (volumes 1-3)
(Harper & Row)

The Great Challenge
(Grove Press)

Hammer on the Rock
(Grove Press)

I Am The Gate
(Harper & Row)

Journey Toward the Heart (Original title:
Until You Die)
(Harper & Row)

Meditation: The Art of Ecstasy
(Harper & Row)

The Mustard Seed
(Harper & Row)

My Way: The Way of the White Clouds
(Grove Press)

Only One Sky (Original title:
Tantra: The Supreme Understanding)
(Dutton)

The Psychology of the Esoteric
(Harper & Row)

Roots and Wings
(Routledge & Kegan Paul)

The Supreme Doctrine
(Routledge & Kegan Paul)

Words Like Fire (Original title:
Come Follow Me, volume 1)
(Harper & Row)

BOOKS ON BHAGWAN

The Awakened One: The Life and Work
of Bhagwan Shree Rajneesh
by Swami Satya Vedant
(Harper & Row)

Death Comes Dancing: Celebrating Life
with Bhagwan Shree Rajneesh
by Ma Satya Bharti
(Routledge & Kegan Paul)

Drunk On The Divine
by Ma Satya Bharti
(Grove Press)

The Ultimate Risk
by Ma Satya Bharti
(Routledge & Kegan Paul)

Dying For Enlightenment
by Bernard Gunther (Swami Deva Amitprem)
(Harper & Row)

Neo-Tantra
by Bernard Gunther (Swami Deva Amitprem)
(Harper & Row)

FOREIGN LANGUAGE EDITIONS
DANISH

TRANSLATIONS

Hemmelighedernes Bog (volume 1)
(Borgens Forlag)

Hu-Meditation Og Kosmisk Orgasme
(Borgens Forlag)

BOOKS ON BHAGWAN

Sjælens Oprør
by Swami Deva Satyarthi
(Borgens Forlag)

DUTCH

TRANSLATIONS

Drink Mij
(Ankh-Hermes)

Het Boek Der Geheimen (volumes 1-4)
(Mirananda)

Geen Water, Geen Maan
(Mirananda)

Gezaaid In Goede Aarde
(Ankh-Hermes)

Ik Ben De Poort
(Ankh-Hermes)

Ik Ben De Zee Die Je Zoekt
(Ankh-Hermes)

Meditatie: De Kunst van Innerlijke Extase
(Mirananda)

Mijn Weg, De Weg van de Witte Wolk
(Arcanum)

Het Mosterdzaad (volumes 1 & 2)
(Mirananda)

Het Oranje Meditatieboek
(Ankh-Hermes)

Psychologie en Evolutie
(Ankh-Hermes)

Tantra: Het Allerhoogste Inzicht
(Ankh-Hermes)

Tantra, Spiritualiteit en Seks
(Ankh-Hermes)

De Tantra Visie (volume 1)
(Arcanum)

Tau
(Ankh-Hermes)

Totdat Je Sterft
(Ankh-Hermes)

De Verborgen Harmonie
(Mirananda)

Volg Mij
(Ankh-Hermes)

Zoeken naar de Stier
(Ankh-Hermes)

BOOKS ON BHAGWAN

Bhagwan: Notities van Een Discipel
by Swami Deva Amrito (Jan Foudraine)
(Ankh-Hermes)

Bhagwan Shree Rajneesh: De Laatste Gok
by Ma Satya Bharti
(Mirananda)

Oorspronkelijk Gezicht,
Een Gang Naar Huis
by Swami Deva Amrito (Jan Foudraine)
(Ambo)

FRENCH

TRANSLATIONS

L'éveil à la Conscience Cosmique
(Dangles)

Je Suis La Porte
(EPI)

Le Livre Des Secrets (volume 1)
(Soleil Orange)

La Meditation Dynamique
(Dangles)

GERMAN

TRANSLATIONS

Auf der Suche
(Sambuddha Verlag)

Das Buch der Geheimnisse
(Heyne Taschenbuch)

Das Orangene Buch
(Sambuddha Verlag)

Der Freund
(Sannyas Verlag)

Reise ins Unbekannte
(Sannyas Verlag)

Ekstase: Die vergessene Sprache
(Herzschlag Verlag, formerly Ki-Buch)

Esoterische Psychologie
(Sannyas Verlag)

Die Rebellion der Seele
(Sannyas Verlag)

Ich bin der Weg
(Rajneesh Verlag)

Intelligenz des Herzens
(Herzschlag Verlag, formerly Ki-Buch)

Jesus aber schwieg
(Sannyas Verlag)

Jesus -der Menschensohn
(Sannyas Verlag)

Kein Wasser, Kein Mond
(Herzschlag Verlag, formerly Ki-Buch)

Komm und folge mir
(Sannyas Verlag)

Meditation: Die Kunst zu sich selbst zu finden
(Heyne Verlag)

Mein Weg: Der Weg der weissen Wolke
(Herzschlag Verlag, formerly Ki-Buch)

Mit Wurzeln und mit Flügeln
(Edition Lotus)

Nicht bevor du stirbst
(Edition Gyandip, Switzerland)

Die Schuhe auf dem Kopf
(Edition Lotus)

Das Klatschen der einen Hand
(Edition Gyandip, Switzerland)

Spirituelle Entwicklung
(Fischer)

Sprengt den Fels der Unbewusstheit
(Fischer)

Tantra: Die höchste Einsicht
(Sambuddha Verlag)

Tantrische Liebeskunst
(Sannyas Verlag)

Die Alchemie der Verwandlung
(Edition Lotus)

Die verborgene Harmonie
(Sannyas Verlag)

Was ist Meditation?
(Sannyas Verlag)

Die Gans ist raus!
(Sannyas Verlag)

BOOKS ON BHAGWAN

Rajneeshismus - Bhagwan Shree Rajneesh und
seine Religion
Eine Einfuhrung
Rajneesh Foundation International

Begegnung mit Niemand
by Mascha Rabben (Ma Hari Chetana)
(Herzschlag Verlag)

Ganz entspannt im Hier und Jetzt
by Swami Satyananda
(Rowohlt)

Im Grunde ist alles ganz einfach
by Swami Satyananda
(Ullstein)

Wagnis Orange
by Ma Satya Bharti
(Fachbuchhandlung fur Psychologie)

Wenn das Herz frei wird
by Ma Prem Gayan (Silvie Winter)
(Herbig)

Der Erwachte
by Vasant Joshi
(Synthesis Verlag)

GREEK

TRANSLATION

I Krifi Armonia (The Hidden Harmony)
(Emmanual Rassoulis)

HEBREW

TRANSLATION

Tantra: The Supreme Understanding
(Massada)

ITALIAN

TRANSLATIONS

L'Armonia Nascosta (volumes 1 & 2)
(Re Nudo)

Dieci Storie Zen di Bhagwan Shree Rajneesh
(Né Acqua, Né Luna)
(Il Fiore d'Oro)

La Dottrina Suprema
(Rizzoli)

Dimensioni Oltre il Conosciuto
(Mediterranee)

Io Sono La Soglia
(Mediterranee)

Il Libro Arancione
(Mediterranee)

Il Libro dei Segreti
(Bompiani)

Meditazione Dinamica:
L'Arte dell'Estasi Interiore
(Mediterranee)

La Nuova Alchimia
(Psiche)

La Rivoluzione Interiore
(Armenia)

La Ricerca
(La Salamandra)

Il Seme della Ribellione (volumes 1-3)
(Re Nudo)

Tantra: La Comprensione Suprema
(Bompiani)

Tao: I Tre Tesori (volumes 1-3)
(Re Nudo)

Tecniche di Liberazione
(La Salamandra)

Semi di Saggezza
(SugarCo)

BOOKS ON BHAGWAN

Alla Ricerca del Dio Perduto
by Swami Deva Majid
(SugarCo)

Il Grande Esperimento:
   Meditazioni E Terapie Nell'ashram
Di Bhagwan Shree Rajneesh
by Ma Satya Bharti
(Armenia)

L'Incanto D'Arancio
by Swami Swatantra Sarjano
(Savelli)

JAPANESE

TRANSLATIONS

Dance Your Way to God
(Rajneesh Publications)

The Empty Boat (volumes 1 & 2)
(Rajneesh Publications)

From Sex to Superconsciousness
(Rajneesh Publications)

The Grass Grows by Itself
(Fumikura)

The Heart Sutra
(Merkmal)

Meditation: The Art of Ecstasy
(Merkmal)

The Mustard Seed
(Merkmal)

My Way: The Way of the White Clouds
(Rajneesh Publications)

The Orange Book
(Wholistic Therapy Institute)

The Search
(Merkmal)

The Beloved
(Merkmal)

Take It Easy (volume 1)
(Merkmal)

Tantra: The Supreme Understanding
(Merkmal)

Tao: The Three Treasures (volumes 1-4)
(Merkmal)

Until You Due
(Fumikura)

PORTUGUESE (BRAZIL)

TRANSLATIONS

O Cipreste No Jardim
(Soma)

Dimensões Além do Conhecido
(Soma)

O Livro Dos Segredos (volume 1)
(Maha Lakshmi Editora)

Eu Sou A Porta
(Pensamento)

A Harmonia Oculta
(Pensamento)

Meditacão: A Arte Do Extase
(Cultrix)

Meu Caminho:
  O Comainho Das Nuvens Brancas
(Tao Livraria & Editora)

Nem Agua, Nem Lua
(Pensamento)

O Livro Orange
(Soma)

Palavras De Fogo
(Global/Ground)

A Psicologia Do Esotérico
(Tao Livraria & Editora)

A Semente De Mostarda (volumes 1 & 2)
(Tao Livraria & Editora)

Tantra: Sexo E Espiritualidade
(Agora)

Tantra: A Supreme Comprensao
(Cultrix)

Antes Que Voce Morra
(Maha Lakshmi Editora)

SPANISH

TRANSLATIONS

Introducción al Mundo del Tantra
(Colección Tantra)

Meditación: El Arte del Extasis
(Colección Tantra)

Psicológia de lo Esotérico:
La Nueva Evolución del Hombre
(Cuatro Vientos Editorial)

¿Qué Es Meditación?
(Koan/Roselló Impresions)

Yo Soy La Puerta
(Editorial Diana)

Sòlo Un Cielo (volumes 1 & 2)
(Colección Tantra)

BOOKS ON BHAGWAN

El Riesgo Supremo
by Ma Satya Bharti
(Martinez Roca)

SWEDISH

TRANSLATION

Den Väldiga Utmaningen
(Livskraft)

RAJNEESH MEDITATION CENTERS, ASHRAMS AND COMMUNES

RAJNEESH MEDITATION CENTERS, ASHRAMS AND COMMUNES

There are hundreds of Rajneesh meditation centers throughout the world. These are some of the main ones, which can be contacted for the name and address and telephone number of the center nearest you. They can also tell you about the availability of the books of Bhagwan Shree Rajneesh—in English or in foreign language editions. General information is available from Rajneesh Foundation International.

A wide range of meditation and inner growth programs is available throughout the year at Rajneesh International Meditation University.

For further information and a complete listing of programs, write or call:

Rajneesh International Meditation University
P.O. Box 5, Rajneeshpuram, OR 97741 USA
Phone: (503) 489-3328

USA

RAJNEESH FOUNDATION INTERNATIONAL
P.O. Box 9, Rajneeshpuram, Oregon 97741.
Tel: (503) 489-3301

SAMBODHI RAJNEESH NEO-SANNYAS COMMUNE
Conomo Point Road, Essex, MA 01929. Tel: (617) 768-7640

UTSAVA RAJNEESH MEDITATION CENTER
20062 Laguna Canyon Rd., Laguna Beach, CA 92651.
Tel: (714) 497-4877

DEVADEEP RAJNEESH SANNYAS ASHRAM
1430 Longfellow St., N.W., Washington, D.C. 20011.
Tel: (202) 723-2186

CANADA

ARVIND RAJNEESH SANNYAS ASHRAM
2807 W. 16th Ave., Vancouver, B.C. V6K 3C5.
Tel: (604) 734-4681

SHANTI SADAN RAJNEESH MEDITATION CENTER
1817 Rosemont, Montreal, Quebec H2G 1S5.
Tel: (514) 272-4566

AUSTRALIA

PREMDWEEP RAJNEESH MEDITATION CENTER
64 Fullarton Rd., Norwood, S.A. 5067. Tel: 08-423388

SAHAJAM RAJNEESH SANNYAS ASHRAM
6 Collie Street, Fremantle 6160, W.A.
Tel: (09) 336-2422

SATPRAKASH RAJNEESH MEDITATION CENTER
4A Ormond St., Paddington, N.S.W. 2021
Tel: (02) 336570

SVARUP RAJNEESH MEDITATION CENTER
303 Drummond St., Carlton 3053, Victoria. Tel: 347-3388

AUSTRIA

PRADEEP RAJNEESH MEDITATION CENTER
Siebenbrunnenfeldgasse 4, 1050 Vienna. Tel: 542-860

BELGIUM

VADAN RAJNEESH MEDITATION CENTER
Platte-Lo-Straat 65, 3200 Leuven (Kessel-Lo).
Tel: 016/25-1487

BRAZIL

PRASTHAN RAJNEESH MEDITATION CENTER
R. Paulas Matos 121, Rio de Janeiro, R.J. 20251.
Tel: 222-9476

PURNAM RAJNEESH MEDITATION CENTER
Caixa Postal 1946, Porto Alegre, RS 90000.

CHILE

SAGARO RAJNEESH MEDITATION CENTER
Golfo de Darien 10217, Las Condes, Santiago.
Tel: 472476

DENMARK

ANAND NIKETAN RAJNEESH MEDITATION CENTER
Stroget, Frederiksberggade 15, 1459 Copenhagen K.
Tel: (01) 139940, 117909

EAST AFRICA

AMBHOJ RAJNEESH MEDITATION CENTER
P.O. Box 59159, Nairobi, Kenya

FRANCE

PRADIP RAJNEESH MEDITATION CENTER
23 Rue Cecile, Maisons Alfort, 94700 Paris.
Tel: 3531190

GREAT BRITAIN

MEDINA RAJNEESH BODY CENTER
81 Belsize Park Gardens, London NW3.
Tel: (01) 722-8220, 722-6404

MEDINA RAJNEESH NEO-SANNYAS COMMUNE
Herringswell, Bury St. Edmunds, Suffolk 1P28 6SW.
Tel: (0638) 750234

HOLLAND

AMITABH RAJNEESH MEDITATION CENTER
Postbus 3280, 1001 AB Amsterdam
Tel: 020-221296

DE STAD RAJNEESH NEO-SANNYAS COMMUNE
Kamperweg 80-86 8191 KC Heerde. Tel: 05207-1261

GRADA RAJNEESH NEO-SANNYAS COMMUNE
Prins Hendrikstraat 64, 1931 BK Egmond aan Zee.
Tel: 02206-4114

INDIA

RAJNEESHDHAM NEO-SANNYAS COMMUNE
17 Koregaon Park, Poona 411 001, MS. Tel: 28127

RAJ YOGA RAJNEESH MEDITATION CENTER
C5/44 Safdarjang Development Area, New Delhi 100 016.
Tel: 654533

ITALY

MIASTO RAJNEESH NEO-SANNYAS COMMUNE
Podere S. Giorgio, Cotorniano, 53010 Frosini (Siena).
Tel: 0577-960124

VIVEK RAJNEESH MEDITATION CENTER
Via San Marco 40/4, 20121 Milan. Tel: 659-5632

JAPAN
SHANTIYUGA RAJNEESH MEDITATION CENTER
Sky Mansion 2F, 1-34-1 Ookayama, Meguro-ku, Tokyo 152.
Tel: (03) 724-9631

UTSAVA RAJNEESH MEDITATION CENTER
2-9-8 Hattori-Motomachi, Toyonaki-shi, Osaka 561.
Tel: 06-863-4246

NEW ZEALAND
SHANTI NIKETAN RAJNEESH MEDITATION CENTER
119 Symonds Street, Auckland. Tel: 770-326

PUERTO RICO
BHAGWATAM RAJNEESH MEDITATION CENTER
Calle Sebastian 208 (Altos), Viejo San Juan, PR 00905.
Tel: 725-0593

SPAIN
SARVOGEET RAJNEESH MEDITATION CENTER
C. Titania 55, Madrid, 33. Tel: 200-0313

SWEDEN
DEEVA RAJNEESH MEDITATION CENTER
Surbrunnsgatan 60, S11327 Stockholm. Tel: (08) 327788

SWITZERLAND
GYANDIP RAJNEESH MEDITATION CENTER
Baumackerstr. 42, 8050 Zurich. Tel: (01) 312 1600

WEST GERMANY
BAILE RAJNEESH NEO-SANNYAS COMMUNE
Karolinenstr. 7-9, 2000 Hamburg 6. Tel: (040) 432140

DORFCHEN RAJNEESH NEO-SANNYAS
Urbanstr. 64, 1000 Berlin 61. Tel: (030) 324-7758

RAJNEESHSTADT NEO-SANNYAS COMMUNE
Schloss Wolfsbrunnen, 3446 Meinhard-Schwebda.
Tel: (05651) 70044

SATDHARMA RAJNEESH MEDITATION CENTER
Klenzestr. 41, 8000 Munich 5. Tel: (089) 269-077

WIOSKA RAJNEESH SANNYAS ASHRAM
Lutticherstr. 33/35, 5000 Cologne 1. Tel: 0221-517199

RAJNEESH INTERNATIONAL MEDITATION UNIVERSITY

Rajneesh International Meditation University offers over sixty-five innovative and dynamic workshops, programs and training courses — and individual sessions — covering the whole spectrum of human possibility, human growth, human flowering.

On beautiful Rancho Rajneesh in central Oregon, Rajneesh International Meditation University is a unique opportunity to explore yourself, to know yourself, to love and celebrate yourself, to soar beyond your self — all in the radiance of a Buddhafield, of a community inspired by the understanding, love and grace of the living enlightened Master, Bhagwan Shree Rajneesh.

"The radiance of the soul, the flowering of the soul, the health of the soul, is what I mean by flowering. And when one has come to flower in the innermost core of one's existence, one knows who one is. That knowing triggers an infinite sequence of knowing; then one goes on knowing more and more about the mysteries of life and death. Just open the first door of self-knowledge and many doors start opening on their own."

Bhagwan Shree Rajneesh
From: *Won't You Join the Dance?*

For information or a complete descriptive catalog:

Rajneesh International Meditation University
P.O. Box 5,
Rajneeshpuram, OR 97741, USA
Tel: (503) 489-3328

"Fall in tune with the
energy of the person . . .
fall in tune so deeply
that his unconscious,
her unconscious,
starts stirring your unconscious,
and in your unconscious,
things start arising
— visualizations.
Those visualizations
will be meaningful . . .
but remember
you are not predicting the future.
So you can use this
for making people
more alert and more meditative,
more responsible
for their lives . . ."

Bhagwan Shree Rajneesh
THE FURTHER SHORE

Rajneesh
Neo-Tarot

A Totally new concept in Tarot — 60 luminous cards inspired by the living Master, Bhagwan Shree Rajneesh.

Each card represents one of life's major lessons. Based on stories from Zen, Sufi, Christian, Hindu, Tibetan Buddhist, Tantric, Hassidic and Greek religious traditions, given new meaning by the clarity and wisdom of Bhagwan Shree Rajneesh.

A booklet of instructions and stories giving the key to the meaning of each card is included.

c 1983 Rajneesh Foundation International

ISBN 0-88050-701-2

$14.95

Please make remittance payable to:
Rajneesh Foundation International
P.O. Box 9, Rajneeshpuram, OR 97741 USA